Modern Political Economics

ONE WEEK LOAN

Once in a   torpor
and a puzz   eeking
explanation   ot only
did the fin   it also
revealed th   *litical
*Economics   d what
the post-20

The boo   heory,
from Arist   ong in
2008. The   f ideas
whose purp   inevitable logic   rasp of
capitalist r   iinacy,
a condition   ics) to
second-gue   eeding
ground of t   *Global
Plan* (1947

This dy   ieticu-
lously the t   lanned
stability, t   ion of
unsustainal   tion of
money in   ng for
Economics   nomic
crash.

Yanis Varoufakis is Professor of Economic Theory at the University of Athens, Greece.

Joseph Halevi is Senior Lecturer at the University of Sydney, Australia.

Nicholas J. Theocarakis is Assistant Professor of Political Economy and History of Economic Thought at the University of Athens, Greece.

Modern Political Economics

Making sense of the post-2008 world

Yanis Varoufakis,
Joseph Halevi and
Nicholas J. Theocarakis

Routledge
Taylor & Francis Group

LONDON AND NEW YORK

First published 2011
by Routledge
2 Park Square, Milton Park, Abingdon, Oxon, OX14 4RN

Simultaneously published in the USA and Canada
by Routledge
711 Third Avenue, New York, NY 10017

Routledge is an imprint of the Taylor & Francis Group, an informa business

British Library Cataloguing in Publication Data
A catalogue record for this book is available from the British Library

Library of Congress Cataloging-in-Publication Data
Varoufakis, Yanis.
Modern political economics : making sense of the post-2008 world / by
Yanis Varoufakis, Joseph Halevi, and Nicholas J. Theocarakis.
    p. cm.
Includes bibliographical references and index.
ISBN 978-0-415-42875-0 (hb) – ISBN 978-0-415-42888-0 (pb) –
ISBN 978-0-203-82935-6 (eb) 1. Capitalism–History. 2. Economics–History.
I. Halevi, Joseph. II. Theocarakis, Nicholas. III. Title.
HB501.V362 2010
330.9–dc22   2010037780

ISBN: 978-0-415-42875-0 (hbk)
ISBN: 978-0-415-42888-0 (pbk)
ISBN: 978-0-203-82935-6 (ebk)

Typeset in Times New Roman
by Glyph International

MIX
Paper from
responsible sources
FSC
www.fsc.org   FSC® C004839

Printed and bound in Great Britain by
CPI Antony Rowe, Chippenham, Wiltshire

Contents

Tables

Figures

Boxes

Three authors, three forewords

Yanis Varoufakis

This book's origins can be traced to 1988 and, in particular, to a sedate corner of Merewether Building (Sydney University's economics department) where Joseph Halevi and I used to loiter until well after all our sensible colleagues had gone home. The conversation monotonously, but also fiercely, negotiated the thorny question of whether one had the right to pursue happiness in a troubled world. Joseph thought that the very idea was preposterous, adopting a position somewhere between Schopenhauer and Comrade Barbuchenko (a fictitious character with whom I identified him). I, on the other hand, having recently escaped England, could not resist a sunnier disposition, one that enraged Joseph.

Then came 1991. The end of the Cold War gave a new twist to our continuing duel. For Joseph it was not just an end of an era but the end of a *raison d'être* – the dissolution of an identity that allowed him to subvert his origins, to exist as a progressive human being and to wage battles against the sirens of racism, of sectarianism and, in the end, of idiocy organised at a planetary scale. For myself, it was a relief that one no longer had to defend the indefensible but, also, a portent of a bleak future both within the microcosm of academic life and more broadly.

As the 1990s unfolded, our debate lost its antagonistic edge and our conversations edged us closer and closer. In 2000, I decided to leave Australia for my native Greece. It was my first decision that Joseph approved of wholeheartedly, perhaps because a similar move was not, and would never be, open to him. Geographic distance brought our narratives even closer together. The *Global Minotaur* storyline, which appeared in 2002 in *Monthly Review*, was our first joint publication and also a marker of a deeper convergence. And when Joseph became, against all prior signs, a gym addict, the foreshadowed union of perspectives was complete.

Soon after arriving in Greece, I met Nicholas Theocarakis, the polymath and a friend-in-waiting. It only took a cruise in the Aegean (during which Joseph, Nicholas and I drank and ate far too much for three days and nights) to forge the Joseph–Nicholas bond. After they passed hours ignoring the splendid scenery in order to debate the most irrelevant and utterly boring minutiae of political economics, it was clear that our trio would, at some point, attempt to inflict some book or other on the world. You are holding the evidence.

Now that the ink is dry and the printer's job is done, it is becoming clear that our book lies at the intersection of a number of failures, some heroic others less so. Capitalism's spectacular failure in 2008, and the unmitigated defeat of the Left that preceded it in 1991, form the bulk of the book's backdrop. Then there are the personal failures of the authoring troika, and a fair share of loss that all three of us experienced, in different contexts, during the book's formative period.

Leaving the personal losses unsaid, the personal failures alluded to above are mostly related to our *condition* as economists. All three of us, though of slightly different vintage, chose economics with high hopes of bringing a *scientific* disposition to bear upon economic life. We embarked on our separate academic trajectories with a conviction that, even if the mainstream of economics had got it wrong, it is not only possible but essential that the light of scientific Reason be shone upon late capitalism. Years before we met, we had attempted to blend mathematical rigour with a progressive political economy approach. We failed in a variety of instructive ways.

Some time in the 1990s, Joseph and I converged on a difficult belief: that *in economics*, error is not just what happens until one gets it right. It is *all* one can expect! Serious, *Inherent Error* is the only thing that can come out of even the most sophisticated economics. The *only* scientific truth economics can lead its honest practitioners to is that the study of capitalism is guaranteed to lead to superstition if predicated upon a determination to extract truth from the theoretical models and their empirical applications.

Our conclusion that all theoretical certainties, upon close inspection, turn into dust was not easy on our minds or hearts. It did not come naturally to us. Yet we embraced it, and even shouted it from the rooftops, once we became convinced of the basic truth therein: namely that a scientific economics is an illusion leading one closer to astrology than to astronomy and more akin to a mathematised religion than to mathematical physics.

Not having been privy to the many years of the rowing between Joseph and I, the interminable quarrels that led us 'effortlessly' to that joint thesis, Nicholas took some convincing. After many conversations and a daylong Athens Summit (that Joseph happily compared to a bygone Cold War institution), the common line was agreed: economic theory is (and can pretend to no other office) a series of *necessary errors* that one must use as a training ground for the mind before turning to an historical, open-ended analysis of capitalism. It is upon that idea that the method of *Modern Political Economics* is founded (see Chapter 10 for a full summary of the method and then to *Book 2* for an historical analysis in concert with our method).

At this point in a foreword, an author would, normally, offer a long list of acknowledgments. Not so here. From the very beginning, we knew that this book will annoy even our dearest colleagues. Not wishing to implicate anyone in what is certainly going to be a disreputable volume, we desisted from communicating any of its ideas in advance. Thus, we shall not be acknowledging the assistance, contribution, insights, collaboration of any colleague. None was sought, no one read any of the book prior to its publication and, thus, no one ought to share the blame.

No one, that is, except for one accomplice who must be exposed: George Krimpas. He read every page, returned a red ink filled manuscript to Nicholas for urgent attention, was exquisitely encouraging throughout, even contributed two important addenda (one at the end of Chapter 6 and one at the end of Chapter 12). All blame for encouraging the authors to get on with the book must go to him, save perhaps for a small portion of the blame that ought rightfully to be directed at Robert Langham for believing in this project from the outset (as he had done before with other less foolhardy projects) and supporting it throughout.

The final acknowledgement must address my personal debt, gratitude and appreciation to Danae Stratou – my partner in everything. The cover is based on one of her photographs. It not only revisits a journey during which we both perished but also echoes a sense of precariousness not unlike that which permeates our post-2008 world.

Joseph Halevi

For me, this book is the completion and the end of 30 years of economic theorising. When push comes to shove, I think that the most relevant economic ideas for the present world are those of the late Paul Sweezy, Paul Baran, Harry Magdoff and Paolo Sylos Labini. As I worked and developed strong friendship relations with all of them (but Paul Baran who passed away too early), I wish to remember them with the deepest respect that world intellectuals command.

A central feature of the ideas of Sweezy, Baran, Magdoff and Sylos Labini was that economic theories must be historically grounded since history is the laboratory of economics. In this context, I should mention also the themes put forward by Michał Kalecki, who significantly influenced the above authors as he was the first economic thinker to have developed the theory of effective demand, which later became trivialised into Keynesian economics. In Kalecki, thanks to his Marxist-Luxemburg background, the problem of effective demand is not resolved by clever financial and policy tricks. Instead the question of profitable market outlets becomes the central internal and systemic contradiction in the advanced stage of capitalism. Wasn't he right all along?

Nicholas J. Theocarakis

Yanis in his foreword reports that it took some convincing before I conceded the main point of this book and decided to go along in publicising our thesis. I still feel uneasy about it, but I do not regret it. For an academic it is a major cognitive dissonance and admission of personal failure to accept that all his training, teaching and work had inadequately prepared him to speak with relevance on his subject-matter as a scientist. It can be always the case that this is indeed a matter of personal failure owing to limited ability, a manifestation of some quirky psychological trait or a sublimation of some life grudge. Maybe it is the ship that has gone astray, not the shoreline. I believe such *ad hominem* arguments will be raised by those who will be annoyed by the book. I welcome reaction infinitely more than indifference.

The disillusion with the scientific pretensions of economic theory was even greater in my case. The largest part of my working life was spent outside academia, with only a foothold in it as an adjunct lecturer, and only for the last five years am I a full-time academic. Having left industry to 'serve' science, it was harder for me to accept that the greener grass was a wasteland. I had been trained as a labour economist in the '80s in Cambridge and this was then a discipline where relevance and subtlety were still practised. My later retreat in the safe haven of the history of economic thought, where my main research interests now lie and where true scholarship is still evident, made me more reluctant to acknowledge the poverty of theory, although more equipped to see how it came about.

Moreover, I quite liked the mathematical constructions of economic theory. I do not find them boring or daunting. (Indeed, none of us do.) What I found boring was inane models expounded in Diamond (and Ashes) list journal articles and departmental seminars with no mathematical interest whatsoever (apart from convoluted irrelevant formalism and adhockery) that pretended to be based on some essential, asocial and eternal human trait or condition that provided the solution to real problems. I found it deeply offensive to see how quasi-rigorous mental gymnastics are increasingly being used to dress up reactionary political positions and end up in justifying policy measures that result in the misery of millions and being hailed as "harsh but necessary" by "embedded economists" – a phrase borrowed from my friend and colleague Thanassis Maniatis – singing in chorus with embedded journalists serving specific class interests. Living in besieged Greece in the last two years made this point even more painful.

Listening to Yanis' recollection of the fall of the Soviet Empire, I must confess that I never felt obliged to justify the indefensible or felt sorry for its demise. I think I saw it then for what it was. But I was taken aback by the viciousness with which the 'free-market system' was used by turn-coat kleptocrats to enrich themselves and turn their vengeance on the people of the 'liberated' states. And I admit that I also failed to see to what extent the countries that purported to be exemplars of 'really existing socialism' served as a countervailing power for the assault on the social rights of the working classes in the West that has been unleashed in the last three decades.

Mainstream economic theory has played a sinister role as an ideological prop for this assault. The practice of presenting political positions as scientific necessities, while paying lip-service to a *wert-frei*, but truly *wertlos,* science, was one of the first reasons that convinced me to reconsider my views on economic theory. The failure of the Left, and concerned economists, to articulate a consistent, cogent and fruitful discourse convinced me that the problem had to do more with the nature of our science than with the choice of the appropriate paradigm. Equally annoying I found the self-proclaimed heterodoxy of alternative schools of thought, where heterodoxy (with the appropriate flavour) was worn as a badge rather than as an intention to do true political economy. Marx, Keynes and Veblen were my intellectual heroes, but I always had a disdain for hero-worshippers.

Another aspect of our science that always worried me was that it pretended that you can ostracise the political element from it. Siding with Protagoras instead of Plato, I believe that you can never argue that politics, and economics, is a science that can be left safely in to the hands of the experts. Scientific pontification in economics is often an attempt to win a political argument with false pretences. The *hoi polloi* may never be able to argue competently about physics, but a democracy requires that those who participate in it must be able to debate political and economic arguments and take sides. This essential political element is what renders inescapable economics' duty to retain an irreducible and significant non-scientific element two and half centuries after its birth.

Meeting Yanis when he came to our Department in Athens was a breath of fresh air and gave hope for optimism. There it was a true intellectual force who wanted to do things about our discipline and our students. We quickly became friends and established a common way of thinking. We collaborated in an article and in a textbook and I joined in his efforts to create a different doctoral programme that served economics as a social science. It was through Yanis that I met Joseph. It was love at first sight. His erudition and profound thinking impressed me and when they proposed that I should be part of their book I was thrilled. This thrill was not to last. The best part of the writing of this book was shadowed by the illness and eventual loss of my long life partner and wife Catherine. Apart from my personal devastation, her loss prevented my contribution to be what I had hoped for, even though I proudly sign the product of a common belief of what we can do with our science and dedicate it to the fond memory of my beloved and truly remarkable Catherine.

1   Introduction

1.1 The 2008 moment

Once in a while the world astonishes itself. Anxious incredulity replaces intellectual torpor and, almost immediately, a puzzled public trains its antennae in every possible direction, desperately seeking explanations of the causes and nature of what just hit it.

2008 was such a moment. It started with some homeowners finding it hard to make their monthly repayments somewhere in the Midwest of the United States, and graduated to the first run on a British bank for 150 years. Soon after, the five grand American merchant banks that were capitalism's pillars had disappeared. Financial markets and institutions the world over were plunged into what was euphemistically termed 'chaotic unwinding'. Governments that had hitherto clung tenaciously to fiscal conservatism, as perhaps the era's last surviving ideology, began to pour trillions of dollars, euros, yen, etc. into a financial system that had been, until a few months before, on a huge roll, accumulating fabulous profits and provocatively professing to have found the pot of gold at the end of some globalised rainbow. And when that did not work, presidents and prime ministers with impeccable neoliberal credentials, following a few weeks of comical dithering, embarked upon a spree of nationalisation of banks, insurance companies and automakers. This put even Lenin's 1917 exploits to shame, not to mention the modest meddling with capitalist institutions of mid-twentieth-century radical social democrats (such as Clement Atlee and Ben Chifley, the post-Second World War prime ministers of Britain and Australia respectively).

What had happened was that the world had finally woken up to the brittleness of its financial system; to the stark reality of a global economic system that was being held together with sticky tape and that most precarious of materials: *self-reinforcing optimism*. From Shanghai to New York and from Moscow to Pretoria the world came face to face with the awful realisation that the 1929 crash was not just a worthy subject for economic historians but, rather, the sort of calamity that constantly lurks around the corner, scornfully laughing in the face of those who thought that capitalism had outgrown its early childhood tantrums.

While these words are being written, the *Crash of 2008* has not, as yet, played itself out. While the first two years after it proved that governments can arrest the system's free fall when they concentrate their minds and loosen their purse strings, a new crisis is looming. For as the public sector takes on its shoulders the sins of the private sector, the latter turns on its saviour with new financial instruments with which to gamble that the saviour will buckle under its new burdens. Thus, the aftermath will remain unknown for many years to come.

What we do know is that tens of thousands of American and British families lost, or are in fear of losing, their homes daily. Migrants abandoned the Meccas of financial capitals, such as London, returning home for a safer, more stolid future. China is in a bind over the trillion plus dollars it holds and seeks new ways of securing its dream run, now that the

West has turned inwards and reduced its imports. More than 50 million East Asians have plummeted below the poverty line in a few short months. Countries that thought themselves immune to the 'Western' economic disease, for example Russia and Iran, are perplexed when their own banks and enterprises are stressed. The job centres and social security offices in Western Europe, just like the famine relief agencies in sub-Saharan Africa, are reporting unusually brisk business. The recession 'we had to have' is upon us. It threatens to mark a new, depressed era.

A world in shock is always pregnant with theories about its predicament. The time has come for political economics to return to a world that had thought it could account for itself without it.

1.2 Why economics will simply not do

Few sights and sounds are less impressive than those emitted today over the airwaves, and in the pages of respectable newspapers, by the privileged commentariat. Having spent the past 30 years confidently informing the world about some 'paradigmatic shift' which, supposedly, had put capitalism on an irreversibly steady growth path, the very same commentators are now gleefully, and equally confidently, 'analysing' the *Crash of 2008*, exuding the air of self-aggrandisement befitting its prophets.

There is nothing new here. Evans-Pritchard, the renowned mid-twentieth century anthropologist, unwittingly pinpointed with brutal clarity how economic commentators weave their narratives. In his 1937 account of how the Azande soothsayers dealt with significant events they had failed to predict, Evans-Pritchard might as well have been writing about contemporary commentators of the *Crash of 2008* (just substitute 'Azande' with 'economic experts'):

> Azande see as well as we that the failure of their oracle to prophesy truly calls for explanation, but so entangled are they in mystical notions that they must make use of them to account for the failure. The contradiction between experience and one mystical notion is explained by reference to other mystical notions.
>
> (Evans-Pritchard in his *Witchcraft, Oracles and Magic among the Azande*,
> 1937, p. 339)

Making a living out of forecasting is, of course, a risky business and we ought to be sympathetic to those who, on the morning after, find themselves with egg on their face. A wise econometrics professor once advised one of us: 'When forecasting some economic magnitude, give them *either* a number *or* a date. Never both!' However, there is a difference between forecasters who simply can get it wrong and forecasters who, like the Azande priests, can only get it right by accident.

On the eve of 15 October 1987, four months after Mrs Thatcher's third electoral victory, which was fuelled by widespread optimism that privatisations and the new spirit of financialisation emanating from the City of London would be leading Britain to a new era of prosperity, Michael Fish, an amiable meteorologist with BBC television, read a letter during his weather section of the evening news. It was written by a concerned viewer who had a premonition that a tornado might hit southern England. Mr Fish famously poured scorn on that suggestion, emphatically saying that Britain had never experienced such a weather extremity and it was not about to. Five hours later, in the thick of the night, a tornado gathered pace in the Bay of Biscay, raced across the English Channel, violently pushed its way across southern England, flattening in the process a significant part of it, including London's splendid Kew Gardens.

A few days after the October 1987 tornado, another calamity hit London. Only this one was not felt on its streets and gardens but in the City, the Stock Exchange and the corridors of Whitehall and of the great financial institutions. The calendar read Monday 19 October 1987, when the world's stock exchanges suffered the worst one-day loss in their history. Originating in Hong Kong, the financial tornado raced across time zones to reach London first before hitting the New York Stock Exchange, shedding just over 22 per cent of the Dow Jones industrial average in a single session.

The hapless meteorologist would have been excused from thinking that economists must have been feeling on 20 October just like he was four days earlier: *humbled*. He would have been terribly wrong for a second time. For unlike him, economists are so steeped in their own 'mystical notions' that every observation they make is confirmation of their belief system. Look at what is happening today. Even though, yet again, the economics profession singularly failed to come even close to predicting the *Crash of 2008* (indeed, poured scorn on economists such as Professor Richard Dale, formerly of Southampton University, who had issued warnings about an oncoming collapse), economists have issued no *mea culpa*, have offered no apologies, have not rewritten their textbooks in light of these momentous events, have not even had the good form to hold a conference on what went wrong with their 'science' (as opposed to what went wrong in the financial sector). Instead, they appear on radio and television, or are invited to speak as 'experts', to *explain* the *Crash of 2008* using the very same methodology that had failed to predict it.

In one sense, this might be admissible. One might legitimately, for instance, want to hear Mr Fish explain the formation of the 1987 tornado even though (or perhaps *because*) he failed to predict it. Meteorologists remain uniquely able to explain their own predictive failures. Who else could do it better? Astrologists? It is in this sense that economists may argue that, though they failed to predict the *Crash of 2008*, it is they who must comment on its causes and nature. So, why be indignant towards economic 'experts' and sympathetic to Mr Fish? One obvious reason is their evident lack of humility. But it is not the main one.

The reason for rejecting the economists' commentary on their own predictive failures goes deeper. The economists' lack of humility is not due to a failure of character. It is rather a reflection of the fact that they have no useful theory of crashes to offer. It is the sub-conscious realisation of that vacuum that results in their hubris. After all, nothing causes scornful self-adulation as surely as deep-seated ignorance. Economists live in a mental world in which capitalism seems like an inherently harmonious system. Their narratives derive from a mystical belief in a providential mechanism that dissolves conflicts automatically, just as the gigantic counter-opposed gravitational forces in the solar system surreptitiously beget *equilibrium* out of potential chaos. In that worldview, a crash is an aberration that is best kept untheorised; something akin to a rogue comet destroying planet Earth.

Mr Fish was guilty of failing to predict a tornado, yet the physics on which he relied has the only sensible story to tell about tornadoes in general and the one that destroyed the Kew Gardens in particular. In sharp contrast, conventional 'scientific' economics, as practised in the economics departments of our great universities, simply has nothing meaningful to say about tumults like that which brought us the *Crash of 2008*.

1.3 The return of political economics

Along with the financial bubble, which eventually burst in 2008, another bubble had been brewing since the later 1970s: a bubble of economic theory founded on the certainties of neoliberalism and propagated by the dynamics of university life. We shall refer to it, for short, as the Econobubble. The crisis of October 1987 had played a crucial role in foster-ing the certainties that led to the Econobubble's growth. The fact that the stock markets recovered quickly after Black Monday was seen as evidence that the new economic order could take in its stride even the most precipitous fall in the price of stocks. The ensuing recession of the early 1990s was blamed on the decline in house prices, following their sharp rise during the 1980s; a mere 'correction' that was nowhere near as poisonous as the crisis of the early 1980s, which had preceded the privatisations and deregulation of the markets (and the Big Bang in the financial sector) whose *raison d'être* was to end such crises by liberating the markets from the shackles of government.

More poignantly, it was not long before the early 1990s slump gave place to a long, glori-ous boom that was only punctuated in 2001 with the collapse of the so-called *New Economy* (Internet-based, dot.com companies, Enron, etc.). That collapse was also short-lived and came with a useful silver lining: while countless IT firms folded, exasperating millions of people who had invested good money in them, the collapsing outfits had bequeathed the world a spanking new high-tech infrastructure, in the form of optic fibre cables that criss-crossed the earth and the oceans, and huge computer storage 'spaces', making a new wave of innovation possible.

In short, the early 1980s inaugurated neoliberalism's golden era, built on a sequence of speculative bubbles leaping from one market to another (as we shall see later in this book). The Econobubble was its theoretical reflection and fuel. The new era was, after all, initially spearheaded in the 1970s by a generation of economists (e.g. Milton Friedman and Robert Lucas in the United States; Sir Alan Walters and Professor Patrick Minford in Britain) and political scientists (such as Professor Robert Nozick) who had been canvassing powerfully for a brave new world of liberated markets only lightly overseen by a minimalist, night-watchman State. The adoption, at least in theory, of these policies first by Mrs Thatcher in Britain and soon after by President Reagan in the United States, and the eventual over-coming of the early 1980s recession (which was credited to these policies), led to a new conventional wisdom that swept the planet. Its highest form was that which, in this book, we term the Econobubble.

Underpinning these views was the conviction that, though markets occasionally fail, gov-ernment meddling in 'our' business must be feared more. The market-based world we live in may not be perfect but it is: (a) good enough; and (b) bent on conspiring to defeat all our democratically agreed efforts to improve upon it. Journalists, academics, private sector economists and government officials embraced the new creed with panache. To those who protested that this meant free market policies which stimulate great inequalities, the answer was either that only 'good' inequality was thus caused (while 'bad' inequality was repressed by market pressures) or that, given enough time, the infamous 'trickle-down effect' will eventually sort that problem too. Economists who resisted the Econobubble were sidelined, often edged out of the profession. Aided and abetted by financial flows that punished any government that delayed the surrender of its economic power to the markets (e.g. that failed to march to the quickstep of privatisation, deregulation of the banking sector, etc.), govern-ments the world over (some of them led by reluctant social democratic parties) adopted the new mantra.

Back at the universities, the Econobubble's dominance spread like an epidemic. Economics syllabi and textbooks were undergoing a momentous transformation. Its greatest victim, after the earlier demise of political economy, was macroeconomics. Indeed, we often heard top economists proclaim the end of macroeconomics, either as we know it or altogether. The idea was that since we now live in a stable world in which all that is required is some intelligent micromanagement, both at the level of firms and in the corridors of government, macroeconomics is passé. The fiction of the *End of History*, which was reinforced by the Soviets' collapse, meant also the end of any serious debate on the dynamics of world capitalism. Whereas in previous epochs, not that long ago actually, economists of all persuasion would debate the state of the world, the wisdom of markets, the importance of planning in developing countries, etc., once economics was taken over by the Econobubble they turned away from all that, confining themselves to 'focused' technical subjects such as Game Theory, the design of auctions and statistical models of movements in exchange and interest rates that lacked any monetary theory behind them which acknowledged (let alone analysed) capitalism's peculiarities.

Thus the 'competitive' economics departments were steadily depleted of anyone who was interested in researching the reasons why labour and financial markets may be ontologically distinct from other markets. Since macroeconomics (the 'holistic' study of an economy) can only be meaningfully distinguished from microeconomics (the piecemeal modelling of individual choices) if labour and finance markets differ from the market for carrots, macroeconomic debate was effectively expelled from the academy. Discussing the Great Depression as a source of interesting insights for today's reality was positively frowned upon, unless confined to economic history seminars for the technically challenged. In fact, reading any article more than five years old was deemed a sign of scientific slippage. Books were only to be used as repositories of already published, recent technical articles. As for macroeconomics, it was kept on the curriculum either out of inertia or only after all real macroeconomics content was bleached out (and replaced by models containing a single person who saved when young and spent when older, before being reborn again to start the 'dynamic' process afresh).

The economists spawned by such an environment, both as students and as professors, quite naturally, have next to nothing meaningful to offer when some systemic crisis occurs. When pressed by inquiring journalists, their answers have absolutely nothing to do with their actual research (how could they, after all?). Instead, as they struggle to say something pertinent, they fall back on the certainties and clichés of the Econobubble. This might have been tolerable in 1987, in 1991 or in 2001. The *Crash of 2008* is different. Now that the financial bubble has burst, we believe the Econobubble is next. It may not burst but it will surely deflate. The world is astonished in ways that the Econobubble can no longer placate.

In a 1998 book, one of us wondered whether the world had settled down and only ideas consistent with the Econobubble had any chance of being admitted into the circles of polite society; or whether 'we live in a new middle ages; a period devoid of clarity but pregnant with new tectonic shifts of economic and social relations which will lead to new heated debates'? This new book was written in the conviction that the tectonic plates have already moved, producing epoch-changing tremors which make a return to a *Modern Political Economics* not merely possible but, in fact, inevitable.

1.4 Why now?

The short answer is that the *Crash of 2008* is attacking social and economic classes that were not affected seriously by the crises of the early 1980s, the stocks' collapse of 1987, the recession of 1991 or the New Economy debacle of 2001. We know, from bitter personal experience, that the early 1980s crisis in Britain (and to a lesser extent in the United States) was perhaps more calamitous for more people than 2008 has so far proven. When four million unemployed were struggling to make ends meet in early 1980s Britain, under a government determined to wreck the social fabric that kept communities together, life was perhaps harsher than now. Nevertheless, that was a crisis which concerned mainly the country's depressed areas (mainly in the north); the working class; a segment of the nation with little or no political influence in London. Mrs Thatcher was the doyen of the south, the queen of the City and its surrounding stockbroker belt, cushioned politically by an electoral system which rendered irrelevant what went on north of Watford or in the depressed mining villages of Kent.

At the same time, the United States middle class was spared the worst effects of that crisis by a president who, while professing the importance of frugal government, embarked upon gigantic spending on weapons of mass destruction to see off the early 1980s recession. And when Black Monday occurred in 1987, it touched only a few people who panicked during that fateful week but left the middle classes largely unscathed. While the 1991 downturn worried the middle classes sufficiently to overturn certain administrations (George Bush Sr being its most prominent casualty), and 2001 shaved a proportion of previously accumulated profits off bank accounts and portfolios, these drops were neither deep nor sustained enough to dent the Econobubble.

In contrast, the *Crash of 2008* is having devastating effects across the neoliberal heartland. In Britain, it is a crisis of the south; probably the first to have hit its richer parts in living memory. In the United States, although the sub-prime crisis began in less than prosperous corners of that great land, it has already spread to every nook and cranny of the privileged middle classes, its gated communities, its leafy suburbs, the universities where the well off congregate, queuing up for the better socio-economic roles. In Europe, the whole continent is reverberating with a crisis that refuses to go away and which threatens European illusions that have managed to remain unscathed during the past 60 years.

All of these people need answers. What happened? How could governments have let it happen? Why did no one warn us? Some of them will become radicalised in ways that we have not witnessed since the 1930s or, more recently, since the Vietnam War. The Panglossian Econobubble cannot survive the wrath of the middle classes any more than the pre-modern faith in fairies, witches and dragons could have survived industrialisation and the scientific revolution.

2008, of course, is too close to interpret fully. However, one thing is certain. The unshakeable belief that the cycle of boom and bust is best kept in check by minimalist states and governments whose first priority is to go with the markets' grain has been destroyed. The idea that particular interest and general interest are mutually reinforcing within the capitalist system is bunk. The Econobubble which has infected the mind of tens of thousands of young women and men with economic nonsense has burst asunder. What will replace it? Humanity loathes ignorance. Either it will turn to a new quasi-religious faith, complete with its own myths, rituals, dogmas and equations, or it will rediscover the rational and aesthetic joys of political economics.

1929 had such an impact. It affected almost everyone. Even the rich, decades later, recalled the horror around them, well after the shockwaves had subsided. With the inanities of free marketeers torn apart by the 1930s depression, the world took eagerly to the writings of young economists who tried to tell a *story* about capitalism's pathology; of its wonders and contradictions; of its unique capacity to produce immense wealth and its equally astonishing tendency to trip and fall over, thereby causing massive deprivation among the innocent. Indeed, the post-war order was designed by people who had previously suffered, or watched while others suffered, the results of the *Crash of 1929*. Men who differed politically, often sharply, were nevertheless united in a determination to do all they could to ensure that such catastrophes would not happen again. They lectured to politicians, designed institutions, preached at universities – all with a single-mindedness that combined the best traditions of political thinking and economic analysis in a concerted campaign against the vagaries of untrammelled markets. They, thence, revived the tradition of political economics. The welfare state, the Bretton Woods agreement, the original (and rather benign) International Monetary Fund (IMF), the fledgling institutions that preceded the European Union were all affected by such people under the influence of the 1929 episode. We call this the *Global Plan* that attempted gallantly to regulate world capitalism between 1947 and 1971.

We feel that 2008 is a new 1929. While we hope that it will not create the same extent of mass deprivation, nor stoke the fires of international conflict, we think that 2008 will lead, just as surely as 1929 did, to the revival of a debate on how to bring some *rational order* into a chaotic world that can no longer rely on the myth of *spontaneous order*.

1.5 A Modern Political Economics for the post-2008 world

Interesting times call for interesting responses. This book is not interested in settling old scores. The temptation for those, like us, who never lost faith in political economics, and were never lured by the easy attractions of the Econobubble (often at high personal cost), is to brag now that the theoretical foe is in dire straits. But, were it to last for longer than a few brief minutes, such bragging would be inexcusable. It would be equally inexcusable to think of the present moment in history as an 'opportunity' to revitalise one's favourite defunct school of thought; some –ism (e.g. Keynesianism, Marxism, neo-Ricardianism…) that the last few decades confined, however unjustly, to the margins of academic economics.

2008 demands of us a grown-up response that eschews dull point scoring between the crashed 'orthodoxy' and its resurgent foes. Just because the *Crash of 2008* revealed to everyone the emperor's nudity, there is no sense in bringing out of the economic theory cupboard of the emperor's older clothes, dusting them down and giving them another airing. The world is simply not interested in newish wine being poured into ancient bottles. It is thirsty for the refreshing stimulus of a genuinely modern political economics.

Our recipe for a modern political economics tuned into the needs of the post-2008 world is simple: *all* of economics must be treated judiciously, critically, with contempt even. This, naturally, does not suggest that we begin from scratch, jettisoning all received economic wisdom. What it *does* mean is that, in writing this book, we start not only without any preconceptions about the rights and wrongs of different economic theories but, moreover, with a commitment to transcend all economic theory. This commitment of ours may strike the reader as a little puzzling, or even apocryphal. However, its point is quite simple. Over the past three centuries, economists have struggled to create 'models' of the economy that are as consistent as Euclidean geometry: every proposition about market societies had to be squared with the initial assumptions about it. Our simple point here is that this approach is bound to obfuscate, rather than illuminate, economic reality.

To give just two examples, some economists tried to explain the value of 'things' in reference to the production costs involved in their manufacture after defining fully the meaning of 'cost'. Others built models in which the values of 'things' reflected their relative desirability, based on a particular (utilitarian) theory of desire-fulfilling actions. The result was two equally logical yet incommensurable descriptions of the world; two theories of the object of study (mainly of prices and quantities) that could not be brought together. When these two schools of thought looked at reality, they did so in search of evidence that the 'other' school, or its model, was inferior. But the more they sought empirical support, the less their own model seemed to make sense. Reality, therefore, became an irritating presence only useful as a source of ammunition to be used against one's theoretical opponents.

This mindset will no longer do. If 2008 and its repercussions are to be understood, we cannot stay fixated within some *system* of economic beliefs. Philosophers worth their salt know well that life despises consistent philosophical systems and busily conspires to punch holes through them. Economic life does the same to all 'closed' systems of thinking about capitalism; not just to the Econobubble. It is high time economists of all schools and shades of opinion recognised this fact too. What this entails is a practical, empirical component in *every* layer of our analysis so as to keep it in constant conversation with reality. Now, the problem with this practical component is that it is bound to disturb any degree of theoretical consistency forged by our analytical reason (i.e. by our techniques). So be it. We are, after all, at a crossroads. One path leads to some satisfying system of interlocking and mutually consistent conjectures. The other leads to a constantly realigning set of incommensurable theoretical propositions which, if perceived astutely, *may* bring us closer to understanding really existing capitalism. We choose the latter.

Another way of putting the above is to describe our political economics as *eclectic* and the models we study (and refer to) in this book as *necessary errors*. Make no mistake: this book does *not* recommend a flight from theory. Theoretical models remain fundamental tools which help the mind remain sharp in its constant war against ignorance. It is just that models *per se* are incapable of helping us approach social reality.

So, how do we proceed from there? How do we converge with the truth about the causes and nature of wealth creation, poverty, growth and depravity in the world around us? How do we approach the *Crash of 2008* and the properties of the post-2008 world? There are three potential avenues that summon us, compelling us to make a choice right from the outset:

1. We may conclude that, since no consistent theoretical system is possible, no truth about world capitalism can ever emerge. Each model is, in this light, no more than an interesting story, a narrative, which may help different people differently in their own haphazard search for meaning.
2. The second avenue is more optimistic about the powers of human reason. It leads to the conclusion that truth is accessible through some sort of Aristotelian moderation; by means of a synthesis of different viewpoints founded on the belief that, in the face of antithetical perspectives or models, the truth must lie 'somewhere in the middle'.
3. The third avenue is the most ambitious. It also asserts that truth is available to the prepared minds which not only accept the tension and incommensurability between alternative models but also celebrate it, indulge it, keenly stoke it and, ultimately, transcend it through a wholesale immersion in historical inquiry.

As the reader may have guessed, it is the third and thorniest of routes that this book takes. In the pages that follow, our book enthusiastically delves into every economic model known to humanity (see *Book 1*) before pitting each against the rest in a quest for theoretical tension that may later, when turning to the history and institutions of capitalism (as we do in *Book 2*), throw light on the darkest aspects of our world's workings. No economic model is left unexamined but, at the same time, no economic model is left standing once we get down to the serious business of discussing the dominance of the US dollar since 1945, the role of Japan, Germany and China in the global economic order, the crisis in Europe, the scope for liberty in an environmentally challenged word, etc. Theory is but a training ground on which we practise before D-day; before, that is, we come to grips (in *Book 2*) with the economic and political reality in which economic concepts take their concrete form in a bid to write history and affect real lives. We call this two-part endeavour *Modern Political Economics*.

Modern Political Economics luxuriates in contradiction. Contradiction is indeed a concept central to every page in this book. Against the simple certainties of those nourished for years on the Econobubble, we savour the seeming paradox of free markets which cannot breathe in the absence of brute state power; we delight in the delicious irony of dictators who cannot resist organising referenda; we assign explanatory power to the fact that the powerful have no objection when the state gives pots of money away, as long as the recipients are not those who really need it; lastly, we are unfazed by the almost tragic sight of a generation of brilliant economists who prided themselves on sticking to scientific methods (which they borrowed from physics before developing them further in technically dazzling ways) but have serious trouble even recognising the capitalist system, let alone explaining its crises and tribulations.

Our provocative stance could be summed up in the motto: *away with theoretical consistency and proper systematisation!* It would be a motto whose purpose is neither to annoy colleagues who have spent their most productive years tailoring their models to meet the demands of logical consistency, nor to appeal to those who think of logic as a constraint on the imagination. Instead, it would be a motto whose simple purpose is to shed rational light on the ways of our topsy-turvy world. *Modern Political Economics* begins with a view that, when analysis leads to contradiction, the answer is not to squeeze the truth out by further logical manipulation but, instead, to allow (as Hegelians might say) *essence to appear*; to make it possible for the *truth* to come out by exposing every theoretical contradiction to historical reality while, at once, viewing what appears to us as reality through the lens of those contradictions.

1.6 A guide to the rest of the book

The two 'Books'

In old-fashioned style, this text is divided into two '*Books*'.

Book 1 is about the major theoretical contributions of political economics as they have taken shape over the past three centuries. Classical and neoclassical political economics are introduced in a manner that distils their essence, ignores superfluous technicalities and homes in on their major contradictions. The narrative seeks to blend two accounts: an account of how the evolution of the economic system spawned the economists' ideas about the former, and a second account of the opposite; of how the economists' ideas influenced economic phenomena. Thus, the important debates are projected against the background of the emergence of conglomerates, the irrational exuberance of the 1920s, the Great Depression, the War Economy and, lastly, the Cold-War era that followed it. Throughout these accounts, the emphasis is on salvaging nuggets of theory and facts that will come in handy when we turn to the main task: to making sense of the post-2008 world. Chapter 10 concludes with a summing up of the different perspectives on political economics; a summary that, surreptitiously, turns into the methodological manifesto of our *Modern Political Economics*.

Book 2 casts an attentive eye on the post-war era; on the breeding ground of the *Crash of 2008*. Its two main, long chapters offer our take on the two main post-war phases: the first we call the *Global Plan*, spanning the period 1947–71. The end of Bretton Woods signals the second period which we call the *Global Minotaur*, with a chronological range beginning shortly after 1971 and coming to a head in 2008. Chapter 13 concludes *Book 2* and sums up our suggestions on how to make sense of the post-2008 world.

A chapter by chapter guide

Book 1

Chapter 2 Condorcet's Secret*: On the significance of classical political economics* today

The chapter begins by distinguishing economic thinking from that of the natural sciences by using Aristotle's failures as a case in point. Whereas his physics and his economics can both be safely described as primitive, the latter contains *lost truths*; insights that contemporary economics has misplaced at its cost. Unlike physicists, who have nothing really to learn from Aristotle about the universe, economists are, at once, bogged down by an *Inherent Error* (that lies in the foundations of all logically consistent economic theories) and prone to lose important truths that their predecessors once understood better. The chapter moves from economics' basic features (the *Inherent Error* and the *lost truths*) to its foundation, which is none other than humanity's capacity to generate surplus. A brief history of surplus is provided before the origins of political economics itself are discussed and linked to what the book defines as *Condorcet's Secret*.

Chapter 3 The odd couple: The struggle to square a theory of value with a theory of growth

The odd couple of the title are value and growth. From the very start, political economics found it difficult to square the two; to create models or accounts of how the exchange value of things was determined in a growing economy. The chapter begins at the beginning, with the French Physiocrats, before moving to Adam Smith and David Ricardo's attempts to tackle this conundrum. The *Inherent Error* makes its first formal appearance in these works, before it returns again and again in the following chapters. The essence of the *Inherent Error* is the impossibility of telling a credible story about how values and prices are formed in complex (multi-sector) economies that grow through time.

Chapter 4 The trouble with humans: The source of radical indeterminacy and the touchstone of value

As if the *Inherent Error* were not enough, economics has to deal with another spanner in its works: humanity's stubborn resistance to quantification; to behaving (at work and elsewhere) like an electricity generator does; in a manner, that is, which allows the theorist to describe its function by means of a mathematical relationship between quantifiable inputs and outputs. This was Karl Marx's pivotal philosophical contribution, which led him to the idea that labour is ontologically indeterminate. To convey the significance of that nineteenth-century thought to our contemporary world (a significance that will become important when discussing crises like those of 1929 and, especially, 2008), this chapter utilises, quite extensively, a narrative based on *The Matrix*; the 1999 film by the Wachowski brothers. The sci-fi analogy illustrates that the input–output type of analysis employed by, among others, John von Neumann and Piero Sraffa, is better suited to a Machine Empire (such as that in *The Matrix*) rather than to a human economy in which workers and employers retain a human core. This is important because, the chapter argues, without the indeterminacy of labour inputs no economy is capable of producing *value*. In short, our economic models can only complete their narrative if they assume away the inherent indeterminacy that is responsible for the value of things we produce and consume.

Chapter 5 Crises: The laboratory of the future

Labour's indeterminacy (see Chapter 4) causes it to acquire two quite different faces or natures. One is a commodity (that workers rent out), the other an activity (which cannot ever be bought or sold, as such). This distinction then causes a similar bifurcation in capital: it too acquires two separate natures (one that takes the physical form of machinery, the other an abstract form of social power). The chapter then presents Marx's view of capitalism as a crisis-prone system on the basis of these bifurcations. In particular, it delves into Marx's explanation of how the same system can produce, in the same breath, growth and depriva- tion, wealth and poverty, progress and regression. Last, the chapter returns to *Book 1*'s main theme; i.e. that economics of all type are afflicted by the same *Inherent Error*. Marx's tussle with the *Inherent Error*, and the unsatisfactory manner of its 'resolution' by the great man and his successors, is the subject with which Chapter 5 concludes.

Chapter 6 Empires of indifference: Leibniz's calculus and the ascent of Calvinist political economics

The chapter introduces the reader to the type of economic thinking that has been dominant for a while and which foreshadowed post-war neoclassical economic theory. From 1971 onwards, the latter underpinned the Econobubble and thus aided and abetted the formation of the *Bubble* which burst in 2008. The chapter traces its origins in nineteenth-century Marginalist political economics, especially those of the British and the so-called Austrian Schools, and emphasises the interesting way in which Marginalism dealt with the *Inherent Error*. In brief, it is argued that the Marginalist school split between two factions: One (the neoclassical) dealt with the *Inherent Error* by ignoring it and by axiomatically imposing 'closure' on their models (while assuming that, in real life, the market would be imposing that 'closure'). The other faction (the continuation of the Austrian school) accepted that the *Inherent Error* precluded theoretical 'closure' (and any analysis that accommodated com- plexity and temporality); they insisted that, because of this source of fundamental ignorance of an economy's 'steady state' (or equilibrium), the only avenue open to us is that which leaves economic coordination to the market mechanism (that is, they recommend letting the state wither and its functions transferred to privateers). The chapter concludes with a pro- vocative description of neoclassical economics as Marginalism's bastard and an association of its method with that of Leibniz's version of calculus. [Chapter 6 comes with an addendum by George Krimpas entitled 'Leibniz and the "invention" of General Equilibrium'; a piece that adds substance to the chapter's allusion to a link between neoclassical economics and Leibniz's mathematics.]

Chapter 7 Convulsion: 1929 and its legacy

The chapter begins with an account of the great scientific discoveries of the mid- and late- nineteenth-century and on how they spawned a transformation in the texture, nature and organisation of capitalism. Technological innovation gave rise to conglomerates and this development changed the manner in which capitalism adjusted to change and reacted to its self-inflicted crises. While a number of important authors had warned about the repercussions of the transition to oligopolised capitalism, their voices were unheard; for they were 'outsiders' – outside both the economics mainstream and the corridors of power. Meanwhile the 'insiders' developed neoclassical narratives which, due to their supercilious attitude to the *Inherent Error*, were becoming divorced from anything even remotely reminiscent of really existing capitalism. The chapter examines, in this context, the uses of *Say's law*, the quantity theory of money and the early manifestations of rational expectations (in models like that of Frank Ramsey). Then came the *Crash of 1929* that had no place in neoclassical models, not only causing a major loss in the insiders' reputation but also giving the insider's insider, John Maynard Keynes, his opening. Keynes's thinking, especially his sophisticated handling of the *Inherent Error*, takes up the chapter's remainder.

Chapter 8 A fatal triumph: 2008's ancestry in the stirrings of the Cold War

During the Second World War, economic policy was in the hands of the New Dealers, who ran the economy on a trial and error basis and in the light of the accumulated experience of trying, not with great success, to kick-start the ailing US economy during the traumatic 1930s. Meanwhile, a group of scientists (mostly of Central European origin) were manning the agencies, laboratories and divisions of the civilian and military authorities whose job it was to solve practical problems (e.g. logistics, planning of transportation systems, price setting) by means of advanced mathematical methods. However, after the war ended, and the Cold War began to take hold, both the New Dealers and the *Scientists* lost out in the struggle for the hearts and minds of academic economics. The winners of that 'game' were a small group of *Formalists*, with John F. Nash, Jr, Gerard Debreu and Kenneth Arrow at the helm. The chapter tells the story of that triumph, which gave neoclassical economics a whole new push, by focusing on the person that the book portrays as the era's most tragic figure: John von Neumann. His 'fate', the chapter argues, was an omen for the type of economics that would prove instrumental in the run up to the *Crash of 2008*.

Chapter 9 A most peculiar failure: The curious mechanism by which neoclassicism's theoretical failures have been reinforcing their dominance since 1950

Economics was in deep crisis well before the world economy buckled in 2008. Students had been turned off in droves by its relentless formalism; economists of renown were lambasting its irrelevance; and the informed public grew increasingly indifferent to the profession's intellectual output. And yet, a delicious paradox hovers over formalist, neoclassical economics: *the greater its theoretical failure the stronger its dominance*, both in the corridors of power and in academia. Tracing the history of this most peculiar failure to the early years of the Cold War, this chapter (in conjunction with Chapter 8) tells a story of how the post-war period spawned a *Dance of Meta-axioms* which kept neoclassical economics both dominant and irrelevant. The analysis focuses on: the decoupling of policymaking from high-end economic theory, to a new type of economics textbook (primarily due to Paul Samuelson); the dexterity with which the resurgent neoclassicism could absorb criticism by interchangeably relaxing and tightening its meta-axioms; the sociology of the profession; and, finally, an audaciously circular mutual reinforcement mechanism (especially evident after the end of the Cold War), which supra-intentionally rewards neoclassicism with institutional power that helps it maintain a strict embargo on any serious scrutiny of (i) its own foundations and (ii) really existing capitalism.

Chapter 10 A manifesto for Modern Political Economics:
Postscript to Book 1

This chapter summarises *Book 1*, its overarching argument, and the method that it proposes for dissecting, and transcending, all shades of political economics. It presents once more the significance of economics' *Inherent Error*, places the notion of *radical indeterminacy* on centrestage and hints at explanations of why economics has proven so helpful to the social forces and institutions that led the world down the road to the *Crash of 2008*.

Book 2

Chapter 11 From the Global Plan *to a* Global Minotaur*: The two distinct phases of post-war US hegemony*

This is the first of two chapters that map out the post-war evolution of global capitalism. It begins with the *Global Plan* which the New Dealers designed during 1944–53 for a world in ruins. For two decades, under the *Plan*, the US sponsored and supported the emergence of two strong currencies (the Deutschmark and the Yen) as well as the industries and trade regions that underpinned them. When, however, US hegemony was threatened by strains on the US balance of payments (caused by the Vietnam war, domestic spending programmes, falling US profits and relative productivity), the hegemon reacted by opting for a controlled disintegration of the *Global Plan*. In this reading, the oil crises and stagflation of the 1970s were symptoms of a change in US policy that led to a new global order: the *Global Minotaur* of the title. During that phase, capital and trade flows were reversed, with the United States attracting the bulk of foreign-produced capital (or surplus value) in return for aggregate demand for the output of the rest of the world. However, this new global 'deal' condemned the rest of the world to a slow burning, often difficult to discern, crisis which was an inevitable repercussion of the constant capital migration to Wall Street. The chapter concludes with a statement by Paul Volcker (Chairman of the US Federal Reserve, 1979–87) that seems to support its main hypothesis.

Chapter 12 Crash: 2008 and its legacy

This chapter completes the story of the *Global Minotaur* (see Chapter 11) by explaining how the mass capital flight into Wall Street (both from the rest of the world and from within the US economy) paved the ground for financialisation, securitisation and, eventually, the creation of *private money* (in the form of CDOs and CDSs) that was predicated upon domestic debt (mainly the subprime mortgages), foreign debt (mainly the sovereign debt of other states) and other capital flows. In this context, a new theory of European integration, and the emergence of the Euro, is offered. The *Crash of 2008* is subsequently placed in the analytical context that unfolded throughout this book's pages. The chapter proceeds to explain how the *Crash* led to the annihilation of the *private money* on which global capitalism had, by that time, become hooked and how governments were forced to step in and replace it with freshly minted public money; only to occasion a fresh wave of *private money*-creation as a resurgent financial sector began to issue new derivatives which, essentially, constituted bets against the governments that saved them. The implications of this dynamic for the future of capitalism, in the United States, Europe and Asia, are discussed. Finally, the chapter concludes with a statement by Alan Greenspan (Chairman of the US Federal Reserve, 1987–2007) in tune with its main argument. [Chapter 12 comes with an addendum by George Krimpas entitled 'The Recycling Problem in a Currency Union'; a pertinent comment on the current debates concerning the future of the Eurozone.]

Chapter 13 A future for hope: Postscript to Book 2

The final chapter is a postscript to *Book 2*. It begins with a reminder (from *Book 1*) that economic theory pushes its practitioners into an awful dilemma: either to stick to the pursuit of logical consistency in the context of 'closed' models, or to remain in contact with really existing capitalism. In this sense, a commitment to *live in truth*, while attempting to make sense of our post-2008 world, comes with a precondition: a readiness to leave behind the 'closed' models of economists. Taking its cue from the analysis of the post-war world in Chapters 11 and 12, the chapter looks into the fundamental choice facing us now: between a resurgent push to recover the very idea of Democracy, and put it to work in an attempt to create a *New Global Plan* that may just save humanity from an ignominious economic and ecological meltdown, or to surrender to the system that seems to be taking shape behind our backs: a creeping Trapezocracy (from the Greek word *trapeza*, meaning bank) which will render our already unbalanced world more unstable, precarious, irrational; and thus shape a future that is simply a considerably nastier version of the past.

Book 1

Shades of political economics

Seeking clues for 2008 and its aftermath
in the economists' theories

2 Condorcet's Secret

On the significance of classical political economics *today*

2.1 Lost truth, *Inherent Error*

Staring into chaos and seeing in it significant patterns is the hallmark of the mad person. It is also the job of the scientist. Theory is a flight from the cacophony of appearances towards some manageable story about the world. When theory resonates with observation, it can lead us to the truth, but it can also lead us astray. By plucking the strings of musical instruments and showing that whole numbers had special properties transcending the limits of both arithmetic and music, the Pythagoreans discovered the magnificent mathematical harmony embedded deeply inside physical objects. But they went too far and their conclusions regarding the structure of the universe were nothing short of absurd. Isaac Newton illuminated the elliptical trajectories of heavenly objects by combining dazzling new mathematical concepts with observation, but held on tenaciously to some bizarre apocryphal views.[1] Gottfried Leibniz gave us the invaluable language of calculus, without which the modern world would have been impossible, but he also thought that his mathematics offered a basis for eliminating conflict from the social world as long as we were prepared to use his formulae to settle disputes.[2]

If the history of science has shown us one thing, it is that *foolish thoughts share skulls with brilliance*; that in the fertile fields of human thinking, insight grows right next to drivel; and that no intellectual pesticide exists that can safely exterminate the one without damaging the other. It has also shown us something further: that *this peculiarity affects social science far more acutely than it does natural science*. For unlike in physics or chemistry, the professionalisation of disciplines such as economics produces a kind of 'progress', which, frequently, leads us to lose sight of important truths that were once better grasped. Let us explain.

Ostensibly, scientific progress ought to be a process by which error is gradually eliminated through the combination of better observation and sharper thinking. This is certainly the process which has allowed physics to wean itself from its false Aristotelian premises before quantum mechanics or Apollo 11's moon landing became possible. However, social science in general, and economics in particular, has a distinct difficulty in emulating that steady elimination of error from its theoretical stock. The first strand of the difficulty is that the errors it discards as it 'progresses' are often entangled with some important truths, which are thus consigned to oblivion. The second, and more crucial, strand of the difficulty is that 'progress' in the social sciences, unlike its natural counterparts, tends to leave unscathed the more serious errors which, untouched by 'progress', remain firmly lodged in our social scientific underpinnings, continually impairing our vision of society.

Why is there this difference between economics and natural sciences? Why do we tend as economists to lose perspective and continue errors in our thinking or jettison important perspectives from our thoughts? First, economists act as social beings participating in the society which they study. They know that their theories tend to legitimise the existing social order or tend to undermine it. Their conclusions are part of politics. Sometimes they argue, pretending to be impartial and disinterested spectators, eschewing value judgements for a value-free (*wertfrei* as the Germans say) science (see Proctor, 1991). Sometimes they are open participants in the political game, arguing that their analysis is the only plausible alternative and that competing paradigms are politically motivated and unscientific and they warn readers of the implications.[3] They derive, however, their categories from the world they live in, and, if in support of the social order, a Panglossian optimism creeps into their results. Once this is done, the doors to alternative approaches are hermetically shut. Excluding the other is more often a political victory than a scientific one. External reasons, that is, those that are not related to the logical coherence of a theory or its ability to explain phenomena, determine the victory of a scientific theory in economics as much as internal ones.[4]

Second, the emulation of natural sciences by economics led economists to opt for a structure of reasoning that is suited to a mathematically structured universe but is inadequate to deal with the inherent complexity of social phenomena.

Put simply, economists in their eagerness to formalise threw the proverbial baby out with the bathwater. Keynes in his *General Theory* (1936, ch. 23, p. 235) spoke of 'Mandeville, Malthus, Gesell and Hobson, who, following their intuitions, have preferred to see the truth obscurely and imperfectly rather than to maintain error, reached indeed with clearness and consistency and by easy logic, but on hypotheses inappropriate to the facts'. Indeed, old insights cannot resurface unless stated in a form that by its construction prevents them from being exploited, while new errors cannot be remedied because it would require a *Gestaltswitch*.

As an example of this twin peculiarity of social science, that is, its penchant for *lost truth* and its imperviousness to *Inherent Error*, let us consider the towering figure of Aristotle. Does a young graduate about to embark upon a glorious research career in physics have anything significant to gain from reading Aristotle's *Physics*? Granted that an engagement with the great texts does no one any harm, the aspiring physicist will not benefit more from reading Aristotle than from Sophocles, Shakespeare or Shelley. The reason of course is that Aristotle's physics was rather primitive and contained no kernels of truth that have not been preserved, and further developed, by modern physics.[5]

Convinced that true knowledge presupposes the search for causes, including *telos* the final cause or purpose, Aristotle sought to explain phenomena, both natural and social, by inspecting their specific *telos*. While his analysis was helpful in explaining the movement of an arrow (namely, the archer's initial location and target), Aristotle's method proved ill equipped to come to grips with gravitational fields, the mysteries of particles or the infinite complexity of fractals. Even when recent developments in physics seem to vindicate one of his hitherto scorned views (e.g. his conviction that there can be no such thing as a vacuum and that the cosmos is filled with some 'all pervading ether'; a view that seems to resonate nicely with the current belief in *dark matter*, *dark energy* and the idea of a universe overflowing with Higgs boson particles), it is an accidental vindication devoid of any compelling reason for our young physicist to turn to the Stagirite's *Physics*.

Aristotle's economics was, arguably, just as primitive as his physics. And yet, a young economist could do far worse than to read his *Politics* and his *Nicomachean Ethics* in search of *lost truth* about the here and now; about the *Crash of 2008* even. To see this, recall Aristotle's theory that as the skilled archer's arrow is darting to its target so does a successful life move towards some *telos*, which for him was *eudaimonia* or true happiness. Human endeavours lacking a *telos* cannot be virtuous and a life without virtue is not worth living.

Moreover, a society that rewards handsomely such unworthy lives is sitting on a knife's edge, ready to fall into a major crisis. To glean the contemporary purchase of this thought, consider two different economic activities: *boat building* and *dealing in CDSs* (or credit default swaps – one of the financial instruments that allegedly brought us the *Crash of 2008*).

Building a boat is, for Aristotle, a virtuous activity precisely because it has an end; a *telos*. The moment the boat is launched into the sea, and begins to slice a purposeful course through the obstinate waves, the boatbuilder's work is done. Closure has been achieved. The *telos* attained. Dealing in CDSs, on the other hand, has no end except to make money. But money, however useful it may be for the attainment of other ends, can never be a proper end in itself, in the sense that it has no *telos,* and no limit, it has no end, or *peras*. When does the trader objectively *know* when to stop making money? At what level of profit can he/she rationally conclude that enough is enough? Aristotle believed that there is no such level; that money-making is endless and, therefore, the activities involved in it cannot be virtuous. Consequently, such an activity, stripped, as it necessarily must be, of a proper purpose, leads to depraved lives (even if supremely … profitable) and failed societies.[6]

Naturally, Aristotle's potential intervention in the current debates on the role of the financial markets, bankers' bonuses, the wisdom of replacing a real economy with a fictitious one, etc. does not answer most of the relevant questions. Nevertheless, unlike his *Physics* which has little to offer the contemporary physicist, a return to his *Politics* and his *Nicomachean Ethics* helps us recover several important *lost truths* about a very contemporary conundrum. Additionally, his writings elucidate the second peculiarity of social science that we mentioned above: its capacity to leave intact *Inherent Error* during centuries of supposed progress. To see this point, consider Aristotle's attempt at a *theory of value*, the first such attempt in recorded history.[7]

Box 2.1 Aristotle's theory of value in the *Nicomachean Ethics*

Now, proportionate return is secured by diagonal conjunction. Let A be a builder, B a shoemaker, C a house, D a shoe. The builder, then, must get from the shoemaker the latter's work, and must himself give him in return his own. If first there is proportionate equality of the works and then reciprocation takes place, the result we mention will be effected. If not, the bargain is not equal, and does not hold; for there is nothing to prevent the work of the one being more than that of the other; they must therefore be equated. (1133a5–14)

All must therefore be measured by some one thing, as was said before. Now, this is in truth need (*chreia*), which holds everything together, since if men did not need anything, or needed them in a different way, there would be either no exchange or not the same exchange; but money has become by convention a sort of representative of need; and this is why it has the name 'money' (*nomisma*) – because it exists not by nature but by law (*nomôi*) and it is in our power to change it and make it useless. (1133a25–31)

Money, then, acting as a kind of measure, equates goods by making them commensurate; for neither would there have been association if there were not exchange, nor exchange if there were not equality, nor equality if there were not commensurability. (1133b16–8)

Aristotle, *Nicomachean Ethics*

Given his characterisation of moneymaking as a non-virtuous activity, Aristotle was by definition philosophically ill disposed to *commodity production*; that is, to the production of goods with a view to selling at a profit (he approved only the sale of goods which *happened* to be produced in excess of the producer's requirements) (*Politics* 1257a30). And yet, his curious mind was fascinated by what appeared as stable economic exchange rates, or relative prices, or, more simply, *values*; e.g. by the observation that five beds would be exchanged, more or less consistently, for one house. As with everything else (from the motion of objects to comedy), he sought to define the phenomenon and to offer a rational account of it (see Box 2.1 and, for a detailed analysis, Meikle, 1995, Theocarakis, 2006 and Pack, 2010).

Consistent with his worldview, Aristotle proposed the theory that market exchanges are directed toward some human *telos*. And that this *telos* is none other than the amelioration of divergent human need within the context of reciprocity. The needs of different people, trading in some markets, are thus mediated, or made commensurate, by a human, or legal, artefact: *money*. But money cannot be the true measure of the value of things, since we can have exchange without money. Money stands as a proxy for the real measure which is *need*. The quantification of need, however, escapes him.

At the end, Aristotle was dissatisfied with this theory, realising that it left a large explanatory lacuna: 'Now in truth, it is impossible that things differing so much should become commensurate, but with reference to need they may become so sufficiently' (*Nicomachean Ethics* 1133b18–20). For a dedicated pursuer of exactness, the phrase 'they may become so sufficiently' (i.e, for practical purposes but not philosophically or scientifically) is tantamount to a declaration of defeat.

It was, undoubtedly, an incomplete, contradictory, unconvincing theory of value. However, even as a failure, it conveys great, timeless insights. *First*, it highlights an *Inherent Error* that subsequent developments in economic theory have never really managed to eradicate: the conviction that a consistent *theory of value* may be derived from primitive data on humanity's steady movement towards some *telos*: human need, preference, social affluence, etc. *Second*, it reminds us of how a truth may get lost as economic thinking 'progresses'; of how the fact that his *theory of value* held little water, and was thus discarded by the Northern European political economists once market societies started taking shape (some time in the eighteenth century), and led to the discarding of an important truth about the difference between virtuous economic activities (e.g. building a boat) and activities which could only be mistaken as virtuous (e.g. profit seeking); a truth that would be laughed out of court in the great business schools of our day, where hordes of young MBA graduates are being trained to think that the games they play, and whose only recognised *telos* is the 'bottom line', equip them to run anything, from a bank or a car manufacturer to a university or a hospital.[8]

To sum up, we believe that, in a world so recently shaken to its foundations by the hubris of the financial sector and the ethos instilled into corporations by high flying MBA graduates, Aristotle's distinction offers a glimpse of a truth that was once better understood and which the recent era has discarded (along with Aristotle's weak *theory of value*) at its peril. Also, we think that it is suggestive of some time-invariant fallacies in the very DNA of economic theory; fallacies which, as we shall argue towards the book's end, are also to blame, at least partially, for the *Crash of 2008* and its aftermath.

Last but not least, Aristotle's dubious excursion into political economy reminds us of how difficult it was to think in fully economic terms *before the emergence of fully fledged market societies*; especially in slave-propelled economies in which the quantity of *commodities* (i.e. goods produced primarily for sale) as a percentage of overall output was too tiny to spearhead a fully fledged political economics. With this thought in mind, we now turn to the historical trajectory that led to the formation of classical political economics. If Aristotle continues to pack insights for our own troubled world, what might the study of that particular trajectory have to offer?

2.2 At the beginning there was surplus

Humanity's *Great Leap Forward* came with the development of farming. While we are understandably proud of our era's remarkable technological progress, none of our contemporary achievements compares with the audacity of certain prehistoric hunter–gatherers who, in response to urgent need caused by Nature's declining capacity to sate their hunger, set about to force Nature's hand; *to grow their own food*. No innovation behind our spectacular gadgets is equal to the impudence of some long dead human who aspired to enslave a mammal, mightier and larger than herself, *so as to drink its milk every morning*. One fails to think of a bolder modern-day initiative than the project of replacing the meagre returns from hunting with the unbounded protein consumption made possible by the *domestication of animals*.

It was these technological innovations which, about 12,000 years ago, put us on the path of *socialised production*. And it was socialised production which gave rise to *surplus*; that is, to the production of food, clothes and other materials in quantities which, over some season, *exceeded* the quantities necessary for replacing the food, the clothes and the other materials that were consumed or depleted during that same season. Surpluses thus provided the foundation of 'civilisation' and the backbone of recorded history. Indeed,

- *Bureaucracies* would not have grown without an agricultural surplus. For, it was surplus production that enabled some people to abstain from the daily toil and take over the administrative duties necessary in the context of socialised surplus production, such as organising the collective effort, directing the division of labour and policing the social norms by which the surplus was distributed between families and social strata.
- The *written word* would have never been invented if there had sprung up no need for bookkeeping in the warehouses housing the grain and other foodstuffs that belonged to different families and clans.
- No *organised armies* would have been possible or, indeed, necessary, without a surplus, as their initial *raison d'être* was none other than to protect the stockpiled food from usurpers (and, on occasion, for looting other people's surpluses).
- The soldiers' *weapons* were forged by the same artisans who fashioned the tools necessary for ploughing the land and harnessing the cows, all in exchange for a cut of surplus food.
- *Biological weapons* of mass destruction too have ancient roots in that distant agricultural revolution. In the presence of so much accumulated biomass (in the warehouses and the adjacent agglomerations of burgeoning numbers of humans and animals living in close proximity), new strands of bacteria evolved. Coexistence with them furnished upon the farmers and their armies a mighty weapon: *immunity*. So, when they set out to conquer more fertile land, the germs they carried on them killed many more of their non-farming hunter–gatherer enemies than those they put to their gleaming new swords.

Crucially, the moment food production came into the picture, the epicentre of *social power* shifted from (a) those who had the right to determine the distribution of caught animals and collected nuts, to (b) those who had gained control over the *production process*. Rituals and norms for dividing spoils and determining hierarchies around the camp fire evolved into rules governing access to land and the division of labour between farmhands, smiths, priests and soldiers. Accompanied by the development of writing and bureaucracies, the practices of the community yielded a collective *ideology* essential to the coordination of the diverse activities necessary for surplus production. Ideology thus emerged as the glue of society that kept socialised production going, minimised the conflicts involved in the distribution of the surplus, underpinned the community's shared myths and fashioned its philosophical outlook.

It was not long before these new ideologies crystallised into *written laws*, complete with the state authority to enforce them. Social strata which gained conventional control over scarce land soon acquired conventional (and later formal) control over others' productive efforts. The power to appropriate segments of the socially produced surplus became inextricably linked to the new legal framework that enabled *some* to claim property rights over land, equipment, technological innovation, animals and even people. It was in this manner that earlier forms of hierarchies and social stratification yielded *social classes*.

Perhaps, the most intriguing feature of our species' social history is the relatively low-key role that explicit violence played within surplus-producing communities. The dominant social classes hardly ever relied on brute force in order to maintain their command over the larger portions of the surplus. Although violence was intermittently utilised in order to shore up their authority, the dominant class only used it when its power was on the wane. Indeed, the power of rulers to compel others (to do what was in the rulers' own interest); the power to appropriate (or 'privatise') a disproportionate part of the collectively produced surplus; the authority to set the agenda; these are not forms of might that can be maintained for long on the basis of brute force. The French thinker Condorcet put this point nicely at a time of another great convulsion of history, back in 1794, when he suggested that 'force cannot, like opinion, endure for long unless the tyrant extends his empire far enough afield to hide from the people, whom he divides and rules, the secret that real power lies not with the oppressors but with the oppressed'.[9]

Condorcet's Secret poignantly illuminates much of what makes societies tick. From the fertile agricultural lands which underwrote the Pharaohs' reign to the astonishing cities financed by surplus production in the Andes; from the magnificent Babylonian gardens to Athens' golden age; from the splendour of Rome to the feudal economies that erected the great cathedrals; in all that is today described as 'civilisation', the rulers' command over the surplus and its uses was based on a combination of a capacity to make compliance seem individually inescapable (indeed, attractive), ingenuous divide-and-rule tactics, moral enthusiasm for the maintenance of the status quo (especially among the underprivileged), the promise of a preeminent role in some afterlife and, only very infrequently, small-scale brute force.

The rulers' *social power* was, therefore, as much a result of their soldiers' spears as it was founded on the *consent of the powerless* to their rulers' authority. It is for this simple reason that social theory matters so much: our way of understanding our social order, our *social theory* in other words, is the primary input into the ways in which our social order is preserved and reproduced. Dynamic societies built their success on two production processes unfolding in parallel: *manufacturing surplus* and *manufacturing consent* regarding its distribution. The 'mind forg'd manacles', as William Blake called them, are as real as the hand forged ones.

2.3 *Condorcet's Secret* and the advent of political economics

Condorcet's Secret took a new twist in the seventeenth and eighteenth centuries when humanity made its *Second Great Leap Forward*; a leap that took feudal societies (featuring markets

---

Box 2.2 The birth of capitalism: *The commercialisation thesis*

From the fifteenth century, improvements in navigation and shipbuilding had made possible the establishment of global trading networks. As the Spanish, Dutch, British and Portuguese traders began to exchange wool for Chinese silk, silk for Japanese swords, swords for spices and spices for much more wool than they had started with, these commodities established themselves as global currencies. Unlike the aristocracy whose wealth was based on the appropriation of locally produced surpluses, the emerging merchant class benefited from taking commodities undervalued in one market and selling them in some remote market at a much higher price: a case of arbitrage. Tragically, the trade in commodities was soon to be augmented by another kind of trade: the trade in slaves whose unpaid labour was to generate more of these global commodities (e.g. cotton in the Americas). At some stage landowners in Britain joined this lucrative global trading network the only way they could: by producing wool, the only global commodity that the British Isles could deliver at the time. To do so, however, they expelled most of the peasants from their ancestral lands (to make room for sheep) and built great fences to stop them from returning – the Enclosures. In one stroke, land and labour had been turned into commodities: each acre of land acquired a rental price that depended on the global price of wool that that acre could generate in a season. And as for labour, its price was given by the puny sum the dispossessed ex-peasants could get for doing odd jobs. The coalescence of the merchants' wealth (which was stockpiling in the City of London, seeking ways of breeding more money), a potential working class (the ex-peasants begging for a chance to work for a wage) and some technological advances spurred on by the ongoing globalisation, eventually led to the invention of a new locus of production: the factory. A frenzy of industrialisation followed.

---

on their margins) and transformed them into fully fledged market societies (featuring pockets of activities that resisted the markets' advance). As feudalism subsided under the inexorable pressure exerted by global commodification and the concomitant technological revolution (see Box 2.2), societies' surpluses grew larger, more diverse (as industrial commodities came on stream) and relied on totally fresh social relations between those who laboured to produce them and those with *social power* over their distribution. The more the world changed in that direction the less able it was to unveil *Condorcet's Secret*.

Under feudalism, direct control over production largely remained in the hands of the peasant–producer, with the master stepping in (through the sheriff) only at the end to claim his share of a surplus that took the form of a pile of corn produced by peasants on communal land belonging to some distant master. It was thus (i) a surplus that all could see, *and* (ii) one whose distribution came *after* its production and was observable by all involved. In that feudal context, therefore, two things were visible to the naked eye: (i) the size and nature of the surplus (e.g. a pile of corn), and (ii) the process of distribution. To put it simply, after having piled up the very corn that *they* had produced, the peasants would watch the sheriff depart with the master's share of a resource he had no hand in producing. Ideology was, of course, important in minimising discontent and legitimising the ruler's authority, but it could not hide completely the peasants' relative powerlessness. This transparency also meant that there was little need for some economic theory that would 'explain' distribution: *the truth about distribution* was plain for all to see and required no *specifically economic concept* in order to be grasped.[10]

Things changed drastically when the market extended its rein into the fields and the workshops and when both land and labour stopped being mere productive inputs but were transformed into *commodities* traded in specialist markets at free-floating prices per unit. The labourers toiling the fields and sweating in the workshops were constantly managed, directed, guided and controlled by the employer. Indeed, the greater the *division of labour* the less well the worker understood how the final product came about.[11] Turning to the employers themselves, their role was nowhere as clear cut as that of the old masters.

Indeed, many of the early capitalists had not chosen to be capitalists. Just as hunter–gatherers did not choose to become farmers, but were led to agriculture by hunger (following the depletion of available prey or naturally growing food), a large number of ex-peasants or artisans had no alternative (e.g. after the Enclosures – see Box 2.2) but to rent land from landlords and make it pay. To that effect, they borrowed from moneylenders (or even from the lord) to pay for rent, seeds and, of course, wages.[12] Moneylenders turned bankers and a whole panoply of financial instruments became an important part of the business of surplus production and of its distribution. Thus *finance* acquired a mythical new role as a 'pillar of industry', a lubricant of economic activity and a contributor to society's surplus production.

Unlike the landed gentry, the dominant social class of yesteryear, capitalist employers, not all of them rich, went to bed every night and woke up every morning with an all pervasive anxiety: would the crop pay their debts to the landlord and to the banker? Would something be left over for their own families after selling off the resulting produce? Would the weather be kind? Would customers buy their wares? In short, they took *risks*. And these risks blurred everyone's vision regarding the role of *social power* in determining the distribution of the surplus between the employer, the landowner, the banker and the worker.

Where the feudal lord knew clearly that he was extracting part of a surplus produced by others, courtesy of his political and military might, the anxious capitalist naturally felt that his sleepless nights were a genuine input into the surplus; that profit was his just reward for all that angst; for the manner in which he orchestrated production. The moneylender too bragged about his contribution to the miracle economy that was taking shape on the back of the credit line he was making available to the capitalist. At least at the outset, as Shakespeare's *Merchant of Venice* illustrates, lending money was not without its perils. Shylock's tragedy was emblematic of the risks that one had to take in order to be the financier of other people's endeavours.

Meanwhile in Britain (see Box 2.3), the labourers were experiencing formal freedom for the first time in their families' long history, even if they struggled to make sense of their newfound liberty's coexistence with another new freedom: the freedom to a very private death through starvation. Those who did find paid work (and these were by no means the majority) saw their labour diverted from the farms to the workshops and factories.[13] There, separated from the countryside of their ancestors by the tall walls of the noisy, smoke-filled grey industrial buildings, their human effort was blended with the mechanical labour of technological wonders like the steam engine and the mechanical loom, participants in production processes over which they had no control and which treated them like small cogs in an endless machine producing an assortment of heterogeneous products many of which they would never get to own (see Box 2.4).

In this brave new world, *Condorcet's Secret* became an impossible riddle. The exercise of *social power* retreated behind multiple veils that no amount of rational thinking could penetrate without new analytical categories; without tools of the imagination that could make sense of the commodification of land and labour; of the new historical forces that diminished the authority of landowners, broke the nexus between political and economic power and produced a new, invisible to the naked eye, grid of *social power* over the ballooning, and increasingly heterogeneous, surplus.

In an important sense, capitalist and worker, moneylender and artisan, destitute peasant and dumbfounded landlord, all had good cause to feel stunned in this new social order; to feel like powerless playthings of forces beyond their control or understanding. Each had something to agonise over and no one could make out, through the new economy's multiple veils, the mechanism by which society's burgeoning surplus was being produced, let alone divided. What made things even more opaque was another bewildering puzzle at the heart of the new social order: its tendency to produce massive new wealth and *at once* unparalleled levels of human misery.

Shocked by the infinite new possibilities for good and evil, wealth and depravity, progress and horror, our eighteenth-century ancestors had questions and demanded answers. How come the increases in the surplus accentuated misery? Was more better? Were the straight highways of progress preferable to the crooked alleys of the ancient towns? What was behind the great societal changes? Was it inevitable that for the surplus to grow the market should be left alone to distribute it without interference from those who sought to serve the General Good? What was the General Good and who had the authority to know it and impose it? Even to begin to fathom these questions, simple observation was no longer enough. The time of *political economics* had come. It is still with us. The *Crash of 2008* left our world floating in a pool of bewilderment. The questions we are asking in the twenty-first century emerged for the first time towards the end of the eighteenth century. The answers given back then by the pioneering political economists still pack important insights about the here and the now.

Box 2.3 Why Britain?

For many historians, it is unsatisfactory to explain feudalism's collapse on external factors, e.g. trade and the rise of global commodities. Some think that the causes were located within Europe. The development of reliable forms of money and the maturation of trade in market towns may have been of equal significance as the increase in global trade. In this account, market societies came into being as local trade in unglamorous commodities was steadily 'liberated' from the fetters of feudal regulation.

Yet other historians object both to the commercialisation thesis and to the above view of the industrial revolution as the outcome of the 'liberation' of local markets. They are keen to avoid assuming what they are trying to explain: to presupposing that capitalism was always there, at least in embryonic form, waiting to be 'released' or 'liberated'. They argue that if this was indeed so, we should be trying to explain what took capitalism so long to emerge (rather than why feudalism collapsed). Additionally, they point out that neither of the accounts of the emergence of market societies above can explain why it happened in Britain and spread to the rest of Europe rather than in the equally commercialised East.

One explanation along this line of thinking begins by focusing on the evolution of land ownership in Britain. Compared to most other parts of the world, land ownership was highly concentrated in England and Scotland. Huge estates made *ex post* surplus appropriation (i e., the plunder of the peasants' produce *after* the harvest was in) very cumbersome and costly. So, the gentry turned to a new method: *charging the peasants a rent independently of the size of the actual harvest*. Peasants were thus transformed into tenants who had an urgent incentive to increase production, reduce cost and sell their produce for a good price at the local market.

Additionally, Britain may have been a more likely breeding ground for the transition to capitalism for a political reason: British landlords, historians tell us, were demilitarised before any other aristocracy. Moreover, the English state was uniquely centralised and wary of the power of the local gentry. Thus, the British aristocracy was becoming increasingly dependent on charging rent, as a means of enrichment, rather than on physical coercion. They used as a weapon not their henchmen's armour but purely *economic* instruments. And as the rent rose, fewer peasants could afford to pay it. Those who were not expelled from the estates were turned into wage labourers employed by other tenants. A whole new economic chain was thus created: The Lords' higher rent pressurised the tenants (i) to cut costs and enter the local markets in pursuit of customers, and (ii) to increase the productivity and reduce the wages of the wage labourers. By the time the landless peasants, who had moved to the towns foreshadowing urbanisation, had been metamorphosed into an army of industrial workers operating the factories, the increases in agricultural workers' productivity made it possible to sustain a large and increasing non-agricultural population.

In summary, the heavy concentration of British agricultural land in a few aristocratic hands, as well as the centralisation of political power in London, created a pattern where both Lords and their tenants became highly dependent on market success for their preservation. By contrast, in France where rents were nominal and the aristocracy continued to rely on the forced expropriation of the peasants' harvest, no such reliance on markets existed. Add to this account the effects of the British domination of the major sea routes and of the rivers of wealth produced by the African slaves in the Caribbean, and a plausible explanation emerges of Britain as the birthplace of the first truly market society. Is it then any wonder why it was also in Britain that political economics became established as the new science of society?

2.4 Epilogue

Our species' *Second Leap Forward* was a chaotic and rather unsavoury affair. Centuries of feudal tranquillity were ruptured. The commodification of land caused massive expulsions, destroyed communities, turned villages into slums, inflamed strife and fuelled intolerance. The commodification of labour spewed out a miserable working class at home and a tragic trade in enslaved humanity across the Atlantic. The smoky new factories, consuming masses of coal, wool, steel and human pain, produced commodities that would conquer the world, combat prejudice, annul communities, inspire scientists, give rise to the new idolatry of possessive individualism and, at the same time, break the back of feudal despotism and bring down its resistance to change. Wealth and misery were, in almost equal measure, artefacts of this revolution. Progress and depravity streamed off the production line in unison.

Box 2.4 Tilting at dark satanic mills

Don Quixote is widely hailed as the last gasp of a bygone era; a romantic leftover who took it to himself to fight for the preservation of chivalry in the face of modernisation. His tilting at windmills is often mistaken as the mindless gesture of an idealist who has lost his marbles. But the windmill was not a random target. It symbolised the machine whose time was approaching. It encapsulated deep-seated anxieties over mechanised labour that could go on and on. The Grimm Brothers tell the story of a pot that will produce anything his owner asks for. Unstoppably. An out-of-control pot that ends up flooding the village with porridge; a precursor of Dr Frankenstein's *Thing*; a mechanical creation that ran amok bringing misery to its creators and innocent bystanders alike. Novelist Margaret Atwood[1] recalls a staging of the opera *Don Quijote*, by Cristóbal Halffter, in which the mills are played by newspaper presses incessantly churning out fabricated news. Long before that, poet William Blake had famously written:

> *And did those feet in ancient time,*
> *Walk upon Englands mountains green:*
> *And was the Holy Lamb of God,*
> *On Englands pleasant pastures seen!*
>
> *And did the Countenance Divine,*
> *Shine forth upon our clouded hills?*
> *And was Jerusalem builded here,*
> *Among these dark Satanic Mills?*

(Blake (1804 [1993]), p. 213)

Blake's dark satanic mills are none other than the industrial revolution's factories. In fact, one of the first factories was known as Albion Flour Mills, built around 1769 by Matthew Bolton and powered by one of James Watt's first 'fire engines' (as the steam engines were then known). The mills that Don Quixote galloped towards were, thus, an early proxy for the workshop, the steam engine, the factory, the robotic arms of automated car assembly plants, the genetic cloning technologies; all those human artefacts that fascinate and scare us, which promise to liberate us but which we fear may, underhandedly, enslave us. In short, it would be a mistake to think that modernity was welcomed with open arms.

Note
1 See her remarkable recent CBC Massey Lecture that she delivered in 2008 under the title *Payback – Debt and the Shadow Side of Wealth.*

Staring into that bleak chaos, Adam Smith discerned patterns of a bright future. Unlike moralists who wailed from the rooftops about the sinfulness of commodification, or the imperative to resist Mammon and return to God, this moral philosopher proclaimed that the cacophony of the globalising industrial world was no more than the birth pains of the impending *Good Society*. The march of the market into all realms of human activity, from food production to moneylending, education, entertainment, housing; the conversion of goods, such as wool, land and labour, into commodities on offer to the highest bidder; this transformation of a world of *use values* into an empire of *exchange values*, was establishing in Smith's eyes a 'system of freedom' as 'natural' as that of the solar system.

Human greed no longer had to be tempered by sermons and moralising. Commodification made competition possible and competition, according to Smith, is a grand conspirator who turns the individual trader's penchant for profit into minimal prices and maximal quantities for all to enjoy. Selfishness, possessiveness and usury could now, all of a sudden, be harnessed as major progressive forces that, in spite (or, possibly, *because*) of their inherent ugliness, would lead society to wholesale wellbeing.

Private vices were thus proclaimed as the initiators of public virtues.[14] Our vices are bound to deliver this miracle when indulged inside a robust, un-tampered yet civil competitive market in which they clash with one another and, like feuding Mafiosi, exhaust themselves until they are emptied of their sinister content. Cleansed from greed, they become sources of purified energy that ushers prosperity into our homes and communities. Thus, the market's unplanned mechanism connives, unbeknownst to all, and led by some 'invisible hand', to spawn a glorious collective enterprise out of the vermin-like intentions of its individual participants.

Smith's story soothed his readers. It gave them hope that beneath all the madness there was reason; that lurking inside the factories' chimneys, which were cleaned nightly by eight-year-old children unlikely to live past the age of 18, there was hope of a better life for all; that the pervasive profit motive was a precursor of finer values. At the time of writing our book, the world is, again, in dire need of soothing. Following the *Crash of 2008*, hundreds of millions the world over have lost their jobs, their houses, their hope. The way Adam Smith found evidence of light in the depths of his age's abyss is instructive for us *today*. Economics is, to an important degree, a kind of storytelling. And storytelling, since at least Homer, played a crucial role not only in stabilising communities but also in spearheading radical change. It is in this sense that studying today the 'stories' told by the classical political economists of yesteryear offers insights into our present woes and possibilities which are simply not available in the pages of contemporary textbooks.

This chapter began with economic theory's predilection for *lost truths* and *Inherent Error*. In the next two chapters, we shall seek out both while perusing the narratives of the French Physiocrats, Adam Smith, David Ricardo, Thomas Robert Malthus and Karl Marx. As we shall see, each one of them understood certain important truths that have since been lost. Our aim is to retrieve these *lost truths* and press them into service in a bid to explain our very own, post-*2008*, world. We shall also revisit economics' *Inherent Error* to which we alluded when using Aristotle as an example; namely, the elemental fact that *no* economic model or theory has a convincing theory of value to offer, while at the same time telling a convincing story about economic growth (i.e. about the dynamic by which a society's surplus is increasing). This realisation will come in handy later when we assess the effects of economists' underhanded ways of *forcing* a consistent theory of value upon their own analysis (which their own premises cannot logically support). Without giving the plot away, it suffices to allude to our forthcoming claim that the valuation of financial instruments (e.g. the CDS), which led to the recent credit crunch and the ensuing economic catastrophe, was based on formulae which assumed away the *Inherent Error*.

Lastly, let us conclude the present chapter with an unlikely historical figure; that of Spartacus. His mythical stature has little to do with the military skills he displayed as the leader of an army of slaves audacious enough to take on the might of Rome. Rather, he personified the liberation of slaves from *Condorcet's Secret*; from the beliefs which had hitherto maintained a culture of quasi-voluntary submission to the *social power* of their Roman owners. Unlike physics, which is not an integral part of that which it tries to explain, social science is indeed part of its own subject matter. As social scientists, we assess existing belief systems but also contribute significantly to them with our proclamations on *how* 'things' are and *what* can be done about them.[15]

Social theory is intertwined with the reality that is its subject matter. In this sense, economics can do two things, sometimes at once: it can solidify the current social order, by supplying reasons why it is 'natural', and thus in synch with justice and the higher values; or it can undermine it, by pointing out its irrationality. It can side with Spartacus or it can side with Crassus. Our objective in the pages that follow is a little subtler: it is to shine a light on *Condorcet's Secret* in its current guise; to illuminate the manner in which *social power* over the production and distribution of the surplus is exercised globally and locally; to show that the *Crash of 2008* and its repercussions cannot be understood without liberating our minds from the illusions that economics has helped to create and which have contributed copiously to the current crisis. To do this, we need to start at the beginning: at the moment in history when the first theories regarding the production and distribution of surpluses appeared on the scene.

3 The odd couple

The struggle to square a theory of value with a theory of growth

3.1 Foreshadowing capitalism: The French Physiocrats

Stockpiles of fine food, superior wine and rare delicacies have always provided the stuff of dreams. Rich and poor, king and peasant, the pious and the ungodly, have all dreamt of a life (or, sometimes, an afterlife) of plenty and an age of abundance that would permanently exile want and scarcity to a distant memory. Roman emperors understood well that their reign depended upon the imported grain surpluses essential for keeping the Roman mob in the style of 'bread and circuses' to which they had been accustomed. Later, while Islam was spreading from Bagdad to Toledo, and the ancient texts of Euclid and Aristotle were being salvaged, translated, studied and improved upon by the Caliphates' sages, paradise was actively imagined not as a state of wisdom and knowledge but as one replete with massive surpluses of rice, flour and honey.[1] Moreover, from the seventeenth century onwards we have a concept of progress in human affairs, particularly in the writings of enlightened mercantilists like Josiah Child, with an expectation of a better life for future generations. 'Power and plenty', a mercantilist motto, had changed perceptions of a life at subsistence level. So, when capitalism exploded upon the scene, sometime in the eighteenth century, the new 'science of surplus', which was necessary to explain the unfolding tumult, was bound to begin by placing stockpiled food at the centre of its inquiry.

François Quesnay (1694–1774), the undisputed head of the French, and indeed first, school of political economics known as *The Physiocrats*, did precisely that, organising his thoughts on the new market economy around the notion of an agricultural surplus. Indeed, at that time, it was almost natural to imagine that surplus only came from the land following the efforts of those who worked it. All other professions, ranging from the priest even to the artisan, seemed to live parasitically off the surplus produced by the tillers of the soil.[2] Even today, the visitor to France gets a whiff of the spirit that gave Quesnay his predilection for placing agriculture at the heart of his economics; a sentimental attachment to traditional food production that is absent in Britain, Germany and the rest of the industrialised north.

Of course, there was nothing new in Quesnay's prioritisation of the agricultural sector. What was *genuinely* path-breaking was that he chose to analyse the production and distribution of agricultural surplus in the context of a *commodified economy* which relied upon markets for the distribution of land, labour and food between the various claimants. It was, of course, inevitable: as the old nexus between political and economic power was breaking down, and economic power was distancing itself from the allocation of ancient privileges; as land and labour were commodifying fast, and increasing portions of the surplus were being traded in markets (as opposed to being appropriated by brute force or conventionally), it was only a matter of time before some thinker would seize the day and come up with an *economic theory* that looks at surplus production and distribution as market-driven phenomena.

At a time when the *Enlightenment* was flexing its considerable intellectual muscles in Europe, and the French Revolution was in train, the new 'science' of society inevitably tried to discover 'natural laws' governing the marketplace, emulating as well as it could physics, chemistry and astronomy. True to form, the Physiocrats thought that market exchanges were subject to objective laws independent of our desires and impervious to the will of peasants and gentry alike. *Physiocracy* literally meant the 'rule of nature'. *In the beginning*, they opined, *there was surplus*, the *produit net*, as they called it; and surplus was a divine gift that, unlike manna from heaven, grew from under our feet. Once men and women received the land's bequest, only then would market exchanges commence, setting into motion laws as dispassionate and rational as those that governed the elliptical trajectory of the Moon around the Earth.

Nowadays, it is absurd to think of economic surplus as made up uniquely of foodstuffs.[3] While it remains true that without an agricultural surplus no urban life would be possible, the identification of surplus with agriculture is nonsensical. As the great factories of China, the high technology companies of Silicon Valley, the German machine tools sector, Japan's car industry and Italy's fine design houses keep delivering the output that modern humans crave, it would be absurd to argue that surplus emerges only from cultivating the land and husbanding animals. However, back in the eighteenth century, industry was still embryonic and the most coveted goods came from the farms. Identification of surplus with the rural sector was understandable.

In the physiocratic analysis, the national economy was approached as an organism dependent on food as surely as the human body depends on nutrients.[4] Quesnay, France's finest medical doctor, could not but look at the economy of France and discern different 'organs' performing intertwined tasks and depending upon each other for keeping the organism healthy. He used a special device to explain this: the *tableau économique,* first published in 1758, the first ever economic model to which the Physiocrats ascribed almost mystical properties.[5] The main 'organs' were three social classes: the *Aristocrats*, the *Peasants* and the urban *Artisans*.[6] Of those three, only one class was deemed life giving: the peasants who tilled the land. The aristocrats collected rents (i.e., part of the surplus) courtesy of their inherited property rights over the land and consumed as food part of that rent, selling the remainder to the towns to buy products from the town-dwelling artisans who could not grow food and were thus labelled 'sterile'. The peasants, the only non-parasitic fertile or 'productive' class, also purchased tools and other manufactures from the towns to which they would have to sell part of their share of the surplus in food and materials. Figure 3.1 captures this circular flow that commences at the point the harvest is brought in.

To sum up, the Physiocrats' analysis involved three social classes and two sectors, of which only one, agriculture, produces a surplus over and above: (a) the subsistence requirements of the population, and (b) the seeds that need to be produced for future production to be maintained. This type of model was novel and proved useful in the centuries to follow. Karl Marx was the first theorist to take up the challenge of developing it further (the infamous *schemas of reproduction*) before twentieth-century theorists John von Neumann, Wassily Leontief and Piero Sraffa turned the same type of model into what is today known as *input–output analysis*.[7]

The physiocratic analysis was ahead of its time. Like all pioneers, the Physiocrats foresaw much that the rest would take ages to discern; but also they erred in thinking that the changes they had detected in the wind had already taken place. They saw land and labour as commodities before they were fully commodified. They foresaw capitalism but insisted in analysing feudalism as if it had already transformed itself out of existence and into a

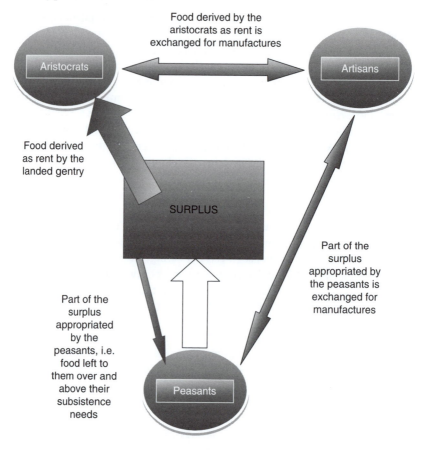

Peasants are the only 'productive' class since their labour is the only type of human effort directly contributing to the generation of the surplus (notice the sole white arrow feeding into surplus). Rent is extracted by the Aristocrats and part of it is exchanged for manufactures with the Artisans, who also exchange with the Peasants qualtities of manufactures for part of their surplus.[8]

Figure 3.1 The physiocratic *tableau économique*.

Box 3.1 The input–output model underlying the Physiocrats' analysis

Input–output models portray economic activity as the production of goods by means of other goods. Each good requires as inputs some of the economy's other goods and, often, some of its own substance, e.g. corn requires tractors but also some leftover corn to be used as seed. Of course, not all goods are necessary for the production of each good (e.g. corn does not require perfume as an input). Additionally, not all inputs are also outputs. For instance, land is not usually produced (except perhaps in the Netherlands where it was reclaimed from the sea). Similarly, labour: while it also depends on produced goods for its reproduction (as workers must eat and be clothed if they are to labour), it is not an output of some production line (unlike in Aldous Huxley's dystopic vision of a futuristic *Brave New World* in which low-grade humans are produced as the output of a particular economic system).

All this can be depicted in the form of a table or *Matrix*, see below, where the rows represent inputs and the columns outputs. The fact that not all inputs are outputs explains why there are more rows than columns. In the example below, we have constructed such a table in accordance with the *tableau*: corn is a necessary input for the production of more corn but not for the production of manufactures. Manufactured tools, in contrast, are required to produce both corn and more manufactures. To be precise, suppose that it takes $\gamma_1(<1)$ units of corn to produce 1 unit of corn, $\gamma_2(<1)$ units of manufactures to produce 1 unit of corn, and $\mu_2(<1)$ units of manufactures to produce 1 unit of manufactures. Suppose also that it takes $\gamma_3(<1)$ units of land and $\gamma_4(<1)$ units of peasant labour to produce 1 unit of corn and $\mu_3(<1)$ units of land and $\mu_5(<1)$ units of artisan labour to produce 1 unit of manufactures. In summary,

	Corn	Manufactures
Corn	γ_1	0
Manufactures	γ_2	μ_2
Land	γ_3	μ_3
Peasant labour	γ_4	0
Artisan labour	0	μ_5

As the Physiocrats were thinking of all this activity as market driven, and of the inputs and outputs involved as commodities, it was 'natural' that they would seek out the 'objective laws' governing the prices of these inputs and outputs. Suppose that:

p_c is the price of each unit of corn
p_m is the price of each unit of manufactured output
r is the rental charge per unit of land
w_p the wage per unit of peasant labour
w_a the wage per unit of artisan labour

Given the input–output table above, the cost of each unit of corn C_c and the cost C_m of each unit of manufactured output equal $C_c = p_c\gamma_1 + p_m\gamma_2 + r\gamma_3 + w_p\gamma_4$ and $C_m = p_c\mu_1 + p_m\mu_2 + r\mu_3 + w_a\mu_5$ respectively. For this economy to generate a surplus, it must be the case that the two sectors manage not only to cover their per unit costs but, in fact, to do a little better than that. While the Physiocrats did not get that far analytically, it is quite straightforward to extend their thinking by suggesting that the condition for this economy to grow, that is to have a surplus, is simply that the price of each unit of output exceeds its cost. Or that, $p_c > C_c = p_c\gamma_1 + p_m\gamma_2 + r\gamma_3 + w_p\gamma_4$ and $p_m > C_m = p_c\mu_1 + p_m\mu_2 + r\mu_3 + w_a\mu_5$. In short, the conditions for a growing economy are:

$$p_c > \frac{p_m\gamma_2 + r\gamma_3 + w_p\gamma_4}{1-\gamma_1} \qquad p_m > \frac{p_c\mu_1 + r\mu_3 + w_a\mu_5}{1-\mu_2}$$

species of capitalism. Their great contribution was to suggest a sectoral economic analysis that identified surplus as the engine of growth and sought to explain its production and distribution in the context of a market society which is divided into three distinct social classes and where money payments to workers and suppliers are *advanced*, thus correctly attributing to *credit* an important role that would not reappear properly in economics for at least a century.

Their Achilles' heel was that they thought in terms of a market society before the market had a chance to fully penetrate society; before labour was separated from the land and therefore, before the labour of landless workers could be commodified and put into 'flexible' use, not only on the land but also in the workshops, in the mines, in the factories supplied by the mines and on the ships in which the surplus would be taken to the four corners of the map. That they thought of surplus only in terms of agriculture was a reflection of their wonderful confusion: of trying to imagine a capitalist present, complete with 'objective laws', before industrialisation and the French Revolution had made it possible. Lest we become too critical of their error, let us not neglect that modern mainstream economics posits an almost socialist society as the foundation on which it erects its theories of contemporary capitalism.[9] Mistaking the present for some imagined ideal that may or may not come to pass is, therefore, not a unique feature of the physiocratic outlook. It is also a very contemporary fallacy. One that, we shall argue, contributed significantly to the *Crash of 2008*.

Box 3.2 A critical celebration of the Physiocrats – by Karl Marx

The analysis of capital, within the bourgeois horizon, is essentially the work of the Physiocrats. It is this service that makes them the true fathers of modern political economy. In the first place, the analysis of the various material components in which capital exists and into which it resolves itself in the course of the labour process. It is not a reproach to the Physiocrats that, like all their successors, they thought of these material forms of existence – such as tools, raw materials, etc. – as capital, in isolation from the social conditions in which they appear in capitalist production; in a word, in the form in which they are elements of the labour process in general, independently of its social form – and thereby made of the capitalist form of production an eternal, natural form of production. For them the bourgeois forms of production necessarily appeared as natural forms. It was their great merit that they conceived these forms as physiological forms of society – as forms arising from the natural necessity of production itself, forms that are independent of anyone's will or of politics, etc. They are material laws, the error is only that the material law of a definite historical social stage is conceived as an abstract law governing equally all forms of society…

  The first condition for the development of capital is the separation of landed property from labour – the emergence of land, the primary condition of labour, as an independent force, a force in the hands of a separate class, confronting the free labourer. The Physiocrats therefore present the landowner as the true capitalist… Feudalism is thus portrayed and explained from the viewpoint of bourgeois production; agriculture is treated as the branch of production in which capitalist production… exclusively appears. While feudalism is thus made bourgeois, bourgeois society is given a feudal semblance.

Karl Marx, (1863 [1963]), 1:44 (vol. 1, ch. 2.)

Returning one last time to the Physiocrats, the fact that in the 1750s, French agriculture had already developed certain capitalist features (e.g. the payment of rent to the landowners), and with an eye to large-scale capitalist agriculture across the Channel, was enough for them to foreshadow a theory of capitalism but not enough to allow them a glimpse of a fully fledged capitalism whose capacity to produce enormous surplus would be grounded not on the land but *in the factories*.

3.2 Re-imagining surplus and value: Adam Smith's musings

The British classical economists, Adam Smith and David Ricardo, shifted the focus from the land to the workshop; from the muddy soil and the horse driven plough to the factory's grey walls and its noisy steam engines. In contrast to the Physiocrats, they lived in a country where the combined effect of *commodification and industrialisation* had a head start compared to France or Germany; a head start that caused its political economists to see before anyone else that which the Physiocrats had failed to recognise: that society's *surplus arises from the use of productive labour in any branch of production*, not only in agriculture, and that, consequently, *surplus is intimately linked to profit*.

Adam Smith went to great pains, from the first pages of his *Wealth of Nations*, to impress upon his reader the idea that the production of pins generates a surplus just as much as the production of wheat does. The realisation that surplus oozes out of every pore of an industrial society, agricultural and non-agricultural alike, placed limitations on the economists' imagination that could only be overcome conceptually and by means of new analytical categories. For, unlike the wheat surplus, which *can* be imagined as a large pile in some warehouse (of a size that exceeds the population's basic human needs), no such visualisation is possible in the case of the surplus resulting from the pin industry. All of a sudden, the theorist had to find some other concept by which to fathom an industrial society's surplus. British political economists chose the concept of *profit* and proceeded to identify it with an advanced market society's heterogeneous surplus.

Their point was simple: if the surplus generated by non-agricultural sectors (e.g. the pin factory) is to be grasped, let alone measured, the profit generated therein is the only sensible indication of a surplus.[10] Consider a bag of pins selling for one Pound. How much of that Pound reflects the bag's 'true' *value*, so that we can compute the residual or profit retained by the entrepreneur? Unless we have a *theory of value*, we have no theory of profit and, consequently, not a clue as to the size or composition of the surplus or of the relative contribution of labour and capital to its production. So here is the rub: to understand the surplus of an industrialised society in profit terms, one needs a *theory of profit* which, in turn, requires a prior *theory of value*.

The deeper reason why a *theory of value* is a prerequisite for a *theory of profit*, and thus for an apt measure of surplus, is simple: a modern economy's total output requires contributions from land, labour, machines and raw materials. In that sense, total income is made up of *rent* (which pays for land use), *wages* (which reward workers for their time) and the remainder, or residual, which is *profit* and which, naturally, the political economists of the time thought of as the reward to the capitalist for embedding machinery into the production process; for undertaking a risky relationship with bankers (without which they could not have made advances to workers and other suppliers); and generally for organising production.

Profit, in that sense, was seen both as a *return to capital* and a *measure of the market society's surplus*. This recognition was tantamount to an acceptance that, before we can talk about the wealth of a nation, we must have something tangible to say about the value contributed by labour to the nation's surplus as distinct to the value contributed by capital and other factors. The trouble is that the conception of profit *both* as capital's value *and* as a measure of the surplus requires a major fudge. Why this is so is a riddle that will occupy many of the forthcoming pages. For now, we just place a marker to which we shall later refer. Let's label this marker the *riddle of value* or economics' *Inherent Error*.

It is not the first time we come across this riddle. In the previous chapter, we mentioned Aristotle's abortive attempt to articulate such a theory and warned of the *Inherent Error* all economic theories have been carrying in their core to this day. Adam Smith understood the problem well but found, in typically brilliant fashion, a way to bypass it: in quite Aristotelian style,[11] he embarked by noting that '[i]f among a nation of hunters, for example, it usually costs twice the labour to kill a beaver which it does to kill a deer, one beaver should naturally exchange for or be worth two deer' (*Wealth of Nations*, 1776, I.vi, p. 65). Put differently, Smith's hypothesis is that in an economy where the *only* factor or means of production is labour, commodities exchange in proportion to the amount of time required for their production. The so-called *labour theory of value* was, thus, born. Alas, what a problematic infant it turned out to be!

Even before stating the basis of his value theory, Adam Smith warned that this early version of the theory was too crude in that it only held for 'that early and rude state of society which precedes both the accumulation of stock and the appropriation of land' (Smith, 1776, ibid.). In industrialised societies, commodity production depends not only on labour but also on machines, raw materials, different types of land, etc. The multi-sector and multi-factor world presented a major complication to Smith which is best explained in terms of a simple example. Imagine an economy similar to that of Box 3.1 featuring two sectors: one produces an agricultural commodity, say corn, the other manufactures or machines. Suppose further that the production of 10 tons of corn requires:

- 1 unit of corn (in the form of seed)
- 2 units of labour
- 3 machines

while the production of 10 machines requires:

- no corn
- 1 unit of labour
- 6 other machines

Assuming that workers consume corn (and no machines), the wage must be expressed in terms of the amount of corn that workers must be paid for 1 unit of their labour. Assume, for simplicity, that the wage is such that 1 unit of labour is rewarded with 1 unit of corn. Clearly, the inputs into the production of 10 tons of corn are equivalent to 3 units of corn and 3 machines whereas those necessary for the production of 10 machines include 1 unit of corn and 6 machines.

Noting that the production of machines is more machine-intensive than the production of corn, which is more labour-intensive, we reach a worrying conclusion: if we are to stay loyal to Adam Smith's *labour theory of value*, we must conclude that *the exchange value of 10 tons of corn* relative to the value of 10 machines (that is, the relative price of corn) *depends on the wage!* Let's see why. According to Adam Smith, given that the cost of 1 unit of labour is 1 unit of corn, the relative value of corn ought to reflect the ratio

$$R_1 = \frac{\text{total labour it took to produce 3 units of corn and 3 machines}}{\text{total labour it took to produce 1 units of corn and 6 machines}}$$

Suppose however that the cost of labour (i.e. the wage) doubles from 1 unit of corn to 2 units of corn per 1 unit of labour. Then, again according to Adam Smith's *theory of value*, the relative value of corn ought to reflect the ratio

$$R_2 = \frac{\text{total labour it took to produce 5 units of corn and 3 machines}}{\text{total labour it took to produce 2 units of corn and 6 machines}}$$

Quite clearly R_1 and R_2 are two very different values, independently of how much labour has gone into the production of each machine. This means that, *if capital intensity differs across sectors, the value of commodities changes as the distribution of income between labour and capital changes* (i.e. as the wage rate changes relatively to the profit rate).[12]

Adam Smith, upon thinking the above thoughts, immediately saw the threat to his project posed by the *riddle of value*. Like all astute storytellers, he wanted to keep to the point and ensure that his story was not more complicated than it had to be. His basic focus was on wealth creation and its determinants. It was a narrative on what, today, we refer to as a *theory of economic growth*; a theory of the dynamics by which society's wealth, or surplus, grows. Smith was keen to get on with the story of how the combined benevolence of the *division of labour* and of *competition* promises to bring about a prosperous society. But the simple calculation in the previous paragraph threw a spanner in the works of the narrative.

To see this from a slightly different angle, recall how the *Wealth of Nations* famously begins with an account of the *division of labour* spearheading the growth of Britain's economic surplus. In his perceptive eye, both the *division of labour* and the resulting *growth* were fuelled by the elixir of *competition*. For, it is competition among egoistic entrepreneurs which promotes the social interest precisely because the entrepreneurs are so indifferent to whatever that might be.[13] Moved solely by the call of private profit, and speared on by their competitors' perceived actions, capitalists are forced to drop prices to an absolute minimum, employ the best division of labour possible, purchase the more productive machinery and

---

Box 3.3 Smith on capital accumulation

Parsimony, and not industry, is the immediate cause of the increase of capital. Industry, indeed, provides the subject which parsimony accumulates. But whatever industry might acquire, if parsimony did not save and store up, the capital could never be greater. Parsimony, increasing the fund which is destined for the maintenance of productive hands, tends to increase the number of those hands whose labour adds to the value of the subject upon which it is bestowed. It tends, therefore, to increase the exchangeable value of the annual produce of the land and labour of the country. It puts into motion an additional quantity of industry, which gives an additional value to the annual produce.

Adam Smith (1776), Book II, chapter iii, p. 337

reinvest all accrued profit back into the enterprise, aware of the cruel fact that their profits are unsafe and that the only insurance policy against future bankruptcy is the perpetual reduction of average costs through unstoppable investment into cost cutting technologies.

Karl Marx, in his usual swashbuckling prose, offered the following faithful interpretation of Smith's more measured turn of phrase:

> Accumulate, accumulate! That is Moses and the prophets! Industry furnishes the material which savings accumulate.[14] Therefore, save, save, *i.e.*, reconvert the greatest possible portion of surplus-value, or surplus-product, into capital! Accumulation for accumulation's sake, production for production's sake: by this formula classical political economy expressed the historical mission of the bourgeoisie, and did not for a single instant deceive itself over the birth-throes of wealth.
>
> (Marx (1867 [1909], p. 652)

Thus, in Smith's story, competition leads to cheap and abundant goods. With profit from arbitrage (i.e. from buying low and selling high) rendered impossible due to price under-cutting between ruthless entrepreneurs, prices go into free fall. As his background was the Britain of the late eighteenth century, rather than Russia since the 1990s, he thought that rivalry was no longer about duels that end in a pool of blood but market stratagems for splashing red ink all over the competitor's accounts.[15] And price cutting was the weapon of choice. As prices gravitated towards what Smith called their *natural* level (another term for the absolute minimum price that is given by the lowest possible per unit cost), society would be blessed with the best remedy for poverty possible: minimal prices and maximum quantities! Miraculously, as if by the providential guidance of some *invisible hand* (*Wealth of Nations*, IV, ii, p. 456) which put society on a course of less moralising, less hunger, less deprivation and, ultimately, greater prosperity. However, if the distribution of these gifts of competition were to change (e.g. if the proportion of the surplus that went to the working class were to rise or to fall), Smith would have to concede that the value of commodities would also change (recall that ratios R_1 and R_2 differ). But then how could he claim that competition succeeds in keeping prices at their 'natural' level?

This complication was clearly one that Smith could do without. So he did what any econo-mist worth his salt does: he assumed it away! More precisely, Adam Smith assumed that the wage share of the surplus, and thus the distribution of income between workers and capitalists, does *not* change while the economy is growing. In this way, he kept his *theory of growth* sepa-rate from his *theory of value*.[16] His manoeuvre around economics' *Inherent Error* came at a price: a silent admission that his narrative cannot explain the wealth of any nation whose social classes experience fluctuations in their share of that wealth. Nevertheless, to his credit, Smith did not pretend to have produced an economics of mathematical exactness and general applica-tion. He told a story about wealth creation and let his readers decide whether, and to what extent, it made sense. If only modern economists had the same integrity they might have avoided spending the last four decades cloaking the profession's *Inherent Error* in multiple veils of pseudo-scientific complexity of the type that contributed so generously to the *Crash of 2008*.

3.3 Value and the social power of non-producers: David Ricardo's anxieties

David Ricardo was unimpressed with Smith's solution to the value question. Writing in the midst of the Napoleonic wars and their aftermath which disrupted corn imports and raised corn prices immensely, Ricardo had witnessed, right in front of his eyes, large-scale changes in the very distribution of wages, rent and profit which Smith had assumed time invariant. Corn prices had risen, subsistence wages paid in corn had followed suit (so that workers could continue to subsist) and that rise had cut deeply into the capitalists' profit. Even worse, these changes, on the back of their negative impact on investment, had clearly retarded overall economic growth causing one of capitalism's early recessions.

Ricardo's anxieties may have been initially caused by the disturbing observation of land-owners gathering 'undeserved' wealth and by his outrage at their campaign to impose *import restrictions* after the war had ended; a campaign whose cynical objective was to extend the gentry's wartime windfall well into peacetime. However, his worries soon acquired a more abstract, theoretical complexion. Taking Adam Smith's narrative on economic growth to its natural conclusion, he predicted that corn prices, and therefore subsistence wages, would rise *inevitably*; even in the absence of wars or tariffs. The reason? As economic growth boosts employment, and more workers require more corn just to show up at the factory gates every morning, more and more land would have to be cultivated. *Ergo*, land of *decreasing fertility* would have to come into production, thereby increasing not only the cost (and thus the price) of corn but, more worryingly, amplifying the difference between the cost of the most and least productive land as well.

This differential (between the highest and lowest cost of corn production) is due to physical attributes of the land (i.e. the different fertility of different plots of land) that neither the division of labour nor the power of competition can do anything about. Indeed, if any-thing, it is a differential that would increase in time as the division of labour advances, competition intensifies, the economy grows and, ultimately, the demand for corn swells. Ricardo's anxiety was that, as this differential expands (i.e. the more relatively infertile land is ploughed to meet the population's expanding demand), an increasing share of the surplus would be siphoned off into the pockets of the landlords and out of the virtuous circle of wealth creation.

Suppose, for example, that the cost of producing one unit of corn on fertile land belonging to Lord Scrooge is $10 but that only a limited output Q is possible on his land. If demand is low enough to be satisfied by production on land similar in fertility to Lord Scrooge's, com-petition between corn producers will keep the price hovering around $10. However, as demand expands, less fertile land will enter production, say at $X per unit of corn (with X>10). Growth means more demand and more demand means a rising X − 10 difference, which is fantastic news for Lord Scrooge and his ilk but a burden on everyone else. The Lord's net revenues, given by $(X − 10)Q, rise at a rate which is analogous to the rate of increase in the price of corn, $X, while, all along, his cost remains the same. This increasing gap diverts towards Lord Scrooge an increasing share of the surplus which Ricardo called *rent*.

But what is wrong with the rich landowners getting richer? Why is it OK for the factory owner to make a profit but problematic when a landowner retains rent? Because profit and rent have different *natures* and play different *roles* in society, bellows Ricardo. While both profit and rent are residuals left over after costs have been met, rent has *nothing* to do with investment, innovation or entrepreneurship but, instead, constitutes a windfall for the land-owner which he owes *solely* to the accident of birth that bestowed upon him property rights over the most fertile land. So, profits and rents are two wholly different species of economic variable, even if identical from an accounting point of view. Turning to their different *roles*, profit incites its claimant (the merchant–entrepreneur–industrialist) to re-invest it whereas rent does no such thing: while rent is a windfall safe from competition (since no amount of innovation by Lord Scrooge's competitors can produce land of equal fertility to his), the industrialist's profit is constantly threatened by wily competitors scheming to eat into it with new products, lower prices, better quality, etc.

So, fear of bankruptcy motivates the industrialist to plug his profits straight back into productive use (better technology, products, division of labour, etc.) while Lord Scrooge, untouched by the angst of competition, hoards his rents or spends it on trinkets and activities, such as patronising the universities and the arts, which do nothing to boost the economy's productive powers. Rents, in this Ricardian perspective, are a brake on growth with a braking power that gets *worse* the stronger the economy's productive forces. From an 'organic' viewpoint, the aristocracy are acting like a reckless virus which attacks its hosts with such virulence that it runs the risk of becoming extinct as a result of killing them all. Unable to limit their ill effects on the healthy organism on which they are dependent, landowners will continue to harvest rents until capitalism's dynamism withers.

That was Ricardo's nightmare. Its lasting legacy is an important contribution to political economics which highlights the chain linking growth, value and the distribution of income between those who produce and those who have disproportionate social power over the output. As it turned out (see below), Ricardo's valiant plunge into the growth–value–distribution nexus pushed him deeply into the messy entanglement that we, in the previous chapter, foreshadowed as economics' *Inherent Error*. And yet Ricardo's economics, while messier than Smith's, packs important insights for *our* time; a time when the world's surplus is harvested to such a great extent by various groups (oil barons, bankers, financial engineers, etc.) whose claim to have contributed to its creation is at least as tenuous as that of the landowners whom Ricardo so valiantly opposed.

Our foray into Ricardo's deeper economic thinking thus begins with his hunch that when rents rise, wages must follow suit, cutting into profits, depressing investment and capital accumulation and, subsequently, trimming down, if not reversing, economic growth. To make his point in a consistent manner, Ricardo took a leaf out of the Physiocrats by evoking a fictitious single commodity economy. The so-called *corn model*! Why was corn placed at the heart of his model of capitalism? While it could have been some other good, corn had its advantages: *first*, it constituted the basic staple diet of the British workers at the time and the battleground on which landowners were fighting a political battle against the rest of British society for the preservation of their privileges.[17] *Second*, in view of corn's political and dietary centrality, it was hard to imagine the growth of Britain's surplus without imagining a growing corn surplus. And because labour was an input into *all* produced commodities (agricultural, industrial, services, etc.), with the wage its reward, expressing the wage in terms of the amount of corn each worker would take home weekly made it possible for corm to be conceived of as an input into all types of economic activity. *Last*, corn's capacity to be its own input (with corn seed being necessary for future corn output) allowed a parallel story to be told, also based on the corn metaphor, about *capital* and its *accumulation* (i.e. a theory of *investment*).

Compare the allegorical utility of corn as a metaphor for capital with that of, say, gold. In principle, there is no reason why gold cannot take centrestage, displacing from our imagination the stockpiles of food, wine and honey with which heaven had been traditionally associated. Although Midas's plight offers a poignant warning against this displacement, it came from a bygone era that preceded commodification and which had been sceptical of the worship of profit. The emergence of market societies from the ashes of the *ancien régime* made possible a freshly legitimate yearning for *money as an end-in-itself*, the best and most graphic depiction of which is Disney's Scrooge McDuck and his ecstatic plunges into a vast pool of golden coins. Nevertheless, despite the rise of Mammon as a legitimate deity and the new possibilities for imagining gold stashes as the stuff of heaven, corn could not be bested as the political economists' *basic commodity*. For, it was not only impossible, even for Scrooge McDuck, to live without it, but it also possessed a mystical capacity that no gold, platinum or diamond could muster: corn required corn (in seed form) for its production while gold and the other symbols of ostentatious wealth could be produced without a smidgeon of their own substance.

Gold was, indeed, dug up by miners who depended on corn, hence gold production necessitated corn as an input; but corn did not need gold at any stage of its production. Generally, corn seemed to enter (through the wage) into the production of *every* commodity, but not every commodity entered into the production of corn. In this view, corn was deemed the *basic commodity* whose production determined how lucrative gold digging might be. This unlikely dependence of the gold industry on its far less glamorous corn counterpart made perfect analytical sense once it was realised that the point about a basic commodity, like corn, is that the rate of profit extracted by its producers determines the rate of profit in the other sectors (including the gold mining sector). Meanwhile, the profit rates of most other sectors (e.g. that of gold) were immaterial to the rate of profit in the corn sector. It was in light of this asymmetry that the corn sector came to be seen as *the* crucial sector and its product could be imagined as a form of all-purpose currency. In other words, choosing corn as his basic commodity gave Ricardo an analytical fulcrum. It allowed him to express the profit rate *in natural terms* bypassing the problem of value in computing the profit rate. Since the profit rate was – through competition – uniform in all sectors of the economy, he could use the profit rate in the agricultural sector as a standard to compute the values in other sectors of the economy.

The British political economists were enamoured of the *corn model* because it allowed them to highlight the conditions for a sustainable (or reproducible) economy and, by extension, the conditions under which an economy grows. Since the overall output of corn cannot be less than the sum of the amounts needed (a) for replanting *plus* (b) for paying the wages of those who work throughout the economy, corn promised to help measure the surplus without assuming (as the Physiocrats had done) that only agriculture is productive and responsible for a market society's surplus. In short, corn promised to deliver the Holy Grail of economic thinking: a combined *theory of the surplus* (and its growth or accumulation) and a *theory of value*.

To see how that combined theory was put together, let us begin with a feature of the *corn model* which greatly simplified any analysis based on it: it left no room for *uncertainty*, save that caused by weather fluctuations. More precisely, in an economy where all payments are made in corn, and corn is at once a consumption good *and* a capital good, it makes no sense to pile corn up (except as a precautionary measure against the possibility of drought or flood). Abstaining from both eating corn and replanting it only makes sense if one is worried about weather fluctuations. So, an uncertain weather aside, any reduction in consumption (i.e. any savings) leads the corn economy to increase investment (in the form of more corn seed to be ploughed back into the land). In this sense, the corn model gave short shrift to any worries that capitalists might hoard profit (i.e. neither consume) instead of investing it. In a corn economy, saving is, therefore, tantamount to investment and abstinence is synonymous with growth: a simple conclusion which fitted nicely into David Ricardo's theoretical project of portraying, and studying, capitalism as an economy where the only threat to growth is rising nominal wages due to the encroachments of rent and to the parasitic landowners who claim it.

The simple *corn model* in Box 3.4 captures Ricardo's core theory of growth and of the distribution of income.[18] Its political-*cum*-economic implication could not be simpler: in a competitive economy, the only impediment to growth is a rise in the wage share of the surplus.

And since workers could not raise wages above subsistence (at a time when masses of unemployed people roved the land and no trade unions or pro-labour government intervention was thinkable), the only threats to growth were increases in the price of wage goods, like grain, and the concomitant hike in landlords' rent. More generally, Ricardo's scheme leads to the conclusion that an increase in real wages reduces net corn savings (since the workers consume more corn) and pushes down both capital accumulation and the profit rate. This is the simple message of the corn model where the distribution between wages and profits governs the pattern of accumulation and growth.

Box 3.4 Growth and the distribution of income in a pure corn economy

In an economy where corn is a one-commodity show (e.g. it is at once an output, an input *and* the currency in which savings, investment, wages, rents and profits are measured and advanced), there is no room for money. To make the analysis even simpler, suppose that corn is the only commodity; and that we have a one-sector economy. Let K be the stock of the economy's corn capital and suppose that S is the corn saved at the end of a period, while D is the quantity of corn that needs to be set aside as seed for next period just to keep corn stocks steady (in more contemporary parlance D is the amount of corn that must be put aside to cover for the corn capital's depreciation. *We have fully circulating capital and the rate of depreciation is equal to 1*). What happens then is that S is invested (since there is no sense in hoarding corn that no one is eating), and constitutes the net increase in corn capital K. In short $S = \Delta K = I$ or $S_t = K_t - K_{t-1} = I$, where I is investment. Growth, in this economy, means a growing stock of capital K which, inescapably, produces a growing surplus.

Taking the analysis further, it is easy to show that, in this pure corn economy, first, profits and wages move in the opposite direction and second, the rate of profit equals the rate of capital accumulation (or the rate at which capital K is increasing).

Letting,

- Q be corn output
- α be the quantity of corn produced per unit of corn capital
- L be the number of labour units involved in corn production
- $\lambda = L / K$ be labour per unit of corn capital (i.e. the amount of labour that each unit of capital requires to work with in order to be productive)
- w the wage per unit corn (i.e. the wage, in corn, that the worker must receive to participate in the production of one unit of corn). We assume that workers do not save and that they consume their wage.
- $W = wL$ the wages (in corn) of all workers put together
- Π the total profits (expressed also in corn) by the capitalists who organise production. All the profits are invested.
- $\pi = \Pi / K$ the ratio of total profit to total capital; that is, the capitalists' rate of profit, we establish the following relations between the different quantities of corn:

$$Q = \alpha K \tag{3.1}$$

$$Q = W + D + \Pi = \lambda w K + D + \Pi \tag{3.2}$$

Combining (3.1) and (3.2) we get:

$$\Pi = (\alpha - \lambda w)\, K - D \tag{3.3}$$

But since corn seed capital is used up each season and the next season's seeds must come from the previous harvest, $D = K$ and (3.3) is simplified as (3.4) below:

$$\Pi = (\alpha - \lambda w - 1)K \tag{3.4}$$

Since the rate of profit is $\pi = \Pi / K$ *equation (3.4) gives*

$$\pi = \alpha - \lambda w - 1 \tag{3.5}$$

The meaning of equation (3.5) is straightforward: the rate of profits π on corn is given by the difference between the output per unit of corn capital α, the wage cost per unit of labour applied to corn capital λw, and the rate of depreciation taken as being equal to 1 because of the assumption of fully circulating capital. Equation (3.5) describes the net surplus of corn per unit of corn capital. The equation defines also the pattern of the distribution of income between the rate of profit and the wage rate. It shows that, for any given value of α and λ, the rate of profit moves in the opposite direction to the wage rate, which, indeed, carries a negative a sign.

Now since all surplus (profits) is saved and invested, and since all wages are spent on consumption $S = I = \Pi$, and

$$S / K = I / K = \Pi / K \tag{3.6}$$

Π / K is π, the rate of profit, and I/K is net investment over corn capital, which, by definition, is the increase in the capital itself. Capital increases only by means of investment.

Since $S = \Delta K = I$, (3.6) becomes

$\pi = \Pi / K = \Delta K / K = g$, where g is the growth rate, or

$\pi = g$

The rate of profit is therefore equal to the rate of increase of capital, that is, to the rate of growth of capital or, in a different terminology, to the rate of capital accumulation. The conclusion is that if all profits and no wages are saved, the rate of profit is equal to the rate of growth.

Conclusion

As the total profit Π is analogous to capital K, the rate of profit $\pi = \Pi / K = (\alpha - \lambda w - 1$ is inversely related to the wage rate w while positively related to labour productivity improvements (i.e. to reductions in λ) and the rate of profits is equal to the rate of growth.

The pressing question however is: how does this theory extend to multi-sector economies? Clearly, a theory of growth in which *the* profit rate is assumed to equal the rate of capital accumulation will simply not do in a multi-sector, or multi-commodity, world. The reason is twofold: (a) there are now *many* different profit rates (one per sector); and (b) there are relative values, or prices, in dire need of explanation. How did Ricardo deal with this *riddle of value* while maintaining a theory of growth?

Influenced by Smith, David Ricardo claims that competition ensures four things at once: *first*, it helps equalise profit rates across all sectors.[19] *Second*, it does the same with wage rates.[20] *Third*, it causes capitalists to save all profits and invest them in capital goods (e.g. machinery, innovations) so as not to fall behind the competition and end up bankrupt due to higher average costs. *Fourth*, it ensures that the prices of all commodities gravitate towards their intrinsic (or true) values and that these values are proportional to the amount of labour expended in their production.

Note that these four feats attributed to competition assumed that the economic system operated on the basis of a long-run Newtonian gravitational field towards stationary positions at which all the forces of competition would have worked themselves out, thereby bringing about the rule of the cost minimising techniques and, with it, the rule of uniform rates of profit. In this way, it was assumed, day-to-day variations in the conditions of supply and demand are just incidental to the fundamental laws of 'economic gravity'. The separation between the determination of the values of commodities and the factors governing the distribution of income between wages, profits and rents makes the latter depend on the relative 'power of the combatants', to use a phrase by Karl Marx. In Ricardo's own words, the crucial element of social conflict lies in that 'the interest of the landlord is always opposed to the interests of every other class in the community'.[21]

To sum up, the first three feats Ricardo had 'expected' of competitive forces (namely, to equalise profit and wage rates plus to instil in capitalists a desire for re-investing all profits/savings) could be seen as plausible and, in any case, underpinned his theory of growth nicely. But things got sticky with the fourth feat: his expectation that *commodity values would reflect the ratio of minimum labour inputs necessary for their production* could not be made consistent with the rest of his theory. Values, it turned out, were bound to depend on the distribution of income between wages and profits unless all sectors and production processes are characterised by identical capital intensity.[22] When they are not, we are back in the grip of economics' *Inherent Error* whose lineage goes back to Aristotle and which we discussed in the previous chapter; an *error* which is reproduced, as we shall argue repeatedly in this book, whenever the theorist tries to embed a consistent *theory of value* within a broader *theory of capitalist economic growth*; an error which, in recent decades, has aided and abetted the policies and strategies that played a hand in bringing us the *Crash of 2008*.

3.4 Relative capital intensity and economics' *Inherent Error*

Adam Smith and David Ricardo shared a conviction that the Good Society could only be brought about by the *automation* and *rationalisation of production*, by a clever *division of human and of mechanical labour*, and by unfettered *competition* that would keep transforming greed into good. In that mindframe, it was thought that society's interests were served best when capitalists retained the right to claim the residual leftover once the factors of production had been paid enough to keep them in production. The reason? Because they would not hold on to it for themselves! Competition, Smith and Ricardo thought, would guarantee that capitalists would have no option but to plough the residual back into the growth cycle, fearful of the vengeance of the market if they did not. The outcome would be bigger and better machines, a cleverer organisation of production, extra research in new technologies and products, development, innovation, etc. All powers to capital so that capital can produce more for less.

The two great thinkers differed on one small detail which, remarkably, was enough to drive a wedge between them: whereas Smith was happy to accept that the distribution of income between the social classes was more or less stable, Ricardo was not. Eager to sound a warning about the deleterious effects of rising landlord rents, he had no alternative but to study the effect of a variable income distribution on growth. But that eagerness unhinged his *theory of value*; a predicament that could only be alleviated if one could argue the unarguable: namely, that the intensity with which machines contributed to output was the same in all of the economy's sectors.

Ricardo's *corn model* was, in summary, a commendably concise theory which helped him make his case against the economic malaise that was the landlords and their increasing power to extract rents. However, any simple model's worth is tested according to its capacity to stay afloat in the high seas, that is, in Ricardo's case, when there are many commodities and not just one kind of input. Thomas Robert Malthus challenged him precisely on that and David Ricardo responded with the book which was to make him famous: *on the Principles of Political Economy and Taxation*, first published in 1817.[23]

Malthus' challenge was to point out (see also note 13 in this chapter) that for the *labour theory of value* to work, each commodity had to be produced by the same technique of production involving the same proportions in the use of the various inputs. Ricardo replied with an attempt to extend the *corn model* to a system with many commodities (see Box 3.5 for the simplest variant). It is, alas, impossible to conclude that his extended model answered Malthus' critique convincingly. The end result is another special case involving identical techniques of production (machines to labour ratios) in every sector of the economy.[24] The best Ricardo could do in response to Malthus was to suggest that his theory was approximately correct. We doubt that this is a sufficient answer; as, we suspect, did he.

Box 3.5 On the possibility of unproductive labour
The extended corn model featuring a luxury good but no machinery[1]

Consider an economy comprising the usual three social classes (workers, landowners and capitalists) and two sectors: one producing corn (the basic commodity[2]) the other gold. Gold is brought to the earth's surface by miners who are paid subsistence corn wages. The landowners own *all* the land, including the mines, which they *rent* to capitalists, some of whom run the farms while the rest operate the mines. Meanwhile, corn is produced by agricultural workers and is both a consumption and a capital good: as a consumption good it is the currency with which both gold and labour are exchanged. As a capital good, it takes the form of corn seeds sown in the soil and functions as a means of further corn production. At the year's end the economy's aggregate corn harvest is divided between:

(a) *Rent*, which is the part of the harvest retained by the landowners who use it to feed themselves and to buy the gold they covet from the capitalists operating the mines.
(b) *Wages*, which is the part of the harvest paid to workers (by the capitalists running the farms) and to the miners (by the capitalists operating the mines).

(c) *Depreciation*, which is the part of the harvest that must replace the seeds sown in the soil the year before.
(d) *Investment*, or the part of the harvest to be ploughed back into the soil so that the next year's harvest is larger than the present one.[3]

In this Ricardian economy, workers and miners subsist on corn wages paid by capitalists. Competition between capitalist farm operators guarantees that they will invest all residual corn (i.e. the profit left over *after* wages, rent and depreciation are accounted for) back into producing more corn next year. As for the mine-operating capitalists, who can only invest by hiring more labour (since this model features no machine tools), they may end up with surplus gold, which will adorn their homes. Thus, all actors will end up with enough corn for subsistence purposes but gold will pile up only in the homes of the landowners and the mine operators.

Suppose now that at the end of each year gold turns into coal dust and is blown away by the wind, as it did in medieval fairytales according to which children, offered gold by visiting night fairies, were left disappointed in the morning with black dust slipping through their fingers. Interestingly, this ritual gold carnage should not affect the system's capacity for economic growth in the slightest! If the harvest generates a corn surplus, due to continued investment in corn capital, growth will carry on (see Box 3.4) and the harvest will be able to feed more and more miners so that gold mining can also be expanded. In this sense, the above is a purely physiocratic model in which economically meaningful surplus comes solely from the land. Of course, things would be different if, instead of gold, corn withered into thin air at the end of each period. Then society would just die. It is in this sense that corn is a basic commodity while gold, despite its infinite and mystical desirability, a mere luxury.

The model above is important because of a very contemporary issue it brings to the fore. Admittedly, post-war consumerism has ensured that there is no such thing as a basic commodity today. Wages pay not just for bread and ham but for a huge array of consumption goods, including items that have till yesterday been branded 'luxuries'. However, the parallel question 'Which type of labour is productive and which not?' is as relevant as ever. The gold-versus-corn allegory suggests that labour is productive not when it is hard or glamorous (recall that, in the above model, gold mining is economically inessential labour even though it may well entail backbreaking work and produce a coveted item) but *when it contributes directly to the reproduction and expansion of society's capital*. In this view, the economic importance of different types of work has nothing to do with its financial rewards, social status, the skills required to perform it or the fatigue it causes the worker. Just like in our simple model, the work performed in the gold sector was irrelevant to surplus generation, even though it was gold, not corn, that adorned the houses of the rich and powerful, so too certain contemporary endeavours may be irrelevant to genuine wealth creation even if they are bathed in the limelight and fêted as hugely important, sophisticated and glamorous. It is even conceivable that the mighty financial sector, along with the glitzy worlds of marketing and fashion, are parasitic to the genuine business that generates wealth.

In conclusion, whether an economic activity is productive or not depends on the ways in which it aids or hinders the multiplication of productive capital – a sobering thought at a time when bankers' bonuses, extravagant marketing campaigns and financial engineering are defended as essential lubricants in the wheels of contemporary capitalism. Notably, this is a conclusion that, as we shall see, 'modern' mainstream economics has no stomach, or mind, for. It constitutes one of those precious *lost truths* that were (as we argued in the previous chapter) once better understood.

Notes
1 The example in this box is inspired by Pasinetti (1983).
2 The notion of the basic commodity has been fully developed by Piero Sraffa (1898–1983) in Sraffa 1960. That book rekindled the critique of the theory of capital that became fashionable at the end of the nineteenth-century – i.e. neoclassical capital theory. Sraffa's contribution effectively rehabilitated classical political economics which, until then, had been referred to mostly as a sort of precursor of neoclassical theory. Sraffa's book put paid to a number of appalling misconceptions: e.g. that Adam Smith's reference to the *invisible hand* was a justification for the theory of perfect equilibrium in all markets simultaneously (i.e. of some General Equilibrium), or that Ricardo's argument about land of diminishing fertility was a form of the neoclassical theory of diminishing marginal productivities (see Chapter 5 below). See also our discussion of Sraffa in Section 4.11 of the next chapter. See also, Eatwell and Panico 1987, J.C Wood (1995), Roncaglia (2000), Kurz (2000). For an admiring view from the opposition see Samuelson 1987.
3 Here we assume that since all production is based on labour and corn is the only capital good, investment only happens in the corn sector.

Box 3.6 Ricardo on the machines *vs* jobs debate

In the third edition of his *Principles*, published in 1821, Ricardo (1817/1819/1821 [1951], chapter XXXI) added an important chapter 'on machinery' and addressed a question that still tries our minds: do machines cause unemployment by displacing labour? His cue came from a workers' movement known as *The Luddites*; an early type of industrial terrorists who destroyed or sabotaged machines in a bid to help workers keep their jobs. Initially, Ricardo had denied that machines posed a threat to employment and advocated the theory of automatic compensation (i.e. that new jobs would be created to take the place of jobs displaced by machines). However, in the 1821 edition, he accepted that such an automatic compensation was unlikely to happen. Interestingly, a strong defence of Ricardo's 1821 position, that machines can reduce wages and output, has been put forward by the leading neoclassical economist of our times, Paul Samuelson (1988 and 1989) in two articles entitled, respectively, 'Mathematical Vindication of Ricardo on Machinery' and 'Ricardo was Right!'.

3.5 Epilogue

Since its inception, physics has undergone many paradigmatic changes, from Euclid to Newton, from Newton to Einstein, from Einstein to the latest attempts to tell a unified story involving energy, quanta, gravity and the mysterious particles contributing to dark matter. With each of these 'shifts', physics moved on from its early simplistic forms to more complex explanatory structures, while retaining the truth of its earlier paradigms. The history of economics could not have been more different.

The *corn model* was political economics' first serious stab at answering, within a single theoretical framework, questions involving (a) economic growth, (b) exchange values and (c) the distribution of income. It was, in effect, a single sector model of capitalism. It is still with us! In all its incarnations over the past two centuries, and despite the remarkable technical advances incorporated into economics since Ricardo's times, the *corn model* remains today central to the way economists think of a growing capitalist economy, often unwittingly.

Economics is, thus, still in the clutches of its original paradigm; of its *Inherent Error*. To this day, the only way we can combine a *theory of growth* with a *theory of value* is *either* by committing intellectual crimes worse than those of Adam Smith (who assumed incredulously a stable income distribution) and David Ricardo (who presumed an identical capital intensity in every sector) *or* by sticking to the (almost physiocratic) single sector model.

The above is, of course, a controversial claim that must (and will) be substantiated in the following chapters. Our simple point for now is a recapitulation of Chapter 2's main theme regarding economics' penchant for *lost truth* and *Inherent Error*. The *Inherent Error* we have discussed: it began with Aristotle, survived the Physiocrats, moved into the *corn model* and, as we shall see, continued to lurk in the theories of Wicksell and in the underpinnings of Ramsey's models. After the Second World War, it resurfaced intact in dynamic theories of growth (such as those of the Roberts Solow and Lucas) and, indeed, lives on within all that passes today, quite scandalously, as 'contemporary macroeconomics'. If we are right, and this is genuinely an *Inherent Error*, *no* economic theory can be *generalised* to a complex multi-sector world resembling our own. This means that economics might be intrinsically ill-equipped to speak to the concrete complexity of the social and historical embeddedness of economic variables.

Box 3.7 The disappearance of money

If we are right in claiming that contemporary macroeconomics is stuck in a single sector (or corn model) mindframe, our theories of money (and by extension finance) are suspended in mid-air. Celebrated economist John Hicks (1985) explained why succinctly. In this type of model, he writes, '[t]here is no problem … about the transmission of saving into investment, for in that model there is no money. Indeed, there is hardly any exchange. One would be quite entitled to think of the landowners (or capitalists) into whose possession the harvest comes just piling it up in their storehouses; then doling it out to those whom they employ, productively or unproductively. Those employed are thus paid for their services, and that closes the matter as far as they are concerned. If they are paid in money, they spend the money on 'corn' consumption, the money just comes back where it was without making a difference. There does not seem to be any harm in leaving [money] out.' (Hicks 1985, pp. 34–5) It seems that an escape from single sector economics was always a strong condition for having anything sensible to say about really-existing capitalism. Alas, such an escape is easier imagined than accomplished …

When as economists we turn a motivated blind eye to this predicament, economics turns dangerous. At best, our theories become glorious irrelevances whose best contribution to humankind is as a warning against consulting economists when formulating socio-economic policies. This is such a pity. For as we have seen in this chapter, despite its intrinsic incongruity, political economics has a unique handle on important truths, for example, the conclusion in Box 3.5 that labour's contribution is linked to the extent that it aids the formation of capital. Economics' dogged refusal to recognise the *Inherent Error* in its bosom leads to the loss of these crucial truths which it, alone, can unearth.

Somewhere around this juncture, the reader may well ask: why can we not retrieve *lost truth* and add new layers of knowledge upon it, bypassing all error and improving economic theory until it becomes socially useful? A noble sentiment no doubt but, alas, a sentiment bound to crash upon the shoals of the economists' iron-clad commitment to be 'scientists', complete with a panoply of *consistent* models. An aspiration to be scientific is, of course, commendable. Who would censure an ambition to be Galileo as opposed to some pontificating ideologue? However, the aspiration to be for economics that which Galileo and Newton were for natural philosophy (as physics was called back then) threatens to produce, instead of enlightenment, a religious fundamentalism-with-equations. The reason is that, unlike in physics, economists have to reckon with an *Inherent Error* that 'natural scientific' inquiry is immune to (thanks to Nature's indifference to our musings). It is an *error* caused by a definite feature of human, market societies: *value can never be independent of the distribution of social power over the surplus produced by human labour and ingenuity.* Social power is *determined* by our valuation of things, of people and of their ideas and, at once, *determines* these values. This infinite *feedback between value and power* lies at the heart of economics' *Inherent Error*, ensuring that all economics that overlooks it, or that tries to 'solve' it by technical means, is bound to produce a profoundly misleading theory of society. One needs to have no Cassandra-like abilities in order to imagine what might happen when such a theory informs the policies of central banks, the fiscal and industrial policies of governments, the financial regulators' practices or, indeed, the curricula of economics graduate schools.

To conclude, this book argues that overcoming economics' *Inherent Error* and procuring a logically consistent *theory of value* within a useful *theory of growth* is more than just difficult. It is impossible! We saw how, in early political economics, this conundrum forced Smith to a fudge involving income distribution and Ricardo to a sleight of hand, namely relative capital intensities. In the following chapters, we shall recount the main nineteenth- and twentieth-century responses to the *Inherent Error* and the new ploys economists used to overcome it. The only reason for telling this story is because *it is important from our current twenty-first-century perspective.* Many of our contemporary troubles stem from the way economic models metamorphosed over the past two centuries without shedding the *Inherent Error* from their foundations. With every such metamorphosis, the models gained in analytical and technical complexity but lost some important truth better understood by earlier forms of economic thinking. Truth was increasingly sacrificed for more elegant clothes, the new knowledge produced proved less and less meaningful and the policies based on them destabilised an already unstable economic system.

Paradoxically, this steady erosion of meaning and truth coincided with the profession's success at augmenting its powers of persuasion. Persuasion in the field of political economics, it seems, depends more on the models' *form* than its *content* or *effect*. Clothes matter more than that which they adorn. And economists have proved to be master designers, accruing considerable discursive success which, in turn, caused them to grow in confidence, to believe their own rhetoric more readily, and to end up peddling knowledge derived from a variant of the *corn model* to a world whose complexity they cannot begin to fathom. Worse still, the 'insights' projected through economics' distinctly single sector lens eased decision makers towards policies and practices that suited them and their constituencies nicely, policies not unlike those which led us to the *Crash of 2008*.

And when the crisis that the models could not have predicted happened, the same models were used to impart 'new' wisdom on what to do next. Unsurprisingly, the remedy offered was worse than the disorder they helped cause in the first place. What else could we have expected of a 'science' built upon an *Inherent Error* which it is hell bent to overlook?

4 The trouble with humans

The source of radical indeterminacy and the touchstone of value

4.1 The red pill

It took Thomas Anderson about five seconds to choose the red rather than the blue pill, and a few more to swallow it. In a triumph of reckless curiosity over the lure of simple pleasures, he turned down the prospect of blissful ignorance offered by the blue pill, opting instead for the cruel reality promised by the red one. But then again, without that heroic choice, *The Matrix* would not have been the box office hit that it was on its release back in 1999. Larry and Andy Wachowski, the film's makers, invite us to witness the reality that Thomas Anderson's choice revealed in all its horror and to follow his subsequent heroics, as well as inner struggle, to alter it.

Upon taking the red pill, Anderson (*aka* Neo) is confronted with the realisation that the world was not as it seemed. His whole life had hitherto been a computer-generated illusion whose only purpose was to cloak the unbearable truth. In the reality that the red pill unveiled, the world had been taken over by machines of our own making decades ago. As in folk tales or works of science fiction past, ranging from the Brothers Grimm's 'sweet porridge',[1] Goethe's *Sorcerer's Apprentice*, Jewish *Golem* tales and Mary Shelley's *Frankenstein* to films like *Blade Runner* and *The Terminator* series,[2] we lost control of our own creations and, when we decided to push the 'off' button, we realised that it was too late: the artefacts had taken over, with an iron will of their own, turning against their creators. Hubris met its nemesis.

What is, however, unique in *The Matrix* is that, in it, our artefacts' rebellion was not just a simple case of creator-cide. Unlike Frankenstein's *Thing*, which attacks humans irrationally out of its sheer existentialist angst, or *The Terminator* series' machines, which just want to exterminate all humans in order to consolidate their future dominance on the planet, in *The Matrix* the emergent empire of machines is keen to *preserve* human life for its own ends – to keep us alive as a *primary resource*. *Homo sapiens*, notwithstanding that it invented human slavery, and despite our unparalleled track record of inflicting unspeakable horrors on our brethren, could not have even imagined the despicable role that the machines would assign it in *The Matrix*: having achieved dominance over humanity through unleashing the usual nuclear holocaust,[3] the machines soon ended up with a Pyrrhic victory in their robotic hands. While the surviving humans were decimated, and no longer a serious threat to their plans for domination, the nuclear explosions darkened the skies and thus precluded the use of solar power as a source of energy for the triumphant machines. Fossil fuels having already been depleted by the Earth's previous tormenters (i.e. humanity), the machines turned to the surviving human bodies as a source of energy. Initially, they just plugged us, kicking and screaming, into power generators which converted our biological heat into electricity.

Strapped onto contraptions that immobilised us to save energy, they force-fed us with a blend of nauseating nutrients suitable for maximum heat generation.

However, the machines were soon to discover that humans do not last long when their spirit is broken and their freedom utterly deprived. Our curious need for liberty was, thus, threatening the efficacy of their human-driven power plants. So, the machines obliged us. They forced not only nutrients into our bodies but also illusions that our spirit craved into our minds. Ingeniously, they attached electrodes to our skulls with which they fed, directly into our brain, a *virtual*, yet utterly *realistic*, life that as humans we could cope with. While our bodies were still brutally plugged into their power generators, feeding them with electricity sourced from our body heat, the machines' computer program known as *The Matrix* filled our minds with an imaginary, illusory yet very 'real' 'normal' life. That way our bodies, oblivious to reality, could live for decades, to the great satisfaction of the machines responsible for generating enough power to sustain their new world. Human oblivion proved a crucial factor of production in the *Matrix Economy*.

The Matrix, being a true blue Hollywood flick, devotes most of its time to some spectacular fighting scenes between the few humans that had escaped to form the Resistance and machines specialising in hunting them down in order to return them to the power generating plants. It does not ask the question that political economics would be compelled to ask: *what kind of economy did these machines build on the basis of human-generated energy?* That they created an economy, there is no doubt. From the few glimpses afforded by the directors, it is clear that the machines erect impressive edifices, produce all the components that they need to address their own wear and tear, build power generating plants, fashion the *Matrix* hardware and software technology necessary for producing imaginary lives in the mind of their human-slaves and, above all else, have a capacity to reproduce by manufacturing other machines as advanced as (and sometimes more advanced than) themselves. Surplus generation is a feature of their fully industrialised economy, as is division of labour, technological innovation and, intriguingly, accumulation.

Box 4.1 Humanity's resistance to utopia: In the words of a machine

In a dialogue between the hero, Neo (as Thomas Anderson renamed himself following his rebellion), and Agent Smith, a sentient program sent to liquidate him, the latter explains why the illusions they fed the humans were not those of a perfect world but rather resembled the often frustrating experiences humans had prior to the Rise of the Machines: 'Did you know that the first *Matrix* was designed to be a perfect human world? Where no one suffered, where everyone would be happy. It was a disaster. No one would accept the program. Entire crops were lost. Some believed we lacked the programming language to describe your perfect world. But I believe that, as a species, human beings define their reality through suffering and misery. The perfect world was a dream that your primitive cerebrum kept trying to wake up from. Which is why the *Matrix* was redesigned to this: [1999,] the peak of your civilisation.'

Wachowski (1998), 140, p. 91

4.2 The *Matrix Economy*

Adam Smith would have marvelled at its division of labour, technological innovation and productive capabilities. David Ricardo would have sought ways to conceptualise its self-reproducing machines as *the* basic commodity (confining corn to the list of 'also run' inputs). However, it is the *Physiocrats* that should have felt most vindicated by *The Matrix*. Just as in their fledgling input–output model (see Box 3.1) labour used the land to produce surpluses in order to maintain farm workers and artisans, so do the *Matrix Economy*'s machines draw on a scarce natural resource (*human bodies* as opposed to the Physiocrats' *land*) in order to sustain economic activity in at least two sectors. On the one hand, the machines seem keen (a) to reproduce themselves by filling the world with a multitude of smarter, more powerful replicas of themselves; and (b) to maintain the actual *Matrix*, the complex system which keeps inert humans alive by means of hardware which keeps their bodies plugged into the *Economy*'s power generators, and software that creates and carefully manages the interactive illusions which are essential inputs in the reproduction of the human resource.

The first break with the political economics examined so far which the *Matrix Economy* demands of us, if it is to be understood properly, is a break with Ricardo's corn model. Recall Box 3.5 where we captured his idea of a two-sector economy, producing corn and gold, where only one of the two goods (corn) could act as capital. The fact that in that model no machines were used in the goldmines, and only corn was necessary for society's actual survival, ensured that only labour expended in the corn sector could be deemed productive. This was the inescapable conclusion of a theory that features no capital other than corn seeds and no mechanical input into the production process. Despite Ricardo's celebration of industrialisation, machines were absent from his analysis.

In contrast, the *Matrix Economy*, fully automated by definition, relies on *both* of its sectors for reproduction: without machines producing machine parts and other machines, there would be no future for the *Matrix*. Equally, without machines maintaining the *Matrix*, which keeps human bodies alive and capable of producing electrical power, *all* the machines would wither and eventually die. In this sense, the *Matrix Economy* features *two* productive sectors, as opposed to Ricardo's model which features only one.

Box 4.2 sketches *sector 1* of the *Matrix Economy* whose purpose would be to design and manufacture general purpose machines, labelled *N*. In effect, while both sectors are productive and indispensible for the survival of the Machine Empire, *sector 1* is the heart of the *Matrix Economy* as its remit is to keep populating the Earth with more machines.

Sector 2 would have been superfluous had the machines been able to tap freely into some energy source. To their chagrin, however, the thick clouds surrounding the planet and the exhaustion of fossil fuels forced the machines to set up and support a separate human-powered generating sector, complete with the *Matrix* hardware–software combination that makes the conversion of human heat into electrical current possible (as well as the 'security' apparatus necessary for combating the small but annoying band of human escapees who are trying to liberate their brothers and sisters from the clutches of *The Matrix*). Box 4.3 describes that sector.

Let us now take a leaf out of the *Physiocrats*' book and, on the basis of the above, produce a 'tableau', or… *Matrix*, by which to capture the interconnections between the two outputs and the three inputs of this economy. The following table or *Matrix* extends the physiocratic tableau or *Matrix* in Box 3.1. What it says is that the production of 1 unit of *N* requires α

Box 4.2 The *Matrix Economy's sector 1*
The machine design and manufacturing sector – N

Sector 1 employs machines replacing worn machine parts, making more machines and, generally, replenishing and adding to the stock of machinery that is the very stuff of the *Matrix Economy*. However, to be capable of performing this task, the *sector 1* machines require assistance from the second sector's output (see Box 4.3). The machines produced by *sector 2* are a different species of automata and prove essential in generating energy supplies for *both* sectors, using as their only raw material heat emitted by human bodies. More precisely,

   Sector 1's output – *N*: *N* refers to units of machines (thought of, for simplicity, as a homogeneous form of robotic device) which are produced in each period on the basis of the following three inputs.

   Sector 1's inputs:

(a) Previously produced *N* units; that is, existing machines (produced by *sector 1* in earlier periods) employed to manufacture the new *N* machine units.
(b) Previously produced output *M* of *sector 2* (see Box 4.3). The *Matrix* technology generated in *sector 2* controls human bodies both physically and emotionally. Without the *M* units produced in *sector 2*, there can be no power to maintain production in *sector 1* (or, indeed, in *sector 2*).
(c) Human body heat – *H*. In this human dystopia, all types of machines (*N* and *M* alike) operate on electricity produced through a combination of the *M* units of *sector 2* and human body heat *H*. The two sectors' requirements of *M* and *H* units may well differ.

Box 4.3 The *Matrix Economy's sector 2*
The Matrix *technology maintenance sector – M*

Sector 2 is the *Matrix*, i.e. all the hardware and software that machines produce and maintain in order to keep human bodies plugged into the power plants that keep the whole *Matrix Economy* going. The machines working and operating the *Matrix* are produced both by machines manufactured within *sector 1* and by processes internal to *sector 2*. Labelling the *sector 2* output as *M*, it is clear that just like *sector 1's* output *N* required units of *N*, *M* and *H* for its production, the same applies to the production of new units of *M* within *sector 2*. Evidently, *sectors 1* and *2* are co-dependent and equally productive (in the sense that the *Matrix Economy* as a whole cannot survive unless both sectors produce incessantly). Summing up,

   Sector 2's output – *M*: *sector 2* generates *M* units of machines per period that squeeze electrical power out of human bodies and which are produced on the basis of the following three inputs.

Sector 2's inputs:

(a) Previously produced N units of *sector 1* (see Box 4.2 above); that is, existing machines produced in *sector 1* are essential in the maintenance of the *Matrix* and the generation of *sector 2's* M units of output.
(b) Previously produced output M of *sector 2*. These are the units of machinery produced within *sector 2* that are essential in the production of further output in this same sector (e.g. self-replicating software).
(c) Human body heat – H. As in *sector 1*, in *sector 2* also human heat must be combined with units M of machines produced within this sector in order to keep the *Matrix* going and, indeed, growing.

units of N, β units of M and γ units of H while the production of 1 unit of M requires δ, ε and ζ units of N, M and H respectively.

Table 4.1 Input–Output *Matrix*

		Outputs	
		N	M
	N	α	δ
Inputs	M	β	ε
	H	γ	ζ

To see what it costs to produce one unit of N we need some additional information on the relative value of these inputs. But what is the meaning of value in this Machine Empire? Suppose that the *Matrix Economy* is run by some *Overlord Program* (OP) which must decide how to distribute the available scarce resources N, M and H between the two sectors so as to maintain a sustainable overall growth rate for both N and M outputs.

The first thing OP must do is to somehow determine the relative weight it wants to assign to each of the outputs and to human body heat (the equivalent in an exchange economy would be its 'price'). OP may have its own priorities in deciding these relative weights or it may be serving a wider agenda. For our current purposes it does not matter how OP came to these weights. Let p be a number which reflects the relative importance it attaches to each unit of N, q the relative importance it attaches to each unit of M and w the relative importance it attaches to each unit of human-driven heat H.

Then, OP estimates the relative importance of the input of N necessary for the production of one unit of N to be $p\alpha$: the α units of N needed times their relative weight; similarly with the other inputs for each of the two outputs. In this manner, OP computes the cost of producing a unit of N and a unit of M as C_1 and C_2 respectively – see the right-hand side of inequalities (4.1) and (4.2) in Box 4.4. With a small amount of arithmetic manipulation, these inequalities lead us to formulae (4.3) and (4.4), which are measures of the surplus per unit of output in each of the economy's sectors.

OP's next 'thought' is that, if the *Matrix Economy* is to be growing in size and quality, each of its sectors must be producing output of greater impact (or 'weight') than that of the inputs consumed in its production. And since the relative importance (or impact or weight) of each unit of N was defined in the above paragraph as p, condition (4.1) must apply if the OP is to ensure that 1 unit of *sector 1* output has an impact greater than that of the inputs used up to produce it.

Box 4.4 An input–output model for the *Matrix Economy*

In the *Matrix Economy* both outputs are also inputs (see Boxes 4.1 and 4.2). Table 4.1 above places the outputs in the columns and the inputs in the rows and explains the technical requirements for the production of 1 unit of N and of 1 unit of M as follows: To produce 1 unit of N (i.e. a single unit of the homogeneous robotic devices that *sector 1* pumps out), the economy needs to devote to *sector 1* α units of N, β units of M and γ units of human body heat H. Equivalently, to produce 1 unit of M (i.e. a single unit of the automata running the *Matrix* and produced in *sector 2*), the economy needs to devote to *sector 2* δ units of N, ε units of M and ζ units of human body heat H. Moreover, we have assumed that the OP, running the whole economy, assigns relative weight p to 1 unit of N, relative weight q to *each* unit of M and relative weight w to each unit of H.

Thus, the cost of 1 unit of N comes to $C_1 = p\alpha + q\beta + w\gamma$, while the cost of the inputs that go into the manufacture of 1 unit of M equals $C_2 = p\delta + q\varepsilon + w\zeta$. For this economy to be able to reproduce itself without fading from one period to the next, inequalities (4.1) and (4.2) must hold as equalities. And if the economy is to grow (as the *Matrix Economy* clearly did), they must in fact hold as inequalities:

$$p > C_1 = p\alpha + q\beta + w\gamma \tag{4.1}$$

$$q > C_2 = p\delta + q\varepsilon + w\zeta \tag{4.2}^1$$

Rewriting (4.1) and (4.2) as (4.3) and (4.4), the OP defines as S_1 and S_2 the surplus per unit of output in each sector.

$$p = p\alpha + q\beta + w\gamma + S_1 \quad or \quad S_1 = p(1-\alpha) - q\beta - w\gamma \tag{4.3}$$

$$q = p\delta + q\varepsilon + w\zeta + S_2 \quad or \quad S_2 = q(1-\varepsilon) - p\delta - w\zeta \tag{4.4}$$

Note
1 These inequalities are analytically identical to the inequalities in the physiocratic analysis of Box 3.1 of the previous chapter.

So far, we have assumed that the OP plucked the relative weight it attached to the economy's three inputs (N, M and H) as if from thin air. Now, we have reached the point where the OP has the capacity to *determine* the relative importance, or impact parameters or simply the relative weights, p, q and w. One way of doing this is to ask a simple question: 'What must I do so as to ensure that the economy's growth is steady and well balanced'? The answer comes in the form of a simple principle (see Box 4.5).

Let us see how all this helps the OP to plan the *Matrix Economy* by means of a numerical example. Suppose that the OP has done its homework and has computed the production

---

Box 4.5 The principle of balanced growth

Each sector consumes certain inputs to generate its output. From the perspective of the machines, who are the *Matrix Economy's* constituents, what matters is the ratio of surplus machine output to machine inputs. That ratio captures their growth rate as a 'species'. To keep their Empire growing sustainably, this ratio *must be the same across the two sectors*. For if it is not, the *Matrix Economy* will end up either with more robots that it can power or with more power than there are robots to sustain.

The relative impact or importance of the machine inputs it took to produce S_1 was $p\alpha + q\beta$ and so the growth rate in *sector 1*, from the machines' viewpoint, is given as $g_1 = \dfrac{S_1}{p\alpha + q\beta}$. Similarly, the *sector 2* growth rate is $g_2 = \dfrac{S_2}{p\delta + q\varepsilon}$. The Principle of Equal Inter-Sectoral Growth articulated here demands that $g_1 = g_2$. It is a condition that helps the OP determine the relative importance of the three inputs which is consistent with steady, harmonious growth for the *Matrix Economy* as a whole. Setting $g_1 = g_2$, the OP ends up with the following equation:

$$g_1 = \frac{S_1}{p\alpha + q\beta} = \frac{p(1-\alpha) - q\beta - w\gamma}{p\alpha + q\beta} = g_2 = \frac{S_2}{p\delta + q\varepsilon} = \frac{q(1-\varepsilon) - p\delta - w\zeta}{p\delta + q\varepsilon} \tag{4.5}$$

Given that the OP is only interested in *relative* weights, it can simplify (4.5) by setting the relative weight of *sector 2* output (that is, the weight q of each unit of M produced by the *Matrix*) equal to one.[1] Then, with $q = 1$, weight p measures the importance of a unit of *sector 1's* output N in relation to the importance of a unit of *sector 2's* output M. For example, if it turns out that $p = 2$, this means that the OP determines that each unit of *sector 1* output is to be given twice the weight, importance or impact of each unit of *sector 2* output. Substituting $q = 1$ in (4.5) we derive equation (4.6), which states the conditions for sustainable growth within the *Matrix Economy*:

$$g = \frac{p(1-\alpha) - \beta - w\gamma}{p\alpha + \beta} = \frac{(1-\varepsilon) - p\delta - w\zeta}{p\delta + \varepsilon} \tag{4.6}$$

Note
1 In economics we usually call this the *numéraire* good. Its choice is usually arbitrary, even though we must be careful not to choose a good that it will turn out to be a free good. Sometimes for mathematical or computational reasons we normalise the sum of prices to be equal to unity. We can find the term used in early mathematical models such as Isnard's (1781, in Berg 2006).

---

requirements of the two sectors as follows: $\alpha = 4/10$, $\beta = 2/10$, $\gamma = 1$, $\delta = 5/10$, $\varepsilon = 3/10$ and $\zeta = 3/2$.

Putting these coefficients into (4.6) and solving for p, the OP comes up with an expression linking p to w (i.e. to the relative importance that the OP assigns to human heat as an input).[4] In other words, the importance of *sector 1* machines relative to *sector 2* machines depends

Table 4.2 The *Matrix Economy*'s steady-state growth path

		Relative weight attached to sector 1 unit output (vs. sector 2 unit output)	Overall growth rate for the Matrix Economy
	w	*p*	*g (%)*
Significance attached by OP to human heat, as an input into both sectors	0	0.740	49.22
	0.1	0.729	27.93
	0.2	0.717	6.26
	0.223	0.714	0
	0.25	0.712	−4.72

on the relative scarcity, as judged by the OP, of the sole primary resource: heat generated by human bodies. Table 4.2 captures the precise relationship between *p* and *w* and, more importantly, explains the determinants of the *Matrix Economy*'s growth rates.

To better understand this relationship, suppose that human heat were a free resource. The machines could squeeze as much heat as they required from their human slaves, so that the relative impact of heat (*w*) would be zero. In this case we would have a fully reproducible economy, and we would care only for coefficients α, β, γ and δ.[5]

The OP would still need to allocate production between the two sectors in order to maximize growth. With *w* equal to zero, the equations in Box 4.5 lead to a precise value for both the relative weight of the first sector's output, *p* = 0.74, and a growth rate for the whole *Matrix Economy*, equal to *g* = 49.22 per cent (which is also the growth rate of each of its sectors).[6]

Let us now ask: what happens with humanity's heat resource? *H* is 'cultivated' in the *Matrix*'s dystopian plantations by its own, specific rules and grows, if at all, at a rate g^H which is contained by human biology (or carbon biology as the machines refer to it sardonically in the film) and can thus be considered exogenous to the *Matrix Economy*. This forces the latter to grow at this exogenous rate.[7] Technically, since g_H is given, we have two equations, two unknowns and, therefore, a solvable problem. The solution comes in the form of two numbers: one for the relative weight *w* and one for the relative weight *p* that if the OP selects, the *Matrix Economy* will grow in a balanced fashion and at the rate computed in the previous paragraph.[8]

The impact of the rate at which heat from human bodies grows on the *Matrix Economy* boils down to the relative weight *w* that the OP assigned to that heat. In this example, the OP finds that if the *Matrix Economy* is to manage just to reproduce itself, that is, neither to grow nor to shrink, this *w* cannot exceed a certain value (*w* = 0.229).[9] In this sense, the machines must ensure that the relative importance of human-generated heat, the *w* parameter, is less than that threshold, if their precious Empire is to grow from strength to strength. This is why in the film they are so keen to put down the human rebellion which, in effect, renders human heat scarcer and raises *w*.

In summary, our most significant conclusion is that the long-term prospects of the *Matrix Economy* depend on the relative scarcity (and, thus, impact factor) of human heat. If human heat does not grow, but declines, the Machine Empire goes into reverse, shrinking unavoidably until, in some future period, no machines are left on Earth.[10] A second analytical result of significance is that positive growth requires that the OP places more importance on each unit of *sector 2* output than on every unit of *sector 1* output; that is, $p<1$.[11] The interpretation of this result is that, while both sectors are productive, they are not 'equally' so. Depending on their relative input requirements, if the economy is to grow sustainably, one of the two sectors produces 'goods' that must be afforded greater priority.

4.3 The value of freedom

Our foray into science fiction has a serious purpose: to offer us a handle on the question of *economic value* and its intimate relationship with *free labour*. Do the machines in the *Matrix Economy* produce *value*? That each machine plays a role in sustaining a growing economy, and that its output is an indispensible component of the world of machinery it belongs to, there is no doubt. But *value*?

Quite clearly, this is a philosophical question. Nevertheless, it is a question which, as economists, we cannot sidestep if we are genuinely interested in understanding the special challenges that a human economy poses for our intellect. The claim here is that to grasp the capitalist economy one needs to seize on the analytical differences between, on the one hand, an economy where humans work *with* machines and, on the other, a fully automated system like that in *The Matrix*. To explain this claim, consider these equivalent questions: do the miniaturised springs and cogs inside an old mechanical watch produce *value* when there is no human to look at the time the watch displays? Would the earthworm's gene which allows it to digest soil at an incredible rate produce *value* if human life on the planet were extinct? Does the sophisticated software inside some computer create *value* in a world where there is no human to use, or benefit from, the computer?[12] More generally, in a *world without humans* (or a world where humans have lost control of their minds completely and utterly, as in *The Matrix*) could we speak meaningfully of *value creation*?

Noting that these are an ontological sort of question akin to 'Do thermostats think?', and that there is no definitive answer to such ontological questions, nonetheless we cannot eschew answering them if we are serious about understanding human economies. The reason we are compelled to take philosophical sides is that our economic theory, whichever we end up espousing, will depend crucially on the answer we shall give, consciously or unconsciously, to this type of question. And since it is always better to choose one's premises, rather than to stumble into a set of premises that one does not even know one has adopted, we shall now state a basic assumption: thermostats do *not* possess what it takes to *think* (but only simulate thinking). For similar reasons, we suggest that, in a world devoid of *free minds*, the cogs and wheels of a mechanical watch, the earthworm's genes, a piece of software, etc. do *not* produce value.

Our position on this is, we feel, philosophically moderate and in accordance with *Ockham's Razor*: why invoke the 'difficult' notion of *value* in the context of systems that feature no humans when the word *function* will do nicely? When watchmakers discuss the wheels, cogs and springs of their object of study, they speak of their function. When computer engineers discuss some fully automated system, they have no use for a term like *value* to describe the role or output of the system's component. They too speak of functions, outputs, inputs, etc.[13] Note that this is exactly what we did above when describing our fictitious *Matrix Economy*. Value, in that context, would have been a superfluous and unnecessarily confusing term. Indeed, it would be quite absurd to speak of the value of each unit of machinery produced by one of the sectors, save perhaps as an allegorical word play.[14]

Recall that in *The Matrix*, humans and their minds were not only present but also essential for that economy's reproduction and growth. However, there was no *free thinking*. Humans' minds were sustained by computer-generated illusions so that their body heat could be 'harvested' by *sector 2* machines. From an economic viewpoint, the analysis proceeded as if there were no *actual* humans inhabiting the system. Indeed, if the machines developed an alternative source of energy, for example, one using tulips, nothing would change in terms of the economics.[15] In this sense, human intelligence is not enough to make a difference, as long as it is wholly under the control of the *Matrix*.

What *would* have made a difference to the economics we set out in Boxes 4.2 to 4.6 is the possibility that some of the economic agents can make *free choices* on the basis of *free thinking*; that is, choices not already preprogrammed into the actors' software or phenotype. To stay with the science fiction genre, and repel any accusation of anthropocentricity, let us imagine that the machines in the *Matrix Economy* were to develop, at some point, a capacity to think freely, just as they did in Philip K. Dick's 1968 novel *Do Androids Dream of Electric Sheep?* Then, the subject of value would rise to the surface not only as a series of issues that a theory attempting to understand this emergent economy *might* potentially address but, in fact, as issues that it *must* speak to.

In short, *value* is only meaningful in the presence of agents capable of (a) *free thinking* and (b) a modicum of *freedom of action*. *Freedom*, in this sense, seems a precondition for a meaningful theory of economic *value*. The bee and the spider build edifices of immense complexity. But they do not create value; nor do machines that are just as preprogrammed as the bee and the spider. In contrast, even an inept human architect (see Box 4.6), because of his/her fascinating capacity to transcend his/her own 'programming' (even if only very occasionally) has the capacity to be *creative*; to churn out *value*.

Whether non-human freedom is possible or not is a fascinating question which, happily, does not affect our inquiry. Perhaps future machines will develop a capacity for free will, an ability, that is, to contribute *autonomously* to the writing of their life's script. For the time being, and until androids can develop consciousness and predestinarian theologians, our concern is with economies in which value, labour and technical change remain under the power of exasperatingly quirky, *aka* free, agents.

4.4 Freedom's lair

The Physiocrats paved the way for a mathematical (input–output type of) economic analysis (see Box 3.1) which proved useful in speculating about the workings of some dystopian *Matrix Economy* (see Table 4.2). But when it comes to human society, what is it that breathes fire into such equations? We just argued that the answer is *freedom of thought and action*. Chapter 2 recounted the emergence of *mass freedom* as a double-edged sword. The peasants

---

Box 4.6 The architect and the bee

A spider conducts operations that resemble those of a weaver, and a bee puts to shame many an architect in the construction of her cells. But what distinguishes the worst architect from the best of bees is this, that the architect raises his structure in imagination before he erects it in reality.

Karl Marx, *Capital*, vol. I, chapter 7 (1867 [1909], p. 198)

expelled from the ancestral lands became free to choose, free to devise newfangled means of survival, free to roam unimpeded. Freedom of movement and action was no longer the privilege of the few. However, at the same moment in history, the multitude became free to starve; free to struggle for subsistence in a mean world which prevented them from combining their own labour with the land. In short, they became, in one sharp swoop, free to choose *and* free to lose everything. It is one of history's great moments when the masses' loss of access to the land made them 'free' to become merchants of their own 'liberated' labour.[16]

That moment in history, as narrated in Chapter 2, gave birth to a new society; a *market society* where labour could be seen as a sort of commodity with a value that fluctuated in response to the same economic forces that determined the value of the other commodities. It was this *dual* and *contradictory freedom* which, we believe, injects 'spirit' into the equations of a human market economy. Prior to the mass creation of free labour, there was no need for economics as we know it. An organic flow chart, similar to the circuit diagrams of engineers, showing the dependencies between different sectors of production would do for Ancient Athens, the Roman Empire, the fiefdoms of China and medieval Europe alike. Just like there is no sense in discussing the production and distribution of value in some futuristic *Matrix Economy*, similarly there was no place for such talk in the slave or feudal economies of yesteryear. This thought is confirmed by the fact that economics did not get off the ground until after the emergence of a market society powered by free labour. Our hunch is that, were the machines to take over in some awful future, one thing they will have no need for is economics. Engineering will suffice.

To establish further the significance of freedom from a purely economic perspective, consider an oil-fired electricity generator and compare it to a human hiring out his/her labour. The generator converts an input (oil in this case) into an output (electrical power). Its capacity can, with some technical skill, be captured by a *well defined mathematical function* which describes with great accuracy the *precise mapping from input to output* (i.e. kilowatts generated for different quantities of oil burnt). Is the human worker amenable to similar analysis? Seen as a potential bio-energy generator, which is how humans were treated in *The Matrix*, such a mathematical function is easily imaginable. Indeed, biologists can readily tell us how much energy, that is, heat, the human body generates given certain inputs (nutrients and water).

But the moment the human animal is seen as one that transforms input into output by a force that involves not only biological processes but also mental ones, the situation changes radically. A function converting inputs (such as nutrient and other consumption goods) into a human output can *seldom* (if ever) be well defined when the said output is not heat or the energy produced by our bodies but, rather, the artefacts of human endeavour. While humans too, just like electricity generators and horses, convert inputs into some sort of output, the mapping from one to the other is hardly ever well defined (or, as the mathematicians would say, a *one-to-one* and *onto* mapping). In layperson's terms, when mental and psychological powers mediate human labour, *many different outputs correspond to the same inputs* and, thus, no mathematical function can describe the relationship between a certain level of input and a precise level of output.

A happy worker, for instance, may produce more output for *given* input than a grumpier colleague. An engineer fearing dismissal may concentrate his/her mind much better, or indeed much worse, when designing an electricity generator (for the same pay and conditions). A disgruntled miner may cause significant damage. An inspired software designer may, like a poet on a good day, produce immense value. The whiff of foreign belligerence may stimulate a worker's creativity in some patriotic burst of moral outrage. Freedom of will and the mysteries of the human psyche throw a spanner in the works of any technical, or mathematical, depiction of the relation between input and human output. A good blues song sung in unison may be as important for the productivity of a group of farm workers as the tools they are using or the prospect of a pay rise. Machines cannot even begin to wrap their software-driven thoughts around this peculiarity of human labourers. Unfortunately, economics has the same difficulty.

To investigate this peculiarity a little more deeply, suppose that a worker's limbs, eyes and ears are surgically replaced sequentially by bionic devices that enhance his/her sight, hearing and dexterity. At which stage will he/she have become a machine? Would such interventions into human bodies bring about the *Matrix Economy* if extended to the whole population? The answer is negative as long as the mental processes remain human; that is, quirky, unpredictable, capable of creativity that transcends algorithmic 'thinking' and constantly threatening to subvert the laws which supposedly govern them. So, *which part of us needs to be replaced before our labour ceases to be free* and some mathematical function can be declared capable of mapping from inputs (into our persons) to our work's output? The answer is, *the core of our free spirit*, wherever that may be located.[17]

Our freedom's lair is, hence, what needs to be invaded and evacuated of all unpredictability, creative thinking and subversiveness before human work can be modelled by the same technical means as that of an electricity generator. In yet another science fiction film entitled *The Invasion of the Body Snatchers*, circa 1953, this is exactly what happens: the alien force does not attack us head on. Instead, humans are taken over from within, until nothing is left of their human spirit and emotions. Their bodies are all that remain, as shells that used to contain human free will. If that task is ever accomplished, and all humanity is taken out of our minds, then and only then will some *Matrix*-like economy become agreeable to a mathematical depiction similar to that of the analysis in Table 4.2. But then again, if that calamity ever hits us, the resulting 'economy' will not be producing any value. All that would be coming out is more and more self-replicating automata that populate an expanding system that is radically free of conflict, unemployment or, indeed, laughter, irony and, of course, *value*. In Kipling's (1901 [1987] p. 270) memorable words: 'When everyone is dead the Great Game is finished. Not before'.

4.5 A most peculiar contract

Let us now return to our mundane world of human workers employed by capitalist employers to produce goods and services for sale to humans. Consider the employer's conundrum: like any other buyer, he/she wants to buy something from the seller: the product of their labour. The only problem is that this is, usually, impossible. Workers cannot sell the product of their labour; for if they could, they would not be workers but enterprising suppliers. At best they can *hire out their labour services* for specified periods of time. So, the employer does the best he/she can and hires *labour time* in the *hope* that, during that time, enough products will be created by the hired workers in order to make the enterprise worth its while.

Paul Samuelson, a celebrated economist on whom we shall be saying more in later chapters, once suggested that *who hires whom* does not matter.[18] The employer brings to the table *capital goods* (machinery and other factors of production) and the worker brings his/her human labour. Like any buyer and seller, they trade and, hey presto, output oozes off the production line. That's true if the work involved is of the sort where the link between input and output is as transparent and straightforward as in the case of the electricity generator. For example, the worker is a weaver weaving in isolation producing an output which is both observable and strictly analogous to the hours spent on the job, as is a truck driver whose 'output' is a direct function of the hours spent behind the wheel.

In these examples, the employer offers the worker *capital goods* that he/she lacks, for example, weaving equipment, sewing machines or the truck, and the worker offers labour in return. What Samuelson seems to be saying is that it makes no analytical difference whether we conceptualise this transaction as (a) one in which the capitalist lays out capital for the worker's labour or (b) as one where the worker lays out his/her labour in exchange for the employer's capital. However, there is a catch here: if there is the slightest uncertainty about the level of demand for the final product, or when there are costs involved in supervising workers and organising their work, the capitalists would have a strong preference for scenario (b) above: they would rather hire out their *capital goods* to the workers and then buy from them their output.

For example, instead of employing them for a wage, why not charge weavers and truck drivers for the weaving equipment and the truck per week, and then, at the end of each week, purchase the textile weaved or pay for the delivery of goods on a per mile basis? As global experience has proven beyond a shadow of a doubt, whenever possible capitalists cease being employers. They, instead, fire their workers and subsequently contract out the work (often to former employees!). Capitalists loathe hiring labour time because it is not something they want to pay for, if they can help it. Indeed, they stop at nothing in search of ways to buy the products of labour *directly*. Just like whole nations may yearn for the migrants' work, while baulking at the idea of hosting migrants, so too capitalists would love to buy labour's input (or output) without having to manage labour.

So, why do they keep hiring workers? Why do they not fire everyone and subcontract all work? The answer, of course, is that more often than not the work involved is not of the sort where the link between input and output is as transparent and straightforward as in the case of the electricity generator. In fact, the production processes which produce genuine value require collaborative work, division of labour and, even, brainstorming. When workers cannot produce output by labouring autonomously, unlike stacks of electricity generators churning away independently of one another, and when the output is collectively, as opposed to individually, determined, it is impossible to single out one worker's output from that of another. Thus, it is impossible to pay them piece rates and the capitalist accepts the inevitable, offering the worker a *labour contract*.

Notice however that labour contracts are very peculiar indeed. Contracts usually specify that the buyer promises to pay price p at time t per unit of good X and the seller promises, in return, to deliver a certain quantity of good X at time t' (where t is usually prior to t'). When this arrangement takes the form of a *labour contract*, one would expect p to be the wage rate and X an amount of labour L. Now, by the above argument, the capitalist will only be interested in a *labour contract* if there exists no well-defined function linking *labour input* units L to its output Q. The reason, we claimed above, is that, if such a function were well defined, capitalists would be able to work out, using that function, the precise amount of output Q that this worker is producing given how much L they are buying from him/her. If so, capitalists would rather they fired him/her immediately, and re-contracted with him/her not as a labourer but as an independent contractor selling Q units of output for price p per unit.

In conclusion, the quantity L that the worker promises to exchange with the employer, as part of this *labour contract*, cannot be the factor of production that the employer wants to purchase! The units of L that the employer hires from the worker are not units that can be

Box 4.7 Of generators and humans

The oil-fired electricity generator: the input *L* that it needs to work, oil, is both *measurable* and corresponds (given the generator's technical specifications) to *specific* levels of electricity output *Q*. A well-defined function $Q = f(L)$ is, in this case, imaginable. Whether the firm pays for *L* units of input *plus* a rental charge to cover for the cost of producing the generator or for *Q*, there is no analytical difference.

    Jill, the worker: her input into production is labour *L*. With the help of capital goods *K* (machines, tools, raw materials, etc.), Jill's *L* produces output *Q*. Suppose that, just like in the case of the generator, *L* is measurable and that there is a well-defined function $Q = f(L)$ that assigns to each level of *L* a level of output *Q*. Again, there would be no analytical difference between a situation in which the firm pays Jill wage *w* for each of her *L* units of input (while providing her the necessary *K* for free) or renting her the *K* units of capital goods, for a given rental price *r*, and then purchasing *Q* directly from her at a pre-agreed price *p*. [In short, $wL = pQ - rK$.]

    Suppose now that (a) the firm *cannot* observe *L* directly *and* (b) there exists *no well-defined function* linking *Q* and *L* because Jill's labour input is *not* observable, the output depends not only on her work but on the combination of the labour input of many workers and, last, because in the context of *social (*as opposed to *atomistic)* production the productivity of human workers depends crucially on social norms and psychological factors that differ ontologically from the inner workings of an electricity generator and, thus, cannot be adequately captured by some mathematical function linking individual labour input to individual output.[1] In this case, there is *no equivalence whatsoever* between (a) a situation in which the firm pays Jill wage *w* for each of her *L* units of input (while providing her the necessary *K* for free) or (b) renting her the *K* units of capital goods, for a given rental price *r*, and then purchasing *Q* directly from her at a pre-agreed price *p*. In this case, the capitalist has no alternative than to be an employer and to offer Jill a labour contract.

Note

1 If such a function existed, then by observing output *Q* the firm would also be observing *L*. In most cases of social production, mere observation cannot help measure either a worker's labour input *L* or her output *Q*. Labour input is hardly ever measurable (How would you quantify Jill's productive effort? Would you plug her into some ergo-metre?) and, also, it is often impossible to tell which part of a collectively produced output is due to Jill's labour and which is due to Jack's, Tom's, Dick's or Harriet's.

technically linked, by means of a simple function (like that in the case of the electricity generator) to the firm's output. For if such a mapping, or function, existed, no *labour contract* would have been offered to the worker in the first place. Workers would be entrepreneurs and capitalists purveyors of capital services, not dissimilar to firms renting trucks and do-it-yourself tools.

    The gist of the argument here is that *all* labour contracts are equally peculiar in the sense that one of the contracting parties, the capitalists, are hiring something that they do not care for in the hope of wrestling from the seller something else, actual *labour input*, which is *not* specified in the contract (simply because it *cannot* be specified). At the end of a successful interview, the new employee shakes hands with the firm's personnel manager and signs his/her *labour contract*. What is he/she promising to offer the firm? It is a number of hours per week of his/her time during which his/her skills and potential effort will be present within the firm's premises and a *vague* promise to work diligently. But since no diligence-o-metre can *ever* be devised (so long as the labourer is human), the only quantifiable part of his/her promise concerns the hours he/she will be spending on the premises.

Now, employers care not one iota for these hours. What they care for is the unquantifiable diligence bit which, unfortunately, cannot be specified. They care for Jack or Jill's unquantifiable, immeasurable, actual *labour input*. This they hope to *extract* during the hours that Jack or Jill will be spending at work. Unlike other contracts which, at the moment of signing, *conclude* the relationship between buyer and seller,[19] the labour contract is the beginning of a wonderful *non-market* relationship. Once Jack/Jill enters the firm, as an employee, he/she exits the market and enters a purely social relationship with other workers and with his/her employers. In this sense, the employer–employee relationship is one of the last vestiges of the *ancien régime* which the market, despite its complete triumph everywhere else, cannot penetrate. No mathematical function can capture this complex non-market relationship and the way it transforms human inputs into the firm's output.[20]

The peculiarity of the *labour contract* results, therefore, from the peculiarity of human labour and its resistance to becoming machine-like. If humans could consent to becoming more like electricity generators, no doubt they would and then the *labour contract* would be no different from any other contract. But, then again, if labour could consent to becoming another species of machinery, it would lose its capacity to produce value. It is a delightful paradox that human labourers *cannot* consent to turn into machines, even if they want nothing more than the sweet oblivion offered by unconsciousness (or, equivalently, the blue pill in *The Matrix*). For, it is this 'incapacity' to abdicate freedom that makes value possible and the task facing economists so different from that facing engineers.

4.6 The rise of the machines

Machines have acquired the governing power over human labour and its products.

This sounds like a snippet from some other science fiction movie in which the machines have, yet again, enslaved us and turned us into a productive resource for *their* benefit. But it is no such thing. It is, rather, a slightly paraphrased version of something Karl Marx wrote in 1844 (in his *Economic and Philosophical Manuscripts*) about the world of his own time.[21] Marx's point was that, even back then, humanity had *already* fallen under the spell of the machines' capacity to generate purchasing power that developed a life of its own. Instead of serving humans to get what they want, it ended up enslaving them, telling them what to want. Thus, indirectly, machines that were initially developed as mechanical slaves for the betterment of men's and women's lives turned into masters. By now the reader will have gathered that Marx's fleeting appearance in Box 4.6 was not incidental. Where Adam Smith and David Ricardo had only alluded to the important role capital goods play in industrial society, Marx was the first political economist fully to incorporate machinery into economic analysis. Moreover, in his usual poetic flourish, he told a story about a machine takeover well before the cinema was invented and *Matrix*-like plots became all the rage.

Of course, Marx did not blame the machines. He never advocated a science fiction scenario in which the machines developed thoughts of their own and, suddenly, turned against us. Even though he was familiar with Mary Shelley's *Frankenstein*, where the artefact developed an alien intellect that eventually haunted its creator, Marx thought that something more prosaic, and more menacing, happened to us: first we built machines to use as elaborate tools. They remained lifeless and dim-witted, mere assortments of nuts, bolts and silicon chips. But then *we* did something extraordinarily stupid: we organised social production around them in a way that made us their willing slaves. In the *Communist Manifesto*, he, along with his lifelong collaborator Friedrich Engels, asserts (using somewhat different words) that we

> conjured up machinery with gigantic productive powers but, like a sorcerer who has lost control of the powers of the nether world he has called up by his spells, we have become their slaves. Instead of capital goods serving humanity, humanity has ended up as a cog in capital's machinery.[22]

His point is that, in a world in which entrepreneurs hire human labour and find themselves in the clutches of the most inhumanly aggressive competition against one another (so eloquently described by Adam Smith in his *Wealth of Nations*), they have no alternative but to accumulate capital: to use bigger and better machines (or, in our days, smaller and better ones) in order to lower costs and thus prevent their competitors from undercutting them. No rest for the wicked! Profit is ploughed back into the manufacture of more machines leaving the entrepreneur no alternative but to espouse the life of a miser; to turn into an archetypal Ebenezer Scrooge, who not only squeezes the life out of his workers but also desists from anything other than subsistence consumption for himself and his family.

So, on the one hand the capitalist lives to serve the propagation of the rows of machines in his factory while, on the other, his workers, wretched, bored and disheartened, attend to them around the clock, making sure that they want for nothing. Capital, in this sense, becomes a 'force we must submit to… It develops a cosmopolitan, universal energy which breaks through every limit and every bond and posts itself as the only policy, the only universality the only limit and the only bond' (Karl Marx, *Economic and Philosophical Manuscripts*, 1844).[23]

Like the human will, which thrives on its own substance, capital too has a self-referential momentum; one that, eventually, makes a mockery of *our* will. While inanimate and mindless, capital quickly evolved *as if* it were in business for itself, using human actors (capitalists and workers alike) as pawns in its own game. Not unlike the human will, capital also instills, in our minds the illusion that, in serving it, we are worthy, exceptional, potent. We take pride in our relationship with it (either as capitalists who 'own' it or as labourers who work it), turning a blind eye to the tragic fact that it is capital which, effectively, owns us all and it is we who serve it.

The German philosopher Schopenhauer castigates as deception the human conviction that our beliefs and acts are subject to our consciousness. Marx castigates us for ignoring the reality – that our thoughts have become hijacked by capital and 'its' drive to accumulate. He asks of us to swallow the red pill and wake up to the fact that capital is the source of our illusions and that their name is *ideology*. But not all news is bad. Indeed, Marx was a master tragedian who saw capitalism as an unfolding drama in which humanity has a chance to awake from a nightmare that is its own doing. We can offer ourselves the option of taking the red pill and, when the circumstances are right, we shall not be able to resist the lure of the naked truth; however hard it may be to stare it in the face.

Authentic radical thinking defers to tradition. Intellectually, Marx was of a Greco-German origin; a child of Ancient Greek philosophy, with Aristotle playing a prominent role and of

---

Box 4.8 Adam Smith on human nature

This division of labour, from which so many advantages are derived, is not originally the effect of any human wisdom, which foresees and intends that general opulence to which it gives occasion. It is the necessary, though very slow and gradual consequence of a certain *propensity* in human nature which has in view no such extensive utility; *the propensity to truck, barter, and exchange one thing for another.*
          Wealth of Nations, (1776 [1981]) book I, chapter ii, p. 25 (our emphasis)

---

the German idealism that struggled to grow in the long shadow cast by his teacher G.W.F. Hegel.[24] From the Stagirite, he inherited a commitment to seeing humanity's purpose, or *telos*, in terms of *virtue*, as opposed to satisfaction, wealth or power. He also derived the idea of the human animal as one that can only achieve individuality while confronted by a wall of 'others' within the *polis*. The notion of the human as a living contradiction, between the 'self' and the 'others', acquired greater significance in young Marx's eyes under the influence of Hegel; for it was Hegel who taught Marx that human freedom is not just about the absence of constraints.

The Greco-German alliance led by Aristotle and Hegel instructed Marx in the fundamental difference between humans and machines; a difference that lies in the deep contradictions lurking *within* our being. It is these irreducible, yet evolving, contradictions which set us apart and bestow upon us the dubious privilege of a unique capacity to create value. Isaac Newton informed us that all matter is subject to contradictory forces which somehow cancel each other out in the process of creating equilibrium. The main condition for a satellite to break loose from the planet's gravity is that its vectorial speed exceeds a certain threshold, so that the centrifugal force defeats its centripetal antagonist: either the satellite's speed exceeds the threshold or it does not. Though we may say that the satellite has been set 'free' if it does, we must be careful not to mistake the metaphorical resemblance between this freedom and the freedom of human agents that the intelligent machines in *The Matrix* are missing, thus rendering the production of value within a fully automated society impossible.

Hegel's objection to the loose use of the term freedom to describe satellites and humans alike was that the human actor is the only 'object' where the telling contradictions lie *within*. Unlike projectiles and robots, human freedom is bound up inextricably with an inner turbulence that demands expression. And human expression comes in the form of body language, speech, writing, art, song, lifestyle choices and creative spurts, even in the manifestations of the inner tussle that draws us sometimes to conformism and at other times to subversive acts. However, to be capable of genuine freedom of expression, we must have something meaningful to express; we must be able to achieve increasing degrees of consciousness as our passage through life progresses.

Aristotle thought that we *became* persons within political society. But not all humans can be part of that socialising *process*. The ones who constitutionally cannot *must* be kept in chains: for *their* sake (since, like children, they are better off under the guidance of superior intellects) as well as for the sake of those capable of genuine freedom. 'Natural slaves', very much like the humans in the *Matrix*, ought to provide the material goods and motive power for the socialising process among the superior beings inhabiting the *polis*. Hegel agreed that freedom was a process but poured tons of scorn over the idea of underpinning the freedom of some with the slavery of others. Our consciousness, he argued, is achieved through reflecting into other people's eyes in the hope of catching a glimpse of who we truly are: 'Self-consciousness attains satisfaction only in another self-consciousness', he wrote.[25] The moment we reflect into the eyes of a person whose will we command as we like, we stare into a void of un-freedom that consumes us. The fear that we may become like the bonded 'Other' impedes our rational thought and sets off a chain of actions whose purpose is to strengthen the Other's chains lest we trade places. But the more we shore up the Other's un-freedom, the more immersed we become in our own fears, the harder it becomes for our consciousness to reflect creatively on that of an Other and, tragically, the further away we get from the possibility of attaining freedom for ourselves. It is in this sense that, for Hegel, the history of human progress is the history of the negation of slavery.

And here lies the grand difference between his take on capitalism and that of Adam Smith. Adam Smith's account, as we have seen, was confined to the universal benefits from the division of labour, from commerce, and from liberty defined as freedom from inter-ference. Human nature was seen as time-invariant and driven by a constant *propensity to truck, barter and exchange* (see Box 4.8).[26] For centuries we lived in societies in which our crypto-merchant propensities were suppressed, waiting it out for the coming of the *Age of Commerce*. When it did come, in Smith's own time, our true and constant nature could at last emerge and fill the planet with gadgets, bargains and all the benefits of unimpeded trade. In that Smithian mindframe, history cannot really teach us anything about ourselves. In his own friend's words, 'Mankind are so much the same, in all times and places, that history informs us of nothing new or strange in this particular'.[27]

But Hegel had other ideas. While also welcoming the coming of the *Age of Commerce*, he placed it in the context of an incessantly unfolding history in which progress in material production was in constant dialogue with progress in human self-consciousness. The miracle of the market was not, for Hegel, so much its capacity to coordinate economic activity but, more importantly, it occurred through the creation of a 'place' where the human will can meet the Other in perfect equality and freedom from all bonds and hierarchies. As buyers and sellers, humans reflect into each other liberated from any compulsion and united only by the prospect of mutual gain. Mutual recognition had found its locus in the marketplace.

Progress is, thus, not just a case of more and better *iPods*, new market niches, greater opportunities for overseas travel and, generally, better access to more material possessions. More importantly, progress is synonymous with the *March of Consciousness*. Whereas Adam Smith focused on market society's capacity to deliver affluence, Hegel concentrated on its ability to help make self consciousness the universal property of humankind. In his own triumphant words: *'Essence must appear'*.[28]

Karl Marx, a truly recalcitrant student, took great pleasure in castigating the unbearable idealism of old Hegel and, often, to rub his face in Adam Smith's political economy. He rejected Hegel's lofty narrative on the *March of the Idea* and the *Progress of Spirit* towards its *Absolute End*, preferring to study reports on wage rates in Scottish mines and wool prices in East India. For a while, he turned his back on German idealist philosophy, feverishly immersing himself in the texts of Smith and Ricardo which he saw as gateways to understanding the subterranean forces that were brutally commodifying the world. But try as he did, young Karl could not shake off Hegel's *dialectic*: the concept of *progress-through-contradiction* that unfolds both *within* and *without* our minds (see Box 4.9). The more he studied British political economy, the more of Hegel he recognised in the world around him.

Box 4.9 The dialectic

Modernism and science share a penchant for dualism. Isaac Newton thought that every action causes a reaction and that the interplay between these opposite forces determines the state of things (from planets to molecules). Sigmund Freud believed that our soul was fraught by a perennial conflict between opposite forces such as *Eros* and *Thanatos*, *Reason* and *Unreason*, *Ego* and *Id, etc.* Thomas Hobbes, John Locke and Adam Smith were all convinced, despite their many differences, of the opposition between the individual and the state. In contrast, Hegel and Marx took a different view on binary oppositions. Rejecting dualism for the so-called dialectic, they criticise dualist accounts for running out of explanatory steam once the opposites are described. In Hegel's dialectical view, the opposites are transient and the conflict between them creative in that it gives rise to something radically new. The opposites appear to him as a necessary aspect of a larger (historical) process that renders their original opposition obsolete. The contradiction itself is, therefore, the determinant of both (a) the outcome and (b) the process that fundamentally alters the constituent opposites of the contradiction.

Consider, for instance, the following riddle: Jill announces that she will mail Jack a present in the next 10 days. But, to keep this a surprise, she stipulates that he will not be receiving the present on a day when he has solid logical reasons for thinking that he will receive it on *that* day.[1] Jack's *analytical Reason* tells him that he will *not* be receiving the present after all! 'If we have not received the present by the last post on the ninth day', his *analytical Reason* muses, 'we will then expect it for certain on the tenth, in which case she cannot mail it on the tenth. *Ergo*, if we have not received it on the eighth day's last mailing, we will then expect it for certain on the ninth (since the tenth day has been ruled out), in which case she cannot mail it on the ninth. And so on. 'Jill will be sending us no present, Jack', concludes Jack's *analytical Reason* pessimistically. But then, Hegel might say, *analytical Reason's* opposite, let's call it Jack's *subversive Reason*, enters the fray (like Newton's reaction to *analytical Reason's* action) with the opposite counsel. 'Don't be silly, Jack', smirks his *subversive Reason*. 'Of course we will be getting the present. If your *analytical Reason* is right, and you believe it as a truly rational person, she knows that you are not expecting a present any day. But then she can mail it on whichever day takes her fancy!' Poor Jack! Convinced by *subversive Reason* that a present is on its way, he wonders on which day it might arrive. *Analytical Reason* goes back into the driving seat and concludes, for the same reasons as above, that no present will be had. At which point *subversive Reason returns*, etc., etc. Hegel's point here would have been that this binary opposition will either be preserved, in which case Jack will go mad, or that it will dissolve giving rise to a more nuanced type of reasoning, one that respects the fact that both *analytical Reason* and *subversive Reason* are right and that they are both wrong and in need of a third type of reason that synthesises the two. In short, having encountered this genuine paradox of reason, Jack has become a smarter boy who understands the pure logic cannot tell him when Jill's present will arrive. Learning to embrace indeterminacy is part and parcel of attaining a higher order of rationality. In the words of French social anthropologist Claude Levi-Strauss,

> ... dialectical reason thus covers the perpetual efforts analytical reason must make to reform itself if it aspires to account for language, society and thought; and the

distinction between the two forms of reason in my view rests only on the temporary gap separating analytical reason from the understanding of life. Sartre calls
analytical reason reason in repose; I call the same reason dialectical when it is
roused to action, tensed by its effort to transcend itself.[2]

For Hegel, the dialectic is at work whenever one human looks into the eyes of another.
The idea is not that of an infinite self-reflection, like the one we would end up with if
we pointed a camera towards a mirror. The machine's eye may reflect infinitely into
itself but its image will not change one iota. In contrast, a human eye, attached to a free
mind, distorts and reinterprets the original image when reflected in another person's
eyes; the see-er sees something *beyond* the original image of herself. She begins to
recognise something about herself that would not be seen in a mirror or camera. And
when one has social power over the other, as in Hegel's celebrated master–slave paradox, the *dialectic of recognition* turns on a more vicious contradiction: Assuming that
the master craves the slave's recognition, but that the slave is programmed (through
fear) to provide anything that the master demands, the offered recognition is worthless
to the master and only a reminder of that which, because he is so powerful, he can
never have.

Marx borrowed the dialectic from Hegel and, from a young age, pressed it into the
service of political economics. Consider, for example, the concept of the individual
which we now take for granted. Marx claims that it could not have existed prior to the
emergence of market societies, before the conflict between the aristocracy and
the bourgeoisie was intensified, and the latter began to eradicate the institutions of
feudalism. As feudalism was subsiding, suddenly it became intelligible as a system
and its death roar furnished thinkers like John Locke and Adam Smith the newfangled
concept of the individual, of individual rights, of freedom from interference. The bitter
opposition between landlord and merchant thus gave birth to a radically new way
of defining persons just at the time when it was being negated by history, i.e. as the
landlords were losing the battle and this particular conflict was becoming a thing of
the past.

Notes
1 For simplicity assume that the Post Office is extra efficient and same-day delivery is
   guaranteed.
2 Claude Levi-Straus (1966 p. 246).

Marx was fascinated by the invasion of the market in every nook and every cranny; by its
insatiable restlessness that led to the commodification of everything; by its tendency to glo-
balise. 'All fixed, fast-frozen relations, with their train of ancient and venerable prejudices
and opinions, are swept away', he wrote (Marx and Engels 1848 [1998], p. 38). The market's
global and local expansion means that 'all new formed [relations] become antiquated before
they can ossify. All that is solid melts into air, all that is holy is profaned...' Behind the
market's drive to conquer, to liberate and to profane, was a particular social class: the
Bourgeoisie. They started as merchants, moneylenders and shipowners before becoming
what we today refer to as *capitalists*. After the momentous events that helped commodify
land and *labour* (see Chapter 2), they were responsible for populating the emergent

industrial society's workshops and farms with waged labour and with newly invented machines. But instead of retaining the role of masters, they soon were to be chased around by the forces they had unleashed, just like the sorcerers' apprentices in *Harry Potter* movies: 'The need of a constantly expanding market for its products chases the bourgeoisie over the whole surface of the globe',[29] Marx surmised Marx and Engels (1848 [1998], p. 39).

As one after the other the realms of human activity surrendered to commodification, under the heavy bombardment of the market's artillery, one bastion of the older, pre-market, regime remained standing: the *human labourer*. However hard capitalists try to turn him/her into a machine, and to extract from him/her 'work' in the same way that they extract effort from a horse or electricity from a generator, it is an impossible task. The worker cannot discard his/her innate freedom even if he/she wishes passionately to be liberated from it; to swallow the blue bill so that the weight of consciousness may be lifted from his/her weary shoulders. The result of freedom's stubborn perseverance is the continued prevalence of the *labour contract*.

Hegel famously pronounced that *no one* can be free in a society which keeps slaves. Marx took this further: no one can be free as long as industrial production is organised around machines that are 'owned' by one group, a minority of capitalists, and 'worked' by another, the majority. If the rationality that allows us to build the machines is the product of history, as Hegel would claim, then capitalism sets limits within which our freedom cannot breathe. The owner-capitalists and non-owner workers are equally at the mercy of the machines that they must both serve. All the world's amazing wealth, every smidgeon of the ever expanding surplus made possible by the *labour contract*, under which 'free workers' labour side-by-side with incredible mechanical slaves, instead of liberating us from want and deprivation seems to deepen our sense of un-freedom and to heighten the feeling of a certain indefinable lack.

This is the first aspect of Modernity's *Grand Irony*. The second aspect is that, as long as human work resists full commodification, society can produce value; but only under circum-stances that also produce crises, like that of 1929 or indeed of 2008. The next chapter tells the story of how these crises are nothing more than a reflection of the unquenchable contra-dictions within our psyche or reasoning caused by the dominant logic of capital. They are also glimpses of hope of a different world in which we become rulers of our destiny, masters of the machines that we brought into the world and designers of a world where a crisis like the *Crash of 2008* will no longer be possible.

4.7 Humanity as a virus

In another scene from *The Matrix* the hero, Neo, is being detained by Agent Smith, the chief algorithm responsible for capturing escaped humans and returning them to the power plant as electricity generators. In an almost human moment, Agent Smith seems compelled to justify to its captive why the machines had no alternative but to take over the planet and treat humans like a renewable resource:

> I'd like to share a revelation that I've had during my time here. It came to me when I tried to classify your species. I've realized that you are not actually mammals. Every mammal on this planet instinctively develops a natural equilibrium with the surround-ing environment. But you humans do not. You move to an area and you multiply and multiply until every natural resource is consumed and the only way you can survive is to spread to another area. There is another organism on this planet that follows the same

pattern. Do you know what it is? A virus. Human beings are a disease, a cancer of this planet. You are a plague. And we are… the cure.

(Wachowski, 1998, #144, pp. 97–98)

The problem with the machine's use of the virus analogy is that it resonates powerfully with our worst fears about ourselves. Humanity's first and second *Great Leaps Forward* turned us from just another nervous species struggling for survival into the Earth's undisputed ruler. After some mindless evolutionary accident endowed us with language (around one hundred thousand years ago) came the first *Leap* (recall Chapter 2) which bestowed upon our ancestors the power to compel the land to yield plants for our consumption and for the consumption of the animals we enslaved for their milk and flesh. Nature's free hand to select its species was now joined by humanity's methodical breeding of plants, animals and germs. It was our first move in a game of planetary take over. Surplus production took hold and grew until artefacts of our Empires, like the Great Wall of China, became visible from space.

The second *Leap* was much more recent and required the liberation of labour from its feudal bonds and its attachment, by means of the *labour contract*, to the newfangled machinery that spread itself and its products across the high seas, the ragged mountains and the endless plains; even into the expanses of space and the minutiae of our own genome. Our collective planetary footprint grew exponentially from almost nothing to that of an enormous Leviathan. While many of our species remain in the clutches of desperate need and in circumstances often worse than those humans suffered a thousand years ago, *collectively* we are producing a great deal more foodstuff, gadgets and machines than we need. Mountains of food and rivers of wine are either binned or stockpiled daily; cars remain unsold; clothes unworn; ships floating idly on the fringes of our great ports. Human labour itself is either too scarce or terribly abundant, impeded from reaching the parts of the global economy where it could be usefully employed. Ever expanding walls obstruct much needed movement in an era that celebrates something it refers to as globalisation. And, meanwhile, the land turns brittle, the rivers reek of poison, the corals are dying and the atmosphere is filling up with noxious gasses.

So, our two *Leaps* helped us take over the planet in a brief ten thousand years. Not perhaps in a manner of our own conscious choosing, but surely and brutally nevertheless. Were we to weigh the total human population plus our livestock and domesticated animals around ten thousand years ago, that is before the first *Leap*, we would find that this aggregate weight accounted for around a tenth of a percent of all the planet's land animals. What do you think the figure is today? It is a stupendous 98 per cent! Paul MacCready, the engineer who computed this astonishing figure, has this to say on the matter:[30]

> Over billions of years, on a unique sphere, chance has painted a thin covering of life – complex, improbable, wonderful and fragile. Suddenly we humans… have grown in population, technology, and intelligence to a position of terrible power. We now wield the paint brush.[31]

The question is what we do with it. Will we confirm the machine's prophetic powers by behaving like a suicidal virus threatening the very biosphere which supports its own life systems? Or will we collectively design our way out of the conundrum? Political economics will, inevitably, play a significant role in determining the answer. However, our economic understanding cannot help much unless it grasps the dialectical nature of our

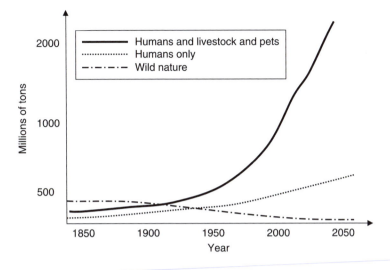

Figure 4.1 Nature's limits.
Source: MacCready, 2004

species (see Box 4.9): namely that, *at the same time*, (a) we possess the properties and display the behavioural codes of a particularly stupid virus; *and* (b) we have a capacity to act as intelligent designers of a rational life on Earth. How this antithesis will play out, and what the future holds for us, depends crucially on securing a firm grasp on the extraordinary human capacity to be both a virus and a god. We have a moral, but also a practical, duty to succeed. Put simply, as a species, we have become too big to fail – much like the banks but only on an even larger scale.

For now, the omens are not encouraging. Our age is one in which two major crises seem to have converged, threatening us, as a species, with the perfect storm. The year 2008 was not only the year of the economic meltdown but also a time when the environmental crisis, caused by our unchecked economic exuberance, has reached something of an apotheosis. And how did we respond? Pathetically, is the honest answer. In the economic sphere, the bailouts and massive government intervention that propped banks up has made it possible for the elites, and the media, to hide their heads in the sand; to pretend that we are back to *business-as-usual*, give or take a little extra regulation of the financial sphere. The year 2009 also marked the sorry failure of the *Copenhagen Conference* whose purpose was, supposedly, to strike a global covenant on how to deal with climate change. We seem to be working hard to vindicate the verdict on our species that the machine bleakly outlined at the beginning of this section.

On a brighter note, every genuine crisis is packed with potential for new pathways to enlightenment and reason. As authors, we stand convinced that 2008 is such a crisis. And that in the new era that began in 2008 it will be possible to prove that, though we often exhibit viral properties, we can be more than a virus: that we can be our own cure. But first we must come to terms with the way our societal structure produces crises *as if* by design. Thus, the next chapter extends the present diagnosis into the first serious account of why crises are endemic to market societies; of why contemporary capitalism sets limits within which humanity cannot preserve, let alone develop, its most endearing capacities.

4.8 Epilogue

The rise of the machines was not planned by anyone. Indeed, nor was music, language, art, arithmetic or money. Every constituent of our culture evolved. This chapter concentrated on the evolutionary pressures on our freedom and our problematic relationship with the technology that has both liberated and enslaved us over the past few centuries. It concluded with a query about our viral properties. The trouble with humans, we surmised, is that, at one level, we surrender unthinkingly to machines and to viral behaviours alike while, at a deeper level, we instinctively resist the loss of freedom that these tendencies entail. This contradiction, as the next chapter argues, offers a powerful explanation of contemporary societal and economic crises.

With the rise of the machines we arrived at the brink of dehumanisation, as Charlie Chaplin's *Modern Times* so eloquently depicted. Rather than inventing our mechanical slaves, we seem to have created our mechanical masters. Our new-found aggregate wealth was purchased at the price of new forms of depravity. Workers and employers alike became appendages to material forces beyond their control. Later on, our minds invented digitisation which, despite its wondrous capacities to free up our imagination and expand surplus further and further, brought us face to face with the spectre of the mother of all false consciousnesses: a virtual reality, as in *The Matrix*, that can potentially lead to the ultimate loss of human liberty; a symbolic reminder of the disconnection between our desires and our capacities that has enriched real estate agents, elevated marketing to a fine art, fuelled financialisation and brought us, eventually, the *Crash of 2008*.

There is, thankfully, a silver lining in all this. Unlike in *The Matrix*, a distinctly human kernel remains at the heart of all our economic activities. And it is this indestructible kernel that is responsible, at once, for the continued production of *value*, for the penchant of our economies for crises, but also for the preservation of a chance for genuine freedom and substantive rationality. It seems to us, as authors, that to confront the challenges of the post-2008 world, humanity needs to find ways of placing value creation under its conscious, rational control. The demeanour of the United States government in the aftermath of both World War Two and, more recently, the *Crash of 2008*, suggests that our perspective is not without historical precedence. After all, in the late 1940s (as Chapter 11 will argue) United States officials set themselves the task of designing, from scratch, a global social economy that worked. Similarly, after 2008, the US Federal Reserve, along with the US Treasury, took it upon themselves to save world capitalism from itself by means of a top-down intervention on a scale never seen before, at least during peacetime.

At this stage it matters not one iota whether one agrees with US policy in the 1940s or in the post-2008 period. Our simple point is that, even the staunchest advocate of free markets, the government of the United States of America, is constantly attempting to *design* a more rational world economy, to which it devotes vast resources. In this book we shall be arguing for interventions, plans and designs that are both bolder and more ambitious. Later chapters will argue in favour of *top-down design* in areas that transcend the financial sphere and touch upon the nexus linking humans and machines, capital and labour, centre and periphery. But before we get more entangled in these intricate discussions, it is important to state our idea simply.

Value, we argued in this chapter, remains relevant as a concept as long as a kernel of freedom remains untouched inside each one of us. The greatest contradiction of our times is that capital accumulation and growth both depend on the preservation of this kernel *and* work inexorably towards its annihilation. The *Crash of 2008* is, to a large extent, but a macro-manifestation of this antinomy. We cannot go on, we argue, like this. If the next economic meltdown due to the irrationality of the global economic system does not bring us down, our incapacity to manage our environment, our population movements, our human and natural resources will. So, if humanity is to be saved from itself, to overcome its tendency to act like an irresponsible virus that destroys its habitat, and to realise its potential as an intelligent designer, our collective task is simple: it is to reach into our deepest recesses, where that stubborn kernel of freedom and reason is hiding, bring it out into the open and use it as the primary raw material with which to fashion a collectively rational design in which the world's machines are well and truly the slaves of the human spirit and their products help us traverse landscapes of the finer pleasures that only creative exertion can yield. Put differently, the time has come to shed our virus-like demeanour and take control of our inventions.

Upon reading these lines, and given the prejudices of our era, one might rightly ask whether it is wise to seek solutions to our species' problems on the basis of some top-down grand design. Is it not the case, one may well ask, that such ambition fuelled the world's greatest authoritarianisms, leading not only to ruined economies and environmental waste- lands but also to the gulag? Indeed, this is very much so. However, we do not hear anyone argue that genetic engineering aimed at eradicating muscular dystrophy is either immoral or pie-in-the-sky because the Nazis embraced (at huge human cost) a combination of Darwinism and genetics (without any tangible scientific success).

Another objection takes the form of the frequently posed question: are unfettered markets not more efficient than any centrally planned system in delivering solutions for a modern world in which freedom-loving people want to live? Not in the slightest. Any half serious investigation of capitalism will reveal that markets were brought about by direct state action and cannot work outside the context of some grand political design enforced and supervised by state power. The dilemma between state intervention and markets is just as false as a claim that we must choose between natural selection and genetic engineering. Granted that a genetic engineer would be criminally negligent were he/she to ignore the manner in which his/her designer organisms would interact with other organisms in the context of natural selection;[32] it would be absurd to suggest that humanity must choose between natural selection and genetic engineering. So, the question is not *if* we want a grand top-down design, both in the realm of genetics and of political economics, but *which one* is best suited to our species interests.

We end this chapter on the human predicament with a diagnosis for the twenty-first cen- tury drawn from two great nineteenth-century figures that, in one way or another, featured prominently in the preceding pages: Marx and Darwin. No one designed capitalism. It simply evolved, liberating us in the process from more primitive forms of social and economic organisation. It gave rise to machines and methods that allowed us to take over the planet. It empowered us to imagine a future without poverty where our life is no longer at the mercy of a hostile nature. Yet, at the same time, just like nature spawned Mozart and HIV *using the same indiscriminate mechanism*, capitalism also produced catastrophic forces of discord, alienation and environmental degradation. It generated acute crises (as the next chapter will illustrate) and produced, in the same stride, new forms of wealth and of deprivation.

In evolutionary terms, capitalism, and in particular the way it hinges production onto the *labour contract*, is too primitive a system. As the next chapter will argue, calamities like the *Crash of 2008* and the collapse of the 2009 *Copenhagen Conference* on climate change are the tip of the melting iceberg. Less well seen is capitalism's wastefulness of human and natural resources, as well as its encroachments on genuine liberty. The main reason? Because capitalism is *one evolutionary stage behind* the productive capacity of the amazing 'machinery' that it, itself, brings into being. Humanity's current task is, thus, to do that which a virus cannot: to *design* our continued evolution and steer its path in a direction of our choosing, if only for the planet's sake.

Box 4.10 Of viruses and humans

This chapter has argued that the origin of all value, as well as the cause of all our woes, is the ontological difference between electricity generators and human labourers; between, on the one hand, the ants and the bees and, on the other, the human architect (see Box 4.6). On one side we have mindless, albeit immensely productive, creations while, on the other, we have quirky but purposefully intelligent creators. This is yet another binary opposition that has caused us much confusion. Charles Darwin's brilliant insight was that this opposition, while real, is not cast in stone, that it can also be dialectically transcended, just like the binary oppositions discussed in Box 4.9.

Following Darwin, we now know that, from the Big Bang onwards, marvellous complexity evolved in the absence of any agent capable of intelligence or comprehension. Life emerged on Earth shortly after the planet stabilised and bubbled along in the form of single prokaryotic cells for a billion years before its first momentous transformation; the fusion of two prokaryotic cells into one brand new eukaryotic one. With the birth of multi-cell life not only was death 'invented' but also the path that led to *our* evolution was cleared. Eukaryotes were the beginning of the division of labour between cells that later developed into muscle, blood, livers and, of course, brains. Two and a half billion years later, we emerged; a mere six million years after our branch in the Tree of Life diverged from that our immediate cousins (the chimpanzees). While our extended family developed no language, and thus no capacity to grasp the ways of Nature so as to produce surplus, we did. The rest, as they say, is history.[1]

But how did this unique human capacity for comprehension, reason and, ultimately, freedom, emerge? What was the impetus of the amazing complexity typifying the structure of our brains which made language, culture, algebra and reality TV possible? Darwin's radical idea was that our intelligence evolved accidentally out of primordial idiocy. That we were the first intelligent designers and that we were ourselves produced, without a blueprint, as a result of a mindless process involving the basic agents of evolution: *replicators* which are no more than *biological or data entities with an attitude*;[2] i.e. with an ability to copy themselves; to adapt in response to the environmental circumstances; and, of course, to mutate.

This simple idea of the unplanned genesis of order and brilliance out of a prehistoric soup of stupid genes has a longstanding symbiotic relationship with political economics. Darwin himself famously admitted that he borrowed the idea of natural selection from Thomas Robert Malthus's argument that death from famine and pestilence played an important role in keeping the number of humans within the limits of the planet's capacity to feed them and that this 'Struggle for Existence' ensured that the behaviours, inventions and ideas that helped men and women survive would be favoured over time, while those that did not would become extinct.[3] But even before Malthus' dismal theories, Adam Smith's radical idea that markets produce virtue in the absence of a benevolent planner (recall Chapter 2) resonated beautifully with Darwin's most basic tenet. From the late nineteenth-century to our days, political economists who took it upon themselves to defend capitalism, from those who purported to regulate, restrain and even overthrow it, embraced the Smith–Malthus–Darwin mindframe, portraying any critic of capitalism as a form of creationist audacious enough to question natural selection.

To this very date, most mainstream economists assume that their defence of the unfettered market system is on a par with biologists' defence of Darwin against the attacks of fundamentalists, creationists and assorted crackpots. This is, of course, a flight of fancy. Darwin himself, in the *Origin*'s first chapter, discusses the methodical selection of species that generations of human agriculturalists and breeders used to interfere with Nature. Since then we took things one step further in developing genetic engineering. No one claims that our capacity to engineer DNA and create new designer organisms in the lab negates natural selection. The difference between us and viruses is that, unlike the latter, we have both a capacity to grasp the laws that rule over our evolution and to affect them directly. The towering question at the present historical juncture is whether we can do something of the sort at a planetary scale before our CO_2 emissions and our toxic wastes destroy our own habitat in a manner that will make a mockery of our claim to be superior to viruses. But this is a political question that evolutionary biology has precious little to say about.

Notes

1 For more on the extent to which history, especially that of capitalism, can be explained by evolutionary theory, see Varoufakis (2008).
2 Daniell Dennett, a philosopher who trained in neuroscience in order to understand the biological processes underpinning human thought, defines viruses as *strings of nucleic acid with attitude* – see Dennett (2001).
3 In the introduction to his celebrated *On the Origin of Species* (1859) Darwin wrote: 'In the next chapter the Struggle for Existence amongst all organic beings throughout the world, which inevitably follows from the high geometrical ratio of their increase, will be treated of. This is the doctrine of Malthus applied to the whole animal and vegetable kingdoms' (1859 [1996] pp. 5–6).

5 Crises

The laboratory of the future

5.1 The two natures of labour

The trouble with humans, as established in the previous chapter, is that our labour cannot be fully commodified *independently of our will*. At work, like in all walks of life, humans can never behave like electricity generators *even if our lives depended on it* (see Box 4.8). Unlike the hiring of a generator, which is a machine fairly unproblematically translating given inputs into a measurable output, the employment of human work is never that straightforward. For, when an employer hires a person's work, the latter cannot be neatly extricated from the worker's subjectivity (recall Section 4.4). Whereas capitalists can do as they like with a generator or a horse, they have no alternative but to tolerate that *core* of the human worker which can never be fully subjugated; a faculty which is impervious to quantification; a will which, ultimately, is uniquely placed to produce *value* because its freedom is non-negotiable and impossible to transfer fully, with or without payment, to another intellect.

Unable to buy the workers' *work*, employers resort to offering them a *labour contract*, specifying pay, hours and conditions, at which point employer and employee embark upon a 'beautiful' relationship (see Section 4.5). The worker's subjectivity is like a thorn in the employer's backside but, at once, proves to be the sole source of the value produced on his premises. Marx read much into this paradox. The opposition between (a) the employer's drive to subjugate an alien force deeply buried in the human worker's psyche and (b) that alien force's frantic struggle for autonomy, defines the *labour process*: the process by which the commodity purchased by the employer is turned into an actual (though uncommodified and uncommodifiable) *labour input* which, in turn, instills value in the produced output.

Through this prism, value is the consequence of a merciless dialectical opposition (see Box 4.10) between the capitalist's yearning to accumulate machines and the worker's inner freedom.[1] At stake is, for the capitalists, their capacity to survive as capitalists and, for the worker, his/her humanity. The fascinating feature of this tussle is that the resistance offered by the worker's inner (human) kernel is as essential for the capitalist as it is despised by him/her. For, if he/she could fulfil his/her employer's greatest fantasy, and turn into an agreeable robot or a type of inexpensive generator, the benefits for the capitalist would be tremendous but only insofar as this is not something that could happen to all workers. A similar acquiescence by *all* workers would take us back (or is it forward?) to a *Matrix Economy* where the machines replicate themselves but no value is created. As long as the capitalists remain human, their interests (as capitalists) would be destroyed by such a development. The saying that 'a vengeful god would grant us our every wish' is tailor-made for capitalists.

Annihilation of the workers' freedom to resist their conversion to mere machinery would also be the capitalists' downfall. In Marx's words:

> If the whole class of the wage-labourer were to be annihilated by machinery, how terrible that would be for capital, *which, without wage-labour, ceases to be capital!*[2]
>
> Labour is the living, form-giving fire; it is the transitoriness of things, their temporarity, as their formation by living time.[3]

Saved by their inability to fully subdue the workers' mental autonomy, and thus destroy the life-giving properties of labour by turning it into a resource like any other, the capitalists remain in control of the production of value. The *labour contract* which enables them to do so embodies the two natures of labour: on the one hand, there is the *commodity* that capitalists hire when shopping at the *labour market*. Marx calls this commodity *labour power*, but it is often easier conceptualised as *labour time*. On the other there is the activity, or lifegiving force, that infuses value into labour's output: the *labour input*.

Labour power, like all commodities, comes at a price (the wage rate) and is sold in preagreed 'packets' measured in hours. Of course, as discussed in Section 4.5, capitalists have no time for *labour power*. If they do buy it, it is only because it confers upon them a legal right, and an opportunity, to extract from workers what they are really after: actual *labour input*. Why extract it and not simply buy it? Because, as we already explained, *labour input*, much like love and talent, *cannot be bought*; because like a beautiful sunset, it can *never* be (at least not in a pre-*Matrix* world) commodified. The only way of getting to it is by buying *labour power* and trying to squeeze *labour input* out of it in the context of the *labour process* (see Box 5.1).

So, labour breathes fire into our social universe but only on condition that a modicum of freedom survives within the mind of the worker. Critically, capitalists are forced to try to adopt a *labour process* (by which commodity *labour power* is turned into activity *labour input*) brutal enough to keep them in business. However, human nature constrains them to a

---

Box 5.1 Labour's two natures

Labour power (the commodity)

This is the quantifiable and commodifiable face of labour. Mental and physical skills, and time on the job. It comprises: '... the aggregate of those mental and physical capabilities existing in a human being, which he exercises whenever he produces a use-value of any description'. (Marx, *Capital*, vol. I, chapter 6) As such, it possesses exchange value (like all commodities) but no real use value.

Labour input (the activity)

This is the unquantifiable aspect of labour which, as such, cannot be the subject of a well-written, water-tight, commercial contract between employer and worker. It possesses plenty of use value (since it is what infuses value into commodities) but no exchange value (since it cannot be bought or sold).

Labour process

The process by which capitalists buy labour power in order to extract labour input. In short, the process by which labour power is transformed *outside* the market (and inside the firm) into labour input.

> For labour, or rather labour power, is not a primary input, on a par with 'land'. Men, like capital, are reproducible, only twiceover: once, when they are born; and a second time, when they enter the labour market. Twice they are born as clay, never as putty. The life horizon of this clay, unlike that of clay-machinery, is exogenously given; and there is not, for men a scrapping rule, whereby an obsolete man can give way, via the surplus which his labour power has created to free capital which can then be reinvested to produce another labour unit. Then, how, do men adapt to a changing world by changing their own value? If we want to go behind the laws of motion, so to speak, to the laws of value of society which underlie them, if we wish to measure the worth to a historical society of labour time, not for the production of surplus but for the reproduction of labour, then we must ask what labour is.
>
> Krimpas (1975)

level of brutality lower than what would be necessary in order to diminish their workers' spirit to such an extent that they become machines. The workers' instinctive resistance to the capitalists' ambition to render their labour mechanical is, in the end, in the capitalists' own interests.

Labour's two natures appear in two separate locations. *Labour power* is traded in the market for labour. *Labour input* is, by contrast, what occurs after workers have exited the market, with a *labour contract* under their belt, and have entered production on the employer's premises. Once they have signed on the dotted line, they have entered perhaps the only locus within capitalism which remains a *market-free zone*: the firm, the factory, the farm, the workplace. While there, their relationship with other workers and with the employer is a purely *social* one that can never be mediated by the market.[4] The labour market's only continuing role, while they are busily employed, is that it offers them the only *fallback position*; their only *outside option*: to resign and gallantly search for another job.[5] Box 5.2 'updates' our theory of how labour contributes to production under the new (dialectical) light of labour's two natures.

The importance of all this comes down to a simple thought: the dual nature of labour offers a useful explanation of where profit comes from. In Adam Smith, for instance competition drives profit to the ground. Prices drop until they reach the level of per unit costs at which point all profit disappears. Naturally, profit only appears fleetingly and disappears the moment the market's gravitational forces 'drag' the system to its natural equilibrium. For Ricardo, profit is something that happens during the transition to capitalism's 'natural state' in which no profits are made, that is, at the point where the whole product is divided between rent and wages, although clearly he dreaded the prospect. Marx begged to differ. He believed strongly that capitalism and profit are synonymous. While in full agreement with Smith and Ricardo that competition wipes out the possibility of making a profit systematically by buying and selling commodities, he was convinced that profit was the elixir that kept

Box 5.2 The labour theory of wages and surplus value

In Box 4.8 Jill, the worker was portrayed as a machine (likened to an electricity generator). Her input into production was labour input L. With the help of capital goods K (machines, tools, raw materials, etc.), Jill's L produced Q units of output of a value analogous to quantity L employed. Each unit of output, thus, had a value of approximately Q/L. However, in the context of labour's twin natures, labour input L cannot be purchased as such. It can only be extracted from Jill's labour power N (measured in contractual hours) that Jack, the capitalist employer, buys at a wage rate of w per unit. His total labour cost in value terms is the product wN, or wN/Q per unit of output. This is the variable capital that Jack must 'spend' on Jill before he gets a chance, during production, to extract her L units of actual labour input.

The value of Jill's labour power: so, what does wN depend on? Marx's answer is consistent with the Labour Theory of Value, according to which the value of a commodity is analogous to the labour input necessary for its production. But what labour inputs go into the production of commodity labour power? Marx's answer turns on the commodities that are necessary for the reproduction of Jill's normal life, e.g. food, clothing, toilet paper, heating fuel. These Jill must buy at the market at a value analogous to the labour input placed into them by strangers. So, suppose that for Jill to be able to report to work every day, and be in a position to work 'normally', she requires, on a daily basis, commodities α_1, α_2,..., α_K. Suppose further that to produce these, other workers, working in places far and wide, must provide the following labour inputs: for the production of the α_1 units that Jill needs, Λ workers had to provide labour units $L_1^{\alpha 1}, L_2^{\alpha 1},..., L_\Lambda^{\alpha 1}$. Similarly, for the production of the α_2 units that Jill needs Ξ workers had to provided labour units $L_1^{\alpha 2}, L_2^{\alpha 2},..., L_\Xi^{\alpha 2}$ ... Finally, for the production of the α units that Jill needs, Ω workers had to provided labour units $L_1^{\alpha K}, L_2^{\alpha K},..., L_\Omega^{\alpha K}$. Letting,

$$V_{\alpha 1} = [L_1^{\alpha 1} + L_2^{\alpha 1} +,\cdots,+ L_\Lambda^{\alpha 1}], V_{\alpha 2} = [L_1^{\alpha 2} + L_2^{\alpha 2} +,\cdots,+ L_\Xi^{\alpha 2}], \cdots,$$
$$V_{\alpha K} = [L_1^{\alpha K} + L_2^{\alpha K} +\cdots,+ L_\Omega^{\alpha K}]$$

we derive, as $V_{\alpha 1}$, $V_{\alpha 2}$,..., and $V_{\alpha K}$, the value of every commodity making up the basket of commodities that Jill must be in a position to afford in order to report to work daily. Thus, the value of the commodity she sells daily to Jack (i.e. the value of her labour power) cannot be less than the sum of these values. In a well-functioning market, the value of Jill's labour power, say, V_{LP} will equal the sum:

$$V_{LP} = V_{\alpha 1} + V_{\alpha 2} + \cdots + V_{\alpha K}$$

Note that the value of Jill's labour power is merely a sum of the actual labour inputs that went into the production of the basket of commodities Jill buys with her wages. It is the magnitude of other workers' aggregate work that keeps Jill going.

The value of Jill's work (or labour): while at work, Jill imparts her own labour units L into the commodity that Jack's firm specialises in, producing thus Q units of output (each of which is, consequently, valued at Q/L).

Surplus value: Jack pays Jill a wage w for N units of commodity labour power: a total of wN which must be (see the definition of the value of Jill's labour power above) such that $wN = V_{LP}$. In return, he receives N units of her labour power, e.g. eight hours of work, which in turn gives him a chance to enter into a social non-market relation with her and extract from her, while she is on the job, an actual labour input equal to L units, i.e. he becomes the owner of the produced Q units of the final product-commodity whose value equals L. The difference between this L, i.e. of the value of the commodity units Jill creates, and the value of her labour power V_{LP} is precisely the same as the difference between the value to Jack of her labour input and the value he paid for her labour power. Marx defines this difference as surplus value[1] and pinpoints it as the source of profit: $S = L - V_{LP}$.

Note

1 In Marx's narrative, it is as if Jill is paid only for a portion of her labour time, receiving the rest as surplus labour. We avoid this exposition because it steals the thunder of Marx's original intuition. For if surplus labour is measurable in (unpaid) hours, this implies that labour input is also measurable (in hours worked). But if it is measurable, then the whole point about the dual nature of labour (which is based on the idea that labour is split between one component that can be quantified and another which cannot) is well and truly lost. For this reason, we adopt a narrative in which the amount of labour input that can be extracted from a given amount of labour power is radically, epistemologically indeterminate and certainly not measurable in hours, kilogrammes or microwatts ... The term 'epistemologically indeterminate' is used to emphasise that, while the individual worker's labour input's magnitude may well be (ontologically) determinate, it is not a magnitude that employers can ever measure with any degree of determinacy. This epistemic indeterminacy is the key to surplus value generation and, by extension, the source of profit.

capitalism dynamic, vibrant and, indeed, alive. Rather than to *explain* profit by invoking some market 'imperfection' (e.g. to claim that powerful firms make profits by restricting competition), he aimed at a perspective which would explain capitalist profit as a *permanent feature* of capitalism at its most 'natural' or 'normal'; that is, even in the presence of the most ruthless competition. His explanation of the source of such systematic profit that competition does not eliminate turns on labour's dual nature.

Unlike other commodities that lack labour's dialectical, or dual, nature, labour allows its buyers to do something they cannot do with any other commodity: *systematically to claim a residual every time they buy and sell it*. This they cannot do with apples, oranges or, indeed, electricity generators. When 'things' are traded, their unitary nature ensures that no profit can be made systematically from *arbitrage* (from buying and re-selling them more dearly); at least not in competitive markets where competition is strong enough. But labour has two natures; its buyer (Jack) buys only one of these 'natures' (*labour power*) not because he cares for it as such but because he is interested in the second nature (*labour input*) that can be neither sold nor bought. Labour's second nature is what the employer is interested in, as it is the life-giving 'force' imbuing output with value. Thus, by driving a wedge between labour's two distinct natures, which can also be expressed as (a) labour's *exchange value* (see V_{LP} in the Box above) and (b) its *use value*, the capitalist reaps *surplus value*. From that, the capitalist pays the landlord the owed *rent* and the banker the owed *interest*. What is left over is the firm's *profit*, a small portion of which the capitalist keeps for his miserly subsistence, and the remainder is ploughed back into the business in the form of investment into more capital whose explicit purpose is to keep per unit costs down and stop competitors from turning him into yet another purveyor of *labour power*.

The size of *surplus value*, and therefore of profit, depends, in this sense, on a purely social process internal to the firm but crucially linked to the whole economy. How many actual *labour units* Jack will *extract* from Jill during the production process is not a technical matter (unlike the electricity generator whose output is linked to fuel inputs in a manner that a qualified engineer can account for fully). It depends on Jack's *social power* over Jill, on the psychological relationship between them, as well as on the social relations between workers governing the ways in which Jill works *alongside* her fellow workers.[6] To offer a simple example, consider what happens when unemployment rises in the sector. It is very likely that Jill will be more fearful of dismissal and, thus, this endows Jack with increased power over her. If this development results in more *labour units L* being supplied by Jill for the same *labour power* purchased by Jack, *surplus value* rises even while all other things remain equal.

The economic effects of labour's dual nature and of the social dynamics this infuses into a market society, know no bounds. Marx identified the value of *labour power*, that is, the wage, with the *labour input* that was necessary for Jill's 'reproduction'. However, he neglected to mention a category of goods essential to the reproduction of Jill's normal life: *the care, support and hard work that her family members contribute to her life*. Alas, these crucial goods are *not* commodities (since they are not 'produced' for sale) and are, mostly, 'supplied' by unpaid female labour. What about the unpaid *labour input* by those shadowy workers which are just as indispensable contributors to Jill's capacity to sell *labour power* to Jack? To see the economic importance of this 'unseen' *labour input*, consider what happens when an economic crisis, like the one following the *Crash of 2008*, reduces wages. When wages are reduced, this means that workers will have to do with fewer of the commodities that are necessary for their 'reproduction'. More often than not, the resulting cuts in their family budgets are compensated for by those who care for them (traditionally their wives/husbands), who must produce more goods at home in order to replace the commodities that the household wage income can no longer purchase. Jill must therefore increase her *labour input* inside her home to replace goods that were hitherto purchased with the wages of her husband and children, as well as her own.[7] Thus, recessions not only intensify the extraction of *surplus value* at the workplace but also of the *labour input* extracted in the domestic sphere by those (usually men) with greater social power over the rest of their families.

To conclude this section, the labour market is the locus of a momentous clash between an irresistible force and an immovable object; a collision between: (a) the inexorable forces of capitalism which commodify everything and anything in their wake, *and* (b) the infinite tenacity with which human nature resists quantification, mechanisation and, thus, full commodification. The result of this contradiction produces the *labour contract* and an economic system that resembles a vast ocean of market activity punctuated by an archipelago of isles against which the mighty waves of commodification crash, but cannot fully overcome. It is on these isles, that is within the capitalist firms, that value is produced by human workers engaged in a *labour process* sequestered from the market. That value, once produced, is tossed back into the ocean of market trades thus generating *surplus value* for the firms' owners, *interest* for the bankers, *rent* for the landlords as well as a source of renewable energy, *profit*, which maintains the ocean's dynamism and overall vigour.

Box 5.3 Labour power, human capital and *The Matrix*

Modern economists talk a lot about human capital and assign an important role to training and education in enhancing it, and thus boosting the value, or more precisely the price, of labour.[1] In the context of the current dialectical analysis, nothing human, including labour, and of course human capital, is a simple, unitary 'thing'. Instead, everything human possesses more than one nature and, often, these 'natures' are at odds with one another (e.g. labour taking the form of both labour power and labour input). Similarly with human capital, which has a double nature too – the commodity form of labour power, as it manifests itself in the labour market, and the form of the human herself, complete with all her hidden talents, aspirations, capacities. The reduction of humanity to sheer labour power, that is, the utter commodification of her time and potential for work, is a process akin to turning men and women into 'things'. During capitalist production, labour power is fused with machines; it *becomes a component of capital*. Marx suggests that

> The worker functions here as a special natural form of this capital, as distinct from the elements of capital that exist in the natural form of means of production.[2]

Once fused with the machinery around her, the worker's human capital is expended during the production process just like the electricity generator's nuts and bolts are subject to wear and tear. But, whereas in the case of the generator there is nothing else going on inside, in the worker's case her inner core, her free will, the kernel of humanity that keeps her ontologically irreducible to an android, is constantly resisting the steady depletion of its potential while, at once, succumbing to it, exhausted, overworked and alienated.

> The individual not only develops his abilities in production but also expends them, uses them up, in the act of production … Universal prostitutions appears as a necessary phase in the development of the social character of personal talents, capacities, abilities, activities …[3]

If human labour becomes no more than human capital as traded in labour markets, we shall have become fully transhuman: a life-form fully integrated within the social universe of capital. *The Matrix* will have become a reality without any need for fancy technology or some takeover by 'emancipated', intelligent machines. Glen Rikovski, in his article 'Alien Life: Marx and the future of the human', agrees that the only spanner in the works, maintaining an irreducible human force within capitalism, is the curious resistance put up by the human spirit against capital's drive to incorporate us fully within its substance; to rid us of all humanity and leave standing only our marketable human capital. This struggle, between human labour and the logic of capital, is within us, Rikovski insists. Capital is an invasive social force that 'possesses' the human, and the intensity of this non-human force to permeate our lives, our souls, increases historically. We are becoming 'capitalised'.[4] In this context, the struggle against seeing people as human capital is not about ethics. It is much more important than that.

Notes

1 It is interesting that in the voluminous literature on human capital – worthy of a *Journal of Economic Literature* (JEL) code by itself (J24) – the question is never asked how human capital becomes productive. It is taken for granted that education or training (on-the-job or not) is productive and hence paid more. The role of education as productivity enhancing is in fact the more benign version of the theory. In other versions, education acts as a signal that separates the able from the not so able (e.g. Weiss (1995)). In more reactionary explanations of wage differentials, the major determinant of inequality is some metaphysical cognitive ability (e.g. IQ) which is responsible for some immutable law of distribution. The most extreme version is the ridiculous *Bell Curve: Intelligence and Class Structure in American Life* (Hernstein and Murray 1994), although most economists do not buy it (see Arrow *et al.* 2000.) It is interesting that a radical critique of the human capital theory that is not repudiated by neoclassicists is that the traits that are valued as human capital are those that make the worker more conducive to manipulation in the labour process (Bowles and Gintis 1975, 1976).
2 Marx, *Capital*, Vol. 2 (1885 [1992]), pp. 445–6.
3 Marx in *Grundrisse* (1857 [1973]), p. 163.
4 Rikovski (2003).

5.2 The two natures of capital

Capital [is] not a thing, but a social relation between persons...[8].

If labour has two natures, so does capital. For if profit is *extracted* by the owner of capital goods (mines, farms, electricity generators, production lines, etc.) in the context of a purely social relation that the *labour contract* sets up between the capitalist and the worker (in the manner described in the preceding section); and if the accumulation of capital is predicated upon this social relation, then capital cannot just be a collection of 'things'. In addition to its 'machine form', capital is something else too: *a social relationship* between capital's owners and workers which has a unique capacity to generate *surplus value* and, in this manner, to feed into the production of more capital.

In this dialectical vein, to own machines or other means of production does not a capitalist make. The sentence written by Marx just before the quotation above states this explicitly: 'Property in money, means of subsistence, machinery and other means of production, do not yet stamp a man as a capitalist if there be wanting the correlative – the wage-worker'. In a *Matrix* society in which labour has lost its dual nature (and has become a production unit not dissimilar to an electricity generator), no capitalist can exist. A technician, a person (or *Overlord Program*) organising the work of a network of machines, perhaps. But to have a genuine capitalist in control of the production process, a human workforce is indispensable. Just as it took the confrontation aboard the slave ship between the European sailor and the African slave to define one as 'white' and the other as 'black' (see Box 5.4 below) so too in the workplace it is only in the eye of the human waged worker that a machine owner can catch a glimpse of himself as a capitalist.

To make this point unambiguously, Marx quotes a story told by E.G. Wakefield (Marx (1867 [1976]), pp. 932–3), of a certain Mr Peel who migrated from England to Swan River, Western Australia. Being a man of means,

Box 5.4 The slave ship and the dialectic of racial identity

While the serfs of Britain were being 'liberated', British, Dutch and French ships were loading enslaved African men, women and children for transportation to plantations on the other side of the Atlantic. Rediker (2007) relates vividly the remarkable story of that voyage.[1] On the initial journey from Southampton or Amsterdam to the shores of eastern Africa, the ship's captain and his officers would painstakingly torture their crew into submission. Often, the ship's crew was treated more savagely than the slaves. Terror tactics were common and the outward voyage was one of utter misery for the sailors who had 'volunteered' as an alternative to being imprisoned for minor offences or, more likely, for debts owed to money lenders.

But once the ship was docked in Africa, and the slave 'cargo' was being loaded, a new fear and a new opposition emerged. Faced by angry, desperate slaves, who would do *anything* to break their chains and jump into the ocean, the captain, his debauched officers and the dehumanised crew found common ground in the fear of a slave uprising. They quickly identified themselves as 'white'. And the slaves, for the first time, identified themselves as 'black'. Thus, the slave trade created new categories, and fresh oppositions, to which these persons had never previously belonged.

Before the 'cargo' came on board, the sailor had considered his captain an alien; a ruthless 'other'. And the Africans, dissenting as they did from different villages and tribes, had never thought of themselves as belonging to the same group. Their new bond was forged by the institution of slavery. Rediker's point is that African-American culture began on the slave ship. In the terms of Hegel's dialectic, the opposition between shipmaster and crew, and the opposition between different African tribes and social groups, were both dissolved by the trade in humans. In its stead rose a new, more totalising, opposition between 'white' and 'black'.

As if to confirm Marx's Hegelian hope about the capacity of the human spirit to overcome even the most totalising of oppositions, Rediker suggests that the frequent battles between sailors and slaves aboard the slave ships necessitated greater security, more sailors and, hence, increased the trade's costs to an extent that made the slave trade uneconomical. This was one of the reasons, though not the only one, why the slave trade was, eventually, abandoned.[2] When it ended, in 1807, the slave ports of the Caribbean were populated by wharfingers: impoverished, diseased sailors who had, between them, been responsible for transporting hundreds of thousands of Africans to a most miserable existence. Once that vicious opposition had melted away, some of them were taken in and looked after by negro women out of pure compassion. Humanity can, ostensibly, resist the most dehumanising of systems.

Notes

1 Rediker (2007).
2 Of course, Marx would add another: That genuine value creation requires free labourers. See the next section where we shall allude to this theory of what happened during the Civil War in the USA.

Mr Peel [...] took with him [...] means of subsistence and of production to the amount of £50,000. This Mr. Peel had the foresight to bring with him, besides, 300 persons of the working-class, men, women, and children. Once arrived at his destination, "Mr. Peel was left without a servant to make his bed or fetch him water from the river".

What had happened? Why did Mr Peel end up with no servant to tend to his whims? The simple answer is that the transported labour force abandoned Mr Peel, got themselves nice plots of land in the surrounding wilderness, and went into 'business' for themselves. Access to land that they could cultivate for themselves allowed Mr Peel's workers to liberate themselves from him and set up their own ventures. It is in this particular sense that Mr Peel, though he took with him money, equipment and a workforce, could not take with him English capitalism. Or, in Marx's words: 'Unhappy Mr. Peel who provided for everything except the export of English modes of production to Swan River!'.[9]

In Chapter 2, we recounted the crucial role that the Enclosures played in driving a wedge between British peasants and the land, cutting them off from its productive powers and, thus, creating a class of potential workers with nothing to do but sell their *labour power*. Mr Peel's British workers, while still in Britain, were therefore tied to his *capital goods* by their lack of access to productive means not belonging to Mr Peel. But once in Western Australia, with its abundant land (stolen as it was from the local Aborigines), they suddenly gained the access they lacked and which, in one brush stroke, ended Mr Peel's monopoly of productive means and, thus, terminated his status as a capitalist.

So, the natural conclusion to be drawn from the idea that labour's peculiar double nature is the source of value is that capital is also two-natured. It appears to us both as a collection of useful 'things' and as a social relationship based on who owns those 'things' – and, crucially, who does not. As if by magic, these two faces are often conflated in the form of *money*. In fact, in everyday parlance, *capital* and *money* are interchangeable terms.

Now, of course, money has been a source of fascination, and of concern, well before capitalism came to the fore. In Chapter 2, we discussed Aristotle's rejection of the thought that moneymaking can be a virtuous activity (since it is an activity that lacks a natural *telos*). In his comedy *Wealth* Aristophanes adds a hilarious narrative on how money sweeps all in its path, homogenising every urge and reducing all value to a single metric or index. While every pleasure and every human drive is subject to 'diminishing returns', money is different [*Plutus*, 188–90]. As Richard Seaford recently put it in his *Presidential Address to the Classical Association* (Seaford 2009), Aristophanes urges us to recognise that

> if someone obtains thirteen talents [a lot of money at that time], he is eager for sixteen, and if he obtains sixteen he swears that life is unbearable unless he obtains forty [Plutus, 193–7]. What, we may add, would have been the point in Homeric society of accumulating a million of those prestige items that embody wealth, such as tripods? Money is different. It isolates the individual, and is unlimited.[10]

A cultural child of the ancient Greeks, Marx could not but be influenced by their scepticism regarding the role of money.[11] Marked by an everyday life overshadowed by permanent money shortages, Marx recognised in it a fascinating, inexorable and at once nauseating force that makes the ugly attractive, the lame mobile, the bad honoured, the dishonest sincere, the stupid talented, the desirous fulfilled. He saw in money a dialectical power to turn incapacities into their contrary; to obliterate natural qualities and

Box 5.5 Capital's two natures

Capital goods (the commodity)

The quantifiable, tangible and commodifiable face of capital. Consists of machines, raw materials, buildings, generators, seeds, computerised robots – in general, all the commodities that have a capacity to contribute to the production of other commodities. As such, capital goods possess exchange value as well as use value. But they lack the capacity to create new value. To explain this antinomy, consider the question: Where does a generator's or a robot's value come from? Consistent with the claim that only free human labour can produce value as such, a machine's value reflects the inventor's creative thinking, the engineer's design skills, the worker's labour that helped manufacture the machine, etc. The machine itself, while employed in the factory, the farm or the warehouse, cannot create new value. It is sterile, in this regard. Although it magnifies Jill's productive capacity no end (allowing her to augment the productive power of her own arms and mind), the machine's 'own' contribution to Jill's final output springs from the value that has already been stored in it by the inventor, the engineer and the machine worker. It is in this context that Marx refers to capital goods as constant capital: 'things' that contain 'crystallised' free human labour units, which are then transferred to the final product made by 'living workers' with the help of these 'things'.

Capital as social power (the relationship)

This is the dynamic, unquantifiable, dialectical face of capital. It is a force that gives the owners of capital goods enough sway over the labour process during which the purchased labour power is converted into labour units. It is the power that denies workers all options except to sell their labour power to an owner of capital goods and, thus, to *consent* to a labour process that extracts, from that sold labour power of theirs, labour units that they could never sell as such (given the peculiar nature of free human labour's inputs). It is the power that Mr Peel suddenly lost when his workers disembarked in Western Australia. His loss, we note, was independent of his ownership of capital goods, which the journey to the antipodes never threatened, and utterly due to the sudden appearance of fresh options for the workers; options that ended Mr Peel's monopoly of capital goods.

   In short, possession of capital goods is a necessary but insufficient condition for capitalism. Capitalism also requires that workers lack the capacity to go it alone. Without a violently unequal distribution of capital goods, its second face, that of capital as power, cannot come into existence. Recalling that *The Matrix Economy* was replete with capital goods (indeed, it featured little else) but lacked a capacity to generate value, it turns out that a genuine capitalism (one that can generate value) requires, in addition to machinery that revolutionises production, free human labourers who have no independent access to these capital goods (or other means of production such as land) and who must submit to an extractive labour process in order to work side by side with the machines.

to replace them with social aspects. In his own words, 'money is the alienated ability of mankind'.[12]

While in one sense it is not too difficult to imagine Aristotle and Aristophanes lambasting the standard contemporary argument that financial markets are worthy because they 'unhook' a person's, a company's or even a nation's, capacity to invest from their own capacity to save, in quite another sense it is impossible to understand the role of money today by studying a pre-capitalist world, like that of ancient Athens, where *capital as power* had not been 'invented'. Marx contributed the important thought that the commodification of land and labour which foreshadowed the rise of market societies (recall the narrative in Chapter 2) gave money and credit a task that goes far beyond the musings above – a role that transcends that of a medium of exchange; of a common currency that can appear magically as a focus of insatiable craving and wholesale reductionism.

Marx's fresh insight was that, once land became a commodity, complete with an exchange value determined through a network of markets, it *craved* to be rented out to persons who took it to themselves to organise production, employing free ex-peasant labour on a fixed retainer that reflected another market-determined value: that of *labour power*. All this organisation of production, based on purchased factors of production, meant that, for the first time in history, substantial sums of money had to be *advanced* to waged workers and often to landlords, long before the harvest was in. In turn, this necessitated a *money market*. Thus, the despised usurers improved their image (see Box 5.6 for a related tale) and evolved into the financiers that have since been doing something more than merely 'lubricating' the wheels of capitalism: they are facilitating the emergence of *capital as power* by lending to fledgling capitalists the money that is necessary to acquire more *capital goods* and *labour power* in exchange for a promise to pay back the original capital plus *interest*. And where would that value come from? It would spring out of the *surplus value* that the *labour process* will extract from *labour power* in the future.

In conclusion, labour's two natures were born at the same time that *capital goods* evolved into *capital as power* and, in short order, took a new money form in the context of a *futures' market* for *surplus value* which, in turn, was only possible due to labour's two natures. Thus, the circle was closed.

5.3 The two natures of capitalism: Wealth and deprivation, growth and crisis

Recall the days of unrestrained growth before the summer of 2008, the collapse of Lehman Brothers in the following September, the sickening amount of money that the

---

Box 5.6 Dr Faustus and Mr Ebenezer Scrooge in the Age of Capital

In the late sixteenth century, Christopher Marlowe told the story of Dr Faustus who famously contracted, using his own blood to sign on the dotted line, to sell his body and soul 24 years hence to Mephistopheles.[1] In exchange he demanded, and secured, a long catalogue of marvellous instant rewards: huge wealth to share with his friends, unimpeded travel to see the world, unlimited power to visit distant times, revenge against enemies, sex with a Helen of Troy lookalike, etc. When his time was up, he regretted his pact and tried to evade the Devil. To no avail. When Mephistopheles appeared in front of him, Faustus enquired why he is not in Hell but right there in Faustus' mortal world, among the living. 'Why, this *is* Hell, nor am I out of it' retorted the evil one, reminding Faustus that if one is in debt one carries it everywhere; just like *he* carries Hell wherever he ventures.

In 1843, a year before Marx wrote his famous lines about the transforming power of money (see above), Charles Dickens published *A Christmas Carol*; the celebrated story of redemption featuring Ebenezer Scrooge; the miser who treated himself with almost the same misanthropic stinginess that he treated everyone around him until, that is, the three ghosts of Christmas (one of the past, one of the present and one of the future) visited him, showing 'videos' of himself as he was, as he is, and as he will be on his deathbed; thus causing him to change his mindset and embark upon a spending spree (primarily on others), eager to 'produce' as much happiness as he could before shuffling off the mortal coil. Intriguingly, Scrooge's story seems like a Dr Faustus in reverse. Faustus encountered an other-worldly figure early on in life, spent recklessly while young, and ended up paying for it dearly at the end. In contrast, Scrooge suffered an awful life at the beginning, not experiencing one moment of pleasure for decades, before, towards the bitter end being confronted by his own other-worldly figure that helped him embark on the redeeming spending spree.

If the two lives are different only in terms of the ordering of behavioural patterns, why was poor Faustus confined to Hell's eternal fires while Scrooge, a man of arguably worse moral standing, achieved redemption (to such an extent that his figure even graces Hollywood animated movies aimed at children)? One explanation, consistent with our narrative on the rise of capital as power through the rehabilitation of usury, is that Marlowe and Dickens were separated by the deep historical chasm which divides a pre-market from a market society. In Marlowe's time, Christians, very much like Muslims today, were banned from charging interest on loans[2] and were taught that it is easier to squeeze a camel through the eye of a needle than a rich person through Heaven's Gate. By the time, however, Dickens was writing up Scrooge, the Protestant Reformation had well and truly put paid to all that and had established the idea that one brings to St Peter one's wealth as testament to his sacred abstemiousness and a password that guarantees safe passage into the delights therein. Jesus' saying 'By their fruits ye shall know them' (Matthew 7:20) had been paraphrased into 'By their accumulated money capital ye shall know them'. All that Dickens had to do to deliver Scrooge to the world, ready for his rise to Heaven, was to find a trick that would convince him to become more like Dr Faustus; that is, to open his purse and let money enter the circular flow of income. For, if Scrooge had been burdened by one mortal sin, given the ethos of the 1840s, it was that he had immobilised his money. Money, as all good banking apprentices know, is only good if it keeps moving. Idle money is a sin infinitely worse than any of Dr Faustus' shenanigans. In fact, today's capitalism might want to turn Faustus into their blue-eyed pin-up boy. If only more young people chose to borrow heavily to spend, spend, spend. If only more capitalists borrowed to invest, invest, invest.

As if to confirm that Dr Faustus had to suffer a terrible ordeal (and fall prey to Mephistopheles' archaic logic) because he was a man ahead of his time, Goethe's version of the story (published in 1832, well before the *Age of Capital* had commenced) affords the troubled Faust the redemption that restores the symmetry with Scrooge's fate, a symmetry in accord with the new market society's reliance on futures' markets in the presence of which the only difference made by a reversal of the timing of pleasure and of suffering is in terms of the rate of interest and who charges it to whom.[3]

Notes

1 The play was staged a number of times between 1594 and 1597 but was first published in 1604 after Marlowe's death.
2 This changed with Henry the Eighth who permitted Christians to charge interest. It is interesting to note that the very word 'interest' bears the marks of this prohibition. Since *usura* (lending on interest, not just on high interest) was canonically forbidden, both parties – the lender and the borrower – pretended that they were part in a common joint venture hence (*interesse*). Much of the modern 'Islamic banking' has its roots in scholastic theology. The Scholastics also made use of Aristotle, 'As this is so, usury is most reasonably hated, because its gain comes from money itself and not from that for the sake of which money was invented' (*Politics*, 1258b2–5)
3 The first part of Goethe's *Faust* was published in 1808. A revised edition appeared in 1828–9. Goethe finished the second part in 1832 the year of his death. It was published posthumously the same year.

US government had to pour into the American Insurance Group (AIG) to prevent the financial crisis from turning into a wholesale catastrophe and the deep recession the world entered ever so quickly afterwards. Things seemed so grand just before the collapse. The few prophets of an impending disaster were laughed out of court. Anyone who warned that things may take a nasty turn was dismissed as an archaic mind incapable of grasping the new paradigm of irreversible growth.

Marx invokes the *dialectic* to explain how things can look at their best just before *The Fall*; of how the collapse is least expected a second before it happens. For him the *dialectic* is just a way of spotting, in any social situation, the potential for qualitative change and teasing it out. He looks to capitalism's strengths for clues regarding its limits; and then immediately turns to its sorrier moments for insights into its next upsurge.

> In our day, everything seems pregnant with its contrary. Machinery gifted with the wonderful power of shortening and fructifying human labour, we behold starving and overworking it. The new-fangled sources of wealth, by some weird spell, are turned into sources of want.[13]

Wealth is created by the *same* process that yields new forms of deep poverty, radical deprivation and heartbreaking want. Labour was, initially, liberated from the feudal bonds in the eighteenth century and, today, from lifelong dependence on social security cheques and restricted trade union practices, only to become free to starve, to become casualised and to commute inordinate distances from shanty towns or depraved suburbs so as to live on poverty wages in the face of exuberant abundance all around.

> The victories of art seem bought by the loss of character. At the same pace that mankind masters nature, man seems to become enslaved to other men or to his own infamy. Even the pure light of science seems unable to shine but on the dark background

of ignorance. All our invention and progress seem to result in endowing material forces with intellectual life, and in stultifying human life into a material force.

(Marx, "Speech at anniversary of the *People's Paper*",
1856 in Marx and Engels (1969), p. 500)

George Bernard Shaw once wrote that 'if a man is a deep writer all his works are confessions'.[14] Karl Marx was one of the deepest. His confession was that he tried to look at the world rationally and the world looked back at him in a way that left no doubt about *one basic truth* that takes the form of a *dialectical contradiction*: the emergent market society was *at once* liberating *and* enslaving human nature. As capitalism's tentacles embraced the globe, its liberating effect came in the form of ridding us of

> all feudal, patriarchal, idyllic relations; [of all the] ties that bound man to his 'natural superiors', and [leaves behind] ... no other nexus between man and man than naked self-interest, than callous 'cash payment'. It ... drown[s] the most heavenly ecstasies of religious fervour, of chivalrous enthusiasm, of philistine sentimentalism, in the icy water of egotistical calculation. It ... resolve[s] personal worth into exchange value, and in place of the numberless indefeasible chartered freedoms, ... set[s] up that single, unconscionable freedom – Free Trade ... [above all else, capitalism compels] ...all nations, on pain of extinction ... to introduce what it calls civilisation into their midst. In one word, it create[s] a world after its own image.[15]

But there is a nasty catch buried deep inside the technology with which capitalism accomplishes its miracles. The increase in agricultural output that quashed the Malthusian nightmare (even if only temporarily), the improvement in communications that linked hitherto isolated communities and nations, the transformation of formless materials into sparkling new gadgets, the creation of new vistas of pleasure for the masses; all these historical achievements of human-made technology were part of a Faustian contract that humanity signed unwittingly. While the rise of the machines helped 'civilise' the world, at least in the image of western merchants, it did so at a price. And the price was wholesale slavery on an unprecedented industrial scale.

First, there were the millions of Africans directly enslaved by the same traders who underpinned the industrial revolution through the establishment of the original trade routes across the high seas (see Chapter 2 and Box 5.4). *Second*, labourers bound to capital, as formally free men and women, by the *labour contract* were just as un-free as the African slaves. *Third*, their supposed masters, whether they were the captains of the slave ships or the captains of industry back in Manchester or Birmingham, were themselves *also* paragons of un-freedom: each and every character in this unfolding global tragedy, African slave, Scottish mineworker, French moneylender, English factory mill owner, were all slaves of a faceless system in which the sole 'beneficiaries' were the proliferating machines. Only the steam engines, the railways, the mechanical looms, the ships, the ploughing contraptions and the telegraphs received loving tender care; from the capitalists, from the 'free' workers, and from the African slaves. Little by little humans were being turned into their appendages, giving rise to some kind of *Matrix* dystopia which endowed automata with intellectual life while reducing human life into a material energy. Meanwhile, except perhaps for the African slaves, the rest were lulled into submission by the illusion of freedom, progress and consumer bliss. The *Matrix* technology of channelling illusions into our brains was not even necessary to settle us down into joyless acquiescence. The commodification of everything sufficed.

In typical fashion, however, Marx saw light in the darkest of black holes. Everything was, indeed, pregnant with its opposite. And as long as the human spirit continues to resist, at some deep level, commodification and the complete obliteration of its quirky attachment to something called freedom, there is hope. The rise of the machines, just when it threatens to become complete and irreversible, causes human society to go into a spasm that contains the promise of emancipation. In *The Matrix*, that spasm was the rebellion of Neo and his comrades. In Marx, it is a spontaneous reaction of the capitalist economy itself to the machines' takeover: 'If the whole class of the wage-labourer were to be annihilated by machinery, how terrible that would be for capital, which, *without wage-labor, ceases to be capital*'![16]

As machines play an increasingly important role in production, they displace human labour. But this means that, while more and more goods, gadgets and trinkets are produced, value per unit of output withers. And as value withers, a human society regulated by the generation and distribution of values enters a period of crisis. This crisis holds, like all ruptures, the promise of the next recovery but also of something excitingly new. The pressing question therefore is this: will the crisis yield nothing more than the raw materials for another spurt of growth that will, in turn, cause the next crisis? Or will it bear the prospect of a different kind of society, one that promises a more rational use of resources and a future free of the terror of the next meltdown? Box 5.7 presents the first full answer in the history of social science, along with its analytical foundations.

Box 5.7 The first theory of crises

The value analysis in Box 5.2 featured no machines. Jill's labour units were the only factor of production. Suppose however that Jill uses capital goods to produce, say corn (consistent with David Ricardo's corn model – see Box 3.5) to the tune of Q tonnes. The value of this corn corresponds to the total amount of labour input units L that have gone into its production. Now, some of these L units have been contributed directly by Jill's labour input, in the form of L^* labour units, and the rest by labour input, which had been previously stored (by some other group of workers) in the tractors, tools, seeds, etc. that Jill uses. Denoting these stored, crystallised or (more morbidly) dead labour input as units C, $L = L^* + C$, i.e. the total sum of units of labour input it took to produce Q tonnes of corn consists of (a) the number of labour input units L^* contributed by Jill and her fellow workers plus (b) the number of previously stored or crystallised labour input units (C) contained 'inside' the used capital goods and transferred to the Q units of corn by the current workforce's efforts – Marx refers to C as constant capital to indicate its sterility (or inability to produce, by itself, new value).

Turning to the costs of production, the employer has paid fully for C but not for L^*. The reason is simple: Having been crystallised into constant capital (the commodity form of capital), labour units C are now a quantifiable commodity that the employer purchases on the open market (often on money borrowed from the money markets) and has no alternative but to pay its full value. Each tonne of corn, therefore, 'contains' constant capital (or capital goods) equivalent to $c = C/Q$, the labour input units that were embedded in it in the past. On the other hand (as we saw in Box 5.2), the employer *cannot* pay for L^*, the labour units of his own workers, since L^* can neither be measured a priori nor traded. Jill and the rest of the workforce that currently contribute their L^* labour units to the Q tonnes of corn are paid for their labour power N, a sum equal to $V_{LP} = wN$ (where w is the wage per unit of *labour power*). So, if that purchased labour power of N units allows the employer to extract L^* labour units that produce Q tonnes of corn, then the 'live' labour cost for each tonne of corn amounts to $v = V_{LP}/Q = wN/Q$. The difference, as defined in Box 5.2, between L^* and V_{LP} is surplus value S and it derives from the production of Q tonnes of corn or $s = S/Q$ on a per tonne basis.

To sum up, Q tonnes of corn are being produced per period whose total value L is given by the sum of labour units contributed by 'live' and 'dead' (or 'crystallised') labour taken together. The machines (along the other capital goods) contribute their C units of 'dead' labour which the employer pays for in full. Live labourers contribute L^* labour units but are not paid for them, as such (since such a payment is rendered impossible in the case of free, alive human labour). Instead, the cost of living labour heeded by the employer amounts to V_{LP} (which, as seen in Box 5.2, are the labour inputs by 'strangers' into the commodities that Jill buys with her wages). The residual labour input units appeared in the form of surplus value S. Consequently, the total value of the Q tonnes of corn is a simple sum:

$$L = L^* + C = V_{LP} + S + C$$

Letting λ be the value of one unit (i.e. tonne) of corn, we have

$$\lambda = v + s + c \tag{5.1}$$

where $v = V_{LP}/Q$ is the value of labour power the employer had to purchase in order to extract from Jill the labour units L^*/Q necessary for the production of one tonne of corn, $s = S/Q$ is the surplus value per tonne of corn that he managed to extract in this manner, and $c = C/Q$ are the 'dead' or 'crystallised' labour input units (i.e. the constant capital) that went into the production of each tonne and which he paid for fully (in the capital markets).

Equation (5.1) completes Marx's theory of commodity value in the context of a market society in which machine labour is combined with free human labour under the control and supervision of the machines' owners. The employment of free labour, explained by the asymmetric distribution of property rights over machines and other factors of production, makes value generation possible and free labour's dual nature gives employers the right and the opportunity to extract surplus value which, of course, they plough straight back into the service of replacing and expanding the realm of the machines.

Let $e = s/v$ be the rate of extraction of labour input units from a given amount of labour power[1] and let $\pi = s/(v + c)$ be the capitalist's profit rate (defined as the amount of extracted surplus value per unit of value invested either on live or on dead capital). The profit rate can then be expressed in terms of the rate of extraction as follows:

$$\pi = s/(v + c) = \frac{s/v}{1 + c/v} = \frac{e}{1 + k} \tag{5.2}$$

where $k = c/v$ is the ratio of constant to variable capital, or the ratio of the exchange value of utilised machines relative to the value of the purchased labour power. Marx defined k as the *organic composition of capital*. However we label it, k reflects the extent of mechanisation of the production process or, equivalently, the degree to which it has become automated. As k increases, machines (or *constant capital* goods) displace free human labour from the production of each unit of a commodity and the economy tends towards its *Matrix Economy* limit.

The upswing: during the period of growth, k rises. Although production burgeons and society is becoming increasingly automated, profit rate π collapses – see equation (5.2). Once near or below zero, a crisis erupts and some firms, the least efficient, go bankrupt.

The downswing: the bankruptcy of few firms increases unemployment ever so slightly. The newly unemployed cut down on spending and this brings on a small reduction in the demand for the hitherto surviving firms. A few additional firms are brought down by this pithy drop in demand. But as the momentum of these events gathers, it is not long before the whole economy descends into a vicious downward spiral.

The depression and the return to growth: when a substantial portion of capital goods and human labour come to a productive standstill, the economy reaches a depressed state where nothing but a boost in the profit rates can help. When no one expects profits to rise, in the depths of that black hole, Marx sees a glimmering light: as competition diminishes (following so many bankruptcies), fewer firms are left to divide an admittedly smaller pie. But their individual shares of that pie grow as long as the number of competing firms falls faster than the pie shrinks. Meanwhile, during these lean and hungry times, the prices of labour power and capital goods drop (as their supply exceeds the demand by the small number of surviving firms). Thus, during the worst of economic times, when capital is diminishing rather than accumulating (i.e. when investment is not even up to replacing 'worn' machines), profit rates paradoxically pick up. In turn they lead to fresh investment as the surviving firms try to convert their newfound profit into long-term market dominance. Their investment spree boosts overall demand and the capitalist economy is dragged out of the mire and on to a path of fresh growth.

The long term: as the economy goes from boom to bust and back again, one possibility is that it will be following a nice wave path with a more or less regular frequency and a steady amplitude (one that resembles trigonometry's sine or cosine waves). Marx's hunch was different. Looking at equation (5.2), and convinced that capitalism was synonymous with a long-term tendency to mechanise everything, he suspected that k, despite any short- or medium-term fluctuations, would rise in the long term. Thus, Marx suspected that profit rates are in long-term terminal decline and, therefore, that capitalism was heading for an apocalyptic end.

Note

1 Of course, Marx refers to 'e' as the *degree of exploitation of labour power* (*Capital*, vol. 1, chapter 9, *Der Exploitationsgrad der Arbeitskraft*, in Chapter 7 of the German edition). The term is not absent from neoclassical economics (see A.C. Pigou, (1920 [1932]), part III, chapter 14 and in the models of monopsony in the labour market) but it is seen as an aberration

when markets are non-competitive, even though recent research within the neoclassical paradigm has shown that the phenomenon of monopsony is more pervasive than it is usually believed (see Manning, 2003). Böhm-Bawerk in his *Capital and Interest: A Critical History of Economical Theory* [1884 (1890)], devoted a whole chapter (Book VI, Chapter I) on what he described as 'exploitation theory' (*Ausbeutungstheorie*) or socialist theory. He accuses a certain author (Guth) that he 'does not scruple to introduce the harsh expression *Ausbeutung* [exploitation] … as *terminus technicus*' (Böhm-Bawerk (1884 [1921], p. 327). Given the emotive tone that exploitation has acquired since Marx's days, we prefer the term *extraction* (in accordance with C.B. McPherson's term in McPherson 1973). One reason we prefer it is its more ethically neutral ring. Another, less important reason, is that it resonates nicely with *The Matrix* and the extraction of heat from human bodies!

Box 5.8 The role of wages and of the unemployed in regulating capitalism's crises

During the upswing, wages rise and this affects the distribution of income between profits and wages. But what causes wages to rise? *Capital accumulation* is the answer. Being the main force field that runs through the capitalist system, the drive to accumulate governs everything; including the tendency of wages to rise during periods of growth.[1] Marx argues (see Chapter 25 of *Capital, vol. I*) that wages rise because the pace of capital accumulation leads to a depletion of the reservoir of labour. This happens because the initial large labour reserves of ex-peasant labour exert a downward pressure on wages that, nonetheless, is growing weaker as capital accumulation causes employment to expand and this 'reserve army' of potential workers shrinks. As wages rise, profits fall and, consequently, capital accumulation slows down. The slowdown means, further, a weaker growth in employment that, in turn, reduces the reductions in the 'reserve army' of labour and a drop in the rate at which wages rise.

During the downswing, the opposite chain of events takes hold: the 'reserve army' sees an increase in its ranks and wages fall. But then profit rates increase, more capital is accumulated, employment rises, the 'reserve army' diminishes again and this restores an upward pressure on wages.

From the above, it transpires that the economic cycle is completely self-contained within the dynamics of capital accumulation. Crises and their overcoming are not caused by outside factors (e.g. war, pestilence, OPEC increases in oil prices, the political interference of government or the skilful policies of the Federal Reserve authorities). Crises are to capitalism what earthworms are to gardens or Hell to Christianity: unpleasant but utterly essential.

The Australia Effect – An illustration

In the deep recession of the early 1980s in the UK, when the 'reserve army' of the unemployed numbered almost 4.5 million, wages did not shrink as Marx might have predicted. Instead, productivity rose and the gap of living standards between the employed and the unemployed skyrocketed. A high-ranking minister of the then Thatcher government, Norman Tebbit, explained in a TV interview his serious worries: the great 'benefit' of the new environment was the spurt in productivity growth caused by the fear in the mind of the employed that they may lose their jobs. This fear grew as the dole queues got longer and more desperate and, miraculously, returned discipline to British workplaces. However, he continued, his worry was that the unemployed were becoming so wretched and poor that, after a while on the dole, they would no longer count as potential replacements of the existing workers. If that were to happen, Tebbit concluded, this 'reserve army' of labour might as well be in Australia, in which case unemployment would no longer boost productivity and profit rates.

Note

1 As we shall see in Book 2, wage growth was always a feature of a growing capitalist economy. Except that this link (between GDP growth and wages) was broken in the USA sometime in the 1970s, and remains broken ever since. This extraordinary phenomenon will be explained in the context of a story according to which the second post-war phase (that was inaugurated after the end of Bretton Woods and the oil crisis of the early 1970s) constitutes a kind of capitalism that has characteristics Marx could never have envisaged. We call this the *Global Minotaur* phase of international capitalism (see Chapter 11).

The above story (in Boxes 5.7 and 5.8) is strikingly modern. Though it is missing some of the crucial ingredients that brought us the *Crash of 2008*, it captures two of its important facets: *first*, that behind the fluctuating prices of houses, shares and derivatives lurks something more tangible and real buried under our society's foundations; something related to the way in which wealth is produced by men, women and machines. *Second*, that we live in a society that combines the most amazing technology with a problematic social organisation of work and property rights over the instruments and fruits of human labour.

Unfortunately, these crucial insights have almost been lost because of dogmatism and the economists' penchant (independently of their political bias) for telling complete, and completely mechanistic, stories. Marx's brilliant political economics did not escape economics' general propensity towards *lost truth* and *Inherent Error*.

5.4 The *Inherent Error*'s return

What does this all mean? Even if we accept that capitalism generates its own crises endogenously, as it does the restorative forces that help it to overcome them, what next? Is capitalism doomed, as the last paragraph in Box 5.7 might suggest? Or is it more like democracy (i.e., a terrible system of government which, nevertheless, remains inter-temporally superior to all available alternatives)? Can it be reformed? Or is it beyond redemption? The time has come to take stock.

The anthropocentric idea at the heart of this chapter arrives at its logical conclusion in the form of the *Fundamental Theorem* below (see Box 5.9). Embarking from a humanist identification of *value* with *freedom* (recall Section 4.3 in the previous chapter), this train of

---

Box 5.9 The *Fundamental Marxian Theorem*

Michio Morishima, a leading economic theorist of the post-war period, in his classic book on Marx[1] has called equation (5.2) the *Fundamental Marxian Theorem* (FMT): A positive profit rate requires a positive rate of extraction of labour inputs from labour power ($e > 0$), with the latter being greater than the profit rate ($e > \pi$). Moreover, the greater the preponderance k of machinery in the production process (i.e. the greater the level of capital accumulation so far) the larger the extraction rate e must be in order to maintain a given profit rate.

Note

1   Morishima, 1973.

---

thought yielded the prediction of a dynamic seesaw between (a) capital accumulation and (b) the profit fluctuations which take capitalism into and out of economic crises.

The dynamic mechanism at the heart of Marx's political economics hinges on the negative relation between profit rates and k in equation (5.2): while the individual capitalist would love nothing more than to swap all his workers with obedient machines, a collapse in the aggregate economy's profit rate would be guaranteed if *all* capitalists managed to displace labour from their businesses, replacing them with machines.

This clash between the capitalists' individual aims and their collective (or class) interest is but another guise, a Hegelian reincarnation, of Adam Smith's similar point about the self-defeating (or *supra-intentional*[17]) consequence of profit maximisation (see Section 3.2 of Chapter 3). But there is a major difference between Smith's and Marx's use of *supra-intentional causality*: in Smith's case the profit motive eliminates profit – for the betterment of capitalist society as a whole. In Marx, however, the drive to accumulate machinery leads inescapably to a crisis of capitalism.

There is bad news and good news here (which is what we might have expected from a student of Hegel!): as k rises, profit rates drop and when they fall below a critical level, a downward spiral begins. Bankruptcies feed into increases in unemployment which, in turn, reduce sales further causing even more bankruptcies. So, the bad news is that *capitalism will not stop accumulating before it undermines itself*; before it condemns, unwittingly, whole generations of workers to long unemployment spells and earmarks their children for a childhood of abject poverty or of a demeaning dependence on the welfare state (or, as is often the case, both). Now for the good news: the crisis prevents the coming of a fully fledged *Matrix Economy*!

Like Sisyphus who pushes the rock *almost* to the hill's top, before it rolls right back, so capitalism's drive to automate production never gets quite to the aimed-at complete substitution of free human labour with machinery. Admittedly, just as Sisyphus *almost* succeeds in his uphill struggle, capital accumulation comes close to dehumanising production, with k rising seemingly unstoppably (think of the almost fully automated car plants of Japan). But before the last remnant of human labour is bleached out of the production line, profits collapse, factories close, machines remain idle, investment ceases. At that point, human *labour power* regains some of its cost advantage (*vis-à-vis* machine labour) given that, in the middle of the recession, desperate people will do desperate things (such as infuse more *labour input*

Box 5.10 The 'scientific' clothes of a political argument and of a teleological hypothesis: Wages, prices and the falling rate of profit

A short-term industrial relations' strategy

Marx was keen to convince organised labour (i.e. trade unions) to campaign for higher wages for two reasons: First, because he thought that, in the *age of inconspicuous wealth*, it was their duty to themselves to improve their pitiful conditions. Second, because a campaign for higher wages was seen as a good 'training exercise' for building solidarity up prior to unleashing a programme for the wholesale redesign of capitalist social relations. To *prove* this point he honed his theory of value in order to demonstrate as a scientific truth that a boost in wages will *not* cause prices to rise but, instead, would depress profit rates.

A teleological hypothesis

Marx hypothesised that, since capitalism would expire without capital accumulation and the profits that keep it going, the fact that more capital goods boost k (the organic composition of capital) and *at once* reduces profit rates means that the high speed train of capitalism is bound to crash against some immoveable wall. The *falling rate of profit*, signalled by equation (5.2), was in Marx's eyes a mathematical truth from which capitalism could engineer no escape.

---

into products while selling their *labour power* for far less). Again like Sisyphus, capitalism picks itself up, dusts itself off and starts pushing the proverbial rock back on the uphill path of renewed growth and capital accumulation.

This theory is, in our eyes, a splendidly narrated tragic tale which captures beautifully the basic contradictions built into capitalism's foundations. The trouble begins when Marx and his spiritual heirs (most of whom he did not deserve) take it too far: when they dress up a particular political agenda as the unique conclusion of scientific analysis. The moment a hunch or prophecy is disguised as 'scientific law', we are thrown back into the realm of economics' *Inherent Error*. And when the latter is exposed, the analysis' genuine insights end up in the *lost truth* basket.

Box 5.10 sums up the short-term political agenda and the long-term prophecy that Marx wanted to promote as a reflection of a 'truth' that could be read objectively and consistently into the laws that governed capitalism independently of the human will, of personal prejudice or, indeed, of ideology. In brief, he wanted to argue that workers must unite initially in order to push wages up and, later, to 'prepare for power' as the capitalists are forced to relinquish it, victims of the allegedly systemic *falling rate of profit*.

Marx understood well that his short-term goal of convincing workers to campaign for higher wages would be undermined by their fear that their struggle might come to naught if firms respond to the higher wage by inflating prices. If *real* wages would remain the same after a long, painful strike, what would be the point? To rid them of that fear, he summoned his Ricardo-inspired *theory of value*: commodity prices, he told the trade unions in a famous speech,[18] do *not* reflect wage costs plus a surcharge to account for the cost of *constant capital* or profits. Under competitive conditions no one can charge a surcharge over the value of 'things'. Values reflect nothing beyond the number of *labour input* units that went into the commodity's manufacture. Consequently, workers' unions could fearlessly push wages up since the result of such action would be a fall in profit rates, leaving prices more or less unaffected.[19]

Turning to his long-term prognostication that capitalism is heading for a Hegelian negation, and as an heir not only to Hegel but also to Aristotle, Marx found it hard to extricate his thinking about capitalism from the idea of a virtuous *telos*. From Aristotle he got his fondness for thinking that virtue can be humanity's only decent *end*. From Hegel he received the idea of history as a dynamic process which proceeds *as if* guided by some ultimate, hopefully virtuous, conclusion. If we add to this philosophical mix Marx's deeply held ethical revulsion caused by the poverty produced by the same system that generates, in his time as in ours, immense wealth, it is easy to see how he was drawn to a form of quasi-wishful thinking; to the prophetic belief that capitalism, fraught as it was with unsustainable contradictions, will negate itself; and that the result of this negation would be something better – a truly virtuous society in which technological progress and human freedom may, at last, grow side by side.

Marx, the archetypical nineteenth-century scholar, believed sincerely that such a weighty truth should be demonstrable (like a mathematical theorem can be) by scientific means. Placing his thinking in historical context, it is worthwhile recalling that, at the time he was forming his view about the dynamics of capitalism, around the late 1830s, Michael Faraday had just made his experimental breakthrough of demonstrating that a changing magnetic field produces an electric field and that, remarkably for the time, an electric field could produce magnetism. This *isomorphism* of two seemingly different natural forces, in conjunction with his deeply held religious belief about the unit of God and Nature, gave Faraday the impetus to pursue an extraordinary scientific project, unifying all forces of nature (light, magnetism, electricity, dynamic motion, etc.) within a single theoretical model. In the 1840s, when Marx was already publishing his early political economics, James Maxwell produced mathematical models of Faraday's experimental results. At first Faraday was annoyed, wondering why his results had to be presented in mathematical form rather than simple prose. Maxwell soon demonstrated why: by using his Faraday-inspired equations he computed the maximum speed of the alternation between electrical and magnetic fields (i.e. the speed at which electricity turns to a magnetic field and vice versa). It was a very large number; approximately 300,000 km per second. At that moment, Maxwell knew that he had achieved Faraday's task: for that was the speed of light, proving that light itself is a form of electro-magnetic radiation.

Maxwell reached that conclusion in 1862, at the same time that Marx was completing the first volume of his *Capital* (which saw the light of day, after painstaking editing, five years later). Maxwell's statement, when lecturing at King's College around that time, that '[w]e can scarcely avoid the conclusion that light consists in the transverse undulations of the same medium which is the cause of electric and magnetic phenomena',[20] was to have a profound effect on Marx. Just as Faraday and Maxwell were discovering a unified, multifaceted force running through Nature, one that was to bring about a sequence of industrial revolutions (including the telegraph, the radio, even today's internet), so was Marx determined to show that there is a force running through every pore of market societies determining our lives, our hopes, our illusions even. It was *capital* both as machinery and as a power relation between persons (recall Section 5.2).

In a bid to emulate the physicists, Marx peered carefully into his simple algebra and tried to find in it incontrovertible evidence about the future of capitalism. The best he could do was equation (5.2). In it he saw evidence that, in the long run, capitalism would run out of steam and give place to something radically different. And since capital as machinery could not and should not be un-invented, the looming new society would be heavily automated but one in which humans were in control of the machines, rather than the other way round.

The problem with the above story is that it emanates from the analysis in Box 5.7, which is framed in terms of a *single* commodity whose value is broken down (into three components, c, s and v). Marx understood perfectly well, and owed this understanding to the Physiocrats (recall Box 3.1) that nothing concrete can be said about capitalism on the basis of an economic model that ignores the interplay between the sector that produces manufactures, or *capital goods*, and the other sectors which produce basic commodities, luxuries, services, etc. In short, Marx knew that his equation (5.2) could not bear the huge explanatory burden he had placed on it. He thus set out, in Volume II of *Capital*, to show that his agenda and prophecies (see Box 5.10) applied equally to a multi-sector capitalist economy.

Let us consider an economy similar to that of Boxes 4.3 and 4.4 of the previous chapter but different in one respect: labour is provided by free human workers. *sector 1*, as in Box 4.3, is the sector producing machinery; the *capital goods* sector. *sector 2*, on the other hand, produces basic goods; the *consumption goods* sector. Box 5.11 relates the conditions that must prevail if this simple two-sector economy is to reproduce itself, neither growing nor shrinking.

Box 5.11 Value and the conditions for growth in a multi-sector capitalist economy

When there are two sectors (capital and consumption goods), equation (5.1) is replicated in each sector as (5.3) and (5.4). Letting λ_1 be the value of one unit of machinery and λ_2 the value of one unit of the consumption good, say corn, we have:

$$\lambda_1 = v_1 + s_1 + c_1 \qquad (5.3)$$

$$\lambda_2 = v_2 + s_2 + c_2 \qquad (5.4)$$

Suppose that this economy is not growing, but it is a 'system' that manages simply to reproduce itself (i.e. there is no investment of surplus value). In this case of simple reproduction, the two sectors will require a quantity of capital goods that just about replaces the capital goods expended: c_1 and c_2 respectively. Hence, the value produced by the capital goods sector, λ_1, must be just enough to produce the minimum capital requirements of the two sectors c_1 and c_2:

$$\lambda_1 = v_1 + s_1 + c_1 = c_1 + c_2 \qquad (5.5)$$

Equation (5.5) must therefore hold if the economy's supply of capital (λ_1) is to equal its demand ($c_1 + c_2$). It states that the value λ_1 embodied in the production of capital goods must be equal to the total demand, measured in value terms, for capital goods. By the same token, the value λ_2 of the consumption goods sector's output must be equal to the value of the total amount of consumption goods demanded. The demand for consumption goods comes from workers' wages, that is, from aggregate variable capital $v_1 + v_2$, and from capitalists consuming their surplus values $s_1 + s_2$, since by assumption there is no net investment in this simple reproduction model. Hence, equation (5.6):

$$\lambda_2 = v_2 + s_2 + c_2 = v_1 + v_2 + s_1 + s_2 \tag{5.6}$$

A closer look at equations (5.5) and (5.6) reveals that they yield the same result:

$$v_1 + s_1 = c_2 \tag{5.7}$$

Equation (5.7) in a restatement of Marx's Fundamental Theorem (see Box 5.9): it states that the equilibrium exchange between the two sectors must be such that the value of the capital goods c_2 demanded by the consumption goods sector equals the sum of the value of variable capital and surplus value $v_1 + s_1$ in the capital goods sector. But that sum is simply the total purchasing power for consumption goods by the workers and the capitalists of the capital goods sector. So, the purchasing power emanating from the capital goods sector must equal the value of capital goods used in the production of all other goods.

So, equation (5.7) must hold if this economy is to manage just to reproduce itself. If it is to grow (in Marx's terminology, to move from *simple* to *extended reproduction*), the same equations apply. The only difference is that they will apply to a growing, or expanding, system where *surplus values* are ploughed back into additional *variable* and *constant capital*.[21]

Let us now use this analysis to see what can be said about the all-important *profit rate*. The difference here (compared to Box 5.7) is that we have two profit rates (π_1, π_2), one per sector, two rates of *extraction* of *labour inputs* from given *labour power* (e_1, e_2), and two *k*s (k_1, k_2) since the *organic composition of capital* will be the same across sectors only by accident. Supposing, as both Ricardo and Marx did, that capital and labour will keep migrating to the sector with a higher profit rate, thus yielding a gravitational force that equalises the profit rates across sectors,[22] we posit that:

$$\pi_1 = \frac{e_1}{1+k_2} = \pi_2 = \frac{e_2}{1+k_2} \tag{5.8}$$

And here is the rub. Unless the *organic composition of capital* is the same across sectors ($k_1 = k_2$), the only way the *profit rates* can be equalised is if the *extraction rates* e_1 and e_2 diverge. But would such divergence not cause workers to keep migrating to the sector in which that rate of *extraction* is lower? And would that labour migration, by achieving equalisation between e_1 and e_2, not drive profit rates apart, thus causing capital to migrate to the more profitable sector? So, it seems that the gravitational forces that should generate equilibrium succeed only in causing a perpetual migration of capital and labour which, as long as one of the two sectors is more capital intensive than the other, will *never* settle down into some equilibrium.

Instead of rejoicing at having found something deep in the foundations of capitalism that generates *flux*, Marx despaired. All of a sudden he realised that a large hole was punched through his *Fundamental Theorem*, namely the argument that a capitalist economy's aggregate profit comes from the total *surplus value* extracted from *labour power*. In one sweep he lost the 'scientific' foundation of both his short-term political campaign and of his long-term prophecy (see Box 5.10): recalling that the relative price of commodities reflects the *labour inputs* necessary for their production only when profit rates are equal, it follows that if profit rates are not equalisable then the prices of commodities will not reflect those *labour inputs*. Therefore, no guarantee can be given to trade unions that a successful campaign to boost wages will leave the general price level unaffected. As for the long-term prospects of capitalism, the idea that a tendency for the rate of profit to fall can no longer be founded on equation (5.2) since, now, there are two profit rates which may well diverge. If they do, capital accumulation will not necessarily bring the economy's overall profit rate down.

To recap, once again a brilliant theoretical attempt to tell a consistent story about (a) the value of things and (b) the way a capitalist economy grows had come unstuck. We can have either a consistent theory about the determination of relative values (if we assume that k, the contribution of machinery to output, is always the same in each sector) or a consistent theory of growth and accumulation. But we cannot have both. Alas, economists (including Marx's followers) have been trying to square this circle ever since, managing only to fall prey to a scholasticism that undermines the serious task of understanding capitalism. Marx's detractors, who craved an opportunity to dismiss him and his vision as pseudo-science, seized upon this incarnation of the *Inherent Error* in order to successfully confine the whole edifice to the wastepaper basket. The result was a great deal of *lost truth* which, in our day and age, can be teased out more readily by studying films like *The Matrix* than economics textbooks.

Box 5.12 The *Transformation Problem* and its implications

The idea that prices reflect underlying values is central to the classical economists' mindset. However, they had to explain *how* the underlying values are transformed into prices. Their standard argument was that the equalisation of profit rates will bring about prices at which each commodity exchanges with others at a rate (or relative price) reflecting the relative labour inputs necessary during their production. In Chapter 3 (Section 3.3) we came across a serious problem with that logic. It transpired that, when machines assist human labour in the production process, an increase in labour costs (relative to cost of the machines) changes the value of all commodities. Adam Smith, as pointed in the last chapter, quickly took his leave from this conundrum by assuming that the wage share of the surplus (and thus the price of labour relative to the price of machines) remains constant. David Ricardo, who did not want to make that assumption, was embroiled in a nasty spat with Thomas Robert Malthus who pointed out that for Ricardo's labour theory of value to hold water, each commodity had to be produced by the same technique of production involving the same proportions in the use of the various inputs. Ricardo meekly replied that his theory could be seen as an approximation.

Marx, who completed Ricardo's model by introducing a productive capital goods sector into the analysis, and also explained how profit can be maintained under strong competitive conditions as a component of surplus value (which in turn is explained by the dual natures of both labour and capital), was not to escape the transformation problem either. As we saw above, see expression (5.8), the only way of maintaining his own theory of value and keep alive the idea of a uniform rate of profit when capital utilisation differs across sectors was to by accept that the rate of labour input extraction is *not* the same across sectors. But then he had to explain why those rates differed.

One potential explanation was to accept that not all capitalists have the same extractive power over labour. That in some sectors more labour input can be extracted from the same labour power than in others. Clearly, this differential extractive power is an obvious feature of really existing capitalism. Corporations do not have the same power over workers as small businesses and some sectors are at the mercy of such corporations more than others. Why did Marx not acknowledge this empirical fact and settle the matter there and then?

The answer is that such acceptance would wreck his main proposition that profit comes exclusively from surplus value. He would have, for instance, to accept that some profit is accounted for by a form of differential power over workers that competition cannot eat into. The road would then suddenly open to the argument that, if some capitalists have more power over workers than other capitalists then, perhaps, they may have some power over other capitalists in the price-setting game. If so, Marx would have to concede that prices do not reflect just labour inputs but also this unquantifiable power over prices. The logical limit of this would then be to acknowledge that an increase in the economy-wide wage rate may indeed lead to an increase in economy-wide prices (i.e. inflation). In effect, Marx would have to apologise to Citizen Weston![1]

Note

1 Citizen Weston was the hapless trade unionist who, during the First International Working Men's Association in June 1865, put forward the view that a wage rise, even if attained by industrial action, might come to nothing if capitalists push prices up. Marx's speech was nothing less than an exercise in lambasting Weston. See Marx (1865 [1969]).

5.5 Lost truth and the return to *The Matrix*

The problem with economics' *Inherent Error* is that it withholds important truths from the future generations that need it most. Marx's determination to silence Citizen Weston, and to provide a fully determinate equilibrium story of capitalism's dynamics, was (at least partly) responsible for the fact that almost no student of economics today is exposed to the narrative in this chapter. The world is a dimmer place for this.

One way of understanding Marx's conundrum is to focus on his exaggerated loyalty to Ricardo. In adopting Ricardo's basic corn model as the scientific kernel of his own theory of value and distribution, Marx inherited a time bomb. A theorist of capitalism much superior to Ricardo, Marx understood perfectly well that commodities do not *actually* exchange according to the relative *labour input* embodied in them; not even in a 'perfect' form of capitalism. He knew better than Ricardo that prices tended to levels reflecting the melange of inputs (including labour) expended during the production process. But he still believed strongly that if we lose the identification of *profit* with *surplus value* at the level of the economy as a whole (i.e. at the macroeconomic or aggregate level of analysis), we will remain innocent of capitalism's essence. Profit spawned capital and capital is the force field running through capitalism, giving it its energy, guiding its path and determining our personal acts and thoughts alike. But none of this would be possible without the wedge driven between *labour power* and *labour input*. In short, without *surplus value*, and thus free human labour, explaining profit, we are back at a *Matrix Economy* or at the terrible predicament of Mr Peel in Western Australia.

While struggling to complete the second volume of his *Capital* (which he never managed), Marx understood the time bomb in his hands and tried valiantly to defuse it. The task was difficult: he had to find a way of salvaging the argument that *profit* comes from *surplus value* while abandoning the simplistic story that prices reflected relative *labour inputs* (see Box 5.7) which is based on, effectively, a model of a single commodity or single sector world. Cognisant of the Box 5.11 analysis (as well as the type of critique in Box 5.12), he dedicated almost the whole of the third volume of *Capital* to articulating the following fresh narrative: imagine that all *surplus value*, extracted from each and every sector, flowed into a common pool. Once there, each capitalist withdraws his share of profit in proportion not to the surplus value his business contributed to the common pool but in proportion to the amount of *capital goods* (or *constant capital*) used in his business (relative to that of the other capitalists).

In this scheme, profit rates can be equalised even when the *organic composition of capital* (the ks) differs across sectors because the rates at which *surplus value* is extracted from workers [the *extraction* rates e_1 and e_2 in equation (4.14)] are also allowed to differ across the sectors. The major implication of this is that the price of a particular commodity no longer reflects the *labour input* necessary to produce *that* commodity. Most strikingly, individual prices can no longer be conceived purely at the microeconomic level: it now takes an analysis of the economy as a whole (i.e. a macroeconomic approach) to explain (a) how aggregate *surplus value* is extracted in each firm and in each sector; (b) how profit is allocated to each sector and firm in proportion to their investment in machines; and finally (c) how this grand allocation determines individual prices.

Did Marx's theoretical remedy hold water? Luigi Pasinetti (1977) thinks so and we agree.[23] Though Marx did not complete the mathematics (and made some technical errors), Pasinetti shows that he was on the right track, foreshadowing a potentially consistent iterative procedure by which to transform *labour inputs*, that is, *values*, into *prices*.[24] Of course, there is always a price to pay for consistency. As shown by Pasinetti, the theoretical cost of establishing a correspondence between *prices* and *labour inputs* (and vice versa) is the loss of Marx's prophecies about the *falling rate of profit*. In short, equation (5.2) no longer holds and nothing concrete can therefore be said about the long-term viability of capitalism. Marx's new distinctly macroeconomic framework rendered his *theory of value* consistent but forfeited any long-term 'scientific' prophecies regarding the future of capitalism.

The problem is that, even if we agree broadly with Pasinetti that Marx managed to deal reasonably well with the *Inherent Error* bequeathed to him by Ricardo, the end result was a mess. Caught up in the Newtonian mechanism of the nineteenth-century, and a Maxwell-like determination to unify all economic phenomena under a single model of a *steady-as-she-goes* capitalism, he squandered his dialectical outlook. While he could have seized the opportunity to argue, with a great deal of supporting evidence (see our argument in Box 5.12), that capitalism is in permanent flux, that disequilibrium is its natural state as long

Box 5.13 The falling rate of profit: Internal and external critiques

Marx was the first political theorist to have practised *immanent criticism*, a scientific method that derives from mathematics and which demands of the theorist that he/she immerse him/herself deeply into the theory under scrutiny. First, one accepts all of a theory's axioms and assumptions and then tests exhaustively their consistency with the theory's conclusions and theorems. Marx did exactly that with the political economics of the Physiocrats, Adam Smith and David Ricardo. Like the connoisseur of tragedy that he was, he suspended disbelief, accepted fully the logic of the political economics he studied. Once firmly embedded in the theory's logic, he proceeded to criticise it from within by highlighting its internal contradictions before, eventually, proposing a way of *overcoming* them. The result was his own brand of political economics. As a devout Hegelian, Marx would have appreciated (however grudgingly) that his own theories could be also subjected to immanent criticism; to an internal critique. As we just saw, Marx's view that the profit rate in capitalism is bound to fall in the long run simply does not stand up to immanent criticism. His own method of recasting the labour theory of value and profit (in vol. III of *Capital*), once rid of mathematical error, leads to the safe result that the *falling rate of profit* cannot be sustained as a theorem.

A second type of criticism, known as *external*, is the one that begins by challenging the axioms, assumptions and general premises of some theory. For instance, one could argue that value can be created in a *Matrix Economy* (even though we are hard pressed to see how we would concur) or that labour inputs can be quantified just as readily as the input into an electricity generator. In the case of the *falling rate of profit*, the potential external criticisms are legion. For instance, it has been argued that the fact that in the past few decades computers play an increasing role in production does not mean that the organic composition of capital (k) is rising since the value of computers is falling so fast. A more telling external criticism brings into the picture the relation between developed capitalist countries with the rest of the world. Take for instance foreign direct investment by American, European and Japanese corporations in the Developing World. Effectively, this is a case of capital goods being exported from high profit countries (where the *organic composition of capital k* is high) to low-profit, low-k countries. Then, profits are repatriated from the latter to the former. Such a migration of capital to developing countries, and of profit to the developed ones, would ensure that the profit rate does now fall even if we accept the truth of equation (5.2).

Now, none of the above (internal or external critiques) means that the profit rate in capitalism does not have a tendency to fall. Indeed, the deeper reason behind the abrupt end of the first phase of the post-war era, in the early 1970s, was an economic crisis due to a secular drop in profit rates throughout the capitalist West (see Chapter 11). The point here is that no 'law' of a falling profit rate can be established theoretically. Human life is not amenable to concrete 'laws' as long as a 'thing' called 'free will' survives within us and we retain a potential for weird endeavours such as art, music, trust and laughter.

as free humans are built into its foundations, and that social power is irreducible to mathematical computations, he went in exactly the opposite way. The philosopher who did so much to unveil the impossibility of treating labour and capital as measurable 'things' ended up struggling with equations in which labour and capital inputs featured as measurable variables. The scholar who acknowledged the fundamental indeterminacy of contradictions invested oodles of intellectual energy in formulating *immutable* laws of change. The revolutionary who rejected idealism foreshadowed the end of capitalism on the basis of a shaky 'scientific' theorem which Karl Popper, a century later, was to refer to as a species of superstition.

In the end, Marx displayed the same tragic determination to 'close' his 'system' that plagued, and continues to plague, *all* of economics. It is, as we shall see in *Book 2*, the same determination that allowed economists and financial engineers to believe their own models and to cause, first, the post-1980 debt-based phase of capitalism (which we call the *Global Minotaur*; see Chapters 11 and 12) and, later, the financialisation bubble that was to gather pace from the mid-1990s onwards until, lastly, 2008 provided that particular tragedy's painful catharsis (see Chapter 12). We make this leap in time, from the nineteenth-century to 2008 to remind the reader that this part of the book is no gratuitous trip down memory lane. Our current task is the serious business of establishing, with no fear or favour, what should be salvaged from traditional political economics for the purposes of our generation's grand undertaking: making sense of the post-2008 world.

Marx's contribution is beyond dispute: he unveiled the contradictory face of capitalism; the two faces of both labour and capital; the manner in which this 'split' makes value-creation possible. He accentuated capitalism's infinite capacity to produce wealth and poverty as if from the same infernal production line. He revealed the curious fact that automation is at once liberating *and* turning humans into the machines' appendages. He illustrated that there are concrete causal links between growth rates, values and prices. From the perspective of our post-2008 world, he helps us become a little more like geologists who peer deep under the surface of things for the subterranean forces shaping the landscape; to look at *value* not as Dollars, Euros and the proverbial 'bottom line', but as a reflection of hard labour performed by real people around the globe who lack, unlike Mr Peel's imported workforce, the option of going into business for themselves; to see wealth not as goodies, trinkets and gadgets for the satiation of impressionable consumers but as the source of power which, while trumpeted for its capacity to impart happiness, ends up a means of subjugating others and, paradoxically, of losing one's self.

Above all else, Marx has this message for our generation: capitalism will cause crises even if peopled by very nice human beings. It will do so even if the individuals running the banks, regulating the markets, presiding over government and its various institutions are truly good people doing their best. It is what capitalism does! Regrettably, all these crucial insights are part of what we call *lost truth*. The catastrophe that was the communist experiment of the twentieth century did much to overshadow Marx's insights.[25] But it was the economics profession that killed them off.

Hell-bent on discovering consistency, and overcoming the *Inherent Error*, the economists that came after Marx learnt from him that, to achieve their objective, they needed to do one of two things: either abandon the search for a believable *theory of value* (as Adam Smith effectively did [recall Section 3.2]) or call off the hunt for a *dynamic model of capitalist growth*. The majority of economists today, the so-called neoclassical mainstream, turned their backs to the notion of a *surplus* whose distribution is determined by the allocation of *social power* among different social groups. Instead they chose to rid political economics of all politics (usually a euphemism for getting rid of any hint of radical politics) and to construct, in its place, a purely Leibnizian view of market societies in which prices and quantities adjust around some equilibrium in a complete social and political vacuum. We shall be turning to their ilk in the next chapter. Then there are economists who *do* care about the way in which the surplus is produced and distributed in a manner reflecting social power. We conclude this section with a brief look at their ways.

Given that a defensible combination of a *theory of stable (or equilibrium) values* and a *theory of stable (or equilibrium) growth* is elusive, one escape route is to ditch the very notion of *value*. Suppose, for instance, that the surplus is imagined not in terms of values [as it was in equations (5.1) to (5.8)] but in terms of some physical output (i.e. in terms of tons of corn, numbers of tractors) resulting from production that goes on simultaneously in different sectors utilising different combinations of inputs. Then, it is possible to select any one of these products and use its price as a reference point or index (a *numéraire* as economists call it). It can be shown that this approach, which was famously presented in 1960 by Cambridge based Italian economist Piero Sraffa, under the apt title *The Production of Commodities by Means of Commodities*,[26] can lead to (a) a uniform rate of profit (where profit is measured in physical terms) and (b) relative prices expressed simply as a ratio between the units of a commodity that correspond to one unit of the *numéraire* product.[27]

Technically speaking, we have *already* shown how all this can be done in the previous chapter. Indeed, equations (4.1) to (4.6) capture Sraffa's approach fully: two products, that are both the outputs and the inputs of the economy; two sectors; three inputs (i.e. the two products plus an additional 'natural resource' not reproduced endogenously); one profit rate; and one ratio of the quantity of the one product that corresponds to one unit of the other. Having ditched the very concept of *value* from the outset, the *Transformation Problem* never gets a look in and a complete theory of relative prices plus a well defined relation between the economy's growth rate and the prevailing wage rate can be established.[28]

Philosophically speaking, however, there is a hefty price to pay for this escape. Recalling that it presupposes the abandonment of *value*, the analysis constrains us to look at production only in terms of the manufacture of physical 'things' by means of other physical 'things', plus *quantifiable* units of some non-producible input. That input, in Sraffa, is *labour input*: a variable that differs from other variables only in that it is only an input and not an output.[29] To spot the hefty price involved in this theoretical move, simply recall the context in which these equations [(4.1) to (4.6)] were formulated: the fully fledged *Matrix Economy* where machines produce other machines and fully enslaved humans play a supporting role as heat generators. Analytically speaking, there is no difference between the role of labour in Sraffa's economic model and the role reserved for us by *The Matrix*.

Box 5.14   Piero Sraffa's model and the spectre of *Matrix Economics*

Sraffa's approach was meant not as a departure from Marx, nor as an abandonment of value theory, but as a simple model by which to criticise the economic approach that will be discussed in the next chapter, and in which all politics is driven out of economics. Sraffa, a left-wing economist who admired Marx and spent almost 30 years of his life editing Ricardo's works, wanted to set aside the *Transformation Problem* (see Box 5.12) and tell a story about price determination, which, however, allows us a helpful glimpse of the role of social power in distributing the surplus between capitalists and workers. By thinking of the wage as a part of the physical product, it is possible to say that a positive extraction rate (or the rate of exploitation) exists when a person receives as a wage less than the size of her physical product. But while this is clearly relevant in backward agrarian societies where horses and humans differed not one bit, what might it mean in a capitalist economy? What is the physical part of the steel output that goes back to the steel worker? No one knows except through a value calculation via prices. But if those prices are determined merely through a physical surplus, then the inputs into production of a horse, an electricity generator and a worker are analytically equivalent: all subject to the same technical, as opposed to social, relation.

To recap, Sraffa's model applies equally to agrarian slave societies,[1] and, of course, to the *Matrix Economy* in which humans are no more than heat generators. By leaving *value* out of the analysis, Sraffa forfeited the option of telling a story specific to capitalism. Once the two faces of labour are lost, the two faces of capital follow and the ensuing economics is no longer able to say anything *specific* about capitalism. Any talk of crisis, genuine dynamics and disequilibrium are thus lost. Nevertheless, we feel that Sraffa understood all this well. His analysis [captured by equations (4.1) to (4.6)] was never meant as a substitute for Marx's dialectical insights but as a critique of Marginalist or neoclassical economics – see next chapter. We do not mention this critique here because of some misplaced necrophilia on our part. Sraffa's critique throws a spanner in the works of those who want to argue that capitalist profits and workers' wages are a reflection of their relative contribution to production. In an age where the working poor are increasing in number and wealth is concentrating in the hands of those who live on income from capital (that is often guaranteed by the taxpaying workers) such a critique is the stuff of power.

Note

1 Possibly also to societies where production is based on gift exchange, e.g. in Papua New Guinea before the introduction by the British of monetary means of exchange. See Chris Gregory, 1982.

5.6 Epilogue

Other cargoes do not rebel!

This is how Benjamin Franklin defined the difference between the trade in slaves and all other commerce at the Constitutional Convention of 1878. Our innate rebelliousness sets us apart from machines and animals, and renders slavery a precarious system. From Spartacus's audacious rebellion and the resistance that African 'cargo' put up onboard the dismal ships transporting 'it' to the Americas, to the anti-slavery movement of the nineteenth-century and Neo's rebellion in the futuristic 'plantations' of *The Matrix*, liberty's call has demonstrated impressive resilience. Industrial capitalism and formal freedom did not evolve together by accident. Capitalism, in fact, does not only tolerate human freedom: it feeds on it (see Box 5.15).

Box 5.15 Capitalism versus slavery and *The Matrix*

For the past few decades a consensus has emerged that global competition demands that labour becomes as amenable to the demands of investors and employers as possible. What if workers agreed enthusiastically? What if they consented to becoming automata at the unconstrained disposal of employers? Chapters 4 and 5 argued that it would be a catastrophic development for capital. Slavery and advanced capitalism do not mix. While it is true that individual employers would rejoice at the thought of slave labour (which explains why a crushing majority of nineteenth-century businessmen were so adamantly opposed to the ban on slavery), capitalism requires free labour that can be hired, used and then disposed of. After the primitive stage of capital accumulation, it was capitalism that turned its back on slavery. The Africans' mounting resistance on the slave ships (recall Rediker, 2007, and Box 5.4), increased the cost of transporting them and contributed to the end of the trade on cost–benefit grounds. And when later the Unionists and the Confederates fought a bitter Civil War (1861–4) over the slavery question, the conflict had little to do with humanist opposition to the principle of slavery.

Indeed, from 1776 until its abolition, America's founding fathers combined moving speeches on liberty with the ownership of slaves. The same Thomas Jefferson who eloquently wrote that '… the whole commerce between master and slave is a perpetual exercise of the most boisterous passions, the most unremitting despotism on the one part, and degrading submissions on the other' (Jefferson 1801, p. 240), refused to free the slaves he owned *even in his will.* Southern plantation owners and Northern industrialists had no qualms about 'clearing the land' from the indigenous population. So it is improbable that humanitarianism was the reason that the Yankees and the Confederates clashed with such ferocity. A closer look at the contemporary debates reveals that the Civil War was about whether or not slavery ought to be allowed in the new territories, basically any land west of Tennessee. Plantation owners wanted slavery to be allowed there while the industrialised Northern states objected strongly for the simple reason that industrialists cherished the freedom to hire and fire free labourers. Their victory in the Civil War created the conditions for full industrialisation and for the modern USA to come into being.[1]

In summary, industrial capital is at odds with slavery because its own reproduction is based on the value produced when labour power is purchased for a price (corresponding to the value of the wages) and then indeterminate labour inputs of greater value are extracted from that labour power in a space (the firm) untouched by the market. As long as this condition is met, many different historical, legal and institutional frameworks can be tolerated: legally imported permanent labour (in countries such as the USA of the Ellis Island era, Australia, Canada but also, today, the Arab Emirates), 'guest' workers (like the ones Germany imported in the 1950s or the ones Australia is importing now on temporary, highly restricted, visas), the pool of disenfranchised labour created by South African Apartheid, the illegal labour power crossing, at great human risk, the border fences and the high seas into the USA and the European Union, etc. The one institution that advanced capitalism has no time for is slavery. While firms would love to turn their workers into will-less automata, a slave economy would be analytically equivalent to the *Matrix Economy* thus spelling capitalism's demise. This contradiction between the interests of individual employers and of the economic system in which they fare is one of the major causes of actual crises. In this account, bankers' bonuses and stock or house price bubbles are mere add-ons that simply make a bad thing worse.

Note

1 In a different context, the emergence of capitalism led, for similar economic reasons, to the demise of the largest slave empire in the world: Brazil, where the slave system was abolished in 1888 just before the establishment of the Republic. The requirements of value production, throughout the New World, demanded labourers who were at the same time free to sign the labour contract and unfree enough to have to sign it. Slavery was, simply, uneconomical.

If only this were the whole story! While liberty exerts a formidable gravitational pull on us and on our social order, an opposing force of similar might is also at work. Our *Will to Freedom* regularly transforms itself into Nietzsche's *Will to Power,* evoking in us an urge to subjugate which then causes an opposite longing: *our tendency to acquiesce in our own subjugation.* The lure of freedom puzzlingly coexists with a penchant for reproducing the conditions of illiberty (others' as well as our own). If Martians were ever to visit, the one thing that would surely strike them as extremely odd is not so much the human capacity for oppressing other humans but the readiness with which these freedom-loving beings consent to oppression. If ever Newtonian thinking applied to human society, it surely manifests itself in this perpetual tug-of-war between the forces of freedom and oppression that fight it out within our own minds.

In Chapter 2 we brought up *Condorcet's Secret* that 'real power lies not with the oppressors but with the oppressed'. In this chapter we added two further vignettes: one was the *Hegelian idea* that *no one is free of oppression* in any society in which *some* are systematically oppressed. The other was Marx's contribution, namely that capitalism is a uniquely tragic system because it oppresses *everyone* in almost equal measure, rather than just the wretched and the meek who used to be at the mercy of the merry aristocracy. Worker and capitalist, man and woman, banker and farmer, the middle classes, even the world's burgeoning squatter population, *each and every one of us is turned into an effective servant of global capital accumulation.* Pressed into the service of the machines, free markets put our society on the path to the *Matrix Economy* where freedom is but an illusion. Even though we are far from such a dystopia, our minds are contaminated by false notions of our 'need' for the latest gadget, the larger house, the bigger mortgage. Philosophically, the *commodity fetishism* that is essential to *capital accumulation*, taken together with the self-perpetuating compulsion felt by those with capital to create more capital, is not too far off the virtual reality of *The Matrix*. Without taking ownership of our bodies, capitalism immerses human minds just as successfully in a virtual reality functional to the needs of the machines.

As in all good tragedies, the possibility of *catharsis* rests on a moment of clarity that follows some deep crisis. At that instant of radical disequilibrium and deep-seated indeterminacy, the protagonists are blessed with a chance of catching a glimpse of their predicament and exposing the most contemporary variant of *Condorcet's Secret.* Only those fortunate to live during such rare moments get a chance to reach, like Thomas Anderson, for the *red pill.* Of course, that moment cannot be willed by the human spirit alone. Since the rise of the steam-powered factories, the telegraph, mass transport and computerised automata, it takes a crisis of capitalism (possibly a string of them) to materialise. The *Crash of 2008* was, in this view, such a moment when the confluence of different economic forces (which we shall investigate in *Book 2*) caused the perfect storm which graced us with the singular opportunity to discover the ways our own belief system has been sustaining an unsustainable social order.

Marx's singular contribution was to point out that such crises may be inevitable. They are not inevitable because capitalists are awful people (even if many of them are), or because the banks have made a killing using other people's hard-earned money (even though they undoubtedly have), but because capitalism is caught in a trap of its own making: as a system it strives to turn us into automata and our market society into a *Matrix*-like dystopia. But the closer it comes to achieving its aim the nearer it gets (very much like the mythical Daedalus) to its moment of ruin. Then it picks itself up, recovers and embarks upon the same path all over again. It is as if our capitalist societies were designed to generate periodic crises. Only this design evolved historically, as both Adam Smith and Darwin would have understood, without a purposeful designer whom we can blame.

Where Marx went badly wrong was in his conviction that capitalism can be scientifically proven to lead to its demise and replacement by a more rational socio-economic organisation in which the two natures of humans will be reunited in genuine freedom from (a) the domination of want and (b) the machines' imperatives. Marx was wrong for two reasons: first, it cannot be shown that this is what will happen, not even in the long run; and second, as John Maynard Keynes famously put it, in the long run we are all dead anyway. And if capitalism wastes natural resources in the same way that it squanders human virtues, then we may not be around on this planet to witness this particular triumph of the *Dialectic* (see Box 4.10).

Rare as they may be, moments of clarity are the stuff of genuine historical progress. Spartacus' moment in history came when he managed to dispel *Condorcet's Secret*; to infuse into the slaves a capacity to see slavery as an unnatural, social, historical construction. Even if his rebellion failed, it continued to resonate through the ages inspiring others to complete the struggle against slavery. The suffragettes, Mahatma Gandhi, Martin Luther King, Nelson Mandela: they all revealed to long-oppressed groups of people the true causation behind their subjugation and, in so doing, empowered them to imagine a world in which such causation is extinct.

Political economics cannot explain how the inspired few can convince us to take the *red pill*. What it *can* do to is to analyse the socio-economic crises which are a prerequisite for that option to emerge. The suffragettes would not have succeeded in pushing forward the idea that women had to have equal political rights were it not for the crisis that occasioned the Great War and brought women into the factories. Similarly, history would have passed Gandhi over had British capitalism not entered into a slow burning, long-term crisis that made the preservation of Empire impossible. Martin Luther King's speeches would not have been heard outside a tiny circle of followers had it not been for the violent discontent caused by a stagnating US post-war capitalism which spawned both the Vietnam War (where blacks were over-represented for the first time in US military history) *and* President Lyndon B. Johnson's Great Society programme for boosting domestic demand among the less privileged consumers.

Knowing the underlying causes of oppression, regardless of whether we are its victims or culprits, is a giant first step towards negating it. In this regard, political economics ought to be rationality's friend and freedom's ally in defusing *Condorcet's Secret*. Alas, in reality, it has been their worst enemy. Rather than convincing us to take the *red pill*, to stare into the blinding sun in defiance of the causes of our predicament, political economics has been embroiled in its own small-minded, farcical concerns. Slavishly copying nineteenth-century physics, it has sought to produce a complete picture of market societies in which all economic variables are 'explained', 'quantified' and 'predicted' with the accuracy of an engineer and the consistency of formal mathematics.

Unable to grasp the importance of humanity's glorious resistance to any force that tries to turn us into inputs no different from coal or electricity, political economics prefers to model capitalism as the locus of predictable change and dynamic equilibrium than as a space of flux, unpredictability and permanent disequilibrium. Even Karl Marx, the scholar who gave us the first decent glimpse of the irreducible dialectical nature of labour and capital, of capitalism's inherent irrationality and of its tendency to erupt in crises; felt the need to seek shelter under mathematical formulations in which everything can be worked out in terms of well-defined functions. Bending the truth to his mechanistic will, he was partly responsible for the authoritarianism that took over the communist movement, turning humanism's greatest hope into one of humanity's worst nightmares.

The trouble with humans is not just that we swing unpredictably from conformism to rebellion and back, but also that we cannot stop ourselves from celebrating our unpredictability *while at the same time striving to repress it*. Our poetry celebrates the fickleness of the human condition while our theory strives to choke it, portraying us as predictable pawns in some predetermined chess game. Of course, sometimes pretend-models are a practical response to the intransigence of reality. But to put them to good use we must never really believe in them. We must always press them to breaking point; drive them to their limits; and watch them disintegrate under the weight of their internal contradictions. And then we must transcend them quickly, never losing sight of the true purpose of our endeavour: to help us rid our societies of systematic idiocy at a planetary level (like poverty in the face of conspicuous wealth; of unemployment when so much work needs to be done; coal burning and the toxification of the atmosphere when investment in green energy would enrich our lives and improve our balances; the list is endless).

Unhappily, all of the above have amounted to significant *truths lost* due to the economics' discipline. Haunted by the dream of some closed, self sufficient system, economics of all types has been returning, like a guilt-ridden criminal, to the scene of its *Inherent Error*: to the aspiration to offer a set of interlocking concepts that are their own cause. Naturally, even to try this logically difficult party trick, all human features (i.e. politics, quirkiness, psychology, social contingency) must be bleached out of economics. Unimpressed by this folly, economic reality treats the economists' 'dream' with the contempt it richly deserves, undermining with mathematical precision the unity of economic models, and preventing them from producing some satisfyingly determinate system.

All our binary oppositions are thus exposed as serious misunderstandings: economics versus politics; microeconomics versus macroeconomics; value versus price; the individual versus the state; the production models in this and the previous chapters versus the 'utility calculus' of the next; each of these notions or models turns out to be both *necessary* and *incomplete*. Each is a *necessary error*, an *indispensible facade*. Economic theory may be our best shot at understanding social reality but is an unsafe friend and an exceedingly poor historian. The best-intentioned economists, with Karl Marx towering above them, begin with a healthy appreciation of the fact their models are nothing but provisional forays into structured thinking. Soon after, however, the models take over and the provisional terms in which they do their work start regarding themselves as conduits of a concrete or material existence. Before economists realise it, their models auto-reify and turn into totalising systems in their own right. As if in a bid to reflect the way in which capital ended up subjugating (*via* the imperatives of competition and capital accumulation) capitalists and workers alike, economic models successfully subjugate the economists, turning them into their appendages.

It seems that the price we must pay for freedom is the same that we must fork out for enlightenment. To understand 2008 and its aftermath we must learn to resist the Sirens of consistent economic models generating determinate 'predictions' on prices and quantities. Resisting in this manner is *our* equivalent of the *red pill*. To allow ourselves to be lured by determinate economic theory is to opt for the *blue pill* that delivers the type of blissful ignorance which passes as mainstream economic theory. While the *blue pill* offers better prospects for a quiet life and professional success, only the *red pill* can tell us about the *Crash of 2008* and the role economic theory played in bringing it about.

6   Empires of indifference
Leibniz's calculus and the ascent of Calvinist political economics

6.1 Lost truths retrieved

The modern world luxuriates in its multiple veils. Capable of being radically unlike what it seems, it is fraught with delicious contradictions and is permanently pregnant with crises, but also with the prospect of their overcoming. However, this 'overcoming' is impeded by *Condorcet's Secret*. To defuse it, society must be ready to swallow the *red pill*. Theory, in this context, ought to be a device for unlearning how to live merrily in deceit. Regrettably, as this chapter will argue, soon after Marx's *Capital* was published, economic theory took a drastically different turn, transforming itself into the most potent *blue pill* in history.

Jean Baudrillard once said wryly that there are two kinds of scholars: those who let dead authors rest in peace and those who are forever digging them up to finish them off. In the preceding chapters, we did something quite different with the texts of early political economics: we plundered them, not in order to score scholastic points against long dead authors, but instead to retrieve *lost truths* in the hope that they may help free *our* generation from the tyranny of contemporary appearances; from, for example, the conventional lie that the *Crash of 2008* was *caused* by rampant bankers, negligent legislators, reckless home buyers and regulators who fell asleep on the job.

The largest nugget of gold retrieved from those texts was the insight that, although history is nothing more than the sum of individual acts, our economic and social reality is shaped by unobserved material forces working their magic behind our backs. Our free will keeps history on its toes and our subjective beliefs motivate our acts but, nonetheless, both are severely circumscribed by unseen material forces. Our subjectivity remains the sole source of value but, at the same time, it is constrained by objective circumstances beyond its immediate comprehension or ambit.

Adam Smith showed how competition may subvert self interest, as if by some *invisible hand*, and David Ricardo distinguished between the activities that produce things *we* value in our market societies from those that are 'objectively' *productive*. But it was Marx who contributed the most shockingly modern and tantalising of thoughts: that, although no one likes a crisis or works to bring it about, *crises are functional to capitalism* in the manner that periodic bushfires help maintain the Australian forests. Rather than avoidable accidents due to an excessive concentration of power in the hands of malicious managers or of corrupt politicians, Marx enabled us to see crises as essential components of capitalism's dynamics. The devastation they wreak to whole generations of workers, shopkeepers, farmers, migrants, etc. is as indispensible to capitalism as Hell is to Christianity.

Even more helpfully, Marx highlighted the pivotal contradiction of the modern era: the faster and surer is economic growth the more profit rates suffer and the closer we edge to the next crisis whose primary *function* is the restoration of the fallen profitability. Where we part ways with Marx, and possibly with the entire economics profession, is in our conviction that *all* economic theory comes much closer to the *blue* than the *red pill*: instead of exposing the inconvenient truths, economics exhibits a natural tendency, often in spite of the economists' best intentions, to obfuscate, to conceal and to lull its practitioners into a false sense of intellectual security; thus becoming a passive accomplice to a life lived almost exclusively in deceit. This chapter is dedicated to the origins of the highest form of that joyless 'condition': the mainstream economics which spawned the Econobubble and provided the ideological cover for the variant of global capitalism which came crashing down in *2008*.

6.2 The *Inherent Error* thus far

How could so many brilliant economists, financial experts, central bankers, etc. get it so wrong? This is a question that reverberated around the world in 2008; just as it had done many times before, 1929 being one of the more memorable occasions. Our hypothesis in this book is that we are staring at a 'systemic' failure, an *Inherent Error*, rather than poor individual judgement on the part of the economists. The root cause of the discipline's *Inherent Error* is, we submit, the determination to forge, come what may, a consistent, unified explanation of both values *and* growth; of distribution *and* accumulation.

There is, of course, nothing wrong with the ambition to discover a general theory that unifies our understanding of

(a) how an economy grows and
(b) how it bestows values upon different 'things'.

But when this ambition can be realised *only* by brutally twisting logic, and by assumptions which violate (rather than merely simplifying) reality, economics turns from an ally in the struggle against ignorance to a species of mathematised superstition.

We have been referring to this *Inherent Error* from the first chapter onwards. Its latest incarnation appeared in Section 5.4 of the previous chapter. It emerged when Marx stumbled upon the useful insight that competition among capitalists *cannot* equalise, across the economy's many sectors, both *profit rates* [the π's in equation (5.8)] and the rates at which *labour inputs* are extracted from *labour power* (the *extraction rates*, the e's, in the same equation). For, if capital moves to the more profitable sector, as is its wont,[1] that will cause the *extraction rates* to diverge. But then, the freshly divergent *extraction rates* will bring about the migration of labour from the sectors with the higher to those with the lower *extraction rate*; a 'correction' that will, however, cause the *profit rates* to diverge, thus spurring a fresh migration of capital. And so on.

Box 6.1 The *Inherent Error's* triptych

- The lure of algebra
- The appeal of closure
- The political utility of determinism

Instead of rejoicing at having discovered one of the reasons why capitalism is synonymous with constant flux, Marx panicked and went into overdrive trying to iron out this 'incongruity'. The *Inherent Error* was, thus, given a new twirl. Why? The reason is threefold, we believe. First, there is what we think of as the *lure of algebra*. To illustrate this 'lure', suppose that one came across two equalities, without knowing what they meant, represented or their connection to some 'reality': e.g. $y = ax^2 + b$; $x = c + dy$. We submit that even the least mathematically minded would experience an inner curiosity to know their 'solution' as a system of equations; even if they were *not*, in any meaningful sense, such a system.

Second, there is the related *appeal of closure*. In Chapter 5 we mentioned the influence on political economics of James Maxwell's astonishing unification of magnetism, electricity and radiation. It is virtually impossible to overstate the mesmeric effect that this 'closure' had on nineteenth-century intellectuals, and not just those who actively engaged in the natural sciences. For, that was the first time in human history that different branches of scientific understanding, hitherto pursued by different groups of scientists (employing different assumptions and methods), suddenly converged (almost by serendipity) to a single model in which a consistent explanation became possible. Thus, an overarching theory of causes and effects explained seemingly disparate phenomena.[2] Its secret was the proof that light, radiation and electromagnetism were mere manifestations of a unified meta-force.

Social theorists of ability and imagination felt compelled to produce similarly unified theories of society. Hegel had already foreshadowed a view of a singular force guiding humanity towards some *telos*,[3] and Friedrich Nietzsche famously posited the Will to Power as the subliminal force lurking behind all that we say and do. But it was Marx who went beyond philosophy and attempted to do for social science what Maxwell had achieved in physics: to *close* the theories of classical political economics by discovering the meta-force whose different manifestations rule over our disparate lives. That meta-force was no other than *capital* (thus the title of his most famous book) and capital was no more than *crystallised human labour*; 'dead' or 'zombie' labour with a twisted logic of its own that was gradually taking over the world at the expense of the living (both entrepreneurs and workers).

To *close* his system, Marx had, just like the physicists, to find a way of leaving no significant 'force' outside his gamut of explanation. Section 5.4 showed that to *fully* explain values, wages and profit rates in terms of capital (and its incessant flow to sectors with higher profitability), Marx saw no alternative but to take the following two steps:

(1) Assume that commodities, courtesy of Smithian competition, trade around their values, which, in turn, reflect the *labour inputs* necessary for their production.
(2) Work out the system's capital accumulation (and profit) rates given these values-*cum*-prices.

In short, *closure* could be bought only at the price of assuming that, at every moment in time, there existed a set of values (one per commodity), a wage rate and a single economy-wide profit (or growth) rate such that, other things remaining equal, the 'system' would be at rest.

We can now begin to see why equation (5.8) gave Marx such grief. For, it revealed a terrible dilemma: either he would have to celebrate the insight that capitalism is typified by constant flux (caused by the continual migration of capital[4] and labour[5] across different sectors); or he should become embroiled in the longwinded project of ironing this flux out of his model. He opted for the latter thus bequeathing us a new variant of the *Inherent Error*: the inauspicious *transformation problem* (recall Box 5.12). Had he chosen the former path, his reward would have been a richly appealing account of the dynamics of capitalism: prices would haphazardly dance around their underlying values (i.e. *labour inputs*) and the trans-formation of *labour power* into *labour inputs* would have retained its true indeterminate nature. Alas, that choice would have led him into politically murkier waters: it would amount to the abandonment of Marx's burning ambition to produce a unified theory of society fea-turing capital as its *unique* meta-force. Why? Because, given that prices would now be irre-ducible to values, the theory would have to allow room for some other determinant of prices, such as the nebulous concept of *power of firms* over consumers[6] and/or over workers.[7]

The *appeal of closure* suggests, at this juncture, the possibility of an interesting compari-son with physics where a similar 'appeal' is just as powerful. Marx was too astute to have overlooked that something was missing from his model of capitalism; that not all forces were reducible to *capital* (even if the latter remained the dominant force running through the world's fabric); that some unaccounted for, translucent, elusive 'dark' force (we call it *power* in the above paragraph) did a lot of the work of determining prices, profits and wages, leav-ing behind an explanatory lacuna. Compare, however, Marx's response to that of the physi-cists when they too discovered that their *Standard Model* could not square (a) their theory of gravitation with (b) their current inventory of cosmic forces and matter.

Upon discovering a gap in their models, the physicists christened the missing ingredient *dark matter/energy* and have ever since been struggling to shine a bright light on it by means of massive new experiments which they are currently conducting in deep coal mines under the North Sea, in endless tunnels dug into the Swiss Alps, aboard space stations, etc. What did Marx, his followers and, indeed, almost every other economist since, do? They went back to their original equations in search of an excuse not to look further; to patch the model up axiomatically with no need to research further the material causes of its incompleteness.

While the *lure of algebra* and the *appeal of closure* explain an important part of the economists' ostrich-like approach, we feel there is much more to the *Inherent Error*. We refer to the third factor contributing to it as the *political utility of determinism*. Take Marx as an early example. He never tried to hide his political agenda, that is, his argument that the working class must strive for higher wages with no fear of price inflation. To bolster this agenda scientifically, he had to keep the question of income distribution separate from the question of value and price determination (recall Box 5.10). Rendering his theory of *value* consistent with his theory of *growth* was, therefore, functional to a precise political agenda. In contrast, the physicists have no such agenda. The discovery that there is simply not enough matter in the cosmos to support their models of gravitation gave them pause, and perhaps a degree of irritation. But neither lasted for more than a few minutes.

Very soon, the fresh evidence of a missing ingredient (which undermined their prevailing theory) appeared to them as a tremendous opportunity for renewed research, furious debate and, poignantly, extra funding at a massive scale. Before long they were happily constructing gigan-tic research facilities. While they too, just like the economists, crave findings that will, eventu-ally, deliver determinacy back into their so-called *Standard Model*, their method of bringing it about involves ingenious new experiments and brand new pieces of hardware with which they scan the universe for clues on what the missing *dark matter* might be and how they can incorporate it in new determinate models. In contrast, economists, whenever their models are found wanting, ignore reality, recoil back into them, and carry on tweaking their axioms until the same tired old models are rendered determinate, naturally at the expense of illumination.[8]

6.3 The defence of the realm

Marx was not immune to the *Inherent Error*. But it was the reaction against his critique of capitalism that elevated the *Inherent Error* to loftier heights, turning it into an unassailable

Box 6.2 Backlash

Powerful interests respond powerfully when challenged. When the first medical studies began to reveal the harm caused by smoking, the tobacco industry went into top gear sponsoring research that cast doubt on the emerging anti-tobacco consensus. It took decades of concerted effort to liberate the truth from such shameless propaganda. (On tobacco and other chemicals see Epstein, 1998.) More recently, the fossil-fuel industries (coal, oil, etc.) began channelling rivers of cash to outfits that dispute the overwhelming scientific data on climate change. These are just two examples of single industries reacting brutally to a perceived political threat. Predictably, the backlash against a challenge aimed at the interests of *all industrialists at once* was of a wholly different scale. At the theoretical level, it took the form of the death of classical political economics. At other levels, its realisation was grimmer (e.g. the murder of Rosa Luxemburg, a talented Marxist economist and humanist political activist, in January 1919).

source of bewilderment and a barrier which hermetically sealed economics off from capitalist reality.

The political economists that followed Marx, and who felt a duty radically to oppose his 'scientific' critique of capitalism, realised that, to achieve their objective, it was awfully easy to shift the 'paradigm' onto vistas within which Marx's view would make no sense. Fearing that Marx was hard to out-manoeuvre on his own analytical terrain (that of classical political economics), the terrain was therefore changed. In effect, they adopted the key counter-insurgency technique of our time: *to kill the fish, drain the lake!*

In analytical terms, this meant a wholesale rejection of the type of political economics upon which Marx had erected his narrative. Classical political economics was thus sacrificed to deny Marx his foundations. The collateral damage, of severing economics' link with figureheads such as Adam Smith and David Ricardo, was deemed acceptable. Thereafter, they were to be revered as symbols honoured more in the breach than in the observance (of their analytical method).

The key theoretical move was the *retreat from value*. From Aristotle's time (recall Chapter 1), prices were imagined as mere ephemeral reflections of something deeper, subliminal, real: of the *value* of things. Smith, Ricardo, Malthus and Marx shared this presumption and thought that prices echoed, however imperfectly, underlying 'objective' values. As the trembling shadows on the Platonic cave's walls vaguely reflect the real persons sitting in front of the fire, so do the rickety prices we pay hazily reflect their 'objective' values; or so the classical political economists thought! By imposing a moratorium on the very idea of value (as something distinct from price), anti-Marxist political economics cancelled the very framework in which Marx's analysis (but also of Smith's, Ricardo's and Malthus's) made sense.

Note the strategy's brilliance: with one small stone it killed off all debate on the role of capital and labour in determining values; on the origin of profit in surplus value; on the analytical importance of the rate at which *labour inputs* (that is, values) can be extracted from given *labour power*, etc. The next task was to devise a theory of prices that does not require any analysis of capitalist reality. The new approach, which became known as *Marginalist* (and soon spawned its so-called *neoclassical* turn – see Section 6.11), offered just that.

Thus capitalism suddenly dropped off the radar screen of political economics. All that remained in view were observable oscillating prices and quantities. The sole institution that stayed at the analytical centre was that of some rarefied market in which our only possible identity is that of buyer and seller. The adoption of this simplistic dualism,[9] within a context of a single surviving institution (the abstract market), made it impossible to think of capitalism as anything beyond a 'natural system' of buyers and sellers. And given that, at least in the late-nineteenth-century, the epithet 'natural' had positive connotations rhyming with 'natural order', 'natural philosophy', etc., it became entirely understandable to think of capitalism as a stable and efficient frame (almost a social counterpart of the solar system) within which human freedom and creativity had the best chance to flourish.

In this new mindframe, Marx's depiction of capitalism as an innately contradictory, illiberal system (and of crises as the inevitable manifestations of these contradictions) echoed as distant, partisan and, to many, slightly paranoid. Capitalism was thus protected by a cloak of theoretical invisibility and the realm of capital was defended most effectively from rational scrutiny. In the process, any hope of coming to grips with the real world around us sustained a major blow from which it has never really recovered. The new Marginalist-*cum*-neoclassical political economics succeeded in monopolising, to this day, the pages of every modern economics textbook on the planet. It informed every finance minister since at least the Second World War. It constrained the imagination of the best willed of politicians. Worse still, it provided the foundations of the post-war Econobubble which did the ideological bidding of the *Bubble* whose demise in 2008 we are now paying for. Where Marx strove to furnish us with an effective *red pill*, the backlash against his worldview created the most insidious of *blue pills*. Sadly, our world remains under its influence. It is for this reason that the present chapter delves into its 'alchemy'.

6.4 A moratorium on value

As with all fresh starts, there was an invigorating quality in the Marginalists' first stirrings. Their utter disregard for everything that went before them is endearing; electrifying even. Recalling how economics' *Inherent Error* began with Aristotle's incongruous theory of value, and continued with the classical political economists' tortuous attempt to square a *theory of value* with a *theory of growth*, the following lines by Ludwig von Mises (a second-generation Marginalist and free marketer – see Box 6.5) are genuinely cathartic. His point is simple: *value is a false concept and the idea that things are exchanged only when of equal value a monstrous fallacy*. The whole notion of value and value equivalence is, through his lens, a counterfeit deity that has caused so many fine minds, from Aristotle to Marx, to flounder in search of a solution to an insoluble, meaningless problem. Away with it, then!

> An inveterate fallacy asserted that things and services exchanged are of equal value. Value was considered as objective, as an intrinsic quality inherent in things and not merely as the expression of various people's eagerness to acquire them. People, it was assumed, first established the magnitude of value proper to goods and services by an act of measurement and then proceeded to barter them against quantities of goods and services of the same amount of value. This fallacy frustrated Aristotle's approach to economic problems and, for almost two thousand years, the reasoning of all those for whom Aristotle's opinions were authoritative. It seriously vitiated the marvellous achievements of the classical economists and rendered the writings of their epigones, especially those of Marx and the Marxian school, entirely futile. The basis of modern economics

is the cognition that it is precisely the disparity in the value attached to the objects exchanged that results in their being exchanged. People buy and sell only because they appraise the things given up less than those received. Thus the notion of a measurement of value is vain. An act of exchange is neither preceded nor accompanied by any process which could be called a measuring of value.[10]

How absolutely true! Suppose we observe Jill swapping a banana for two of Jack's apples. If Jill thought that her banana was of the same value as Jack's two apples, why did she bother to swap? Clearly, she must have thought that his two apples are of greater value to her than her one banana. (And, at once, he must think the opposite.) The operative words here, of course, are *she* and *her*. Von Mises' message is that only one thing matters at the market-place: *subjective appraisal*. Apples, bananas or, indeed, software and space shuttles, do *not* come complete with some pre-packaged value hinging on the production cost and splendidly independent of the buyer's judgement. It is the very divergence in the subjective judgements of buyer and seller that motivates trading.

So, asks von Mises, why bother with the idea that, when a bargain is struck, something other than the price offered by the buyer and accepted by the seller needs to be equalised? Why look into the shadowy world of unseen *values* when the world of *prices* is bathed in sunshine and contains all we need to understand the marketplace? Moreover, if the retreat from value helps eliminate the *Inherent Error*, it is surely a blessing. But does it eliminate the *Inherent Error*? Unhappily, it does not, as we shall establish in the rest of this chapter. Though a defensible price theory based on subjective appraisal becomes possible, it does so in the context of an economy that either features no machines (i.e. no capital goods) or one in which all time and space are compressed into a single point!

As we shall be arguing, the retreat from value led instantly to the disappearance not only of any meaningful handle on capitalist dynamics but also of capital and the idea of change altogether. The price of eliminating value was high. Political economics, at the (false) prom-ise of the elimination of the *Inherent Error*, was lured into purveying an official view of capitalism that left room neither for capital nor for the flux that is its hallmark. In a crisis-prone world, crises became theoretically impossible.

6.5 Prices without values: Staying poised on the margins of utility

Von Mises, and the Marginalists before him (see Box 6.5), had their own firm ideas of what to put in place of the discarded value theory: *a purely subjective theory of prices*. Whereas clas-sical political economics was trying to unlock the mystery of price by delving into the produc-tion process, the neoclassicists turned to the psychic universe of the buyer, to his/her desires, preferences and, ultimately, to the combination of goods over which he/she is indifferent.

The basic idea behind this *price theory* was simple: as long as there are many potential buyers in the market for lemons, the price of a lemon is proportional to the 'satisfaction' of the buyer who purchased the *last* lemon sold (or, in their terminology, the *marginal* lemon). Not only is *every one of us* valuing lemons differently (as von Mises suggested above), but, in addition, each person values *every particular lemon* differently (depending how many he/she already has).

In the new *Marginalist* language, it was the lemon *on the margin* (or the *marginal* lemon) that determined the price of *all* lemons. No matter how much Jack values lemons, if the greengrocer chooses to sell lemons to Jill too, the price Jack will pay will reflect Jill's (lower) valuation of lemons. Shielded by competition from the seller's avarice, Jack retains a private surplus[11] since he pays a price proportional to Jill's utility from the last lemon bought.[12] A case where, so to speak, the tail (i.e. the *marginal* lemon) wags the dog (i.e. the whole market). Or, as superannuated postmodernists would enjoy saying, the answer is blowing on the margin.[13]

To make this point clearer, it helps to pit this Marginalist explanation against its classical counterpart by putting an identical question to both camps: *why does our society price a video game much more highly than clean air?* The classics would, in one voice, fall back on the *labour theory of value*: air, however critical it may be for the preservation of life, requires no human effort to be supplied. Until humanity succeeds in turning the atmosphere into a noxious gas, air will be supplied *effortlessly* and, hence, it will have no exchange value. Consequently, no one will be able to sell air canisters (except to scuba divers or astronauts) at a positive price. On the other hand, a video game takes countless hours and a great deal of human effort to design, program, debug and distribute. All this human *labour input* bestows value upon video games that the market then translates into a significant price.[14]

Note how the utility from air or from the video game played no role in this, otherwise fine, classical price theory.[15] The reason is of course that the classicists looked exclusively into the production process for clues regarding the price of things. The Marginalists, however, turned their eyes away from the production process, seeking instead the origin of prices in the individuals' private *subjective appraisals* of (or private *utility* from) different goods.[16] First, they note that the utility of air is infinite for all those of us who wish to continue living, or at least as high as the satisfaction we get from remaining alive. Second, they contrast this thought to the reality that, as long as our bodies are immersed in a relatively clean atmosphere, we do not care at all for one extra (or one less) cubic centimetre of air. In short, the *marginal* unit of air offers us, in itself, precisely zero utility. And since price reflects the utility of the *marginal* quantity, air is free of charge (except, again, to scuba divers for whom air's marginal utility can be steep).

As for the video game, the product is indivisible (in that you cannot play the game if you have at your disposal less than one unit of it) and so the *marginal* video game is the last copy of the game sold. Let's say that it was Jack who bought that *marginal* copy and suppose that he values it enough to want to play it, rather than delete it immediately from his gaming console. Then, it is evident that Jack's subjective appraisal of (or utility from) this video game is positive (and, quite possibly, considerable). And since price reflects the utility contributed by the last unit sold (the *marginal* unit) to its buyer, that is, to Jack, the price of video games that he and everyone else pays is positive (and perhaps substantial) while, at the same time, the price of the air they breathe is exactly zero, despite air's infinite contribution to their total utility.[17]

Underlying this price theory is the so-called *equi-marginal principle*; (see Box 6.3). Alfred Marshall, one of Marginalism's stalwarts (see Box 6.5), put it as follows: 'When a boy picks blackberries for his own eating, the action of picking is probably itself pleasurable for a while; and for some time longer the pleasure of eating is more than enough to repay the trouble of picking'.[18] Marshall's point here is that we crave that which we lack but, as we get more of it, the craving subsides and we are less prepared to work for it. In other words, as we 'stock up' on some good, we experience *diminishing marginal utility*:[19] 'But after he has eaten a good deal' Marshall continues, 'the desire for more diminishes; while the task of picking begins to cause weariness, which may indeed be a feeling of monotony rather than of fatigue'. So, when should the boy stop picking berries?

Box 6.3 Neoclassical Price Theory
Utility, the equi-marginal principle and the introduction of Leibniz's calculus into economics

Suppose that all you care for in life is an abstract notion of preference satisfaction called *utility*. Suppose also that all activities in life can be mapped on to some index of private utility. Then, it is a truth of mathematics that you should always act in accordance with the following rule known as the *equi-marginal principle*: continue with some action as long as your marginal utility (i.e. the contribution to your net utility from the last unit of the said activity) is greater than the related marginal dis-utility (i.e. the losses in utility caused by that last unit of the activity). Cease and desist (from that activity) the instant marginal utility equals marginal dis-utility!

Now note that the notion of marginal utility has an important mathematical interpretation: If the utility from apples is denoted by function $U(a)$, where a is the number of apples Jill eats and U her utility from that experience, then an increase in U caused by eating δa extra apples equals $\delta U = U(a+1) - U(a)$. The proportionate rate of change in utility, following an increase in apple consumption, is given by ratio $\delta U / \delta a$. When the number of extra apples tends to zero (i.e. when Jill eats an extra small bite of an apple), δU tends to the first order derivative of function $U(a)$ subject to a. This is the language and notation of *Gottfried Leibniz (1646–1716)* in which *marginal utility* becomes synonymous with $U'(a)$ or $\dfrac{dU(a)}{da}$. Thus, Leibnizian calculus, as opposed to the calculus simultaneously discovered in the 1680s by Isaac Newton, found its central place in political economics; a place that it has not lost since.

Note: The significance of the fact that it was Leibniz's calculus, rather than that of Newton, which became ensconced within Marginalist political economics is discussed towards the end of this chapter.

According to the *equi-marginal principle*, he should stop when the last (or marginal) berry gives him the same utility that it denies him. In Marshall's own words:

> Equilibrium is reached when at last his eagerness to play and his disinclination for the work of picking counterbalance the desire for eating. The satisfaction which he can get from picking fruit has arrived at its maximum: for up to that time every fresh picking has added more to his pleasure than it has taken away; and after that time any further picking would take away from his pleasure more than it would add.

To see how a general theory of prices emerges from this simple thought, consider some abstract commodity X that Jill buys at the supermarket. Suppose the price is fixed at $10 per unit of X and Jill wants to spend at most $30 on X. How many units of X should she buy? If Marshall is right, and the first unit of X gives her a great deal of utility, the more she buys the less she values the *marginal* (or last) unit and the less, therefore, she is prepared to pay for it. Suppose that Jill gets 30 units of utility from the first unit of X (let's call them *utils* for short), 20 utils from the second unit of X, 5 utils from the third unit of X and, lastly, 2 utils

---

Box 6.4 Dr Faust and the *Equi-Marginal Principle*

In Goethe's version of Dr Faust the good doctor is portrayed as an intellectual deeply discontented with the limitations of his knowledge regarding the big questions, the dearth of his powers over circumstances and the ingrained unhappiness that is the human condition. Mephistopheles (an incarnation of the Devil) finds an opening in Faust's yearning and offers him a deal 'he will furnish Faust with all he seeks until the moment Faust reaches the pinnacle of happiness. Then he shall claim his soul.' Faust accepts the covenant, thinking that human happiness can never peak. But, after using the dark powers afforded to him to tame the combined might of Nature and War, Faust experiences a singular moment of exaltation. Mephistopheles, with some justification, thought that the moment of reckoning had come and Faust's soul was now his. However, when he ventured to claim his prize, heavenly angels impeded him in recognition of Faust's perennial suffering.

In this section's terms, Faust had imagined that the marginal utility from knowledge and power never vanishes, whereas Mephistopheles, like any self-respecting Marginalist, was convinced that all good things are subject to vanishing marginal utility. Goethe was unaware of Marginalism, whose early glimpses would appear two decades later in German-speaking lands with von Thünen's work, but it is probably fair to argue (in line with our point in Box 5.6 of the previous chapter) that he was writing during an era ripe for an intellectual takeover by the logic of the merchant. As we shall see in the following chapters, the equi-marginal principle came to encapsulate that logic well, especially in the second part of the nineteenth-century.

---

from the fourth unit of X. At the same time, suppose that every time she pays $10 for anything she loses 5 utils.[20]

Given the above information, the answer is simple: Jill will buy 3 units of X, her overall expenditure on this good will amount to exactly $30 and her net utility from this purchase will equal 40 utils. The key to this answer lies in the equi-marginal principle (see Box 6.3 above): Jill will surely purchase the first unit of X, since she gets 30 utils from it at a cost of $10 which, in utility terms, comes to 5 utils. How about the second? The second unit of X gives her 20 utils at a cost, again, of 5 utils. A bargain too! However, the third unit of X is touch and go: for it contributes 5 utils to Jill and costs her 5 utils also. She will buy it, as it is just about worth it, but this is where she will call it a day.[21] For, a fourth unit would cost her the standard 5 utils but would only deliver a pitiful 2 utils.

The general price theory that can be derived from this simple computation, based on the *equi-marginal principle*, boils down to the following thought: *the price of a good reflects its marginal utility*. Different units of X give Jack and Jill different utilities. However, price does not care for all this diversity of per unit utilities but, rather, it gravitates to a level reflecting the utility generated by the last (or *marginal*) unit bought by either of them, that is, the *marginal utility*. In fact, it is possible to tighten this 'theorem' further by turning a mere 'reflection' into a firm equality. In Jill's case, the 'loss' of $10 was worth 5 forfeited utils; or $2 per util. Thus, Jill demanded 3 units of X because her marginal utility (expressed in dollars) was $10 and so was her marginal dis-utility. The general theory, therefore, can now move from the statement *'The price of a good reflects its marginal utility'* to the more 'scientific':

$$\text{Prices equal marginal utilities, or } p = MU$$

To avoid the accusation of premature rejoicing, the above needs to be slightly complicated. Jill, so far, chose between different quantities of a single good. What if she faced the more complex task of choosing between combinations of different quantities of many goods? After all, Ricardo and Marx got into considerable trouble when they tried their hand at extending their intuitions from the corn model to a multi-sector or multi-commodity setting. In contrast, it only took a little of Leibniz's calculus for the Marginalists to show that, in their theoretical universe, the *equi-marginal principle* applied with equal force to the multi-commodity case. The new mantra simply transforms the statement *prices equal marginal utilities* to the even more scientific:

$$\text{The ratio of prices equals the buyers' ratio of marginal utilities, or } \frac{p_x}{p_\gamma} = \frac{MU_x}{MU_\gamma} \qquad (6.1)^{22}$$

Having consigned production-based theories of value to the dustbin of social science, the Marginalists had now devised their own overarching theoretical scheme: a *price theory* built upon a *utility calculus* that was meant to match people's subjective appraisal of scarce 'things' with the rates at which they were bought and produced.[23] Just as Marx had tried to explain his world in terms of a single, overwhelming force that shapes everything around us (*capital*), so did they. Only in the place of *capital* they put the whimsical notion of *utility* and replaced *capitalism* with the more anodyne concept of *interlocking markets*.

Box 6.5 The Marginalists

Marginalism sprang out during the nineteenth-century independently in England, France (and French-speaking Switzerland) and in parts of German-speaking Central Europe.[1] Of these three groups, it was the German speakers who did a lot of the early running, strongly politicising the project in the process. Their aim, at least initially, was not just to cancel Marx's influence but, more broadly, to oppose the whole tradition of the German Historical School,[2] which was, during the nineteenth-century, maintaining a tight hold on German academia. The crushing majority of the German-speaking Marginalists were not German but residents of the Austro-Hungarian Empire. To distinguish them from the German, largely *Historist*, academics of the time, it soon became customary to refer to them as the *Austrian School*. This was a term coined by the leader of the 'younger' German Historical School, Gustav Schmoller. Later on, once the stranglehold of the Historical School on German universities had been loosened, the Austrians turned their talents to opposing the ideology and practice of socialism worldwide, particularly in the writings of Eugen von Böhm-Bawerk and Friedrich von Wieser. Unlike the French Marginalists (especially Walras who were quite left-leaning in their political sympathies), or the English Marginalists (whose focus was more on the analysis than the politics), the Austrians remained on the barricades till well after the Second World War (with Ludwig von Mises, Friedrich Hayek and their disciples playing a central role in founding centres that would help shift American and European politics to the right).

Ironically, the first 'Austrian' Marginalist, Hermann Heinrich Gossen (1810–58) was not Austrian at all but German (Prussian). Gossen started the ball rolling by being the first to write, in 1854,[3] about the theoretical importance of marginal utility as a potential determinant of price. However, it was (the authentically Austrian) Carl Menger (1840–1921) who is generally considered the grandfather of Marginalism. With his 1871 book *Grundsätze der Volkswirtschaftslehre* (translated into English as *Principle of Economics*) he struck the first serious blow for the Marginalist mantra. Following that influential tome, Menger made two further contributions with which he staked important claims to a Marginalist theory of capital (1888) and money (1892).[4]

The Englishman W. Stanley Jevons (1835–82) was, quite independently, telling a similar story in a book published in the same year.[5] Coming from a wholly different background from Menger, he followed closely Benthamite Utilitarianism (strangely absent from Menger or Gossen) and sought a mathematical theory of economics.

Meanwhile, at approximately the same time, in 1877, the Frenchman Léon Walras (1834–1910) working in Lausanne was publishing (1874 and 1877) mathematical models that attempted to map out the *simultaneous* determination of *all* prices. With a utopian socialist mindset (which included the conviction that all land ought to be nationalised to rid society of the scourge of the landowner and finance state expenses from rents), he was also responsible for discovering the work of a much older compatriot of his, Antoine Augustin Cournot (1801–77), who was technically light years ahead of the rest (especially *vis-à-vis* the determination of prices when firms act strategically) but who insisted that Marginalism should not endeavour to grasp all prices at once for fear of a theory of capitalism that would legitimise awful abuses, including the destruction of the environment – see this chapter's Epilogue for more on this remarkable foresight!

Turning back to the Austrians, it was Eugen von Böhm Bawerk (1851–1914), who along with his friend Friedrich von Wieser (1851–1926), expounded in 1889 an interesting Marginalist account of capital.[6] Seven years later, in 1896, Böhm-Bawerk published his analytical challenge to Marx. Having spotted Marx's capitulation to the *Inherent Error*, he exposed the transformation problem (see Box 5.12) in a volume entitled *Karl Marx and the Close of his System* (1896).[7] It was a publication that played a key role in the discrediting of value theory that preceded the Marginalists' success in persuading economists worldwide to retreat from value.

Meanwhile, in England, Francis Ysidro Edgeworth (1845–1926), having taught himself mathematics and physics, expounded the Marginalist calculus of utility first in an article entitled 'Hedonical Calculus' published in the philosophical journal *Mind* in 1879 and then in a notoriously badly written but, at the same time, hugely influential book entitled *Mathematical Psychics: An Essay on the Application of Mathematics to the Moral Sciences* (1881). It was in those works that Edgeworth conscripted the notion of *indifference* in order to frame geometrically (but also logically) the conceptual underpinnings of Marginalist price theory that, to this day, undergraduate students of economics have to learn. Imagining that there are combinations of commodities over which we are indifferent, he showed that the slope of the line that they form (the so-called *indifference loci* or *indifference curves*) is the geometrical equivalent of the ratio of marginal utilities in equation (6.1) above.[8] And since price equals that ratio, the secret of prices lies in these indifference shapes. Thus persons, individuals, decision makers, etc. are depicted as bundles of preferences that are bisected by areas of indifference whose shape determines the prices of everything: from corn and tractors to labour and video games. The present chapter's title reflects this vision: *a world populated by autonomous regions of indifference whose geometry determines the price of everything.*

A little later, in 1890, Alfred Marshall (1842–1924) published perhaps the first textbook on economics with a distinctly Marginalist bent. Unlike Edgeworth's book, his *Principles of Economics*[9] was a pleasant read and did a great deal to popularise the Marginalist way of economic thinking.[10] Indeed, it was the first book to feature the now ubiquitous demand and supply diagram. Four years later, Phillip Wicksteed (1844–1927), an accomplished theologian and Dante scholar, published two books that were to cement further the case for Marginalism: *An Essay on the Coordination of the Laws of Distribution* (1894) and *The Common Sense of Political Economy* (1910).[11]

In 1906, Vilfredo Pareto (1848–1923), an Italian whose economics was to influence Italian Fascist dictator Benito Mussolini, published a book that changed utility forever. The book was entitled *Manual of Political Economy*[12] and in it Pareto proposed a new interpretation of utility that completely de-politicised and de-psychologised the concept. The idea was that utility no longer had to be thought of as a measurable variable, like electricity or pressure. From then on economists conceive utility functions, mainly, as a *list* reporting on how Jack and Jill rank their possible 'experiences'; e.g. *Jack: theatre-cinema-bar* and *Jill: bar-theatre-cinema* means that while Jack prefers to go to the theatre and his last preference is to go to a bar, Jill places the cinema last and the bar first. Meanwhile, Jack's and Jill's utilities can no longer be compared, since no metric or measure is involved. In this manner, Pareto allowed Marginalists to ditch all psychology and ethics since the end of measurable utility also meant the end of all private psychology and, of course, the demise of the concept of Jack's and Jill's average utility as an indicator of their collective interest. While this de-socialisation strengthened Marginalism's claims to political, psychological and ethical neutrality (and, therefore, raised its 'scientific' status), it rendered impossible (as Kenneth Arrow was to prove beyond doubt in 1951)[13] any further pretence that Marginalism may have had to telling a story about social utility; that is, about what lies in the public interest.

Marginalism was not immune to major splits. Walras, Marshall, Edgeworth and Pareto were, unintentionally, to create a more stringent, austere and ultimately successful variant of Marginalism: *neoclassicism*. We tell the story behind this new sect in Section 6.10 below (see also Box 6.16). For our purposes here it suffices to conclude that, by the 1910s and 1920s, political economics was dominated by three opposing camps.

A. The Marginalists who turned neoclassical and who, very soon, were to dominate all academic economics.

B. The Marginalists who did not espouse neoclassicism, mainly Austrian economists like Ludwig von Mises (1881–1973) and Friedrich von Hayek (1899–1922), and who turned out to be the most sophisticated defenders of unfettered capitalism well into the twentieth century.

C. An assortment of leftists (mostly Marxists), and so-called institutionalists, e.g. Thorstein Veblen (1857–1929), who believed neither in the merits of unbridled capitalism nor in the promise of socialism. During the last few years of the nineteenth-century and in the early twentieth century, there emerged a rich literature on business cycles and on the way in which the rise of large corporations, including financial institutions, amplified them. It involved Marxists, like Lenin (1870–1924), Rosa Luxembourg (1871–1919) and Rudolf Hilferding (1877–1941), non-Marxists, such as Gustav Cassel (1846–1945) and Albert Aftalion (1874–1956), as well as scholars like Joseph Schumpeter (1883–1950). Their economic analysis focused usefully on the transformation of capitalism that followed the second industrial revolution and its greater tendency towards volatility and crises. However, the writing was on the wall for economics: marginalism had already spawned neoclassicism; a form of economics whose dominance was purchased at the expense of any serious engagement with the institutions and historical contingencies of really existing capitalism.

Then, 1929 happened! And the economics establishment (comprising mostly the Marginalist-*cum*-neoclassical school) was taken aback by the occurrence of, what they thought was, a zero probability event: The Great Depression. Soon after, the figure of John Maynard Keynes (1883–1946) cast a long shadow over all schools, but in particular over A and B above who were unprepared for capitalism's major crash. While schooled totally in the Marginalist-*cum*-neoclassical tradition, Keynes broke from it violently, treating its model of capitalism with contempt. It was left to camp B above to keep nineteenth-century Marginalism's homefire burning from 1929 to the end of Bretton Woods in 1971. During that period (1929–71) a different, four-way, opposition was emerging in the West: the one between the New Dealers, the *Scientists* and the *Formalists* (see Chapter 8). After 1971, however, neoclassical economics made a comeback. But that's another sad story to which we return in Chapter 12.

Notes

1 This box gives necessarily a simplified view of the 'Marginal Revolution'. There are many interpretations of what really happened in the 1870s and who the real Marginalists are. We have, for example, a theory of diminishing marginal utility even before Adam Smith by Daniel Bernoulli (1738). William Forster Lloyd and Nassau W. Senior in the UK can be considered proto-Marginalists but especially anti-classical. In France the engineer Jules Dupuit wrote in 1844 'On the Measurement of the Utility of Public Works,' and applied marginal calculus. For a collection of articles see Black, Coats and Goodwin, 1973 and Howey, 1960.

2 The tradition which held that there were no formally deducible 'laws' of the social economy the discovery of which could be delegated to deductive reasoning (e.g. proof of theorems). Carl Menger entered the *Methodenstreit* (debate over method) with the leader of the 'younger' Historical School, Gustav von Schmoller. When the latter wrote in 1883 in his *Jahrbuch*

a scathing critique of Menger's *Untersuchungen über die Methode der Sozialwissenschaften, und der politischen Oekonomie insbesondere* (Investigations into the method in social sciences and political economy in particular) (1883), Menger replied with his *Die Irrthümer des Historismus in der deutschen Nationalökonomie* (1884). (The errors of Historism in German political economy).

3 Hermann Heinrich Gossen (1854 [1983]): see the excellent introductory essay by Nicholas Georgescu-Roegen in the English edition.

4 Menger (1888, 1892).

5 *The Theory of Political Economy*, 1871. He may have a precedence claim since he read a brief sketch of his theory in Section F of the British Association in 1862. Published as Jevons (1862 [1866]). Jevons was possibly the first Marginalist to have realised that once value is reduced to price, and price is explained only in terms of marginal utility, there is no longer any room left in one's economics for a theory of production as something separate from a mirror image of a theory of utility creation. Alfred Marshall (see below) later rejected that view and put considerable effort into embedding a theory of production into Marginalism. The extent to which the latter escaped Jevons' insight (regarding the impossibility of a substantive theory of supply) remains arguable. Philip Wicksteed, the most Jevonsian of British economists, were to write later that only demand curves exists: 'But what about the 'supply curve' that usually figures as a determinant of price, co-ordinate with the demand curve? I say it boldly and baldly: There is no such thing. When we are speaking of a marketable commodity, what is usually called the supply curve is in reality the demand curve of those who possess the commodity; for it shows the exact place which every successive unit of the commodity holds in their relative scale of estimates. The so-called supply curve, therefore, is simply a part of the total demand curve.' Wicksteed (1914 [1933]), p. 785.

6 Friedrich von Wieser's (1889 [1893]). Eugen von Böhm-Bawerk (1889 [1891]).

7 Böhm-Bawerk (1896 [1898]). See also Sweezy, 1949.

8 Strangely enough even though Edgeworth invented the notion of the indifference curve we had to wait for Vilfredo Pareto to derive its geometrical intuition and thus populate our textbooks with the all too familiar concept of indifference curves. Pareto, however, did not believe in the concept of a cardinal utility.

9 Even though the term 'economics' was not suggested by Marshall – it has been used even by Petty ("Oconomicks" 1662 [1899], p. 60) and Hutcheson ("Oeconomicks", 1753, iii.1, p. 243) – the *Principles* was the textbook that popularised the new name of our science. Marshall has used the term in *The Economics of Industry* (1879) co-authored by his wife Mary Paley. The term was there to stay. Jevons in the preface to the second edition of his Theory of Political Economy (1879) writes 'Among minor alterations, I may mention the substitution for the name Political Economy of the single convenient term Economics. I cannot help thinking that it would be well to discard, as quickly as possible, the old troublesome double-worded name of our Science. Several authors have tried to introduce totally new names, such as Plutology, Chrematistics, Catallactics, etc. But why do we need anything better than Economics? This term, besides being more familiar and closely related to the old term, is perfectly analogous in form to *Mathematics, Ethics, Æsthetics*, and the names of various other branches of knowledge, and it has moreover the authority of usage from the time of Aristotle. Mr. Macleod is, so far as I know, the re-introducer of the name in recent years, but it appears to have been adopted also by Mr. Alfred Marshall at Cambridge. It is thus to be hoped that Economics will become the recognised name of a science, which nearly a century ago was known to the French Economists as *la science économique*. Though employing the new name in the text, it was obviously undesirable to alter the title-page of the book' (Jevons, 1879, p. xiv).

10 Marshall could be all things to all people. The book was unencumbered by mathematics in a prose attractive to the educated layman offering relevance instead of obfuscation. Diagrams and technical material were pushed to footnotes, notes and appendices satisfying the technically trained. Instead of offering an arcane mathematical model of General Equilibrium, Marshall opted for partial equilibrium in a language full of 'if's and 'but's brimming with

useful examples from everyday life. Marshall was also responsible for the professionalisation of economics creating the first ever academic degree in economics (the economic tripos in Cambridge). See Groenewegen, 1995.

11 A profound difference between the Austrian and English varieties of Marginalism, especially after the Great War, is purely political. As Maurice Dobb explained in his *Theories of Value and Distribution since Adam Smith* (1973) the Austrians were motivated by fervent opposition to Marxism and the rise of the European social democratic parties, the German one in particular. In contrast, the English Marginalists were not particularly motivated by antagonism to the fledgling Labour Party.

12 Pareto (1906 [1909] [1927] [1972]).

13 Arrow (1951 [1963]).

6.6 A most contemporary dogmatism: The birth of today's economic mantra

It was not long before the Marginalists' *equi-marginal principle* spawned an economic epic. At first there was the verse: 'marginal utility, you determine price with no timidity'. Or something like this... then the plot thickened. If competition is rampant, prices must also reflect the seller's marginal dis-utility. Think about it: if the last widget made brought the producer greater utility (in the form of revenue) than the dis-utility from producing it, wouldn't the producer make yet another widget? They surely would, as the net utility from it would also be positive (albeit lower than before). But when would they stop making more and more? The answer is, courtesy of the *equi-marginal principle*, that they will cease when the last widget finally gives them as much utility (from the collected revenue) as the dis-utility it causes them (from the drudgery involved in making it). So, if competition between producers keeps prices constant for each producer, and price at once reflects the buyer's utility *and* the seller's dis-utility, the marketplace is a structure of finely balanced marginal utilities and dis-utilities, resembling the counter-opposed forces that keep the great European cathedrals upright.

The epic's first stanza was thus completed. One can almost visualise the pristine architecture of a market resembling a complex building, a Notre Dame or a Sydney Opera House, with its beams and arches and multiple layers all supporting each other to create a harmonious, solid structure of beauty and poise, their marginal utilities and dis-utilities united in resplendent mutual support. Crucially, identities do not much matter in this architecture. The laws of their special type of structural relationship are the same in all parts of that edifice, regardless of whether agents purvey oil, snake oil, coins or, indeed, the promise to do someone's laundry. It matters not whether they are men or women, black or white, landowners or farmhands, waged workers or shareholders. Each appears as a different pillar and every such pillar, larger or smaller, plays its role in keeping the whole together. The new mantra could, indeed, be a hymn to radical egalitarianism.[24]

When we start humming it (as anyone who wants to be schooled in economics must), we experience a soothing withdrawal from the disconcerting dialectics of Hegel and Marx, a move back from Schopenhauer's bleakness, a repudiation of Kierkegaard's worrisome portrayal of freedom-as-anxiety. Its melody engenders a return to a reassuring dualism where persons are nothing but buyers or sellers, often both at once. It exudes a sense of having 'arrived' at the best of all possible worlds. As epics come, the flagrant dualism on which it turns is more *The Sound of Music* than *Iliad*, more *Barber of Seville* than *Tosca*.[25] However, its mathematical simplicity makes it beautiful and, importantly, its universal reach lends itself to a general theory of almost everything. It is only when one realises its implications about more pedestrian matters that its totalitarian effects are felt. Box 6.6 summarises the main ones.

We have already seen how the first two dogmas flow naturally out of the *equi-marginal principle*. Competitive prices equilibrate the buyer's satisfaction engendered by the last unit bought with the discomfiture involved in producing it. Though no value theory is permitted here (recall the Marginalists' moratorium on value), the implicit ethics are crystal clear: without passing value judgements, and in the absence of any direct comparison of Jack's utility with that of Jill, when Jack buys the last widget Jill makes at, say, $10, his dis-utility from handing the $10 over equals his utility from that widget and, simultaneously, Jill's dis-utility from labouring to produce that (marginal) widget precisely equals the utility she experiences upon pocketing Jack's $10. Can one imagine of a fairer deal?

Suppose now that some do-gooder, unconvinced of the ethicality of the transaction, and worried that Jill's income is too low to live decently, intervenes in favour of Jill by, for instance, passing some law that specifies a minimum price of $15. Since no one can force Jack to buy as many widgets as he did before, his expenditure on Jill's widgets will fall. While Jill will want to sell quite a few more widgets at the new minimum price, her sales will plummet and both Jack and Jill will be worse off. The outside intervention, having interfered with the 'natural' order, has reaped a bitter harvest completely at odds with the do-gooder's best intentions. It is, at this point, useful to note that this third dogma (see Box 6.5 above) applies independently of what the mysterious word 'widget' signifies. It could signify a vegetable, a mineral, an electronic device or, indeed, it could denote Jill's labour.

In Marginalism's dualist account, where only buyers and sellers are featured, labour is no different from any other 'thing' that one buys or sells. All material notions, such as physical *surplus*, *capital goods* (e.g. machines), etc., have been pushed aside and the single force left running through the theory, explaining all prices and quantities, is *utility* (that is, *subjective appraisal*). But then labour can no longer feature as in any way different from other physical items, processes, etc. *Everything* is reducible to utility and, as such, nothing can or ought to be excluded from the force of the *equi-marginal principle*. So, if competitive prices are fair, wage labourers cannot be wronged so long as the labour market is populated by many competing employers.

Box 6.6 Seven Marginalist dogmas

Competitive markets ensure that

1. buyers pay a price reflecting their utility from the last unit purchased;
2. the price is fair in that the seller is rewarded in proportion to her dis-utility experienced during the production or supply of the last unit sold;
3. any attempt to alter prices by extra-market intervention will make someone worse off and will, ultimately, frustrate any good intention that motivated it;
4. prices are pieces of information and information wants to be free;
5. the general price level will depend on the quantity of money;
6. unemployment can only be voluntary; and
7. appropriate investment is inevitable.

Anyone who crosses this 'natural' order is playing with fire. A trade union striking for higher wages; a meddling government imposing minimum wages; even a strong social convention that places a moral burden on employers to keep wages above the marginal disutility of the labourers' marginal hour; they are all examples of folly that do both employers and workers a major disservice. Only God can suspend Natural Law. It is called Providence. Humans, in contrast, can only try mimicking God and pretend to providential powers that they patently lack. Natural Law philosophers and environmentalists alike would concur. Who wouldn't? The question, of course, is whether capitalism is no more than a set of markets and whether markets are the social equivalent of some 'natural order'.

But this is not a question that Marginalist political economics ever asks. Nor did Adam Smith, for that matter. Yet, there is a difference. Whereas Smith advocated free markets at a time of autocratic rule, guild-controlled prices and embryonic capital markets, and expressed his advocacy rhetorically and by means of deep philosophical arguments, Marginalists tried to show that their statements about free markets could be *proven* as if by symbolic logic; without any empirical evidence, in the absence of historical evidence, axiomatically. They agreed with Smith that the market was the nearest society has ever come to producing a 'natural' order. But whereas Smith saw the market system in Newtonian terms, as a dynamic solar-like system governed by objective gravitational forces, the Marginalists' tended to another physical parable: that of a finely balanced, static architecture; an electromagnetic field in stasis at best. At least Smith's world contained movement, gravity, even the possibility of a recalcitrant asteroid that may cause Earth a great deal of damage. The Marginalists' static viewpoint, heavily in tune with Leibniz's version of calculus (see Section 6.11 below), proved conducive to the most unbending of dogmatisms.

Take for example the fourth dogma in Box 6.6: Unbridled competition *guarantees* prices that reflect the gains of buyers and the costs of sellers at the margin of their transactions. Market prices are suddenly not just a source of useful information but the *only* source. Nothing can double-guess markets and anyone who thinks that it is possible to regulate them, in order to avert trouble, is committing a mortal sin against Logic and Nature.

This obsession with prices is understandable. Value, utility, even capital are profoundly unobservable. But prices are numbers that even a small child can see and make sense of. Computer screens can beam a myriad prices into every home and every smart phone. When the price of a little-known rare earth metals shoots up, people take note, even if they have no idea what that metal is used for. Those who possess it economise its use and those who do not, try to establish whether known deposits of it may be concealed on their patch. It is as if the whole world is energised to conserve and produce more of that substance.

In a celebrated paper, Friedrich von Hayek (1945) persuasively restated the *Austrians'* main point (recall Box 6.5) that the 'economic problem' is not, as many textbooks say, to allocate resources cleverly between competing uses but, that it is

> rather a problem of how to secure the best use of resources known to any of the members of society, for ends whose relative importance only these individuals know. Or, to put it briefly, it is a problem of the utilisation of knowledge which is not given to anyone in its totality.[26]

When knowledge is dispersed (e.g. when no one knows for sure how much Jack cares for a widget or precisely Jill's dis-utility from labouring to produce a widget), prices are the best source of insight into the missing information. When the price for widgets goes up relative to that of other goods, it is *as if* producers all over the world are given the signal to make more widgets while consumers are told to economise.

In this line of thought, as long as price movements are unimpeded, they help people coordinate their actions as best as possible. But when some do-gooder, or tyrant who fancies himself a superior organiser of economic activity, interferes with prices (e.g. by imposing caps), the result is the same as demagnetising ocean faring ships' compasses during a mighty storm. 'Free' prices are compasses that demand non-interference from human hands if they are to deliver to humanity their best possible service. They are packed with information and information wants to be free. Anyone denying it that freedom does untold damage to everyone.

The reason inflation is seen as such a fiend by mainstream economists is that it muffles price signals. When all prices start surging at once, their paths begin to feed off each other, spiralling quickly and erratically upwards. As the tide picks up speed, inflationary swirls affect some sectors more than others and some boats, caught up in the swirl, rise sometimes faster than others and, later, more slowly. In the tumult, the subtle information that is normally emitted by the natural ebb and flow of relative price changes is lost. Inflation makes it very difficult to know whether an increase in the price of widgets really means that society has found new uses for them and whether, therefore, widget producers should respond by producing more or fewer of widgets.

And what causes inflation? Too much money, is the mainstream answer. In economies with gold coins, miners could affect prices by striking a new vein of gold. For if more coins chase after the same (more or less) number of goods, more coins correspond to each unit of every good. Prices, therefore, rise. When the Spanish Conquistadores returned home from South America with vast quantities of looted gold, Spanish inflation shot up.[27] Since the emergence of paper money, the *quantity of money* is determined by some state-controlled central bank. Yet again, the state is to blame: in our monetised societies, the story continues, inflation is caused by imprudent governments that mint too much money in order to service their destructive interventions.

Seen through this prism, the US government's momentous intervention in 2008 and beyond sends cold shivers up the Marginalist's spine. Indeed, to save the financial sector from complete implosion, the US government infused an ocean of printed money into the American economy. Those of a Marginalist disposition can be excused for predicting that the sky must, sooner or later, fall on our heads with an inflationary thud that the world has not seen even in its darkest nightmares. One can even understand how this way of thinking led some Marginalists, like von Hayek, to the conclusion that, since the state should be prevented from such experiments that can easily blow up the market system, it is a mistake to allow the government to print money, let alone to have a monopoly over money issues. Let anyone print their own money, suggested von Hayek,[28] and allow the market to select which currency we shall use, just like it coordinates everything else by assigning the 'right' price signals to all useful things.

Before we dismiss this idea as ridiculous (can you imagine an economy where Jack and Jill each prints his or her own money?), let us remind ourselves of how the US government, under both Republican Bush and Democrat Obama, was *forced* in 2008 and beyond to adopt a fiscal stimulus that can only be compared to the *Great Flood*: for a decade or more, prior to 2008, financial institutions were busily creating the fabled toxic derivatives. We shall say a lot more about those in the following chapters. For now, it suffices to make the simple point that these derivatives (which the markets referred to with a variety of bewildering acronyms: CDS, ABS, CDO, etc.) were pieces of paper of debatable (and incalculable) value that private banks bought in droves. While the bonanza lasted, banks then used their stock of derivatives as if it were a stock of money. So, those who issued the derivatives were, in effect, issuing a form of private money.

Indeed, much of the liquidity that fuelled the *Bubble* which burst in 2008 was caused by this type of Hayekian money. Tragically, it turned out that the market mechanism did the opposite of what von Hayek had hoped: instead of assigning the 'right' prices and coordinating activity 'efficiently', it fuelled a frenzy of unproductive financial activity that fed into, and off, a serious inflation of house and derivative prices. When it all blew up, the government had no alternative but to pick up the pieces. The question then on everyone's lips was: how did such a fundamental development (the creation of private money under everyone's noses) occur without any regulator stepping in? The answer is, we submit, to be found in the mantra in the current section and, in particular, on its success at becoming, sometime in the mid-1970s, the official ideology of both the state and the markets: unregulated markets can do no wrong!

Good epic poetry flows effortlessly. One story feeds into the next and they all blend seamlessly into a cosmogony that the audience quickly gets addicted to; similarly here. Beginning with the simple story about the nature of prices, and the universal scope of the *equi-marginal principle*, the Marginalist epos picks up speed. It casts an eye upon the twin scourges of contemporary capitalism, inflation and unemployment, and deconstructs them with clean swerves of its steely theoretical sword. Inflation would vanish if only governments were prudent, so that the quantity of money they allow to flow into the markets and unemployment is dismissed as a mirage. If people are jobless, it must be either because they just do not wish to work (for the currently available wage), or because someone (more likely than not an officious government) interfered when they should have known better.

Can they be serious? Unemployment a mirage that no government should (or could) do anything about, except make it worse? Were the *Grapes of Wrath* a piece of groundless fiction? Evidently! The Marginalist logic behind this outrageous aphorism can be quite compelling (like that of all fundamentalisms): a scarce commodity (i.e. one whose supply is finite) must bear a positive price (reflecting the marginal utility of those potential consumers). Only if it is *not* scarce will everyone's marginal utility from it (and, therefore, its price) be zero. *Ergo*, if its price is *not* zero, it must be scarce and, hence, in a competitive market there can be no unsold units of that commodity. Seen as another commodity for sale, there exists some price for labour (i.e. wage) at which all units for sale will find a willing buyer (i.e. employer). So, if chunks of labour remain unsold on the shelves of job centres and outside the factory gates, the Marginalist knows why: wages are stuck at unsustainable levels because of non-economic, outside, intervention due to trade unions, state interference and, possibly, bothersome social norms that make unemployed workers reluctant to undercut the wages of those already in employment.

Thinking in this manner leads to an inescapable conclusion. If the wage is non-zero, and free to rise or fall depending on demand and supply, all those who want to work for that wage will, in equilibrium, find a job. At the same time, in the boardroom, companies will decide to borrow and invest more, thus raising employment, when the price of money, that is, the interest rate, comes down. If the government tries to increase the number of those in employment further by borrowing and spending, all it will achieve is more inflation and higher interest rates. As all prices rise at once, no firm will interpret the rise in the price of its own good as a signal to produce more. So, it will not increase output. Instead of stimulating the economy, the government will have muffled price signals, spoiling the market's capacity to coordinate itself. Moreover, the parallel rise of interest rates (as the government borrows more from the private sector) will depress private investment into the things we need, producing less employment and a general paralysis of the market system.

In this vein, if we *truly* want to ensure that anyone who wants work will find it, all society need do is to afford the market the 'freedom' to lower wages and interest rates to a level consistent with the *equi-marginal principle*. When that happens, labour's price will reflect both its marginal utility to the firm and its marginal dis-utility to the worker. Money, at the same time, will be borrowed at a price consistent with the utility from spending your last dollar today relative to the utility from the thought of having an extra dollar tomorrow. Any wage or interest rate higher than that offends the *natural order* of things. Government fiscal stimuli, trade unions, minimum wages and unemployment benefits appear to the Marginalist believer not only as impediments to wellbeing but, perhaps more importantly, blasphemous (in a cosmic, if not theological, sense)!

6.7 A captive market: Marginalism-in-action

Marginalism reduces to a calculus of pure exchanges. But capitalism is a lot more than a set of pure exchanges of one thing for another, as we argued in Chapters 4 and 5. Thus, the one realm where Marginalism seems perfectly at home is the world of collectors. Exchanges are part of the collector's mindset and a means by which collections are enriched, not to mention an activity that carries its own utility. Additionally, and by definition, collectibles are out of production and this renders them a perfect case study for a price theory that pays no attention to the *actual* production process (recall Section 6.5), save for the dis-utility involved in supplying some factor of production. Collectibles, therefore, offer Marginalism an opportunity to exhibit its wares at their best.

The best way of illuminating Marginalism's limits is to look carefully at the one case we know in which Marginalist theory works seamlessly,[29] and which comes as close to a real economy without invalidating Marginalism's insights. It was recorded by R.A. Radford, a British army officer unfortunate enough to have been captured by the Germans early in the Second World War, thus spending a long period of incarceration in a prisoner of war (POW) camp somewhere in southern Germany. A formally trained economist, Radford was delighted to see *Marginalism-in-action* everywhere he turned his eyes within his camp's barbed wire. So impressed was he with his discipline's account of life in the POW camp that, at war's end, he published a delightful article narrating the spontaneous birth and development of a complex POW exchange economy, complete with goods markets, money markets, credit markets and even futures' markets.[30]

Box 6.7 Natural unemployment

In the 1970s, free-marketers returned to prominence after the shock of 1929 had consigned them to the margins. The old Marginalist dogma on unemployment (see the sixth dogma in Box 6.6) was given a makeover. Any level of unemployment prevailing while price inflation remains constant was labelled *natural unemployment*. Even if 30 per cent of the population are without work, as long as inflation is not increasing, most economists would refer to that unemployment rate as *natural*. As with all things 'natural', the gods are angered when humans try to interfere with them. The ancient Greeks called it *hubris*. And so mainstream economists tend to think that if our 'natural' rate of unemployment is too high, the only remedy is lower wages or greater labour effort for the existing wage levels.

Radford begins his story with what happened after the initial shock of being captured by the enemy subsided and once the first Red Cross parcels started arriving at the camp. Economic activity, he tells us, began in earnest. Initially, each section (British, French, Soviet, Canadian, etc.) bartered items among themselves, for example, coffee for chocolate. Soon after, money emerged, in the familiar form of cigarettes, so that exchanges could be made even in the absence of the rather rare double coincidence of wants. Almost at the same time, some entrepreneurial men recognised the scope for improving their material circumstances (i.e. profiting, in the economists' language) through *arbitrage*. The first obvious opportunity for arbitrage arose as a result of the perennial cultural difference between the French and the British: the price of tea (expressed in cigarettes) was, quite naturally, higher in the British than in the French section, where coffee was more highly prized (reflecting different relative marginal utilities). But once *arbitrage* began, and the British prisoners started 'exporting' coffee to the French section in return for tea, both prices (of tea and coffee) eventually equalised between the two sections.

With quite a few prisoners acting as middlemen and with the development of *Exchange and Mart* notice boards (on which buyers and sellers would post their offers and orders; e.g. 'I am selling 2 bags of tea for 5 cigarettes. Talk to Jim, English section, 5th row, top bunk'), prices converged and no significant profit could be made from spot trading: competition had pushed prices to the lowest possible level and swaps served the purpose of a more efficient allocation of given goods. It is not at all far-fetched to suggest that these equilibrium prices reflected the relative valuations of the marginal units (or, equivalently, the ratio of marginal utilities). Thus, life in the POW camp confirmed the first two dogmas in Box 6.6. In fact, as Radford's article demonstrates, many of these dogmas proved approximately correct in the POW camp setting.

Market enthusiasts despair at the moralistic criticism of middlemen and of the idea of profiting from mere buying and selling. While most people find it hard to accept the notion of thousands of young people making oodles of money by sitting in front of a computer screen all day buying and selling unseen commodities in a virtual global market, free marketers take a different stance. Their moral defence of arbitrage is simple: arbitrage eliminates price fluctuations and engenders a kind of radical egalitarianism, as everyone ends up paying similar prices for similar goods. The removal of price and output variability allows for better planning, more investment and a stable environment that is conducive to growth. They also add, for good measure, that unfettered trade leads Jill to the greatest utility possible, given Jack's utility level. By focusing on the utilities *at the time of the exchange*, Marginalist thinking eliminates the possibility of subjecting the politics and ethics of arbitrage to serious rational scrutiny. It is for this reason that banks' trading practices prior to 2008, and even afterwards, were typically defended, deploying Marginalist language, as 'a nasty job that someone must do' on behalf of all of us.

In Radford's POW camp, while the arbitrageurs (especially the non-smokers) were also intensely disliked by many, it was unarguable, at least at one level, that most prisoners benefitted from the spontaneously created exchange economy that the traders kept going. For their aggressive arbitrage ensured that the person who craved tea the most would have to give up the fewest (and least valuable) of his other items to get it. In this sense, only a dogmatic market-hater would object. Nonetheless, as Radford makes clear, the moral concerns were not absent. Setting aside the larger ethical and political questions involved,[31] the prisoners' commanding officers were often worried by 'market failures'. For instance, there were the many cases of malnourished heavy smokers;[32] or situations that threatened the men's morale when the spontaneously generated credit and futures' market collapsed. Crises, it seems, were a common occurrence even in this type of exchange economy were no one could be unemployed, supplies

Box 6.8 The futures' trader: A morality tale

One trader in food and cigarettes, operating in a period of dearth, enjoyed a high reputation. His capital, carefully saved, was originally about 50 cigarettes, with which he bought rations on issue days and held them until the price rose just before the next issue. He also picked up a little by arbitrage; several times a day he visited every *Exchange and Mart* notice board and took advantage of every discrepancy between prices of goods offered and wanted. His knowledge of prices, markets and names of those who had received cigarette parcels was phenomenal. By these means he kept himself smoking steadily – his profits – while his capital remained intact. Sugar was issued on Saturday. About Tuesday two of us used to visit Sam and make a deal; as old customers he would advance as much of the price as he could spare us, and entered the transaction in a book. On Saturday morning he left cocoa tins on our beds for the ration, and picked them up on Saturday afternoon. We were hoping for a calendar at Christmas, but Sam failed too. He was left holding a big black treacle issue when the price fell, and in this weakened state was unable to withstand an unexpected arrival of parcels and the consequent price fluctuations. He paid in full, but from his capital. The next Tuesday, when I paid my usual visit he was out of business.

Credit entered into many, perhaps into most, transactions, in one form or another. Sam paid in advance as a rule for his purchases of future deliveries of sugar, but many buyers asked for credit, whether the commodity was sold spot or future. Naturally prices varied according to the terms of sale. A treacle ration might be advertised for four cigarettes now or five next week. And in the future market 'bread now' was a vastly different thing from 'bread Thursday.' Bread was issued on Thursday and Monday, four and three days' rations respectively, and by Wednesday and Sunday night it had risen at least one cigarette per ration, from seven to eight, by supper time. One man always saved a ration to sell then at the peak price: his offer of 'bread now' stood out on the board among a number of 'bread Monday's' fetching one or two less, or not selling at all – and he always smoked on Sunday night.

Radford (1945)

were unaffected by forecasts and demand was given. In response, the senior officers repeatedly intervened in order both to ameliorate the market's failures and to prevent future ones.

The *quantity theory of money*, Dogma 4 in Box 6.6, was also confirmed, as the general price level fluctuated with the quantity of cigarettes that came into the camp. However, the fluctuations were neither proportional nor predictable. News from the front had uneven effects and caused large waves of optimism to alternate with mass pessimism. Prices oscillated erratically and, at times, the market mechanism broke down, which meant that many prisoners ended up with stocks of items they did not want while lacking that which they needed. To limit these occurrences, the senior officers came up with an interesting plan: they attempted to introduce a new currency which would be less volatile than cigarettes and which would also help prevent the malnourishment of the heavy smokers.

Around D-day, food and cigarettes were plentiful, business was brisk and the camp in an optimistic mood. Consequently the Entertainments Committee felt the moment opportune to launch a restaurant, where food and hot drinks were sold while a band and variety turns performed…. Goods were sold at market prices to provide the meals and the small profits were devoted to a reserve fund and used to bribe Germans to provide grease-paints and other necessities for the camp theatre… To increase and facilitate trade, and stimulate supplies and customers therefore, and secondarily to avoid the worst effects of deflation when it should come, a paper currency was organised by the Restaurant and the Shop. The Shop bought food on behalf of the Restaurant with paper notes and the paper accepted equally with the cigarettes in the Restaurant or Shop, and passed back to the Shop for the purchase of more food. The Shop acted as a bank of issue. The paper money was backed 100 per cent; and hence its name, Bully Mark. The Bully Mk was backed 100 per cent by food; there could be no over-issues, as is permissible with a normal bank of issues, since the eventual dispersal of the camp and consequent redemption of all BMks was anticipated in the near future.

Radford, R.A (1945)

At first, the camp's 'central bank', that is, the Shop–Restaurant authorities (akin to the Federal Reserve–Treasury nexus in the USA or the equivalent Brussels–Frankfurt duet of the European Union) set the exchange rate: *one BMk was to be worth one cigarette.* At first, the new currency system worked well. The currency was pegged (or tied) to food, not ciga-rettes. As long as the Red Cross food parcels kept coming, the Restaurant was well supplied by prisoners, in exchange for Shop items, and prices were stable. But during a 'recession' caused by a reduction in incoming food parcels, confidence in the BMk was shaken and the currency began its steady devaluation to oblivion. In the end, it could only be used to buy dried fruit from the almost deserted Restaurant. The monetary dynasty of the cigarette had re-established itself once again.

The new but ill-fated currency was a 'political' instrument that the senior officers devised to intervene without however charging headlong against the torrent of market forces. But the 'authorities', especially the Medical Officer, did not think it was enough to stop prisoners from over-trading. It was their considered opinion that monetary intervention should be sup-plemented with standard regulatory measures for limiting the market's vagaries. The author-ities, thus, came up with price bands above or below which no trade was allowed. Technically, this meant that the *Exchange and Mart* notice boards came under the aegis of the Shop whose staff saw to it that advertised prices diverging from the 'recommended prices' by more than 5 per cent were removed forthwith.

While the Shop–Restaurant institution was at the height of its power, the regulatory regime worked well, using its oligopoly power to keep prices stable. But when the crisis which destroyed the Restaurant and devalued the *BMk* hit, prices 'wanted' to move much more quickly than the officers were willing or able to allow. An increasing number of notices were being removed from the official notice boards and, predictably, a black, unregulated, market emerged. The imported 'recession', therefore, led not only to the collapse of the currency system but also to the demise of price controls.

By the summer of 1945, the parcels stopped coming and the market crashed. Radford concludes his eloquent account in an almost utopian fashion:

On 12th April [1945], with the arrival of elements of the 30th US Infantry Division, the ushering in of an age of plenty demonstrated the hypothesis that with infinite means economic organisation and activity would be redundant, as every want could be satis-fied without effort.

Marx would not have put it differently.[33]

6.8 Beyond Manna from Heaven: Marginalism on wages and profit rates

In R.A. Radford's POW camp, the items bought and sold were 'exogenously' provided; a kind of *Manna from Heaven* (or from the Red Cross, more accurately).[34] The exchanges between prisoners were, to a large extent, an inessential pastime. Even so, as Radford reported, energetic trading caused enough consternation and grief to create a widespread demand for some central intervention to avert crises, restrict over-trading and deal with the ethical dilemmas caused by the new market ethos in the camp.

Once we move from the communities of prisoners or stamp collectors to fully fledged capitalist economies (in which people not only swap pre-produced 'items' but also work beside machines, enter into joint production, save for the future, borrow to invest and even go on strike for better wages), Marginalism finds itself totally out of its depth. When it tries its hand at analysing capitalism-proper, its otherwise perfectly sensible analytical statements about pure exchanges turn into absurd and dangerous dogmas (see Box 6.6); doctrines which both contributed to the crises of 1929 and of 2008, not to mention our inability to understand the causes of such calamities.

When arbitrage involves trading between actual producers and speculators, or the trading of financial 'products' that have a potential to siphon off the credit on which material production depends, the stakes rise far beyond anything we saw in the previous section. Box 6.8 contains a fictitious, but also chillingly accurate, tale of how a middleman's activities can harm struggling producers. Yet, as we shall see immediately afterwards, the ethical dimensions introduced by projecting Marginalism onto a world of human labour are eclipsed by theoretical troubles which make Marx's duel with the *Inherent Error* look like a benign sideshow.

Chapters 4 and 5 made a big deal of the centrality of free labour in human economies. The POW camp featured next to none of it.[35] This is precisely why its 'economy' was almost adequately captured by the dogmas emanating from a straightforward application of the *equi-marginal principle* (Box 6.6). But when *material production* enters the scene, the radical inadequacy of these dogmas emerges in full ®*Technicolor*. Before we argue this controversial point, let us revisit Marginalism's price theory and, in particular, its pronouncements on the price of labour (i.e. the wage) and the reward to capital (i.e. the profit rate). With the Marginalist claim to a universal theory of price in mind (see Box 6.9), we begin with the *equi-marginal principle* and its derivative all-encompassing price theory in equation (6.1).

Suppose that Jill agrees to wash Jack's shirt in exchange for 2 bags of tea. To have agreed to this deal, equation (6.1) reports that the following must hold:

$$\frac{MU^{Jill}_{Leisure}}{w} = \frac{MU^{Jill}_{teabag}}{p_{teabag}} \Rightarrow \frac{w}{p_{teabag}} = \frac{MU^{Jill}_{Leisure}}{MU^{Jill}_{teabag}}$$

$$\frac{MU^{Jack}_{not\ washing\ shirt}}{w} = \frac{MU^{Jack}_{teabag}}{p_{teabag}} \Rightarrow \frac{w}{p_{teabag}} = \frac{MU^{Jack}_{not\ washing\ shirt}}{MU^{Jack}_{teabag}}$$

$$\frac{w}{p_{teabag}} = \frac{MU^{Jill}_{Leisure}}{MU^{Jill}_{teabag}} = \frac{MU^{Jack}_{not\ washing\ shirt}}{MU^{Jack}_{teabag}}$$

$$(6.2)$$

Box 6.9 Of famine and arbitrage

In a small settlement somewhere in Africa, ten families grow wheat, which they take to the nearby market every year. The minimum income they need to stave off starvation is, say, $100 per family per annum. Output depends on the weather and the weather can be *good*, *normal* or *bad*. If it is *good*, a bumper crop of 150 tonnes is harvested. If the weather is *normal*, the harvest comes to 100 tonnes. But if the weather is *bad*, the harvest shrinks to only 50 tonnes. *During normal years*, their 100 tonnes fetch $10 per tonne at the local market. *In the good years*, however, they have 150 tonnes to sell and, therefore, must reduce their price to $8 to find buyers. *In years with bad weather*, they only bring to the market 50 tonnes and so price rises to $19. Summing up, in normal years, the settlement's income is $1000 (or $100 per family), in good years it goes up to $1200 ($120 per family) whereas in bad years it falls to $950 ($95 per family). So, over a cycle of three years (one good, one normal and one bad), average family income is $105; that is, just above starvation levels.

Suppose that during a good year, a middleman arrives and offers them the following deal: 'you take the 100 tonnes to the market and sell it for $10 per tonne, like you would in a normal year. As for the remaining 50 tonnes, you sell them to me for $8.50 per tonne. If you turn this offer down, and take all 150 tonnes to market, you will make much less money since the price would drop to $8.' Naturally, the villagers agree. But then the bad year comes, and their crop is only 50 tonnes, the middleman sells the 50 tonnes he had stocked up during the good year and, therefore, ensures that aggregate supply is that of a normal year (100 tonnes). The market then sets a normal price of $10. The middleman's gain is: 50 tonnes × $10 minus 50 tonnes × $8.50 = $75. How do we interpret his role:

Interpretation 1: Like all middlemen, his contribution to society is price stability. By buying during the bumper season and selling off when the harvest is lean, he irons out price and output fluctuations over a period of variable weather conditions. Bakeries and the wider public, who need a constant supply and predictable prices, benefit from his trading. As for his moral rectitude, the farmers did not have to accept his offer at the end of the good year. It was a free trade, one to which they consented.

Interpretation 2: He is a scoundrel who capitalises on the fact that he has money with which to trade. Without producing anything, he pockets a net profit of $75 when the harvest is bad while, in the process, condemning the poor farmers he trades with to starvation, as their average income now dips below the $100 per family starvation level.[1] Looked at intertemporally, the middleman's profit was bought at the cost of the farmers' suffering.

Note well that both interpretations are soundly founded on the facts. Economic analysis has no analytical means by which to privilege one of the two interpretations above on the grounds of its scientific superiority. This is another example why economics is, and can only be, political economics.

Note

1 In the good year, the middleman has helped the villagers boost their income from $1000 to $1422 (by buying 50 tonnes from them for $8.50). But during the bad year, he sells these 50 tonnes at the marketplace and the villagers (who only bring to market 50 tonnes too) now see their income crash from $950 (which is the income they would have drawn from their 50 tonnes if the middleman did not sell his 50 tonnes, thus preventing price from rise from $10 to $19) to a measly $500. During these two years (one good and one bad), the village's average total income falls, because of the middleman, from $2150 (or $1075 per annum or 107.5 per family per annum) to only $1922 or $96.1 per family per annum – well below the starvation level.

Box 6.10 A thoughtful Marginalist on how labour may differ from all other commodities

Alfred Marshall was one of the more thoughtful Marginalists. He tried to moderate some of Marginalism's more extravagant claims and to temper the Marginalists' propensity for mathematising that is, by nature, not quantifiable: Most economic phenomena, wrote Marshall do not lend themselves easily to mathematical expression'. We must therefore guard against 'assigning wrong proportions to economic forces; those elements being most emphasised which lend themselves most easily to analytical methods' (Marshall, 1890 [1920], *Mathematical Appendix*, p.850). Nevertheless, it is instructive that even he thought that labour was, analytically speaking, no different from electricity generators, corn or androids. Was there a difference between selling 'things' and selling one's labour? Yes, Marshall thought, but not in the deeper ontological sense that we espoused in Chapters 4 and 5. He wrote:

> When a workman is in fear of hunger, his need of money (its marginal utility to him) is very great; and, if at starting, he gets the worst of the bargaining, and is employed at low wages, it remains great, and he may go on selling his labour at a low rate. That is all the more probable because, while the advantage in bargaining is likely to be pretty well distributed between the two sides of a market for commodities, it is more often on the side of the buyers than on that of the sellers in a market for labour. Another difference between a labour market and a market for commodities arises from the fact that each seller of labour has only one unit of labour to dispose of. These are two among many facts, in which we shall find, as we go on, the explanation of much of that instinctive objection which the working classes have felt to the habit of some economists, particularly those of the employer class, of treating labour simply as a commodity and regarding the labour market as like every other market; whereas in fact the differences between the two cases, *though not fundamental from the point of view of theory*, are yet clearly marked, and in practice often very important.[1]

Note that the emphasis in the last sentence is ours. It highlights the point that Marshall, even though sensitive to the workers' special bargaining disadvantages, did not think (as we did in the previous two chapters) that labour was profoundly different to other commodities. In that regard, Marshall's take on labour was like that of the other Marginalists.[2]

Notes
1 Marshall (1890 [1920]), v. ii § 3, pp. 279–80.
2 In his *Principles* (Book VI, Chapter iv) Marshall offers a number of reasons why labour is different from other commodities including the role of upbringing and education and the fact that 'when a person sells his services, he has to present himself where they are delivered. It matters nothing to the seller of bricks whether they are to be used in building a palace or a sewer: but it matters a great deal to the seller of labour, who undertakes to perform a task of given difficulty, whether or not the place in which it is to be done is a wholesome and a pleasant one, and whether or not his associates will be such as he cares to have.' (1890 [1920] VI, iv§5, p. 471). This led to the theory of 'compensating wage differentials.' In fact, since the worst jobs are highly correlated with low pay the theory suggests that inequality of wages should have been even greater if 'psychic' wages were not taken into account.

It is only a matter of some manipulation to show that equation (6.2) translates into a simple statement (see Box 6.11):

> Wages reflect the ratio of the marginal utilities of both employer and worker.

Moving from barter (1 clean shirt for 2 teabags) to a monetised economy (like that in the POW camp once the BMk was established), the above Marginalist theory of the wage becomes even simpler. As long as workers are competing against one another:

> The utility of the money wage per unit of labour equals the employer's utility from marginal unit of labour.

Note how the above analysis is indifferent to Jill's actual *labouring*. Whether Jack is paying 2 teabags in exchange for a clean shirt or for Jill's *labour input* is one and the same thing. *Labour inputs* are, therefore, treated as no different from 'things'. In Chapter 4 we argued that this amounts to a flight from human economies where labour is impossible to objectify even if the worker wants nothing more. But let's set this aside, for the time being, to illustrate Marginalism's *internal* inconsistencies. For, even if we were prepared to accept (which we definitely are not!) that *labour input* is a 'thing' for sale, like all other 'things', the Marginalist theory of the wage (and of profit) leaks like a sieve.

Marginalism's main point is that, when workers compete against each other in the labour market, wages reflect two things:

(a) the marginal labour unit's *output*, and
(b) the employer's extra revenue from that output.

Box 6.11 The Marginalist calculus of wages

Suppose that for every *util* Jack forfeits when paying Jill (in tea, cigarettes or dollars) he gets 3 *utils* when she washes his shirt for him. Then, by equation (6.1), Jill must receive one of her *utils* from her 'wage' for every 3 *utils* she forfeits when washing Jack's shirt. Let the dis-utilities be thought of as the 'price' paid by Jack and Jill. Jack pays the 'price' of forfeiting two teabags (p_K) and Jill pays the 'price' of labouring to wash his shirt (p_L). They do this in exchange of the following utilities:

- Jack's utility for not having to wash his marginal shirt = MU_K
- Jill's utility from the two teabags = MU_L

Re-writing equation (6.2), using the new notation, we derive:

$$\frac{MU_k}{p_k} = \frac{MU_L}{p_L} \quad \text{or} \quad \frac{MU_k}{MU_L} = \frac{p_k}{p_L} \tag{6.3}$$

And since the ratio p_k/p_L can be thought of, simply, as a measure of the wage (relative to the worker's disutility), it turns out that the equi-marginal principle is telling a simple story identical to that it tells regarding all prices – recall equation (6.1).

Indeed, the employer's marginal utility from labour (which determines the wage, according to the *equi-marginal principle*) is no more than the product of (a) and (b). Marginalists refer to (a) as the *marginal productivity of labour* (denoted by MP_L) and to (b) as the employer's *marginal revenue* (*MR*). The product of (a) and (b) is known as labour's *marginal revenue product* (*MRP_L*). Summing up, the theory concludes that (as long as workers compete against one another) the wage stabilises at a level equal to labour's *marginal revenue product*.

> The money wage equals the product of labour's *marginal productivity* and the employer's *marginal revenue*, known as labour's *marginal revenue product*, *MRP_L*
>
> OR

$$w = MP_L \times MR = MRP_L \qquad\qquad (6.4)$$

An identical logic is deployed in explaining capital's price, or rate of return, or profit rate or whatever we may wish to call it. Capital, just like labour, is seen as a 'thing' for sale and equations (6.3) and (6.4) are repeated, only this time in terms of the capitalist's marginal dis-utility from providing capital (which is due to deferring consumption into the future), the *marginal productivity of capital* (*MP_K*), etc. The gist of the matter is that:

> The price of capital, which is the same as the profit rate π, equals the product of capital's *marginal productivity* and the firm's marginal revenue; that is, capital's *marginal revenue product* (*MRP_K*)
>
> OR

$$p = MP_K \times MR = MRP_K \qquad\qquad (6.5)$$

All of the above is a complicated way of telling a terribly simple story: both capital and labour are rewarded by a payment reflecting the capacity of the *last* unit of capital or of labour to add to the firm's net revenues. As for the *quantity* of capital and labour the firm will engage, the answer (again courtesy of the *equi-marginal principle*) could not be simpler: capitalists will recruit more labour units until the wage rate exactly equals the capacity of the *last* unit of labour to add to the firm's revenues. Similarly, they will keep 'hiring', or enlisting, more units of capital until the cost of each unit of machinery equals the capacity of the *last* unit of machinery to add to the firm's revenues.

6.9 Marginalism and the *Inherent Error*, part 1: The trouble with capital

A theory that cannot see the profound, ontological, difference between *labour input* and some material, quantifiable input like electricity is unsuitable for the purposes of illuminating capitalism's ways. At least this was our argument in the preceding two chapters. Interestingly, even if we were prepared to recant and enthusiastically accept Marginalism's basic premise (that labour is ontologically no different from electricity), it turns out that the resulting (Marginalist) analysis of capitalism is incoherent *on its own terms*! Indeed this section explains how the Marginalists' ambition to elucidate all prices in terms of the *equi-marginal principle* proved an open-ended invitation for economics' *Inherent Error* to return. And when it returned it did so with unprecedented vengeance. It inflicted so formidable a retribution, wrecking Marginalism's scientific claims with abandon, that under normal circumstances we should not be discussing Marginalism at all, except perhaps in a book on heroic intellectual failures. But, regrettably, our circumstances are far from normal.

We live in a world in which Marginalist economic thinking is the secular religion. It provides the rhetorical framework in which *all* the important debates are couched. Central bankers and hedge fund managers, presidents and prime ministers, ambitious opposition politicians and even many trade unionists, influential journalists and well meaning environmentalists: they *all* formulate their thinking and policy proposals within the straitjacket of Marginalist thinking. With their imagination severely circumscribed by the Marginalist framework, they acquiesce to a narrative conducive to catastrophic practices. And none of these are more catastrophic than those concerning the markets for labour and capital. This is why the present section puts under the microscope Marginalism's claims regarding wages and profit rates, and explains how the *Inherent Error* returned to destroy the logical coherence of its claims.

Marginalists, as we have seen, delegate all social explanation to subjective appraisals or utility. But if production is to be defined as the costly generation of utility, professional comedians are producers. Fair enough. But what of the friend who makes us laugh around the dinner table? Is he/she a producer too, even though he/she may be having just as much fun as we are? And if so, what is his/her capital? Could it be his/her stock of jokes? Perhaps. But then what is the difference between his/her utility from making us laugh (his/her notional wage) and his/her profit? These simplistic questions echo Marginalism's difficulty to distinguish between production and consumption, capital and labour, wages and profit. They may sound frivolous but they pack important insights into why the dominant economic thinking of our day finds it so hard to recognise that which most sensible people already know and, worse, remains blind to the less visible causal relations surrounding us (see Box 6.12 for an example).

In the last section we became acquainted with Marginalism's main theory of distribution which, in fact, could be framed in quasi-ethical or political slogans:

> each according to the market value of her marginal product! All powers to marginal productivity and to the price the final product can fetch at the marketplace! Labour and capital earn their keep in proportion to the revenue generated for the firm by their last unit!

Note that, in this context, only one determinant of wages and profit rates lies outside the firm: the price of the final commodity, which determines the market value of the marginal product of both capital and labour. As long as capitalism is competitive, nothing else that goes on in the economy at large (and which is independent of the final product's price) matters in the determination of wage and profit rates.

Ignoring any external critiques (such as those in Box 6.13 below), how *coherent*, or *internally consistent*, is this view? Not much, we shall be arguing. Starting at the level of the individual firm, suppose that Jack and Jill are employees working in the bread industry. Jack works for the *Sliced Bread Co.* and Jill for the *Wholesome Bread Co.* Suppose, however, that the *Sliced Bread Co.* is antiquated and uses old electric ovens whereas the *Wholesome Bread Co.* uses modern low-energy industrial microwave ovens. There is only one way the *Sliced Bread Co.* can survive: by having Jack work harder than Jill in order to compensate for its slower, more expensive, ovens. At the end of the day, one of our two workers works harder than the other and yet both the products of their labour sell at the same price and both collect the same wage. Because of the difference in the machines used, Jack's payment per unit of labour supplied is lower than Jill's. But because the political economics built upon the

Box 6.12 The discovery of domestic labour

Are women who give up their jobs to raise their children producers? If they enjoy doing it, they can be said to gain utility directly from the activities involved, in which case they may be thought of as consumers. In contrast, if they loathe changing nappies but do it for the future rewards of parenthood, they are investors. Producers even! But does this mean that only disgruntled stay-at-home mothers are producers, while the perfectly blissful ones are not? Surely this is absurd. For centuries housework was considered a woman's *duty*, if not her *calling*, *pleasure*, *purpose in life*. No one thought of them as *producers*. Marginalism, alas, did not help in this regard, since it could not tell the difference given its recourse to the definition of production as a form of utility generation. Feminists, on the other hand, protested that women were called housewives so as to hide the fact that they were unpaid producers of housekeeping services (some cheerful, others desperate). This later view seems to resonate better with our times. What has changed? Marginalism cannot say. However, deploying the perspective of the last two chapters (which makes room for the dialectical overcoming of binary contradictions), a useful answer emerges. According to one such argument,[1] the emergence of a new economic sector that provides many housekeeping services for a price reflecting the cost of waged labour (e.g. domestic cleaners, professional nannies and contractors undertaking various housekeeping chores) has brought into light women's unwaged work. Marginalism, by focusing exclusively on the utilities of the contracting parties, has no way of seeing, let alone recognising, this type of social dynamic.

Note
1 See Himmelweit (1995).

equi-marginal principle [e.g. equation (6.5)] leaves no room for the difference in qualities or vintages of capital goods, nor for the differences in labour inputs extracted by the firm from a given number of hours worked, it cannot explain why Jill's effort is paid (per unit) more generously than Jack's. In short, this difference cannot be attributed to the marginal productivity of the labour that the two firms hired from Jack and Jill.

Marginalists respond to this criticism in two ways. The first one is to argue that, in the long run, the *Sliced Bread Co.* will have to upgrade its ovens or close down. When this happens, Jack and Jill will be working as hard as each other in order to bake bread of similar market value. Be that as it may, a theory that works only as long as firms are assumed to utilise machines of identical quality, vintage, capacity, etc. is profoundly unconvincing. Marginalists, naturally, understood this point and felt compelled to reconfigure their theory in order to allow for heterogeneous machinery. What follows is their second response to what is, unsurprisingly, a very old riddle:[36]

For equation (6.5) to work, the stock of capital (K) must be conceivable as a homogeneous variable; something like an army of capital units must be lined up and the output of the marginal (or last) unit noted. Leading Marginalists confessed that this is not possible. Machines are, by nature, heterogeneous and their physical quantities indivisible and therefore impossible to line up so neatly. Thus, no amount of technical ingenuity can reduce a firm's capital stock to a single variable. In contrast to land holdings and labour hours worked which

---

Box 6.13 On the impossibility of a sensible microeconomics

Microeconomics is Marginalism's pampered firstborn. On the basis of the equi-marginal principle, a whole new political economics was founded that sought to determine the price of everything at the level of individual agents. Indeed, if prices reflect buyers' marginal utilities, then a general price theory is possible that focuses not on the economy as a whole (which is what the classical political economists did) but on the individual. That this is at best a tendentious claim can be gleaned from our example with Jack and Jill baking bread for different employers. If Jack's employer could, however temporarily, make him work harder for the same pay, and during the same period, as Jill, then it must be true that how much labour effort, or labour inputs, will enter production depends on how successful management is in making Jack and Jill labour harder for the same pay and hours. Management experts dedicate their lives to this task. Beyond the techniques that they develop (often employing psychology), there is also another important factor that all self-respecting managers understand well: the fear of dismissal and its connection with the prevailing rate of unemployment: the more widespread unemployment is the lower the wage per actual labour unit provided (as Jack and Jill increase their work's tempo fearful that if they do not the likelihood of joining the dole queues increases). And it is not just the overall level of unemployment that matters but also its spatial distribution. So, if the *Sliced Bread Co.* is in an area of deeper and graver unemployment than that the *Wholemeal Bread Co.* is located at, the result may be that Jack's wage per labour unit is even lower than Jill's, even if everything else (e.g. the technology of the two companies, the marginal productivity of the two workers) were identical. But then if the determination of a price (like the wage) depends on macro-variables (like unemployment) and their spatial variations, then no microeconomic analysis of the wage is secure. By extension, profit rates may be irreducible to microeconomic phenomena which renders a satisfying microeconomics chimerical.

---

can be added up reasonably easily, how does one add up a truck with an industrial robot to come up with the firm's (or, worse, the sector's) aggregate quantity of capital? How can the different machines littering the factory floor be lined up, one unit after the next, before working out capital's marginal productivity?

It was Knut Wicksell (1901) who came up with a possible solution:[37] He argued that a firm's capital stock, while hopelessly heterogeneous and indivisible, can still be turned into a smooth variable by calculating the price of each machine and then constructing a measure of capital stock based on these market prices. For example, if a firm uses a truck worth $50 thousand, a computer system worth $25 thousand and a drilling device worth $15 thousand, then its capital stock is, simply, $90 thousand. Instead of lining up units of machinery (before we work out the contribution of each of these units to production), the idea here is to line up each dollar of capital stock equivalent and find out what was its contribution to total output.

Wicksell's next suggestion was that machines ought to be seen as the crystallisation of human labour and land; a line similar to Marx, except that Marx did not see land as a contributor to capital formation. Capital is then acquired by a conscious decision by the capitalist to postpone his consumption. He could have spent his $90 thousand on a new car but chose to invest it instead in capital goods. Also, he could have chosen to spend less (more) on machines and more (less) on labour or land. Thus, in Wicksell's thinking, the capitalist

---

Box 6.14 Knut Wicksell on capital

We have already pointed out that capital itself is almost always a product, a fruit of the cooperation of the two original factors: labour and land. All capital goods, however different they may appear, can always be ultimately resolved into labour and land; and the only thing which distinguishes these quantities of labour and land from those which we have previously considered is that they belong to *earlier years*, whilst we have previously been concerned only with current labour and land directly employed in the production of consumption-goods. *But this difference is sufficient to justify the establishment of a special category of means of production, side by side with labour and land, under the name capital*; for, in the interval of time thus afforded, the accumulated labour and land have been able to assume forms denied to them in their crude state, by which they attain a much greater efficiency for a number of productive purposes… .

[Wicksell (1901[1934], pp. 149–50). First emphasis original, second emphasis ours.]

---

performs a crucial, two-fold task: he strikes a fine balance between consumption and savings and also between the different bundles of land, labour and capital that can produce output. Captains of industry, in this reading, preside over the economy's parsimony and over the various sectors' choice of production techniques (e.g. how much labour-saving technology to utilise). Their profits are their reward for these important tasks. But above all else, it is a just reward for postponing consumption; for saving.

It follows that, since the capital stock is now measured in dollars, and capital accumulation (or investment) is a form of savings by the capitalist, his/her (and capital's) rate of return cannot be (sustainably) different to the rate of interest r. In terms of equation (6.5), the rate of profit *is* the rate of interest (i.e. $\pi = r$). As this rate fluctuates, capitalists adjust their utilisation of capital relatively to that of labour and land. When r falls, capital utilisation rises and machines play a greater role in the production of each unit of output; and vice versa. These fluctuations will continue until, at the given interest rate, the supply of capital (or savings) becomes equal to the demand for capital (or investment).[38]

Problem solved? Hardly: Wicksell's method requires a strict separation of the *quantity of capital* (measured in dollars) from the *price of capital* (also measured in dollars), which corresponds to the market value of the output due to the last or marginal unit of capital. It is not difficult to see that this separation is very hard to achieve, except in very special cases. The conundrum here is plain to see: if the physical capital's magnitude depends on its price, how can its price be explained by its magnitude? This is the analytical equivalent of a cat chasing after its own tail *ad infinitum*. There are only two cases in which Wicksell's solution makes sense and avoids this infinite loop (or regress):

Case 1: A single good economy (e.g. Ricardo's corn economy, where corn featured both as the consumption and the capital good) in which, however, the capitalist can select from an infinite number of capital intensities, each with its own mix of capital and labour employed (a menu of intensities that the capitalist will choose from depending, as already shown, on the rate of interest).

Case 2: A multi-good economy with infinite potential capital intensities but where the *same* product must be produced with *exactly the same* capital intensity by each and every firm. This condition is *sine qua non* because, without it, we lose the inverse relationship between (a) the interest or profit rate and (b) the quantity of capital.[39] And if this relationship vanishes, Marginalism's theory of capital formation disappears.

It is now abundantly clear that we are back to square one: to the *Inherent Error*! The very same *error* that struck Marx when he discovered that his basic value theory (on which he based his whole political agenda) required a uniform *organic composition of capital*; i.e. identical capital intensities in every sector. Both Cases 1 and 2 above inflict the same calamity upon Marginalism's price theory; namely, the verdict that a theory of prices erected on the *equi-marginal principle* cannot extend to a genuine multi-product economy!

The blow to Marginalism's political agenda was no smaller than that in the case of Marx. Marginalists invested heavily in linking capital intensity, profit rates and the rate of interest in a manner consistent with the view that, in competitive capitalism, labour and capital receive their just desserts which reflect their marginal productivities and relative scarcity. But we have just discovered that in realistic settings (with different capital intensities across different firms, sectors, product lines, etc.) neither the profit nor the interest rate can express the relative scarcity of capital or its marginal productivity (see Box 6.15 for more on this).

Put simply, Marginalism has no convincing story to tell about the determinants of profits. The corollary is that it has no persuasive explanation either regarding wages. In the Marginalist conception of capitalism there are markets, prices, utilities but no profits. The price that the economics profession paid by espousing Marginalism is that it could no longer tell the difference between capital's physical quantity and its returns to the capitalists. A theory of capitalism without a theory of capital was a unique achievement of political economics.

6.10 Marginalism and the *Inherent Error*, part 2: The trouble with time, scale and composition

Marginalism's ideological aim was to defend the capitalist realm from critics like Marx, whose own ideological aspiration was to portray capitalism as a conflict-ridden, crisis-prone, irrational system that curbs human freedom and turns us into ghosts possessed by their own inventions. To do this, Marginalism set out first to prove that Marx's own theoretical scheme was wrong (recall Böhm-Bawerk's (1896 [1898]) work) and, at once, to prove *as a mathematical theorem* that Adam Smith was right; that, as long as markets are competitive and unhindered by non-entrepreneurs (state institutions, trade unions, even conservative social mores), the common good is best served by the institutions of a market society.

Marginalism's *first step* in constructing its *Grand Proof* was mathematically to derive the prices and quantities a 'free' market would generate. Its *second step* was mathematically to define the common good as a function whose maximisation would coincide with societal bliss. Finally, the *third step* that would complete the *Grand Proof* is the demonstration that the prices and quantities discovered in the first step in fact do maximise the function specified in the second step, subject to society's available resources. Unfortunately, Marginalism's great expectations were dashed as insurmountable theoretical problems beset the first and second steps above.

Beginning with the *first step*, a defensible theory of competitive pricing and quantity proved impossible. Antoine Augustin Cournot (see Box 6.5) had realised this problem as far back as 1838. In his impressively far-sighted book *Researches into the Mathematical*

Box 6.15 The loss of measurable capital

In Chapter 4 we objected strongly to the idea that human labour inputs are measurable on a single, quantifiable scale. Our point there was that if labour could be thus measured, the world we live in would tend to some dystopia, like that in *The Matrix*. Marginalists had no such qualms. Eager to use calculus in order to work out the price of everything (on the basis of marginal utilities), they assumed that *labour input* is no different from electricity: that it can be quantified and therefore bought and sold as readily as AC/DC power. Alas, economic theory proved its vindictiveness by forcing Marginalists to pay the ultimate price for their hubris: the loss of a meaningful measure of capital.

This is how it happened:[1] Marginalism aimed at eliminating the classical political economists' separation of value (or price) from distribution; to argue that the distribution of national income between landowners, workers and capitalists is not a political matter but reflects their respective factors' contribution to society's utility from physical output.[2] Just like apples have a price that reflects their marginal utility to the buyer, so do machines have a price that reflects their marginal utility to the firm (or their marginal productivity). The problems began when that view had to be spelt out analytically: for when production uses both capital goods (K) and labour (L), even speaking of capital's marginal productivity requires that we imagine the existence of a well-defined production function telling us which combinations of quantities of capital and labour (K and L) yield every possible level of output Y. Something like $Y = F(K, L)$.

By the end of the nineteenth-century, neoclassical economists like Wicksteed, Wicksell and Walras have understood the grave significance of this.[3] To argue that the last or marginal unit of capital contributes to output a quantity whose value reflects the price of (or return to) capital (i.e. the profit rate), it must be the case that some units of output (Y) must be due to capital and the rest to labour; that there is no residual (i.e. units of Y that are due neither to K nor to L nor to both at once). For this to make sense, the production function $F(K, L)$ must have a special property which, in mathematics, is called *homogeneity of the first degree*. In plain language, this means that, if the quantity of both factors is doubled, output must double too. And if only one of the two factors (capital *or* labour) is augmented, then the output will rise but the rate of that increase will diminish. It is these diminishing and strictly separable marginal productivities of capital and labour that allow Marginalists to think of the demand for capital as a decreasing function of its price and of the demand for labour as a decreasing function of the wage. Then and only then can it be said that the *marginal revenue product of capital* (MRP_K) is the price of capital (which is the same as the rate of profit π, which, in turn, must be equal to the rate of interest r) and that the *marginal revenue product of labour* (MRP_L) is the wage rate.

In this manner, through the marginal productivities of the factors of production, Marginalist political economics drove a wedge between the quantity and the price of capital and unified price theory with a theory of income distribution. To see this, it suffices to note that the prices of the factors (i.e. the profit and wage rates) represent also the shares of the firms' income accruing to capital and to labour. The *theory of income distribution*, therefore, loses all the political dimensions that it had under classical political economics and becomes a branch, or a by-product, of Marginalist price theory.

In this unified theory of prices and income distribution, the rate of interest r plays two roles at once: (a) it determines the capital intensity in each firm (since the higher r is the more firms will substitute labour for machines); and (b) it equilibrates savings and investment (since a drop in r will reduce savings and increase investment until the two balance out).

To see the importance of this theoretical resolution (beyond its political utility of claiming that profit is a fair reward for capital's contribution to production, just as much as the wage is for labour), suppose that (for some reason) business confidence drops and, consequently, investment falls. This should push the interest rate down (as some savings will not be invested), a development that has two simultaneous effects: first, it cheapens machinery and, therefore, encourages firms to replace labour with capital units; second, it reduces savings. The first adjustment boosts the demand for machines (thus creating new investment and employment in the capital goods sector) while the second adjustment increases consumption (and thus demand). If all goes well, the economy should bounce back and confidence will be restored. Crises? What crises?

Alas, note how the harmonious operation of the benign markets described above is predicated upon the assumption concerning the homogeneity of the production function $F(K, L)$. This assumption (that *all* production functions must be *homogeneous of the first degree*) is equivalent to assuming either a single commodity economy or one in which every product is produced by the same capital utilisation intensity. The question then becomes: *what light can Marginalist political economics throw on an economy where each product is produced by firms which employ different mixes of capital and labour?* Not much!, is the honest answer. Once capital's marginal contribution to output cannot be measured *separately* from labour's contribution (since hardly any relation between a firm's inputs and output is homogenous), its price cannot be determined by the marginal revenue product of capital (MRP_K). But then, if capital cannot be priced, there is no measure of the quantity of capital either. No quantity of capital, no theory of investment, savings or interest rates. One after the other, Marginalism's chips fall, leaving behind very little that can pass as a theory of capitalism.

Notes

1 The main point made below originates in the works of Cambridge economists Piero Sraffa, Joan Robinson and Luigi Pasinetti. Their argument occasioned a bitter debate with American economists like Robert Solow and Paul Samuelson, whose location in Cambridge Massachusetts meant that this debate became known as the *Cambridge Controversies*. For a fascinating account, see G.C. Harcourt (1972). For a more recent review of the debate see Avi J. Cohen and G.C. Harcourt (2003). Note that recourse to General Equilibrium models, where no aggregate notion of capital is required, does not save the day, since this reformulation does not preserve the relationship between the price of capital and its scarcity.

2 Of course, the marginal productivity theory is political in a much more important sense. It argues that despite vast inequalities in income between the owners of factors of production, the distribution of incomes in a perfectly competitive economy is just. As John Bates Clark put it 'what a social class gets is, under natural law, what it contributes to the general output of industry' (1891, p. 312). See also his 'Distribution, Ethics of' [Clark, 1894]. Moreover, the marginal productivity theory also has a corollary that the ensuing allocation of resources is efficient, since if marginal products were not equated across jobs, a more efficient allocation could prevail by moving the worker from the job with the less- marginal product to a job with a higher one (see Dorfman, 1987). Thus we have the best of all possible worlds: an economy which is efficient and just. QED.

3 Wicksteed has pointed this out in his *The Coordination of the Laws of Distribution*, in 1894. He produced the necessary conditions for the production function for the law to hold. As Alfred W. Flux pointed out in 1894, the production function must be homogeneous of the first degree so that Euler's theorem must apply. To see it clearly, if the product is 'exhausted' into the rewards of factors of production, and each factor of production receives the value of its marginal product, we must have for a production function $Q = F(K, L)$ that $Q = rK + wL$, where Q is output, K and L the units of capital and labour and r and w their rewards. We assume that price $p = 1$. Then if $r = \dfrac{dQ}{dK}$ and $w = \dfrac{dQ}{dL}$, we must have

$$Q = \frac{dQ}{dK}K + \frac{dQ}{dL}L.$$ But this is not a general function; it must obey the law of constant returns to scale. Walras wanted to steal Wicksteed's contribution and complained that it was all there in the second edition of his *Elements* and hence he included an appendix in the third edition with an unjustified and virulent attack on Wicksteed, which because of its vehemence was removed from the 4th edition. (« Note sur la réfutation de la théorie anglaise du fermage de M. Wicksteed » Appendix to the 3rd (1896) edition of the *Elements* [Appears in Walras (1954)]) Wicksell in his *Lectures* (1901[1934]) took another path. He suggested that when competition is worked out, firms produce at the minimum average cost where the necessary conditions for the exhaustion of the product apply. Hicks in his *Theory of Wages* (1932) provided the mathematical proof of this. The exhaustion of the product is still with us and it is responsible for the ubiquity of the Cobb–Douglas production function, which in its canonical form $Q = AK^{\alpha}L^{1-\alpha}$ is homogeneous of the first degree. In fact when Wicksteed first proposed the theory – which he thought that 'would hold equally in Robinson Crusoe's island, in an American religious commune, in an Indian village ruled by custom, and in the competitive centres of the typical modern industries' (1894, p. 42), he met the sarcasm of Edgeworth (1904 [1925], p. 31) who wrote: 'There is a magnificence in this generalisation which recalls the youth of philosophy. Justice is a perfect cube, said the ancient sage; and rational conduct is a homogeneous function, adds the modern *savant*. A theory that points to conclusions so paradoxical ought surely to be enunciated with caution'.

Principles of the Theory of Wealth,[40] he analysed the mathematics of competition between two or more firms. His first discovery was that no mathematical analysis can *ever* explain prices and quantities when firms are allowed (as they are in real life) to choose both their output level *and* the price they charge. Put simply, it was like trying to solve a system of two equations in four unknowns.

Cournot, therefore, chose to study what would happen when competing firms chose their output and left the price to the market to determine (i.e. as if firms brought their produce to some market where an auctioneer auctions off the good's total supply). Even then, there was a problem. When firm A tries to decide how much to produce, it cannot predict the price it will be selling at without knowing the output of firm B. So, firm A cannot know which output would maximise its own profit. But this applies also to firm B. Clearly, competitive output selection is like a game where what one does depends on what one thinks others will do. Before long, too much over-thinking takes over and leads to hopeless indeterminacy: firm A's output will depend on what it thinks B will think that A will expect B to think that A will predict *ad infinitum*. Cournot's masterstroke was to work out (i) A's profit maximising output given its prediction of B's output; and (ii) B's profit maximising output given its prediction of A's output. These two equations formed a nice system in two unknowns: an eminently solvable problem yielding one output level for A, one for B and a price that corresponds to the total of these two outputs (assuming we know how much consumers are prepared to pay for a given total supply).

There was a snag; however, and Cournot was, in our estimation, painfully aware of it: it was difficult to explain *how* the market would converge to this price and output. Cournot hypothesised that each firm sets some output level on the basis of its prediction of its competitors' output. That estimate would only prove accurate (for every firm) by some freak accident. When, as is more likely, a firm observes a discrepancy between *its estimate* of the competition's output and *their actual* output choice, it adjusts accordingly both its estimate and its own output. For example if A had overestimated B's output, it will have also underestimated the market price. With this new information under its belt, A now adjusts its price estimate upwards and, correspondingly, boosts its output. But then, B will also adjust its output once it observes A's adjustment. The question then is: how do we model mathematically this adjustment process? First blush it sounds like a technical question that can be answered by some clever technical fix. But it is not.

The problem is that when A is about to adjust its estimate of B's output, and alter its own output level, it must know that this adjustment will cause B to readjust. So, unless A knows in advance B's own reaction to A's reaction, A does not know how to react *ad infinitum*. In short, the problem has been elevated onto a higher order without being solved. Initially there was uncertainty regarding what the competition would do. Now the uncertainty moves to the level of worrying about how one's output adjustment, caused by one's shifting estimates of the competition's output, will alter the competition's estimates. In essence, the mathematical problem is getting more and more complicated, rather than edging towards a solution.

Cournot understood this and decided to deal with the developing Gordian knot in Alexandrian fashion. He drove his analytical sword through it by assuming that firms do not over-think things. That, mechanically, whenever B's output proves higher than A had expected, A boosts its estimate of B's output by a certain arbitrary factor falsely assuming that B will keep output steady. If B does the same, it can be shown that the two firms will edge towards an equilibrium at which the market will rest. Of course, the theoretical price to pay here is that the firms' behaviour can be modelled only if their managers are lobotomised: prices and outputs can be partly explained[41] *only if firms are assumed to hold false beliefs about the repercussions of their decisions.*

More than a century later, through the work of celebrated game theorist John Nash Jr we discovered how deeply ingrained this problem is. Nash's analysis, *circa* 1950, revealed that Cournot's problem could be solved even if the firms' rationality was fully restored. But then, something else would have to be sacrificed: time! In Cournot's own scheme, as described above, firms chose and kept adjusting their output *in real time* on the basis of their irrational, or myopic, estimates of the competition's output. In Nash's framework, firms were allowed to be fully rational (at least as rational as Nash) but the solution could only be worked out mathematically in a time-vacuum; that is, in the absence of any opportunity to *adjust* their output since the radical lack of time forces them to select their output once and for all.

Thus, caught in between Cournot and Nash, the Marginalist theorist faces two successive dilemmas: to determine prices he/she must ditch quantities, or *vice versa*. Then, he/she must either abandon the idea that firms act rationally in their pursuit of profit or discard time itself. The task of producing Marginalist models of markets featuring firms that are rationally operating in real time is equivalent to the task of squaring the circle.[42]

The *second step* of the *Grand Proof* was meant to depict the common good by means of a function that increases in proportion to society's welfare. Marginalists, having already identified the private good with some individual utility function, thought that a social utility or welfare function (reflecting the common good) could be put together by somehow aggregating these separate private utility functions. Yet again, their ambition was thwarted as the transition from private interest (the individual utility functions) to the common good (the overarching social welfare function) proved impossible to achieve in a politically neutral (or 'scientific') manner. It was not just hard to synthesise private utilities into an overarching function whose maximisation would coincide with the best interests of society: it was, in fact, impossible![43]

With the demise of its first two steps, the planned *Grand Proof* could never reach its third and final step; at least not without some serious sleight of hand. So, a sleight of hand was used! Marginalists (with some exceptions), frustrated by their inability to deliver the *Grand Proof*, chose to behave *as if* it had been delivered; to assume that which they had hitherto been trying to prove on the basis of whatever axioms it took to prop up their claims. Thus, *neoclassical political economics* was born; probably the most significant fraud in humanity's intellectual history.

6.11 Marginalism's bastard: The birth of neoclassical political economics

Faced with the impossibility of mathematically deriving prices and quantities on the one hand and a metric of social welfare on the other, some Marginalists understood the limitations of their utility calculus. Mainly of an Austrian persuasion (most notably Ludwig von Mises, Friedrich von Hayek and Joseph Schumpeter),[44] they even gallantly tried to use this failure to the advantage of their claims on behalf of untrammelled markets and against the encroachments of collective agencies, trade unions, governments, etc. For example they interpreted the impossibility of determining competitive prices and quantities as follows. If no degree of mathematical sophistication can pin down the 'right' prices and quantities, how can a government or other form of collective agency work them out? How could a socialist economy, or even a national health service, ever price things? Thus, the market mechanism is indispensable *because* of the radical indeterminacy of prices and quantities. It, and only it, can help society grope its way towards (analytically undiscoverable) prices that emit useful signals which stand a chance of coordinating economic activity. No human brain, committee of brains, or super-computer can calculate them. Similarly with social welfare: the impossibility of reliably working out what society wants (even if we know *exactly* what each of its members wants) means that *no one* (however well meaning and sophisticated he/she might be) can know what is in the common interest, let alone know how to bring it about. *The state, even if run by wise angels, can never serve the public interest!*

The downside of this rhetorical exploitation of Marginalism's analytical breakdown in the hands of its own version of the *Inherent Error* was that it denied Marginalists the right to pose as social physicists, complete with sophisticated, determinate mathematical models. And while the likes of von Mises, von Hayek and Schumpeter did not mind, the rest did. Thus, a new strategy surfaced: the use of mathematics, not in order to describe how markets converge to some price or quantity (which proved impossible) but to discover under which assumptions a model of markets could be penned, which (a) works 'perfectly' and (b) is consistent with Marginalist analysis. This was a twist of enormous significance.

Up until that moment, all of political economics was, in one way or another, trying to explain really existing capitalism or, at the very least, real world markets. Its abstractions were meant as devices by which to come closer to a description of reality. They resembled the blueprints of engineers who use technical and mathematical means in order first to describe some mechanism and then to improve upon it. But this new, *neoclassical* turn in political economics had a wholly different aim, a radically distinctive method and, naturally, a novel effect: it signalled a mass retreat from temporal reality. It was akin to a retreat into some pre-agrarian mindset.[45] The end result was a Marginalist economics whose purpose was to create a model of a single moment during which a thin-as-a-needle 'market' allocates resources with absolute efficiency. The task of illuminating the markets we know, and the capitalism we live in, was dropped unceremoniously.

It is crucial to mark well this transition from the engineering approach to a purely formalist mathematical approach. Using mathematics in order to describe a phenomenon unfolding in real time (like the weather, the motion of a pendulum or the workings of an electricity generator) is one thing. But creating a fully abstract model of that dynamic phenomenon, which only hangs together if its dynamics are radically excised, is quite another.

Neoclassical economics, as this variant of Marginalism became known, defends its method with the argument that it is perfectly legitimate to work out on paper a model of an efficient market and then compare it to the actual, far less efficient, markets around us. The idea is to discern the facets of the real market that differ from the model market as a guide to the institutional changes which, if introduced into the real market, might improve its workings. The reason why such a defence borders on pure nonsense is that comparisons are only meaningful if they compare like with like. However, Section 6.9 revealed that the only way of creating a determinate mathematical model of market prices and quantities was by *assuming away either time or rationality*. What good will a comparison do when on the one hand we have a real market and on the other a model market which is either frozen in time or is populated by firms unaware of their effect on their competitors (not to mention that capital and labour are never present in a form that is even vaguely familiar to us)? It is like trying to improve upon the design of an airplane by juxtaposing a video tape of a flying prototype against a model of the same aircraft built on the assumption that it must remain still in mid-air!

Despite the neoclassical turn's absurdity, its discursive power proved stupendous.[46] More than a century after its inception, it retains a stranglehold on almost every economics textbook on the planet. If Marginalism marked a retreat from any account of capitalism that takes labour and capital seriously, neoclassicism marked a complete withdrawal from the scientific method. Indeed, it resembled more the evolution of a religious sect into a global religion. Where did it draw its power from? How did it turn its own, much vivified, version of political economics' *Inherent Error* into a source of power? In Box 6.1 we referred to the triptych underpinning the *Inherent Error*'s discursive power: the *lure of algebra*, the *appeal of closure* and the *political utility of determinism*.

Neoclassicism satisfied the first condition, as had Marginalism before it (the broader church from which it emanates). Indeed, by branching out from algebra to calculus and then, in the 1940s and 1950s, to topology and probability theory, neoclassicism could count on an even stronger lure than the one provided by plain algebra. But it was the *appeal of closure* that enticed the majority of most Marginalists to become neoclassicists. Neoclassicism's promise to rid Marginalism of the problem of indeterminacy proved the strongest drawing card. Consider, for instance, Marginalism's original insight: Jill buys a quantity of X from Jack such that her marginal dis-utility incurred by paying Jack equals her marginal utility from getting the product; meanwhile, Jack sells a quantity such that his marginal utility from the sale, that is, his marginal revenue (which is the utility he gets from the money he made from the last unit sold) equals his marginal dis-utility, or marginal cost. Now, the problem with this, to which we alluded in the previous section, is that when Jack is competing with other sellers for customers like Jill, he cannot know what his marginal revenue will be *unless he knows what the other sellers will do* (e.g. what price they will charge, what quantity they will produce, etc.). This is the source of indeterminacy which stopped Marginalism from offering a determinate model of prices and quantities.

What does one do when one comes up against a theoretical impasse? The honest person, for example, the Austrians mentioned at the beginning of this section, admit to their theory's indeterminacy and move on. Ignorance is acknowledged and, in fact, theorised. The neoclassical economists, on the other hand, do something extraordinary: they *assume they know!* How can anyone get away with such insolence, and portray it as scientific to boot? The answer is: by an application of the most contorted logic! First, the neoclassicist asks us to imagine that Jack is just a tiny drop in a vast ocean. Compared to the sector's total output, his output is minute, minuscule, insignificant. Thus, none of his competitors cares about how much output he produces. Whichever level he achieves, it will be like a single grain in a huge silo. So, Jack's competitors do not even bother to predict his output.

This is fine. Most of us are but specks of dust in the wider scheme of things. But then the neoclassicist asks us to take things one step further. To imagine that *no competitor is interested in what any other competitor does*, as each is just as pathetically unimportant as Jack. In this vision, the market is a tranquil archipelago of lone *empires of indifference*; of isolated buyers and sellers in which no one has the power to affect the price and, indeed, no one is remotely concerned with anything anyone else does. Each takes the price that the market sets as a given and no one needs to think twice about what others think that one thinks that… With prices treated as manna from heaven (or from the market's mysterious ways), the *equimarginal principle* is back in business: Jack and Jill take the market-given price and simply select the quantity that sets their marginal utility equal to their marginal dis-utility. Then the market, *as if* providentially, ensures that *that* price is the one clearing the market, that is the price that teases out of firms an output level that is just what is needed to satisfy demand (at that price).[47] It is called *perfect competition* and it is a model, or narrative, that underpins every aspect of neoclassical economics.

Shakespeare's *Macbeth* became king by murdering, however reluctantly, the incumbent and then, famously, adding crime upon crime in a desperate, and ultimately futile, bid to stay afloat. Neoclassical economics' story is not too dissimilar. Once it had pushed intellectually honest Marginalists out of the limelight, its long list of successive crimes against common sense helped it reproduce its discursive power. Its initial transgression was (see previous paragraph) the enlistment of *perfect competition* for the purpose of ridding its models of real rivalry between competitors, and thus for determining prices and quantities. It was not enough. The discursive power it furnished was soon to wither at the hands of three challenges to its persuasiveness.

First, a query appeared about the coherence of perfect competition in the presence of *economies of scale*. Second, there was the question of how prices change when preferences or technologies shift. Third, and most threatening, was the concern about how prices are set in a multi-sector economy. On each occasion, neoclassicism added a major offence against common sense to its initial transgression in order to see off the challenges.

The *first challenge*, relating to *economies of scale*, was quite devastating in itself.[48] Take a sector with strong returns to scale; for example, electricity generation. When in embryonic form, the costs of setting up a grid are enormous. But as the grid grows, the cost of plugging an extra house or business to the network declines fast. It is not hard to see why in such industries it is impossible even to imagine *perfect competition*. Since size matters, little insignificant Jack cannot last long in such a sector, for his costs would be cripplingly high and Jill would rather she used candles than pay him for electricity. It is, indeed, not hard mathematically to show that in sectors characterised by economies of scale (e.g. cars, telecommunications, airlines), a small number of firms will trump the rest and a natural oligopoly (if not monopoly) will emerge. And since in such markets it is impossible to argue that sellers lack any capacity to influence price, the indeterminacy regarding prices and quantities cannot even be assumed away. Neoclassicism's response? *To shrug its shoulders and move on assuming that there are no economies of scale. Anywhere!*

The *second challenge* combined powerfully with the third to blow a gigantic hole in neoclassicism's armour. Neoclassicists set up a model capitalism featuring many *perfectly competitive* markets each at a state of rest or equilibrium. Suppose now that, beginning with such a miraculously harmonious state of rest, something changes. For example, Jill's desire for tea rises and she goes slightly off peanut butter. The initial equilibrium will be destabilised. At first, the demand for tea will rise, ever so slightly, and the demand for peanut butter fall. One would think that the price of tea must now rise and that of peanut butter decline, reflecting the new relative scarcities and marginal utilities. Will equilibrium be restored and, if so, what will the new prices be? It is not hard to see how tough this question is.

Multi-market economies are notorious for the interconnections between their constituent markets. When the price of tea edges upward, the overall demand for tea will decline and so should the demand for complementary goods, for example, milk, sugar. At the same time, the fall in the price of peanut butter will reduce the demand for its substitutes (e.g. marmalade or honey) and boost the demand for bread. The chain reaction is potentially endless and penetrates all sorts of different markets (including specialised labour markets where, for example, the demand for the labour of workers in peanut plantations will subside). Will it end in some new economy-wide equilibrium? Which prices will be left standing if and when the dust settles?

At first, the Marginalists who looked at this problem hoped that some mathematical fix could provide answers to the question of how prices adjust towards a new General Equilibrium. We now know that no such fix can be had; that it is not merely a hard problem to crack mathematically but that it is impossible. The first to suspect so was Léon Walras (first mentioned in Box 6.5). In his 1874 *Elements of Pure Economics*,[49] Walras conceded defeat but also managed to snatch a famous theoretical victory from its jaws. He proposed the following thought experiment in order to help us understand how equilibrium prices might be calculated for each product in each market.

Suppose that all potential buyers and all potential sellers of each good are online, each in complete isolation from everyone else. A computer program (perhaps the *Overlord Program* from Chapter 4)[50] sends an email to all with a price for every good. Their job is to think carefully and send one email each back listing the quantity of every good that they want to buy or sell at the specified prices (recall the *exchange and mart* notice boards in Radford's POW

Box 6.16 Thou canst not stir a flower without troubling of a star

This verse by Francis Thompson (1859–1907) was quoted by J.R. Hicks in his 1934 article entitled 'Léon Walras' on the occasion of celebrating one hundred years from Walras' birth. Hicks is using it as an allegory for Walras' grappling with the way a small change in some preference or production technique can destabilise the whole edifice of market prices everywhere.

camp, Section 6.7). The computer program then compiles all this information (a simple addition) and ends up with data on total demand and total supply for each good *given the list of prices it has specified*. Then, the program sends a fresh email to everyone with new revised prices that it computes by slightly reducing the price of the goods whose supply exceeded demand and *vice versa*. This process continues until, one hopes, the program hits upon a list of prices such that demand equals supply for all goods.[51] Then and only then do the sellers send their goods to a central warehouse from which they are dispatched to the buyers, *amazon. com*-like. Walras defines this catalogue of final prices as an economy's General Equilibrium.

There are two important features of the above procedure that we need to note. First, it is entirely consistent with the neoclassical notion of *perfect competition*, in which Jack and Jill choose their quantities given a certain price over which they exercise no control whatsoever. Here too, buyers and sellers receive a list of prices, which they have no way of influencing, and must choose their quantities based on those computer- (or god-) generated prices *as if* they are alone in the whole universe. Second, no real time is allowed in this analysis. To see that real time is absent, revisit the rules of the 'game': in each round, the program sent its list of prices and the agents replied with their chosen quantities *given those prices*. Then the program revised the price list and had another go at balancing the demand for and supply of each product. However, *the program did not allow any actual trading until the final price list was compiled*. For if sales were allowed before a General Equilibrium was discovered by means of this algorithm, the poor program would never have a chance of discovering it![52]

The fact that convergence to the General Equilibrium takes time to achieve, as the program keeps sending fresh emails with revised prices, does not mean that *real time* is allowed to unfold. In an actual economy, trading is taking place in *real time* all the time. Shops and consumers do not wait until demand and supply are harmonised everywhere before they can trade with one another. Recall that this was precisely *how* equilibrium came about in the POW camp of Section 6.7. Indeed, in the real world, *the trading that goes on before the equilibrium is reached is the reason why equilibrium is reached*, as buyers and sellers alter their own decisions (how much to buy or sell, what price to advertise at, etc.) to take advantage of the imbalances between demand and supply. Arbitrage would not help steer a market to equilibrium otherwise.

Now, Walras' rule that no trading is allowed until the General Equilibrium is established (because, if it does, no equilibrium *can* be theoretically established in his model) is analytically equivalent to an admission of *defeat*: his analysis cannot handle real time or, equivalently, it cannot model the way in which trading determines the path leading to equilibrium prices. But notice the victory that was salvaged from the wreck: suddenly, neoclassical economists acquired the keys to a sparkling new narrative device which afforded them the opportunity of filling up countless blackboards and pages with equations depicting a list of prices capable of equilibrating every single market on the planet, if imposed somehow (in a static world, of course).

The fact that these prices are meaningless outside the context of a world where the space–time continuum is condensed into a point the size of a proton[53] made no difference. Neoclassical economics had achieved closure by means of advanced mathematics. With the *lure of algebra*[54] and the *appeal to closure* in the bag, all that neoclassicism was missing (before it satisfied the third part of the triptych that makes the *Inherent Error*'s irresistible) was the *political utility* of its proposed determinism. Luckily for neoclassicism, the magnitude and vivacity of that utility was, in fact, such that neoclassicism's *Inherent Error* produced a great triumph and, thus, has managed to leave an indelible blot on Western Civilisation's thinking about itself.

As we saw in previous chapters, capitalism's champions have, since Adam Smith, claimed that it is a *natural*, not a particular, *system*. Critics such as Marx objected, suggesting instead that there is nothing natural about capitalism, that it is, in fact, a pretty unnatural and irrational way of organising life on this planet. Yet, the two 'camps', prior to the rise of neoclassicism, could converse freely on the matter, based on an assessment of really existing capitalism. But once neoclassicism came to the fore, through the works of Walras, Edgeworth, Pareto and their twentieth-century successors (see Box 6.16), capitalism disappeared from view and debate about it withered. Instead, all that was left were models featuring bundles of utility preferences (the 'persons'); bundles of measurable productive factors (the 'firms'); and prices consistent with a naturalistic 'equilibrium' between the choices of these two types of 'bundles'. What kind of serious debate on capitalism could this new framework support? None, is the answer.

By the beginning of the twentieth century, the neoclassical method had dominated academic political economics almost completely. This domination translated into a decree that 'self-respecting' economists approach capitalism as a 'natural' system. Consequently, in the decades that followed, up to 1929, the wake of neoclassical economics left behind it a profession busily churning out technical studies of fictitious markets; studies which acted as mere *diversions* from the real task of studying capitalism. So, when the Great Depression broke out in 1929, the economics profession was caught unawares (exactly as it was in 2008). So startled were economists that they tried to ignore it. Paul Samuelson, possibly the greatest post-war neoclassicist, recalled as a freshman in Chicago in 1935 that 'everything I was taught and I read disagreed with what I saw outside the window of the university'.[55] It could not have been otherwise. For the 'beauty' of neoclassical political economy was precisely that: its model of the world was so far removed from capitalism that it shielded economics from any engagement with the capitalist economy.

Evidently, the utility of this feat is immense for those with an interest in keeping capitalism out of serious theoretical scrutiny. Capitalism appeared in the economists' eyes as a complex entity no less natural than Creation had appeared in Leibniz's imagination (see Box 6.16 below). At a time of fledgling trade unions and powerful political movements challenging capitalism's efficiency and desirability from Chicago to St Petersburg, the best defence of the realm came in the form of countless bright young economists being quick-marched headlong into academic obscurantism and socio-economic irrelevance. Instead of acting as the *avant garde* that would prise out the truth regarding the causes and nature of the crisis about to hit humanity in 1929, political economics had been turned into a form of secular religion; a Homeric lotus plant; another example of *Condorcet's Secret*; the ultimate *blue pill*.

Then, 1929 happened. Just like in 2008, the world realised, to its consternation, that the one 'science' whose remit it was to shield society from such calamities had proved the Greatest Crisis' keenest handmaiden.

6.12 Epilogue

Capitalism's admirers and detractors agree on one thing: no other development in history (save perhaps for the meteorite that ended the dinosaurs' reign) has whipped up a tidal wave of comparable flux. Following the transition to capitalist market societies, 'all that is solid melts into air';[56] all that was tranquil turned into a seething magma brewing perpetual upheaval. In that inexhaustible surge of *creative destruction*,[57] the use of calculus was inevitable. The mathematics that provided the analytical tools for mapping out change, and shifting our thinking from the statics of Euclid to Kepler's elliptical dance of the planets and to the equations of streaming fluids, was not going to be denied its chance to tell a story about the oscillating prices and quantities of market societies.

From the moment Adam Smith invoked some *invisible hand* that would counter-intuitively bring harmony where the massive forces of demand and supply cannot be contained by the *Collective Will*, the writing was on the wall: calculus would sooner or later emerge as the economists' basic tool just as surely as it had surfaced in Isaac Newton's mind as a tool for answering basic questions about the manner in which fantastic gravitational forces cancelled each other out to produce a beautiful solar system.

Now, the classical political economists saw themselves as Newtonians, but without the calculus. Temporal change was their prime concern and economic modelling was all about working out the requirements for sustainable growth. Ricardo's corn model and Marx's schemas of reproduction were studies in the mechanics of never-ending sectoral change, while their conception of a positive profit rate (kept equal across the various sectors by perpetual migration of people and machines towards the most profitable sector) was that of the economy's motive power; the force that could propel it into the future. Why did they utilise no calculus? Because their idea of a growing capitalist economy was utterly compatible with linear mathematics. Based on the labour theory of value, they had no need for utility differentials (i.e. for infinitesimal differences) as determinants of prices and could build their growth models by assuming fixed proportions (e.g. it takes two farm workers to drive a cow-pulled plough and three such ploughs to cultivate a field that yields 500 bushels of wheat).

The sardonic irony of political economics is that the mathematics of infinitely variable change, that is calculus, was put to work by Marginalism in a manner that obliterated temporal change altogether. But then again, the very origins of calculus are stigmatised by a dispute which, in a sense, foreshadowed this strange development. While Isaac Newton created calculus to study temporal change, his German contemporary Gottfried Leibniz crafted an identical mathematics for freezing time out of the analysis of change. Box 6.17 tells the story of the two great scholars who invented calculus independently but who conceived it in violently contradictory ways.

Marginalism can claim a first in bringing calculus to political economics. Its first bold step was to ditch all theories of value and replace them with a theory of price determination which associates prices with *utility-on-the-margin*. '(T)he marginal approach', wrote Piero Sraffa,[58] 'requires attention to be focused on change, for without change either in the scale of an industry or in the "proportions of the factors of production" there can be neither marginal product nor marginal costs'. Indeed, no change, no marginal utility and, thus, no *equimarginal principle* and no Marginalist theory of prices.

However, marginal change does not require time, as Leibniz had so vividly demonstrated. For he devised calculus as a tool for studying the geometry and organisation of timeless spaces, reflecting his religious belief in an omniscient God for whom time held no secrets. Unlike Newton, who projected everything against the background of the constantly shifting sands of time, Leibniz studied the way that one quantity varied with another within the universal mosaic cast by the Almighty. This is precisely what Marginalist economists also did: they pitted Jill's utility against her consumption of cookies and hypothesised about the manner in which the former changed with respect to the latter, rather than with respect to time.

There was a reason why most Marginalists, though not all, sided with Leibniz and not Newton, one that had nothing to do, at least initially, with any religious bias. In principle, all Marginalists were ever so keen to model temporal economic change; indeed, to this day many of their young begin their careers with ambitious plans to do exactly that.[59] Alas, as Section 6.10 argued, time proved deeply hostile and unaccommodating to Marginalism's

Box 6.17 The two faces of calculus: Newton's *Flux* versus Leibniz's *Mosaic*

The feud between Isaac Newton (1643–1727) and Gottfried Wilhelm Leibniz (1646–1716), over who could legitimately claim to have invented calculus, was as acrimonious as it is well researched.[1] One explanation is that the two men could not see eye to eye because of cultural, temperamental and political differences.[2] However, there is another explanation that is of greater significance from a social science perspective: both men were heavily into theology but their theologies were at odds. For Newton, God created the world and immediately placed it under the dominion of temporal change. The universe, thus, comprises *fluids* or objects in constant *flux* under the crushing influence of gargantuan gravitational forces. God is all powerful, gravity is his force of choice and the fixed time–space dimensions his canvas.

Leibniz, on the other hand, had a different interpretation of God's greatness: rather than all-powerful or omnipotent, Leibniz's God was extremely smart, omniscient. Thus, God could foresee everything that would happen at the moment of Creation. It was as if the world were his wind-up toy and all he had to do was wind it up and watch it do its 'thing' without the need to intervene. For if he did have to intervene, as the doctrine of Providence was widely interpreted within Catholicism and Lutheranism, then it must have been the case that the original design was less than perfect. In this scheme, time is not of great significance; at least not more so than the other dimensions (e.g. length, width, depth) since the great architect in the sky can see through it just as well as a terrestrial builder can discern the straight edges of one of his walls.

In contrast, Newton felt that God's greatness is confirmed by the harmony that he can extract from gigantic forces that only he could have conjured up. Interestingly, Newton used the word *flux* interchangeably to denote change and time which, in his thinking, were the only intransigent givens in God's universe. Creation happened when God chose to set the world in motion and to unleash forces that only he could tame. Providence, which comes in the form of occasional corrective interventions, was, in this sense, confirmation of God's power and of his divine penchant for stretching his own infinite limits.

These theological differences affected the two men's mathematics immeasurably. Newton began thinking about calculus in the 1680s in the context of his astronomical endeavours: how can we define the motion of a planet at a given instant? How might we mathematically represent the time and trajectory through which a planet has been moving? Johannes Keppler (1571–1630) had already shown that the radius linking a planet to the sun sweeps up equal areas in equal lengths of time and, for this reason, the planets orbit around the sun along elliptical paths. Newton set himself the task of working out mathematically the precise area contained by a section of an ellipse *so as to calculate the time it takes a planet to cover a certain distance.* Standard geometry was not helpful in this regard. Differential calculus, which Newton called the *Science of Fluxions*, was the technique he invented in order to answer these questions regarding *rates of actual temporal change.* Thus, he discovered *differentiation* (by which he computed the direction of the orbiting planet) before moving to *integration* (the computation of the area of the ellipsis along which the planet travelled).

Leibniz invented the same kind of mathematics but in a completely different context and in accordance with his own theology. Consider a great medieval cathedral and focus on one of its magnificent arches. What is the area enclosed by that (non-linear) arch? That was Leibniz's starting point, from which he went on independently (from Newton) to invent calculus too. Just like Newton, he was effectively interested in computing the precise area enclosed by a non-linear curve. His method was to splice it up in many infinitesimally tiny areas (pixels we might call them today) and then add them together. The result of this aggregation was integration and then its opposite (i.e. the working out of the arch's equation given an estimate of the area enclosed by it) differentiation. Technically speaking, Leibniz invented integration first before proceeding to differentiation whereas Newton's discovery started with differentiation and then moved to integration. Alas, their difference was far weightier than one of order.

While Newton and Leibniz, in the end, invented the same calculus (albeit using different symbols), since they were studying problems of identical geometrical structure, it did not look the same to them. For Newton was studying a solar system in perpetual motion caused by opposing gravitational fields while Leibniz was measuring the area of a static surface impervious to temporal change. If Newton's well documented loathing of Leibniz was truly based on intellectual differences, it was because Leibniz was refusing to acknowledge the centrality of *flux* and *time* in God's design, insisting instead on aggregating static bits of area. As for Leibniz, he considered Newton's obsession with the metaphysics of time a sort of denial of God's infinite intelligence.

Notes
1 See for instance Hall (1980).
2 At the time of the feud, the King of Hanover, who had hitherto been Leibniz's employer, was about to be crowned King of England. Leibniz was as keen to ensure his King's continued favouritism as Newton was eager to ingratiate himself with the new King of England. This was a clash that Newton won hands down.

theoretical aspirations. At that point, Marginalism split into two tendencies. Section 6.11 presented our account of this split and we do not wish to repeat it here, save for a fleeting mention of Austrian thinkers, such as von Hayek, who never fell for the neoclassical turn and consistently treated with disdain the Leibnizian calculus. However, the bulk of Marginalists could not resist the neoclassical turn. One of neoclassicism's greatest testified towards the end of his life: 'For several years I worked with a zeal, tenacity and resourcefulness that modesty will not allow me to describe. And to no avail. The shrewdest hypothesis was contradicted by evidence, the most brilliant conjecture crashed upon the shoal of inconsistency'.[60] These elegant words sum up the feeling of many honest neoclassicists who attempted the Sisyphean task of harnessing real time within models of foresightful customers, enterprising capitalists and work-averse workers. One reason why Austrians like von Hayek were feted by the economics profession in the 1980s was this kind of feeling of resignation amongst neoclassicism's grandees.

In this light, Marginalism's embracement of calculus along the lines penned by Leibniz was imposed on its practitioners, rather than an act of free intellectual or ideological choice. The smarter Marginalists could no doubt foresee, even before embarking on their analytical journey, what a source of constant irritation time would prove, at all levels of analysis. In terms of this book's overarching claim about the *Inherent Error* at the heart of economic theory, the use of calculus gave rise to a new metamorphosis of the *Inherent Error*: To tell a consistent story about price determination in a multi-market economy along the Marginalist lines of differential calculus, time had to be dropped. Marginalists faced a dilemma just as terrible as that encountered by Marx before them: either analyse a single-person model economy unfolding in real time (a type of Robinson Crusoe world in which the same person is employer, worker, consumer, producer, investor, etc.[61]) or analyse a multi-market, multi-person market system that is frozen in time.

This chapter began with a summary of Marx's conundrum – how, in order to keep *capital* as the unique force running through capitalism and explaining everything in its wake, he had to leave out of his analysis all other forces, such as *market and social power*. By contrast, Marginalists, at least those of them who insisted on 'closing' their models, had to bar all type of Newtonian forces from their analysis. This meant that Leibnizian geometry was all they were left with. To see this better, consider the type of theory they were getting involved with: a theory mapping a uni-directional, one-way, trajectory from (a) preferences and constraints to (b) actions and choices. Naturally, for such a theory to have the remotest chance to produce determinate conclusions (or predictions), preferences must be constant enough.

Suppose, for instance, that Jill's preferences over fish and meat change all the time, possibly in response to sensations felt every time she tastes fish and meat. Suddenly not only are the choices determined by the preferences but the preferences are also influenced by the choices. The theory is paralysed instantly by the breakdown of the one-way system (from Jill's preferences to her actions) and can yield no conclusion about what Jill will actually do *unless we feed it with precise information on how Jill's eating of fish and meat affects her preferences over fish and meat*. Moreover, if Jill's preferences are mimetic, and she is influenced by what Jack is doing (in ways that go beyond the effect of Jack's choices on the prices that Jill must pay), again her preferences are in flux once time is allowed to move along its temporal vector and the Marginalist model demands a precise formula by which to link Jack's actions to Jill's preferences. Given that this information is inaccessible to even the best psychoanalyst, it is incontrovertible that Marginalism breaks down the moment preferences change in real time and under the influence of experience.

Marginalists 'dealt' with this problem by assuming that Jill's utility does not change in time.[62] In their textbooks they refused to say so explicitly, hiding behind lesser assumptions, for example, that preferences stay still within the timeframe during which the theory's predictions of her purchases are current. But this was not enough. When *all* the deleterious effects of time (some of which were discussed in Section 6.10) are taken onboard, it is not difficult to see why time had to be expelled altogether; how the dominance of Marginalist political economics brought to the fore the full weight of Leibnizian economic calculus that students of economics must now endure the world over. Indeed, the textbook theory of both consumer and producer choices is no more than a Leibnizian study of convex utility spaces.[63]

With temporal change ostracised from political economics, and an Empire of Preference ensconced at the heart of its analysis, neoclassicism came to reflect Leibniz's theology for purely secular, self-interested, opportunistic reasons. What was the tipping point beyond which Marginalism rushed into neoclassicism's embrace? When did the failure to take the measure of temporal variation motivate Marginalists to turn their considerable energies to the task of 'closing' the entire menu of prices and quantities by ostracising time? Such paradigmatic shifts occur at multiple points in time and usually involve different scholars in different places. But for the purposes of our narrative, we shall answer the question by focusing on two French Marginalists (first mentioned in Box 6.5): Cournot and Walras. Our story will be that Marginalism bore neoclassicism when Walras' project defeated that of Cournot.

Cournot was convinced that the explanatory cart should never be put before the explanatory horse; that we must first understand how particular prices *move* before we establish the definitive economy-wide catalogue of prices which, if they prevailed, would produce *equilibrium*. Walras sympathised with Cournot but understood that the old man was championing an impossible task: no model of foresightful agents competing in real time could ever be 'closed'. This was a hunch that we now know as fact, courtesy of post-war Game Theory.[64] So, Walras chose to cut to the chase: to compute the General Equilibrium prices by means of a method that guarantees the impossibility of even discussing the way that the market mechanism might engender these prices. His was a flight from temporal variation to a purely Leibnizian construction: *neoclassical economics*.[65] The bulk of the Marginalists followed him. Edgeworth had already begun moving in the same direction. Pareto provided important principles along the way. Marshall dithered but in the end did little to stem the tide.

By the 1920s, Leibniz's conquest of the queen of the social sciences was complete. Economics' *Inherent Error* combined nicely with Marginalism's ambitions to deliver neoclassicism; a type of economics which exhausts its intellectual capacities in search of harmonious states (i.e. prices consistent with a General Equilibrium); an analytical project which assumed that everything can be known in advance of any real action; a kind of equilibrium that can just float in a timeless universe; a world where the troublesome problem of temporal convergence has withered by an act of divine will. Its power was based on the lure of its calculus, the appeal of the Leibnizian 'closure' of its models and, last but not least, the immense political utility of its determinism. Through its lens, capitalism and its market mechanism appeared no different from Leibniz's vision of God's creation: a wind-up toy that the Creator sets off and then does not even bother watching since its temporal workings are, in his Grand Plan, predetermined. Perhaps it would not be too far-fetched to regard neoclassical political economics as the nearest thing to a Calvinist utility calculus.

Nothing good could come out of this flight from historical time, except some well-remunerated careers and a plethora of mathematically laden arguments against the critics of capitalism. One of the old Marginalists, Cournot, arguably the very first Marginalist, had predicted the dire results of Marginalism's propensity to turn neoclassical. We know this because of letters he exchanged with the young Walras many years later.[66] Walras had written to Cournot to express his appreciation of the old man's contribution to his own thinking and in order to portray their different approaches as two sides of the same coin.[67] Cournot politely begged to differ. First, he complimented his younger correspondent by suggesting that their difference 'is a question of method. Mine seems faster, yours goes at a slower pace, which suggests it goes at a surer pace.' But further down he could not contain his consternation:

> But I fear that your curves... will lead to pure *laissez faire*, that is to say, for the national economy to deforestation of land, and for the international economy to the overwhelming of the plebeian races by a privileged race in conformity to Mr Darwin's theory.

How foresighted Cournot was (unlike the capitalists in his own model)! Walras' economic analysis, unbeknownst to him, became the foundation for an ideological attack on *any* form

Box 6.18 Calvin, Leibniz, Walras and… Voltaire: Neoclassical economics as a political theology

John Calvin (1509–64) was an influential French protestant theologian made famous by his original interpretation of the scriptures and, significantly, his striking tenet of predestination. The idea was simple: if God is omniscient, nothing we do can surprise him. *Ergo*, our deeds are transparent to his mind's eye even before our birth. If so, a God determined to separate those who will be admitted through Heaven's pearly gates from the rest for us, for whom unceasing damnation beckons, will have made his selection before our birth. Taken to its logical conclusion, this thought leads Calvinists to the belief that our lives are predestined at the singular moment of Creation.

Calvinist predestinarians have a point that resonates powerfully with that of Leibniz (see the previous box). Consider, for instance, Heaven. According to the scriptures, Heaven can be thought of as the lack of scarcity. When we pass through its gates, we leave behind all our (inner or outer) conflicts over scarce resources. Heaven is a scarcity-free zone. But how could this be? Theologians have traditionally invoked an infinite time horizon in order to help us imagine a world without scarcity. Facing an infinite future, Heaven's dwellers can expect eventually to experience anything they crave and, thus, have no reason to feel stress or experience any sense of lack. Or have they? We think they still have cause to crave. For while one may hope to do anything one wishes for *sooner or later*, one could not, such that something would have to be given up so that something else can be chosen. Thus, do everything at once. For instance, one could not climb a mountain *and* read Shakespeare simultaneously. At each point in time, there would be a trade-off and a choice would thus have to be made; scarcity survives even in an infinite Heaven. Surely, this contradicts the idea of Heaven as the absence of constraints and as a scarcity-free vacuum.[1]

So, for Heaven to be characterised by *a radical absence of scarcity*, it is necessary that Heavenly time is quite different to the type of time that we are used to, i.e. to the sort of time that Newton had in mind. Put differently, Heavenly time must be closer to Leibniz's conception than to Newtonian time, which ticks along an infinitely long but also infinitesimally thin time line. Indeed, to allow us to do everything at once, and thus genuinely free us from scarcity, Heavenly time must be infinite also in 'width'. In such a Heaven, there would be no need for trade-offs in the sense that one could do an infinite number of things at once and forever. In another sense, at every instant there would be an infinite amount of time. Then, indeed, there would be no scarcity whatsoever.

Interestingly, once time has been made infinitely 'wide', there seems no good reason to retain its length. If Heavenly time were infinite in width, then (we have already surmised) the heavenly dwellers could have unlimited experiences simultaneously. Why would it then be necessary (even desirable) that time's length is also infinite? An infinite width should, clearly, suffice. A better conclusion is that of Leibniz: in a Heaven were scarcity is wholly absent, time loses its dimensions. It can, indeed, be thought as a single point with infinite mass. And since Heaven happens to be God's realm, God's mind does not think temporally. His creation, the universe we inhabit, may appear to us as structured along a time–space continuum, but to the Almighty it appears as a speck of dust that he created for the reason that artists do things: for the sheer pleasure of it. In this context, Leibniz's deployment of calculus to work out the geometry of the cosmos, while largely disregarding its temporal dimension, makes perfect theological sense.

Returning to worldly matters, Calvin's idea that God had determined, prior to Creation itself, who amongst his creatures would be saved and who damned, armed Calvinists with a compelling drive that gave their theology a galvanic force that strengthened trade, bolstered manufacturing, influenced politics, accelerated capitalism's march and, last, shaped neoclassical political economics.[2] When Walras froze time, in his famous mind experiment, whose purpose was to imagine the set of prices that would bring about a General Equilibrium, he was subconsciously ushering in a form of Calvinist political economics, expressed in the language of Leibniz's mathematics. The difference, of course, is that Walras and his fellow Marginalists had allowed themselves to fall into this camp because of the difficulty in incorporating Newtonian time in their Marginalist models, possibly against Walras' socialist-leaning politics. While Leibniz chose his mathematics to be in accordance with his theology, Walras and the neoclassicists fell into theirs as a result of the unholy alliance of economics' *Inherent Error* and the analytical-*cum*-ideological imperatives of Marginalism.

Meanwhile, another Frenchman, Voltaire (1694–1778) had hit the nail on the head: once you assume an omniscient God, absurdity is the inevitable outcome. Having spent a couple of years as an exile in Britain, Voltaire had come to appreciate Newton's version of calculus and optics. Back in France, and while his mistress Émilie le Tonnelier de Breteuil, the Marquise du Châtelet, was busily translating Newton's *Principia* into French, Voltaire wrote his masterpiece *Candide, ou l'Optimisme* (Candide, or Optimism), first published in 1759. It was a delightful satire of Leibniz' view of a world created in a time-vacuum by an omniscient God. The story features Pangloss, young Candide's tutor, who appears as an enthusiastic disciple of Leibniz. Voltaire pours oodles of scorn on Pangloss in order to ridicule Leibniz's absurd conflation of cause and effect, the inevitable result of denying Newtonian time its true significance in order to retain a belief in an omniscient God.

More than a century later, yet another Frenchman, Antoine Augustine Cournot (see Box 6.5) was to imply a similar critique against Walras and the direction towards neoclassical economics that he was pointing to (see below for Cournot's devastating letter to Walras). What Cournot seems to be implying is that, once you assume an omniscient market, political economics becomes an obscurantist discipline that is fraught with inconsistency and produces nothing useful except to those who are keen to shield capitalism from rational scrutiny.

Notes
1   The notion of scarcity of time was introduced by the precursor of Marginalist economics Hermann Heinrich Gossen (1854) but it has dropped out of sight for at least 120 years.
2   The most famous book on Calvinism's role in fomenting the rise of capitalism was Max Weber's (1905) *The Protestant Ethic and 'The Spirit of Capitalism'*. For a more recent historical account see MacCulloch (2009).

of regulation or political interference with the workings of capitalism. Others also believed that the market knows best. But it was this neoclassical depiction of a multi-sectoral market economy in perfectly static harmony (or General Equilibrium) that provided the dominant mantra. While unworkable as a narrative of change, of even a source of insight on how an increase in the demand for coffee affects coffee prices in real time, its political utility was tremendous. It gave the *Inherent Error* its most sinister guise but, at once, it upgraded *Condorcet's Secret* to a mighty defender of the realm. For once, neoclassicism had taken over from both classical political economics and early Marginalism, the grim truth about the true determinants of our subjective beliefs, and actions dropped out of our collective radar screen. We could no longer recognise the actions which, like a riot of small rivers, converge in real time into oceanic social forces inexorably working towards both growth and instability; wealth and wasted potential for alleviating suffering; great innovations and environmental degradation; and, last but not least, new capacities and the steady withering of our substantive freedom.

Humanity was always torn between staring painfully into discomfiting truths and luxuri-ating in blissful ignorance. The *blue pill* always stood for our understandable readiness to be lulled by the comforting explanations; to turn a blind eye to systemic failures; to believe at a time of steady growth that crises are a thing of the past; or to think, during a crisis like today's, that the problem is not capitalism itself but the sinfulness of bankers, the over-reliance on complex financial instruments, the irresponsibility of home owners and the sloppiness of regulators.

Cournot's hunch, at a remarkably early stage in the development of contemporary capi-talism, was that Walras' type of political economics was to become the most potent, the most dangerous, *blue pill*; that it would lull the world with a Panglossian portrayal of capitalism and would silence the Cassandras, whose tragedy was that the more sensible their warnings the less discernible their voices. Meanwhile, the surer the economics profession was becom-ing of capitalism's Panglossian properties, the nearer it edged to the *Great Convulsion*. A mere 19 years after Walras' death, the world was to do something that shattered the Leibnizian portrait of a harmonious capitalism. The year 1929 was but a first rude awaken-ing. Cournot's *j'accuse* to Walras continued to resonate through history well beyond the 1930s. It is just as poignant now, in our post-2008 era, shedding precious light on the awful confluence of environmental and economic crises to have hit humanity. It qualifies as one of history's greatest, and least known, prophecies.

Addendum to Chapter 6

Leibniz and the 'invention' of General Equilibrium

by George Krimpas

Leibniz is the inventor of *pre-established harmony*, the origin of modern General Equilibrium theory. Yet his sin is lighter than that of the radical neoclassics who gave life to the Walrasian project: his world had *telos*, a sort of timeless yet directed dynamic which makes his ultimate Panglossian conclusion all the more intriguing, if not plainly suspect. Ever worried and inse-cure, a perennial place server, Leibniz hid his eventually most popular (though not best) essay in the care of his gullible patrons: *La Monadologie*, written in French (1714); he prob-ably did not believe in it. The text is composed in short numbered articles, in all ninety of them. Given the claim stated above, it is tempting and may be useful, just before dipping into it, to freshly re-imbibe Debreu (1959) or, perhaps best, Koopmans (1957). The *Monadology* then exudes an eerie feeling of *déjà vu*, thus (the *italics* are original, **bold** and (.) are added):

1. La Monade, [Unity] dont nous parlerons ici, n'est qu'une **substance** *simple*, sans parties, qui entre dans les composés. [*The Monad, of which we shall here speak, is nothing but a simple substance, which enters into compounds*].
2. Et **il faut** qu'il y ait des substances simples, **puisqu'**il y a des composés: car le composé n'est qu'un *aggregatum* des simples. [*And there must be simple substances, since there are compounds; for a compound is nothing but a collection or* aggregatum *of simple things.* (Comment: Notably, the Monad's logical existence is here **deduced** from the as yet undefined 'aggregatum')].
3. Or la, ou il n'y a point de **parties,** il n'y a ni **étendue**, ni **figure,** ni **divisibilité** possible. [*Now where there are no parts, there can be neither extension nor form [figure] nor divisibility.* (Comment: These Monads are the real atoms of nature and, in a word, the elements of things. All it gets as positive predicate is '*simple* substance')].

Wherefrom do these Monads come, by what *process* do they turn up, or down? From no-where and no-how:

4. Il n y'a aussi point de **dissolution** à craindre, et il n'y a aucune manière concevable par laquelle une substance simple [the Monad] puisse **périr** naturellement. [*No dissolution of these elements need be feared, and there is no conceivable way in which a simple substance can be destroyed by natural means*].
5. ... il n'y en a [aussi] aucune manière concevable par laquelle une substance simple [the Monad] puisse **commencer** naturellement, puisqu'elle ne saurait être formée par composition [*...there is no conceivable way in which a simple substance can come into being by natural means, since it cannot be formed by the combination of parts (composition)*].

So the Monad is just 'there', it cannot 'dissolve' or get itself 'going', there is no before or after to it, it is just is-ness and a simple one at that. Thus:

6. Ainsi, ..., les Monades ne sauraient commencer, ni finir, que tout d'un coup, ..., commencer que par **création** et finir par **annihilation** [*Thus ... a Monad can only come into being or come to an end all at once; ... it can come into being only by creation and come to an end only by annihilation ...* (Comment: they are 'here' or 'not here' by creation or annihilation – whence the necessity of a creator or annihilator)].
7. Il n'y a pas moyen aussi d'expliquer, comment une Monade puisse être altérée, ou changée dans son **intérieur** par quelque autre créature; puisqu'on n'y saurait rien transposer, ni concevoir en elle aucun mouvement interne ... les Monades **n'ont point de fenêtres,** par lesquelles quelque chose y puisse entrer ou sortir [*... there is no way of explaining how a Monad can be altered in quality or internally changed by any other created thing; since it is impossible to change the place of anything in it or to conceive in it any internal motion ... The Monads have no windows, through which anything could come in or go out. ...* (Comment: The Monad is an ironclad windowless 'fortress-unto-itself, nothing can go in – or out – for now, but wait!)].

Creation and annihilation are then clearly 'exogenous', the no-windows condition ensures that the Monad's, so to speak, 'integrity', is sacrosanct. But to what **purpose** – indeed, **whose** purpose, 'are' they, if they just 'are'? They must be capable of 'something', thus:

8. Cependant il faut que les Monades aient quelques **qualités,** autrement ce ne serait pas même des **êtres** [*Yet the Monads must have some qualities, otherwise they would not even be existing things. ...*(*Comment*: the Monad must be **distinguished** by some qualities, otherwise it would not even 'be')].

9. Il faut ... que chaque Monade soit **différente** de chaque autre [*Indeed, each Monad must be different from every other.....*(*Comment*: it must be **different** from another, otherwise they would be **indiscernible** from each other thus the same – and further)]:

10. ...tout être crée est sujet au **changement,** et ce changement est **continuel** dans chacune Monade [*...every created being, and consequently the created Monad, is subject to change, and further that this change is continuous in each.* (Comment: **all** created things are subject to change, so the Monad must not be just different but continuously different)].

11. Il s'ensuit que les changement naturels des Monades viennent d'un *principe interne* [*It follows from what has just been said, that the natural changes of the Monads come from an internal principle, ...* (*Comment*: an **'internal principle'**, exogenous but 'embodied' in the Monad by its creation, it is the 'governor' of the Monad's qualitative change)].

12. Il faut aussi qu'outre le **principe** du changement, il y ait un **détail** de ce qui change [*But, besides the principle of the change, there must be a particular series of changes [un detail de ce qui change], which constitutes, so to speak, the specific nature and variety of the simple substances. ...* (*Comment*: the principle of change must have something to bite on)].

13. Ce détail doit envelopper **une multitude dans l'unité,** ... par conséquent il faut que dans [la Monade] il y ait une pluralité d'**affections** et de rapports [*This particular series of changes should involve a multiplicity in the unit [unite] or in that which is simple. For, as every natural change takes place gradually, something changes and something remains unchanged; and consequently a simple substance must be affected and related in many ways, although it has no parts, ...* (*Comment*: this 'detail' is a very packed affair, no less than a 'synthesis' of the one and the many, and to make this possible the Monad must contain a **plurality of 'affections' and 'relations'**)].

Thus a lot, perhaps too much rather than too little, seems to be going on inside this mere so-simple 'being': the Monad is also in some wise a 'becoming', in what wise?

14. **L'état passager** ... dans [la Monade] n'est autre chose que ce qu'on appelle la *Perception* [*The passing condition ... in [the Monad] is nothing but what is called* Perception (Comment: **perception** then is but a fleeting thing – in mental 'time')].

15. L'**action** du principe interne qui fait le changement ou le **passage** d'une perception a une autre, peut être appelé *Appétition*: **l'appétit** parvient à des **perceptions nouvelles** [*The activity of the internal principle which produces change or passage from one perception to another may be called* Appetition. ... desire [l'appetit] ... attains to new perceptions. (Comment: time is a working dimension, there is input [appetite] and output [perception], and again and again 'continuously'; perchance there is net output or surplus hence 'growth', once again mental)].

18. On pourrait donner le nom **d'Entéléchies** a toutes les Monades créées, car elles ont une certaine perfection (ἔχουσι τὸ ἐντελές), il y'a une **suffisance** (αὐτάρκεια) qui les rend

sources de leurs actions internes et pour ainsi dire des Automates incorporels [*All simple substances or created Monads might be called Entelechies, for they have in them a certain perfection* (echousi to enteles); *they have a certain self-sufficiency* (autarkeia) *which makes them the sources of their internal activities and, so to speak, incorporeal automata.* (*Comment*: the Monads then have **purpose,** therefore **potential** toward fulfilment, they are sufficient 'own' sources of their purpose, they are self-sufficient mental 'automata'. This is important: by the continuous sequential repetition of the cycle **Appetite into Perception** their 'becoming' is led on and on – until; let us dare call this 'Maximization'].

22. Et comme tout présent état d'une substance simple est une **suite** de son état précédent, tellement que **le présent y est gros de l'avenir** [*And as every present state of a simple substance is naturally a consequence of its preceding state, in such a way that its present is big with its future.* (*Comment*: thus their 'being' is itself sequential, their present is pregnant with their future].

To repeat, at any fleeting 'moment' there is 'perception' but the action behind this lies in 'appetition' and this in turn begets 'novelty', thus the present is 'pregnant' with the future. But this brings the monad to the frontier of reason, or at least its 'imitation':

26. La **mémoire** fournit une espèce de *consécution* qui imite la **raison** [*Memory provides the soul with a kind of consecutiveness, which resembles reason...* (*Comment*: perception, though fleeting, leaves a trace, there is a 'storage unit' in the Monad, it records the past in sequential 'structured' form, this structure **'imitates' reason,** the 'laws' of which will turn up below, articles 31 and following)].

At which point Leibniz the metaphysician happily turns to logic of which he was master – but only to produce yet more metaphysics, no less than the ultimate delicate subject: the necessity and sufficiency of the **existence of God**:

31. Nos raisonnements sont fondés sur *deux grands principes* celui de la *contradiction* [*Our reasonings are grounded upon two great principles, that of contradiction, ...*]
32. Et celui de *la raison suffisante, ...,* pourquoi il en soit ainsi et non pas autrement [*And that of sufficient reason ... why it should be so and not otherwise...*]
33. Il y a aussi deux sortes de *vérités*, celles de *Raisonnement* et celles de *Fait* [there are two kinds of truth, the truth of logical inference and the truth of fact. (*Comment*: here note **the next step** carefully)]
36. ... la *raison suffisante* se doit trouver **aussi** dans les *vérités ... de fait ...* qui entrent dans la **cause finale** [*But there must also be a sufficient reason for ... truths of fact ... which go to make its final cause.* (*Comment:* the principle of sufficient reason must cover **both** truths of reason and of fact; but truths of fact 'enter' into the final cause, which is to say ultimate purpose or **telos**: it is in this way that 'teleology' provides the link between being and becoming, toward qualitative potential, and eventually the link between being and morality, thus duty, reward and punishment – which is where Candide comes in, but this is looking far ahead)].
38. Et c'est ainsi que **la dernière raison des choses** doit être dans **une substance nécessaire**: ... et c'est ce que nous appelons *Dieu* [*Thus the final reason of things must be in a necessary substance, ... and this substance we call* God (*Comment*: Thus **telos**, or final reason, **must** be based or reside in a **necessary** substance, which we call God)].

39. Or cette substance étant **une raison suffisante**; ... *il n'y a qu'un Dieu, et ce Dieu suffit* [*Now as this substance is a sufficient reason ... there is only one God, and this God is sufficient* (*Comment*: 'but this necessary substance being also sufficient', it follows that there is but one God and that this God is sufficient)].

With God thus present in the scheme of things, all looks decidedly cheerful, from everything being [almost] too small everything now is [almost] too large:

41. Dieu est absolument parfait; ... la *perfection* est absolument infinie [... *God is absolutely perfect*; ... *perfection is absolutely infinite*. (*Comment*: **perfection is infinite**, Leibniz knows well what he is talking about)].

43. Dieu est non seulement la **source** des existences, mais encore celle des **essences**, ou de ce qu'il y a de réel dans la possibilité [... *in God there is not only the source of existences but also that of essences, in so far as they are real, that is to say, the source of what is real in the possible.* (*Comment*: God being perfect guarantees that the possible may beget the real, whose name is 'essence')].

45. Dieu seul a ce privilège qu'**il faut qu'il existe s'il est possible** [*Thus God alone has this prerogative that He must necessarily exist, if He is possible.* (*Comment*: for his own **privilege** is, because of his perfection, that God must exist because he is possible; and how is he possible? – because, answers the rationalist Leibniz, perfection, like infinity, is **thinkable**)].

This being settled, what does God's **perfection** further lead to? – but to a **perfect order** in general, thus:

48. Il y a en Dieu la *Puissance*, qui est la **source** de tout, puis la *Connaissance* qui contient le **détail** des idées, et enfin la *Volonté*, qui fait les **changements** selon **le principe du meilleur** ... Mais en Dieu ces attributs sont absolument **infinis ou parfaits**; et dans les Monades créées ou dans les Entéléchies ce n'en sont que des **imitations**. [*In God there is* Power, *which is the source of all, also* Knowledge, *whose content is the variety of the ideas, and finally* Will, *which makes changes or products according to the principle of the best.* ...*But in God these attributes are absolutely infinite or perfect; and in the created Monads or the Entelechies there are only imitations of these attributes.*

(*Comment*: Given God's perfection, His 'being' includes the **Principle of the Best**; His creations, however, namely the Monads, can only **imitate** this)].

49. La créature est dite *agir* au dehors en tant qu'elle a de la perfection. Ainsi l'on attribue l'*action* a la Monade, en tant qu'elle a des perceptions **distinctes**. [*A created thing is said to* act *outwardly in so far as it has perfection... Thus* activity *is attributed to a Monad, in so far as it has distinct perceptions.* (*Comment*: The Monad may **act** outside of itself only to the extent that its perceptions are (clear and) **distinct**; to that extent their 'windowless' being can nevertheless, so to speak, shed light outwards)].

50. Et une créature est plus parfaite qu'une autre, en ce qu'on trouve en elle ce qui sert à **rendre raison *a priori* de ce qui se passe dans l'autre**, et c'est par là, qu'on dit, qu'elle agit sur l'autre. [*And one created thing is more perfect than another, in this, that there is found in the more perfect that which serves to explain a priori what takes place in the*

less perfect, and it is on this account that the former is said to act upon the latter. (*Comment*: But perfection is an ordinal thing, measured by the degree of dinstinctness; so a more rather than less perfect Monad is the one whose distinct-er ideas may 'justify' or 'make sense' **on *a priori* grounds** of what goes on inside another Monad; the light shed by the less imperfect Monad is thus allowed to penetrate the more imperfect Monad's closed windows)].

51. Mais ... ce n'est qu'une influence idéale d'une monade sur l'autre, qui ne peut avoir son effet que par **l'intervention de Dieu**, en tant que dans les idées de Dieu une monade demande avec **raison**. Car puisqu'une monade créée ne saurait avoir une influence physique sur l'intérieur de l'autre, **ce n'est que par ce moyen** que l'une peut avoir de la dépendance de l'autre. [*But ... the influence of one Monad upon another is only ideal, and it can have its effect only through the mediation of God, in so far as in the ideas of God any Monad rightly claims that God, ... For since one created Monad cannot have any physical influence upon the inner being of another, it is only by this means that the one can be dependent upon the other.* (*Comment*: But this can only be an 'ideal' influence; and it can only occur through the intervention of God; and that intervention requires that there is reason for it – the application, so to say, of a Monad for God's intervention must be grounded in reason before being granted; and there is no other means of procuring 'interdependence' among Monads)].

52. Et c'est par là, qu'entre les créatures les actions et passions sont **mutuelles**. Car Dieu comparant deux substances simples, trouve en chacune des raisons, qui l'obligent à y **accommoder** l'autre. [*Accordingly, among created things, activities and passivities are mutual. For God, comparing two simple substances, finds in each reasons which oblige Him to adapt the other to it.* (*Comment*: It is thus and only thus that Monads' actions and passions become mutual; God finds a reason to accommodate one to another)].

56. Or cette *liaison* ou cet **accommodement** de toutes les choses créées, **a chacune et de chacune a toutes les autres**, fait que chaque substance simple a des rapports qui expriment toutes les autres, et qu'elle est par conséquent **un miroir vivant perpétuel de l'univers**. [*Now this connexion or adaptation of all created things to each and of each to all, means that each simple substance has relations which express all the others, and, consequently, that it is a perpetual living mirror of the universe.* (*Comment*: And this liaison or accommodation – or perhaps **mating,** since Leibniz wrote and meant in French – makes of each Monad a living mirror of the universe as it is the embodiment of all the relations possible, which therefore 'express' all other Monads)].

58. Et c'est le moyen d'obtenir autant de **variété** qu'il est possible, mais avec le plus grand **ordre**, qui se puisse. [*And by this means there is obtained as great variety as possible, along with the greatest possible order*].

59. Aussi n'est-ce que cette hypothèse (**que j'ose dire démontrée**) qui relève comme il faut la grandeur de Dieu. ... [c]ette **harmonie** universelle, qui fait que toutes les substances expriment toutes les autres par les rapports qu'elle y a. [*Besides, no hypothesis but this (which I venture to call proved) fittingly exalts the greatness of God ...this universal harmony, according to which every substance exactly expresses all others through the relations it has with them.* (*Comment*: And this is the only hypothesis, now he claims demonstrated, which properly allows for the greatness of God. This Universal Harmony such that all Monads express all others though their relations between all pairs of them)].

Follow some clarifying remarks as to the tightness or looseness of the blessed **liaison**, they are a function of the distinctness of each Monad's **ideas**, a measure of its distance from the infinite, which is to say God. And the good doctor, Hippocrates, is invoked with a saying, σύμπνοια πάντα – the togetherness of breath, alluding to a distinct idea we may call **sympathy**.

One might think that Leibniz could have stopped here and that perhaps so should we. But one would miss a crucial final step of the teleology, namely the **moral** aspect or conclusion of it all. So we shall follow him to the end without asides and minimal annotation:

69. Ainsi il n'y rien d'inculte, de stérile, de mort dans l'univers, **point de chaos**, point de confusion qu'en apparence. [*Thus there is nothing fallow, nothing sterile, nothing dead in the universe, no chaos, no confusion save in appearance.* (Comment: There is no chaos, confusion is only apparent)].

71. Tous les corps sont dans un flux perpétuel. [*All bodies are in perpetual flux*].

72. Il y a souvent métamorphose. [They often **metamorphose**].

78. L'âme ...et le corps ...se rencontrent en vertu de **l'harmonie préétablie** entres toutes les substances, puisqu'elles sont toutes les représentations d'un même univers. [*The soul... and the body ... agree with each other in virtue of the pre-established harmony between all substances, since they are all representations of one and the same universe* (Comment: Body and soul meet or perhaps *liaise* by virtue of **pre-established** harmony)].

79. Les âmes agissent selon les lois des causes finales par appétitions, fins et moyens. Les corps agissent selon les lois des causes efficientes. Et les deux règnes, celui des causes efficientes et celui des causes finales, sont harmoniques entre eux. [*Souls act according to the laws of final causes through appetitions, ends, and means. Bodies act according to the laws of efficient causes or motions. And the two realms, that of efficient causes and that of final causes, are in harmony with one another* (Comment: Souls act on the principle of final cause; bodies act on the principle of efficient cause; and the kingdoms of the twin types of cause are in harmony with one another)].

82. Quant aux Esprit ou Ames raisonnables ... [Now on the matter of Spirits or Reasonable Souls ...].

83. ... les Esprits sont encore des images de la Divinité même, ou de l'Auteur même de la nature: capables de connaître le système de l'univers et d'en imiter quelque chose par des échantillons architectoniques. [*...minds [esprits] are also images of the Deity or Author of nature Himself, capable of knowing the system of the universe, and to some extent of imitating it through architectonic ensamples,...* (Comment: Going up the hierarchy of distinctness of ideas, Spirits are further able to know the system of the world, by imitating God, though only in architectonically constructed samples)].

84. C'est ce qui fait que les Esprit sont capables d'entrer dans une **Manière de Société** avec Dieu, et c'est qu'il est à leur égard, non seulement ce qu'un inventeur est à sa Machine (comme Dieu l'est par rapport aux autres créatures) mais encore ce qu'un Prince est à ses sujets, et même un père a ses enfants. [*It is this that enables spirits (for minds)] to enter into a kind of fellowship with God, and brings it about that in relation to them He is not only what an inventor is to his machine (which is the relation of God to other created things), but also what a prince is to his subjects, and, indeed, what a father is to his children.* (Comment: Thus Spirits are in a Manner of Society with God, who then is like a Prince to them or even as Father to his Children)].

85. D'où il est aisé de conclure, que l'assemblage de tous les Esprits doit composer la ***Cité de Dieu***, c'est à dire le plus parfait Etat qui soit possible sous le plus parfait des Monarques. [Whence one may conclude that the class of Spirits (or minds) must compose the City of God, that is to say the most perfect state under the most perfect monarch].

86. Cette Cité de Dieu, cette Monarchie véritablement universelle, est un **Monde Morale**, dans le Monde Naturel ... [C]'est aussi par rapport à cette Cité divine qu'il y a proprement de la **Bonté**. [This City of God, this truly universal monarchy, is a moral world in the natural world, ... It is also in relation to this divine City that God specially has goodness, ... (*Comment*: The City of God is a Moral World; and it is in this City that there is properly Goodness)].

87. Comme nous avons établi une Harmonie parfaite entre deux Règnes naturels, l'un des causes Efficientes, l'autre des Finales, nous devons remarquer ici encore une autre **harmonie** entre le règne **Physique de la Nature** et le règne **Moral de la Grâce**, entre Dieu considéré comme Architecte de la Machine de l'univers, et Dieu considéré comme Monarque de la Cité divine des Esprits. [*As we have shown above that there is a perfect harmony between the two realms in nature, one of efficient, and the other of final causes, we should here notice also another harmony between the physical realm of nature and the moral realm of grace, that is to say, between God, considered as Architect of the mechanism [machine] of the universe and God considered as Monarch of the divine City of spirits [or minds].* (*Comment*: Beyond the harmonies so far established there is then also the Harmony between Nature and Grace, that is between God the Architect and God the Monarch of the divine City of Spirits)].

88. Cette Harmonie fait que les choses conduisent **à la Grâce par les voies mêmes de la Nature** ... pour le châtiment des uns, et la récompense des autres. [It is this harmony which dictates that Grace is achieved according to Nature ... for the punishment of those ones and the reward of those others].

89. Dieu comme Architecte contente en tout Dieu, come Législateur; et qu'ainsi les **péchés** doivent porter leur **peine** par l'ordre de la nature; et que de même les **belles actions** s'attireront leurs **récompenses.** [God as The Architect and God as the Legislator-Judge are mutually content; thus sins will receive their pain according to the order of nature; and so good actions will attract their reward].

90. Enfin sous ce gouvernement parfait il n'y aurait point de bonne Action sans récompense, point de mauvaise sans châtiment: et **tout doit réussir au bien des bons**, de ceux qui ne sont point des mécontents, qui se fient a la Providence, après avoir fait leur devoir, et qui aiment et imitent, comme il faut, l'Auteur de tout bien, se plaisant dans la considération de ses perfections suivant la nature du *pur amour* véritable, qui fait prendre plaisir à la félicité de ce qu'on aime. C'est ce qui fait travailler les personnes sages et vertueuses et se contenter de ce que Dieu fait arriver par sa volonté secrète, conséquente et décisive; **en reconnaissant que l'ordre de l'univers surpasse tous les souhaits des plus sages et qu'il est impossible de le rendre meilleur**; non seulement pour le tout mais encore pour nous même, si nous sommes attachés, non seulement comme à l'Architecte et à la cause efficiente de notre être, mais encore à notre Maitre et à la cause finale qui doit faire tout le but de notre volonté, et peu seul faire notre **bonheur.** [*Finally, under this perfect government no good action would be unrewarded and no bad one unpunished, and all should issue in the well-being of the good, that is to say, of those who are not malcontents in this great state, but who trust in Providence, after having done their duty, and who love and imitate, as is meet, the Author of all good, finding pleasure in the contemplation of His perfections, as is the way of genuine 'pure love,' which takes*

pleasure in the happiness of the beloved. This it is which leads wise and virtuous people to devote their energies to everything which appears in harmony with the presumptive or antecedent will of God, and yet makes them content with what God actually brings to pass by His secret, consequent and positive (décisive) will, recognizing that if we could sufficiently understand the order of the universe, we should find that it exceeds all the desires of the wisest men, and that it is impossible to make it better than it is, not only as a whole and in general but also for ourselves in particular, if we are attached, as we ought to be, to the Author of all, not only as to the architect and efficient cause of our being, but as to our master and to the final cause, which ought to be the whole aim of our will, and which can alone make our happiness.]

We refrain, if only for purely aesthetic reasons, from annotating or interpreting this phantas-magoric statement of Enlightened Calvinist ideology, the message should by now be clear.[1] So FINIS, and a pause. We use it to submit an apology and then raise two questions.

First, the apology: why torture our readers with an admittedly questionable metaphysical argument [Kant, for example, wouldn't have any of it], no less in the [Anglo-Saxon] 'enemy' language, namely French? And why do it in this tortuous way? The first part of the answer is related to our reference to Leibniz in relation to the style of mathematics reasoning, (see Box 6.17), as against the 'engineering' approach of Newton, and the implications thereof: we wish to provide more evidence as to the quality of that important difference. This leads to the choice of the original French as the appropriate medium for showing the difference. There are of course multiple translations of *The Monadology* in English, just try Google; the most convenient hardcopy compendium, which includes it, may be Garber and Ariew, G.W.Leibniz, *Discourse on Metaphysics and Other Essays* [Leibniz (1991)], yet: it *just ain't*. We have instead used the Livre de Poche edition of *La Monadologie* in the original French [Leibniz (1714 [1991]). Further, in confession as well as apology, and though the text is both concise and brief, we opted as 'quotation' from it for a severely truncated subset of the text as originally written. This is certainly not a potted version but it may be worse, omis-sion is a surgical thing. But so is abstraction. We hope that our good faith with the post-surgical truth will not be taken for granted. We also hope that the minimalist comment and emphases [in **bold**] will properly mark out the pivotal swings in the argument. To the extent that you bother, a bit of linguistic sweat is better than gulping delivered fast food. Now the two questions.

The first question is 'existential', why bother with philosophy at all, whether in French or for that matter in Chinese? The simple answer is that political economy is, as we have argued at some length, not a 'science' but rather a branch of moral philosophy, that it is a 'moral science' [a term often used by Keynes, a bastard linguistic concoction as only historical Cambridge could devise], so it is practical and useful to know rather than guess what the philosophical underpinning of any structured set of propositions which we call a 'model' rests on. But this simple answer, though we believe true, is not of much import, the neoclas-sical high church will suavely shrug it off. So, and so to say for oeconomy, we may skip the answer altogether, best by twisting the question: why bother with metaphysics when we have mathematics instead? Indeed. Because mathematics *is* [at least] '*like*' metaphysics, though obviously of its own very distinctive kind. For mathematical 'objects' and meta-physical 'objects' share the same reality, which is to say unreality. It is the narrowness of the rules, not only the narrowness of the objects, which make the difference, whereby there is usually less mathematical than metaphysical nonsense. But taking mathematics as perfectly superior substitute of metaphysics is taking the guts out of the ultimate 'existential' question, the so-what of things. Economists may think that the [philosophical] distinction between positive and normative has settled the matter [few, knowing it based on an inadequate philosophy, disagree]; and like medieval monks being copyists but only of mathematics, they have invented all sorts of new distinctions of unmeaning. But on this topic it is perhaps more economically politic to confine preaching to the converted.

The second question is why bother with Leibniz's philosophy in particular? His take on the 'meaning' of the calculus, (see Box 6.17) above, is sufficient reason. But there is another, stated in the first sentence of this box: that *he 'invented' the notion of pre-established harmony*. Now this concept is awfully awkward. Harmony taken by itself is an unquestionably good thing, the whole and the parts and conversely the parts and the whole can, at worse, live with it. Economists are not in general knowledgeable in etymology, Harmony is the name of the capping stone of an arch, it 'arms' the forces of gravity with a transmission mechanism which keeps the edifice, once erected, in place together, the name was subsequently copyrighted to that which is notionally designed to turn up as music, if ever a transient thing. Undoubtedly, harmony – what's in a name, call it instead 'equilibrium' – is a good thing, so the question is: *can it be established rather than pre-established? Or is it condemned to be pre-established in order to be established?*

Here comes to rescue us the complete methodological rule of 'science', if you do not like the answer then change the question; better still, shift the questioner instead. It is, after all, only the metaphysicians who insist on *final* causes and impose them on the so sufficient sufficient causes. Just get rid of metaphysics and its final cause. Stick to the sufficient cause and the answer to the question is settled, or so the mathematical metaphysicians contend. And they found it, they *proved* the existence of harmony under sufficient conditions. The so-what question remained in limbo, *a non-question that may not be asked*.

Leibniz was bolder. What is it that you, the participant-beholder, want harmony-equilibrium for? Is there a *moral* purpose, if so declare it. If not go your speculative kindergarten ways. The dialectic of simultaneously being and becoming, that either you are in equilibrium or you get into it, is impossible, unless you are both in it and becoming with it, a permanent, indeed evolutionary steady state. What are both sufficient and final conditions for this preposterous claim? Simply God. Radical neoclassic piety is only apparently more humble, the Market will do. The proverbial little boy contemplating the bare-arsed king was however astonished: and 'who' will set prices? His name was [and is, wonderfully] Kenneth Arrow. So: if metaphysical rubbish will not do, will mathematically clothed rubbish do better?

Ending the pause we now sum up: Leibniz posited a metaphysical object which he called the Monad, defined by negations and gradually beefed up to its ultimate purpose, that of being in communion with God. In the process of this buildup of a moral system he invented the necessary logical truth of pre-established harmony and then used it to characterize its eternal stability. The radical neoclassics reinvented or rather subinvented Leibniz and his *Monadology* by substituting a mathematical object for his metaphysical one: a point set in space is a sterilized monad in new clothing, direction is even ideally timeless, axiomatic continuity and convexity lead to the possibility of the bounding-separating hyperplane doing its touchy-feely job, existence of a General Equilibrium is thus deduced from these so cunningly sufficient conditions, Q.E.D.

We may conclude with an impious remark: we find the Leibniz version that God is the Market more plausible than the neoclassical version that the Market is God.

To put a different scent to this farewell we may now change tack and invoke yet another facet to his *persona*, that of Leibniz the geopolitical strategist. In the service of his lord of Hanover he authored a memorandum of advice addressed to no less than the King of France, then Louis XIV, *Le Roi-Soleil* himself. The major proposition was that France should refrain from land-war in Germany and turn instead to conquering the world, in the following logical steps: first, the great Christian Prince should liberate the Christian Greeks from the infidel, then from that springboard France would go on to conquer Egypt, this would give her mastery of the Red Sea and thus open the road to India, whereby Britannia would be sent back to her foggy island; in the process sparing Leibniz's German master. Of course, though not himself a rationalist philosopher, Napoleon later had similar thoughts but then it was his proper job, and it was also by then too late. But it was not too late for Captain Mahan (1890) who, writing his *Influence of Sea Power upon History*, unearthed Leibniz's memorandum and presented it extensively. As happens, a copy of Mahan's book landed on the desk of Admiral von Tirpitz who endeared the prospect of overseas empire to Bismarck's successors and crucially the Kaiser, with the result that the German naval programme threatened the British sponsored balance of power and brought the civilized world to August 1914 and thence to the American century.

For a mere rationalist philosopher this is not bad going. He was a Slav careerist at the close of the age of adventure [the 'Leibniz' without the German 't' was his own version of Lubenicz], a proper successor to Parmenides rather than Plato or Aristotle, both of whom he felt free to use and abuse, a superb logician, that is one with imagination. Perhaps the reason we like him so is that our own, so to speak, UADPhilEcon patron saint, Bertrand Russell, has left us with a superb monograph, published in the symbolic *tournure de siecle* year 1900: *The Philosophy of Leibniz.*

Finally, and without his knowledge or permission, we wish to dedicate this brief speculation on the origin of General Equilibrium theory to Frank Hahn, who so mightily and so honestly contributed to its edifice. The dialectics of honesty being so unpredictable, and Horace being his middle name, he was not content with repeating Arrow's question but did positive demolition work on the body of the neoclassical order. For the institutional distinction he was so grudgingly spared we offer a libation to the merely 'sufficient' body which might have bestowed it.

Notes

1 The editorial culprit here is Nicholas Theocarakis. Fearing that a non-French speaking readership could not follow Leibniz's great text he inserted in italics the translation of Robert Latta [Leibniz (1714 [1898]) and marked as *"Comment"* George Krimpas' minimal paraphrases of the French text, sacrificing his wishes for the sake of readability. Translations without italics are by Krimpas.

7 Convulsion

1929 and its legacy

7.1 The Surge

Establishment theory is never abreast of the times. It is either premature or belated; either antiquated or too hasty to pronounce on what lies ahead. When it does not confuse the present with an unfeasible future it limps behind the march of history in a futile struggle to catch up with it.

While Marginalist political economics was morphing into neoclassicism, the world was transforming itself beyond recognition. Neoclassicism became the establishment's Official Mantra precisely at a time when capitalism was moving further and further away from the neoclassicists' portrayal of capitalism as a tranquil, timeless, radically egalitarian archipelago of preference bundles.[1] Early in the nineteenth-century, steam power began to move out of the dark satanic mills, pushing locomotives and steel ships to far flung places. In the 1830s, when his beloved wife died a few hundred miles away from where he was, oblivious to her suffering, a Calvinist painter resolved to end the tyranny of distance. To this end he harnessed electricity, and the internet's precursor was born.[2] In the 1860s Maxwell's discoveries of the wonders of electromagnetism (recall Section 5.4 of Chapter 5) were applied to the invention of everything that we now identify as modern technology; Dmitri Mendeleyev's periodic table of chemical elements gave rise to the chemical industry; Henry Bessemer's magnificent steel cauldrons and Carl Wilhelm Siemens' open hearth furnaces produced plentiful cheap steel.

In short, while Marginalist political economists were fiddling their way into the clutches of neoclassical stasis, industrial magnates were tapping into the nineteenth-century's scientific surge, grabbing what they could from the scientists' laboratories and the engineers' workshops. In the process they fashioned not only new industrial products but, significantly, *a new network of corporate power* which gave birth to the world that we now live in. They looked into the abyss, they shone into it a bright light borrowed from science and like Prospero they bellowed: '*This thing of darkness I acknowledge mine!*'[3]

On a cold January day, in 1903, a crowd of New Yorkers assembled at Coney Island's *Luna Park*. They did not come to enjoy the rides or the popcorn but to witness a grotesque happening: Topsy, the elephant who had not taken gracefully to captivity, was to be electrocuted by Thomas Edison (1847–1931), the great inventor who at the tender age of 22 had manufactured an electric voting machine, before going on to turn night into day with his electric light bulb, to capture music and then reproduce it mechanically on his phonograph and to arrest scenes from our lives on film (or *motion pictures* as he called them). So, what business did such an inventive man have killing an elephant in public?

The answer helpfully illuminates the spirit of the *Second Industrial Revolution*. Edison epitomised the new entrepreneur at the heart of a brand new phase in capitalist development: an inventor who innovated in order to create monopoly power for himself, not so much for the riches that it provided but for its own sake; for the sheer glory and the sheer power of it all; an entrepreneur who inspired, in equal measure, incredible loyalty from his overworked staff and loathing from his adversaries; a friend of Henry Ford who also famously played a key role in bringing machinery into the lives of ordinary people while, at once, turning workers into the nearest a person can come to a machine.

Topsy's execution was symbolic of the new game in town. Edison's success took a lot more than his penchant for useful inventions. He was a master at profiting from their mass production once he had established property rights not only over the invention but also over the whole network of its dissemination. His invention of the light bulb, for example, was only the first step in creating electricity-generating stations and the network of wires that took that electricity into every American home before lighting up the bulbs produced *en masse* by his own factories. Without control of the generation and distribution of electricity, his bulbs would not have made him King of the Electron. Thus occurred the, so-called, *War of the Currents* against his great adversary: George Westinghouse.[4]

In a tussle over whose standard would prevail (that has since then become all too common in other realms),[5] Edison and Westinghouse bet on different types of electrical current: Edison on DC (direct current) and Westinghouse on AC (alternating current). Both knew that this was a winner-takes-all game. So they fought tooth and nail. Poor Topsy was mere collateral damage, as were a number of other animals that Edison and his employees electrocuted in a bid to besmirch AC by demonstrating its lethality, and thus drum up public support for the safer, albeit dearer, DC.

Although an opponent of the death penalty, Edison set his employees working on an AC powered electric chair (first used on a human in 1890) solely for the purposes of marketing DC and persuading the authorities to ban AC as too dangerous.[6] To grasp the stakes for which Edison and Westinghouse where playing, it helps to recall that in 1887 Edison owned an empire of 121 power stations in the United States delivering DC to customers. The realisation that DC was economically inferior to AC was a devastating blow.[7] By 1903, all could see that the game was up and AC had won, courtesy of its very low distribution costs. Topsy's execution was Edison's last bid to turn the tide against his corporate competitor. Never one to miss out on the opportunity of promoting more than one product line at once, Edison pushed for another of his inventions during that January day at Coney Island: he had Topsy's electrocution captured frame by frame using another invention of his that would soon spawn another major industrial sector: the movie camera.

Men like Edison, Westinghouse and Ford were part of the *avant garde* of a new era in which capital could no longer be thought of, in Ricardian style, as heaps of saved corn, to be ploughed back into the fields. The new machines, from light bulbs and locomotives to the telegraph and the phonograph, transcended the labour-saving function of the early steam engines and mechanical looms of the first industrial revolution. Innovations were producing new sectors almost every year and were bent on breaking down the simplistic divide between consumption and capital goods.[8] The naive models both of classical and Marginalist-*cum*-neoclassical political economics could simply not keep up with the surge of capitalist development.

7.2 The Outsiders

Wilful obscurantism was never the political economists' aim. That was the doing of the *Inherent Error* to which they were betrothed. Word had got to them that the world was getting more complex, faster than ever before. But, sadly, their theory could not keep up with events; at least not without dropping the ambition to maintain a consistent explanation of value *and* change in the context of models featuring multiple, interlocking (not to mention multiplying) sectors. Inevitably, political economics faced a stark choice: either ignore reality's transformation altogether, or break with theoretically consistent modelling. Neo-classicism opted to turn a blind eye to the world, losing itself in its 'Calvinist' models which featured enough Leibnizian calculus to keep a good scholar nicely insulated from the vagaries of the real world until retirement. Section 7.3 revisits this pristine tradition, which continues unabashed to this day. For now, we concentrate on the widening cracks inflicted upon classical political economics by the second industrial revolution and its repercussions.

The rise of the corporations which transformed the world during the second industrial revolution encouraged a number of thinkers to pose the forbidden question: *what if savings are not what determines investment and, thus, growth?* In Ricardo's *corn model* (recall Chapter 3), such a question would be nonsensical: what is the point of not eating corn in the current period if one does not intend to keep it as seeds for planting in the next? Granted. But when we move to a multi-sector economy, especially to the brave new world of Edison, Siemens, Westinghouse and Ford, it is not at all clear that skipping dinner will necessarily increase the economy's productive capacity. Is this how Edison enhanced his capital? Through abstinence?[9] Of course not. Though abstinence was a necessary condition, and this only if you lack financial backers, it was not sufficient in the slightest. Had it not been for the technological innovations *and* the political posturing that allowed him to turn his inventions into monopoly power, the impact on the economy of his thrift would have gone unnoticed. Plain savings do not guarantee that railway lines will be laid, ammonia will be harnessed in the production of fertilisers and electricity will carry messages to Australia.

Another way of asking the same 'forbidden' question is this: commodities are, by definition, items produced for exchange. Their sellers will pocket an income that will, subsequently, finance their own purchases. *Why do we assume that the demand thus created will be sufficient to absorb all the produced commodities?* Again, in a Ricardian single-commodity world this is not a question that can be asked. As long as people get hungry, produced corn will be 'demanded' and the only question remaining concerns the proportion of corn output that will be saved and invested. Ricardo assumed that what applied to his *corn model* applied to the world at large: that produced commodities would find a market; that supply would manufacture its own demand. This conviction is known as *Say's Law*, named after French economist Jean-Baptiste Say (1767–1832), though its origins are lost in the mists of time.[10]

David Ricardo and most of his followers were utterly convinced of *Say's Law* validity and, thus, of the impossibility of a shortfall in aggregate demand. Crises were, consequently, seen as temporary aberrations. Though at least three influential political economists (Say himself, Malthus and Marx – see Box 7.1) questioned this 'law', it was the second industrial revolution and the rise of immense corporate power that raised serious concerns over its validity. For if the likes of Edison, for any reason, withheld one of their major investment sprees, it would be a flight of fancy to *assume* that increased investments by the small business sector would automatically make up the shortfall in aggregate investment. When corporations grow gargantuan, their investment drive is hard to replace and the moguls' confidence in each others'… confidence acquires a new importance.

The new industrial terrain posed another issue that late-nineteenth-century thinkers had no excuse to ignore: the role of prices in the era of corporate empires. In Adam Smith, as in Ricardo and indeed Marx, arbitrage was assumed to perform its magic reliably and ensure

Box 7.1 Say's Law or the Law of the Markets: The Inherent Error's alter ego

In 1803, Jean-Baptiste Say wrote: 'It is worth while to remark that a product is no sooner created than it, from that instant, affords a market for other products to the full extent of its own value'.[1] Classical political economists[2] such as David Ricardo (1772–1823), John Ramsay McCulloch (1789–1864), Nassau William Senior (1790–1864), Robert Torrens (1780–1864) and James Mill (1773–1836) interpreted this pronouncement as a 'law', the gist of which was that economic crises cannot be prolonged, and certainly not turn into depressions. Why? Because price and interest rate reductions will cause demand to bounce back and unemployment to be eliminated.

Of all the classics, it was their precursor, David Ricardo, who pushed the case for *Say's Law* most powerfully: 'Too much of a particular commodity' he wrote, 'may he produced, of which there may be such a glut in the market, as not to repay the capital expended on it; but this cannot be the case with respect to all commodities',[3] This dictum was phrased in a manner that stops all debate on the matter. Fascinatingly, the first voice to be raised in favour of a more nuanced approach was by Say himself. For Say was not a true believer in his own 'law'. He criticised Ricardo's denial that there could be periods of crisis during which investors lose confidence and, instead of investing their accumulated money, choose to hoard it. In such cases, Say advocated public works as a short-term remedy of unemployment.[4]

More famously, Thomas Robert Malthus (1766–1834) engaged Ricardo in a debate on the causes of the recession of their times by questioning, with his usual deference, Ricardo's belief that *Say's Law* applied all the time. In essence, Malthus was arguing that capitalism could not generate enough demand for the products churned out by the factories and that, for this reason, some source of additional demand had to be arranged for. Ricardo replied angrily[5] and Malthus never pushed him too hard on the matter, failing fully to articulate exactly what was wrong with *Say's Law*. For, underneath their disagreement, ran a conflict that had little to do with economic analysis and everything with pure, undiluted politics.

Malthus was a defender of the landowning class, convinced that their prosperity was essential for the nation's wellbeing. His argument was couched in terms of a presumption that the landowners' rents served a useful purpose: to be spent on consumption and luxury goods that industrialists would not indulge in. The thinking here was that, while industrialists were constantly fearful of their competitors' increasing ingenuity, innovation and lower costs, and therefore abstained from consumption in order to invest as much as possible, the landowners faced no real competition, courtesy of the historical accident that they owned the more fertile land that no entrepreneur could conceivably produce, let alone more cheaply. Malthus felt that, for this reason, the landed gentry's rents provide the missing demand that allows capitalism to absorb its own industrial output.

Ricardo, on the other hand, was the landowners' sworn enemy and thought that their prosperity was not only undeserved but, worse still, a drain on capital accumulation.[6] In this context, *Say's Law* was a device by which Ricardo could strengthen his political case for repealing the Corn Laws; a piece of legislation that impeded corn imports into Britain, kept the price of food (and thus wages) up and boosted the aristocracy's rents. Malthus' questioning of it was, in Ricardo's mind, nothing but a political gesture on behalf of the rentiers that had to be opposed ferociously.

A few decades had to pass before *Say's Law* was to be subjected to rigorous criticism. The critic was Karl Marx. Chapter 17 of his *Theories of Surplus* Value, written in 1862–3, is entitled *Ricardo's Theory of Accumulation and a Critique of It* and subtitled *The Very Nature of Capital Leads to Crises*, [Marx (1862–3 [1968]), pp. 493–509]. Starting with the salvo that the Law is 'the childish babble of a Say, but it is not worthy of Ricardo', Marx goes on to argue that:

> In the first place, no capitalist produces in order to consume his product .... Previously it was forgotten that the product is a commodity. Now even the social division of labour is forgotten. In a situation where men produce for themselves, there are indeed no crises, but neither is there capitalist production. Nor have we ever heard that the ancients, with their slave production ever knew crises, although individual producers among the ancients too, did go bankrupt ... A man who has produced, does not have the choice of selling or not selling. He must sell. In the crisis there arises the very situation in which he cannot sell or can only sell below the cost-price or must even sell at a positive loss ... During the crisis, a man may be very pleased, if he has sold his commodities without immediately thinking of a purchase. On the other hand, if the value that has been realised is again to be used as capital, it must go through the process of reproduction, that is, it must be exchanged for labour and commodities. But the crisis is precisely the phase of disturbance and interruption of the process of reproduction. And this disturbance cannot be explained by the fact that it does not occur in those times when there is no crisis ... The general nature of the metamorphosis of commodities – which includes the separation of purchase and sale just as it does their unity – instead of excluding the possibility of a general glut, on the contrary, contains the possibility of a general glut.

Marx was, evidently, open to the idea of a 'general glut', a crisis, a depression even. However, as we saw in Chapter 5, his eagerness to 'close' his model, to maintain the consistency of his theory of capitalist dynamics with his *labour theory of value*, forced him in the arms of the *Inherent Error*; in a form of analysis that buys consistency at the expense of sacrificing the complexity of a capitalist system, i.e. a model that effectively returns us to a single sector economy or one that cannot accommodate any type of socio-economic power not captured in the mechanics of capital accumulation. In this sense, Marx's theory of crises, while *the* major breakthrough in the way we conceptualise capitalism, remained wedded to the Ricardian idea that, eventually, crises are self-annulling; that the rise in unemployment suppresses wages; the fallen wages reinvigorate profit; profit is automatically invested; and *hey presto* demand is restored.

Notes
1 Jean-Baptiste Say (1803 [1850]), p. 134. It is in the famous Chapter XV of Book I, the French title thereof being *Des Débouchés*.

2 Not all of these economists subscribed to the Ricardian theory of value. Senior and Torrens were not classical in this sense. But they would agree on the validity of *Say's Law*.
3 See Chapter 21 (esp. p. 292) of David Ricardo's (1817/1819/1821 [1951]).
4 See Baumol (1997).
5 'You often appear to me to contend not only that production can go on so far without an adequate motive, but that it has actually done so lately, and that we are now suffering the consequences of its stagnation.' Quoted in Blaug 1962 [1997], p. 170. In Ricardo (1952), p. 16, Letter 442 (9 July 1821).
6 See Mark Blaug, *ibid.*

that, at least in the medium run, no commodity would be selling for anything above its value. That, for instance, if demand for a widget were to fall, widgets would exchange at a lower price and this would somehow limit the reduction in the quantity of widgets produced and sold. Flexible prices were seen, in short, as capitalism's shock absorbers. But in an era of increasing market power, such as the one over which Edison and Westinghouse were squabbling (see previous section), it is not at all clear that competition would convert a drop in demand into an analogous drop in price. Everyone could see that when (to remain with the same example) the demand for the electricity produced by one of Edison's or Westinghouse's power plants dropped (e.g. because of a fall in wages during a downturn), electricity prices were hardly dipping unsurprisingly, since the new moguls faced next to no competition within their well guarded territory.

What would be the effect of these two departures from the classical theory? What if prices do not fall readily whenever demand subsides and what if, even when they do, demand does not bounce back to match the available supply? The immediate worry caused by these queries is that capitalism may be prone to a depression from which it will find it hard to extract itself. For if the prices that Edison, Westinghouse, Coca-Cola, Ford, McDonalds, etc. charge tend to be inflexible, due to the market power of the corporations, this means that a fall in demand will result in substantial reductions in their production; which also means that employment will fall much faster when, for any reason, demand dips. And if *Say's Law* proves hollow, even if these corporations respond to the recession with an increase in output, this does not necessarily mean that customers will be found to absorb the bulk of the fresh output. On their part, moguls of industry who, rationally, suspect that this will transpire, may hoard their past profits rather than invest during a recession. But then such a decision by the big movers and shakers of the second industrial revolution will guarantee a depression.

These were not just idle concerns. The nineteenth-century was littered with moments of intense panic and acute recessions connected to the failure of large corporate investments and the collapse of banking outfits. In 1847, the end of the first boom in railway building in Britain caused the financial markets to crash. In 1873 a six-year-long depression began in the United States as a result of the bursting of a speculative bubble over the building of railroads following the end of the American Civil War. When a major bank, Jay Cooke & Co., could not sell several million dollars of Northern Pacific Railway bonds, it collapsed, thus spearheading the depression. A mere three years after the US economy had recovered, another recession began in 1882 which was to last three years. In its midst, a major investment firm and the Penn Bank (of Pittsburgh) went under, together with around ten thousand businesses. In 1890, London based Barings' Bank's investments in Argentina proved unsafe, thus causing the bank's near collapse. Though the Bank of England intervened to save Barings, the loss in business confidence reverberated around the world and nearly plunged capitalism into another depression. Alas, the recession was not to be denied. For, in 1893, another financial bubble which had also begun with railway overbuilding in the US burst, gave rise to a run on gold reserves, a precipitous rise in unemployment (from 4 per cent to 18 per cent), a series of industrial strikes and a change in the US political terrain. The depression lasted until 1896 when a new gold rush raised the economic tempo, thus ushering in a period of rapid growth which lasted until 1907; at this point, a fresh financial crisis, involving a 50 per cent drop in the New York Stock Exchange, whipped up mass panic, widespread unemployment, business closures, etc. Indeed, it was the *Crash of 1907* which led to the creation of America's Central Bank in 1913, the Federal Reserve System, with an explicit remit to prevent similar occurrences.[11]

In light of such tumult, the questions in the penultimate paragraph were painfully pertinent. Remarkably, the professional economists of the era, caught up in the niceties of their neoclassical models (recall Section 6.11, previous chapter), did not address them. It was the *outsiders* who tried to answer them: men, and one woman, who continued the tradition of classical political economics outside the ivory towers of the great universities but wholly immersed themselves in the anxieties and concerns of everyday people.

The first *outsider* in our list was *Friedrich Engels* (1820–95), Marx's comrade in theory and in life. After Marx's death, Engels became increasingly aware of the cleavage between the dynamics of Marx's business cycle and the historic importance of the rise of corporations. In the new world fashioned by large business, Engels sees the seeds of an impending depression, possibly one spearheaded by speculation, bubbles and the now familiar excesses of financial markets.

[A] change has taken place here since the last major general crisis. The acute form of the periodic process with its former ten-year cycle, appears to have given way to a more chronic, long drawn out, alternation between a relatively short and slight business improvement and a relatively long, indecisive depression – taking place in the various industrial countries at different times. But perhaps it is only a matter of a prolongation of the duration of the cycle. In the early years of world commerce, 1845–47, it can be shown that these cycles lasted about five years; from 1847 to 1867 the cycle is clearly ten years; is it possible that we are now in the preparatory stage of a new world crash of unparalleled vehemence? Many things seem to point in this direction. Since the last general crisis of 1867 many profound changes have taken place. The colossal expansion of the means of transportation and communication – ocean liners, railways, electrical telegraphy, the Suez Canal – has made a real world-market a fact. The former monopoly of England in industry has been challenged by a number of competing industrial countries; infinitely greater and varied fields have been opened in all parts of the world for the investment of surplus European capital, so that it is far more widely distributed and local over-speculation may be more easily overcome. By means of all this, most of the old breeding-grounds of crises and opportunities for their development have been eliminated or strongly reduced. At the same time, competition in the domestic market recedes before the cartels and trusts, while in the foreign market it is restricted by protective tariffs, with which all major industrial countries, England excepted, surround themselves. But these protective tariffs are nothing but preparations for the ultimate general industrial war, which shall decide who has supremacy on the world-market. Thus every factor, which works against a repetition of the old crises, carries within itself the germ of a far more powerful future crisis.[12]

Engels is, effectively, telling us that the *Inherent Error*, which in Marx takes the form of the continuing relevance of the Ricardian *corn model*, impedes a decent analysis of the present and, in particular, blinds us to the very real possibility of a 'more powerful future crisis'. To remain faithful to 'the precision of the natural sciences', advocated by Marx in the preface to his *Critique of Political Economy*, means to remain oblivious to real, evolving capitalism. For unlike physical (even biological) processes, capitalism's path is predicated upon a human element that infuses it with radical indeterminacy. At the level of the production process, it is the irreducibility of human labour to an electricity generator type of device that is responsible for both the creation of value and the impossibility of pinning down analytically the value of things (recall Chapters 4 and 5). Meanwhile, at the level of investment and corporate management, once firms grew into conglomerates, the Edisons, the Fords, the Gates, etc. acquired an importance that cannot be accounted for by simplistic models. Suddenly, the prospect of much faster growth became real but, at once, so did the prospect of a massive collapse.

At around the same time, John Atkinson Hobson (1858–1940), a liberal intellectual energised by the Second Boer War in South Africa, made a connection between the new phase that capitalism seemed to be entering, with the rise of corporate power, and *imperialism*; in particular with the *Scramble for Africa* in which Hobson took a keen interest. Hobson is the second of our outsiders in this section. For although he was a lecturer at the London School of Economics, his critique of *Say's Law*, and his ensuing political economics, was reportedly the reason his economics was scoffed at by established economists. Soon after he published his eminently influential 1889 book,[13] he was instructed to confine his lectures to literature before being pushed out of academia altogether.

In his important book, Hobson recognised that the second industrial revolution was working against *Say's Law* in that the accumulation of vast capital in the hands of a relatively small band of industrialists was giving capitalism a propensity towards under-consumption (or, equivalently, over-production); that is, capitalism developed a tendency to produce a great deal more than it could absorb. With Europe's industrial working classes never far off the verge of extreme poverty, the gleaming new products of the second industrial revolution could not be readily soaked up. New markets had to be found and this is what caused the clash between European powers for control of faraway places, from Africa and East Asia to Latin America and the Middle East.

Box 7.2 Imperialism's new clothes

Even though a liberal, Hobson seems to have influenced his fellow liberals less than he did the Marxists. Karl Kautsky (the German Social Democratic leader) and Vladimir Lenin (the eventual leader of the Russian Revolution) were much impressed by Hobson whose views helped them break away from Marx's conception of capitalism as a system of competitive markets. In its stead they developed a view of monopoly capitalism, reflecting the rise of the corporations, which was then, in the manner suggested by Hobson, linked to neo-imperialism. Lenin makes the point powerfully that the capitalism of Smith, Ricardo and Marx had been and gone:

> Free competition is the basic feature of capitalism, and of commodity production generally; monopoly is the exact opposite of free competition, but we have seen

the latter being transformed into monopoly before our eyes, creating large-scale industry and forcing out small industry, replacing large-scale by still larger-scale industry, and carrying concentration of production and capital to the point where out of it has grown and is growing monopoly: cartels, syndicates and trusts, and merging with them, the capital of a dozen or so banks, which manipulate thousands of millions. At the same time the monopolies, which have grown out of free competition, do not eliminate the latter, but exist above it and alongside it, and thereby give rise to a number of very acute, intense antagonisms, frictions and conflicts. Monopoly is the transition from capitalism to a higher system.[1]

In a lecture delivered on 14 (NS 27) May 1917, a few months before the Russian Revolution, Lenin explains how peace and the smooth functioning of monopoly capitalism at home can only be purchased at the price of wars of conquest abroad:

Peace reigned in Europe, but this was because domination over hundreds of millions of people in the colonies by the European nations was sustained only through constant, incessant, interminable wars, which we Europeans do not regard as wars at all, since all too often they resembled, not wars, but brutal massacres, the wholesale slaughter of unarmed peoples.[2]

Notes

1 See Chapter 7 of Vladimir Lenin (1917 [1948]). *Imperialism, the Highest Stage of Capitalism.*
2 Lenin (1929 [1964]), p. 401.

In 1913, Rosa Luxemburg (1871–1919; see also Box 6.2, previous chapter) took Engels' and Hobson's points to their natural conclusion: the new developments in capitalism, brought about by the second industrial revolution, repudiated Ricardo's repudiation of the possibility of a 'general glut'. *Say's Law* was no more and a 'general glut' became not only possible but inevitable. It is tempting to think that, through Luxemburg, Malthus got his revenge on Ricardo (recall Box 7.1). But it would be only very partially true. Luxemburg's point is not that a portion of the surplus has to be given over to unproductive people (e.g. Malthus' aristocracy or, in our societies, to unemployed artists or surfers refusing to work) who will then spend it and, unintentionally, generate the missing demand which will alleviate, even preclude, the crisis.

Her point was, rather, that in a world ruled by few, large corporations, the drive to produce more and better capital goods, innovations, etc., is not kept in check by the automatic disciplining mechanism of prices, wages and the interest rate. The likes of Edison will keep accumulating capital as if in a frenzy. And when that capital runs out of opportunities to yield decent returns, a period of gross over-investment will more likely than not give its place to a total investment crunch; the first step into a treacherous bog from which market societies may not be able to extricate themselves. Six years before her brutal murder, Luxemburg wrote:

[I]f … the capitalists do not themselves consume their products but practise abstinence, i.e accumulate, for whose sake do they produce? Even less can the maintenance of an ever larger army of workers be the ultimate purpose of continuous accumulation of capital. From the capitalist's point of view, the consumption of the workers is a consequence of accumulation; it is never its object or its condition, unless the principles (foundations) of capitalist production are to be turned upside down. And in any case, the workers can only consume that part of the product which corresponds to the variable capital, not a jot more. Who, then, realises the permanently increasing surplus value? ... the capitalists themselves and they alone. And what do they do with this increasing surplus value? ... They use it for an ever greater expansion of their production. These capitalists are thus fanatical supporters of an expansion of production for production's sake. They see to it that ever more machines are built for the sake of building – with their help – ever more new machines. Yet the upshot of all this is not accumulation of capital but an increasing production of producer goods to no purpose whatever.[14]

Reading these lines in the works of Engels, Hobson and Luxemburg one thing becomes clear: the writing had been on the wall for a long while. Capitalism was at once gathering pace and preparing for a large scale calamity. These *outsiders* could sense the approaching storm. They saw how small-scale crises were becoming more frequent, deeper, eerier; and how the amplifying intercourse between the financial markets and the burgeoning corporations was increasing volatility. They witnessed the way in which over-investment, especially in railways, caused the first ever cases of demand–scarcity in the history of humanity and helped fuel hideous conflicts in Africa and elsewhere. They issued their warnings with clarity and passion. But their *outsider* status muffled their voices, except when finding expression in the literature and boisterous gatherings of the revolutionaries.

Meanwhile, extreme serenity ruled in the amphitheatres of the *insiders*; of the academic political economists whose university job description it was to keep their finger on capitalism's pulse. Alas, their fingers were too busy penning equations in which crises were simply impossible.

7.3 Great Expectations

Well before 1929, *validity* had eclipsed *truth* in the insiders' works. Their Marginalist ambition to reduce every price to some marginal utility led them straight into the arms of the *Inherent Error*'s best-laid trap; to the dreadful neoclassical dilemma of *either* allowing for many commodities *or* for time, but *never* for both in the same model.[15] Whenever a scholar ignored this limitation, and tried to include both, the model punished him/her mercilessly. After a promising beginning, his/her best theoretical moves would unravel into an indeterminate model, a vague set of relative prices and an ambiguous collection of quantities. It was the theoretical equivalent of invading Russia: a brisk start, followed by the inevitable slow down, before the powdery snow of good intentions was covered in blood and wholesale retreat became the only hope. In the case of the insiders, retreat meant the hasty return to models featuring either a single sector or an imaginary setting where time and space occupied a single, mass-less, point.

Since the ontological furniture of the insiders' models could not include complexity *and* time, the insistence on explaining relative prices as ratios of marginal utilities meant one thing: that any connection with really existing capitalism had to be abandoned. Curiosity and mathematical prowess were thus channelled exclusively to a rigorous investigation of the logical consistency of models that were either static or fit solely for a corn-only economy, or an economy like that created by the shipwrecked Robinson Crusoe.[16] The neoclassicists' optimal strategy for answering questions about crises, recessions and the prospects of capitalism during the second quarter of the twentieth century was to duck them. And the best tactic for doing this was to turn a blind eye to the deepening chasm between their own models and the reality of intense financialisation unfolding in unison with the rise of the great corporations.

The more neoclassical economists could smell the fear of real people in the run up to 1929, the better they became at ignoring such human frailties. Outside their university corridors, prices rose and fell as if some irregular tide, ruled by unruly gravitational forces, was stringing them along. Speculative exuberance gave its place to panic, panic dissipated for a while before picking up again and unemployment oscillated like a yo-yo. Neoclassicism was unable to tell a story about any of this while gallivanting around as the ultimate and purest of price theories.

Nevertheless, however well insulated academic economists might have been from economic reality, *some* semblance of realism had to be projected, if only in order to impress their academic superiors. A theory of the general direction of dollar, or nominal, prices had to be incorporated into their Marginalist theory of relative prices. But not at any cost! Their fledgling theory of average prices could not be allowed to sully their basic price theory. It should leave untouched the underlying, the foundational, theory of relative prices. So they ended up grafting a neoclassical theory of *average prices* on top of their Marginalist theory of *relative prices*.

The trick was to assume that any changes in *average prices* would leave *relative prices* untouched, so that the latter could continue to reflect ratios of *marginal utilities*, as stipulated by the *equi-marginal principle* [recall equation (6.1), Chapter 6]. And to defend this farfetched assumption of money neutrality, the *insiders* of political economics (the neoclassicists as we call them here) invoked an older theory of inflation (or deflation) known as the *Quantity Theory of Money*.[17] One of its first advocates was philosopher David Hume (1711–76), Adam Smith's inspiration. Based on observations from Spain and elsewhere on the effects of a rapid increase in gold and silver coinage, Hume declared that wealth is not related to the quantity of money as such. When extra gold is discovered, or looted from foreign lands, economic activity rises initially in response to the larger quantity of money that is now circulating. However, pretty soon prices rise and any initial boost in activity fades. All that remains is the higher prices.[18]

This take on money suited the neoclassicists' aim to the ground. Its presumed neutrality allowed them to articulate a theory of the average level of prices, and its rate of change, which does *not* meddle with their basic theory of how many slices of bread trade for a croissant or for one hour of Jack's labour.[19] The price of one croissant, and one hour of Jack's labour, as expressed in the equivalent number of bread slices, was therefore declared independent of the quantity of money circulating in the economy. All that changes when money floods in or out is that, suddenly, more or fewer coins, or banknotes of a higher or lower face value, correspond to each slice of bread.

To see the logic of this, but also its severe limitations, let us revisit Radford's POW camp of Section 6.7 (see Chapter 6). There, money was literally carcinogenic: all transactions were denominated in cigarettes, except for the brief period when the senior officers tried to create, with some success, a fictitious currency with which to replace cigarettes. Radford's (1945) narrative empirically supports the *Quantity Theory of Money* in that, in most cases, average prices (expressed in cigarettes) fluctuate with the actual quantity of money (i.e. of cigarettes) in the POW economy. When more cigarettes were contained, relative to other goods, in the incoming Red Cross parcels, prices expressed in cigarettes rose while, at the same time, the relative prices of, say, tea and coffee remained largely unaffected. At least within the confines of the POW camp, the *Quantity Theory of Money* seemed to be working as the neoclassicists had wanted it too.

Interestingly, Radford mentions another determinant of average prices: expectations about the quantity of money. When news came in of an impending influx of cigarettes, average prices would skyrocket. At other times, when the prisoners expected an aerial bombardment (and thus disruption to Red Cross deliveries) average prices deflated. So it seems that, quite naturally, expectations matter a great deal. And here is yet another rub. In a complex, dynamic capitalist economy, in which goods are produced, rather than fall from the sky manna from heaven-like, expectations concern not only the level of prices but also the level of aggregate investment and, concomitantly, of aggregate demand. Of course, none of this applies to the POW camp. But it does apply to really existing capitalism.

To see this, in Radford's POW economy, average prices, say P, fluctuated with the quantity of cigarettes (i.e. money), say M, because two other variables were not affected by the latter: the quantity of goods Q available for trade between prisoners in each period and the number of deals struck every hour δ. In general, whenever a quantity of money M is used to sell a quantity of goods Q, average prices P are given as:

$$P = (M \times \delta)/Q$$

(7.1)

The idea here is that average prices P (i) rise with the quantity of money M (when the number of goods Q and the speed δ with which they are traded remain constant); (ii) rise with the number of deals δ struck per period (when the quantity of money M and the quantity Q of goods available for trade remain fixed); and (iii) fall when the quantity Q of goods available for trade rises (assuming a constant quantity of money M and a constant number of deals struck every hour δ).

At the POW camp, it made sense to assume that variables δ and Q were unaffected by fluctuations in M. For example, if Louis had a quantity of tea which he wanted to swap with Bob's unwanted quantity of coffee, the transaction would go ahead, even in the absence of cigarettes (i.e. money). If the 'money supply', that is, the quantity of cigarettes M, were larger or smaller, this would affect solely the number of cigarettes corresponding to each ounce of tea or coffee (i.e. average prices) but not to the ratio of these two numbers (i.e. the price of tea relative to the price of coffee). In terms of equation (7.1), M's fluctuations only influenced average prices P because this was a POW camp in which δ and G were independent of M.

In a POW economy, variables δ and Q can be assumed independent of M because production and investment are truly exogenous. Bob's coffee was produced in Ethiopia and Louis' tea in French Guiana *independently of the expectations of Radford and his fellow prisoners*. The quantity of these goods, Q in equation (7.1) had nothing to do with the price determination mechanism and the expectations formation process. The prisoners' expectations were as likely to affect the quantity Q of goods to be traded in the camp as their weather forecasts were likely to affect the weather: *not in the slightest!*

In summary, the only expectations that changed anything in Radford's little POW economy were the prisoners' forecasts concerning the number of cigarettes M. These particular expectations entered equation (7.1) exclusively and helped determine average cigarette prices P, with often lasting effects on P. The reason is that when they predicted a rise in the number of cigarettes (of *M*), they immediately predicted a rise in average prices *P*. Thus, their estimate of the purchasing power of the cigarettes (or, put differently, the cigarettes' *exchange value*) fell. Smokers would then indulge their habit more liberally and, in this manner, part of *M* would go up, literally, in a puff of smoke! Consequently, *M* would drop and prices stabilise.

In short, even though the number of cigarettes *M* circulating was almost as exogenous as the amount of coffee, tea and chocolate, expectations over average prices had an impact on it. Something of an 'automatic stabiliser' worked its minor miracle in the camp, ensuring that greater expectations regarding the supply of cigarettes yielded a smaller increase in prices than one would have expected (in the absence of smokers). And *vice versa*: deflationary expectations (i.e. the prediction of reductions in the supply of cigarette-money) did not depress prices as much because the very prediction that more coffee would soon correspond to the same number of cigarettes gave smokers an incentive to cut down![20]

What about expectations on the quantity *Q* (of tea, coffee and other goodies) and the speed of transactions δ? Did they matter? Only in a very limited manner. Although fluctuations in the prisoners' expectations on *Q* and δ could affect the price level *P* [through equation (7.1)], such effects were temporary and dissipated once the *Q* and δ variables were observed. Moreover, Radford's comrades were not dim. They shared common knowledge that their expectations could not, in the medium term, affect the actual level of *Q* and δ. This common knowledge allowed the prisoners to operate like true believers of the *Quantity Theory of Money*; that is, of the theory that average prices move in tandem with the quantity of money.

The question then becomes: is it sensible to assume such common knowledge outside the barbed wire of a concentration camp? Is the simplistic *Quantity Theory of Money* valid in a capitalist economy? We think not. For, when *Q* must be produced within the society generating the expectations which encourage some to invest, and this investment is predicated upon an expectation of profit, it is no longer the case that variables *Q* or δ are exogenous and that they are *necessarily* unaffected in the medium and long run by expectations regarding *Q* and δ. On the contrary, business trades on nothing else but hopeful forecasts. Great expectations concerning *Q* and δ lead to bountiful investment which reinforces these expectations, in all their greatness. And vice versa: dismal forecasts may well precipitate a collapse in *Q* (and subsequently in δ) which, also in a circular fashion, will confirm the empirical validity of the awful prognoses. None of this flies in the face of Reason. Instead, it is what Reason prescribes (see Box 7.7 for a comprehensive presentation of this argument).

The reader may well stop us in our tracks at this point and ask: why did the neoclassical economists not see this? Are you cleverer than them? No, we certainly are not. Our conviction is that the whole Marginalist project was like a huge tanker that could not be turned around even if those at the helm saw the folly in the chosen course. The reason was the *Inherent Error* and, in particular, the guise it adopts when all prices must be reduced to ratios of marginal utilities.

As we argue in Box 7.3, the only way of allowing expectations about the future to matter, while keeping to a Leibnizian calculus, is to allow for time to enter the model. But this means that, to make room for time, the model economy cannot contain more than one person or more than one commodity. But then, once back in the bosom of the *corn model* or the Robinson Crusoe economy, expectations cannot possibly influence output, employment, investment. For, when Robinson Crusoe is working alone, his expectations may bear upon

Box 7.3 From cornfields to Wall Street
(via the neoclassical version of the Inherent Error*)*

In a single-commodity world, like the corn model, the notion of price makes no sense (since there is nothing to trade it with). However, there do exist two 'prices' in this single-minded economy: the price of labour (e.g. the amount of corn paid per hour of work to labourers) and the price of savings or the interest rate. Ignoring the wage for now, savings (S) are, naturally, always equal to investment (I), since corn is saved today only in order to be ploughed back into the soil tomorrow. The increase in future production due to this act of abstinence is its reward.

Suppose that for every kilogramme of corn saved (in the form of seeds), production rises in the next period by a factor of $(1 + r)$, where $0 < r < 1$, r is the economy's rate of interest, which is also its growth and profit rate (recall Box 3.4 from Chapter 3). To extend this model in such a way that it becomes a proper Marginalist theory of the interest rate, while incorporating a theory of both general and relative prices, we need two things: first, we need a second commodity that will make (analytical) room for relative prices to be explained in terms of the equi-marginal principle. Second, we need to add some form of money into this economy, so that we can differentiate between the general price level (or average money prices, e.g. the average of prices expressed in dollars or cigarettes or whatever token we choose to play the role of money) and the relative prices.

Note the severe difficulty with both of these steps: if we are to introduce a second commodity (e.g. machines in addition to corn), this is tantamount to introducing a second sector or market; one that is interlocked with the corn sector. In a Marginalist context, this is fine as long as there is no time involved. But how can we preserve the notion of the interest rate, r, without time? As we have argued in Section 6.11 of the last chapter, time and multiple commodities cannot co-exist within a logically coherent Marginalist framework and, for this reason, neoclassicism fudged the problem by basing its inferences concerning capitalism on, effectively, a single-person or a single-commodity model. This strategy reached its culmination when neoclassical theory tried to tell a story about general or average prices and ended up with a seemingly complex story that, nonetheless, was built upon the flimsiest of foundations: on a model that, in order to preserve time (and thus maintain the notion of the interest rate), had silently dropped any pretence to allowing for multiple commodities.

Put differently, the neoclassical theory of inflation/deflation that prevailed prior to 1929 was extracted from the Marginalist story that, so as to carry the explanatory burden, had surreptitiously dropped its own theory of relative prices. And when asked about relative prices, and their determinants, the jolly theorist would reply: 'But they are not influenced by movements in general or average prices, are they'? Where did their confidence come from? It came, we think, from the faith that there is no difference between Radford's POW camp and a capitalist economy; from the belief that, like in the POW camp, output is independent of expectations and demand is always abundant enough to absorb the produced output. As for investment, it is assumed to be unidirectionally determined by savings that are, in turn, determined by the rate at which present consumption is deferred to the future.

The best-known examples of the era are the models by Knut Wicksell (1898) and Irving Fisher (1911). The first thing the reader of these treatises notes is, indeed, the absence of multiple commodities. Both Wicksell and Fisher tell their story in terms of aggregate variables, such as the quantity of money (M), the rate of interest (r), average prices (P) and total output (Q). Wicksell's initial assumption is that there exists a *normal or natural* interest rate $r*$ such that, when it prevails, the demand and supply of savings are equalised; that is, investment equals savings ($I = S$).[1] Wicksell acknowledges that banks can destabilise this 'equilibrium' by creating more credit (e.g. by giving out more paper loans through a reduction of their reserves) or by restricting it. When this happens, the quantity of average prices P respond accordingly.[2]

Fisher's 1911 theory[3] differs from Wicksell's in that the money M changes (just as it did in the POW camp when the inflow of cigarettes fluctuated) and distinguishes between two types of money: currency or primary money M (i.e. money in people's pockets) and bank deposits M'. Unlike Wicksell's model, Fisher's predicts that the money or nominal interest rate will not fall when more money is pumped into the economy. Instead, bank deposits (M') will rise faster than the quantity of cash (M) and the nominal interest rate will rise but not enough to keep the real interest rate (i.e. the nominal rate r minus the rate of increase in average prices P) at its original level.

Regardless of these niceties, one thing remains constant in both models: relative prices and total output! Why? By assumption! Since there is no room for relative prices in this type of neoclassical model, due to the Marginalist-*cum*-neoclassical version of the *Inherent Error* (and the impossibility of including both time and relative prices, i.e. multiple sectors, in the same Marginalist analysis),[4] Wicksell's and Fishers' analyses could not possibly leave room for instances when changes in the quantity of M may affect both average prices P *and* the economy's relative prices. Instead of admitting that their theory has *nothing* to say about relative prices (since their theories could not logically sustain more than one sector), the two authors did what all neoclassicists worth their salt have been doing ever since: they took it for granted that relative prices will not be affected! This is no different from astronomers who rule out the possibility of an eclipse not because their theory leads to this conclusion but because they lack a theory of eclipses.

Such was the state of theoretical play just before the storm; the theoretical ammunition with which humanity was armed prior to 1929 in order to understand the role and impact of Wall Street on its daily life. Not the best of defences against the oncoming tempest.

Notes
1 See Knut Wicksell (1898 [1936]).
2 Wicksell's mechanism by which a rise in M affects P is this: suppose that the banks reduce the money or nominal interest rate r such that $r < r*$. The quantity of money M in the economy will increase and capitalists will borrow and invest more. Thus the quantity of capital K will rise. As a result, resources will be shifted from the consumption goods sector to the capital goods sector and the price of capital K will also rise. Meanwhile, no more consumption goods will be produced (since resources are abandoning this sector) at a time of increased demand (following the rise in demand for consumption goods by capitalists, whose capital is

now rewarding them better). The result of this will be an increase in the price of consumption
goods, pushing average prices, P, upwards. QED.

3 See Fisher (1911).

4 For an insightful depiction of the neoclassical variant of the *Inherent Error*, as it applies to
the quantity theory of money, see Visser (1974), pp.168–74 in particular.

his decision to go fishing today (e.g. if he foresees a storm) but not on his investment
decision (e.g. on how much of his time to invest in making a better fishing rod, at the
expense of catching fewer fish today). Similarly, in a populous corn economy, while an
expectation that the end of the world is nigh may affect the rate at which corn is saved for
the future, there can be no uncertainty that if a lot of corn is saved today perhaps this will
lead to a glut of corn tomorrow (i.e. a crisis caused from ending up with large quantities of
unsold corn).

At the risk of repetitiveness, we shall restate our simple point here: the *insiders* failed to
see the *Crash of 1929* coming, blinded not by inadequate analytical skills but by the demands
of their theoretical project. Once the Marginalist-*cum*-neoclassical approach came up against
the *Inherent Error*, it had no alternative but to choose between *time* and *complexity*. It
dropped complexity and, as a result, its models could not possibly account for any influence
expectations may have on savings, investment, output and employment. Hence, the *insiders*
were left with models in which crises were impossible since relative prices were disconnected from average prices and expectations continually affected the latter but never the
former. Thus, the price neoclassical economists forked out for the mathematical closure of
their utility calculus was the mother of all empirical failures.

Perhaps the best guide to the theoretical *cul-de-sac* that was 1920s neoclassicism is a
wonderful little Marginalist exercise in Box 7.4. We include it here for two reasons: first,
because its author, Frank Ramsey, was a young mathematician of astonishing accomplishment not only in mathematics but also in philosophy; second, because of the way this model
was interpreted by the economists. Ramsey worked on a mathematical exercise in pinning
down the optimal level of investment in an 'economy' featuring no markets, a single-commodity
and, effectively, a single person. The economics profession interpreted it, and used it, as a
parable for the workings of capitalism. That this model was hailed as the last word in neoclassicism's attempt to explain the ups and down of average prices, a year before the *Crash
of 1929*, is, we believe, an education in itself.

Concluding this section, we go out on a melancholy note. Crises are not a happy time and
1929 was one of the unhappiest. Just before it struck, the best way of capturing the political
economists' sum of understanding of the workings of capitalism would come in the form of
a sentence beginning with: *we have no clue!* The point of the rest of the book is that *nothing
has changed since then. Absolutely nothing!* Whereas other sciences have moved in leaps
and bounds, the insiders of our discipline remain wedded either to single-commodity and
Robinson Crusoe models (featuring amazingly complex dynamics) or to wonderfully complex multiple-commodity (or General Equilibrium) models in which time sits still. Neither
variety of model allows us a glimpse of an expectations-driven world in which our expectations are capricious, not because we are not smart enough to form them rationally,
but because capitalism is indeterminate.

Box 7.4 The unbearable lightness of calculus on the cusp of 1929
The melancholy tale of Frank Ramsey

If we had to name one person that captured the fatal lure exerted by neoclassicism on brilliant minds during the optimistic 1920s, we would choose Frank Ramsey (1903–30). Ramsey was a brilliant mathematical logician with a depressive streak. After studying mathematics at Trinity College, Cambridge, he spent time in Austria seeking solace in Freudian psychoanalysis as well as acquainting himself with Ludwig Wittgenstein's gruelling book on logic's limitations, the *Tractatus Logico-Philosophicus*. In 1924, he returned to Cambridge where, with John Maynard Keynes' help, he secured a fellowship, before gaining a University lectureship two years later. A committed atheist, he was acutely aware of the perils of the ascent of fascism and Nazism, possibly due to his heavily politicised progressive interlocutors at Cambridge; among them Piero Sraffa (the Italian leftwing economist mentioned extensively in Chapter 5) and Ludwig Wittgenstein, whose path-breaking philosophical thesis translated by Ramsey was submitted as a doctoral dissertation in Cambridge with Ramsey as his supervisor.[1]

Encouraged by Keynes (his original sponsor at Cambridge) to apply his exemplary mathematical talents to economic questions, Ramsey came up with three distinct contributions whose influence on neoclassicism persists to this day. We shall focus on one, his last, as a paradigm of how the use of calculus, courtesy of the *Inherent Error*, leads even the brightest and the most sensitive soul to models that (a) have no link to capitalist reality but (b) are used by neoclassicists to tell stories about reality that confuse, disorientate and, ultimately, increase the risk of economic disaster.

In his 1928 paper entitled 'A mathematical theory of saving',[2] Ramsey tried to do that at which Marginalist economics had proven so abysmal: to extend calculus to models incorporating time. Since the *Inherent Error* does not budge however brilliant the analyst who chooses to confront it, to tell his temporal story Ramsey had to confine it within the realm of a single sector 'economy'. So, this is what Ramsey asks of his reader: imagine a first born; let's call him Adam. He starts life all alone with only his labour as a weapon against scarcity. He puts himself to work to produce corn which he must, once the harvest is in, divide between the quantity that he will eat and the rest which he will save for planting in the next period. Adam is remarkable in two ways. First, he is immortal. Second, as time goes by, another miracle occurs: Adam divides and multiplies (exponentially) into clones of himself.[3]

The question Ramsey put to himself was this: what proportion of their produce should Adam and his clones consume and what proportion should they save? If Adam was in full control of his decision, the answer would depend, among other considerations, on the extent to which Adam empathises towards his clones, as well as on the empathy felt by clones for future (currently unborn) clones. The more the current generation cares for the unborn future generations, the more they save. Additionally, a question of distribution between the different generations might emerge (e.g. Adam requesting a higher proportion of output in the future if he has invested heavily at the outset). To remove these complications, Ramsey introduces another assumption:

neither Adam nor his clones decide on how much should be consumed or saved per period. Or on how they will divide the spoils. No, the decision is that of a benevolent God (or Central Planner, or the Overlord Program in the *Matrix*-like economy of Chapter 4) who supervises this 'economy' and who determines the saving decision of each version of Adam with a view to maximising the intertemporal utility of Adam and of every cloned Adam well into an infinite future.[4]

Ramsey's analysis turns on two differential equations: the first one determines *intertemporal investment*, or the rate at which uneaten corn (i.e. capital) accumulates. Ramsey assumes that, in each period, this rate, i.e. investment, depends on (a) the corn output not consumed and (b) the amount of corn that is necessary to replenish expended corn seeds in the current production period (note how similar all this is to the logic of Box 3.4). The second equation determines *intertemporal savings*, and results from Ramsey's assumption that God is a dedicated Marginalist who decides on the basis of the *equi-marginal principle* applied intertemporally. In other words, just like Jill decided, in the previous chapter, how many cherries to pick *as if* by setting her marginal utility equal to her marginal cost, in Ramsey's case God wants to make sure that Adam's (and his clones') consumption of corn, at every moment in time, is such that his marginal utility of current consumption equals his marginal cost.

Now, Adam's marginal utility from eating corn in the current period is straightforward. But what is his marginal cost, in the absence of money or some other commodity? Given that there are no prices here, God does his sums on the basis of *opportunity cost*: Adam's cost from eating one kilogramme of corn now is the utility he loses at the thought of the kilogrammes of corn that he is giving up in the next period (i.e. the corn output that he would have had available in the next period had he planted the current kilogramme of corn now, instead of devouring it). Ramsey's assumption in this regard is that this marginal cost of consumption depends on Adam's sympathy towards his future self (i.e. how much utility he gains today at the thought of an increased utility in the future) as well as on the rate at which consumption has been growing so far and, of course, on the production function that turns today's saved corn into tomorrow's additional harvest.

With these assumptions under his belt, Ramsey came closer to solving his two differential equations in two unknowns: investment (or capital accumulation) and savings. Of course, to render the mathematics manageable, he had to introduce a host of simplifying assumptions (e.g. a smooth, concave utility function for the various Adams, a production function that allowed for no economies of scale, in accordance to our musings in Section 6.10 of Chapter 6, etc.). When all was said and done, Ramsey produced a 'solution' reporting on the combinations of the level of capital stock (i.e. corn seeds) and of consumption that were consistent, in every period, with maximum intertemporal utility for Adam and his clones.

Ramsey's mathematics was impeccable. What was less so was the use the economists put it to after his premature death. Taking it for granted that Ramsey's model is a useful abstraction for understanding really-existing capitalism, neoclassical economists employed it in order to make pronouncements on sensible policies on investment![5] Mistaking an assumption for a theorem, they drew the conclusion from Ramsey's model that increased savings always feed into higher growth and that capitalism was best equipped to oversee this transformation of current abstinence into future prosperity. They extracted such wise counsel for governments and parliaments on the basis of a model featuring one good, no markets and a benevolent (also unaccountable) God-like planner. The way in which they managed to convince themselves that this interpretation of Ramsey's elegant model was pertinent to the state of capitalism in 1928 beggars belief.

This is, we suggest, one of history's best examples of the misuse of mathematics. And its significance is painfully contemporary. For, if one looks at the macroeconomics literature *circa* 2007, that is, a year prior to our very own 1929, one will be struck by their resemblance to Ramsey's analysis; the only difference being that in the newer generation of Ramsey-like models (known as *overlapping generation* General Equilibrium *models*), Adam and his clones do not live forever. Perhaps every economic meltdown is preceded by a flourish of models featuring no markets and an almighty central planner!

Notes
1 Ramsey did not supervise the *Tractatus*. For peculiar reasons, after Wittgenstein had already written the *Tractatus*, he remained in Cambridge doing doctoral work with Ramsey as his supervisor. Eventually he was allowed to submit the *Tractatus* as a doctoral dissertation with Moore and Russell as his examiners.
2 See Ramsey (1928).
3 If at the outset, the number of people in this 'economy' is 1 (i.e. Adam), by time t the number of Adam-like agents equals e^{nt} where n is the cloning rate.
4 Note that the fact that they are all clones is very convenient since we can now assume that, at any time, all 'individuals' have identical preferences. In this manner, we have removed all complexity caused by heterogeneity: they all want the same thing and, since God decides on what each will get, all distributional concerns disappear. Each gets an equal share of corn dedicated for present consumption and no disagreement is possible on the basis that some get more utility than others from present consumption, relative to the utility of anticipating future consumption.
5 The standard neoclassical model taught in graduate classes today is the so-called Ramsey–Cass–Koopmans model after the contributions by David Cass (1965) and Tjalling C. Koopmans (1965). This is the veritable neoclassical model since Solow's growth model assumes an exogenous savings ratio and leaves room for someone to choose the Golden Rule savings ratio. The model we describe here is closer to the canonical version, which is the staple model in growth classes today. Ramsey thought it ethically indefensible to give a discount factor for future generations, so he assumed a 'bliss point' that the social planner had to reach in an optimal manner, even though later in the article he examined the possibility of relaxing this assumption. Keynes had to add his own comments to make the point understood by the less mathematically-privileged-readers. Keynes has also written a beautiful obituary (Keynes, 1930 [1972]).

In the weeks leading up to 1929, just as in the run up to 2008, insiders failed to grasp the simplest of truths: that economies capable of flying high on the high-octane fuel of great expectations is just as likely to crash when the expectations turn sour; that Reason cannot predict these turning points; that it cannot do this because there is more than one thing that *may* happen, rationally (see Box 7.7); and that when Reason fails, contingency rules. Insiders are scornful of contingency. They have an understandable urge to pin things down. Unfortunately, some things cannot be pinned down, except through intellectual subterfuge.

Intellectual honesty requires that we acknowledge capitalism's radical indeterminacy: its capacity for growth, when optimism rules, and for catastrophe, whenever the tide goes out on happy forecasts. Regrettably, honesty is not the stock in the economists' trade. Keeping the *Inherent Error* alive trumps the need to deal with *Condorcet's Secret* every time. Modelling the capitalism of Edison, Ford and Siemens as if it were analytically indistinguishable from Radford's POW camp was functional to many careers, and to a few bankers, robber barons, etc., but lowered society's resistance to the oncoming depression.

Unlike bad astronomy, which can have no dire effects on humanity at large, bad economics is lethal. By steeling policymakers against any suggestion of an impending Crash, neoclassicists played an important role in bringing about the very war that created the POW camp in which the neoclassical story found its most propitious habitat – a twist that, while utterly incapable of lessening the tragedy of the Second World War, at least allows us to 'feel the irony' in its wickedest form.

7.4 The Fall

> Men who have created new fruits in the world cannot create a system whereby their fruits may be eaten. And the failure hangs over the State like a great sorrow. [A]nd in the eyes of the people there is the failure; and in the eyes of the hungry there is a growing wrath. In the souls of the people the grapes of wrath are filling and growing heavy, growing heavy for the vintage.[21]

Novelists, unencumbered by our *Inherent Error*, captured the spirit of the fall with prose that we can only envy. As George Stigler (1911–91), a committed neoclassicist, once admitted: 'We [economists] cannot tell a nation to stop turning beautiful trees into waste paper, but we can weigh the ashes'.[22] And what a mountain of ashes we had to weigh after 1929! A whole generation was cast to the wastelands of poverty, unemployment and malnutrition before it was thrown again, this time onto the killing fields and furnaces of the Second World War. Hopes and dreams that were powered by the faith in markets went up in smoke overnight. The very idea of progress through thrift and betterment via personal virtue died in that fateful year. What replaced them was gloom, hopelessness and a war whose enormity was such that its survivors sought solace in the thought that it might be the war which ends all wars.

Back in the early 1920s, the American worker was told that the cure to poverty had been found: 'Hitch yourselves to the bandwagon of the brave new capitalism that Edison, Ford and the financial markets are shaping, and you will thrive. Turn your back to the poisonous recipes of the Russian Bolsheviks, and life will be good. Put behind you the divisive ideas of class conflict, and prosperity will come. Ignore the sirens of redistributing an existing pie, and your pie will get larger and larger. In short, live the New American Dream. We can all get rich. Together. All it takes is hard work, confidence in Wall Street, and trust in the corporations nesting in its listings'.

For a while, it seemed a plausible dream. A worker who in 1921 started investing $15 from his weekly wages on blue chip shares could look forward to having, by 1941 (judging by how things were going from 1921 to 1929), a nice portfolio of shares worth $80,000 and a healthy monthly dividend of $400. These were not empty promises: by 1926, our thrifty worker's initial nest egg of $780 (put together by buying $15 of shares weekly) had grown to almost $7,000. Three years later, just before the bubble burst, his shares were worth a heart-warming $21,000 (see Figure 7.1). But then, the dream turned sour. In short order,

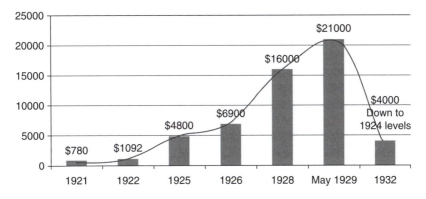

Figure 7.1 Reward from investing $15 per week in Wall Street during the swinging 1920s.

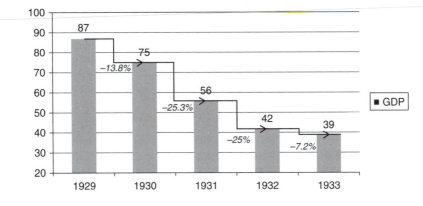

Figure 7.2 GDP in billion dollars.

forty billion dollars disappeared from Wall Street. Our parsimonious friend's shares fell and fell and fell. By 1932, they were down in value to $4,000. Had he instead stuffed his weekly $15 inside his mattress, he would have amassed more than double the sum in the same 11-year period.

After the initial shock, expectations of a quick recovery grew. 'Surely, things would get better, wouldn't they?' They did not. Instead, what desperate people from all walks of life got, up and down the country, were false dawns. Within months of Wall Street's collapse, newspapers, economists, even President Hoover himself; all predicted that the economy was about to perform a Phoenix-like trick. It did no such thing. National income in the United States continued to fall precipitously. In 1930, it fell by almost 14 per cent in dollar terms; in 1931 by another 25.3 per cent; and when everyone thought the bottom had been reached, it shed yet another 25 per cent. By 1933, all the gains capitalism had made during its most vibrant years had fizzled out (see Figure 7.2). Banks hit the wall in droves for four years running (see Figure 7.3).

Poverty was back and seemed a lot crueller in view of the broken promises of the optimistic 1920s. Much of the middle class, that had only recently climbed out of relative

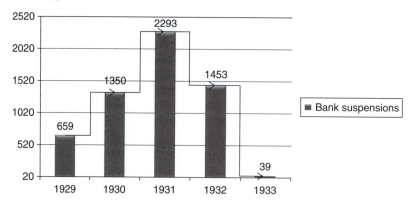

Figure 7.3 The great banking disaster.

deprivation, was dragged back into the mire of helplessness, unable to fathom how their slow, painful social climb could have hit such a slippery patch.

Meanwhile Washington was clueless. Herbert Hoover, the hapless President at the time, had one ear trained on the economists, who were assuring him that the self-correcting stabilisers of the market economy were about to kick in, and the other on the people's desperate cries for help. His administration responded like a distressed shopkeeper. On the one hand, it tried to do what every shopkeeper does in lean times: tighten the belt. The idea of doing something with the state's monopoly on money was alien to them. Capitalist economies were running what was, in essence, a common currency, much like today's Euro in the 16 countries of the Eurozone. It was called the Gold Exchange Standard (see Box 7.5 below) and it prevented governments from doing what the US, British, Chinese, even the Australian governments did in 2008: to pump money into the economy in a bid to arrest the decline into deflationary chaos.

Box 7.5 Midas loses his touch
The Gold Standard and the Great Depression

If money is nothing but tokens in which to express relative prices, why not adopt the shiniest tokens money can buy: gold coins. And because paper money is easier to issue and use, including cheques and other forms of IOUs, why not fix the value of a country's currency on some given amount of gold. The first such system in modern times has its roots in 1717 when Sir Isaac Newton, who, at the time, was moonlighting as Master of the [English] Royal Mint, edged silver out, giving gold a leading role.[1] Formally, the Gold Standard was adopted in Britain in 1819. The United States dropped silver in favour of gold in 1834 by fixing its price at a little over $20 per ounce. That price survived until the Great Depression. In 1933, the US government decided to unshackle itself from that price and the Gold Standard was confined to the annals of history. Other countries started joining the Gold Standard from 1870 onwards. Its first major test was the Great War (known after 1945 as the First World War); a test that it failed miserably. As the belligerent states were going broke, printing money to finance the war effort, they abandoned any pretence to keeping to the promise of selling gold at the prescribed rate.

In 1925, during a period of generalised growth and confidence, a new Gold Standard was created, the so-called Gold Exchange Standard, with a view to creating confidence in the currencies, minimise inflationary pressures and support trade through a system of fixed exchange rates. Effectively, the GES was meant to put in place an international single currency, supported by gold held in London and Washington. Countries such as France, Holland, Greece and Italy could hold gold, Dollars or Pounds, as collateral for their own currencies, but Britain and the USA would hold only gold.[2] All currencies would be, in theory, tradable for gold at the specified fixed prices.

The theory behind the GES, which motivated governments to join in, was that it represented the monetary system most in synch with the Quantity Theory of Money – recall Section 7.3. Since glitter cannot turn to gold, and gold reserves grow only as fast as miners hit new veins, tying the quantity of money to the physical quantity of gold meant that average prices would be kept on a leash.[3] Moreover, trade flows would automatically stabilise price levels between countries that grew at different speeds. When, for example, Edison lit the night and, as a result, American companies could work longer and faster; or when Henry Ford revolutionised the production process, the US economy began to grow faster than the French or the British. Since the quantity of money M is fixed at a planetary scale, equation (7.2) tells us that a rise in US output (Q) would bring average US prices (P) down. But that drop would heighten demand for American goods in France and Britain and depress Americans' imports from these countries. Countries with a balance of trade surplus would then, according to the GES scheme, see their holdings of gold rise, at the expense of the deficit countries. With more gold in their economies, M would rise and average prices P would follow, thus restoring the previous balance. This is Hume's price-specie flow mechanism in his 1752 Essay 'Of the Balance of Trade'.

Exogenous fluctuations in the quantity of money M were imagined to have an impact similar to that in Radford's POW economy. When new gold was found in California, as it was in 1848, M was expected to rise, P to tag along and domestic producers initially to respond by producing more output Q. Soon, however, because US exports would fall as a result of higher prices, an outflow of gold from the American economy was anticipated that ought to push M, P and Q down again. At least that was the theory. In practice, there were many wrinkles to the Gold Standard story that only historical analysis can reveal. Various tricks were used to prevent an outflow of gold in times of trade deficits or to avoid having to impede an inflow of gold when experiencing a trade surplus. The commonest trick was to take liberties with interest rates and government borrowing. Under the GES, the rules clearly stated that a deficit country, seeing that its gold reserves were shrinking, should increase interest rates to control spending (consumption plus investment), to reduce average prices P, to stimulate exports and, thus, to eliminate the trade deficit.

However, a number of deficit countries simply refused to increase interest rates when faced with a trade deficit. For example, when Britain was experiencing a balance of trade deficit with the rest of the world, rather than allow its gold holdings to flow to the countries with which it was in deficit, as the rules specified, it found an ingenious way around the problem: it appropriated India's trade surplus, thus causing an flight of wealth from India to the City of London; a flight that seriously retarded growth in India, fuelled poverty even among hard-working Indians and incited additional dis-content in the subcontinent. Meanwhile, many surplus countries chose to issue securi-ties (i.e. increase government borrowing), rather than push interest rates down to avert an inflow of gold. In this manner they killed two birds with one stone: they limited the amount of gold or money circulating while, at the same time, allowing for an inflow of gold from other countries.

The overall effect of these policies, with which the rules were bent, was to exacer-bate the volatility of output and investment. When the system's shock absorbers were interfered with, any shock to the system (e.g. one caused by a fall in investor confi-dence, bad weather affecting agricultural production or even a new gold rush in Australia or California) was amplified. And even though average prices were impres-sively stable, the effect of these shocks was most painfully felt in the real economy: employment and production fluctuated a lot more during the Gold Standard era. In the USA, the official average unemployment rate in the 1879 to 1913 period was almost six per cent; a large figure for a young, innovative capitalist economy. Furthermore, when the shocks were large, the system was suspended (in England, the Pound-to-gold convertibility was suspended during the war-torn 1797–1821 period and during the Great War and its aftermath, 1914–25; in the USA, the Civil War saw another suspension of the Gold Standard, from 1862 to 1879). While the Gold Standard returned after the dust had settled in the battlefields, it met its match in the *Crash of 1929*. The Fall was its undoing and Midas finally lost his touch in the dustbowls of the American Midwest, the soup kitchens of Amsterdam and the hunger marches of British workers.

Notes

1 During the same period in France, a Scot, John Law (1671–1729), who took control of the finances of the State started an experiment with paper credit that eventually ended in disaster. It took 300 years after his birth before his proposals were adopted not by a French Regent but by the American President Richard Nixon (See the sympathetic but brilliant monograph of Antoin E. Murphy, 1997).

2 The return of Britain to the Gold Standard effected by Stanley Baldwin's Chancellor of the Exchequer, Winston Churchill, prompted Keynes to write in 1925 *The Economic Consequences of Mr. Churchill*.

3 Indeed, as in Radford's POW camp, the global economy too experienced surges in average prices when Australian and Californian miners literally struck lots of gold.

Despite his economists' advice, President Hoover knew he could not just sit idly by. So, he did what many a beleaguered leader did: he turned against the foreigners. In June 1930, a bill was rushed through Congress raising tariffs on imports in an ill-fated attempt to increase demand for domestically produced goods. When other countries retaliated, things got worse and the malaise spread out further afield.

By 1933, official US unemployment had climbed to 25 per cent, more than 5,000 banks had folded, fired workers were singing 'Brother can you spare a dime'? and hundreds of thousands of farmers had lost their land, congregating all over the country in slum-cities, which became known as *Hoovervilles*. Stung by the insinuation, President Hoover created a federal loan agency whose purpose was to stimulate home building and to help those who had not yet lost their house to foreclosure, to keep it. It was like rearranging deckchairs on the sinking Titanic. Wages, employment, profits, national income and morale, were in free fall.

In the 1932 Presidential election, Franklin Delano Roosevelt swept to power with his promised New Deal. One of his first measures was to take the USA out of the Gold Standard. The politicians' love affair with the crude *Quantity Theory of Money* had been ended by the Crash's uncompromising cruelty.[23] The problem with the dogmatic adherence to the *Quantity Theory of Money*, which made the Gold Standard so attractive to economists convinced of the wisdom of their own models, was that it tied the Federal Reserve's (i.e. the US Central Bank) hands with regard to interest rates. Instead of reducing interest rates to inflate an economy in ruinous deflation, the Fed was keeping to the Gold Standard's scenario that ruled out the use of monetary policy as a tool for propping up domestic demand. Why? Because their 'model', as a result of the latest incarnation of the *Inherent Error* (which we discussed extensively in the previous section), made no room for a crisis like this. Having assumed away the possibility of a Great Depression, of a *General Glut*, of a *Shattering Fall*, etc., they had no tool in their toolbox for such an eventuality.[24] Roosevelt's decision to follow Britain and the Scandinavian countries, who had lessened the Depression's impact by bailing out of the Gold Standard in 1931, was not so much wise as inescapable.

While the economic crisis was psychologically devastating for a rising economic power-house wallowing in the debris of its previous optimism, the rest of the world's developed economies were feeling the pain too. In Canada and Australia, two economies that largely supplied raw materials to the industrial centres in Europe and the USA, industrial production crashed by more than 40 per cent from 1929 to 1932. In Britain, unemployment jumped from 1 million workers in 1929 to 2.5 million in 1930, touching an extraordinary 20 per cent of the total workforce, which meant that in some industrial regions unemployment had topped 70 per cent. In 1931 Britain was forced to quit the Gold Standard but the respite was not tangible. A year later, unemployed Northerners marched to London, walking for two months through the streets of every major town and setting off the 1930s newest institution: the *hunger marches*.

The fall took a couple of years to be properly felt in continental Europe. Some countries fared worse than others but the fall visited them all. In France, while its impact was relatively benign, it was still strong enough to bring people onto the streets and give rise to the first socialist, Popular Front, government. Interestingly, the opposite political effect came to pass in Holland where the crisis was deeper and longer, possibly due to the government's stub-born adherence to the Gold Standard (which it abandoned as late as 1937). There, the political upheaval caused by demonstrations and violent clashes on the streets led to the formation of a pro-Nazi government. Speaking of Nazis, the fall's most significant dimension is the way it reverberated, and twisted, the social economies of the three countries which were to form the fateful axis: Germany, Italy and Japan.

Germany was already in economic strife, even before 1929. Forced to pay massive war reparations to the victors of the Great War (aka First World War), a condition that John Maynard Keynes had immediately criticised as a recipe for disaster,[25] it depended heavily on its only silver lining of the era: the US loans that were aimed at helping with Germany's recovery. But when 1929 struck, the American loans dried up and thus the Wall Street crash had an impact on Germany more immediately than elsewhere in Europe. By 1932, unemployment had exceeded by far the already dismal levels of the USA and Britain. Coupled with monetary collapse, and the related loss of the middle class' savings, the ground had been paved for Hitler's rise to power in 1933, not without a helping hand from industrialists who looked to him as a bulwark against the political left.

The idea that Hitler might not turn out to be 'that bad', which motivated the Weimar Republic's head, President Hindenburg, to invite him to form a government, was partly due to recent Italian and Japanese experiences. In Italy, Benito Mussolini had already become Prime Minister in 1922. His administration combined political fascism with pro-market and pro-industry economic policies quite in tune with neoclassical political economics, Vilfredo Pareto (see Box 6.5, previous chapter) being one of his early influences. Fascism's seemingly paradoxical idea, of using repressive political means in order to impose 'free' market solutions on a corporatist state, appealed to industrialists with a burning desire to maintain their control over factories, farms and private property in general. During a period when unemployment and the evident collapse of capitalism allowed workers to imagine an alternative to capitalism, captains of industry could count on the fascist and Nazi parties to do that which they had shown a certain talent for: putting the lid on trade union activity.

The fact that the Soviet Union was untouched by the crisis,[26] despite its many other ills, added to the urgency with which many industrialists romanced the fascists in Italy and their counterparts elsewhere. When the crisis reached Italy, major industries found themselves on the brink. The Fascist government instructed the banks to step in. When the banks could not bear the burden, around 1931, the state moved in. Nevertheless, three major banks failed and the state had to bail those out too, by creating a number of institutions whose purpose was to keep the banking sector afloat. Careful not to antagonise the industrialists, Mussolini's government kept pouring money into the banks, and instructing that the banks finance industries of all shapes and sizes, without nationalising them.

Another nail in the Weimar Republic's coffin in 1933 was the Japanese experience with autocratic political rule. The *Crash of 1929* caused the Japanese economy to shrink, between 1929 and 1931, by 8 per cent. Not a fall but, still, a recession that worried Japanese Prime Minister Takahashi Korekiyo. His response ought to be familiar to the post-2008 reader: his government increased spending (on armaments) and devalued currency (to boost exports). The combined effect of these two policies helped Japan both to upgrade its military[27] and to overtake British-produced textiles in the world market.

By 1933, when Hindenburg was deliberating on whether or not to pass the baton to Hitler, Japan had already overcome its mild crisis. Hitler's ascent to power confirmed capital's expectation that his rule, however distasteful in other ways, might restore demand, increase profitability and, most importantly, keep workers and their political organisations in their place. As the Panzers and the Messerschmitts began to roll off the production lines, and the imposing Autobahns unfolded through the German *Länder*, the German economy recovered fast, bestowing upon Hitler the kudos which allowed him to drag his people into the most murderous escapade in history; an escapade which, in a twist of tragic irony, dragged the whole world out of the Great Depression. For while Roosevelt was striving valiantly to kick start world capitalism, through his New Deal's social programmes, its effectiveness was limited.

Throughout the 1930s, the 'recovery' was in the eye of the beholder. Always around the corner, permanently precarious, either unseen or faltering, it never made its presence felt in a manner similar to that in Hitler's Germany or Korekiyo's Japan. In 1937, as confidence was beginning to return to the land of the free, another recession took the wind out of American capitalism's sails.[28] The Great Depression did not loosen its grip on the liberal capitalist nations before the Second World War had exacted its many pounds of flesh on humanity. At the war's despicable heights, the politicians were sufficiently unshackled from economic dogma to throw caution to the wind, spend as if there were no tomorrow, create the largest spurt in production and innovation the world has known and, in the process, slay the dragon of 1929. Figures 7.4 and 7.5 confirm that it was possible to ditch the *Quantity Theory of Money*, more than double the national debt in a few short years and, thus, boost production without increasing average prices. Indeed, Figure 7.4 shows that during the war years, 1942–45, when the Roosevelt administration invested oodles of cash into the Military–Industrial Complex, and in doing so increased national debt to more than 120 per cent of national income, average prices rose by 13.4 per cent. This was a modest figure, just below the level of inflation during the 1950–55 period (during which, see Figure 7.4, spending came down fast) and much lower than the 1945–50 period during which, if anything, government spending (and thus national debt) was falling even faster.[29]

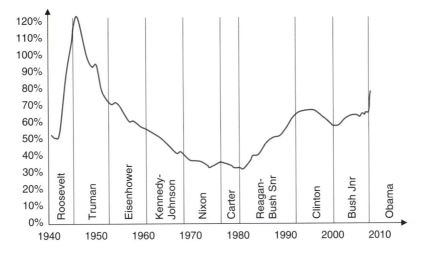

Figure 7.4 US National Debt as a proportion of US National Income (GDP) per Presidency (1940–2010).

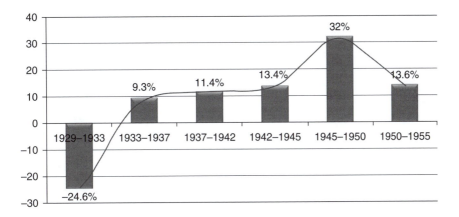

Figure 7.5 Annual rate of inflation in the USA (1929–55).

In the end, the war that was to create Radford's POW camp illustrated that the conventional wisdom peddled by the insiders of political economics[30] did not apply to the War Economy for precisely the same reasons that it applied beautifully to the POW camp.

7.5 We are damned if we know...

> Can we prevent an almost complete collapse of the financial structure of modern capitalism? ... The immediate causes of the world financial panic – for that is what it is – are obvious. They are to be found in a catastrophic fall in the money value, not only of commodities, but of practically every kind of asset ... Debtors of all kinds find that their securities are no longer the equal of their debts.

The above words could have been written in 2008. And once the massive bail-outs of 2008 and 2009 had stabilised the financial sector, and governments began to buckle under the crushing debt burden transferred to their treasuries from banks and large corporations, the following words would have been equally apt:

> Few governments still have revenues sufficient to cover the fixed money charges for which they have made themselves liable. Moreover, a collapse of this kind feeds on itself.

They are, of course, the words of *John Maynard Keynes* (1883–1946), in 1932.[31] The *Crash of 2008* has ensured that Keynes requires no special introductions. Though his star had until recently looked as faded as a pair of flower-embroidered 1960s jeans, capitalism's recent troubles have brought back in vogue the thinker who shone the brightest light on the dark and failing world of the 1930s. The post-2008 shock remains so strong today that even establishment figures, who habitually used 'Keynesian' as a term of abuse, are climbing into their attics in search of a yellowing copy of his *General Theory*; a book they were, in all likelihood, compelled to read at a time when *We were all Keynesians*, to coin President Nixon's famous, but ever so insincere, words.[32]

Keynes brought to the debate two unique virtues: first, he was an insider's insider; second, he was the first insider intellectually brave enough to free himself of the *Inherent Error*. This was a powerful combination. Others (recall the *outsiders* of Section 7.2) also said things not dissimilar to Keynes' pronouncements. But the effect was different when they came from an archetypal insider. Furthermore, Keynes went beyond even the most radical outsiders' criticisms. Keynes, unencumbered by the ideological baggage of radicals, such as Friedrich Engels, Lenin and Rosa Luxemburg; emotionally detached from the plight of the multitude; and worried primarily about the preservation of his elevated way of life,[33] cast a dispassionate gaze upon the world of financialised capitalism from within. The intellectual heir to Alfred Marshall, the renowned Marginalist who taught him at Cambridge, Keynes was not pinned down by any sense of misplaced loyalty to Smith or Ricardo or Marx.

So, once he broke from Marginalism (see in particular his Chapter 2 of the *General Theory*), he was free as a bird to pick his own flight of fancy in search of insights into what on earth was going on during his testing times. Critical of the classical tradition for seeing everything through the prism of the *corn model*, and scornful towards the neoclassical attempt to understand capitalism as if it were a blown up version of Robinson Crusoe's little island world, Keynes allowed himself the luxury to think things over. It was perhaps something that only an English patrician, aided and abetted by fine, inquisitive and radical foreign minds at Cambridge (people like Piero Sraffa and Ludwig Wittgenstein), not to mention the Fabians of the Bloomsbury Circle, would have had the audacity to do: to consider the possibility that *all* of the economists before him had missed the central point about capitalism: that their assumptions had hitherto helped cloak an already complex reality in a veil of obfuscation, rather than help unveil the truth about capitalism through the development of useful abstractions.

Perhaps most remarkable was the simplicity of his conclusion about the epistemic limits of economic theory: *we are damned if we know!* These are, of course, not the words that he used, but we are confident that they convey optimally his main point. If we were to put it more 'scientifically', we would say that Keynes' critique of all that went before him in political economics boils down to a realisation that the *Inherent Error* is buried deep inside the foundations of political economics. Yes, the very same *Inherent Error* that we have been exposing throughout the preceding pages, sections, chapters.

Put differently, Keynes understood that *any* model of capitalism intent on telling a quantitatively consistent story of what determines both *value* and *growth* is earmarked for failure and bound to lead to a view of capitalism that encourages the most damaging of economic policies. So, his proposal for getting out of the Depression was as austerely simple as his pronouncement on the limits of economic theory: *arrest the Fall by having the state reflate the sinking ship!* The immediate implication was, of course, the abandonment of *Say's Law*, the suspension of the *Quantity Theory of Money*[34] and a willingness to extend the authorities' role from that of guardian of the currency's 'honour' to saviour of capitalism – from itself!

Such radical thinking had to begin somewhere. It began when Keynes broke ranks with his peers by doing the unthinkable: by revisiting the spat between Ricardo and Malthus and taking the side of the clergyman. In no uncertain terms, in the midst of the Great Depression, he wrote: '[I]f only Malthus, instead of Ricardo, had been the parent stem from which nineteenth-century economics proceeded, what a much wiser and richer place the world would be today'![35] With this inflammatory statement, Keynes was adopting neither Malthus' stand in favour of aristocratic rentiers nor his theological views about the redemptive power of suffering.[36] Rather, Keynes embraced Malthus' scepticism regarding (a) the wisdom of seeking a *theory of value* which is consistent with capitalism's *complexity* and *dynamics*[37] and (b) Ricardo's conviction that persistent depression is incompatible with capitalism.[38]

Keynes alone among the profession's insiders dared agree with Malthus and with the outsiders of Section 7.2 that capitalism may go through phases when the worst scarcity we face is not that of capital, labour or raw materials, but an awful scarcity of demand for already produced goods. Not because people do not crave them, but because they lack the means to buy them. However, his explanation of why *effective demand*[39] may be scarce was different from that of Malthus, Hobson, Engels and Luxemburg (see Box 7.6). Whereas they focused on under-consumption, Keynes's diagnosis was that capitalists are wimps; that they abandon ship at the first sign of troubled waters; the moment economic turbulence is in the air, they bail out; they stop investing. And this propensity of investment to fall *on a whim* is the cause of depressed times.

> The modern capitalist is a fair-weather sailor. As soon as a storm rises, he abandons the duties of navigation and even sinks the boats which might carry him to safety by his haste to push his neighbour off and himself in.[40]

In a letter to left-wing playwright George Bernard Shaw (1856–1950), a year before the publication of *The General Theory of Employment, Interest and Money* (abbreviated to the

Box 7.6 Keynes on Malthus and the Outsiders

In existing conditions — or, at least, in the conditions that existed until lately — where the volume of investment is unplanned and uncontrolled, subject to the vagaries of the marginal efficiency of capital as determined by the private judgement of individuals, ignorant or speculative, and to a long-term rate of interest that seldom or never falls below a conventional level, these schools of thought are, as guides to practical policy, undoubtedly in the right. For in such conditions there is no other means of raising the average level of employment to a more satisfactory level. If it is impracticable materially to increase investment, obviously there is no means of securing a higher level of employment except by increasing consumption.

Practically I only differ from these schools of thought in thinking that they may lay a little too much emphasis on increased consumption at a time when there is still much social advantage to be obtained from increased investment. Theoretically, however, they are open to the criticism of neglecting the fact that there are *two* ways to expand output. Even if we were to decide that it would be better to increase capital more slowly and to concentrate effort on increasing consumption, we must decide this with open eyes, after well considering the alternative. I am myself impressed by the great social advantages of increasing the stock of capital until it ceases to be scarce. But this is a practical judgement, not a theoretical imperative.

See Chapter 22 of the *General Theory of Employment, Interest and Money*.[1]

Note
1 Keynes (1936), p. 325.

General Theory), Keynes boasted that the book he was in the final stages of preparation would knock away 'the Ricardian foundations of Marxism...'.[41] His aim was not so much to criticise Marx but to get at Ricardo, Say, Walras and all 'respected' (i.e. bourgeois) economists who took for granted that a dollar saved would be a dollar invested. By evoking the parable of the modern capitalist as a fair-weather sailor, Keynes raised an important analytical point regarding investment.

Economists before him mistakenly assumed that investment

> comes from believing that the owner of wealth desires a capital-asset as such, whereas what he really desires is its prospective yield. Now, prospective yield wholly depends on the expectation of future effective demand in relation to future conditions of supply. If, therefore, an act of saving does nothing to improve prospective yield, it does nothing to stimulate investment.[42]

But why would rational capitalists not anticipate any prospective yield when savings rise? Most economists, especially after the end of the Second World War (for reasons that we shall discuss in the following chapter), misunderstood, and continue to do so, *to this day*, the answer that Keynes gave to his own crucial question.

They think that Keynes questioned the rationality of investors; that he interpreted their capricious investment decisions, their tendency towards sheepish herd behaviour, as a sign of 'bounded rationality',[43] a polite term for irrationality; that, inundated with too much information, investors miscalculate and, as a result, panic when the stakes are high and the world begins to behave in unanticipated ways. In contrast, this book is confident that Keynes' argument had nothing to do with the irrationality of entrepreneurs. Indeed, we suggest that his analysis of capitalism's propensity to failure is perfectly consistent with the rational capitalists doing their best for themselves. To see this, we ask the reader to consider the following interaction.

Jack and Jill play a game involving 20 matches resting on a table. Jack is invited to come to the table first to collect at least one and at most two of these matches and then sit down again. Then Jill is asked to do likewise (to collect one or two matches) before Jack has another go, and so on until all matches are collected. Whoever collects that twentieth match wins a prize. What should Jack's strategy be at the outset if he wants to win? The answer is: pick two matches at the beginning and sit down. Then, whatever Jill does in the next rounds, pick the number of matches necessary in order to ensure that, when it is his turn to play, he sits down after collecting the fifth, eighth, eleventh, fourteenth, seventeenth and, lastly the twentieth match.[44]

The point of this game is that it represents the type of interaction that capitalists are *not* involved in. In this game, Reason furnishes *the* rational course of action. As long as Jack is rational he knows what to do. His Reason carves a uniquely rational path through the thick jungle of conjectures and shows him the way to 'victory'. Once he and Jill have worked out what rationality tells them is the road to victory, the game holds no secrets and their behaviour during it becomes utterly predictable.

Of course, Jack may well be less than rational, in which case we, as theorists, may mispredict his behaviour and overestimate his returns. He may miscalculate at the beginning and choose only one match, giving a smart Jill the chance to usurp the dominant strategic position and beat him. Keynes was never interested in portraying investors like a blundering Jack. His point was not that they fail to use their rationality in order to work out rationally their best investment strategies but, instead, that the 'investment game' is radically different from our 20-match game; so different that *the optimal strategy cannot be rationally worked out*, unless investors are equipped with the gift of telepathy. Box 7.7 gives an example that captures better the nature of the interaction in which capitalists find themselves.

The essence of Box 7.7 is that, unlike Jack's task in the 20-match game above, the pure light of Reason does not, by itself, dissolve the dilemma to invest or not invest. The outcome of an investment decision depends not only on how well the investment project is implemented but also on how many other investors, in the economy at large, will choose to invest;

---

*Box 7.7 When *Reason* defers to *Expectation**

Suppose that 100 strangers (who have no way of communicating with one another) are playing the following game. Each must email us a number between 0 and 1 (including 0 and 1). Once we collect all their emails, we compute their payments as follows: assuming that player i emailed us number X_i, she or he will receive a number of dollars equal to $d_i = 1000 \times (1 - 3m + 2X_i)$, where m is the *maximum* value of X chosen by someone in this group of 100 people. What number X would you choose if you were one of the participants?

Unlike the game with the 20 matches, this is a hard problem lacking a ready answer. Not because people are not rational enough but because your best answer depends on a complex web of expectations that cannot be rationally dissected without the benefit of telepathy. Let's see this in more detail.

The best outcome for everyone, *the happy scenario*, is that each emails us the number 0 and wins $1000. [NB when everyone sets their X equal to 0, then m, the maximum number emailed, is also 0 and $d_i = 1000$.] Do you have any incentive to email us a number greater than 0 if you predict that all 99 of your co-players will set their X equal to 0? No, you do not. [NB For if you did something of the sort, then your choice of X, X_i, would become the maximum emailed number, m, and your own reward would diminish since, in this case, $d_i = 1 - X_i$] Does this mean that the best strategy is to email us the number 0? Not necessarily. It depends on everyone's expectations in a situation when no one, however rational, can predict what these expectations will be.

The truth of the matter is that your best strategy here depends on your estimation of the degree of optimism among your group of co-players. Optimism here means that everyone expects m to approximate 0. If this is what you think is going on, you will have a cast iron reason to email us the number 0, or very close to it (recall the argument in the previous paragraph). And if everyone does this, you will receive your $1000 each. But then again, what if you predict that someone in the group will email us, say, number 0.9. It is easy to show that your best response to this expectation is that you also choose 0.9! But, the reader may ask, why would anyone choose 0.9? Well, because if someone predicts that someone else may fear that there is one person in this group who will choose 0.9, then that 'someone' will have a dominant strategy: *choose 0.9!* And if everyone is anticipating this, then each player will be emailing us the number 0.9; the tragic conclusion being that, instead of a $1000 credit in your bank account, all you get is a measly $100.

This game offers an example when Reason, caught up in an infinite regression, cannot work out what to do. However hyperrational you and your co-players may be, and regardless of the confidence that one has in everyone else's rationality, there is no guarantee whatsoever that you will succeed in securing a decent payoff. In effect, what we have here is multiple, equally hyperrational, potential outcomes of individual decision making, each corresponding to a different agglomeration of group expectations. It is the stuff of true human drama played out on a stage where the *Power of Prophecy* makes its triumphant entry: on this truly social stage, when people believe that good things will happen, they do. Equally, negative expectations bear negative consequences.

This thought resonates powerfully with the experience of a complex, dynamic capitalism where, at the first scent of an impending recession, capitalists go on an investment strike and the recession occurs, confirming their gloomy forecasts. It also echoes John Maynard Keynes' famous description of investment decisions as a realm '... where we devote our intelligences to anticipating what average opinion expects average opinion to be.'[1]

Note

1 See Chapter 12 of the *General Theory* (1936, p. 156).

for if there is a surge of investment, each investor flourishes. And *vice versa*. So, the decision to invest depends on average opinion among investors and this average opinion is not anchored on some objective logical process of reasoning (e.g. as it is in the twenty-match game) but is, instead, self-referential; like a cat chasing its own tail, investors' beliefs are chasing the average beliefs of investors – *ad infinitum*. And when this happens, predicting the future is not a matter of good scientific analysis but of serendipity.

In Chapter 1 we foreshadowed the above point by indicating that forecasting economic variables is drastically different from forecasting the weather. Meteorologists have a hard job but nowhere near as hard as that of investors. If a number of competing meteorologists are getting more scientific, and thus better at their job, their estimates will be converging. If only capitalists could be blessed with such a simple life! The following parable offers a feel for the incomparable complexity facing those unlucky enough to bet their bacon on whether the 'economy' will improve, and whether aggregate demand will rise or fall.

Imagine a planet, say Ambience, where the weather is determined not only by objective natural forces but also by what a majority of the planet's meteorologists expects it to be. Fluctuations in weather conditions may occur that are independent of average opinion but average opinion determines the long-term outlook. Suppose further that Ambience's inhabitants have a strong preference for fair weather punctuated once or twice a week by a downpour that would serve agriculture and replenish the water table. Lastly, imagine that the punishment inflicted upon each meteorologist who wrongly predicts clear skies is great (and larger than it would be when reality contradicts their forecast of bad weather).

Does rationality compel Ambience's meteorologists to converge on a weather report of 'fair weather with the occasional downpour'? Not at all. Although rationality tells them that it would be nice if this is precisely what each of them predicted (since such an average opinion would be self-confirming and everyone would be better off), rationality does not instruct them to consistently issue this rosy report. Since storms can happen unexpectedly, for natural reasons unrelated to the meteorologists' average opinion, it is not irrational for some meteorologist, let's call her Jill, to predict a storm soon. But then it is also plausible that some other meteorologist, let's call him Jack, may begin to fear that Jill is toying with the possibility of an unexpected weather deterioration. Then Jack, reasonably, fears that Jill's foreboding may cause some other meteorologists to imagine that a considerable proportion of their colleagues will become pessimistic about the weather. What does rationality compel Jack to do in this situation?

The clear answer is: *to downgrade his own expectations and issue a less rosy report*. And if the rest get a whiff that some people are thinking like Jill and Jack, their weather reports may get gloomier too. Rationally, weather forecasts will, in this manner, be growing more and more pessimistic, and in a never-ending circle, Ambience will be increasingly covered with black clouds brewing heavy weather. Intriguingly, once this slide into darkness begins, rationality not only fails to impede but, instead, it amplifies its severity.

Keynes likened the economic climate in which investment decisions are made, to Ambience's. In a corporatised and financialised capitalism, if capitalists are fair-weather sailors it is because rationality compels them to be exactly that. Since the sea that they are sailing is bound to turn nasty on them if only their fellow captains start fearing that the average opinion in their ranks turns pessimistic, they have solid reasons to fear the weather more than real sailors who are at least comforted by the thought that oceans' vindictiveness is not amplified by their fellows' pessimism.

In truly interactive worlds, like Ambience's weather or Earth's market societies, loose talk ought to be avoided with the same stringency that central bankers adopt before commenting on interest rates in the presence of journalists. If one describes a growth spurt as a bubble, it may burst just because one called it a bubble. In such a precarious world, the state of the economy is a figment of our mood. Keynes' mistake was to mis-label his unique insight. In a famous passage on the matter he allowed his prose to overshadow his point. The invocation of *animal spirits* has, ever since, been thought to imply that Keynes was proposing a theory that explained economic crises on the basis of investors', or speculators', irrationality, on the basis of their propensity to be lured by their 'animal spirits' away from cool, level-headed, rational calculation:

> Even apart from the instability due to speculation, there is the instability due to the characteristic of human nature that a large proportion of our positive activities depend on spontaneous optimism rather than mathematical expectations, whether moral or hedonistic or economic. Most, probably, of our decisions to do something positive, the full consequences of which will be drawn out over many days to come, can only be taken as the result of *animal spirits* – a spontaneous urge to action rather than inaction, and not as the outcome of a weighted average of quantitative benefits multiplied by quantitative probabilities.
>
> (*General Theory*; ch. 12, emphasis added (1936, pp. 161–2))

The use of the term *animal spirits* was, we believe, a major own-goal.[45] For, his opponents (i.e. the economists who are unwilling and unable to liberate themselves from the *Inherent Error*) have latched on to this term as 'proof' that Keynes' analysis of capitalism is interesting only to the extent that capitalists are fickle, impulsive, less than rational. It is a small step from there to argue that all we need to avoid crises, and thus confine Keynes to the scrapheap, is a little more rationality.[46] Moreover, it is a term that left Keynes open to the (largely correct, but for different reasons) accusation of paternalism: Keynesianism was portrayed as a rational theory that worked only as long as the people whose behaviour it was explaining were assumed less rational than the theorist.

Had Keynes spoken not of *Animal Spirits* but of *Rational Indeterminacy*, or of a *Probing Reason*; even better, had he enlisted Hegel's *Cunning of Reason*, he would have made it harder for the lurking neoclassicists to insinuate that Keynesian economics is concerned with an economy populated by lesser intellects (see Box 7.8). Perhaps then, the focus would have been on his essential theme that the behaviour of (a) rational capitalists, (b) rational workers and (c) rational consumers is irreducible to some formula involving well-defined mathematical expectations; not because of a rationality deficit that prevents lesser mortals from performing the necessary mathematical calculations, but because of a *scarcity of telepathy*.

Regarding investment, we have already seen his argument: no amount of intelligence can help guarantee, unaided by the right mood, the level of investment necessary to keep the factories going at full capacity. Similarly with workers: if investment is not guaranteed at maximal level, nothing can reassure them about their job security or the purchasing power of their wages. So, when endowed with some bargaining power, either at the individual or the trade union levels, workers have good cause not to use it like an Australian mine owner does in negotiations with Chinese coal buyers; but to use it instead in order to lessen the impact of a *future* reduction in employment, an increase in prices, etc.

Consumers too face similarly intractable unknowns. Every decision to make a substantial purchase requires confidence in a decent job and a future income stream. Neoclassical economics textbooks tell their readers that Keynes posited a theory of irrational consumers who, unlike Frank Ramsey's planner (always striking the optimal balance between present and future consumption – see Box 7.4), myopically consume a given proportion of their income. This is one interpretation, which builds on the false claim that Keynesian economics works only for an economy of clueless automata. It is not ours. Our interpretation is that when rationality does not suffice to tell one what to do, one gets on with it regardless. One adopts some rule of thumb, follows it, adjusts it by trial and error and hopes for the best. This is the only rational course of action when engulfed in the deep ignorance of what lies ahead, as one is when living in really existing capitalism. Thus, Keynes' theory of consumption, which links it to income in an *ad hoc* way, is a mere reflection, not of the difficulty but indeed, of the *impossibility* of choosing how much to save and how much to consume with the mathematical precision of Ramsey's planner.

In conclusion, all our economic decisions, connected to *investment, labour supply* and *consumption*, are veiled in an uncertainty ontologically different from the one we have concerning tomorrow's earthly weather. If we want a physical parallel, our conundrum is that of weather forecasters on planet Ambience, where uncertainty can give rise to periodic bouts of pessimism which, in turn, create the circumstances for, but never the certainty of, a depression.[47]

Box 7.8 The *fallacy of composition*
Rational Expectations and the Inherent Error

In the reading of Keynes proposed here, economic agents are fully rational. They act sensibly in the pursuit of their objectives and in accordance with their forecasts of an unknowable future. That their estimates can be systematically wrong is not due to their less than perfect rationality but, rather, to the fact that Reason cannot see into the future consistently when that future is co-determined by everyone's forecasts. Thus, the future's inevitable opacity causes deep insecurity in the mind of not only investors but also consumers, workers, etc. When something untoward happens, this rational insecurity may feed on itself: agents begin to form pessimistic expectations that are then confirmed simply because of the reductions in both consumption and investment that they motivate. Like Laius was killed by his son just because he believed the prophesy that this would happen,[1] so do capitalists may bring about a crisis if they simply believe that a crisis is looming.

Keynes' recommendation was that we stop thinking of capitalism as we do of Robinson Crusoe's economy and that we distinguish what is good for the whole from what is good for the one. In the case of Crusoe, it is of course a tautology that thrift is *always* good for his little economy's growth and for the building up of stockpiles for a rainy day. Similarly for the shopkeeper who must reduce costs instantly the moment sales dip. But these examples of micromanagement are, according to Keynes, disastrous if they are to be used as a parable for clever macroeconomic policy during lean years. He referred to this as the *fallacy of composition*: mistaken conclusions about how a complex system works drawn from observations of the workings of its constituent parts. For example, the conclusion that because thrift is *always* good for Crusoe it must also *always* be good for the United States or the Chinese government. When a complex capitalist economy enters a downward spiral like the one described in the previous paragraph, thrift makes things far, far worse. Then, the only glimmer of hope is the state. Uniquely able to step in and pump money into the economy, it is our only chance of ending the 'beggar thy neighbour' logic during a recession. This is exactly what the Second World War did (see Figure 7.4) and how the post-war economic golden age came about.

By the 1970s, and the end of the first post-war phase (see Chapter 11), Keynesianism was in retreat. At the theoretical level, the challenge took the form of the so-called Rational Expectations Hypothesis (REH), which helped restore neoclassical economics to the prominence that Keynes so rudely interrupted. The main point of the REH was this: 'We cannot rationally expect a policy to succeed if its success depends on people failing to understand its logic'. Take, for example, David Hume's famous parable in which a dying poor farmer bequeaths a barren land to his lazy sons but succeeds in having them plough it well and deeply (and thus boosting its productivity) by hinting at a hidden treasure somewhere deep inside their newly inherited land. This is an example of a 'policy' that works because the agents do not understand its logic. The REH, correctly, argued that economic policy cannot succeed in the same manner. That, even if investors, consumers and workers are fooled some of the time, they cannot be fooled all of the time.

But this is not a criticism of Keynes. For Keynes, as we argued in the preceding pages, never doubted that people are rational. Nor did he ever argue that crises are due to irrationality or that the state must restore growth by using people's misunderstanding of the way the economy works. Indeed, if this were what Keynes proposed, the state's intervention would either bring about no recovery whatsoever or the achieved recovery would wither the moment people find out how it came about! No, Keynes made his case convinced that it was valid for a world in which everyone is supremely rational; even one in which everyone read, and understood, his *General Theory*! For, even if all knew everything that there was to know, and could crunch the numbers and see through the models with the incisiveness of the best economist, rationality cannot preclude a dismal equilibrium, in which nasty prophecies are self-confirming (recall the game in Box 7.7).

Indeed, each rational citizen would welcome a government intervention that lifts everyone's spirits, fully aware of the inability of individual Reason to lift them alone. Latching on to the sight and sounds of the government's opening purse strings, everyone's depressed spirits begin to lift for good rational reasons. Almost immediately, output and employment rise, reinforcing the rising expectations. Investors, workers and consumers remain just as rational during this upturn as they were during the worst of the recession. The difference now is that their rationality is laced with some optimism which causes them to engage in more rapid economic activity which uses existing productive capacity, creates more wealth, generates higher capital accumulation and sets the scene for sturdier long-term growth. Optimism, which Reason alone cannot guarantee, is therefore self-confirming and proves just as much a prerequisite for growth as savings are in Ricardo's and Ramsey's models.

Last, it is instructive to note why neoclassicists in the 1970s (to this day) think of their REH analysis as a blow on Keynes: it is because of the *Inherent Error* from which they do not want to escape! Chapter 6 showed that neoclassicism can only achieve closure if it drops *time* or *complexity* (i.e. multiple sectors). In macroeconomic debates, it is thus forced to drop complexity which is another way of saying that neoclassicism makes a *strategic choice* to focus on single-product or single-agent models. This is tantamount to ignoring, by design, Keynes' *fallacy of composition*. For if they choose to see capitalism through the prism of a Robinson Crusoe model, is it any wonder that their assumption of a rational Crusoe guarantees that his own demand will be enough to absorb his own output fully? It is, therefore, obvious that, since the REH concerns exclusively a Crusoe-type economy, it leaves Keynes' theory unscathed. So, why did it come to pass as a telling blow against Keynes, whose whole point was that capitalism cannot be explained by models which set its complexity aside?

The sad answer is that Keynes' thought was brought to the masses by textbooks penned by neoclassical authors, first and foremost Paul Samuelson.[2] They retold Keynes' theory using neoclassical diagrams, curves and equations that reduced Keynes' glorious narrative to a single sector version model of capitalism; the very model of capitalism that Keynes had no interest in.[3] This bastardised Keynesian model was, later, slaughtered by the hand of the REH. It is like rewriting Shakespeare's *Hamlet* using no more than one hundred words and then taking the bard to task for prose's paucity.

Notes

1 Laius was King of Thebes. When the Delphi Oracle prophesied that his baby son would murder him and marry his wife, Jocasta, he ordered that the baby be taken into the woods and murdered. The allotted child murderer desisted and the young prince, Oedipus, was sent to Corinth where he was raised with no knowledge of his origins. On a trip to Thebes, Oedipus clashed with Laius, in what can be thought of as the first recorded case of road rage in history, and killed his father. A typical case of the *Power of Prophecy*.

2 See Paul Samuelson (1948), *Economics: an introductory analysis*.

3 For the best account of this bastardisation, see Axel Leijonhufvud (1968).

7.6 No redemption

Cycles may cause uncertainty, but at least soon after they reach their trough, they move up again. The *Crash of 1929* did *not* fit the pattern. Instead, it soon turned into the Great Depression. Every prediction of its passing proved premature; every sign of light a mirage. Global capitalism's inability to activate the self-correcting mechanisms that should have buoyed it, along with its recalcitrance to the state's faltering interventions in the 1930s, gave Keynes pause. While livid with the neoclassicists' chimeras, he remained unenamoured of theories featuring economic cycles, Marxian or otherwise. He just did not buy the argument that the Depression was the turning point of a redemptive economic cycle.

Come to think of it, Keynes had a point. Why assume that *all* that goes down must come up again? While this is true about the sun, it certainly was not the Titanic's experience. Of course, if one is determined to see life in terms of cycles, it is not hard to do so. Indeed, one may argue that the Black Death killed millions of the bacteria that caused it and, for good measure, it also 'corrected' Europe's 'supply' of bonded farm workers. The ruthlessness of the *ancien régime* brought about its own 'correction', in the form of the storming of the

Bastille and, later, of the guillotine. The hubris of the European Empires was 'righted' by the chemical weapons in the killing trenches of the Great War. Everything is corrected, eventually. Life finds its strange redemption in death and death is essential for the evolution of life.

Keynes was not impressed by any of this cyclical stuff. The type of theory imparted in Box 7.9 was not his cup of tea. There was, in his view, nothing redemptive about high unemployment. Bankruptcies played a good and proper revitalising role under normal circumstance. But when they came as an avalanche, rooting out all manner of firms, efficient and

---

Box 7.9 Redemptive cycles

Ibn Khaldun (1332–1406) was the scholar who carefully described cycles of power and crisis. Based on his close study of the history of the Arab states of Spain and Northern Africa,[1] he outlined an account of how socio-economic power stems from the evolution of *asabiyyah* within small social groups. *Asabiyyah*, a term that has been variously translated as solidarity, group feeling, cohesion, etc., emerges as a result of the need to co-operate, to follow strict norms of rectitude, to remain close together in order to fend off need and danger. *Asabiyyah* thus confers power and success to the groups within which it takes root. These groups then rise to power in the cities and found great city states. However, their success is pregnant with the seeds of its destruction. In four or five generations, the rulers lose touch with their subjects and *asabiyyah* begins to recede. The rituals of power, the hubris that comes with absolute authority, the gratification afforded by amassed riches, all conspire to sap the rulers' vigour. When *asabiyyah* has faded beyond a certain threshold, the rulers discover that their authority and power has weakened. Strife and anarchy follow, hope diminishes and optimism fades. Then some other group that developed *asabiyyah* elsewhere takes over and the cycle continues. In brief, crises are due to the natural tendency of *asabiyyah* to fade, and, once they reach their crescendo, they help revive *asabiyyah* by bringing another group to power.

In political economics, the idea of redemptive crises was first canvassed by Karl Marx. Chapter 5 discussed this extensively. Here, it suffices to quote from our epilogue to that chapter:

> As a system, capitalism strives to turn us into automata and our market society into a *Matrix*-like dystopia. But the closer it comes to achieving its aim the nearer it gets (very much like the mythical Icarus) to its moment of ruin. Then it picks itself up, recovers, and embarks upon the same path all over again. It is as if our capitalist societies were designed to generate periodic crises.

Taking a brief leave from political economics or history, we note that the idea of a seesaw applies to nature just as it does to society. Its first mathematical form dates to 1925–6 and the Lotka–Volterra system of differential equations.[2] Vito Volterra (1860–1940) was intrigued by the way populations of Adriatic predator fish were in constant, cyclical flux. When their prey was plentiful, the predators' numbers rose. However, this put the prey population under pressure and, once it had fallen under a certain level, the predators' numbers went into decline. When the decline reached a given level, then the prey population would rebound and the whole cyclical process would start again. In a paper published in 1926, Volterra captured this dynamic nicely by means of a system of differential equations. Meanwhile, Alfred Lotka (1880–1949) had come up with the same system of differential equations in order to codify certain chemical oscillations.

Besides the many applications to ecological modelling, chemistry, medicine, epidemiology, etc., Richard Goodwin (1913–96) employed this type of model to mathematise Marx's economic cycles.[3] Two differential equations were used: the first one determined the rate of change in the economy's employment rate as a decreasing function of the workers' share of the aggregate surplus. The second equation modelled the rate of change of the workers' share of the aggregate surplus as proportional to the economy's employment rate. These two differential equations, once combined into a system, gave out nice diagrams of total output and total wages which (a) exhibited long-term growth, but (b) were always lagging behind the economy's full productive capacity and followed an oscillating path – diagrams which, effectively, demonstrated that long-term growth is consistent with periods of recession during which both wages and output fall. The fall in wages, during these crises, has a redemptive effect on output and helps revitalise growth.

Joseph Schumpeter (1883–1950), also influenced by Marx's cyclical story, made the point that capitalism's tendency to produce large corporations with significant monopoly power gives rise to periodic violent plunges. But these plunges help the system renew itself. Corporations that grow too big and, thus too complacent, are usurped by hungry, innovative upstarts. The dinosaurs become extinct and new more vibrant 'species' of firms rise to the surface. Crises are, in this sense, a crucial part of the capitalist growth story. In the post-war economics literature, Hyman Minsky (1919–96) extended this very basic idea to financial markets. Minsky's starting point was Keynes' argument in the *General Theory* that: 'Speculators may do no harm as bubbles on a steady stream of enterprise. But the position is serious when enterprise becomes a bubble on a whirlpool of speculation. When the capital development of a country becomes a byproduct of the activities of a casino, the job is likely to be ill-done'.

Minsky's contribution[4] was to suggest, pretty much along the above lines, that periods of growth and financial stability reduce both interest rates and the rate of defaults on loans, This encourages investors to take increasing risks, a bubble builds and then bursts, with the inevitably disagreeable effects on the rest of the economy. This pushes interest rates up, causes financial markets to become more risk averse, asset prices are kept in check and the course is set for another period of low risk taking, stability, etc. Once financiers get used to this, a new propensity towards risk taking surfaces and the cycle repeats itself. Minsky's simple, but important, point reminds us of what happens when cars get safer: *we tend to speed more.* So, even though accidents become rarer, when they do happen they tend to be more lethal.

To finish off as we started, we refer the reader to philosopher Martin Hollis (1938–98) and his last book entitled *Trust within Reason*.[5] Taking Ibn Khaldun's main point to a more modern capitalist setting, Hollis argues that the stronger the bonds of trust the more a market society progresses. But the more it progresses, along the lines of *possessive individualism*, the more penny-pinching, or instrumentally rational, its citizens become in their dealings with one another. And the more instrumental their relations become the less trustworthy they are. Thus, the social bonds on which markets rely are loosened and a socio-economic crisis becomes inevitable. As the encroachments of the second-hand car merchant's logic erodes the bond of trust that makes markets tick, and which commercial society continues to need in order to coordinate economic activity efficiently, cracks appear in capitalism's facade and crises are our bitter reward.

Notes
1 Ibn Khaldun (1967). The Greek historian of the second century BCE Polybius (1922, VI.9) was among the first to describe the concept of political *anacyclosis*.
2 See Lotka (1925), and Volterra (1926).
3 See Goodwin (1967).
4 See Minsky (1986 [2008]).
5 See Hollis (1998).

wasteful, innovative and old hat, entrepreneurial and antiquated, bankruptcies turned into a scourge. In particular, Keynes was convinced that nothing good can ever come out of expanding poverty, condemning whole generations to a life on the dole, throwing to the wind skills that took years to hone. His diagnosis was that capitalism, at least in 1929, was like a car whose engine's spark plugs died unexpectedly, leaving the vehicle stranded and unable to change its own spark plugs. The more it sat idle on the street the less likely it was that it would start again sometime soon. Someone had to open the bonnet, get her hands dirty and change the faulty plugs. And since there is no one else outside the markets with the power to act but the state, it is the state's job to take the initiative.

The pressing question that Keynes set himself the task to answer was simple: what does it take to prevent a depression? Or to end it once it has taken hold? Before grappling with it, he encouraged his readers to undermine economics' *Inherent Error*; to desist from consistent explanations of value and growth that are founded on some imagined underlying bedrock of reality unalloyed by humanity's indeterminate nature. He incites us to ignore both the Ricardian and the neoclassical sirens, which are trying to enchant us with stories of objective labour values or subjective utilities, and to accept that a monetised capitalist economy is floating on a cloud of conjecture that is irreducible either to input–output matrices (recall Chapters 3 and 4) or to production and utility functions (Chapter 5). Keynes argued that money matters. Not just as a 'veil' thrown over a bartering transaction that would have happened anyway in the absence of money, but as a determinant of a new type of relation: the financial relation between investors and banking institutions.

When trying to secure a loan, capitalists do not speak of the productivity of their machinery, or of their workers, but of the returns on money loans to the lender. The gross unknowability of the future gives finance its role. While industrialists are banking on plant and equipment, and are at the mercy of fluctuations in demand for their products, financiers open their purses only if their expected returns are somewhat safer than those of the industrialists. Whereas industrial capital's rewards depend on conventional profits, earned from making things and then selling them, the financial speculators profit when their assets appreciate. But what determines asset prices and the total amount of capital available to industry?

The answer is delivered by a price mechanism embedded in the financial markets and only very lightly attached to capital's physical 'productivity'. In these money markets, participants engage in a grand game of mergers and acquisitions, based totally on mood and hunches. They buy and sell profusely, creating a torrent of share trades and spun-off bundles of capital assets, firms, subsidiaries, etc. And what does their mood depend on? It depends on the estimated level of *aggregate demand* which will underpin their moody asset prices with real profits that are made in the real economy; an estimate that no amount of scientific expertise can pin down (for reasons explained in the previous section).

During periods of growth, capital assets are worth sums that reflect the optimism that underwrites the ongoing growth, not the actual growth rate itself. Thus, financial investments are often much more profitable than long-term capital investments on plant, equipment and human labour, and the value of firms is a multiple of their actual income stream. Keynes remarks that this makes productive investment difficult to come by: 'Investment based on genuine long-term expectation is so difficult to-day as to be scarcely practicable'. (Kynes 1936, pp. 156–7).

Moreover, the higher financial assets rise the more catastrophically they fall when, for whatever reason, expectations deflate. Once financial profits overtake the more mundane type of profit made from actual production, the idea that profit seeking will always lead to investments that enhance a society's surplus in the medium or long-term is in terminal jeopardy:

> There is no clear evidence from experience that the investment policy which is socially advantageous coincides with that which is most profitable ... The measure of success attained by Wall Street, regarded as an institution of which the proper social purpose is to direct new investment into the most profitable channels in terms of future yield, cannot be claimed as one of the greatest triumphs of laissez-faire capitalism – which is not surprising, if I am right, in thinking that the best brains of Wall Street have been in fact directed toward a different object.
>
> (Kynes 1936, p. 159)

And when the bubble bursts, we find that all the king's horses and all the king's men cannot be put back together again simply by reversing its causes. As governments found out to their consternation in the 1930s, and are rediscovering in the post-2008 period:

> [W]hilst the weakening of credit is sufficient to bring about a collapse, its strengthening, though a necessary condition of recovery, is not a sufficient condition.[48]

At the time that he was writing the *General Theory*, Keynes' colleagues still believed in capitalism's automated shock absorbers; namely, that a rise in unemployment would push the wage rate down and stimulate employment. And that a similar process, working through lower interest rates, would encourage investment. Keynes was scornful of their touching faith in markets and wrote the *General Theory* as a rejoinder to it. Common sense confirms that, although downward pressure on wages naturally delights capitalists, the level of the wage is not what keeps them up at night. During good times and bad, they toss and turn in their beds wondering what the future holds regarding the demand for their wares. Especially during recessionary times, the news that wages have fallen may horrify them, signalling a further drop on medium-term demand that cancels out the good news of lower labour costs. Similarly with interest rate reductions: welcome as they are by industrialists labouring under their obligations to bankers, such news may push them deeper into despair if interpreted as an omen of a deepening recession.

These thoughts led Keynes to a major departure from received 'wisdom', both classical (mainly Ricardian) and neoclassical. It is not that savings determine investment but exactly the opposite is true: *investment determines savings!* And what determines investment? The short, honest answer is: *we are damned if we know!* Let down by Reason, which has insufficient raw materials by which to forge a decent, well defined, mathematical expectation of what an investor stands to gain from throwing a sum of money at some asset or project, investors try to smell the air; to get a whiff of what others in their position might do. Mathematics, under the circumstances, is at a loss to produce anything other than models whose utility is aesthetic rather than scientific – recall Box 7.7.[49] Psychology thus makes a noisy entrance into Keynes' economics, not because he thinks that capitalists are irrational but, as we argued previously, because rationality does not come up with the goods. For when Reason is stumped, *anything goes*. And as if this were not enough, the plot thickens further when the markets of actual goods and services are dominated by corporations with a capacity to influence prices. Box 7.10 introduces that additional wrinkle to an already complex world.

Box 7.10 Investment: The joker in the pack

In single sector models, both classical and neoclassical, savings are automatically translated into investment in physical capital and, thus, into future output that will, again automatically, be absorbed either through consumption or through further investment. Thus, (as is also true in the Ramsey model of Box 7.4) growth is bolstered by thrift. But in complex, financialised economies there is no automatic translation of a dollar saved into a dollar spent on corn seeds, machines, labour, etc. Fear that aggregate demand may fall will *cause* it to fall as both investment and employment dry up.

Consider a simple economy with two sectors: machines and chocolate. The latter cannot be used for investment purposes and a machine cannot be eaten. Suppose now that, for some reason, a recession begins to bite. As unemployment rises, demand for chocolate drops, resulting in unsold chocolate. What will happen next? Will the economy bounce back unaided? Polish political economist, and one of Keynes' interlocutors, Michał Kalecki (1899–1970) suggested two possible scenarios:[1]

(1) The slump in the chocolate sector reduces the price of chocolate more than it does the price of machines. Chocolate output thus falls and an excess capacity of chocolate is realised. The profit margins of chocolate producers fall and unemployment amongst chocolate workers rises. As their income declines, chocolate demand falls further. Thus, while the wage has dropped, and the potential for profits have risen as a result, in practice profits have fallen. If unemployed workers migrate to the machine sector, wages will fall there too. But will this fall in

wages suffice to cause capitalists to invest in more machines? The answer is: only if capitalists operating in the machine sector expect that their collective investment in machines will rise sufficiently to push total demand back to levels that justify the investment. But this is the sort of game outlined in Box 7.7: a game with no unique rational resolution. The ensuing uncertainty may well impede any investment in the machine sector, let along the level of investment that is required to lift the whole economy out of the mire.

(2) The slump in the chocolate sector reduces demand for chocolates and machines symmetrically. The rise in unemployment pushes money wages down but the real wage does not change much since both wages and prices have fallen together. Will the fall in the real wage stimulate investment and employment? Not necessarily. It will only do so if capitalists imagine that it will. But there is no rational reason to imagine that this is what will or will not happen. Anything goes and so, in the end, it depends on the prevailing mood.

Keynes' argument was, the reader will recall, that, while not impossible, there is no guarantee that a drop in wages will act as a signal for greater investment. The only way to imagine that this is what *must* happen is to think in terms of the *Inherent Error*'s neoclassical version. More precisely, to become confident that a wage drop will stimulate investment one needs to assume that, other things being equal, every capitalist behaves as if she is the only capitalist in the economy. For, only then can the capitalist overcome the radical uncertainty caused by the fact that no capitalist can, by herself, raise aggregate investment to a level that makes it worth her while to invest. But no capitalist is daft enough to think this way. Keynes referred to this type of thinking as the *fallacy of composition* (see Box 7.8).

Kalecki's important emendation to this thought was the introduction into the picture of the role of corporate power first discussed seriously by the outsiders (see Section 7.2). Ever since capitalism was dominated by large firms, with the market power to set prices significantly above costs, firms began to count on a positive mark-up; that is, a sustainably positive difference between price and average cost. Kalecki postulated that labour's share of the surplus did not fluctuate significantly over the economic cycle. The reason he gave was that, during a recession, wages fall as a share of national income when the corporations' mark-ups fall and rise when their non-labour costs (e.g. raw materials, energy) decline. Thus, wages remain more or less constant during a downturn. This means that, even if Keynes exaggerated the relative unimportance of the falling wage as a stimulus of investment (see the previous paragraph), there was an additional reason why we should not expect that recessions will be overcome by a fall in wages.

The combined effect of Keynes' and Kalecki's arguments was to promote the radical view that fluctuations in output cannot be blamed or credited to changes in wages. But if the changes in output are not due to fluctuations in the workers' share of national income, what are they caused by? By fluctuations in investment, conclude Keynes and Kalecki in one voice. So, if we want to understand the fluctuations in economic activity we must understand first the fluctuations in investment. However, and this was the poignant theoretical break, investment fluctuates in a manner that undermines any attempt to explain it by means of a determinate, 'closed' model. In short, reason is too feeble to determine the level of investment in a capitalist society. Part of the mystery of investment's penchant to cause crises, by its sudden disappearance, is that it is so indispensible and yet so capricious.[2]

Notes
1 See Kriesler (1997).
2 Kalecki makes this point well: 'The tragedy of investment is that it causes crisis because it is useful. Doubtless many people will consider this paradoxical. But it is not the theory which is paradoxical, but its subject – the capitalist economy'. *Essays in the Theory of Economic Fluctuations*, (London 1939), p. 149. Quoted in Dobb (1973), p. 222.

7.7 Epilogue

If the last chapter ended with a triumph, of Leibniz over Newton in a bewildering post-humous contest for the soul of Marginalist economic modelling, this chapter ends with a deconstruction. The attempt to turn political economics into a form of social physics pro-duced an economic ideology that was well and truly discredited in 1929 by the facts on the ground. But facts never speak for themselves and this is why Keynes's epic tome, which followed in 1936, proved invaluable.

With considerable patience, piercing boldness and uncommon erudition, the archetypal English insider told a stunned world the plainest of truths about itself: when it comes to market economies, *we are damned if we know what breathes fire into the equations of invest-ment and consumption.* In a state of permanent cluelessness about what capitalism has in store for itself, we must come to terms with the unalloyed truth that no amount of intelli-gence, mathematical prowess or statistical wizardry can help us second-guess capitalism. For it is in capitalism's recalcitrant nature to unexpectedly and violently pull the rug from under the feet of the most accomplished statistical model, the shiniest mathematical theory, the boldest codification of its functioning.

In its approach to natural phenomena, Reason first measures and quantifies before fash-ioning determinate models which causally link together the quantified variables. They are the weapons it arms us with so that we can pierce our veil of ignorance to gain a glimpse of an objective reality that lies on the other side. Unfortunately, capitalism is not a natural phe-nomenon and these weapons prove inept in the fight against our ignorance of its ways. When deployed to explain investment, consumption and employment, models work only during the lull between 'discontinuities' or 'turning points'. Unable to predict these turning points, models condemn to nasty surprises those who end up believing in them. Ironically, the poli-cies they recommend are most likely to bring about the disagreeable turning points to which they are themselves oblivious.

The deeper cause for the radical uncertainty endemic to market societies is that, unlike in nature, capitalist economies are largely governed by the prevailing mood; outcomes hinge on an agglomeration of human opinion about these very outcomes. Keynes raised the fine point that, in this setting, the never-ending causal circle between average beliefs and actual outcomes engenders an infinity of possible outcomes, each of which is fully compatible with Reason. The resulting plethora of potentially rational outcomes rules out some firm predic-tion that Reason can home in on. Rational men and women, thus, have no alternative but to follow hunches, adopt rules of thumb and, generally, be very jittery in their economic dealings.

In his masterly book *The Great Chain of Being*, published in the same year as Keynes' *General Theory*, Arthur O. Lovejoy (1873–1962) suggested that Enlightenment thinking never really transcended religion; that a direct line continues to connect our modern, scientific view of the universe to theology.[50] As a result, we still have a tendency misleadingly to think of the cosmos as a series of predetermined stages; to think 'axiarchically' that of all the countless ways that the whole of reality might be, only one is the way reality is. In the natural sciences, Darwinism, relativity theory and quantum mechanics are beginning to break this chain, imparting a view of a radically open universe.

In this far less accomplished book, we have been suggesting that political economics has not managed a similar transition from a closed to an open universe. To paraphrase Lovejoy's title, we are stuck with another tradition: the *Great Chain of Economics' Inherent Error*, which runs like an invisible thread and threat through the whole gamut of humanity's faltering attempts to understand exchange value and economic growth. In the preceding chapters, we traced this chain from Aristotle to the classical political economists and to neoclassicism. Karl Marx was the first thinker to object to it by stressing the irreducibility of human activity to some quantifiable resource input (recall Chapter 4). However, he did not sever the chain because, as he became enthralled with the possibility of adorning his political agenda with a cloak of scientific objectivism, he himself succumbed to the *Inherent Error* (see Chapter 5) and gave up his great insight about the irreducibility of human labour. It took the aristocratic irreverence of Keynes to break, once and for all, our discipline's *Great Chain*.[51]

Where Marx had concentrated on *labour* as the one economic force that capitalism can never fully quantify, subjugate and objectify, Keynes focused on two other, more bourgeois, human activities resisting objectification: acts of *consumption* and *investment*. Because our medium-term situation is always a collective creation crucially depending on the current mood, spending on consumption and capital goods is motivated by factors that cannot be objectified, quantified or reduced to some mathematical expectation (either at the level of the individual or the social). Any such modelling attempt is bound to fall foul of the very nature of the game we play – recall Box 7.7.

But can we do without models? After all, the human mind cannot be stopped from associating variables; from trying to discern connections between interconnected phenomena. In this sense, we have a stark choice between models that are consciously drawn up and models which operate at a subliminal level, impervious to rational scrutiny. Nonetheless, this is no reason to remain victims of the *Inherent Error*. In the epilogue to Chapter 5, we summed up our theoretical 'manifesto' thus: 'Each... model turns out to be both *necessary* and *incomplete*. Each is a *necessary error*, an *indispensible facade*.'

Keynes understood this well. A master of technique, he studied every model that came his way, even waxing lyrical about depictions (e.g. Ramsey's 1928 model) that clearly disagreed with his take on capitalism. He toyed with models of his own making (mostly Marginalist, in view of his background) which he used to concentrate and sharpen his analytical thinking. However, when it came to characterising reality, and recommending measures to make it more palatable, he shoved the models to one side as if in accordance with Lovejoy's (1936: 8) advice: 'Man must become habitually mindful of the limitations of his mental powers, must be content with that "relative and practical understanding" which is the only organ of knowledge that he possesses'. When confronted with the spectre of the Great Depression, Keynes produced both a simple diagnosis and a clear-cut policy prescription.

The diagnosis was that such is capitalism: a system with an inbuilt tendency for invest-ment seizures that can be triggered by all manner of mood swings among investors and consumers alike. With spending in decline, demand goes into free fall, people delay pur-chases in the hope that tomorrow the price will be even lower than today, bankruptcies escalate, debts grow larger,[52] liquidity disappears and a war of all against all sinks all boats. A crisis that began through no one's fault is turning everyone into an accomplice of the dynamic which drags society into a deep, dark hole from which it cannot hope to be extri-cated without help from its organised polity: the state.

While his peers sought enlightenment in models of predetermined business cycles, or blamed government for causing the depression (see Box 7.11), Keynes remained pragmatic and mercurial. In place of the imponderable mysticism of the models of his fellow econo-mists, Keynes sought to offer a demystified analysis appropriate for a depressed age in which the principal doctrinal beliefs had proven both wrong and destructive. Analytically attuned to the demands of his time, Keynes felt no need to fit the facts to his theory because his theory was not a hermetically closed doctrine. With the freedom that his open-ended theory afforded him, he came to his simple, liberating, astute recommendations: first, the straight-jacket that was the Gold Standard, along with the ideology that supported it, had to go, since it was limiting the ability of governments to refloat the sinking boats, and liquidity had

---

Box 7.11 Neoclassical Revisionism and the role of the Federal Reserve, then and now

Refusing to accept that 1929 was damning for their mindset, neoclassicists tried val-iantly to fit the facts to their theory. Unwilling to imagine that markets could generate endogenously a calamity of this magnitude, and convinced that the smoking gun always points to government failure, they put the blame on the US Federal Reserve, or Fed for short. The chargesheet opines that in 1929 the Fed failed to respond to a major contraction in the quantity of money. So, a 'normal' panic at the stock exchange caused a crisis of liquidity and, because the Fed failed in its task to keep the quantity of money constant (recall the neoclassicists' espousal of the *Quantity Theory of Money*; see Section 7.3), banks began to fail and the Great Depression became inevitable. One of the most prominent proponents of this explanation is Ben Bernanke, who as fate would have it, found himself at the helm of the Fed in 2008. His energetic stoking of the US economy with hitherto unseen amounts of liquidity, as a means of staving off a post-2008 depression, is consistent with his interpretation of the causes of 1929.[1]

While it is of course true that in 1929 the Fed's penny pinching attitude to the quan-tity of money did much to fuel the spate of bankruptcies that spearheaded the depres-sion, the above argument neglects that the Fed was labouring under strict limits, set by the rules of the Gold Standard, on how much credit it could create at a time of crisis – recall Box 7.5; the very rules that neoclassicism supported to the full on the basis of its very own version of the *Quantity Theory of Money*.

Note
1 See Bernanke (2004). *Essays on the* Great Depression. Princeton, N.J.: Princeton University Press.

to be replenished. Second, liberating monetary policy from the constraints of the *Quantity Theory of Money* was insufficient as an effective 'antidepressant'. As 2008 and its aftermath are confirming daily, when the rot starts, pumping liquidity into the banking system is simply not enough. Keynes was adamant about this: '[W]hilst the weakening of credit is sufficient to bring about a collapse' he wrote in Chapter 12 of the *General Theory*, 'its strengthening, though a necessary condition for recovery, is not a sufficient condition'.

So, what does it take to give recovery a chance? The simple answer is: *government expenditure on activities that directly increase employment.* Money in workers' pockets finds its way into the circular flow much faster than money given to banks or to the rich. While factories and farms remain idle due to low demand, this increase in the quantity of money will have no effect on prices as long as it is an injection that helps lift the spirits, improves the mood of spenders (consumers and investors alike), raises demand, boosts output and, thus, more money ends up chasing after more commodities.

The importance of an optimistic mood does not come in more arresting form, but nor are the limitations of sentiment more arrestingly illustrated than in the *General Theory*. While optimism is essential for growth, growth can only happen in economies with the capacity to save and the technology to produce the machines that amplify the powers of labour. Marx alerted us to the central role played by the capitalists' self-reproducing hunger for *surplus labour* which, in turn, relies on the dialectical and, therefore, indeterminate nature of both labour and capital. He assumed that all profits are reinvested because he wanted to prove that even a perfect form of capitalism (in which capitalists consume nothing) is subject to periodic downturns. Keynes took us a step further than Marx in suggesting that saving is driven by a similar metaphysical urge for abstract wealth; for an unknowable future return by which to shield one's self from the vagaries of chance and unforeseen circumstance.

In strong contrast to Marx, Keynes did not believe even in the theoretical possibility of a perfect capitalism in which profit is automatically ploughed back into the economy's productive capacity. More importantly, by breaking the *Great Chain*, Keynes delinked abstract wealth from surplus value and split the abstract nature of monetary wealth from the means by which it is attained in the sphere of production. His tool? – the idea that *effective demand is indeterminate* and the financial sphere is much more than a neutral monetary veil thrown over the 'real economy'. If Marx was the definitive Newtonian, for whom capitalism was following a predetermined path made inevitable by objective gravitational forces, Keynes was a one-man 1927 *Solvay Conference*.[53] In a letter to Kingsley Martin, editor of the *New Statesman*, Keynes wrote: 'The inevitable never happens. It is the unexpected always'. In essence, we cannot rely on endogenous forces to lead us to redemption either in the short run, as neoclassicists insisted, or in the long run, as Marx had hoped. Capital is just as untameable as labour and the result is 'interesting times', as the Chinese might say.

Keynes was not the only thinker to part ways with the *Inherent Error* in the mid-war period. Austrian Marginalists, who never bought the neoclassical turn, were also worried that political economics, in its quest for consistent models of capitalist economies, were jeopardising capitalism's survival chances. Friedrich von Hayek (1899–1992), the most prominent of the Austrians, was convinced that neoclassicism offers excellent ammunition to those who want to wreck the free market. Since it has to ditch time in order to portray capitalism's complexity, neoclassicism imparts not a model of a dynamic capitalist economy but, rather, a hellish picture of stagnation. Markets, in Hayek's mind, are irreplaceable because of the *impossibility* of second-guessing capitalism. People change their minds all the time about what they want, fashions come and go, technology is an ever-accelerating roller-coaster: there is just too much economic information around us even for angels in authority to harness it. In this context, the anarchic market is the only institution that can create some order out of this chaos. Nevertheless order which is thus created is created *spontaneously* or, otherwise phrased, *unpredictably*. Unsurprisingly, no economic model (i.e. a human being's design) can capture this process; for if it could, then the market would not have been spontaneous (and, by deduction, irreplaceable).

There is a close resemblance between Hayek's and Keynes' espousal of indeterminacy. The impossibility of knowing the future, even probabilistically, was central to both men's thinking. The decisive significant difference, however, was that, unlike Keynes, Hayek remained a true believer. Not in economic models but in the ability of capitalist markets to deliver the best of all possible outcomes. Unlike Keynes, who worried that neoclassicism was blinding state officials to their duty to save capitalism from itself, Hayek was inimical to any role for the state, whose 'mingling' he saw only as destructive of creativity, prosperity and liberty. The clash of these two perspectives was to indelibly mark public discourse for decades. Underneath the fine points and the powerful arguments of both sides lies a simple question of faith.

Hayek and his free marketeer followers espouse the concept of flux and, like Keynes, do not believe that Reason can second-guess temporal change when the latter depends on the synthesis of billions of individual acts. Change is good. It is the natural habitat of the

---

Box 7.12 Austrian Revisionism and the role of the Federal Reserve, then and now

Just like the neoclassical revisionists (see Box 7.11), Friedrich von Hayek blamed the Great Depression on the hapless Federal Reserve. But, unlike the former, his criticism was that the Fed created too much money in the 1920s, the result being easy credit, low interest rates, heavy borrowing and the creation of a bubble in assets (stocks, bonds, land values). Then, mindful of the dangers that this bubble entailed, the Fed tightened credit and the money supply in 1928. But it was too late. The bubble did not deflate slowly but, instead, blew up. The moral of the story is that governments should not be trusted with any type of economic role, not even with the guardianship of the nation's currency. In an astounding 1976 treatise,[1] he advocated the end of central banks and the granting to private banks of the right to issue their own money, which would then compete for people's allegiance at the market place.

Following the *Crash of 2008*, a large number of commentators gave an identical explanation. Noting that the Fed had set interest rates at historically low levels since 2001 (in a bid to prevent the bursting of the so-called dot.com bubble from spilling over into a recession), they argue that between 2001 and 2008 the low interest rates helped stoke up a bubble in all sorts of assets, including the securitised subprime mortgages. When that bubble broke, the post-2008 recession was inevitable. Alan Greenspan, the long-time Chairman of the Federal Reserve (from 1987 to 2007), has recently issued a rejoinder suggesting that interest rates are too much of a blunt instrument either to cause an assets' bubble or to prevent its formation.

Note
1 Friedrich von Hayek (1976). *Denationalisation of Money*.

human condition. However, only change that is brought about by voluntary individual action qualifies. It is Hayek's article of faith that change brought about by collective agency, by central authorities (e.g. increased government spending during a crisis), must be frowned upon, especially when it is democratically endorsed. The deeper reason behind this faith is the simple idea that we are surrounded by a world determined to outsmart our collective efforts to control it!

Why are our collective efforts to shape the world doomed? Because it is so chaotic, and it evolves simultaneously in so many different places at once, that it cannot be planned. They (orthodox economists and politicians) are convinced that, as in biological evolution, whatever we may think of the evolving world, any attempt to resist its 'motion' will make us look like King Canute trying to stop the tides by the power of his will.[54] However, here lies a contradiction: although they argue that nothing that is in humanity's interest can be made to happen by government or some other form of collective agency, almost anything can be accomplished through individualistic, decentralised action. But if the social world is uncontrollable by humans, if it can be counted on to 'bite back' at our best efforts, how is it that they are convinced that free enterprise and the *Invisible Hand* will be exempt from the world's vengefulness? Can they seriously argue that spontaneous order will tame global warming?

Keynes had little time for the rantings of the faithful; whether they were free floating free marketeers, treasury officials believing in their model's validity, or Marxist revolutionaries caught up in their own certainties. He had especially little time for rantings that were heard loudly far and wide not because of their plausibility but because they resonated nicely with the built-in tendency of privilege to reproduce itself. Above all else, he was convinced that economics had done serious damage to the mindset of members both of officialdom and of the public. And he set himself the task to reprogramme it away from the *Inherent Error*.

> Unfortunately the popular mind has been educated away from the truth, away from common sense. The average man has been taught to believe what his own common sense, if he relied on it, would tell him was absurd.[55]

But it was not Keynes who changed the mindset. It was the carnage of the Second World War that sidelined, at least for a while, political economics and its *Inherent Error*. In the US, the War Economy was run by a band of pragmatic policymakers who had cut their teeth during the New Deal in, or never far away from, the wastelands of the 1930s. Partly informed by Keynes, and mostly guided by the war's appalling imperatives, they combined central planning with private ownership of factories and farms to produce an unprecedented spurt in investment, growth and technology. They learnt how to manage prices, to socialise capital accumulation, to redistribute the surplus in order to maintain social cohesion at a time of national emergency. Above all else, they learnt that capitalism was too important to leave to the capitalists; that, as Marx had put it in 1852, the capitalist class'

> own interests dictate that it should be delivered from the danger of its own rule;... [that] in order to save its purse it must forfeit the crown, and the sword that is to safeguard it must at the same time be hung over its own head as a sword of Damocles.[56]

While the war was raging, a group of scientists and applied mathematicians, mostly *émigrés* from Central Europe and Scandinavia, were applying their skills to the micromanagement of the war economy. They were devising optimal transportation systems (for efficiently ferrying arms and supplies to the four corners of the planet); setting prices of production (that the government was imposing on industrialists); planning the air force's bombing raids for maximum effect; breaking enemy codes; optimising the navy's logistics; and, last but not least, dabbling in the Manhattan Project that was to culminate in the atom bomb. For the first time in the history of economics, men of incredible scientific skill moonlighted in solving real, practical economic problems.

At war's end, and with the Depression behind them, but never far from their minds, policymakers in Washington were busily planning for the peace on the basis of a discursive cosmopolitan Keynesianism, a New Deal pragmatism and the prospect of receiving practical guidance, at the microeconomic level, from the scientists who were manning the various planning divisions of the US military, government, transportation authorities, etc. Indeed, the work of the scientists briefly promised to change political economics from a field of pure ideology, if not theology, to an engineering-like discipline with practical uses. Alas, it was not to be. As the next chapter will argue, our scientists were soon to be routed by a resurgent neoclassicism.

When the Cold War took over from its piping hot predecessor around 1950, a new formalism combined (a) the *Inherent Error* of the pre-Keynes neoclassicists with (b) a new type of (axiomatic) mathematics. The combined effect was to sideline the brilliant scientists who remained committed to a practical, engineering approach to economic problems. Thus, from the 1950s to the early 1970s economics was savagely bifurcated: on the one hand, government continued to conduct economics policy based on its discursive Keynesianism and New Deal pragmatism. But, on the other, academic economic theory was engulfed in a resurgent neoclassical formalism that swept everything in its path. Students of economics were bewildered, and many still are, by the chasm separating so-called *microeconomics* from *macroeconomics*. The cause of their puzzlement is historical and can be traced to this post-war bifurcation.

The great bifurcation ended in the early 1970s, together with the first phase of the postwar era.[57] Neoclassicism, having already 'captured' theoretical economics, extended its grip into the corridors of power. From then onwards, neoclassicism was to rule the roost in academia and in government at once. In 2008, we paid the price of this reunification under the aegis of the *Inherent Error*'s most insidious form.

8 A fatal triumph

2008's ancestry in the stirrings of the Cold War

8.1 The New Dealers

> I should like to have it said of my first Administration that in it the forces of selfishness and lust for power met their match. I should like to have it said of my second Administration that these forces have met their master.
>
> President Franklin D. Roosevelt, Campaign Address at Madison Square Garden, New York City. 'We Have Only Just Begun to Fight', 31 October 1936.[1]

If speeches are deemed great for their capacity to encapsulate an era's spirit, President Roosevelt's 1936 Campaign Address was one of the greatest. It conveyed with immediacy and pathos the disgust that middle America felt for the deceit of the bankers, the glorified spivs and, generally, Wall Street; the professionals to whom they once looked up, whom they trusted with their savings and whom, following the fall of 1929, they held responsible for the wholesale anguish with which their hard work had been repaid.

Regrettably, the truth was less heroic than the New Deal's rhetoric might have us believe. Neither was Roosevelt's first term in office (1932–36) the 'moment' when 'the forces of selfishness and the lust of power met their match', nor was his second term (1936–40) the time when 'these forces met their master'. In truth, when Roosevelt and his team of New Dealers came into office to clean up the mess of 1929, they had no plan to energetically confront Wall Street[2] or to tackle the Great Depression using, as Keynes was to recommend four years later, the lever of government expenditure.

Indeed, from the outset, the New Dealers followed a 'natural' conservative instinct which told them that all problems begin with government, the greatest of these being government deficit. Astonishing as it may now sound, their first priority in the depths of the Great Depression was to slash outgoing President Hoover's deficit by cutting the salaries of civil servants and the benefits of army veterans.[3] It was only *after* 1936 that Roosevelt accepted the premise that government's top priority ought to be to kick-start growth by means of a spending stimulus.

The change of heart did not come, as some Keynesians like to think, from the publication, in that year, of the *General Theory* but from two harsh empirical observations during the 1932–36 period: first, that the spending cuts of the first term had disastrous effects and, second, that only countries where public spending rose exponentially experienced significant recovery (e.g. Germany and Japan). Even when the President's change of heart came, it was half-hearted and, thus, anaemic in its impact. Had it not been for the Second World War,

Roosevelt's Presidency would have gone down in history as the administration that failed to lift the curse of the Great Depression.

Be that as it may, Roosevelt's 1936 speech was a moment of high drama that represented the sharpest critique by a US president of untrammelled markets and of the ideology (including the political economics) which had kept them so. In fact it took seven decades, and a fresh version of 1929, before another US president would dare hurl similar words at Wall Street, its ideologues and their assorted fellow travellers:

> Instead of learning the lessons of Lehman and the crisis from which we're still recovering, [many in the financial sector a]re choosing to ignore those lessons. I'm convinced they do so not just at their own peril, but at our nation's. So I want everybody here to hear my words: we will not go back to the days of reckless behavior and unchecked excess that was at the heart of this crisis, where too many were motivated only by the appetite for quick kills and bloated bonuses. Those on Wall Street cannot resume taking risks without regard for consequences, and expect that next time, American taxpayers will be there to break their fall [T]he old ways that led to this crisis cannot stand. And to the extent that some have so readily returned to them underscores the need for change and change now. *History cannot be allowed to repeat itself.*
> President Barack H. Obama's address on financial reform,
> 14 September 2009[4] (emphasis added).

In the same speech he added:

> So I want everybody here to hear my words: we will not go back to the days of reckless behaviur and unchecked excess at the heart of this crisis. Those on Wall Street cannot resume taking risks without regard for consequences, and expect that next time, American taxpayers will be there to break their fall Taken together, we are proposing the most ambitious overhaul of the financial system since the Great Depression.

In his *Liberalism and its Discontents*, Alan Brinkley[5] incisively narrates how, once in power, Roosevelt's New Dealers jettisoned their critical assessment of capitalism. It is like reading a more recent book written for our times. A sense of recurring *déjà vu* prevails as one turns its pages. From Obama's first days of administration, his appointments foreshadowed a

---

Box 8.1 The 'menace' of financial reform

The moment President Obama announced his intention to regulate Wall Street, his administration was lambasted as overbearing, statist, socialist. As the following quotation confirms, there is nothing new under the sun:

> Every demand of the simplest bourgeois financial reform, of the most ordinary liberalism, of the most formal republicanism, of the most shallow democracy, is simultaneously castigated as an 'attempt on society' and stigmatised as 'socialism'.
> Karl Marx in *The Eighteenth Brumaire of Louis Bonaparte*, 1852

remarkable repetition of history. A Democratic administration swept into office on a wave of expectation, sourced, just as in 1932, at grassroots' discontent with Wall Street and the overarching ethos of financialised capitalism; it composed its actual policies to reflect not an agenda for sweeping change, trimmed down by pragmatism, but rather an agenda that was timid from the start, fearful of the label 'socialist' (see Box 8.1) and independent of any serious critique of financialised capitalism. Most tellingly, those appointed to key economic positions had been deeply immersed in the economists' *Inherent Error* before their appointment and had in fact played key roles in unleashing Wall Street from the tenuous restrictions placed upon it by their 1930s New Deal political ancestors.[6]

While it is true that the New Dealers did, in the end, increase government intervention later into the 1930s, they did so when they were left with no alternative and, even then, did so with the utmost reluctance. Similarly, Obama's administration was only moved to curtail the excesses of Wall Street when inactivity emboldened the banks to use taxpayers' money in order to lobby against their regulation; even to bend the US Supreme Court to their will with a monstrous judgement that promised immeasurably to increase the banks political gravitas.[7]

Contrasting the era of *Napoleon Bonaparte* with that of *Napoleon the Third*, Karl Marx wrote: 'Hegel remarks somewhere that all great world-historic facts and personages appear, so to speak, twice. He forgot to add: the first time as tragedy, the second time as farce'.[8] While it is perhaps too early to declare the post-2008 political reaction to the latest financial collapse a farce (even though we very much fear that it will prove so), it is pertinent to focus on the reaction to the original tragedy from the perspective of political economics. A false impression came to pass that Keynesianism became the official mantra as soon as the *General Theory* was published. In truth, it did not. Only after the end of the Second World War did the New Dealers, who remained in power well into the Cold War, adopt a strange form of Keynesianism that John Maynard Keynes would never have condoned. Its purpose was theoretically to dress up their brand-new post-war plan for a new global order (see Chapter 11).

Returning to 1932, the New Dealers showed no sign of an interest in having the state guide aggregate investment, break up monopoly power or plan aggregate demand centrally.[9] What they did try out was price and wage controls. In 1933, President Roosevelt set up the *National Recovery Administration* (NRA) and armed it with the power to regulate prices and wages in major industries in a bid to stem the deflationary spiral. The idea was not to break up the cartels but to supervise the prices they charged and the wages they paid.

Even though the NRA failed quite spectacularly, the idea behind it proved popular and, in 1936, Roosevelt campaigned forcefully in its favour, invoking the threats to liberal capitalism posed by large corporations and the perils of 'organised money' (see this chapter's opening speech quote). Once re-elected, however, the New Dealers quietly ended attempts to regulate prices and wages, to control the corporations and, more generally, to alter the structure of American capitalism. Price and wage regulation only made a comeback, this time with considerable success, during the war but was lifted again in 1945. At war's end, the New Dealers' project extended beyond the borders of the USA and helped shape a new *Global Plan* that was to survive until the early 1970s.

In the meantime, while Roosevelt's New Dealers were tiptoeing in search of policies with which to defeat the Great Depression, without stepping too harshly on the toes of corporate capitalism, the younger and more academically minded among them immersed themselves in Keynes' *General Theory*. A good example is a spontaneous reading group formed just before the war by three Rockefeller Fellows at Harvard. They were John Kenneth Galbraith (1908–2006), the Frenchman Robert Marjolin (1911–86) and Paul Samuelson (1915–2009).

Galbraith was to spend the war as Roosevelt's '*Price Czar*',[10] determining the price of all major commodities; Marjolin was to become initially Jean Monnet's deputy at the French *Commissariat général du Plan* and then the first Secretary of the Organisation for European Economic Co-operation (OEEC) (the OECD's precursor) whose ambit was, at first, the management of the Marshall Plan and, later, the coordination of the political efforts to forge that which is known now as the European Union; Samuelson was the third recipient of the Nobel Prize in Economics, and the first who did not share the honour, and the author of the most famous economics post-war textbook of all time.[11]

While these three were scrutinising Keynes's *magnum opus*, other Harvard contemporaries were busy drafting policy papers. *Paul Sweezy* (1910–2004), for instance, who was to become the American Left's leading political economist, was already publishing papers on particular aspects of the crisis, prognosticating new trials and tribulations for American capitalism. Most New Dealers had been hoping that the post-Depression recovery would feed on itself until full employment was restored. But it was not to be. The sharp recession of 1937 destroyed such hopes as unemployment leapt once more from 14 per cent to 19 per cent. Both Sweezy and his mentor, Joseph Schumpeter, were exercised by the new crisis. In 1938, Alvin Hansen (1887–1975), then the most prominent Keynesian economics professor at Harvard, wrote his *Full Recovery or Stagnation?*[12] and a number of young economists, graduate students and instructors at Harvard and Tufts, signed their *An Economic Program for American Democracy*.[13]

In that climate of heightened intellectual activity, both Schumpeter and Sweezy put forward different explanations of capitalism's tendency towards stagnation.[14]

Schumpeter's explanation focused on the system's political constraints while Sweezy's Marxist take concentrated on the contradictions embodied in capitalist economic development.[15] Clearly, for anyone interested in debates regarding the response of the New Deal generation to the challenges of the *Depression* and its aftermath, Harvard was the focal point and Keynesianism, laced with doses of Schumpeter and Marx, was the mind-frame.

The war added new urgency and discursive layers to these men's thinking. Some of them went straight into public service as planners, analysts, etc. Galbraith, as mentioned above, became the fixer of all major relative prices in the US War Economy, earning the nickname *Price Czar*. Sweezy joined the army in the fall of 1942 and was assigned to the *Office of Strategic Services* (the CIA's precursor), serving under his former Harvard professor and colleague Edward Mason. He was soon to be dispatched to London to join the *Research and Analysis* program of the OSS there, under economist, Chandler Morse, with a view to keeping an eye on British economic policy on behalf of the US government. In this context, he was meeting regularly with James Meade, another famous economist working at the time for the British Economic Warfare Agency.

By that stage, it was clear to all that the Second World War would lead to a major reorganisation of global capitalism, in which the US would claim a leading role. The young New Dealers were destined for significant roles in this *Global Plan* (see Chapter 11). Indeed, the politicians and policymakers above them, whose hands were on the levers of real power, were practical men who came to the conclusion that, in view of 1929, the peace economy ought to be planned just as meticulously as the War Economy was. They themselves had felt the Great Depression in their bones and were marked for life by the experience. Having joined the Roosevelt administration with a clear commitment to economic planning whose aim was to guide markets to socially desirable outcomes, their later experience of running a fully planned War Economy produced a mindset ripe for the demands and challenges of the post-war era.

Book 2 begins with an account of the resulting *Global Plan*; our term for the first post-war phase spanning the years 1947 to 1971. It is instructive to consider here the ideological and analytical background of three of its architects. James Byrnes (1879–1972) had risen the hard way within the law profession (without even receiving a law degree) and was exasperated by the demise of many of his peers after 1929.[16] His visionary position on the Marshall Plan, including his insistence that the Europeans must put forward specific developmental plans for their own backyards, was directly caused by his conviction that planned capitalism was the only alternative to catastrophe. James Forrestal (1892–1949), despite having personally weathered the storm rather well (making CEO at *Dillon Read* by 1938), repeatedly explained how the Great Depression had turned him into a passionate New Dealer. His wartime experience of running, and planning for, the US Navy was crucial to his post-war contribution to the *Global Plan* (see Chapter 11). Finally, George Kennan (1904–2005), whose rise to prominence is credited to the longest telegram in history,[17] became another strong advocate of direct US investment in Europe's and Japan's industries (the significance of which we discuss in Chapter 11) because of a combination of (a) his experience of the Great Depression (and its stubborn resistance to market solutions); (b) a careful study of the war economies of the Soviet Union, Germany and the US; and (c) a deep appreciation of the importance of European economic development for the US.

In summary, the United States came out of the war with New Deal policymakers at the helm whose plans for the post-war peace coincided with those for winning the Cold War. While these plans reflected several brands of Keynesianism, as seen mainly through the prism of pre-war Harvard, they were founded on the practical experience of running the War Economy which prepared them well for the tasks of effectively managing global demand and recycling surpluses among the major centres of capitalism; a task at which governments had failed miserably during the 1920s and 1930s. As we shall see in *Book 2*, the experience of the Second World War emboldened New Dealers to design global policies as different from their pre-war equivalents as post-1945 fighter jets were from the propeller-driven biplanes of 1939.

8.2 The scientists

While the War Economy was being planned at the top by pragmatic New Dealers, a group of mathematicians-turned-scientists were busy solving practical problems on behalf of the military. One such scientist was a Dutchman named Tjalling Koopmans (1910–85). Having embarked on a distinguished mathematics career at age 17, Koopmans penned a famous theorem in theoretical physics in 1934 (still referred to in the literature as the *Koopmans Theorem*) before completing his physics doctorate in 1936 at the University of Leiden. When the Second World War broke out, Koopmans moved to the United States where he was immediately employed by the Combined Allied Shipping Boards to write algorithms for allocating shipments between sources and destinations in a manner that minimised cost and delays. Koopmans based his work on a previous formulation by John von Neumann (1903–57), the doyen of European mathematicians also working closely with the US military, and the practical solutions he offered were the beginning of what mathematicians today refer to as *linear and dynamic programming*.

Soon after the war began, a military–scientific establishment came into being in the US, brimming with mathematicians and scientists whose technical skills were finding immediate applications. In addition to Koopmans, George Dantzig (1914–2005) is another apt example. Also employed by the US Air Force on linear programming projects, Dantzig later delivered the definitive method (called 'simplex') for planning the efficient allocation of given resources.[18] However, Koopmans' significance (at least from the perspective of this book) lies at a higher level. On the basis of his programming work, Koopmans was inducted into the Cowles Commission whose motto was *Science is Measurement*[19] and its purpose to put mathematics, statistics and the 'hard' sciences in the service of economic policy. Koopmans, as it will transpire below, in his capacity as Cowles' heart and mind, played a leading, albeit unsung, role in the transformation of political economics during the Cold War, if only because of the people he hosted at the Cowles Seminars. First and foremost among the latter was no other than John von Neumann himself.

To grasp the significance of von Neumann's 1944 Cowles Seminar, we must first look back to his scientific origins that stretch well before 1944. Von Neumann was probably the

---

Box 8.2 The Cowles Commission for Research in Economics

The Cowles Commission was founded in 1932, in the shadows of the Great Depression, by Alfred Cowles III (1891–1984), a Yale economics graduate and businessman much frustrated by economics' inability to turn itself into a 'proper' science, especially by its spectacular predictive failures during the Great Depression. Unaware of the *Inherent Error* in its foundations, Cowles believed that economics could be elevated into an exact science if only it enlisted better and fresher mathematical and statistical minds.[1] To this effect, he invested a considerable amount of his personal fortune to create the Commission named after himself and his family. From the outset, the Cowles Commission focused exclusively on quantitative economic theory and econometric modelling of the US economy.

In 1939, the Cowles Commission moved from Colorado Springs to the University of Chicago. During 1943 to 1948 it was directed by Jacob Marschak (1898–1977), an odd choice given his early leanings towards socialist planning. However, Marschak accepted the agenda of steering Cowles firmly and enthusiastically in the direction of mathematical and econometric modelling, perhaps because at the time various social-ist economists also moved in that direction (e.g. Oskar Lange, 1904–65). In 1948, Tjalling Koopmans took over. The next three years were to help change economics for good; the list of Economics Nobel Prizes awarded to people that cut their teeth at Cowles tells the story powerfully: Tjalling Koopmans, Kenneth Arrow, Gerard Debreu, James Tobin, Franco Modigliani, Herbert Simon, Lawrence Klein, Trygve Haavelmo and Harry Markowitz (the first researcher to produce a mathematical model that provided the foundation of the mathematics behind the determination of the prices of complex financial products; the very prices that crashed so spectacularly in 2008).

By 1955, deep hostility from the University of Chicago Economics Department saw the Commission move to the East Coast, and Yale University in particular, where it was rebranded as the Cowles Foundation.

Note
1 Alfred Cowles III was himself an active researcher. In 1939, he published a monograph on the stock exchange and later papers in well-respected journals like *Econometrica* and the *Journal of American Statistical Association*.

most gifted mathematician ever to have graced both pure and applied mathematics. A Hungarian of Jewish origin, von Neumann was awarded two doctorates simultaneously at the age of twenty-three: one in mathematics (set theory) and one in chemistry. By his mid-twenties, he had achieved celebrity status in the mathematics community of Central Europe. Influenced by the popularity of *formalisation* in the 1920s, he pursued the line first advocated by David Hilbert (1862–1943) whose assistant von Neumann was at Göttingen in 1900 – namely, that a mathematician's proper task is to pinpoint the axioms on which *all* of mathematics rests.

In that vein, von Neumann tried, with considerable success, to axiomatise theories ranging from *set theory* in mathematics (1926) to *quantum mechanics* in physics (1927).[20] Every year he would publish a number of papers on diverse topics but with a common concern for establishing an axiomatic, formalist foundation for the issue at hand. As an interesting sideline, he published a paper in 1928 which effectively invented Game Theory and was later to become the foundation of his 1944 classic text of the same title, co-authored with Oskar Morgenstern.[21]

In 1930, at a conference in Königsberg, whose stated purpose was to celebrate 30 years since the commencement of David Hilbert's grandiose project of pinpointing *the* single set of axioms on which *all* of mathematics would sit, a young man delivered a now infamous paper.[22] His name was Kurt Gödel (1906–78) and his result has come to pass as the *Incompleteness Theorem*. It singlehandedly demolished Hilbert's project by proving arithmetic to be incomplete. Gödel had worked within the confines of classical logic in which the 'law of the excluded middle' (i.e. that formal logical propositions are either true or false) is a fundamental axiom. However, he proved that, in *any* formal system, there exists a proposition such that neither it nor its negation is provable.

Perhaps out of incredulity at the young man's audacity, no one in the audience grasped the significance of Gödel's momentous result. Except, that is, for another young man who sat there in awe of what he was hearing: von Neumann! Unlike the others sitting around him, von Neumann immediately grasped the meaning of what he had heard. Reportedly, he left that auditorium a changed man, having recognised the pointlessness of his engagement with formalism. Judging not only by his own account but also by the direction of his work thereafter, it is clear that Gödel's paper had a profound effect on him, so much so that he instantly lost interest in formalist mathematics and turned his attention to practical problems where mathematics could prove genuinely helpful.

Between 1930 and 1933 von Neumann was oscillating between Europe and the US, teaching mathematics and physics intermittently at Princeton but also retaining several appointments in Germany. By 1933, Hitler's rise to power in Germany and his own appointment to one of the six mathematics chairs at the newly founded *Institute for Advanced Study* in Princeton[23] had conspired to keep him in the US, and at Princeton, for the rest of his life. From then until the beginning of the Second World War, von Neumann focused on algebras that now bear his name. Things changed rapidly with the Japanese Imperial Navy's attack on Pearl Harbor in December 1941.[24]

Von Neumann entered the military–scientific establishment on the back of his hydrodynamics, a branch of mathematical physics crucial to the modelling of explosions. His preoccupation with hydrodynamics predated the war and originated in the interesting demands it placed upon his mathematical skills (as explosive events required solutions to complicated non-linear partial differential equations) and soon became a major participant in the *Manhattan Project*, which resulted in the atom bomb.

When the bomb ended the war in the Pacific theatre, von Neumann moved on to the design of both the hardware and software of the Cold War and the arms race the latter spawned. As an associate of RAND corporation, and with strong links with both the CIA and the Pentagon, he was a key developer of the rocket technology necessary for delivering nuclear warheads, in particular of the hydrogen bomb that had been recently developed. Additionally, he deployed Game Theory, one of his many brainchildren, in the planning of nuclear strike scenarios, MAD (Mutually Assured Destruction) being the best known of them all. In all this, his non-linear mathematical skills came in particularly handy as did his readiness to seek numerical solutions; a readiness that was to lead him to major contributions to computing science[25] and artificial intelligence.[26]

Box 8.3 The RAND Corporation

The Research and Development (RAND) Corporation started life at the conclusion of the Second World War in Santa Monica, California. The idea for its institution belonged to General H. H. 'Hap' Arnold, chief of staff of the Army Air Corps (which later became the US Air Force). Initially, it was a mere division of the *Douglas Aircraft Company*, which, in 1967, merged with *McDonnell Aviation* to form the *McDonnell-Douglas Aircraft Corporation*. In 1997 this leading aircraft manufacturer, and high technology weapon maker, was taken over by *Boeing*. RAND's first director was Franklin R. Collbohm, a Douglas engineer and test pilot.

Arnold's original rationale for setting up RAND was to extend beyond the war years the closely knit wartime relationship between the scientific community, the military and US government policymakers, as epitomised by the Manhattan Project (which delivered the Atom Bomb) and the subsequent nuclear weapon industry. Under the tutelage of Collbohm, RAND became the attractor of the ultimate roll call of mathematical economists, some of whom recruited from the ranks of the Cowles Commission (see Box 8.2). They included future economics Nobel Prize winners John Forbes Nash, Jr. and Kenneth Arrow (both of whom are discussed extensively below), and also Herbert Simon (1916–2001), a major contributor to procedural decision making, Paul Samuelson (see the next chapter for more), Thomas Schelling (b. 1921), whose two books *The Strategy of Conflict* and *Micromotives and Macrobehavior* remain monuments of intellectual achievement[1] and Edmund Phelps (b. 1933), a more recent Nobelist with an important presence in the transformation of political economics in the 1970s.

RAND had a finger in many different pies, from computing and artificial intelligence to pure mathematics and political analysis. However, in the public mind it became firmly associated with the design of nuclear war strategies on the basis of Game Theory, the theory 'invented' in the 1920s by John von Neumann. Indeed, all the main contributors to mathematical economics that used Game Theory methods worked, at one time or another, at RAND: e.g. John F. Nash, Jr., George Dantzig, Anatol Rapoport, Melvin Dresher. Practically every great thinker of these disciplines worked at RAND. Their motto: *thinking the unthinkable*.

After RAND physicist Bruno Augenstein (1923–2005) had developed the plans for intercontinental ballistic missiles (IBMs), which were to be the centrepiece of the Cold War arms race, the US Air Force sought recommendations for ways to deploy them.

The call was answered again by RAND associates, in particular Albert Wohlstetter (1913–97) and, of course, John von Neumann. The result was the aptly-named doctrine of MAD: Mutually Assured Destruction; the basic idea being to authorise in advance maximum escalation of a limited nuclear war, in the hope that this would present the ultimate deterrence to a nuclear aggressor. MAD became the cornerstone of US defence strategy and Wohlstetter, in his later years, became the mentor of the George W. Bush administration's neoconservatives, e.g. Paul Wolfowitz and Richard Perle, who were instrumental in the 2003 invasion of Iraq. The fact that Donald Rumsfeld, the US Secretary for Defence at the time of the Iraq invasion, and Condoleezza Rice, that administration's last Secretary of State, were both trustees of the RAND Corporation speaks volumes of its centrality during the post-war era.

Whether MAD succeeded in averting nuclear holocaust during the Cold War, or whether our species survived by a fluke *in spite of it*, is something that future historians must pronounce upon. However, another set of RAND policies, concerning a tragic conventional war, backfired famously. For it was RAND's considered opinion that the Vietnam War – that led two successive US administrations (one Democrat, the other Republican) to the deadly mire that was not only to cause untold suffering among the Vietnamese people and the US soldiers but, additionally, to end the New Dealers' *Global Plan* in 1971 – should be escalated; (see Chapter 11).

We finish this brief history of RAND with one exceptional case of scientific brilliance combined with uncommon courage: Harvard-educated economist Daniel Ellsberg (b. 1931). Students of economics encounter his name in the context of a dazzling experiment that demonstrated how problematic it is to assume, as neoclassical economists habitually do, that people act *as if* in order to maximise expected utility (or utility on average, where the averages are computed by means of the probabilities of various potential outcomes) – recall Chapter 6. In effect, Ellsberg demonstrated experimentally that when people are faced with *genuine uncertainty* (as opposed to risk), i.e. when even the probabilities of potential events are ambiguous, they tend to behave in ways that are meant to curb that ambiguity often at the expense of average, or expected, utility.[2]

What is less well known is that Ellsberg was a RAND scientist who became deeply enmeshed in US government policy, namely the nuclear arms race, the prosecution of the Vietnam War, etc. Because of his unquestionable credentials as a RAND employee and a leading Cold Warrior, he had access to the so-called *Pentagon Papers*: a vast set of highly classified documents that proved beyond doubt that *every* US administration knew that the war was unlikely to be won and that casualties would be legion. Shocked by what he read, Ellsberg started attending anti-Vietnam war meetings. In 1969, in one of these meetings, he encountered a soldier who was determined to go to prison as a stand against the prosecution of a mindless war. Coming so close to a flesh and blood conscientious objector, a person ready to risk everything just in order to 'do the right thing', caused Ellsberg's epiphany which prompted him to become the US government's most famous dissident. With the assistance of another RAND employ, he spent countless nights photocopying the documents one by one. After his attempts to interest legislators in their contents failed, he leaked them to the *New York Times* and the

Washington Post. The first explosive extracts were published in June 1971.[3] Subsequently, Ellsberg was fired from his job and was subjected to a court trial in 1973 under charges that would have him spend more than 110 years in gaol. However, his high-profile case, rigorous defending by top attorneys and some clear evidence of government subterfuge (including a covert campaign to vilify and even injure Ellsberg), led to his acquittal. To this day, RAND has not forgiven him.

Notes

1 See Schelling (1960 [1980]), (1978 [2006]).
2 See Ellsberg (1961). Interestingly, and possibly unbeknownst to Ellsberg, his experimental result came close to John Maynard Keynes' rejection of the notion that, in an uncertain world, rational people do not behave as if maximising some self defined function involving mathematical expectations.
3 By coincidence, two months later, on 15 August 1971, President Nixon announced the end of the *Global Plan* phase of the postwar period (see Chapter 11).

In his 'spare' time, between other more lethal assignments, von Neumann found the energy and time to make contributions to economics that would have been considered worthy of adulation even if their initiator had accomplished nothing else. Setting aside, for the moment, his contribution to Game Theory, von Neumann penned a short-ish paper in 1937 (re-printed in 1945),[27] by which he staked a worthy claim to classical-economist status. The paper presents a mathematical model of a growing multiple-sector economy featuring prices that are consistent with the overall growth rate. Recalling the *Holy Grail* of political economics, that is a model of a *growing* economy comprising *more than one sector*, the question arises: did this model lay the *Inherent Error* to rest? Had the *enfant terrible* of the *Manhattan Project* and RAND managed to solve the problem which hitherto eluded all economists?

Unlike Ramsey's 1928 single–good model (see Box 7.4 of the previous chapter), von Neumann packed an amazing amount of economic complexity into his mathematics. He made room for umpteen products, presumed that commodities are produced using as inputs previously produced commodities, allowed for many different production processes (each generating multiple products and by-products) and even different degrees of production intensities for each process. Moreover, having abandoned formalism in 1930, von Neumann was not interested in a theory that abstracted from historical time. So, his model 'economy' moved from one period to the next, *ad infinitum*, using at time t the previous period's $(t-1)$ outputs as inputs into the fresh round of production.

None of the above was virgin territory. Many an economist before von Neumann had specified such a model 'economy' but, then again, none had managed to provide a determinate solution for it. Von Neumann did! When referring to a 'solution', we mean a determinate answer to the question: is it possible to prove the *existence* of (a) an overall *growth rate* for this 'economy' and (b) a set of *relative prices* that are consistent with that growth rate? Von Neumann's paper will be etched in gold letters in the history of economics because he answered that question in the affirmative. Utilising a mathematical technique called *Brouwer's fixed point theorem*, he offered an *existence proof* that holds on condition that a number of (admittedly restrictive) assumptions are respected.

Box 8.4 Brouwer's Fixed Point Theorem

Luitzen Brouwer (1881–1966) was a mathematical philosopher at odds with David Hilbert, John von Neumann's original mentor. Much opposed to formalism and mathematical logic, and convinced that the principles of logic cannot be valid independently of the subject matter to which they are applied, he promoted the alternative method of *intuitionism* – a notion much influenced by his contact with the philosophy of Arthur Schopenhauer (1788–1860), a fascinating sceptic of the powers of human logic. However, in 1907, after completing his thesis, Brouwer decided that in order to make his mark in academia first he had to demonstrate his mathematical skills. To do so he proved and published, in 1910, his famous *fixed point theorem*. David Hilbert, in spite of their ongoing methodological duel, appreciated Brouwer's work and helped him secure a position at the University of Amsterdam. Once safely ensconced in academia, Brouwer returned to his pursuit of intuitionism. Soon after, von Neumann would also part ways with Hilbert's formalism, under the influence of Gödel (see above). Just before doing so, he used Brouwer's to produce a general solution for all zero sum games, as part of his 'invention' of Game Theory – see his 1928 paper on the subject.

Brouwer's fixed point theorem proves under what conditions some function $F(x)$ will possess at least one *fixed point*; i.e. a value for x such that $x = F(x)$. More precisely, Brouwer proved that *any* continuous function $F(.)$ mapping from the unit sphere in an N-dimensional Euclidean space on to a similar space must have such a fixed point. For example, $x = 1$ is a fixed point of quadratic function $F(x) = x^2$ and $x = 0.739$ is the fixed point of function $F(x) = \cos(x)$. To visualise Brouwer's fixed point theorem-in-action in more than two dimensions, imagine you get hold of a full cup of coffee and shake it. The theorem suggests that, however you move the cup, there will be at least one point, or molecule, in the coffee, the fixed point, that remains fixed (i.e. in the same place), unwilling to follow the movements of the coffee around it. Mathematically speaking, this is the same as imagining each coffee molecule to be a continuous function $F(.)$ of its original position and that the moving coffee, after you shake the cup, is contained within the cup's given space dimensions. Brouwer proved that, since that space is sufficiently closed (i.e. satisfies the properties of the unit sphere in an N-dimensional Euclidean space), at least one coffee molecule will be unmoved by your shaking of the cup; i.e. there exists a location x such that $x = F(x)$.

In his 1928 Game Theory paper, von Neumann used Brouwer's fixed point theorem to prove that in zero-sum games[1] the set of all possible strategies contains one fixed point; i.e. a best reply to itself. In this sense, if Jill were to use this (fixed point) strategy against Jack, it would be wise for Jack also to adopt it against Jill. Nine years later, when penning his growth model, he used the same type of mathematical device to prove the existence of a set of relative prices that are fixed while everything around them changes (as the economy grows). In both cases, the trick was to reduce the mathematical model of the 'game' (in the 1928 paper) or of the model 'economy' (in the 1937 paper) to a single function F possessing a fixed point.

The proof was tantamount to proving the existence of mutually best strategies or of reproducible relative prices: in the Game Theory context it meant that the discovered 'solution' comprises 'reproducible' strategies (in the sense that it is in the players' interest always to adopt them), while the 'solution' of the growth model reported reproducible relative prices, i.e. relative prices that, if one plugs into the economy at t, they pop up again intact at $t + 1$. In this sense, his two economic theorems discovered stationary or fixed points not dissimilar to the coffee molecule that stays put while all the other molecules in the swirling cup of coffee are going haywire.

Ironically, John von Neumann ended up employing anti-formalist Brouwer's piece of formal mathematics in order to provide good, non-formalist advice along engineering principles: in the case of zero-sum games, advice about what to do when caught up in them, and in the case of the growth model, advice as to which prices must prevail if the 'economy' is to grow at a given, sustainable rate.

Note

1 A zero sum game is any interaction between people such that one's gains is another's loss. Neumann (1928) and Neumann and Morgenstern (1944) provide a general solution for all zero sum games. However, most economic interactions are *not* of a zero sum form, since they include the prospect of co-operative outcomes in which mutual gains are possible. For more, see Hargreaves-Heap and Varoufakis (2004).

So, was the *Inherent Error*'s spell on political economics dispelled? Regrettably, it was not. Before explaining why not, it is pertinent to begin by pointing out that von Neumann's model, unlike Ramsey's, is neither Marginalist nor neoclassical. Indeed, it features no desire-driven consumers, no well-defined utility or production functions, no use of the *equimarginal principle*. Instead, its central 'players' are *commodities* that are jointly produced by means of other commodities in ways described by fixed coefficients of production (e.g. a unit of corn requires $\alpha<1$ units of corn, β units of machines and λ units of labour). Moreover, it leaves perhaps the most important economic variable outside its ambit: the *wage rate*, which is assumed exogenous to the model.[28]

Written in German, the 1937 paper did not mention Walras' General Equilibrium in the title, for the simple reason that the model was a million miles removed from Walras' neoclassical logic. Instead, the author promoted his wares as 'an economic system of equations and a generalization of Brouwer's fixed point theorem'. However, when the same article reappeared in an English translation in 1945 it was miraculously relabelled: *A Model of General Economic Equilibrium*. Though neither Walras[29] nor neoclassicism got a mention in the paper itself, this new title encouraged many mistakenly to think of it as a piece of neoclassicism.

In fact, judging by the model's main features, it is obvious that von Neumann's model was much closer in spirit to the classical tradition of Ricardo and, more precisely, to Piero Sraffa's analysis.[30] Just like Sraffa's model, von Neumann's manages to capture a complex economy with a potential for surplus generation, which keeps it on a steady growth path. Naturally, von Neumann's model shares with Sraffa's the property of being equally as consistent with a slave economy as it is with a fully fledged *Matrix Economy* (recall Chapters 4 and 5), where machines produce other machines in a world where humans are altogether absent (or have been diminished to a primary commodity, as in the *Matrix*).

In short, the price that von Neumann's model had to pay to maintain a semblance of realism (i.e. of growing multiple sectors) was that it had to leave out of the analysis

(a) any theory of what determines wages (and thus the profit rate) and (b) any kind of distinctly human activity, whether the latter involved labouring or planning for the future. Marx and Keynes would not be pleased with these omissions, as the model leaves no room for value generation (see Chapter 4) or, indeed, for any meaningful role for the money and credit markets (see Chapter 7). Money again features at best as an add-on veil, of the sort that Keynes disparaged,[31] while his prices fail to capture the fact that commodities acquire *value* (as opposed to some 'function' within a mechanical system) only because of quirky human inputs irreducible to some technical specification.

Be that as it may, von Neumann's model comes close to the maximum amount of light any mathematical model can cast upon a complex, growing economy. There is nothing strange about the fact that his model, despite the fine mathematics, offers severely limited insights about capitalism. With the *Inherent Error* lurking behind every theoretical turn, a theorist with an engineering (as opposed to a formalist) approach to economic modelling must leave something important out of his mathematics in order to make the model work. Good theory must, and can only be, incomplete, as Gödel taught von Neumann back in 1930. Good neoclassicists, who respect the demands of the *Inherent Error*, leave out either *time* or *complexity*. Von Neumann followed the more classical tradition of leaving out other things, such as a theory of the price of labour.

As our book's argument unfolds, it is becoming increasingly clear that the mark of the useful economist is that which he/she chooses *not* to explain within his/her proposed theory. Unlike the second-rate neoclassicist who, like a spoilt child insists on appropriating everything at once, wise political economists understand the importance of focusing on the parts of the picture that can be grasped, and acknowledge that not every part of the picture can be illuminated by the same source of analytical enlightenment; that their theory will result in *unavoidable lacunae*; that it will contain *necessary errors*. The question then becomes: what do we leave out? The trouble with neoclassicists is that when they do not sideline *complexity* they sideline *time*; and vice versa. Von Neumann, in contrast, was not prepared to sacrifice either. Instead, he chose to let wages be determined by other means. It is up to us to imagine what these may be: historical precedent, evolving social norms, anthropological factors outside the ambit of a mere political economist, etc.

In conclusion, Chapters 4 and 5 argued that human activity is *essential* in the generation of value but, also, that there can exist no well-defined mathematical expression linking the number of labour hours available to the quantity of labour input entering the production process. In Chapter 6 we took this further by highlighting the indeterminate nature of any analysis that focuses on human desire and its effect on prices. Lastly, in Chapter 7, aided and abetted by John Maynard Keynes, we claimed that in financialised capitalism, the pursuit of profit is of a nature that disallows *any* determinate mapping from given facts (e.g. production technologies, consumer preferences, quantity of money) to well-defined expectations about aggregate demand, investment and, finally, the state of the economy as a whole. In this context, it would have been absurd to expect of von Neumann, or any other talented model builder, to do the impossible: to pin down, within a determinate model, all important economic variables.

Von Neumann's willingness to leave unanswered the question of what determines the distribution of income is another sign of his genius. This, in many ways disagreeable, man graced political economics with something that the discipline had never really enjoyed: *a competent engineer's attitude*. Having consciously denounced the formalism at which he had once excelled as a very young mathematician, von Neumann turned to a practical question: *what should relative prices be in a complex, growing economy?* That he could not answer this question fully is due to the stubborn *Inherent Error* in our discipline. At least, he came as close to an answer as is feasible.

At the risk of over-simplification, von Neumann's model was the contribution of an applied mathematician who, unburdened by the fixations of the neoclassical formalists, removed from the New Dealers' daily grind in the corridors of power, and oblivious to the Harvard Keynesians' dilemmas, dedicated a short portion of his time to the exploration of the mathematical properties of a crisis-free economic system. Having satiated his curiosity, von Neumann moved on to other projects as part of his submersion, first, in the wartime US military–scientific establishment, and, later, in its Cold War offspring.

8.3 The formalists

Tjalling Koopmans, in his capacity as head of the Cowles Commission in Chicago, issued two invitations, one in May 1945 and one in October 1950, that were to alter the course of political economics in ways that affect us all to this day. The first invitation was issued to John von Neumann to present a Cowles Seminar in May 1945. Von Neumann accepted the invitation and delivered a paper on 25–26 May based on his game theoretical *magnum opus*, *Theory of Games and Economic Behavior*, which had seen the light of day less than a year before (co-authored with Oskar Morgenstern). Koopmans' personal bond with von Neumann's bond was twofold: they had both originated from a European mathematical (but also cultural) milieu and they utilised similar mathematical tools (e.g. linear programming) as part of the war effort.[32]

Von Neumann's paper, and in particular the *fixed point existence theorem* at its heart (see Box 8.4), made a great impression on the mind of young participants and led, a few years later, to a series of seven follow-up papers consistent with von Neumann's type of analysis. They were delivered in 1949 by five different scholars.[33] However, von Neumann's influence was ended abruptly by another presentation organised at Cowles by Koopmans five years later, in October 1950. After that seminar, von Neumann's trace literally disappears from mathematical economics and his engineering attitude to economic questions is replaced by an ironclad formalism not previously seen since before 1929. In effect, neoclassicism had returned from the cold just as the Cold War was gathering pace. What exactly happened? Who gave that October 1950 seminar and why did it have such a profound impact?

Let's cast our gaze back to 1945 and recall how John von Neumann had paved the ground for two types of glamorous, impressive, and potentially useful applications of mathematics to economics: (a) Game Theory, and (b) Growth models for economies consisting of multiple sectors. Both fields reflect his break from formalism (*circa* 1930) and an exclusive focus on mathematical applications of a distinctly practical value. More precisely, his Game Theory was intended solely as a source of good advice to decisions makers operating in strategic contexts (from chess players to businessmen, generals, government, etc.). It was *not* meant as an all-encompassing theory of strategic behaviour.[34] Similarly, his growth model was not at all about explaining *all* economic variables endogenously but, rather, strived to outline the general conditions for equilibrium growth, leaving important variables (e.g. wages and rents) outside the analysis' scope. In short, *incompleteness* was the price von Neumann was prepared to accept for practicality. Moreover, he understood well that it was not a daunting price since incompleteness is, unavoidably, part and parcel of all analytics (recall his 1930 encounter with Gödel).

The Cowles Commission participants were quite happy to go along with von Neumann's research agenda, as the early 1949 string of papers on his type of Game Theory (see note 31) confirms. Kenneth Arrow, in particular, made two presentations of his own at Cowles during 1949 in which he ably explored facets of von Neumann's game theoretical models, enthusiastically and diligently. Interestingly, he never actually published these papers, even though they were undoubtedly of publishable quality. Moreover, nothing in that work prepares the reader for the work that was to make Arrow famous a few years later.

Arrow's fame came from his joint work with Gerard Debreu; a young French mathematician who had arrived in 1949 at Cowles, straight from Paris. In contrast to Arrow, Debreu was never taken by the von Neumann approach; his engineering attitude to economic issues was not his cup of tea. During 1949, and while Arrow and the rest at Cowles were excitedly pursuing the research agenda inspired by von Neumann, Debreu listened, read and kept largely quiet. Then, something happened that energised him (and also put an end to his friend Arrow's engagement with von Neumann's Game Theory). That *something* was another pivotal seminar that Koopmans organised at Cowles. The calendar read: October 1950.

The 12 October 1950 Cowles Seminar featured a young, quivering mathematician, utterly oblivious to the lasting impact his stuttering delivery was going to have on political economics for the next half century (and possibly beyond). That youngster was none other than John F. Nash Jr, the Princeton doctoral student who, with four short papers written between 1950 and 1953, reshaped Game Theory and made it a central player in the social sciences.[35] It is our contention here that, in the process, he also changed the whole of political economics with a force unprecedented in the discipline's history.

Sitting in Nash's audience, Gerard Debreu immediately realised that the speaker was throwing him a lifeline; that Nash's paper offered an opening for his own brand of formalist mathematics in a context *ostensibly* similar to what others at Cowles were doing but, in reality, far removed from the engineering spirit of von Neumann. Debreu, we repeat, had never 'wasted' his time dabbling in von Neumann-type Game Theory *because he was genuinely uninterested in using mathematics to answer practical questions* (such as, 'How should I play this game?'). So, when Nash rose to speak, Debreu saw his chance to shine; to pursue a purely *formalist project*, unburdened by any practical concerns, whose purpose would be to present *complete* mathematical theories of everything economic; and to do all that using mathematics that did not strike one as too dissimilar to that of John von Neumann.

The rest, as they say, is history. Debreu and Arrow emerged from Nash's seminar and in a few short months applied what they had heard to hammer out their own *existence proof* in the context of a multiple-sector model economy: one that effectively brought back from the dead Walras' (fully neoclassical) idea of a General Equilibrium complete with determinate prices for everything, including labour input and capital goods (recall Chapter 6). This they accomplished by procuring General Equilibrium's ultimate mathematical proof; an *existence proof* that showed under which conditions a set of relative prices exists such that *all* markets (including that for labour) are in equilibrium.

This *existence proof* was to mark a new neoclassical turn in political economics; a turn that altered the discipline's course and returned neoclassical obscurantism to the throne from which it had been removed by the combined forces of the fall of 1929, the analysis of John Maynard Keynes, the engineering brilliance of von Neumann and, last but not least, the experiences of economic policy during the New Deal and the Second World War.

The story of how Nash's 1950 paper energised Debreu who, in turn recruited Arrow to his cause, is an epic tale of intellectual conquest. We shall devote the rest of this section to tell it as well as it can be told within our space limitations. Evidently, Debreu is the key protagonist in this tale. Unlike both von Neumann (who had long given up on formalism) and Arrow (who had never taken it up previously), Debreu came to the US and to Cowles in 1949 (on a Rockefeller fellowship) with a strong background in the mathematics of the French Bourbaki tradition.[36]

Bourbakist mathematicians chose wilfully to ignore Gödel's incompleteness theorem by interpreting mathematics as a self-contained, self-referential discipline and their own role as cartographers whose purpose was to proceed from basic axiomatic structures to more derivative ones ('binmen of mathematical knowledge' was an unflattering term used by competing mathematicians to describe them). In this vein, they sought to create axiomatic theories of some abstract 'structure'. This boils down (a) to the deduction of the logical consequences of the axioms that define that 'structure' and (b) to the exclusion of all hypotheses inconsistent with these axioms.

When Debreu was studying mathematics during the war at the *Ecole Normale Superieure*, his favourite instructor was Henri Cartan (1904–2008), one of the Bourbaki school's founding members. Upon arriving at Cowles a few years later, he was greeted by Marshall Stone who, in addition to holding the econometrics chair at the adjacent University of Chicago, was also the primary devotee and propagandist of the Bourbakist school in the US. Given Stone's key influence with the Cowles crowd, Chicago was probably the most hospitable town for a young Bourbakist like Debreu. Moreover, the Cowles Commission at the time was experiencing an intellectual existentialist crisis. Having started life as a hub of mathematical statistics and econometrics, its patrons soon realised that the application of such means to economics is fraught with difficulties. In short, the *Inherent Error* was rearing its ugly head. Not only were their statistical models failing to procure useful estimates but, additionally, the von Neumann type of mathematics was frustrating for those who sought complete explanations; models that did not leave important variables (e.g. wages and profits) outside their ambit.

By 1949, the year of Debreu's passage to the US, Koopmans was already reorienting Cowles away from statistics and towards mathematics in the hope of breaking the *Inherent Error*'s back. This reorientation created useful elbow room for a mathematician schooled in the Bourbaki tradition who also happened to have some interest in economics.[37] However, it was not until that fateful seminar in October 1950 that Debreu could breathe a sigh of relief and feel sufficiently energised to stamp his imprint on economics. As explained above, until then, the analytics that prevailed at Cowles were of the Koopmans–von Neumann, practically minded, type. Everyone at Cowles, including his eventual friend and collaborator Kenneth Arrow, was mimicking the great Hungarian's method which precluded, by design, any ambitions to build universalisable, complete theories.

All this changed, we are claiming, with Nash's presentation. But what did Nash say in that seminar that had such a profound effect? The answer is that Nash's presentation marked a complete break with von Neumann's idea about the very purpose of mathematical modelling and the legitimate uses of the new mathematical topology which von Neumann was the first to import into the United States. Von Neumann thought that what mattered was the extent to which the use of *fixed point theorems*, and the like, provided firm advice to decision makers.

To illustrate, consider the so-called *Bargaining Problem*, which was what Nash talked about at Cowles. Imagine two or more people bargaining over how to divide some notional pie (an asset, a resource or simply a sum of money). If they come to an agreement, each collects the agreed portion. If not, no one benefits. This problem is central to economics since all trade involves potential gains which, depending on the agreed price, are distributed differently between buyer and seller. Von Neumann studied carefully the *Bargaining Problem* but concluded that it cannot be 'solved', that it was indeterminate. He left that project behind, convinced that mathematical analysis cannot recommend to a bargainer how to negotiate with a view to maximising his/her portion.

Unfazed by von Neumann's conclusion, Nash began his Cowles presentation by announcing that he had cracked the *Bargaining Problem*. To an astonished audience, he outlined an
unquestionably brilliant solution. Nevertheless, Nash's 'solution' was of a wholly different
type from what von Neumann would have described as a solution. In fact, Nash 'solved' it by
first declaring that he will *not* be studying the bargaining process at all. Instead, he stated a
number of axioms (which he believed a rational agreement ought to respect) and then proved
that only one potential agreement respects all these axioms at once. Note that the 'strategic
neglect' of the bargaining process is tantamount to a radical absence of any advice on how
one ought to bargain. In this sense, Nash solved the *Bargaining Problem* by divorcing the
analysis from any meaningful, practical advice that the theory could offer a bargainer.

Box 8.5 Nash's unique solution to the *Bargaining Problem*

In his 1950 paper,[1] Nash proved, against the grain of opinion among social scientists,
that all bargaining situations feature a unique solution: rational bargainers, Nash suggested, will settle for the division of the 'pie' that precisely maximises the product of
their utility functions. Suppose that during a negotiation Jack offers Jill x per cent of
the 'pie' but she rejects it demanding a higher share of, say, y per cent, and threatening
Jack that, unless he relents, she will abandon the negotiations with probability p. Jill's
rejection is deemed credible if she prefers, on average, the prospect of getting y per
cent (>x per cent) of the pie with probability $1-p$ rather than x per cent of the pie with
certainty. Next, let us define distribution A to be an *equilibrium of fear agreement* as
follows: when Jill offers A to Jack, and he credibly rejects it in favour of some alternative distribution B, then Jill can credibly reject B (for all possible Bs) in favour of her
original offer of distribution A. Nash first proves that bargainers will *only* settle for an
equilibrium of fear agreement and then proves that there exists only one such agreement: his proposed solution to the *Bargaining Problem*. This result is made even more
remarkable by the aesthetic beauty of the proposed agreement: it is the distribution of
the pie that maximises the product of Jill's and Jack's utility functions:

$$\bar{x} = \underset{\bar{x}}{\arg\max}\left[\prod_{i=1}^{N} U_i(x_i)\right]$$

The downside of this result is this: it only holds water if we can assume that Jill and
Jack can potentially share *common knowledge* of the probability of no agreement p
with which Jill threatens Jack in order to get him to agree to her preferred distribution.
But how can they, given that Jill has an incentive to overrepresent it? As rationality
alone cannot bring about such common knowledge, something closer to telepathy is
necessary. Note that this argument is not too different to the Keynesian rejection of
the idea that investment decisions can be made on the back of rational computation
of mathematical expectations (see Box 7.7) and Chapter 4 of Hargreaves-Heap and
Varoufakis (2004).

Note
1 See John F. Nash, Jr, (1950). 'The *Bargaining Problem*'.

One can easily imagine how the Bourbakist Debreu must have felt in the face of this delicious departure from the scientific, almost engineering, attitude of von Neumann to a rarefied world where economic problems are dealt with in the context of axiomatics alone. Add to this the fact that Nash had based his proof on a version of *Brouwer's fixed point theorem* due to Shizuo Kakutani,[38] and a clear picture of the seminar's effect on Debreu surfaces. Though Debreu never refers to Nash in his seminal work, it is instructive to read what he had to say, many years later, in his 1983 Nobel Prize acceptance speech (entitled *Economic Theory in the Mathematical Mode*), on how Nash was the trigger that occasioned the wholesale retreat from von Neumann-type mathematical economics and the elevation to prominence of his own radical brand of axiomatic formalism:

> In the year I joined the Cowles Commission, I learned about the Lemma in von Neumann's article of 1937 on growth theory that Shizuo Kakutani reformulated in 1941 as a fixed point theorem. I also learned about the applications of Kakutani's theorem made by John Nash in his one-page note of 1950… Again there was an ideal tool, this time Kakutani's theorem, for the proof that I gave in 1952 of the existence of a social equilibrium generalizing Nash's result. [39]

Debreu, here, is confirming that Nash's abstract formulation of the *Bargaining Problem* allowed him to see how he could appropriate von Neumann's mathematical techniques (the *fixed point theorems* that the Hungarian had brought to the economists' attention) and press it into the service of Bourbakism; of a purely formalist approach inimical to practical problem solving. This is not merely an assertion. Debreu himself confirmed it in a speech he gave in 1991 in which he makes his research agenda abundantly clear: to produce models characterised by internal consistency.

> The benefits of [the] special relationship [between physics and mathematics] were large for both fields; but physics did not completely surrender to the embrace of mathematics and to its inherent compulsion toward rigour… In these directions economic theory could not follow the role model offered by physics theory. Being denied a sufficiently secure experimental base, economic theory has to adhere to the rules of logical discourse *and must renounce the facility of internal inconsistency*[40] (emphasis added).

This is as close as one can come to a UDI (a *unilateral declaration of independence*) from an economics whose purpose is to deal with the incongruities of real economic relations, involving really existing humans. In terms of this book's theme, it is a manifesto for killing off the *Inherent Error* even at the expense of the last drops of realism; for surgically separating economic theory from the reality that is capitalism. Put it another way; Debreu, for reasons sourced not in his politics but in his commitment to Bourbakist formalism, reinvented the spirit of neoclassicism; that is, the commitment axiomatically to impose an equilibrium on a timeless exchange economy featuring given utility and production functions.

In May 1951, Debreu presented his first seminar paper at Cowles. In it we find a model wholly consistent with his roots in the Bourbaki mathematical tradition, derivative of Nash's approach to Game Theory, and diametrically opposed to von Neumann's agenda. Its central contribution is the transplantation of Nash's axiomatic approach from Game Theory to neoclassical General Equilibrium: a fresh, Bourbakist, axiomatic formalisation of an economy which finds itself in a static 'General Equilibrium'.[41]

By 1954, he and Kenneth Arrow (who had, after Nash's presentation, also abandoned von Neumann-like models), produced their famous *existence proof*. Their theorem showed that under several axioms or conditions that their 'economy' must respect,[42] there exists a unique set of non-negative prices (one per commodity) which (were they to prevail) would equilibrate supply and demand in every market. This is known as the proof of the existence of a General Equilibrium or, more grandly when accompanied with the proof that it is also Pareto optimal as, the *First Fundamental Theorem of Welfare Economics*. It was to be the main of three theorems which changed economics forever, ushering in the currently dominant type of mathematical formalism which typifies the 'good' economics departments. By 1957, Koopmans had also jumped on the bandwagon (with a famous paper included in his *Three Essays on the State of Economic Science*), two years before Debreu would publish his definitive book with the weighty title *Theory of Value*.[43]

Thus began the post-war neoclassical dominion which, in a few short years, extended its reach from Cowles and RAND to academia, on the back of neoclassicism's highest form: the combination of (a) Welfare Economics (which is no more than the realm of Debreu and Arrow types of analysis) and (b) Game Theory (of the variety that Nash ushered in at Cowles in October 1950). Meanwhile, economic policy was running itself, only slightly attached to an Americanised form of Keynesianism. During the decades from 1950 to 1970, the theoretical apparatus informing Washington policymakers and the theories of the formalists might as well have resided on different planets.

In short, throughout the first post-war phase (which we refer to below as the *Global Plan* – see Chapter 11) capitalism was managed, globally and locally, in the practical spirit that developed during the war and its aftermath by the New Dealers and their counterparts in Europe and Japan. It was only when the *Global Plan* phase of post-war capitalism collapsed in 1971 that the resurgent neoclassicism, which owed its resurrection to Nash, Debreu and Arrow, began to influence macroeconomic policy. By the 1980s, its stranglehold over the whole of economics was unbreakable. And when 2008 struck, economics, having become hostage to formalist neoclassicism, was just as dumbfounded as it had been in 1929.

8.4 A tragic figure at a sad crossroads

In his 2002 book *Machine Dreams: Economics Becomes a Cyborg Science*, Philip Mirowski offers an engaging account of John von Neumann's continuing influence in economics.[44] While we agree that almost all research fields currently ploughed by mainstream economists were either invented or heavily re-jigged by von Neumann, we have a different interpretation of the great man's legacy: for, we see him as *the* tragic figure in the plot that is post-war political economics, with John Nash in a powerful supporting role also riddled with tragedy.[45]

Teachers of Game Theory and economics mention von Neumann's name reverentially but never fail to add that the great man, despite having invented all the ingredients of 'modern scientific economics', 'failed' to take them to their logical conclusion; that this task was left to younger men like Nash, Debreu and Arrow who fashioned what today passes as the last word in economic analysis (the mighty combination of Nashian Game Theory and General Equilibrium *Theory* mentioned above). They often point out, for instance, that when the young Nash visited von Neumann at his Princeton office, bearing a copy of the famous paper that he was to present at Cowles in 1950 (and publish in the well-respected *Econometrica* soon after), the great professor made some polite noises about its calibre but, in effect, dismissed it as trivial. This dismissal is given one of two interpretations: either von Neumann failed to recognise its importance, or he did recognise it but lacked the grace to acknowledge that the young Nash had surpassed him. It is our contention that neither interpretation holds water.

Starting from the second allegation, we think it absurd to question von Neumann's graciousness when in the presence of another high-calibre intellect. Admittedly, he was never an easy or pleasant character. Upon hearing that his former director from the *Manhattan Project* years, nuclear physicist and father of the 'Bomb', J. Robert Oppenheimer (1904–67), had publically opposed the construction of hydrogen bombs, advocated nuclear disarmament and expressed regrets over his own involvement in inventing the nuclear arsenal, von Neumann quipped: '[he] is confessing to the sin in order to claim the glory'. Nevertheless, von Neumann was always ready to recognise another person's scientific contribution, regardless of political or other differences. Indeed, as explained in the previous section, upon hearing Gödel's presentation in 1930, he was not only impressed but also became furious for not having proven the incompleteness theorem himself. Nonetheless, this 'fury' never stopped him from acknowledging, assisting and even celebrating the man who had beaten him to it.

As for the claim that he did not recognise the importance of Nash's claim to have 'solved' the *Bargaining Problem*, anyone who has read both Nash's paper and any of von Neumann's work will be hard pressed to maintain that his reaction was due to miscomprehension. There is no doubt that von Neumann knew inside-out the mathematics behind Nash's solution. The *Kakutani fixed point theorem*, which Nash used to prove his theorem, was a mere generalisation of *Brouwer's fixed point theorem* (see Box 8.4). And, as we saw already, not only was Brouwer von Neumann's contemporary back in Europe but, in addition, von Neumann had paved the way for Nash to use that type of theorem by having employed it himself both in his own Game Theory (1928,1944) and in his growth model (1937). Indeed, von Neumann had met with Kakutani at the *Institute for Advanced Study* before the war, while Kakutani was being hosted by German mathematician Hermann Weyl. In 1948, at the behest of von Neumann, Kakutani returned to the *Institute* before being appointed to a chair at Yale University in 1949. The notion that von Neumann did not comprehend the Kakutani theorem and its implications in Nash's 1950 paper is ludicrous.

So, why did von Neumann dismiss Nash's result as trivial? Our answer is simple: because it was his considered opinion that it *was* trivial. Moreover, we think he was completely justified in reaching that conclusion. For, unlike the young Nash who was, at the time, struggling to make an impression, and thus gain a PhD in the cut-throat Princeton environment, von Neumann was immersed in practical (albeit often highly objectionable) projects and had no time for formalist gymnastics. To him, Nash's solution to the *Bargaining Problem* could offer no advice to bargainers and, therefore, it was a trivial result. He may even have felt, justifiably, that, had he cared enough, he could have produced this result on the back of an envelope between main course and dessert during some dull dinner party.

Von Neumann's candidature for tragic status transcends the insinuation of some alleged failure either to follow or to acknowledge Nash's game theoretical achievements. Consider his 1937 growth model. Soon after Debreu, with Arrow's able help, pushed the discipline away from von Neumann's concern for combining *complexity* with *time*, von Neumann's analysis was totally eclipsed. Courtesy of Nash's unconscious prodding, Debreu and Arrow brought back into vogue hermetically 'closed' (Leibnizian) models purchased at the cost of fully abstracting from a world of temporality and flux.

Save for a few polite references to his implicit contribution to their brand of General Equilibrium (including some kind words from Arrow), these days few, if any, students are taught von Neumann's model. Instead, economists treat the Arrow–Debreu General

Equilibrium model as the ultimate source of theoretical legitimacy for all types of mainstream economics (pure and applied). Is this proof that Arrow and Debreu succeeded where von Neumann had failed (despite having built all the building blocks that these 'upstarts' needed to build their models)? Certainly not.

Since the neoclassical resurgence that began in 1950 with Nash, Debreu and Arrow (in that very order) *success* in economics has been inversely related to genuine enlightenment (see the next chapter). Von Neumann's economics was all about the growth path of a multi-sector economy. He was not interested in some thin-as-a-needle, nebulous, axiomatic economy that lasts for a fraction of a second, and whose equilibrium is therefore static and only of interest to a seminar of Bourbaki-minded mathematicians. Cognizant of the ubiquity of incompleteness, he would rather have a workable, dynamic model with many sectors which does not explain all prices at once, than a General Equilibrium model that explains everything as long as no one dares ask questions such as: how will these prices materialise? What are the forces that guide, in real, historical time, an economy onto its potential equilibrium growth path?

To sum up the argument so far, something at once interesting and supremely saddening happened to economics in 1950. Instead of the momentous intellectual battle that one might have expected within economics between New Dealers (e.g. Galbraith) and *Scientists* (e.g. von Neumann), a short paper presentation by a young mathematician (John F. Nash Jr) was taken up by two other mathematical formalists (Gerard Debreu and Kenneth Arrow) to form a research agenda that, in the end, confined both New Dealers and *Scientists* to the profession's margins. The result was a hollowing out of political economics; the bleaching of any content pertinent to capitalism that had managed to creep into economics between 1929 and 1950. And all that at the time of capitalism's historic transformation into what Chapter 11 will refer to as the *Global Plan*.

If this section portrays John von Neumann as the era's tragic figure, it is not only because we genuinely believe that he was, but also because we wish to highlight the major turning point for economics that coincided with the beginning of the Cold War. Our point here is that even eminent cold warriors, like von Neumann, were discarded from the new post-war 'intellectual order'. In effect, it was not a left versus right, pro-state versus pro-market tussle. The tragedy of it all was that the joint defeat of the New Dealers and of the *Scientists*, at the hands of the new neoclassicism, deprived post-war economics of all useful knowledge that had been learned the hard way during the hideous 1930s and 1940s.

As humanity was licking its war wounds and hoping for a more rational world order, and as the global economy was changing in weird and wonderful ways, political economics was returning to a supercharged form of neoclassicism, rushing headlong to practical irrelevance. All hope that the preceding harsh years of crisis and war had bestowed upon our species some decent insights into capitalism went up in smoke as the formalists turned inwards into a world of symbols designed to be infinitely removed from the reality of capitalism.

The only saving grace was that, unlike its 1920s predecessor, the new post-war formalists acknowledged freely that their theories could not be of use to anyone with an interest in making the world a better place. Indeed, Nash, Debreu and Arrow had the nous and the decency to warn their students that one should never confuse that which they found theoretically *interesting* with that which decision makers might find *useful* in the pursuit of socio-economic objectives. In Gerard Debreu's own words: 'the theory… is logically entirely disconnected from its interpretations'.

The question with which this chapter passes the baton to the next is simple: *why? How come the accomplished New Dealers and the brilliant* Scientists *fall prey to such an unlikely predator?* Granted that the mathematical formalism of Nash, Debreu and Arrow was aesthetically pleasing and logically fascinating, it is not straightforward to imagine how it could have disposed of, and with such ruthless efficiency, the type of thinking that (a) worked wonders in restoring economic growth (during the war and its aftermath) and (b) brought an engineering mind-frame to economic analysis. We reserve our answer for the next chapter.

8.5 Epilogue

Formalism's triumph, at the expense of the New Dealers and *Scientists* alike, was largely unintended. None if its agents intended to expunge the New Dealers or to purge von Neumann's models from the practice and textbooks of economics. Their triumph was supra-intentional and possibly one that they regretted at a personal level; at least in relation to von Neumann's sidelining. It is, therefore, of interest to conclude this chapter with a comment on the formalists' *own* motivation for pursuing their particular line of work, leaving the causes of their inadvertent triumph for the next chapter.

John F. Nash Jr, who started the ball rolling, was determined to solve the insoluble; to cut the most convoluted of Gordian knots; to provide *the* rational agreement to *all* negotiations. Having come to Princeton from a more lowly college, it was his way of making his mark on a university campus sporting the likes of Einstein, Veblen, von Neumann and Gödel. His audacity was his strength. First, he borrowed the Marginalist portrayal of rational agents.[46] Second, he acknowledged that it is impossible to explain the negotiation process stroke-by-stroke, demand-by-demand, offer-by-offer, bluff-by-bluff. So, from the outset, he abandoned any ambition to tell a (Newtonian) story of how bargaining *gravitates towards an agreement*. With these two moves he thus came down on the Leibnizian side of the methodological argument that we touched upon in Chapter 6. Third, with temporal change evicted from his model, all he had to do was to find a *fixed point* (recall Boxes 8.4 and 8.5) in the set of bargaining strategies. This proved a technical problem and was treated with a technical remedy.[47]

Nash's focus was on an abstract case of some people squabbling over a fixed pie. But when Debreu heard him deliver his paper in 1950, he realised that Nash had opened a five-lane avenue to something much more ambitious: to the complete characterisation of all prices in *any* complex multi-sector model economy.[48] All that Debreu and Arrow had to do was reformulate Walras' depiction of a multi-market system in a way that allows the relevant equations to resemble Nash's bargaining strategy sets. The moment they managed that, Nash's technique (the *fixed point theorem* which he used to produce a unique agreement) delivered a unique set of equilibrium prices – one for each commodity.

Our plain claim is that the troika of pioneering formalists (Nash–Debreu–Arrow) were motivated purely by an honest curiosity to see how far they could take this type of analysis; to discover precisely what sacrifices they had to make in order to overcome the *Inherent Error*. In this regard, their work confirmed our point (in Chapter 6) that, to keep *complexity*, Marginalism must ditch *time*. Nash, Debreu and Arrow simply discovered the extent of 'closure' that is possible in a time vacuum. Left at that, their contribution would have been an interesting addendum to the story of political economics. Alas, it was not left at that…

In the years that followed, especially after the collapse of the *Global Plan* in 1971, their work was plundered by lesser intellects. Causing distaste even among the formalist pioneers, the magpies of political economics who got to work in the 1970s[49] cherry-picked bits and pieces from the pioneers' models to produce logically incoherent accounts of real economies *evolving in real time*. Pristine models that become brittle and collapse the moment the clock starts ticking were desecrated and used to tell banks and regulators stories about inter-temporally dynamic optimal decision making. Thus, formalism morphed into a form of fraud.

We finish this chapter with a question that leaps through time and lands smack in the middle of our current predicament: *where did the financial 'engineers' of the 1990s and the naughties find the courage to bury tenuous assumptions* (about various crucial parameters) *in equations that were then used* ad nauseam *to price derivatives, thus contributing, in the run-up to 2008, to the roaring trade in toxic assets?* The answer we shall be giving ties up the formalists' early 1950s triumph to the *Crash of 2008*. And it is this: *they found it in the formalist economic models which ended up, from 1970 onwards, influencing policy and imparting a false sense of relevance when, in reality, they were designed for a timeless uni-verse.*

The *Crash of 2008* can be seen, through this prism, as the *Inherent Error*'s postmodern revenge. Sadly, it was a revenge that affected the innocent a great deal more than it hurt those who built lucrative careers on misrepresenting the logical games of a Nash or a Debreu as guides by which to navigate the stormy waters of late financialised capitalism.

9 A most peculiar failure

The curious mechanism by which neoclassicism's theoretical failures have been reinforcing their dominance since 1950

9.1 Neoclassicism's audacious resurgence: Five causes

It would, of course, be quite absurd to pin the radical transformation of post-war political economics entirely on some seminar presentation at the Cowles Commission in the fall of 1950. However striking the new axiomatic method, it could not possibly explain how a small grouping of formalist mathematicians appropriated the stature of the New Dealers (who drew much inspiration from John Maynard Keynes) while at once usurping the authority of the *Scientists* (who counted John von Neumann among their leading lights). Only a mighty convergence of historical trends, institutional prerogatives and discursive power can explain neoclassical formalism's never-ending theoretical triumph.

This chapter presents a joint hypothesis of how *a political economics designed to be entirely useless* came to dominate economic thinking across the world for six decades running. Our exegesis concerns the grandest paradox in the history of science: *how a particular type of theory grew in influence in proportion to the immensity of its theoretical failures!* Is this possible? Can consistent failure prove a source of strength, rather than spell the end of influence? In the house of political economics it can and it does! At least, this is our claim in the following pages.

Our explanation turns on five distinct, though highly integrated, causes, or processes, underpinning this most peculiar failure:

(a) the progressive decoupling of policymaking from high-end economic theory which began at a time when the Cold War was developing particular ideological demands
(b) a new type of economics textbook that provided neoclassical formalism with the necessary mass appeal
(c) the dexterity with which the resurgent neoclassicism could absorb criticism by interchangeably relaxing and tightening its meta-axioms (we label this process the *Dance of the Meta-axioms*)
(d) the sociology of academic economics
(e) an audaciously circular mutual reinforcement mechanism (especially evident after the end of the Cold War) which supra-intentionally rewards neoclassicism with institutional power that helps it maintain a strict embargo on any serious scrutiny of (i) its own foundations and (ii) really existing capitalism.

9.2 Worlds apart

Our first explanation of the resurgence of formalist neoclassicism in the Cold War era is precisely its complete disconnection from the economic reality of that very era. Put bluntly, neoclassicism benefitted in its discursive struggle against the New Dealers and the *Scientists* by being a world apart from capitalist reality and its management by the post-war elites. We get a glimpse of that chasm by noting that, unlike the US military which utilised the best scientists available during both the Second World War and the Cold War, the US government showed no similar penchant for entrusting economic policy to the 'best' academic economists of the time; at least not to those practising in the top universities or their derivative high-powered institutions (such as Cowles, RAND and the like).

A quick perusal of those serving on the President's *Council of Economic Advisers* (CEA) is instructive on the matter.[1] From 1946, when the CEA was instituted by President Truman, to the end of the 1960s, it was usually headed by New Dealers (whom we discussed in the two previous chapters) immersed in the type of activity associated with the planning of the post-war international order which we label the *Global Plan* and which we discuss in detail in Chapter 11. For now, we focus on the almost complete divorce of the Cold War economic policy that led to the *Global Plan*'s architecture, from the highest form of economic theory during the Cold War. This curious divorce will help explain, in part, the steady elevation of post-war neoclassicism on a higher plane where dominance would be sustained by its disconnection from actual policymaking, its successes and failures.

The CEA's first chairman, Edwin G. Nourse, was initially an engineer who specialised in agricultural economics with little or no schooling in the finer aspects of high-end economics. Nourse famously advocated that the US reduce its production of armaments and shift productive resources towards civilian projects. On this 'guns versus butter' issue, he was opposed by his vice-chairman, Leon H. Keyserling (a New Deal lawyer with some economics graduate work under his belt). Keyserling argued that such a trade-off was a dangerous mirage since military expenditure, at a vast scale, would permit the US economy to expand, thus effecting an overall improvement in living standards. Keyserling's position was fully in tune with that of the designers of the *Global Plan* (whose role we discuss in Chapter 11): James Forrestal, James Byrnes, George Kennan as well as Dean Acheson. Nourse's position, in contrast, was at odds with this *Global Plan* and led Acheson unceremoniously to replace him with Keyserling.[2]

It is quite telling that Acheson, a lawyer, saw fit to make momentous decisions about, among other, purely economic matters (e.g. the design of Bretton Woods, the Marshall Plan, the recommendations of CEA, etc.) with only cursory advice from the mighty economists of the time (with Keynes being the solitary exception). The post-1949 years were a fascinating age for economic policy on a grand scale made all the more interesting by the marginalisation of academic economists.[3] Perhaps an explanation lies in the massive blow that 1929 had delivered on the discipline's stature; as well as in the New Dealers' confidence which grew during the war as employment and growth were being restored without a great deal of help from academic economics.

Acheson's career is illuminating in this regard: having entered the administration in 1941, as Roosevelt's Assistant Secretary of State, he spent three years coordinating economic warfare against the Axis.[4] In 1944, he made use of this accumulated experience to play a leading role in preparing the ground for the *Global Plan* and its post-1947 implementation. He emerged as the commander-in-chief of the Marshall Plan, and, by 1949 (after making Secretary of State) held the unofficial title of the Cold War's master architect.[5] Meanwhile, scientists-*cum*-economists, such as von Neumann, were better employed at RAND (developing anything from computers to the hydrogen bomb) while the more theoretically adept New Dealers had returned to their university careers. In none of their grandiose projects did men like Acheson feel the absence of academic economic wisdom.

Keyserling was replaced in 1953 by Republican appointee Arthur F. Burns, who had (as the Korean War was receding) advocated a shift away from the *Global Plan* towards less extravagant spending on defence and a departure from Keynesianism. However, the 1953 recession put paid to his proclamations and, thus, an Americanised form of globalised Keynesianism acquired bipartisan status. Though Burns was a Columbia-trained economist, with some research in business cycles, his tenure at CEA, as well as in the Federal Reserve later (which he headed from 1970 to 1978), bears only a weak connection with his economics. Like his predecessors, his policy positions reflected a take on the position of the US economy that had little or nothing to do with what was considered, at the time, cutting edge economic theory.

Between 1956 and 1969, the CEA reflected an impressive consensus on economic policy based on practical measures in complete accordance with the *Global Plan*. Between December 1956 and January 1961 the post was held by Raymond J. Saulnier; also a Columbia-trained economist, who had made a career in banking, railroads, the stock exchange and several large companies. In 1961 he was succeeded by Walter W. Heller who had begun his career in the war's aftermath by helping re-establish West Germany's currency, and later as one of the Marshall Plan's designers.[6] Perhaps the most accomplished economist to have held that position was Arthur Okun, a Yale professor, well known among Keynesians for having studied the relationship between unemployment and economic growth.[7]

To sum up, if one had to infer something about the state of economic theory during that time from the curricula vitae and position papers of the aforementioned CEA chairmen, one's task would be hopeless. Post-war economic policy was, by and large, institutionally (though not theoretically) Keynesian, rooted in the New Deal, and intimately linked to a *Global Plan* that started life in the ruins of 1945 and acquired a new complexion during the Cold War. By contrast, high-end economic theory had, after 1950, shunned both the New Dealers and the *Scientists* (see previous chapter). The turn from von Neumann-like dynamic modelling to the timeless formalism of Nash, Debreu and Arrow meant that academic economics was positioning itself as a wilfully impractical discipline whose utility had to be sought beyond any applications it might have in designing real policy for really existing economies. What was that utility? *Ideological*, is our answer.

At this juncture it is helpful to recall that the Cold War pitched not only two sets of destructive nuclear arsenals against one another but also two opposing ideologies. The ideological aspects of the Cold War were, naturally, multifarious, ranging from political philosophy to the arts, but contained one strand that both sides (Washington and Moscow) privileged above the rest: *economic justification*. Lest we forget, the European 'front' was in political flux, with left-leaning parties brandishing impressive economic arguments in favour of planning with a view to achieving, at once, greater efficiency and less inequality (while frequently invoking the memories of capitalism's collapse during the 1930s). Additionally, the Developing World was up for grabs. As the era of de-colonisation got underway, and the superpowers were jostling for position on the new fluid geopolitical map, the liberation movements paid a great deal of attention to the theoretical war between those advocating a socialist central plan and those who favoured capitalist market mechanisms. The emerging elites of Asian and African nationalist movements were genuinely interested in economic theory as a source of insights into the growth and distribution strategies that they ought to adopt once the imperial fist was forced to unclench. Economic models were, in this sense, political instruments almost as sharp as diplomacy and military manoeuvring.

In this Cold War tussle, the formalism that Debreu and Arrow built upon Nash's method proved an invaluable ideological weapon. While the global economy was being planned meticulously and energetically by the New Dealers in Washington, the Cold War necessitated a clear *ideological* red line between the two great camps – one that, *at the level of ideology*, allowed for a discursive distinction between (a) the grubby authoritarian planning of Gosplan-inspired leftists; and (b) the spontaneous order generated by decentralised markets where liberty and self-interest combine to promulgate the Good Society. Debreu and Arrow's new formalism fitted that narrative like a glove.

To see why, consider the essence of Debreu and Arrow's General Equilibrium model and suppose, for a moment, that a group of Martians were to use it in order to familiarise themselves with the West prior to boarding their spaceship. What would they expect to find upon landing? A tranquil and supremely civil market society in benevolent *stasis*; totally free of wasteful conflict; populated by persons resembling *Empires of Preference* – subjects identical in every respect except for their preferences, incomes and endowments (recall Chapter 6). A world, in other words, where no one exercises power on anyone, discrimination and exploitation are nonsensical words and even crying or laughter is pointless. A society where the only relations among persons are pure market instantaneous exchanges; rationality reduces to the efficiency with which predetermined preferences are satiated; work is (ontologically) no different from play; and the *labour contract* is indistinguishable from any other kind of contract (so that it makes no difference whether the asset-holding employer is hiring the worker's labour or the worker is hiring the employer's asset). Finally, the Martians would expect to find an economy perpetually producing at its 'frontier', squeezing the maximum 'welfare' out of given resources, without the need for any bureaucrat or recourse to anything other than voluntary and mutually advantageous swaps between free, consenting agents.

The fact that our Martian tourists would probably sue the publishers of such a, fictitious, *Lonely Planet Guide to Earth* is neither here nor there. For the Nash–Debreu–Arrow depiction of capitalism was designed to bear the same resemblance to reality as Napoleon's empire building project to Beethoven's Third Symphony. Such designer unrealism resonated beautifully with the *Cold Warriors'* ideological project. For it depicted capitalist 'reality' as an egalitarian, harmonious system worth fighting a nasty Cold War for. To boot, the extremely elegant mathematics it came packaged in added much sought out 'scientific' legitimacy.

Did the Cold War *Scientists* not offer elegant mathematics too? Sure they did. For example, von Neumann's 1937 growth model was also a mathematical gem. But it did not have the same ideological utility since it depicted the economy in a manner that could also apply to a centrally planned, Soviet style, multi-sector economy.[8] Unlike Debreu and Arrow's General Equilibrium, von Neumann's model was depicting productive sectors whose inputs and outputs were harmonised in a manner consistent with equilibrium growth. A Soviet planner could claim that it was precisely his job to effect such a growth path by carefully centrally calibrating the relative prices to match the growth rate. In contrast, Debreu and Arrow paid no special attention to production and, instead, placed consumers at their model's heart; a 'narrative' choice with much higher propaganda value at a time when the *Cold Warriors* were keen to depict their adversaries as production-centred deniers of the importance of consumer freedom.

Does any of this mean that Gerard Debreu, or Kenneth Arrow, or John F. Nash Jr for that matter, were responsible for the ideological uses to which their formalism was put? Not guilty, we say. For they never hid their view that the formalist models built to their own specifications were irrelevant from the point of view of policymaking.[9] Whenever lesser neoclassicists tried to interpret their work with a view to making pronouncements on what ought to be done (i.e. on policy), they were scolded for confusing that which is (theoretically) interesting with that which is (practically) useful. Debreu, in particular, faithful to his Bourbaki roots, noted in the preface of his *Theory of Value* (1959: viii) that '[a]llegiance to rigor dictates the axiomatic form of the analysis where the theory, in the strict sense, is logically entirely disconnected from its interpretations'.

The question thus returns: how did this type of economic theory, which (even according to its founding father, Gerard Debreu) is entirely ill-equipped to interpret the real world, come to dominate economics? Our answer is: it did so on the back, exclusively, of its *ideological utility* in the context of the Cold War. Its self-referential nature and total disconnection from the reality of the post-war world counted as an asset, rather than as the liability that it was at the scientific level. It passed the test set for it by the Cold War environment because of its elegant depiction of capitalism as a timeless, 'natural' system founded on an implicit radical egalitarianism and an abundance of free individual choices.

Nevertheless, even the considerable ideological utility of post-war formalism cannot explain its wholesale takeover of political economics and, in particular, its never-ending staying power. We have already foreshadowed in Section 9.1 that it took four more ingredients to dominate and to maintain that dominance. The second ingredient was a textbook that educated the post-war generation on all matters concerning the workings of capitalism. We examine it in Section 9.3 below with a view to explaining how it became the first truly global textbook on economics, thus influencing millions of youngsters who came in contact with political economics either at the level of some senior high school course or during undergraduate college training. Its importance lies in the manner in which it erected a believable narrative on capitalism's workings *on a hidden foundation of Nash–Debreu–Arrow formalism*; a truly incredible feat. Then, in later sections, we return to the inner crevices of academic political economics where neoclassical formalism was evolving in peculiar ways, puzzlingly gathering evolutionary fitness in proportion to its irrelevance.

9.3 The Text

Every creed requires its popularising Text and so the new post-war neoclassical formalism found its own. The first edition appeared in 1948; its author none other than the multitalented Mr Paul Samuelson.[10] During the Cold War, Samuelson's *Economics* sold countless copies and introduced millions of students all over the globe to the charms and tribulations of neoclassical economic theory. While Debreu and Arrow's General Equilibrium occupied the high echelons of post-war economics, Samuelson's textbook (the Text hereafter) was spreading the formalist mantra in high-school classrooms and university amphitheatres worldwide.

Samuelson was an unquestionably brilliant, prolific and highly energetic participant in every debate that had mattered since 1945. Like John Kenneth Galbraith, his Harvard contemporary, and the rest of their small circle of fellow students (including Marxist Paul Sweezy), Samuelson was deeply marked by the Great Depression. In Chapter 1 of the first edition of the Text (Samuelson 1948: 3), he introduces his reader to the subject of 'economics' with a warning which, in our post-2008 times, sounds exceedingly prophetic:

> When, and if, the next Great Depression comes along, any one of us may be completely unemployed – without income or prospects… There is no vaccination or advance immunity from this modern-day plague. It is no respecter of class or rank… From a purely selfish point of view, then, it is desirable to gain understanding of the first problem of

modern economics: the causes on the one hand of unemployment, overcapacity, and depression; and on the other of prosperity, full employment, and high standards of living. But no less important is the fact… that the political health of democracy is tied up in a crucial way with the successful maintenance of stable high employment and living opportunities. It is not too much to say that the widespread creation of dictatorships and the resulting World War II stemmed in no small measure from the world's failure to meet this basic economic problem adequately.

Nothing in the above resonates with this section's opening remark, that the new formalist creed found its popularising Text in Samuelson's book. These are words that prepare the reader for a head-on assault on real world economics; for an approach whose purpose is to delve into the workings of capitalism, rather than a journey into some obscure mathematical universe. Nor did Samuelson change his mind when the *Crash of 2008* hit us. In November 2008, a month after Lehman Brothers collapsed, unleashing the greatest crisis since 1929, Samuelson had this to say:

> Deregulated capitalism is a fragile flower bound to commit self-suicide.[11]

John Maynard Keynes would not have put it differently (recall Chapter 7). Reminiscing about his first fledgling steps as an economist, it is clear that Samuelson's motivation for studying economics was to make a difference; to rise up against the (neoclassical) departments of economics establishment who preached the infallibility of markets while all around them the victims of unregulated capitalism were piling up.

> When I was a freshman at the University of Chicago, I was a good student. I got good grades and I had great teachers… Frank Knight (1885–1972), Paul Douglas (1892–1976) and so forth. However, everything I was taught and I read disagreed with what I saw outside the window of the university. At least one-third of the population had no jobs at all. It was exactly the same story in Germany. In 1933, Franklin Roosevelt gained power. Herbert Hoover was as unpopular as George W. Bush is. Adolf Hitler came to power in Germany. Hitler spent money endlessly preparing for a war of revenge and that ended the big unemployment in Germany by 1939. The same thing happened in the United States under Franklin Roosevelt… through public works expenditures, through the agricultural support programs.

Indeed, the Text itself is replete with statements concurring with the view of its author as a New Dealer; a theorist with centrist views who believed strongly in the need for planning, for state intervention, for collective action that supports, guides or even constrains the market.[12] Though often dismissive of Karl Marx (he once referred to him as a minor post-Ricardian), the Text ostensibly parts company with the usual Cold War anti-Marxism by expressing the view that: 'It is a scandal that, until recently, even majors in economics were taught nothing of Karl Marx except he was an unsound fellow' (9th edn: ix); or that 'Marx was wrong about many things – notably the superiority of socialism as an economic system – but that does not diminish his stature as an important economist' (15th edn: 7). His courteous attitude to the Cold War enemy even led him to include, in the Text's thirteenth edition (as late as 1989, months that is before the collapse of the Soviet Union), that: 'the Soviet economy is proof that, contrary to what many sceptics had earlier believed, a socialist command economy can function and even thrive' (13th edn: 837).

Additionally, the Text explicitly set out to bring Keynes to the lecture theatre; to teach his main contributions in a manner that integrates the great man's insights with the rest of the economics students had to learn. Indeed, the macroeconomic part of the Text can easily pass as Keynesian, at least in terms of its language and emphasis on the employment of fiscal and monetary policy to manage demand and, therefore, stave off the scourge of unemployment.

So, why are we arguing that the Text proved an essential ally to the spread of the new formalism at the expense of *relevant* economic thinking? How could it be that a scholar of Samuelson's ability and predilection for relevance is accused of aiding and abetting the slide towards the neoclassical formalism that started life with Nash, Debreu and Arrow? The mere fact that Samuelson was fond of, and good at, mathematical modelling is neither here nor there. After all, John von Neumann was even keener on mathematics (and a vastly better mathematician than Samuelson) and yet this book exonerates him of any complicity with regard to the formalist takeover of economics (portraying him, instead, as its tragic victim).

The reasons for taking a different view of Samuelson's role, and for presenting his Text as a major accomplice in Cold War economic formalism, can be traced all the way to his doctoral thesis (published in book form in 1947, a year before the Text's first edition).[13] It is entitled *Foundations of Economic Analysis* and is nothing less than a masterpiece of a combination of mathematics and neoclassical political economics. Unlike von Neumann, Nash and Debreu, none of whom had any schooling in economics prior to dabbling in it, Samuelson had an impressive command of all the economics that preceded him, from Adam Smith onwards. His thesis exudes an urge to synthesise all that accumulated knowledge by means of mathematical tools. Its author presents himself as the latest link in a chain that starts, effectively, with the classical economists, moves on to Alfred Marshall (a major textbook writer in the tradition of J.B. Say and J.S. Mill and purveyor of mathematical–economic reasoning) and continues to Keynes, Marshall's student. Perhaps, though, his approach is closer to Pareto in spirit and form.[14]

Samuelson's ambition was, clearly, to bring Keynes back to the Marginalist-*cum*-neoclassical fold, from which the Englishman had escaped in a bid to explain the Great Depression. He ached to reunite the great Anglo-French tradition, so that Walras, Pareto, Marshall and Keynes could be brought back under the umbrella of a general theory provided by the ambitious Mr Samuelson.[15] For if he succeeded in doing this, Samuelson believed passionately, the deep chasm between microeconomics (which was always Marginalist in spirit and, mostly, neoclassical in practice) and macroeconomics (which was born when Keynes cut off his neoclassical roots in order to understand the Great Depression) would fade and economics might, at long last, claim its legitimate place in the pantheon of the sciences.

While ostensibly wishing to reunite Keynes and Marshall, thinking that Marshall's Marginalist mathematical syntax ought to become the foundation of Keynesian macroeconomics, it must be pointed out that Samuelson's interpretation of Marshall was not as safe as it might have been. Marshall may have used mathematics but was highly suspicious of its influence on economic thinking. In an anxious moment, Marshall had warned that most economic phenomena 'do not lend themselves easily to mathematical expression'. Economists must therefore guard against 'assigning wrong proportions to economic forces; those elements being most emphasised which lend themselves most easily to analytical methods'.[16] Unlike Keynes who clearly heeded this advice, Samuelson *chose* to disregard it.

In the introduction to his *Foundations*, Samuelson considers Marshall's advice as well as his dictum that the economist ought to avoid putting literary propositions into mathematical form. Once considered, the old man's advice is rejected outright: '[T]his dictum should be exactly reversed', is young Samuelson's considered conclusion. In his opinion, literary propositions that take no mathematical form are vacuous and, moreover, the effort of converting essentially mathematical propositions into a literary form is wasteful and involves mental gymnastics of a peculiarly depraved type. It is this interpretation of the role of mathematics in social science that prepared Samuelson for the role he was to play during the 1950s and beyond as the key legitimiser, at the level of introductory economics courses, of neoclassical formalism.

To illustrate, let us consider briefly the way Samuelson presents Keynes' thought in the Text. The belief that genuine insights are to be deduced chiefly from the mathematical depiction of some concept led him to teach Keynes to generations of students as follows:

> We begin by writing down the equations and draw the geometry which define the macro economy. Then we prove, as theorems, a number of propositions regarding the importance of government intervention in maintaining a certain level of effective or aggregate demand.

This method was miles away from Keynes' own. For, as we saw in Chapter 7, Keynes' greatest contribution was to alert us to a disarmingly simple truth:

> in a complex, financialised capitalist economy, it is impossible to derive, by reasoning, the well defined mathematical expectations which one needs to 'close' a macro-economic model.

This discrepancy between Samuelson's and Keynes' take on Keynesianism was to mark political economics forever. Samuelson was inspired to proceed with his own interpretation after reading a review of Keynes' *General Theory* published in *Econometrica* by John Hicks (Hicks, 1937). In that review, Hicks presented a simplification of Keynes's argument based on a simple mathematical model. It was meant as an abstraction that offers *some* (but not all of the) insights relevant to Keynes' point in the form of a simple system of equations. Samuelson transcribed this model in his Text in diagrammatic form, except that he failed to transfer along with it Hicks' conviction that not everything of importance in Keynes' argument could be conveyed in that manner. It has gone down in history as the ISLM model.[17] From that moment onwards, generations of students were educated by Samuelson to think that this type of geometry was the be-all-and-end-all of Keynesian thinking. This model formed the basis of what in the third edition of *Economics* in 1955 Samuelson felt confident to describe as 'the neoclassical synthesis'.[18]

Thus, a type of model utterly alien to Keynes (both to his thought and to the manner in which he arrived at his policy recommendations) came to be identified, in the eyes of millions of students, as Keynesian macroeconomics. As Chapter 7 went to pains to point out, taking much of its inspiration from Axel Leijonhufvud's excellent 1968 book, the very attempt to squeeze the thread of Keynes' thinking through the eye of a mathematical model's needle was to deny its substance; to bastardise it; to hollow his argument out. To remind the reader of our Chapter 7 argument, it suffices to mention Keynes' underlying answer to the question of how investment (and thus effective or aggregate demand) is determined: *we are damned if we know* (recall Section 7.5).

The essence of Keynes's analytical argument was that, because of irreducible complexity, agents (e.g. investors, consumers, workers, capitalists) labour under deep-seated uncertainty. Reason cannot cut through the forest of interdependent beliefs and, therefore, expectations become self-fulfilling. In mathematical terms, this means that there exists no sufficiently narrow set of rational expectations that either agents or economic theorists can go to work with. Consequently, recessions happen when agents fear they will. And if nothing impedes the mutual reinforcement between awful economic outcomes and glum forecasts, recessions can spawn nasty depressions.

Not an iota of the above rationale, which was at the heart of Keynes' own thinking, made it to the Text's pages. Samuelson, by contrast, directed his readers, contrary to Marshall's wise counsel, towards assigning exclusive emphasis to 'those elements being most emphasised which lend themselves most easily to analytical methods'. In so doing, he ensured that the generations of students who acquainted themselves with Keynes through the Text remained forever blind to the great man's most basic, and uniquely useful, insight. It was like introducing schoolchildren to *Hamlet* without the Ghost or, even more like it, to *Oedipus* without the power of prophecy.

Neoclassical formalism had, thus, done its ugly deed at the level of introductory economics: it appropriated Keynesianism while bleaching out of it the only content that mattered and which might have armed the post-war generation with an intellectual defence mechanism against disasters such as 2008. To see why this appropriation, and debasement, of Keynesianism was such a significant victory for neoclassicism, recall the manifestation of our *Inherent Error* in the context of neoclassicism. In Chapters 6 and 8, we saw how the *Inherent Error* forced both pre-1929 and post-1950 neoclassicism into a stark dilemma: *complexity* or *time*? A dynamic single sector economy or a multi-sector economy in temporal stasis? Well, Samuelson's portrayal of Keynesian thinking through the prism of the ISLM model in effect sacrificed Keynes' complexity (the result of which is irreducible uncertainty and temperamental levels of investment) on the altar of neoclassical closure.

Indeed, even casual perusal of any version of the ISLM model confirms that it is no more than a depiction of a single-sector economy (with a homogeneous output symbolised by Y and an undifferentiated price level P). But once complexity is jettisoned, and we are back to a *corn model*, Keynes' point about scarce aggregate demand makes no sense, as *Say's Law* is restored to its throne and the *Quantity Theory of Money* rules OK (recall Chapter 6). The only way that aggregate or effective demand can be scarce in this single sector world is if you bring into it, from the outside, *rigidities*. And this is what Samuelson did.[19]

Rigidities came in different forms but always in an *ad hoc* manner, ushered in from the 'cold' so to speak. Workers and business people were, for example, patronised by the assumption of *money illusion*;[20] trade unions were blamed for resisting wage cuts during the downturn; investment was assumed to be inexplicably stuck at some arbitrary level that would not rise even when interest rates fell, etc. When students asked 'Why does output get stuck below the level corresponding to full employment?' the answer came in the form of one or more of these rigidities; rigidities that *had* to be invoked since Keynes' own explanation had been ruled out the moment Samuelson decided to ignore a complex, financialised form of capitalism in favour of his single sector, fully neoclassical ISLM framework.[21]

Samuelson understood well the importance of his Text. Nasar (1995) reports that he once said: 'I don't care who writes a nation's laws – or crafts its advanced treaties – if I can write its economics textbooks'.[22] He also understood that its influence was amplified by his thoughtful participation in debates with those opposing the new neoclassical formalism's creed.[23] Moreover, his own research accomplishments at the top end of neoclassical economics perpetuated the myth that there was a clear path linking what the beginners were reading in the Text to both (a) the Nash–Debreu–Arrow type formalists and (b) the debates between formalists and dissidents (e.g. Keynesians, Marxists, neoliberals of the

Austrian school). This impression was of course illusory but it played a vital role in broadening the appeal of the new, formalist, Cold-War-era neoclassical political economics.

So, while John F. Nash Jr, Gerard Debreu and Kenneth Arrow were taking over academic economics, the 'masses' were being educated by Paul Samuelson's Text that

(a) echoed the new mantra of seeking truth *in* the mathematics (as opposed to von Neumann's determination to use mathematics as tools);
(b) exuded a feeling that economics is reducible to 'closed' mathematical models which leave nothing (except preferences) for history, philosophy or the rest of the social sciences to explain; and
(c) was sufficiently 'liberal' to pass for a non-ideological, impartial manual successfully incorporating Keynes's thought within its simplistic mathematics.

To sum up, Samuelson 'reunited' Keynes with his old master, Marshall, by pushing him, kicking and screaming, back to the simplistic Robinson Crusoe model of nineteenth-century Marginalism-*cum*-neoclassicism. His Text paraded a version of Keynesianism that was depleted of Keynes' essential thinking. It discussed government policy but only in an abstract context that was, ultimately, disengaged from Keynes's logic or from the logic that had underpinned the actual policymaking of the New Dealers. As for the *Global Plan*, the post-war period's most significant feature (see Chapter 11), Samuelson had next to nothing to say.[24]

None of these failures mattered. The Text flourished commercially and conquered ideologically its millions of readers by giving them the false impression that they owned, and had read bits of, a textbook which (a) covered the whole of gamut of economic thinking, and (b) was politically broadminded and scientifically rooted to what was going on both at the level of economic policy *and* at the higher echelons of economic theory (e.g. at the postdoctoral level).

More significantly, the false impression imparted by the Text was never really tested. Most of its readers would move on to other things, retaining only a false memory of having encountered Keynesian economics through the Text. As for the tiny minority who moved on to graduate economics, they would soon swap one virtual reality, the Text's, for another (that of Nash–Debreu–Arrow). In contrast to Samuelson's Text which, at the undergraduate level, taught them to ignore *complexity* in order to have something to say about a macroeconomy's likely (or equilibrium) state (recall the ISLM, one-sector, approach), graduate economic teaching pushed them into the Nash–Debreu–Arrow realm where *complexity* was regained at the expense of *time*.

The *Inherent Error*'s demand that neoclassicists embrace *either complexity or time* (but never both at once) suddenly played out along the borderline between undergraduate and graduate studies. While in a state of undergraduate bliss, economics students were kept innocent of *complexity*. But the moment they crossed the borderline into graduate economics, they were immersed in the language and rituals of the Nash–Debreu–Arrow formalism where *complexity* was regained by means of a comprehensive moratorium on *time*. Thus it became possible to entertain the illusion that they were one-time masters of both *time* and *complexity*, conveniently forgetting (perhaps in order to minimise cognitive dissonance) that there was never a time when they managed to hold on to both at once.

Ironically, the Text's undoing was the revenge that life took upon its bastardised version of Keynesianism. For while the New Dealers' *Global Plan* was going strong (from around 1947 to 1971), the world seemed in tune with the Text's ostensibly Keynesian policy recommendations: signs that unemployment was rising inspired Washington to raise spending or reduce taxes. Increases in average prices were met with the opposite response, often accompanied by increases in interest rates. It all seemed like a choreography that reflected the movements of the IS and LM curves in Samuelson's Text.

However, once the *Global Plan* got in trouble (in the late 1960s and early 1970s), for reasons that Samuelsonian neoclassicism was oblivious to (and which we discuss in Chapter 11), Washington policymakers dropped it like a hot potato. Not by choice, but rather because of the collapse of the Bretton Woods system (which regulated exchange rates until August 1971) and the subsequent inflationary spiral (that got out of hand after the 1972 oil crisis), they were compelled to dump the *practice* of maintaining effective demand through increased government spending, lower taxes, etc. At that point, Samuelsonian macroeconomics (e.g. the ISLM model) lost its *raison d'être*. And once the practice of effective demand management, through fiscal policy, was dropped, the ideological utility of Samuelsonian Keynesianism went into freefall. It did not take long before it was shelved.

All that was necessary to bring Samuelson's version of Keynesianism down in the theoretical arena was to say: if Samuelson and Patinkin (see endnote 19 to this chapter) are right that assorted *rigidities* are the reason why output and employment get stuck stubbornly at some level, then to hell with them (the rigidities, and possibly the scholars too!). Noting that all this was happening at a time (late 1960s, early 1970s) of a rising unemployment that was not responding well to the usual Samuelsonian treatment (of looser fiscal policy; e.g. higher government spending), the same Samuelsonian view pointed to an obvious policy. If the wages' downward rigidity is to blame, then let's get rid of the trade unions who are responsible for it. Let workers lose their jobs, if this is what it takes to correct for their *money illusion* and help further with the removal the offending rigidities. Surely once the rigidities have been flushed out of the system, unemployment would disappear, wouldn't it?

When the deed was done (i.e. the influence of labour unions shrunk almost to nothing and unemployment rose to levels not seen since the 1930s), it was only a matter of time before Samuelson and his variant of neoclassical Keynesianism was politely pushed to the margin. By the mid-1970s, Samuelsonian Keynesianism, and its recommendation of massaging aggregate demand through fiscal policy, was gone. All that was left standing in the economics curriculum, even at the undergraduate level, was the neoclassical formalism that began life at the Cowles Commission in October 1950. A mathematical project designed to have nothing to say about capitalism was the only game left in town; the only source of inspiration for policymakers. Paul Samuelson's two-decade-long effort of attaching a 'practical' variant of Keynesianism to this neoclassical project ended with the ejection of the former as global capitalism moved into a new, more turbulent phase; the phase we call the *Global Minotaur* (in juxtaposition to the post-war *Global Plan*).

This is the prelude to the story of the post-1971 world which led us to the *Crash of 2008* (see Chapter 12). A monstrous misrepresentation of Keynes, due largely to Paul Samuelson's well-intended Text, paved the ground for a radical, intransigent Right to embark on a long march that was to demolish all the institutional restraints created after the Great Depression in order to prevent another 1929. In a sense, one branch of (Samuelsonian) neoclassicism built a straw man version of Keynes, recasting Keynes in its image by denying the substance of his thinking. Twenty or so years later, when the political and economic tide had changed, another neoclassical sect (lacking Samuelson's memory of the Great Depression and his sensitivity to the pain it had exacted) demolished it. Once the *Global Plan* was ready for the fall, and the *Global Minotaur* was ready to claim its place, all it took was a small gust of neoclassical hot air.

Since the 1970s, macroeconomic thinking is under the spell of a new dominant creed that has no time for the New Dealers, the *Scientists*, or for that matter for Samuelson, Nash, Debreu or Arrow. Underpinned by a *bastardised* form of the formalist neoclassicism which emerged victorious out of the Cold War, the new classical macroeconomics (as they became known) provided, from the mid-1970s to 2008, an ironclad free-market ideological cloak for the practices and policies that led the world to the *Crash of 2008*. From the perspective of this chapter, it is interesting to note that, while the dominant economic paradigm during the *Global Plan* phase (1947–1971) was a bastardised form of Keynesianism built upon a neoclassical formalist foundation, the *Global Minotaur* phase that followed (1971–2008) can be described as a bastardised form of neoclassical formalism founded on an underlying pre-1929 free-marketeering ideology. With the enthusiasm of the resurgent neophyte, and the inexorable power of the *Global Minotaur* behind it, the new creed provided the ideological and 'scientific' cover that was necessary to demolish all the checks and balances that the Great Depression had imposed on capitalism. The *Crash of 2008* would not have happened without it.

9.4 Neoclassicism's three meta-axioms

In this section, we investigate the social dynamics within academic economics which helped cement formalist neoclassicism's dominance in the discipline after 1950. It offers a hypothesis on the sociology of mainstream political economics that is consistent with our preceding narrative about the manner in which, both before and after the demise of Samuelsonian Keynesianism, neoclassical formalism has been providing the foundation of the *über*-ideology for the whole post-war era.

Our starting point is the acknowledgement that, in spite of its bountiful ideological utility, the new formalism's incapacity to explain real-world economic phenomena detracted from its persuasive power. The question we now want to address is: why did this lacuna of explanation not detract from neoclassical formalism's discursive power? The simple answer is that the said lacuna was filled by countless academic economists who laboured diligently to extend the theory's scope.

Lured partly by the mathematics' elegance and partly by the great rewards on offer (in terms of career prospects in universities and institutions like RAND), a small army of mathematically inclined economists got down to work with a view to refining the original, awfully 'stiff', Nash–Debreu–Arrow models and set out to provide a *complete* explanation of everything social (not just economic) *within* this unitary, formalist research programme.[25]

Over the next six decades, they produced an abundance of models, faithful to the Nash–Debreu–Arrow template, which seemed not only to carry the original method much further afield but, indeed, to explain (almost) everything under the sun: less than perfect markets; psychologically complex behaviour; the political economy of vested interests; the formation of social norms; the ways in which policymakers can be captured by vested interests; even the rationalisation of revolutionary ideology (Roemer, 1985). Consequently, whenever a critic mentions, as this book does, the new formalism's disconnection from reality, or its ideological bias, a heavy box-set of countless articles, explaining the whole gamut of human behaviour (economic, social and political) is likely to be thrown at him/her, with a cover letter denouncing the critic's ignorance of the new, ever expanding, frontiers of formalist neoclassical political economics.

The mass production of models that expand the theory's reach has done wonders (a) for the career prospects of the bright young minds engaged in this activity, and (b) for dispelling the view that the Nash–Debreu–Arrow project is irrelevant to anyone interested in the real world. So, are we wrong in claiming that the post-1950 dominant economic paradigm never managed to overcome its divorce from reality? The opposite is true, we allege. Indeed, we claim that the charge of irrelevance is more pertinent today than it has ever been (Arnsperger and Varoufakis, 2006; Varoufakis and Arnsperger, 2009)

Before we explain this claim, we need to address an intriguing rejoinder: *that main-stream economics is not really neoclassical!* Indeed, the majority of economists seem to converge on this view. Even some critics of neoclassicism think that the mainstream has moved on from formalist neoclassicism.[26] So, are we barking up the wrong tree? We think not. Naturally, as the term was coined much later, it is of course true that neoclassicism's nineteenth-century pioneers (e.g. Walras, Marshall, Pareto – see Chapter 6) would not have even recognised the term neoclassical. As for the contemporary crop of mainstream economists, the fact that they detest the epithet neoclassical[27] is neither here nor there. After all, neither would the inhabitants of the Eastern Roman Empire have appreciated the label 'Byzantine'; nor would late nineteenth-century Britons have conceived of their society as 'Victorian'. Such epithets have analytical value analogous to their capacity to illuminate certain eras and mind-frames. Similarly with the epithet 'neoclassical'; its value stems from its capacity to encompass a way of thinking about the economy that began in the nineteenth-century and continues to this day.

This is not mere semantics. In our quest for a useful explanation of how economics came to be as 'unprepared' for 2008 as it had been in 1929, a closer look at what constitutes neoclassicism (both pre-1929 and post-1950) is helpful. But in providing a definition for it, we take a second leaf out of the historians' book: their terms 'Byzantine' or 'Victorian' may well be overarching but, at the same time, are deployed carefully so that their use does not invalidate their subject matter's *dynamic complexity*.[28] In the same vein, we too are keen to define neoclassical economics in a manner that respects the undisputed fact that its axioms and theoretical practices have been evolving, changing and adapting from the very beginning. For that reason, we shall eschew any definition based on a fixed set of neoclassical axioms.[29]

We ask: granted that neoclassicists' axioms and methods are in constant flux (inter-temporally but also across different models and fields), is there some analytical foundation which: (a) remains time and model invariant, and (b) typifies a distinct approach to political economics? This is equivalent to searching for invariant *meta*-axioms: higher-order axioms about axioms which underpin *all* of neoclassical economics, irrespective of the actual axioms' fluidity or the malleability of its focus. We propose three such meta-axioms as the foundation of all neoclassicism.

The first two meta-axioms delineate the various assumptions defining the type of human agency populating the formalists' models. Effectively, they are the meta-axioms which 'fix' the character of agents, the meaning of rationality, the nature of persons' beliefs, the socio-economic and legal rules within which they function, etc. In the pioneering models of Nash, Debreu and Arrow, the first two meta-axioms were posed in an asphyxiatingly rigid format. Agents appeared *thin-as-needles*, bereft of any of the characteristics that make us human; markets were rarefied; the state was nowhere to be seen; money was conspicuous by its absence; the actions of one person did not influence anyone else directly (no sympathy, no envy, not to mention solidarity were possible), except through the price mechanism; everyone knew everything there was to know; companies could not even add one cent to the price of their product, without losing *all* their customers; and so on.

Evidently, such models had no purchase on reality, as was their creators' wont. However, this type of analysis could not spread its influence beyond a narrow band of academics unless *something* was done to make them easier on the casual observer's eye; to extend the formalist analysis to more 'realistic' settings. That 'something' came in the form of a mass production of refinements and extensions which, as mentioned above, led to a proliferation of models incorporating all the missing features. Methodologically speaking, they constituted exercises in relaxing the iron grip of the first two meta-axioms.

Alas, there was a hefty price to pay for this relaxation: *radical indeterminacy*. The relaxation of the first two meta-axioms complicated the mathematics to such an extent that the models became unsolvable. The *Inherent Error* was always around the corner, waiting to exact its Pound of flesh on the hapless economists who dared cross it. To 'close' their models, to button them down, the theorists had to turn to the third meta-axiom, a blunt instrument with which to crush all subtlety and beat the model into submission. In short, the third meta-axiom *imposed* a 'solution' *on* the model, as opposed to demonstrating how the model's premises rationally yielded its 'solution'.

Let us now investigate these three meta-axioms in some detail. Box 9.1 presents them in brief while Boxes 9.2, 9.3 and 9.4 offer more detail.

Box 9.1 Neoclassicism's three meta-axioms, in brief

1st meta-axiom – methodological individualism

All explanations are to be sought at the level of the individual agent. In nineteenth-century Marginalist accounts (see Chapter 6), the idea was that all 'action' is due to choices made by Robinson Crusoe-like individuals whose sole concern was their individuated preference satisfaction, with preferences treated as prior to the offered explanation. To this day, this has been the universal feature of all neoclassicism. However, in recent years there have been some important amendments to this script. For example, some formalists have dismissed the 'whole' individual from the centre of their theories, replacing her with strategies. In this sense, one's strategies acquire a life of their own, evolving and mutating in a Darwinian manner and reminiscent of Richard Dawkins' (1976) 'selfish gene'. Such models maintain the thrust of methodological individualism by, on the one hand, splitting the social atom into its 'constituent' parts (e.g. strategies, beliefs) and, on the other, placing these parts, as opposed to the whole person, centre stage. The most important repercussion of this weaker version of methodological individualism is that it leaves room for the actual person under study (e.g. the consumer, the entrepreneur) to evolve and to develop a mutually influential relation with the social structure within which she acts. (See Box 9.2.)

2nd meta-axiom – methodological instrumentalism

The 'individual' agent must have reasons for action. The second meta-axiom insists that these reasons must be exclusively instrumental; i.e. the means must serve pre-specified ends which are definable in terms of some mathematical function of 'success'. In its simplest form, harking back to nineteenth-century utilitarianism, the idea here is that persons are motivated by given preferences to which they are fully betrothed and which, therefore, carry the burden of explanation of agents' behaviour. A weaker version of this meta-axiom has also appeared in the literature. When the theory studies not the whole person (see the weaker version of the first meta-axiom mentioned above) but a subset of it, e.g. a person's strategies or beliefs that have acquired a life of their own, the index of success that guides behaviour can no longer be the person's preferences. So, it takes on a different format, i.e., the pre-specified 'interests' of the strategy or behaviour under study in the context of its Darwinian 'struggle' against its 'competitors'. (See Box 9.3.)

3rd meta-axiom – methodologically imposed equilibrium

This is the linchpin of the neoclassical method; its last resort 'mechanism'; its nuclear weapon against the *Inherent Error*. What it does is to 'close down' a model using brute force when 'closure' cannot be achieved by rational means. As the last section of Chapter 6 demonstrated, neoclassical models cannot handle *time* and *complexity* at once. Therefore one of the two must be dropped unceremoniously. But even then, 'closure' is often not possible unless some additional hidden assumption, at odds with common sense, is introduced through the back door. With the advent of the Nash–Debreu–Arrow axiomatics, this enforced 'closure' took the form of exceedingly abstract devices inaccessible to anyone not intimately familiar with the model's mathematical formulation (See Box 9.4.).

Meta-axiom 1: Methodological individualism

Consider the analytic–synthetic method of a watchmaker faced with a strange mechanical watch. First, he/she takes it carefully apart with a view to examining the properties and function of each of its tiny cogs and wheels. Then, he/she screws it back together. If a reassuring ticking sound ensues, this must surely mean that the fragments of knowledge imparted by the *separate* study of *each* of its parts were successfully synthesised into a macro-theory of the watch.

This parable of an ideal reductionist, analytic–synthetic economic approach has been implicit in neoclassical theorising since the first stirrings of Marginalism. While the term *methodological individualism* was first coined later by Joseph Schumpeter (1908), it featured well before its christening as the bedrock on which Marginalist political economics (recall Chapter 6) was founded. Marginalists, in a determined bid to break from the political economics of Adam Smith, David Ricardo and Karl Marx, turned the exclusive focus on the individual agent into the litmus test of 'scientific' economics.[30] In that mind-frame, individuals are the equivalent of the watchmaker's cogs and wheels: parts of a whole to be understood *fully* (complete with determinate behavioural models) and *independently* of the whole that their actions help bring about. In an important sense, *methodological individualism* is the outright rejection of the *dialectic*, in any shape or form (recall Box 4.10, Chapter 4). Thus, any socio-economic phenomenon under scrutiny is to be explained *via* a synthesis of partial knowledge derived at that individual level.

But there is a snag: the *dialectic* cannot be so easily dismissed. Unlike the world of mechanical watches, society consists of 'parts' which are not readily separable. A pulley or a cog can be fully described in isolation from the other mechanical parts with which it was designed to work harmoniously. Indeed, the 'relations' between the watch's parts are straightforwardly revealed, to the trained eye, through close inspection of the parts' shape, size and other physical properties. In the social world, however, not only are the relations between its 'parts' not deducible from primitive data concerning these parts alone (e.g. from data on persons' means and ends) but, also, it is simply impossible to understand the parts' properties in isolation from one another.

When Aristotle spoke of the human being as a *political animal*, or when Hegel narrated his *master–slave paradox*, they were dwelling on this radical difference between the constituents of society as opposed to the parts of mechanical systems (regardless of their complexity). Indeed, this was the basis for the argument in Chapter 4 on the irreducibility of human labour to some *labour input* and in Chapter 7 concerning the impossibility of capturing investors' expectations by some well-defined mathematical function.

Reading the neoclassicists texts, old and more recent ones, reveals an interesting oscillation between strong methodological individualism, which insists that all explanation must be reducible to knowledge derived from isolated selves (an archipelago of Robinson Crusoes); and a weaker version which acknowledges that the individual is indefinable outside its social and relational context.[31] Our explanation of this oscillation will be (see next section) that, while thoughtful neoclassicists are mindful of the logical conundrum awaiting them if the analysis of persons excludes their relations to other persons (and, thus, to the surrounding institutions), they are *forced* inevitably to fall back on a strong version of methodological individualism.

Forced by what? By the ambition to 'close' their models, we suggest.[32] Human relations are notorious for their resistance to determinate modelling. Put simply, the mathematics of defining a person in terms of his/her relations to others, in addition to his/her means and ends, is of an order higher than most economists would want to engage with and, worse, offer no determinate solution (i.e. behavioural prediction).[33] Importantly, this is no mere technical difficulty awaiting a technical fix. Rather, it reflects the *impossibility* of a deductive methodological individualism which treats human relations as primitive data.[34] It is for this reason that neoclassicism gravitates towards strong methodological individualism, while alluding to its weaker version when in more philosophical mood.

Box 9.2 sums up neoclassicism's first meta-axiom and its two main variants of methodological individualism typifying neoclassical economics of *all* types:

Box 9.2 The first meta-axiom's strong and weak variants
The primacy of the part over the whole

Strong methodological individualism – D

All explanations are to be synthesised from separate, autonomous and prior explanations at the level of the individual. A strict explanatory separation of structure from agency is imposed, with an analytical trajectory that moves unidirectionally from full explanations of agency to derivative theories of structure. In this variant, agency feeds into structure (which is merely the crystallisation of agents' past acts) with no feedback effects from structure back into agency.

Weak methodological individualism – d

As above with the difference that feedback between structure and agency is permitted, even though the explanatory force remains in the realm of agency.

Since the 1940s, and the publication of Samuelson's Text, all textbook economics is founded on variant **D** of the first meta-axiom (see Box 9.2), as are the foundational texts on the mainstream's main theorems: General Equilibrium, Game Theory, the New Classical Economics of the 1970s and 1980s, etc. However, in the last two decades or so, a new crop of highly interesting models appeared, which turn on **d**.[35]

In the next section we shall be arguing that the interplay between **D** and **d**, rather than signifying a retreat from neoclassicism, is part of a complicated dynamic which reinforces its dominance and can be grasped only when all three meta-axioms are considered at once. Therefore, we now turn without further ado to the other two meta-axioms.

Meta-axiom 2: Methodological instrumentalism

Methodological individualism is vacuous without a theory of what motivates individuals. Contrary to the impression given by microeconomics textbooks, greed was never a foundational assumption of Marginalism-*cum*-neoclassicism. While it is true that its models may have been traditionally populated by hyper-rational bargain hunters, never able to resist an act which brings them the tiniest increase in expected net utility, the latter can just as readily result from bars of gold as from reductions in Developing World poverty.

Closer to the truth, regarding neoclassicism's foundations, is the claim that it relies on the axiom of *instrumental* (or means-end) *rationality*: agents are rational to the extent that they deploy their means efficiently in the service of *current, pre-specified* and *sovereign ends*. However, we have already explained why we shun any definition of neoclassical economics which turns on some specific axiom. By the term *methodological instrumentalism* we signify a meta-axiom encompassing all strands of motivation within neoclassical political economics (from Jevons and Marshall, see Box 6.5, to *Evolutionary* Game Theory[36]).

Under both **S** and **s**, rationality loses its *substantive* meaning. **S** turns rationality into a capacity to achieve the highest possible level of preference-satisfaction, so much so that there is no longer any philosophical room for questioning whether the agent will/should act on his/her preferences.[37] Bounded 'rationality' is also permitted, under both **S** and **s**, when the computation of optimal decisions is costly and/or time consuming. Last, under **s**, substantive rationality is wholly absent (since humans are not even the object of study in these models) and yet the analysis is fully instrumental as behaviour is selected (or abandoned) on the basis of fully specified exogenous rules.[38]

Before proceeding to neoclassicism's final meta-axiom, it may be of interest to note that both strands above, **S** and **s**, can be traced to the philosophical scepticism regarding the limits of Reason of David Hume (1711–76), Adam Smith's mentor.[39] The origins of **S** lay in his famous division of the human decision-making process into three *distinct* modules: *Passions, Belief* and (instrumental) *Reason. Passions* provide the destination while *Reason* slavishly steers a course that attempts to get us there, drawing upon a given set of *Beliefs* regarding the external constraints and the likely consequences of alternative actions.[40] As for **s**, and neoclassicism's 'evolutionary turn', it too draws its energy from Hume's *Treatise* and in particular from the argument that, when instrumental Reason is given insufficient 'data' from which to derive useful advice on what action Jack and Jill should take (recall Keynes's argument in Section 7.5 and Box 7.7), conventions or customs emerge that fill the vacuum. Their evolution proceeds along the lines of an adaptation mechanism which selects practices according to their efficacy, namely the agents' predetermined passions.[41] Where **s** diverges sharply from Hume is in its incompatibility with the one thing he cared greatly about: the (un-modellable) feedback effect between, on the one hand, forecast, action and outcome;

Box 9.3 The second meta-axiom's strong and weak variants
Well defined motives

Strict methodological instrumentalism – S

Behaviour is driven by some well-defined function mapping the combination of all feasible agents' behaviours onto some homogeneous index of individuated 'success'. The latter reflects agents' preferences which are given, current, fully determining, and strictly separable both from (a) belief[1] (which helps the agent evaluate the alternative future outcomes) and (b) the means employed.

Weak methodological instrumentalism – s

Behaviour is, again, explained in terms of an homogeneous index of 'success', on to which behaviours are mapped. However, the focus of study is no longer the decision maker but rather each element of her complete set of feasible actions (*aka* strategies). The models are, in this sense, populated by competing alternative strategies or behaviours (rather than decision makers) whose fortunes are determined not by instrumental rationality but by some 'replicator dynamic'; that is, by a difference or differential equation which 'selects' the strategy or behaviour that 'does better' than its 'competitors' in terms of some exogenously given set of individual 'welfare' criteria.[2]

Notes
1 The strict separation of belief from preference can be relaxed, as in the case of psychological Game Theory – see Hargreaves-Heap and Varoufakis (2004), Chapter 7. Weak methodological instrumentalism, see *s* below, accommodates such departures from *S*.
2 See Hargreaves-Heap and Varoufakis (2004), Chapter 6, for more.

and, on the other, the normative beliefs that are born endogenously[42] and which fashion our view of that which we call our 'self-interest'.

Meta-axiom 3: Methodological equilibration[43]

Most political economists, with the possible exception of Keynes and the Austrians, revolve around the search for equilibrium states or paths. What distinguishes neoclassicism is that, in the absence of any plausible explanation of how the system under study is supposed to edge closer to equilibrium, equilibration is *imposed axiomatically*. This practice is best described as a meta-axiom, since it takes many different axiomatic forms which, nonetheless, are consistent with the definition of strong methodological equilibration below:

The classical economists, also beholden to equilibration, traditionally espoused e: in brief, they wished to demonstrate in a Newtonian manner how a market or an economy would *converge* to its equilibrium state.[44] All nineteenth-century Marginalists shared, at least initially, the same ambition and refrained from **E**, investing their skills in devising logical explanations of the path to equilibrium.[45] But then, due to the *Inherent Error* and the indeterminacy that it caused, such convergence could not be proved. It was, therefore, assumed! In terms of the Box 9.4 definitions, this signalled a transition from e to **E**.

Box 9.4 The third meta-axiom's strong and weak variants
Equilibrium at all cost

Strong methodological equilibration – E

Once the model is specified, a set of equilibria is deduced from the available primitive data (e.g. motivation, constraints, production possibilities, adaptation mechanisms, etc.) and the focus of study is restricted (usually by some hidden axiom) to that set. Thus, only behaviour consistent with the model's equilibrium or equilibria is admitted. Finally, sensitivity analysis is introduced to discern the equilibria at which small, random perturbations are incapable of creating centrifugal forces able to dislodge behaviour from that state or path.

Weak methodological equilibration – e

The set of equilibria is arrived at through a process that unfolds either in logical or historical time by means of a pre-specified selection mechanism which forms part of the analysis' primitive data.

Thus a number of Marginalists crossed the Rubicon into neoclassicism, Walras being the obvious example. They did this by abstracting from the historical process that leads in real time, if at all, to equilibrium. Following Nash's approach to the *Bargaining Problem* and strategic interaction in general (recall his October 1950 Cowles Commission presentation), and then Debreu and Arrow[46] who extended Nash's audacity to the study of General Equilibria, the slide from **e** to **E** was given a new twist. Once the Nash–Debreu–Arrow formalism had established itself, **e** was well and truly eclipsed by **E**.

The highest moment of this radical shift was the celebrated proof by Debreu and Arrow that a complete set of prices could be found such that the 'economy' would be in a state of General Equilibrium; a proof purchased at the cost of historical time (and, thus, of any logical argument regarding how that General Equilibrium might emerge).[47] Its significance presupposes the espousal of neoclassicism's third meta-axiom, and in particular its strong version **E**. Without it, the model's existing ingredients (e.g. the assumed type of agency, including its constraints and capabilities) procure precisely zero explanatory power. For unless we accept that a timeless equilibrium is the only state of the model that we ought to focus on, the proof of its existence is immaterial. It is at that point that the third meta-axiom's strong version enters the fray, secures 'closure' and lends discursive power to the theory.[48]

Later, once the Nash–Debreu–Arrow project had more or less produced its important theorems, the race was on for *refinements* and extensions that would dazzle the world with intricate explanations that expanded the new formalist paradigm's domain. Alas, the more that domain expanded, and the assumptions relaxed (to usher in greater realism into the analysis), the closer the 'refiners' came to the trap laid for them by the lurking dragon of radical indeterminacy. To slay it they relied on **E**, the strong version of the third meta-axiom. Equivalently, they smuggled into the analysis an array of (increasingly indefensible) assumptions about the 'outcomes' until some sufficiently narrow band of predicted 'outcomes' would result. In the end, they arrived at 'solutions' that were all but axiomatically imposed, courtesy of **E**, while the actual phenomenon they were supposed to explain was assumed away.

But if the means (**E**) defeated the end (to generate understanding, as opposed to imposing a 'solution'), why did they proceed in this manner? Why impose **E**? Because, the short answer is, formalism without formal results is pointless and none of the prestigious technical journals of the time (e.g. *Econometrica*) would have succumbed to its charms; at least not once the initial excitement with the Nash–Debreu–Arrow results wore off. But then the question becomes: how did they get away with the sleight of hand that is **E**?

Our contention is that their success hinged on a controlled oscillation between **e** and **E**; between narratives that relied only on **e** (to tell stories in the context of single sector 'economies') and accounts that turned on **E** (when it became necessary to demonstrate that their method was not confined just to single good, single person or single sector economies). With the dexterity of the able magician, who keeps his/her audience's eye off the critical move, they made sure that the shifting between **e** and **E** went unnoticed.

In the next section, we examine this perpetual 'shifting' between **e** and **E**, labelling it the *Dance of the Meta-axioms*. Its function, we shall argue, is to deflect criticism by switching between the weaker and the stronger versions of all three meta-axioms depending on the criticism at hand: whenever a potential critic questions the realism of the formalist model under scrutiny, he/she is met with various 'refinements' built upon weakened versions of the first two meta-axioms (a shift from **D** and **S** to **d** and **s**). Then, once the criticism has been defused, the strong version of the third meta-axiom, **E**, is rolled out to curtail the resulting indeterminacy. But when fresh criticism threatens to question the plausibility of **E**, new rejoinders appear to the effect that **e** may be enough. However, to demonstrate that **e** may suffice, the theorists must strengthen the first two meta-axioms (replacing **d** and **s** with **D** and **S**), thus annulling the sophistication that their relaxation had made possible. A truly brilliant manoeuvre: while the meta-axiomatic goalposts are constantly moving, the critics stand next to no chance of scoring.[49]

9.5 The *Dance of the Meta-axioms*

Models are an open invitation to meddle with assumptions, and formalist neoclassical models have been no exception. Since Nash's 1950 paper, we have had six decades of such meddling. Some of these amendments were so extensive that many, including economists who had previously been most critical of neoclassicism,[50] began to discern a fundamental shift from neoclassical formalism. In evidence, they cite the noteworthy relaxation of the assumptions about what people are like[51] and, more generally, the observation that the traditional neoclassical core (e.g. General Equilibrium) seems to have been sidelined by non-formalist pursuits, for example, experimental economics, simulations, neuroeconomics, evolutionary models, etc.

This section cautions against such a verdict. It suggests that neoclassicism's stranglehold over the economics mainstream is as strong as it has ever been. Indeed, the more it seems to 'loosen up', the greater its power over the hearts and minds of economists, politicians and business. This claim is based on the observation that, at close inspection, the centrifugal forces occasioned by dissatisfaction with the original formalist neoclassical position, after initially pushing the mainstream away from the neoclassical nucleus, eventually subside, turning centripetal. At that point, they return the analysis either to the original neoclassical position or, even worse, to a position at a higher plane of neoclassical abstraction on which the original 'problem' not only remains unsolved but is, indeed, amplified and potentially more misleading.

The dynamic mechanism at work is outlined below in diagrammatic form (see Figure 9.1). We term it the *Dance of the Meta-axioms* featuring the following simple steps: Starting from the *original formalist neoclassical position* **1**, some theoretical *challenge* **c** is issued (either from within neoclassicism or from without); for example, the opinion that economics assumes too much rationality on behalf of investors, or that it underplays the importance of social norms.

In some cases, the challenge is *ignored* outright (arrow **i**) while in others it is *addressed* (arrow **a**) *via* a relaxation that occurs within one (or both) of the first two meta-axioms. At that stage, because of the by now all too familiar *Inherent Error*, the analysis hits an invisible *Wall of Radical Indeterminacy* and the profession recoils in horror. To 'close' the model, either it *retreats* to the original position (**1**) or it *backslides* (arrow **b**), *via* a severe tightening of the third meta-axiom (the shift from **e** to **E**), to some new position **4**; a position where the

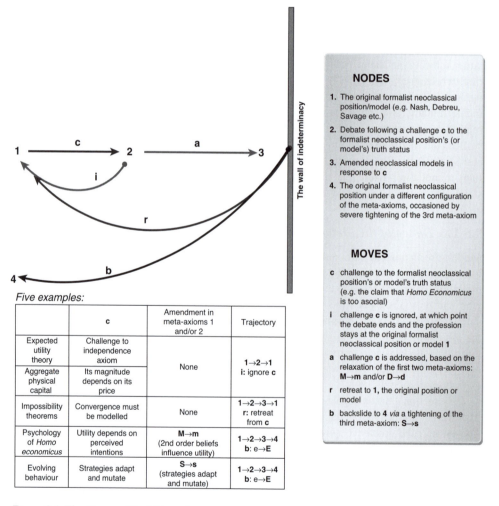

NODES

1. The original formalist neoclassical position/model (e.g. Nash, Debreu, Savage etc.)

2. Debate following a challenge **c** to the formalist neoclassical position's (or model's) truth status

3. Amended neoclassical models in response to **c**

4. The original formalist neoclassical position under a different configuration of the meta-axioms, occasioned by severe tightening of the 3rd meta-axiom

MOVES

c challenge to the formalist neoclassical position's or model's truth status (e.g. the claim that *Homo Economicus* is too asocial)

i challenge **c** is ignored, at which point the debate ends and the profession stays at the original formalist neoclassical position or model **1**

a challenge **c** is addressed, based on the relaxation of the first two meta-axioms: **M→m** and/or **D→d**

r retreat to **1**, the original position or model

b backslide to **4** *via* a tightening of the third meta-axiom: **S→s**

Five examples:

	c	Amendment in meta-axioms 1 and/or 2	Trajectory
Expected utility theory	Challenge to independence axiom	None	1→2→1 i: ignore **c**
Aggregate physical capital	Its magnitude depends on its price		
Impossibility theorems	Convergence must be modelled	None	1→2→3→1 r: retreat from **c**
Psychology of *Homo economicus*	Utility depends on perceived intentions	**M→m** (2nd order beliefs influence utility)	1→2→3→4 b: e→E
Evolving behaviour	Strategies adapt and mutate	**S→s** (strategies adapt and mutate)	1→2→3→4 b: e→E

Figure 9.1 The *Dance of the Meta-axioms*.

original problem (that **c** sought to address) seems assuaged when, in truth, its intractability is greatly intensified.

The remainder of this section illustrates this hypothesised dynamic by evoking a number of challenges (**c**) to core neoclassical models that occurred during the post-war era. These it groups in three main categories. We begin with important challenges which were ignored outright (**i**). Next, we look at challenges of note which were addressed (**a**). From some, the profession retreated (**r**) while others occasioned a backslide (**b**) to a new, more complex neoclassical position even more theoretically problematic than the original.

Essential to our hypothesis is the argument that (*i*) because of the *Inherent Error*, none of these challenges could penetrate the resulting *Wall of Radical Indeterminacy* while retaining their allegiance to the neoclassical meta-axioms; and (*ii*) the profession, after dallying with complications of its foundational neoclassical models, returns to a position (**1** or **4**) which, at the expense of explanatory power, remains as loyal to the meta-axioms as ever.

Ignored challenges: The 1→2→1 *quickstep*

Here we look at challenges to neoclassicism which, while poignant and irrefutable, were unceremoniously ignored. We begin with an example concerning the foundational model of men and women which, in the early 1950s, was adopted by Nash–Debreu–Arrow formalism.[52] The proposition that rational men and women act *as if* in order to maximise some mathematical expectation of their utility was first challenged, at the macroeconomic level, by John Maynard Keynes (see Chapter 7). However, in the 1950s, it was confronted both experimentally and logically in the form of two separate but equally devastating critiques: that of Maurice Allais (1953), whom we first mentioned as the author of the first economics book that Gerard Debreu read even before leaving Paris for Chicago (see note 36 of the previous chapter) and Daniel Ellsberg (1956, 1961), the RAND employee who was to expose the folly of the Vietnam War (recall Box 8.3). Together, these challenges disproved the empirical validity of *Expected Utility Theory* and challenged the logic of its foundational axioms.

Since then a cottage industry of laboratory experiments has confirmed the former while a series of fascinating alternatives to *Expected Utility Theory* have been published in the mainstream's top journals.[53] And yet, to this day, *Expected Utility Theory* reigns supreme both in the lecture theatres and in *every* form of neoclassical theorising, from rational expectations models to each and every application of Game Theory.

Turning to Game Theory itself, questions were eventually raised about the plausibility of presuming that rational agents must always select behaviour consistent with Nash's notion of equilibrium. In the context of static games it became apparent that *disequilibrium behaviour* could be fully rationalised.[54] Similarly, it transpired that behaviour not predicted by the models (usually referred to as *out-of-equilibrium behaviour*) could be just as rational in finite dynamic games as the equilibrium path proposed by Nash and his disciples.[55] As for games that unfold indefinitely through time, the devastating force of the *Inherent Error*, and the ensuing indeterminacy, was felt in the form of the so-called *Folk Theorem* which confirms that, in real time interactions that last for an unspecified period, *anything goes*.[56]

And yet, today, *all* applications of Game Theory (from theories of the way central banks behave to models of corporate rivalry, labour economics and voting models) ignore these challenges, *assuming*, against the theory's own pronouncements, that behaviour will remain on some narrow equilibrium path.[57]

Perhaps the best known case of a challenge ignored is the debate presented in Section 6.9 that has come to be remembered as the *Cambridge Capital Controversies* (see, in particular, Box 6.14). The issue there was Marginalism's stubborn insistence that, with price taking agents, returns to capital reflect capital's marginal productivity. Piero Sraffa, Joan Robinson and Luigi Pasinetti, the reader will recall, objected to the fact that a highly damaging reflexivity was buried deep in the Marginalist position: while it is possible to speak meaningfully of homogeneous apple juice, even of homogenous 'abstract' labour, it is impossible to treat capital goods as homogenous (in view of their different types and vintages) and, consequently, to measure an economy's capital stock independently of its price. But then, if physical capital's magnitude depends on its price, how can its price be explained by its magnitude?

Geoff Harcourt (1972) sums up the course of this debate and how it petered out once the neoclassical corner effectively threw in the towel.[58] And yet, today, no trace of this debate is to be found in any mainstream economics curriculum. The challenge has been ignored and the mainstream has continued to assume that the profit rate (i.e. capital's price) is explained, uni-directionally, by the revenues due to the last morsel of an aggregate physical capital whose magnitude is independent of that return.

Around the mid-1970s, once the *Global Plan* shrivelled and died and the *Global Minotaur* began to show its teeth (see Chapter 11), formalist neoclassicism threw off any remnants of Samuelsonian Keynesianism (see previous section), returned to its pre-1929 free-marketeer posture and extended its dominion to policy debates. Since then, the *Cambridge Capital Controversies* debate has been written out of the textbooks, lest a smidgeon of doubt entered students' minds about the scientific infallibility of the new (but at once very, very old) neoclassical creed.[59] For an *ideology* that owed its re-birth to the Cold War, and the struggle against Soviet despotism, it is ironic that it borrowed a typical Soviet method: expunging its foes from the history books.

Retreat: The 1→2→3→1 move

Not all valid and poignant challenges came from critics of neoclassicism. Some of the strongest ones emanated endogenously and, perhaps for this reason, were taken seriously by the economics profession. The best example is the Nash–Debreu–Arrow edifice itself. While its architects had no qualms in admitting that it was part of their proof *not* to have an answer to the question of *how* or even *whether* their 'solution' (either the agreement between bargainers or the set of prices that equilibrates the economy) will materialise, neoclassicism could not avoid such questions forever, especially in the lecture theatres.

Confronted with eager undergraduates, teachers found themselves almost compelled to rely on deeply unsatisfactory heuristics. In the case of bargaining, stories were told that involved positing a bargaining process with stages in which concessions were motivated by different amounts of fear of disagreement.[60] Similarly, in the case of the competitive price mechanism, tales of equilibration were allowed to linger on the basis of an analytically untested faith that prices *must* adjust until excess demand vanishes.

While these equilibration narratives had (and could have had) no basis in the axiomatics of Nash–Debreu–Arrow, they seemed ever so obviously correct to students as to silence dissenting voices; except, of course, those of the *leading* neoclassicists, who understood only too well the analytical folly intrinsic in the offered narratives. Nevertheless, with one exception (namely, Debreu)[61] even they craved some demonstration of convergence from their axiomatically derived, and thus inherently static, equilibria; a demonstration with which to replace the incongruous lecture theatre tales.

Thus, a challenge was issued, from *within* neoclassicism, to model convergence explicitly, in the context of General Equilibrium and in Game/Bargaining Theory. Indeed, once neoclassical formalism, especially after the mid-1970s, entered undergraduate curricula, it became impossible to maintain an embargo on real-time explanations. At a time of oil crises, of stagflation (i.e. the co-existence of high inflation and increasing unemployment), of painful industrial disputes, etc., an inability to say something meaningful about disequilibrium prices, or on costly delay before reaching agreements, would have weakened neoclassicism's hold.

So, neoclassicists responded with an avalanche of models purporting to plug the various holes. In effect, they set out to tilt at the windmills of the *Inherent Error* in search of ways to combine *complexity* with *time*. Unschooled in the fate of earlier attempts to do precisely that, they mobilised hundreds, if not thousands, of the best minds in the context of a research agenda that was, by its very nature, predestined to fail. In Game Theory, this agenda took the label *The Refinement Project*.[62] Elsewhere, it came in different guises (e.g. Computable General Equilibrium, General Disequilibrium Theory).

Beginning with Nash's bargaining theorem, the best example of an attempt to narrate the process that leads to the theory's predicted agreement is due to Ariel Rubinstein. In his 1982 paper, he argued that Nash's solution could be shown to be the limiting case of a bargaining process in which rational bargainers issued alternating demands.[63] As for costly delays in reaching agreement, they could be explained by asymmetrical information on each other's eagerness to settle (see Rubinstein, 1985). Meanwhile, in General Equilibrium theory, some promising preliminary work hinted at ways in which the groping process towards an equilibrium price vector could be modelled (for an early attempt see Arrow, 1959). Of course, it was not long before it transpired that both projects were doomed. The bad news for the neoclassical project, in both cases, came from Hugo Sonnenschein, a University of Chicago economics professor.

Starting with General Equilibrium, Sonnenschein (1972, 1973) single-handedly destroyed the one belief shared by all mainstream economists: that, all other things being equal in a complex multi-sector economy, excess demand for some commodity will force its price to rise. Sonnenschein startled the profession by proving that, contrary to conventional wisdom, excess demand for some commodity could *never* guarantee that its price would rise. This was a crucial moment when a fully fledged, technically superb, neoclassicist came to a logical conclusion which, unbeknownst even to him, confirmed Keynes' hunch; the hunch that multi-sector, complex economic systems do not behave as we would expect a single sector economy to.

Indeed, Sonnenschein's result meant that even if we have all the information we need regarding the demand and supply of each product, we cannot synthesise this information so as to define the level of aggregate or effective demand in the economy as a whole. In short, our argument regarding economics' *Inherent Error* and, of course, Keynes' related notion of the *fallacy of composition*, found its expression in the form of a neoclassical theoretical proof!

The implication was startling to all who could understand the mathematics involved and their meaning for political economics. As a testimony to the supreme honesty of the pioneering formalists, its poignancy was confirmed by their leading lights (see Mantel, 1974; Debreu, 1974). The combined meaning of what has become known as the *Sonnenschein–Mantel–Debreu theorem* (SMD thereafter) was that:

(a) convergence to General Equilibrium is *impossible* to model, and
(b) it is no longer possible to guarantee the General Equilibrium's uniqueness.[64]

Moving on to bargaining theory, the idea that delay in reaching agreement can be explained by asymmetrical information, within the context of the Nash–Rubinstein approach to bargaining, was also dispelled by work in which Hugo Sonnenschein played a central role (see Gul and Sonnenschein, 1988). If we add to this a series of devastating critiques of the logical coherence of extending Nash's method to dynamic interactions (i.e. multi-stage games)[65] the neoclassical literature itself reached a simple conclusion: there is no reason to believe that a bargaining process between rational agents is amenable to mathematical modelling that generates some firm prediction of what agreement they will reach.[66]

Taken together, these two contributions of Hugo Sonnenschein and his associates had a single, inescapable, implication for the post-war all-conquering neoclassical formalism: *we are damned if we know how a multi-sector economy works!* In more 'scientific' language, *the highest form of neoclassicism had nothing meaningful to say about either price and or contract formation.* In the language of the 'trade', Sonnenschein armed us with two devastating *impossibility theorems* (one that rules out a determinate story about how prices are formed, the second declaring invalid the Nashian method of homing in on some rational outcome of negotiations).

Intriguingly, it was neoclassicism which challenged itself to come up with a response to the convergence issue and it was neoclassicism which procured these two impossibility theorems, which *prove* that it could not meet its own challenges. Put the same argument in terms of the previous section's meta-axioms, and the point is that the best and brightest challenged themselves to shift neoclassicism's highest form away from a reliance on version **E** of the third meta-axiom and towards its weaker version **e**. Alas, all such efforts crashed against the *Wall of Radical Indeterminacy* (see Figure 9.1).

Sonnenschein's two impossibility theorems had an illustrious predecessor: the first, and best known, impossibility theorem due to Kenneth Arrow himself. The previous chapter told the story of how, after attending Nash's Cowles Seminar in October 1950, Gerard Debreu impressed upon Arrow the importance of moving away from von Neumann's scientism and, instead, applying Nash's formalist method to the reconstruction of Walras' model of General Equilibrium. What we did not mention was that, at the same time, Arrow worked on another project too, almost in his spare time: the project of investigating (using Nash's toolbox once more) the possibility of synthesising individual preferences (i.e. individual utility functions – see Chapter 6) into a single, well-defined function whose maximisation coincides with the pursuit of the *General Good*; a function known by economists as the *Social Welfare Function.*

Arrow's work led him to a surprising result: it is *impossible* to synthesise private preferences into social preferences without violating some very basic rules that this 'synthesis' ought to respect. Noting that any synthesis of individual into social desires is tantamount to a political process that gives the state the requisite legitimacy to act on behalf of its citizens, Arrow's result is overwhelmingly meaningful. For what it says is that the only way a society (comprising different individuals portrayed as bundles of ordinal utility preferences) can be guaranteed to know what it wants from its state is to have a dictator telling it![67]

This extraordinary result, known as *Arrow's Impossibility Theorem*, is possibly one of the most significant results to have come out of the social sciences during the twentieth century. Once digested, there are only two conclusions that it leaves room for. Either we must accept that the liberal democratic state can *never* act on our behalf (since our collective will cannot be determined, even if each one of us has well defined preferences);[68] or we must ditch the Marginalist-*cum*-neoclassicist model of men and women.[69] The one thing we cannot do is to carry on pretending that neoclassical political economics can offer government advice on how to serve society.

In conclusion, by the time neoclassicism was to fully dominate economics departments (sometime in the 1970s), it had already spawned, like a spider weaving a web out of its own substance, *three impossibility theorems*. These theorems ruled out, in the context of a minimally complex society,[70] any logically coherent neoclassical explanation of (a) the notion of a *General Will*; (b) the process by which prices come to some General Equilibrium; and (c) the way in which rational agents reach agreement on how to distribute benefits and burdens among themselves.

The crucial question is: what happened next? The answer is depressing for anyone who believes in the power of Reason: neoclassical economists, discomfited by the power of their own method's resplendent impossibility theorems, chose to ignore them; like small children, they swept them under the carpet and continued to 'play' as if nothing had happened. In terms of our diagram in Figure 9.1, what ensued was a multifarious retreat (arrow **r**) back to position **1**. Just as in the case of the *Cambridge Capital Controversies*, the challenge of the *three impossibility theorems* came to naught, even though they rose within the neoclassical tradition.

The actual retreat (arrow **r**) took various forms. Most common was the retreat behind single sector or representative agent models (i.e. the *corn model* and the Robinson Crusoe economy) in which the weak third meta-axiom (**e**) suffices. What is, however, of great interest is the *repeated* deployment of the *1→2→3→1 move*. When facing questions about the determination of value in a world of many agents and sectors, the profession responds by showcasing the original Nash–Debreu–Arrow analysis, complete with the strong version of the third meta-axiom (**E**). If questions are then asked about convergence, dynamics, growth, etc., the weaker version (**e**) comes into play and the emphasis shifts silently from Nash–Debreu–Arrow to single sector and/or single agent models. And if anyone, at this point, impertinently protests that the world comprises multiple agents and sectors, his/her neoclassical interlocutor dusts off the original Nash–Debreu–Arrow and brings on **E**. And so on.

This continual *move* back and forth between **e** and **E** keeps out of sight the theoretical failure to rise to the original challenge **c**. In fact, which of the two versions of the third meta-axiom is deployed depends on the question the neoclassicist feels compelled to answer: If he/she is put on the spot to explain action (e.g. moves, offers) in real time, he/she will deploy **e**. But if he/she needs to articulate a theory of prices (competitive or bargained, e.g. in neoclassical macroeconomics, labour economics, industrial organisation), he/she returns to **E** and the glittery existence proofs founded upon it. Above all, the surreptitious, never-ending move from **e** to **E** to **e** to… *ad infinitum* keeps out of sight the neoclassical failure to rise to its own challenges, and thus out of the mainstream economists' agenda.

Backslide: The 1→2→3→4 shuffle

In this section we offer two examples of what we call the *backslide* (arrow **b** in the diagram) which, following a failed foray into greater plausibility and sophistication, returns the theory not to its original position (node **1**) but to a state once removed from it (node **4**) where the original position's weaknesses are both *better hidden* and *much amplified*. Our two examples concern, first, the attempts to give *Homo Economicus*[71] a (much needed) richer psychology and, second, neoclassicism's so-called *evolutionary turn*.

Let us begin with the major breakthrough in economic psychology marked by two classic papers: Geanakoplos *et al.* (1989) and Rabin (1993). Jill is now psychologically sophisticated in her interactions with Jack and cares not only about what he will do but also about his motives. To illustrate, consider a *prisoner's dilemma* played only once between Jill and Jack and suppose that both are instrumentally rational, that is, each is motivated only by the idea of maximising her or his *own* payoffs in the *Matrix* below. It is easy to see why standard Game Theory predicts mutual defection. Since Jill's best reply is to defect, regardless of whether she expects Jack to cooperate or not, she will do precisely that. And the same applies to Jack. Thus, while they would both be better off if they cooperated (securing 2 utils each) their 'greed' for utils drives them to defection (and 1 util each): a typical case where instrumental rationality is self-defeating and leads to social or collective irrationality.

Now, game theorists get to their predictions of how games will work out by assuming *commonly known rationality* (CKR). This means the following: Jill knows that Jack is instrumentally rational (i.e. motivated only by the idea of maximising his own payoffs in the *Matrix* (Table 9.1) below); and vice versa. Moreover, Jill knows that Jack knows that she is instrumentally rational; and vice versa. Further, Jill knows that Jack knows that Jill knows of his instrumental rationality; and vice versa. And so on *ad infinitum*.

Of course, in the simple *prisoner's dilemma* above, CKR is surplus to requirements; the game is so simple that Jack and Jill know what to do (i.e. defect) independently of their expectations of what their opponent will choose; as long as they care only about their own payoffs, each will defect. Thus a determinate prediction (i.e. 'solution' or equilibrium) is arrived at. However, in more complex games, CKR becomes necessary (though rarely sufficient) to reach some firm prediction.[72]

Now suppose that CKR is in place in the simple game above. Regardless, both players predict that the other will defect. In standard neoclassical analysis, there is nothing more to say: *mutual defection* is unavoidable. However, in a psychologically enhanced version of the game, intentions matter. Consider two different thoughts which might be underlying Jill's prediction that Jack will defect:

(a) 'Jack is defecting *because* he is expecting me to defect too.'
(b) 'Jack is defecting *even though* he is expecting me to cooperate.'

Should Jill feel the same when entertaining thought (a) compared to how she feels when entertaining thought (b)? Not under CKR! Let us explain: because of CKR, she knows that Jack knows that she is best off defecting, whatever he does. So, under (b), where Jack expects Jill to cooperate, he cannot explain his prediction that she will cooperate on the basis that she is irrational (for that would contradict CKR). So, why else would he expect her to cooperate? The only rational explanation Jack can come up with is that he thinks she is trying to be kind to him. And how does he repay her 'kind gesture'? By defecting, and thus pushing Jill's payoff to the lowest possible level.

Table 9.1 The prisoner's dilemma

	Jack cooperates	Jack defects
Jill cooperates	2, 2	0, 3
Jill defects	3, 0	1, 1

In short, thought (b) upsets Jill in a way that thought (a) does not. Indeed, under (a) Jill assesses Jack's defection as psychologically neutral.[73] Is it not reasonable to imagine that Jill will be happier with the *mutual defection* outcome under (b) than under (a)? We think it is. But then there are two utility pay-offs corresponding to the bottom right cell of the game's *Matrix* depending on whether Jill's second order expectations are captured by (a) or by (b).

Summing up the above paragraph, it turns out that the *same* outcome (*mutual defection*) has different utility implications for Jill depending on whether she labours under (a) or (b). In other words, her second-order beliefs influence her utility from a given outcome. The analytical significance of the above is that (a) it enhances the analysis' realism (by restoring the motivational role of perceived intentions) and (b) it allows us to rationalise cooperative behaviour unceremoniously dismissed by standard neoclassical theory.[74] There are two morals to this story.

First, neoclassicists are right when arguing that *Homo Economicus* can be 'trained' better to resemble a real person through a relaxation of their first two meta-axioms.[75] The second moral, however, is more sobering: *indeterminacy kicks in with a vengeance causing a back-slide to an even less defensible position than the original.* The reason is that civilising the neoclassical agent threatens to wreck the very fabric of the analytical framework. What we term the 'backslide', arrow **b** in the diagram, is merely a reaction to this threat.

To see this more clearly, our point here is that complicating Jill and Jack's psychology leads to a vicious form of indeterminacy never encountered before. Up to now, indeterminacy has appeared in this book in a relatively mild form: a theoretical model's failure to produce a prediction of what will happen given its own premises; for example, a model of markets that could not be solved for the prices that equilibrate demand and supply; or a model of Robinson Crusoe in which his utility function and other information on his means could not produce a prediction of how much time he would spend fishing (as opposed to resting). But here, the indeterminacy we face not only translates into an inability to predict outcomes but, fascinatingly, implies the loss of the interaction's very definition as well. For once, Jill is allowed to care about Jack's intentions; our simplistic *prisoner's dilemma* above ceases even to be a well-defined game!

Note that before Jill knows the utility value, to herself, of the *mutual defection* outcome, she must first interpret Jack's motivation for defecting, that is, she must have a view of what she thinks that Jack expects of her. Suddenly, Jill and Jack's motivation (i.e. pay-offs) can no longer be defined a priori. They now depend on a combination of their first- and second-order beliefs (or their beliefs about one another's beliefs). And when motives 'infect' utilities directly, as they do here, the only way of writing down the game's pay-offs is if we know the players' beliefs a priori. But we can only know them a priori if we make the a priori assumption that their (first and second order) beliefs are aligned! But this is tantamount to putting the cart before the horses; of imposing equilibrium (the third meta-axiom) in order to define the interaction itself!

So far the third meta-axiom was used to squeeze a theory of *social structure* (or social outcomes) from a given model of *individual agency*. Here, the third meta-axiom is used to define both the *individual agency* and the corresponding *social structure*. Thus nothing non-trivial results from the analysis and the whole framework becomes possibly the grandest tautology the human mind has ever portrayed as a social theory.

In summary, after having given Jill and Jack a more realistic psychology (based on the notion that they care not only about outcomes but also about one another's intentions), the hapless neoclassicist lost sight of the game's very structure. To retrieve it (i.e. to be able to specify the utilities from each of the interaction's four potential outcomes), he/she was forced to backslide to the strongest imaginable version of the third meta-axiom. To an **E** on steroids.[76]

The above illustrates nicely the backslide (**b**) in the preceding diagram. A fascinating challenge (**c**), emanating from another field (psychology, in this example), was taken on gallantly by neoclassicism (arrow **a**) but the ensuing indeterminacy defeated its best intentions and forced it onto the back foot. The indeterminacy proved so radical that it jeopardised not merely the model's 'closure' (i.e. whether a unique solution could be found) but, indeed, the model's very structural coherence.[77] A major tightening of the third meta-axiom saved the day, via a logically indefensible leap of faith,[78] returning the analysis not to its original position (**1**) but to another position (**4**) once removed from it. Interestingly, at that new position (**4**), the theory is rationally less defensible than before but, simultaneously, possesses more discursive power![79]

The evolutionary turn of neoclassical economics is our second and final example of a major *backslide*. Evolutionary biologists[80] demonstrated that, in a hypothesised world of insects and birds, behaviour converges automatically onto equilibria that are analytically equivalent to those of neoclassicism; seemingly with no need for the **E**, the strong variant of the third meta-axiom. Understandably, neoclassicism was thrilled by this discovery, feeling that its stance was, at last, vindicated.[81] In place of the farfetched **E** variant of the third meta-axiom, with which they themselves never felt at ease, neoclassicists could now appeal to a Darwinian rationale. Even critics of neoclassicism began to suspect that this evolutionary turn was a sign that the mainstream was being weaned from its neoclassical, formalist past.[82]

Alas, the truth was, once again, less heroic. A closer look at the reportedly Darwinian rationale (with which the evolutionary turn to replace the rigid **E** variant of the third meta-axiom) reveals that it is just another reincarnation of **E**. The announcement that, following its evolutionary turn, neoclassicism had ceased to be neoclassical proved terribly premature. The hopes of many,[83] that neoclassicism would, at last, evolve into a quasi-Darwinian, technical albeit pluralist, complexity-friendly and, ultimately, more scientific socio-economic discipline, crashed against the *Wall of Radical Indeterminacy* (see Figure 9.1). Let us explain why we say this.

All evolutionary models turn on two mechanisms: an *adaptation mechanism* and a *mutation generating mechanism*. The adaptation mechanism produces, via some type of natural selection (or *replicator dynamic*), convergence, regularity and predictability. In contrast, the mutation generating mechanism is responsible for a constant inflow of unpredictable variety. To model these two mechanisms mathematically (something that, of course, Darwin was not in the slightest interested in), we need the following joint assumption that

(a) the two mechanisms are independent of each other, and
(b) mutations are authentically unpredictable (or, more precisely, identically and independently distributed (iid) random events).

While this combination of (a) and (b) may be plausible in biology, it is certainly not so in the social sciences. Humans have the curious habit of combining conformity (i.e. of individually copying the relatively successful behaviour of others) with

(i) individual acts of subversion caused by some theory regarding the rules that govern their society (i.e. an ideology), and

(ii) collective or coordinated acts of subversion intended clearly to undermine established social conventions and norms (e.g. confronting patriarchal notions of propriety, bourgeois norms of property rights). The conjunction of (i) and (ii) constitutes, in evolutionary terms, behavioural patterns consistent with highly correlated mutations linked inextricably to the *adaptation mechanism*.

In short, (i) and (ii) disestablishes the joint assumption (a) and (b), without which the evolutionary models cannot take a mathematical, formalist expression. Put simply, they cannot be 'solved', which means we are back in the clasps of radical indeterminacy. While evolutionary thinking is essential in order to understand nature and society, evolutionary *models* are insufficiently evolutionary. At least not as long as humans remain irreducible to either an electricity generator or to a random number generator (recall, respectively, Marx in Chapter 4 and Keynes in Chapter 7) and human history is influenced systematically by our capacity for reflection, dialogue and political action (a capacity antithetical to the assumption of mutations as exclusively random iid events).

To their credit, a number of evolutionary theorists have understood this well and tried to respond analytically.[84] However, they quickly reached a now familiar conclusion: that once the mutation probabilities are interdependent with the social *adaptation mechanism, we are damned if we know what history has in store for us.*[85] This is similar, both in spirit and analytically, to the *Folk Theorem* mentioned above which, in indefinitely repeated games, shows that almost *any* conventional behaviour can become disestablished and any alternative may take its place if 'subversives' coordinate their mutation probabilities appropriately and in response to the current behavioural conventions.

In conclusion, the *Wall of Radical Indeterminacy* has, once again, defeated neoclassicism's efforts to rise to a new level of sophistication. Its attempt to infuse some realism into its models, this time by borrowing heavily from evolutionary biology, caused the set of (evolutionary) equilibria to divide and multiply *ad infinitum*.[86] And what did the economics mainstream do in the face of such infectious indeterminacy? Yet again they recoiled behind the strong version **E** of the third meta-axiom (by insisting that mutations *are* random iid events[87]). By now, such a response ought to cause us no surprise since the only other alternative would be to drop mathematical modelling and to concentrate either on simulations or on empirical work (or both).

While some gallant evolutionary economists did focus on simulations, they soon realised that the mainstream left them behind, preferring to perform the *1→2→3→4 shuffle* which took it back to a neoclassical position that is just as unsophisticated as the original (since the insistence that humans are incapable of coordinating their 'mutations' effectively returns us to a world of pseudo-rational fools). And yet, this fresh theoretical failure enhanced neoclassicism's discursive power no end. For it made it possible to push the claim onto the vast majority of their 'audience' (who lack the technical sophistication to discern the subtle criticisms raised above) that its theorems can now be supported by an evolutionary narrative.[88]

The reader may, at this juncture, protest that our argument is turning conspiratorial; that it presupposes a plot by a large number of practitioners, guided by common interest and persecuted clinically at the individual level through some fancy footwork, to confuse students and the public at large into accepting untruths about neoclassicism's theoretical achievements. Such a claim would be absurd. In the next section we shall argue that neoclassical formalism's domination (including practices such as the *Dance of the Meta-axioms* above) evolved spontaneously, without any conscious planning either at the collective or the individual level. In brief, no conspiracy was necessary.

9.6 A priesthood evolves

This chapter began with the observation that, while the post-war order was based on a very definite design (the *Global Plan* of Chapter 11), the fledgling Cold War of the late 1940s created considerable demand for an ideological break from any type of economics which lends credence to collective agency, social and economic planning, state interference in the social economy, etc. The new neoclassical formalism that began life in 1950 fitted the bill beautifully (see Section 9.2). In addition, it relied on higher mathematics beyond the grasp of most economists. And since exclusion is the shortest road to discursive power, the small circle of practitioners who were conversant in it saw their careers soar.

Younger economists producing models of that ilk soon found themselves in demand by top journals and Ivy League departments alike. The era's anti-Marxism helped substantially in this regard. The creation of imaginary economies where labour could not be distinguished from other commodities; the neoclassical models' inherent radical egalitarianism; their constant references to *equilibrium, markets, welfare* and, above all else, *efficiency*; the impressive mathematics deployed both on paper and on the blackboard; these were the ingredients of formalism's success in an academia jostling for position in the sun under the Cold War's cloudy skies.

As for the *Dance of the Meta-axioms* of the previous section, it too materialised spontaneously. Consider a graduate student who wants to make his/her mark. Suppose further that he/she is intellectually honest and curious, so much so that, although he/she yearns for recognition at one of the top (formalism-dominated) departments, he/she nevertheless refuses to ditch *complexity*, insists on civilising *Homo Economicus* and on modelling some aspect of social intercourse that has hitherto remained outside formalism's scope. He/she embarks hopefully down that road, encouraged by the flexibility of the first two meta-axioms which he/she manipulates for months, or even years, in order to allow into his/her models the type of phenomenon he/she wants to study. And here is the rub: once committed to this type of modelling, he/she sooner or later realises that no determinate 'solution' can be had; that the mathematics has become terribly complex; that something radical must be done to get it sorted out; that unless it *is* done, he/she will never get the paper published or the thesis passed. Only then, in a Faustian moment of moral panic, does our well meaning theorist realise what the price for 'solving' his/her model is: it is the loss of its very soul on the altar of 'closure'. Technically speaking, it is the adoption of **E**, the strong version of the third meta-axiom.

Determinacy is thus bought at the price of tightening up the third meta-axiom and returning *Homo Economicus* to strict isolation from his/her brethren, of dropping all *complexity* in order to keep *time* and vice versa, of relinquishing meaningful social norms, and of losing social and historical contingency. In brief, the *Inherent Error* ensures that determinacy develops particular imperatives which whip our well-meaning young economist back into the pen. Before he/she knows it, his/her survival instincts drive him/her back to the fold of the original Nash–Debreu–Arrow fictitious pure-exchange economies in which a view of really existing capitalism is as viable as a fire under a mighty waterfall. Having already invested huge intellectual energy, his/her best years and often a large sum of money (e.g. tuition fees and, more importantly lost opportunities and earnings) on coming that far down the analytical (and career) track, it takes a brave and tragic theorist to desist and call it quits. Those who do are never heard of again; those who do not, rise through the ranks.

So, he/she bites the bullet and 'closes' his/her model through the strongest form of the third meta-axiom. Then, after he/she gets his/her teaching position, or is consulted by government officials, he/she is put on the spot with requests for a commentary on how the real world works. The *Dance of Meta-axioms* is what he/she subconsciously performs in response to his/her influential audience's demands. His/her reward is a career in a profession where success is as divorced from the theory's truth status as the theory is from real economies. Before he/she knows it, he/she has entered an evolved priesthood, complete with its mystical beliefs and adorned with decorative mathematics, striking rituals and a well-determined system of rewards and punishments.

This is the reason why we began this book with a quotation (which we reproduce below for convenience) from a famous anthropologist who explained the resilience of a priesthood's influence even when their predictions are consistently proven wrong:

> [The] Azande see as well as we that the failure of their oracle to prophesy truly calls for explanation, but so entangled are they in mystical notions that they must make use of them to account for the failure. The contradiction between experience and one mystical notion is explained by reference to other mystical notions.
>
> Evans-Pritchard (1937, p. 339)

Political economics possesses exactly the same defence mechanism from internal and external criticism. Trading in a completely self-referential belief system, it accounts endogenously for its own explanatory failures.[89] No empirical test, however skilfully devised, can test the theory's non-falsifiable meta-axioms. So, when some of our theorist's models fail to predict reality (which is more often than not), its failure is accounted for by appealing to a model built on the same meta-axioms which failed to produce a sound prediction in the first place. The meta-axioms themselves are never put on trial, and the profession is thus constantly entangled in a ceaseless search for some new model that fits the data better. In the midst of all this, the idea of discussing the logic of really existing capitalism does not even get a look in.

As a matter of fact, political economics is worse than the Azande priesthood in one particular respect: unlike the Azande, in which the failed mystical notions simply spawn new mystical notions of a complexity similar to the old ones, in neoclassically dominated political economics every theoretical failure spawns a new model which, while just as flawed as the previous one, is considerably more complex (mathematically speaking). In this important sense, our priesthood's discursive power increases exponentially through time in proportion to the technical complexity of their narrative. So, their theoretical failures succeed in shielding them with skyrocketing efficiency from external criticism by shrinking fast the circle of people who are both willing to criticise the mainstream and able to 'read' the offered analysis.

So, within the profession, and at a personal level, successful economists find it quite natural to continue with their familiar (and personally lucrative) practices, since, in a never-ending circle, their failed method accounts fully for its own theoretical failure. As long as they stay within the meta-axioms, and apply their considerable technical skills to fashioning increasingly fancy models, which push their theoretical weakness onto increasingly higher levels of abstraction (amplifying them in the process), their work will get published in the journals that 'matter', filling up their pages, and the blackboards of the good universities, with equations 'without the need', in the famous words of Ronald Coase (b. 1910), an economics Nobel prize winner (1991), 'to find out anything about what happened in the real world'.[90]

It is in this sense that no conspiracy is necessary to explain the *Dance of the Meta-axioms*: neoclassical formalism's evolutionary fitness is shored up by an automated process which works best when no formalist is aware of it.

9.7 Capitalism and neoclassicism: A supra-intentional affair

How does mainstream political economics get away with what is, after all, a very thinly disguised form of fraud? Even if Alan Kirman (1989) and Ronald Coase (1994) are right that professional economists have long stopped caring about the truth-status of their wares, does the world not notice their grand failure? Of course it does, at least intuitively. Students are abandoning economics majors in droves; the number of critical voices within the profession grows;[91] and as for the public, official economic 'wisdom', especially after the *Crash of 2008*, causes derision or merriment.

Meanwhile, while mainstream economics is dwindling, the neoclassical stranglehold over it remains as strong as ever. Exactly as the Azande parable predicted, the same neoclassical priesthood who had ruled out a crisis like the *Crash of 2008* shamelessly returned to explain it after the event, employing tweaked up versions of the same, bankrupt neoclassicism which helped bring us the *Crash of 2008*. How do they do it?

In the previous section, we sketched out an explanation of what goes on *within* the economics discipline. But there is a second reason relating to neoclassicism's immense ideological utility, namely the current socio-economic order. The demise of the Cold War did not diminish neoclassicism's ideological utility one bit. If anything, its capacity to rule out *any* systemic analysis of capitalism has increased its stock in the political exchange since 1991.

Lest we forget, since the ninteenth century, capitalism's champions have claimed that it is a *natural*, not a particular, *system*. Its critics (i.e. the Left) have objected that there is nothing natural about capitalism; that it is predicated upon a *particular* grid of political, legal and coercive power which could (and should) have been otherwise. Methodologically, this disagreement translates, simply, into whether human social economies (as opposed to the *Matrix Economy* of Chapter 4, or some fictitious archipelago of preferences, as in Chapter 6) can be fruitfully theorised by models that keep *social structure* separate from *individual agency*.

Imagine, for a moment, that this separation is feasible. It would amount to a recognition that there is something *essential* about human nature which makes it possible to theorise individuals fully before theorising their social context. If this premise is accepted, it is straightforward to imagine a market mechanism as a neutral network that allows fully formed individuals to link up and engage in mutually advantageous intercourse. This view is functional to the further view of capitalism as a *natural system*. In other words, the combination of neoclassicism's first two meta-axioms is, ontologically, in tune with a defence of capitalism as *natural system*.

Of all the brands of political economics, Marginalism uniquely claims that a complete theory of *agency* (e.g. the equi-marginal principle determining Jack and Jill's choices in Chapter 6) can be devised prior to the development of a theory of *structure* (e.g. of the economy's set of prices, of notions of the General Will or Good, of aggregate demand). It is, thus, not an accident that believers in capitalism's virtues are drawn to Marginalism like bees to a honeypot. Once there, the transition to fully fledged neoclassicism is a prerequisite for entry into the respectable economics departments. Nonetheless, this does not mean that economists who make it into the inner circle of the profession are not curious to see what will happen to their theory if they breach the structure–agency separation.[92]

Indeed, many have attempted just that and produced riveting debates in the process. As we noted in the previous section (e.g. the example of psychological games and evolutionary models), mainstream economists built whole careers by tampering with neoclassicism's first two meta-axioms and, in that manner, produced an extraordinary variety of interesting narratives. Unfortunately, the narratives proved too multifarious (what we term *radical indeterminacy*) for the liking of the leading journal editors. At that juncture, their creators faced a dilemma: continue a critical approach to capitalism or get published; accept indeterminacy or revert to the strong variant of the third meta-axiom. Those who chose the former effectively chose to end their careers as top-flight economists.

In this sense, the profession's ostracism of *any* analysis that ventures beyond the three meta-axioms is tantamount to *a decree that every single mainstream economist accepts capitalism as a 'natural system'*. Consequently, what we are left with is a profession churning out technical studies of fictitious markets which act as mere *diversions* from the real task of studying capitalism. Of course, the utility of this feat, for those who have an interest to keep capitalism out of serious theoretical scrutiny, is immense. Capitalism appears in the public's eyes as a complex entity no less natural than the physical universe; it is, we are told, an entity to be analysed with the clinical impartiality of a social physicist, exploited by financial engineers, tamed by 'independent' central bankers and only occasionally criticised by a few superannuated neoclassical economists.

To conclude, neoclassicism takes no political side as long as it relies solely on its first two meta-axioms. But when the third meta-axiom is introduced, it leaps off the political fence and lands squarely on the neoliberal side of the political spectrum. Simply put, neoclassicism comes equipped with an automated trap for those who dare use its power in order to do the 'right thing' and to employ its means in the context of a broad-minded social science agenda. It lures them in on the basis of the flexibility of the first two meta-axioms, based on promises such as 'anything goes' and 'there is no limit to the sophistication or political ideology of *homo economicus*'. However, once they are committed to this type of modelling, it instructs them in no uncertain terms (often using journal editors as omnipotent interlocutors along one's tenure track) that their model is worthless unless it boils down to determinate predictions (that is, to a small number of equilibria). Only then, in a feat of moral panic, does the well-meaning theorist realise the exorbitant price he/she must pay to save his/her life's work: the loss of the merest of possibilities of critically discussing capitalism.

Furthermore, recent neoclassicism and contemporary capitalism have given rise to a similar ontological claim: according to influential commentators, neither any longer exists! They are portrayed as gradually transcending into something altogether 'different'; of having, in fact, 'transformed' themselves out of existence.[93] Evidently, the 'capitalism-has-disappeared' line of argument is jointly functional to capitalism *and* to the dominance of neoclassical political economics. It is functional to capitalism because it helps it remain invisible, shielding it from systematic criticism. And it is functional to neoclassicism because it justifies its insistence on the three meta-axioms.

While the world is struggling, following the *Crash of 2008*, to make sense of the tumult visited upon it by a *particular* strand of globalising capitalism, the latter's best defence comes in the form of thousands of young economists being quick-marched headlong into academic obscurantism and socio-economic irrelevance. Instead of acting as the *avant garde* that will prise out the truth about the causes and nature of the current crisis, they are conscripted to this perpetual feedback mechanism that mutually reinforces (a) the current economic order and (b) the neoclassical core of mainstream economics.

Future social historians, we suspect, will mark this out as our era's most fascinating, *and* most tragic, evolutionary social dynamic. In contrast, historians of social theory will see it as the crowning glory of *Condorcet's Secret*.

Box 9.5 When formalism is applied to economics it turns political. And when it is applied to finance it becomes ruinous

Gerard Debreu is a rare breed of economist. Always alert to his theory's limitations, he steadfastly struggled to stop his followers from implying that his work is more useful than it is. Whenever a colleague dared use results derived from the Nash–Debreu–Arrow framework in order to draw policy implications, Debreu would strike him down with a stern reminder that the theory is too removed from reality to have any policy implications. Faithful to his Bourbakist lineage, he disassociated himself from anyone who wanted to draw him into the political debates between New Dealers and free marketeers, between social democrats and conservatives. Referring to the two General Equilibrium theorems he and Kenneth Arrow famously penned, Debreu (1986, p. 1266) wrote:

> Foes of state intervention read in those two theorems a mathematical demonstration of the unqualified superiority of market economies, while advocates of state intervention welcome the same theorems because the explicitness of their assumptions emphasises discrepancies between the theoretic model and the economies that they observe.

While it is undoubtedly true that the Nash–Arrow–Debreu theorems could easily be bent to the demands of various competing political viewpoints, is it wise to deduce from this that neoclassical formalism is apolitical?[1] We do not believe so. For while its theorems can, indeed, be interpreted differently by readers of different political persuasion, the Nash–Debreu–Arrow method unintentionally blinds all who adopt it to capitalism's particularities. And this is perhaps the greatest ideological interference *any* method could ever aspire to.

Furthermore, there is the question of formalism's unintended consequences in the sphere of finance. In Chapter 12 we shall discuss the role of financial 'products', e.g. the now infamous credit default obligations (to mention one example), in precipitating the *Crash of 2008*. For these 'products' were assigned prices on a particular assumption that comes very close to the strong version (**E**) of the third meta-axiom: the assumption that defaults (i.e. people not being able to repay their mortgages) would not occur in waves; that there would be almost zero correlation between them. The question that the world was asking in the aftermath of 2008 was: *where did the finance theorists who constructed these 'products' find the confidence to assume that default correlations would be low enough to stave off catastrophe?* Our answer will be that they found it in the same place where neoclassicists found the confidence to impose the strong variant (**E**) of the third meta-axiom every time they needed to 'close' one of their models.

Note
1 Gerard Debreu, in an interview in March 1996, argued precisely this: he did not accept that his mathematical models took any political position. He insisted that they could be used by Marxists and libertarians alike: 'Moi, j'adopte simplement l'attitude suivante: que les hypothèses qui portent à des conclusions on peut en faire ce qu'on veut: si cela satisfait les économistes libéraux et les marxisants, parfait! Je ne peux rien demander de mieux. Intellectuellement vous êtes emporté par le courant des idées et vous allez dans la direction où il vous porte'. [As for myself, I take the following view: we can make whatever we like with the assumptions that lead to conclusions. If this satisfies the liberal economists and the *marxisants*, that's fine! I couldn't ask for more. Intellectually you are carried away by the current of ideas and you go to whichever direction it takes you] (Bini and Bruni, 1998).

Box 9.6 Neoclassicism's 'slash and burn' strategy

Has capitalism, as a system, withered to the extent that it is absurd to speak of mainstream economics as its ideological reflection? This ought to be an empirical question. However, the delicious paradox here is that the economists most likely to argue that capitalism has withered (and, therefore, that neoclassicism cannot possibly constitute a reflection of its spirit) are the ones who are least likely to provide such data. This is not an accident. It is a mere manifestation of what Robert Sugden, in his critique of how Darwinian natural selection was adopted by game theorists (Sugden, 2001), refers to as the mainstream's 'slash-and-burn' strategy. A strategy consisting of transplanting into neoclassical political economics ideas and concepts that were developed elsewhere on the back of hard empirical work (e.g. in evolutionary biology). However, the mainstream economists who adopt them do so for the purposes of sprucing up their existing models *without a smidgeon of an interest in the empirical work that would have been required to make the transplantation intellectually viable.*

9.8 Epilogue

Neoclassical political economics draws its immense narrative power from

(a) its demonstrable ambition to explain *all* social phenomena (including non-market outcomes) with the help of three meta-axioms rooted in historical efforts to explain, and ethically cleanse, capitalist activity, while denying that they are so rooted; and

Box 9.7 Wither capitalism?

Neoclassical political economics takes the same position on capitalism that it does on neoclassicism. According to that view, neoclassical economics and capitalism have evolved so much that the terms are now meaningless. Section 9.5 has dispelled the myth that neoclassical economics has withered. But what about capitalism? Can it be argued, reasonably, that technological and social changes have caused a serious rupture in the foundations of capitalism? That what we think of as modern capitalism is so different to the capitalism of Marx and even Keynes that it makes little sense to continue referring to it as capitalist, and subjecting it to the critique of the preceding chapters?

It is true that many commentators nowadays question the term 'capitalist system' on the basis of empirical evidence that the economy is dematerialising, the working class is shrinking inexorably, the nation-state is dwindling in front of our eyes and almost anyone with access to the Internet also enjoys access to capital goods. The argument goes that, as the economic foundation of society shifted during the nineteenth-century from agriculture to heavy industry, it has shifted again towards the end of the twentieth century. On the one hand, the collapse of the USSR and its satellites opened up the whole world not only to globalisation in terms of goods but also, more importantly, to unhindered capital and information transfers. On the other hand, commodity production tilted against heavy industry and in favour of the 'information' or the 'knowledge' economy in which weightless goods, such as computer software, account for a galloping share of aggregate exchange value.

Thus, it is claimed, as the working class shrinks and physical capital loses out to the stock of 'knowledge', the traditional nexus of capital and labour breaks down. The increasing affordability of ultra-modern capital goods renders unnecessary the capitalist's intermediation. Whether in an affluent suburb, a depressed working-class area, or even in the Developing World, a standard laptop computer with an Internet connection is accessible to almost anyone. We are, therefore, all graced with sufficient access to the means of production so as to render passé past definitions of capitalism.

If all this is true, political struggle is no longer centred upon the control of means of production, distribution and exchange, but instead revolves around the production, distribution and accumulation of 'knowledge'. In this brave new society, all we have is networks of interdependent social power. It may not be a fair world but nor is it one that can be made more intelligible by sticking to the antiquated notion of 'the capitalist system' or 'the systemic logic of capitalism'. In fact, as this argument concludes triumphantly, the causes of social justice or equity are best served by a theoretical perspective able to make sense of this new social reality, which cries out for a scientific investigation of power, interplay and interaction. And what is that perspective? The latest version of neoclassical political economics that, courtesy of Game Theory and its offshoots, seems to be the best show in town.

There are two problems with this suave tale. *First*, the neoclassical analysis of this new world of interaction and information feedbacks is not all it is cranked up to be (see previous sections). *Second*, the role of physical capital has hardly changed over the past century or so. Indeed, *neither the economy nor capital are dematerialising*. Although there is no doubt that the relative value of weightless products (e.g. software) is increasing fast, they are no less material in their nature than locomotives or steel. 'Ideas' have no exchange value whatsoever in the New Economy (even if they are great ideas) unless they take the form of a *privately traded commodity*, one that can be packaged individually and sold to a subset of those who want it in a manner that prevents the rest from getting their hands on it without paying.[1] Additionally, *neither the working class nor its capitalist counterpart are vanishing*: while the proportion of blue-collar workers is diminishing in the First World, information technology (IT) disperses production capabilities to countless people who could not sensibly be called capitalists, and pension funds sprinkle specks of capital on to the majority of employees, the worldwide proportion of waged workers (who enjoy neither any significant unearned income nor access to productive means of their own) is rising at a time when control of large corporations, as well as of total wealth, is being more and more concentrated in the hands of fewer and fewer people.

Last, *it is untrue that the new technologies are dissolving the traditional separation of capital and labour*. The New Economy workforce has changed markedly, at least culturally, in comparison to their blue-collar mothers and fathers. Information and communications technology has made it possible for them to work anywhere, even from home, using affordable machines. Their skilled labour is the primary raw material with which they manufacture products of great commercial value. But does this mean that the chasm separating them from the owners of capital has been bridged? Of course it does not. However skilled they may be, they lack the capital that is necessary to set up a viable competitor to, say, Microsoft. Like all profitable sectors in the capitalist past (e.g. the steel industry), the New Economy is also characterised by increasing returns to scale the result of which is high ownership concentration (i.e. oligopolistic capitalist property rights) and continuing reliance on wage labour, often made cheaper through outsourcing. Even a passing glance at the financial press gives the open-minded reader a strong impression of a process of capital formation that has its own logic; a logic that extends well beyond that of the individual entrepreneurs pulling the strings daily.

To sum up, we claim that political economics must transcend neoclassicism if it is to begin to *see* capitalism, let alone explain it, because: (a) the capitalist system encompasses the market system, but remains irreducible to it, (b) it produces an historically realised ideology just as surely as it generates colourful industrial products, designer labels and numerous gizmos, and (c) neoclassicism *is* this ideology's highest theoretical incarnation.

Note
1 Whether the commodity in question is a computer program comprising billions of electrons or the blend of steel, plastic and glass we call a car, it is still a material commodity. Thus all claims that we are moving towards a Platonic realm where ideas are taking over from material output can be safely laughed at. The stock exchanges of the world have already had their laugh, reflecting the fact that the bulk of funds gambled in the late 1990s on the so-called 'New Economy' were generated in the good Old Economy: oil, cars, steel, mining, transport and, of course, banking. The recent price hikes of material commodities, the worldwide renaissance of the steel industry, the rise of the price of oil (in short, the sky-high surge of Indian and Chinese industry) have put to rest any remaining turn-of-millennium messianic narrative on 'dematerialisation'.

(b) an audaciously circular process of mutual reinforcement. Faithful to its constitutive meta-axioms, which it juggles continuously in a manner that hides their implications (and, often, their logical incoherence), neoclassicism retains its hold over the economics mainstream *and* rules itself out of engagement with the logic of really existing capitalism. The latter, supra-intentionally, rewards neoclassicism with institutional power which helps it maintain a strict embargo on any serious scrutiny of its own foundations.

In the terms of this book's ongoing narrative, neoclassical political economics dares press into its own service the discipline's *Inherent Error*. Unlike other strands of political economics, which were embarrassed and weakened by the *Inherent Error*, neoclassicism has feasted on it, gaining in power and stature from its amplification.

It seems almost indelicate to point out that, while this feedback mechanism remains opaque and unexamined by the mainstream's critics, contemporary economic reality and neoclassical political economics will remain strangers who reinforce each other's dominance as long as:

(a) mainstream economics remains innocent of the logic of capitalism, courtesy of its meta-axioms, and
(b) the logic of contemporary capitalism spreads faster and deeper when economics' meta-axioms help it remain invisible.

Quite possibly, never before has intellectual history fashioned an ideological triumph of this magnitude out of a sequence of sorry, yet powerfully motivated, theoretical failures.

10 A manifesto for *Modern Political Economics*

Postscript to *Book 1*

10.1 It works just as well if one doesn't believe in it…

Niels Bohr (1885–1962), the Danish physicist behind quantum mechanics, had a horseshoe pinned above the door of his country home. Upon seeing it, a visiting colleague once told him he could not believe that horseshoes warded off evil spirits. Bohr famously replied: 'I agree. I have it there because I was told it works just as well if one doesn't believe in it' (Pais, 1986: 210).

Bohr was joking. But his joke, unbeknownst to him, is on us, on the house of political economics. Since formalist neoclassicism scored its triumph in the 1950s, and then took over macroeconomics in the 1970s, no sensible politician or entrepreneur *really* believes that economic theory offers anything other than an interesting yet deeply impracticable commentary on capitalism. No one *deep down* thinks that the economists' recommendations do, on average, more good than harm when taken seriously.

Nonetheless, economists 'practise' their trade anyway and politicians speak *as if* their proclamations are founded on solid, scientific economic truths provided by economists. The powers that be pay heed to economics seemingly convinced that 'it works even if no one really believes in it'.

That it works, there is no doubt. But not in the way a science is meant to. No, it works in the same way organised superstition functions to shore up a priesthood attached to a ruling cohort whose power is enhanced the more the superstition spreads through the community. In Chapter 2 we referred to this as *Condorcet's Secret*. Stunning careers are built upon its shenanigans, Nobel Prizes (of sorts) are awarded to its practitioners, countless students are trained to think in its logic (even if fewer and fewer are choosing to major in it); the end result of all this activity being a more unstable capitalism and less comprehension of its instability.

We wrote this book on the conviction that the calamitous events of 2008, which will reduce the life prospects of a whole generation, were due to two interrelated bubbles: the financial *Bubble* and the Econobubble. The former requires no introductions. Its bursting in 2008 brought financialised capitalism to its knees and, once governments bailed it out, the crisis spread to the rest of the economy where the weakest suffered the most.

Less well known is the role in all this of the *Bubble*'s strongest ally: the Econobubble, a frothing of economic theory founded on the certainties of free market faith and propagated by the dynamics of formalist neoclassical economics which took hold in 1950 and came into their own during the time of the *Global Minotaur* (see Chapter 11).

Now, after the world's governments took it upon themselves to save the financial sector, and transferred the immense costs of the bail outs to those who lack the clout to be bailed out themselves, the Econobubble is returning. With no compunction, the same theorists who proclaimed the end of capitalist crises prior to 2008, and a new paradigm of perpetual growth (guaranteed by unregulated markets where everything is privatised), are now the authorities which propose to 'explain' to the masses the *Crash of 2008*.

The Azande sorcerers would have been proud of them! Today's economic priesthood enjoys, in relative terms, living standards that their pre-modern counterparts could never have imagined. Never before have predictive failures of such catastrophic magnitude shored up such enormous social power on behalf of those who make it their business to furnish the failed predictions. And much like Bohr's horseshoe, they do not even require that the purveyors, or indeed anyone else, believe in them …

Box 10.1 The knowledge machine of Laputa
(from Jonathan Swift's Gulliver's Travels, 1726)

The first Professor I saw, was in a very large Room, with Forty Pupils about him. After Salutation, observing me to look earnestly upon a Frame, which took up the greatest Part of both the Length and Breadth of the Room; he said, 'perhaps I might wonder to see him employed in a Project for improving speculative Knowledge, by practical and mechanical Operations. But the World would soon be sensible of its Usefulness; and he flattered himself, that a more noble, exalted Thought never sprang in any other Man's Head. Every one knew how laborious the usual Method is of attaining to Arts and Sciences; whereas, by his Contrivance, the most ignorant Person, at a reasonable Charge, and with a little bodily Labour, might write Books in Philosophy, Poetry, Politicks, Laws, Mathematicks, and Theology, without the least Assistance from Genius or Study. He then led me to the Frame, about the Sides whereof all his Pupils stood in Ranks. It was Twenty Foot square, placed in the Middle of the Room. The Superficies was composed of several Bits of Wood, about the Bigness of a Dye, but some larger than others. They were all linked together by slender Wires. These Bits of Wood were covered on every Square with Paper pasted on them; and on these Papers were written all the Words of their Language, in their several Moods, Tenses, and Declensions; but without any Order. The Professor then desired me to observe, for he was going to set his Engine at work.' The Pupils at his Command, took each of them hold of an Iron Handle, whereof there were Forty fixed round the edges of the Frame; and giving them a sudden Turn, the whole Disposition of the Words was entirely changed. He then commanded Six and Thirty of the Lads to read the several Lines softly, as they appeared upon the Frame; and where they found three or four Words together that might make Part of a Sentence, they dictated to the four remaining Boys who were Scribes. This Work was repeated three or four Times, and at every Turn, the Engine was so contrived, that the Words shifted into new Places, as the square Bits of Wood moved upside down.

Six Hours a-Day the young Students were employed in this Labour; and the Professor shewed me several Volumes in large Folio already collected, of broken Sentences, which he intended to piece together; and out of those rich Materials to give the World a Compleat Body of all Arts and Sciences; which however might be still improved, and much expedited, if the publick would raise a Fund for making and employing five Hundred such Frames in *Lagado*, and oblige the Managers to contribute in common their several Collections.

[Swift (1726 [1995]), pp. 173–5]

10.2 The *Inherent Error*

Could a different type of economic theory from that which rose to dominance after the war deliver enlightenment? No, is our unequivocal (and highly unpopular) answer. In Chapter 1 we foreshadowed this controversial contention by suggesting that, while economic theory is our best shot at understanding social reality, it is an unsafe guide and an exceedingly poor historian. The reason is the *Inherent Error* that no economic theory can shed, however well intentioned its practitioners and sophisticated its approach.

During our trek through the thick foliage of political economics, time and again we saw how each and every attempt at systematising our thinking about *value* and *growth* ended in tears. At the conclusion of every inquiry (e.g. David Ricardo's, Karl Marx's, Piero Sraffa's, or indeed Alfred Marshall's and Léon Walras') we were met with an awful dilemma: choose either a consistent theory of *value or* a theory of *growth*; sacrifice *time* to gain *complexity or* vice versa; treat capitalism like a series of production sectors bereft of consumers *or* like an empire of subjective consumer preferences where production is a species of consumption. To paraphrase the Marx Brothers, this 'science' of ours, economic theory, may *look* like an intellectual *cul-de-sac*; its practitioners may *behave* as if caught up in an intellectual *cul-de-sac*; but do not let that deceive you: economic theory *is* an intellectual *cul-de-sac*.

The cause of this failure is the *Inherent Error*; the inevitable logical inconsistency of any system of ideas whose purpose is to describe capitalism in mathematical or engineering terms. This is not, however, an intellectual failure as such. It is a mere reflection of capitalism's essence, which only appears to us as logical inconsistency when we try to transplant into political economics a mind-frame confined within some fixed 'geometry'. Imagine a theorist that tries to explain complex evolving ecosystems by means of engineering models. What would result but incongruity and a mindset bent on misunderstanding the essence of the *explanandum*; a flight from that which craves explanation?

Political economists are that kind of theorist: nuts-and-bolts mechanics trying to defeat indeterminacy and to replace it with 'closure'; tragi–comic figures struggling to impose a mechanical template upon evolving systems. No matter how skilled as engineers, and irrespective of how adept we are at machining our tools precisely, our efforts are doomed. If anyone doubts that, it is worthwhile looking at what happened when economists accepted the challenge of incorporating evolutionary mechanisms into their study of capitalism's historical dynamics. The exciting logic of Darwinian evolution (according to which complex patterns arise spontaneously from very simple underlying mechanisms) was emptied of all content and thrown onto the pyre of the *Inherent Error*.[1] Like a latter-day Midas, everything that the mainstream economist touches turns into a glittering, barren 'thing', bereft of life and explanatory potential.

This is the stuff of unintended consequences of efforts to transplant a 'scientific' approach to political economics. The best-intentioned political economists begin with a healthy appreciation of the fact that their models are nothing but provisional forays into structured thinking. David Ricardo, Karl Marx, Alfred Marshall and John von Neumann are excellent examples. However, they are inevitably led astray by the very ambition to model economic phenomena by means of 'closed' accounts of all the variables within. As we explained in preceding chapters, this ambition ensures that, before long, the models take over and the provisional terms in which they do their work start regarding themselves as direct reflections of a concrete reality.

Before economists know it, their models auto-reify and turn into totalising ideologies. As if in a bid to reflect the way in which machines ended up subjugating capitalists and workers alike, economic models successfully subjugate the economists, turning them into their 'staff'. The remarkable turning point, around 1950, which spawned formalist neoclassicism, gave rise to a different category of political economist: the logician who, having liberated himself from any interest in capitalism, is quite happy to spend his working life enmeshed in an abstract universe that he knows to be as beautiful as it is irrelevant.

His abstraction, however, proved functional to the post-war socio-economic order which rewarded handsomely lesser scholars; economists who, against the grain of the abstraction's internal logic, utilised it in order to dress up particular policy recommendations with a cloak of fraudulent 'scientific objectivity'. The rest were, meanwhile, confined to the unloved margins. Convinced that they must produce a 'better' model than the one used by the powers that be, the 'dissidents' followed a good instinct to a path that led nowhere. For as long as they seek truth in well-specified models, they too (just like their mainstream rivals) are at the *Inherent Error*'s mercy.

If our diagnosis is correct, the point is not to replace one form of modelling with another. It is, rather, to accept the limits of economic theory; to come to terms with the *Inherent Error*; to use our engagement with economic theory as a training ground in which to practise before D-day; before, that is, we attempt to wrestle with our economic and political reality. In this sense, *Book 1* was the training ground and *Book 2* is our very own D-day.

Attempting to make sense of the post-2008 world, which will be our task in the remainder of this book, would be futile without a serious engagement with economic theory. Equally, the truth about our world does not reside in the theory, its mathematics, or its overall logical structure. On the one hand, we must engage (as we did in *Book 1*) with every single model furnished by the political economists. But then, before tackling the real issues confronting the real world, we must see each and every one of these models as indispensable but *incomplete* mental exercises; as *necessary errors* on the road to the possibility of enlightenment.

In short, economics' *Inherent Error* cannot be defeated by the power of our Reason. Reason can only overcome it by reaching out to, and engaging with, History.

10.3 Shameful subterfuge: Or how to poison the minds of the young

We finished Chapter 6 with the magnificently prophetic words of Antoine Augustine Cournot. 'Cournot's hunch', we wrote there,

> at a remarkably early stage in the development of contemporary capitalism, was that Walras' type of political economics was to become the most potent, the most dangerous, *blue pill*. That it would lull the world with a Panglossian portrayal of capitalism and would silence the Cassandras whose tragedy was that the more sensible their warnings the less discernible their voices. Meanwhile, the surer the economics profession was becoming of capitalism's Panglossian properties the nearer it edged to the *Great Convulsion*.

How right Cournot was! In the 1950s, Gerard Debreu and Kenneth Arrow, drawing upon John F. Nash Jr, proved their 'welfare theorems' which were to mark the *Formalists*' triumph. It was no more than a formalist proof that Walras' type of General Equilibrium exists on paper (under particular restrictions). Nothing more, nothing less. But let's see how that proof was interpreted by a prominent economist of our era, as if in order to confirm Cournot's ancient premonition. The economist in question is *Olivier Blanchard*, a Frenchman who headed the MIT Department of Economics (which Paul Samuelson had set up almost single-handedly), wrote one of the leading textbooks by which our young learn macroeconomic theory, and is currently Chief Economist of the IMF (the International Monetary Fund).

Blanchard had this to say about the Nash–Debreu–Arrow formalist project and the theorems it spawned:

> More than 200 years ago, Adam Smith explained that in a market economy individual egoisms combined to bring about the best possible outcome for the community. This proposition was so surprising and so full of consequences that it became necessary to understand its nature and its limits. Thanks to Walras at the beginning of the 20th century, and furthermore thanks to economists like Arrow or Debreu fifty years later, and especially thanks to a huge effort of abstraction and to powerful mathematical tools, the conditions of Adam Smith's theorem have been clarified.[2]

Leaving aside serious doubts that Adam Smith would approve of what Walras and the formalists allegedly did in his name,[3] Blanchard goes on to interpret the Nash–Debreu–Arrow theorems as follows:

> Having clarified the necessary conditions required to satisfy the Adam Smith theorem, research has been directed almost entirely into investigating what happens when the conditions are not satisfied. Namely, why some markets work badly, and what type of institutions have to be put in place in order to improve their working.

Note the leap of undiluted faith from the formalist model to the real world. Blanchard's claim is that the formalism can help us understand why some *real* markets work badly. It is as if Gerard Debreu had never issued his legendary warning that 'the theory … is logically entirely disconnected from its interpretations'.

The whole Blanchard argument is a complete *non sequitur*. *No* investigation of the circumstances under which a Walrasian General Equilibrium will *not* obtain can illuminate the causes of real market failures. Why? Because the theory hangs together only under assumptions that push it onto a universe in which real capitalist markets could not, physically, exist. Is it not the duty of a leading textbook writer to spell this out? Anything less, we submit, is intellectual poison, especially for the young minds who treat a famous textbook writer as an authority on the subject matter.

Alan Kirman (1989), one of formalism's leading lights, sums up our conclusion thus:

> In conclusion, then, it is worth repeating that recent theoretical work has shown how little the Walrasian model has to say about aggregate behaviour. Economists therefore should not continue to make strong assertions about this behaviour based on so-called General Equilibrium models which are, in reality, no more than special examples with no basis in economic theory as it stands.

Does Olivier Blanchard not know this? He ought to, and we think he does. But such is his ideological inner drive to argue that his policy recommendations are founded on a bedrock of good mathematics, that he is being economical with the truth. More disturbing even than this naked act of dishonesty is what Blanchard and his merry colleagues do in order to arrive at their policy recommendations (e.g. the ones he pushes onto the world community as Chief Economist at the IMF). Given the utter inability of Walrasian or Nash–Debreu–Arrow theorems to say anything tangible about the real world, they return to the single sector or Robinson Crusoe types of economies. There is nothing like strong (often austere) economic policies derived from false premises to inspire sheer horror in the hearts and minds of those in the know.[4]

10.4 Modern Political Economics: The primacy of radical indeterminacy

Book 1's driving force can be described as an *impossibility theorem*. Because of the *Inherent Error*, we have argued, all models become inconsistent with some crucial aspect of really existing capitalism. When theorists try to squeeze consistency out of their models, the result is failure. While such failure can leave their job prospects unaffected (or even, sometimes, enhanced), eventually it deprives the theory of persuasive power. And when, eventually, the logical incoherence is revealed, the theory is rejected wholesale, the proverbial baby being thrown out together with the bathwater. The result is that which we termed *lost truths*.

For example, Ricardo's insistence of squaring his value theory with a theory of growth led to Malthus's devastating critique; Marx's desperate attempt to close his model led to the *transformation problem* and the contorted logic required for its resolution; the Marginalists' insistence of explaining all prices and quantities by means of the equi-marginal principle forced them, eventually, to stick to Robinson Crusoe-like economies, etc. The trouble with these failures was that, once their logical incoherence became apparent, and the political order no longer had uses for them, they led the following generations of economists to drop them wholesale, together with the important insights contained within. And if this has not happened just yet with neoclassicism, because of its continuing political utility, eventually it will.

In the past eight chapters, *Book 1* has been consistently pounding this simple point: that the *Inherent Error* plaguing all of economic modelling is also responsible for the fact that today's crop of economists are oblivious to *lost truths* – insights about capitalism that were, once, better known by their predecessors. So, whereas even right wing economists at the turn of the twentieth century benefited significantly from Marx's thought (e.g. Joseph Schumpeter who has acknowledged his gratitude to Marx for the development of his idea of 'creative destruction'), today's crop has no access to such truths. Oblivious to the lessons learnt by previous generations of political economists, they march straight into their own Waterloos.

What should we do, in view of this repetitive process of theoretical failure, caused by different manifestations of the *Inherent Error*, and followed by the loss of important truths? This book has a recommendation so simple and yet so controversial: *adopt Sisyphus's optimal strategy!* That is, stop pushing the rock up the hill. The might of the *Inherent Error* cannot be overcome either through Reason or by the Power of our Will. The impossibility of the task should not give us extra energy to tackle it but ought to grant us pause to think of that which constitutes our real task: to explain the real world and, if possible, to improve upon it.

But this means a complete disengagement from the *Inherent Error*, which is the same thing as a retreat from the project of discovering the truth about capitalism within some determinate abstraction; within some 'closed' model. In methodological terms, this is equivalent to abandoning rigid meta-axioms even if the price we have to pay is *radical indeterminacy*. Would the latter constitute a serious defeat? As the previous chapters have shown, it constitutes no such thing: for even when we impose the most stringent of meta-axioms, radical indeterminacy cannot be avoided. Why then pay the price exacted by the meta-axioms

	Agency		Regularity		
	Strong Meth. Ind. (D)	Strong Meth. Instr. (S)	Strong Meth. Equilibration (E)	Spontaneous Order (O)	Reducibility of human action (R)
Ricardo - Sraffa	✗	✗	✓	✗	✓
Marx	✗	✗	✓	✗	✗
Marginalists	✓	✓	✗	✗	✓
Marginalists-cum-Neoclassicists	✓	✓	✓	✗	✓
Austrian Marginalists	✓	✓	✗	✓	✗
Keynes	✓	✓	✗	✗	✗
MPE	✗	✗	✗	✗	✗

Figure 10.1 The six meta-axioms of political economies.

(i.e., total historical blindness and a sequence of serious violations of logic) when, in truth, they do not even deliver us from indeterminacy?

Chapter 9 defined the currently dominant variant of political economics in terms of three meta-axioms (recall Section 9.4). Figure 10.1 above extends this definition to all variants of political economics in this book. The first three columns correspond to neo-classicism's three meta-axioms. Naturally, the fourth row which corresponds to Marginalism-*cum*-neoclassicism reports ticks in these first three columns. The difference with Marginalism (the third row), neoclassicism's original starting point, is that the Marginalists who never espoused the neoclassical penchant for imposing equilibrium (as opposed to explaining convergence toward equilibrium, e.g. Cournot) did not adopt meta-axiom **E** (notice that there is no tick in the third, row third column cell). And since economists of the Austrian persuasion and John Maynard Keynes also locate their roots in that form of Marginalism, while steadfastly refusing to *assume* equilibrium a priori, they too 'get' ticks in the first two rows, but not in the third.

In contrast, David Ricardo, the neo-Ricardian Pierro Sraffa and Karl Marx, like all classical economists, make no assumptions about individual *agency*, and thus get crosses (see the first two rows under **D** and **S**). Of course, courtesy of their imposed assumption that inter-temporal equilibrium prevails in the macro-economy (as the rate of profit tends to equalise across the different sectors; and supply equals demand for all produced commodities), they get ticks in the third column (**E**).

To sum up so far, the first two columns (meta-axioms **D** and **S**, carried intact from Chapter 9) typify an individualist approach to *agency*. In such accounts, *structure* is to be explained by an *agency* located in individual action that is instrumental and comes prior to *structure*. The next two columns concern the manner in which the theorist comes to firm conclusions about *regularity*, without which no firm predictions can be made (and regardless of whether the agency boxes are ticked or not).

There are two ways in which we can extract *regularity* from a theoretical model: the most common one is through the strong meta-axiom of methodological equilibration (**E**), that is, by assuming equilibrium not only exists but, additionally, that it is the only state of the economy worth studying. Interestingly, both neoclassicists and classical economists, including Marx, took that step. In Chapter 5 we argued that this was a pivotal choice by Marx, motivated by his political agenda and one that led to a logical impasse that has plagued many of his followers ever since. Chapter 9, on the other hand, demonstrated neoclassicism's grand (though very peculiar) failure as a result of combining the first three meta-axioms (**D**,**S** and **E**).

Meta-axiom **E** is, arguably, so strong and logically unwarranted, that a number of Marginalists refused to espouse it. The first to refuse **E** was Cournot, who even sounded a warning to the effect that humanity might embark upon a lethal path if **E** is endorsed together with **D** and **S**. Beyond Cournot, the Austrian school turned **E** down, perhaps because of the fact that their point of origin was a critique of Marx's espousal of **E**. Nevertheless, since they were just as politically driven as Marx (even though they were trying to make precisely the opposite point to his), they too craved *regularity*. For without *regularity*, no theory has firm predictions. And without firm predictions, how can a political economist advocate particular policies?

For this reason, the Austrian School came up with an interesting alternative to **E**: the idea of a *spontaneous order* that is 'as good as it gets'. They begin their narrative by endorsing the first two meta-axioms (which define human ontology and the way we must conduct economic 'science') but they reject the notion that some equilibrium will result. For if it could, human Reason might be able to work out what that equilibrium would be, and then socialism might be justifiable (as a system that imposes that very equilibrium).

To render socialism wholly indefensible, they had to argue that equilibrium is neither possible nor desirable. Thus they put forward the hypothesis that, due to the irreducibility of human knowledge to some well-defined mathematical function, no central plan and no collective agency (i.e. a state, a municipality, a club) can generate social outcomes. The best humanity can hope for is the social outcome that will emerge *spontaneously* if people and markets are 'left alone'. Thus, the Austrians sought *regularity* in the *spontaneous order* resulting from free intercourse (a meta-axiom we label **O** in Figure 10.1) between persons (who are to be theorised on the basis of the first two meta-axioms, **D** and **S**).

The Austrians were not the only ones to reject **E** while embarking from an individualist perspective consistent with the first two meta-axioms (**D** and **S**). John Maynard Keynes was another such thinker. The difference was that he was not a believer! Indeed, his best work reflects the 'we are damned if we know' logic, as outlined in Chapter 7. In short, Keynes did not believe in the *inevitability* of *any* kind of *regularity*, of either the equilibrium (**E**) or the spontaneous order (**O**) types. For this reason, Figure 10.1 awards him only two ticks, courtesy of his roots in his teachers' (and in particular Alfred Marshall's) Marginalism.[5]

We end our discussion of Figure 10.1 with the last column which captures whether the 'mind-frame' of the thinkers in each different row is predicated upon human reductionism, upon, that is, a readiness to think of men and women, indeed of children too, as analytically equivalent to machines, to a mathematical mapping of outcomes to some index of preference satisfaction, or, at best, to the algorithms running our magnificent computers.

The British classical economists embraced human reductionism clearly and knowingly. Adam Smith and David Ricardo left no room in their political economics for economic insights that are uniquely due to the indeterminacy of human nature. In their economic writings, humans appear as machine-like, preprogrammed creatures.[6] The first political economist to have based an important *economic insight* on the irreducibility of the human person to a quantifiable, machine-like entity, was of course Karl Marx (recall Chapters 4 and 5). But so did the Austrians and, of course, Keynes (thus the crosses in the respective cells in the last column).

The Austrians rejected the idea that information equals knowledge and that it is a technical matter to aggregate it all into one large, hard disk-like device. They rejected the notion of some economy-wide equilibrium because they rejected the idea that human knowledge is like grains of sand to be piled up by a process of mechanical aggregation. Similarly, Keynes opposed the view that investors and consumers predict the future in a manner ontologically no different from performing a technically difficult computation. For reasons that are related to their appreciation of the *Inherent Error*, both the Austrians and Keynes thought that there is no such thing as a sufficiently narrow set of rational expectations that agents, if clever enough, could home in on.

In summary, Karl Marx, the Austrians and John Maynard Keynes set themselves apart from the rest of political economists by treating the indeterminate human element as a crucial analytical datum. Of these three, however, only Keynes felt sufficiently liberated from his own ideological imperative to present an argument in favour of, or against, capitalism. He took it for granted that he liked capitalism and did not need to prove its superiority or desirability. What concerned him was capitalism's capacity for self-suicide; period.

In this spirit, Keynes embarked upon his *General Theory* in order to furnish practical advice on how to manage capitalism's depressive character effectively. For this reason Figure 10.1's penultimate row (dedicated to Keynes) features no ticks in the last three columns: Keynes, having rejected that human reasoning can be reduced to the operations of an algorithm, did not trust capitalism to equilibrate or regulate itself.

Which brings us to Figure 10.1's last row, the one enigmatically labelled **MPE**. This is our column and its purpose is to act as a brief manifesto for our *Modern Political Economics*. It is a simple four-word manifesto: *no meta-axioms please.* 'Closed' models are destined to fall prey to the *Inherent Error* and the *Inherent Error* is what stands between us and a decent grasp of reality. The only scientific truth about capitalism is its *radical indeterminacy*, a condition which makes it impossible to use science's tools (e.g. calculus and statistics) to second guess it. The more we feel we have capitalism's number, the closer we get to the moment when it will astonish us with (what our 'closed' models told us was) an almost zero probability event. When the improbable becomes fact, our only hope is that the casualties will not be too numerous.

But what are the sources of the *radical indeterminacy*? Keynes partially answered that question. In multi-sector, financialised capitalist economies, consumers and investors lack the data that would allow them, even if they possessed God's own computing capacities, to construct a determinate mathematical expectation of what the future holds. Like ships with de-magnetised compasses sailing on a starless night, they tend to follow one another along self-confirming paths. *Even if captained by supremely experienced sailors*, they may make it safely to port or they may all be led astray, ending up marooned on shoals from which they cannot extricate themselves.

In summary, because of the impossibility of uniquely rational answers to pressing questions, such as 'How much should I save?' and 'Should I invest now?', consumption and investment are at the mercy of the *Cunning of Reason* (which Keynes mislabelled *animal spirits*). But there is another source of *radical indeterminacy* that Keynes ignored, possibly because he was unwilling to recognise its location in the veins of a class of people upon whom he was conditioned to look down: human *labour* which (as Karl Marx taught us) is the life-giving force that runs through capitalism bestowing value and even life upon mere 'things', albeit only as long as it remains *indeterminate*; irreducible, that is, to an electricity-like force. It is this vivifying, indeterminate energy that creates *capital* out of mere machines, a relatively newfangled force with the astonishing capacity both to liberate and to enslave the humans that work it and, with equal force, the humans that own it.

In brief, without a grasp of the *dialectical nature of both labour and capital* it becomes impossible to understand:

(a) the dynamics of a capitalist economy *and*
(b) the ways in which irrepressibly free humans become increasingly enslaved by their artefacts.

Our hypothesis is that to make sense of capitalism we need to capture (a) and (b), and to combine them with Keynes' successful escape from the *Inherent Error*. The task is equivalent to introducing into political economics, as 'data', the two sources of *radical indeterminacy*:

 (i) the irreducibility of labour input, and thus capital, to some well defined metric; *and*
(ii) the irreducibility of human forecasts to a well-defined mathematical expectation function.

As long as (i) and (ii) are combined with a determination to assume neither *equilibrium* (which was Marx's error) nor *spontaneous order* (as is the Austrians' religious wont), we stand a chance of grasping our present moment in history. Moreover, the events of 2008 are better understood as our collective punishment for the economists' greatest sin: the assumption that *radical indeterminacy* can be tamed by means of formalist meta-axioms at one level and simple pricing formulae at another level, the one on which financialisation procured its splendid fantasies.

10.5 Epilogue: Making sense of the post-2008 world

To make sense of anything, let alone of something as complex as the post-2008 capitalist reality, two lethal enemies must be evaded. One is *relativism*, the philosophical rejection that anything *can* be known objectively about the reality 'out there'. The other is *determinism*, an ambition to create some 'closed' system of mutually consistent components that provide each other's cause.

Relativism, in its various guises (ranging from ancient Greek *Sophism* to contemporary *Postmodernism*) rejects theory as anything more than yet another (slightly more pompous) narrative. *Determinism*, on the other hand, stakes a claim to having reduced reality to its bare essentials; and then of having put it back together in the form of a 'closed' model of reality. Our brand of political economics appropriates the epithet *modern* to reflect (a) our disavowal of postmodern *relativism* and (b) our repudiation of *determinism*, primitive modernism's trademark.

> *Question:* Is there an objective economic reality 'out there' to be understood rationally?
> *Answer:* Absolutely!

> *Question:* Can we understand it by means of determinate abstractions or 'closed' models?
> *Answer:* Absolutely not!

To broaden our point, let us for a moment dip into Niels Bohr's world of quantum mechanics. In that weird and wonderful universe, where everything is pregnant with its contradiction, a photon can pass through two different gates at once. Light can behave like a string of particles one moment and like a mass-less wave the next. Quanta turn out to be deeply indeterminate, in the sense that it is ontologically impossible (as opposed to just difficult) to determine *at once* where they are, their mass, and the speed at which they are travelling. And as if that were not enough, the unfolding phenomena (on which our macro world is built) can never be approached by determinate models (not even by models incorporating randomness and probabilities). Why? Because our attempts to observe them alter the very phenomena in radically unpredictable ways.

In physics this is known as the *Heisenberg Principle*. In political economics, a similar idea appeared in Chapter 7 as the *we are damned if we know* principle. The reader may even recall our parable (see Box 7.5) of macroeconomic forecasting as weather prognostication on a planet where the weather responds to our average weather forecasts. In that world, much like in that of quantum mechanics, no determinate model can tell you what will happen. To entertain genuine rational expectations is to expect the unexpected.

The point of dipping into quantum mechanics is to demonstrate that to admit to radical indeterminacy is not to yield to the sirens of *Postmodernism*, whose objective is to lull us into a renouncement of the idea of a reality 'out there' and the loss of any ambition to approach it rationally. Just like physicists have not given up on their attempts to understand the microcosm of quanta, we have no intention of forfeiting the ambition to rationalise capitalism.

But how should we do that? *Book 1* has presented different theories, often enthusiastically, but concluded that each was, at best, a *necessary error*. Was it a waste of time? Do we now have to make sense of the post-2008 world without any genuine assistance from theory? Have we returned to the beginning, no wiser than when we started? We leave it to the poet to find the perfect words to answer these questions on our behalf:

> We shall not cease from our exploration
> And at the end of all our exploring
> Will be to arrive where we started
> And know the place for the first time[7]

Our study of 'closed' models in *Book 1* did, indeed, lead to their rejection. But, though we may feel we have returned to our point of embarkation empty-handed, the truth is that we can now recognise in it features that before were opaque to our eyes. We are now able to know the 'place' in a profound way like never in the past. Yes, we labelled all models *errors*; but we also called them *necessary*. Without them, our discussion of capitalism would not differ from that of second-rate journalists. The models in the preceding chapters yielded false views, like the one we get when looking from an angle at a stick that is half submerged in water. From our viewpoint, it looks bent. From another viewpoint, it also looks bent, only the discontinuity seems to come at a different angle and to occur at a different point in relation to the stick's apparent mid-point. Physicists refer to this as the *parallax*. The stick is real and straight but, while submerged, and depending on our standpoint, it looks bent.[8]

In Box 4.10 we summoned the *dialectic* as a device for overcoming unhelpful binary oppositions on the way to coming to grips with the underlying reality. We do the same here to suggest that capitalism is like the proverbial parallax stick and our models of it, the *necessary errors*, are different viewpoints. Each leads to an erroneous conclusion but when taken together they have the potential to *become* the raw materials which our Reason can synthesise into a decent grasp of reality.

In this vein, to make sense of the post-2008 world we need to transcend our models, not eliminate them. It was important that, first, we looked at their meta-axioms and, thus, understood their architecture and the particular error toward which each of the meta-axioms pushed us. Now that we have a good sense of the limits of fixed geometry explanations, we are free to break, cleanly and resolutely, from all meta-axioms, in the same way the human mind, at some point, realises that the half submerged stick is straight, even though our eyes tell it differently.

How does our Reason overcome the appearance to grasp the reality when all of its 'viewpoints' are partial and, effectively, misleading? The simple answer is this: it combines the contradictory views from the different observation points by means of a reasoning process irreducible to the empirical evidence derived at each viewpoint. A pluralist disposition (i.e. one that causes us to devour all sorts of different models *without becoming hostage to any of them*) therefore becomes the foundation of a rational, modern, political economics.

Thus we arrive at our next task. Equipped with the necessary, but erroneous, viewpoints provided by the different shades of political economics in the preceding pages, we shall now attempt to synthesise them into a theory of 2008 and its aftermath; to an understanding of late capitalism that is the equivalent to the realisation that the stick is straight.

Almost certainly, our conclusion will be more jagged and far less convincing than the physicist's rational overcoming of the parallax view. But we take solace from the fact that capitalism generates complexity of a higher order than anything a stick and a volume of water can produce. Our ambition is, anyhow, no greater than to take a wobbly first step towards a worthy path. Hopefully, others will follow down that path, along a thoroughly modern political economics leading to a helpful rationalisation of our stunningly irrational socio-economic order.

Book 2

Modern political economics

Theory in action

11 From the *Global Plan* to a *Global Minotaur*

The two distinct phases of post-war US hegemony

11.1 A *Global Plan* is born

The *Crash of 2008* began in the United States for reasons that could be clearly traced to its serially profligate financial sector. It broke out at a time when the United States government was labouring under a gargantuan deficit and the economy at large was plagued by the mother of all trade deficits with the rest of the world. Any other country with a brittle fiscal position, a heavily indebted citizenry, a large trade deficit and an oversized financial bubble that burst with a tremendous bang, would be facing an exodus of capital, people, resources. And yet, the *Crash of 2008* caused a flight *to* the US dollar.

Put differently, the United States of America is not 'any other country'. To wrap our minds around its special place in the world, and the paradoxical manner in which crises caused within attract to it capital from without, we need to begin our inquiry around 70 years earlier.

The United States of America came out of the Second World War as the major and, in fact, if one excludes Switzerland, the *only* creditor nation. For the first time since the rise of capitalism, all of the world's trade relied on a single currency, the dollar, financed from a single epicentre, Wall Street. While half of Europe was under the control of the Red Army, and Europeans were openly questioning the merits of the capitalist system, the New Dealers, who had been running Washington since 1932, realised that history had presented them with a remarkable opportunity – the opportunity to erect a post-war global order that would cast American hegemony in stainless steel. It was an opportunity that they seized with glee.

Their audacious scheme sprang from the two sources that lie behind every great achievement: *Fear* and *Power*. The war endowed the United States with great military and economic power. But, at the same time, it acted as a constant reminder of American failure to come properly to terms with the legacy of 1929 before the Japanese navy unleashed its bombs and torpedoes over Pearl Harbor. The New Dealers never forgot the unexpectedness of the Great Depression and its resistance to 'treatment'. The more power they felt they had in their hands the greater their fear that a new 1929 could turn it into thin ash running through their fingers.

Even before the guns had gone silent in Europe, and before the Soviet Union emerged as a dragon to be slain, the United States understood that it had inherited the historic role of reconstructing, in its image, the world of global capitalism. For if 1929 nearly ended the dominion of capital at a time of multiple capitalist centres, what would a new 1929 do when the whole game revolved around a single axis; namely the dollar?

In 1944 the New Dealers' anxieties led to the infamous Bretton Woods conference (see Box 11.1 below). The idea of designing a new global order was not so much grandiose as it was essential. At Bretton Woods a new monetary framework was designed placing the Dollar

Box 11.1 The Bretton Woods Conference
Setting up the Global Plan's monetary framework

While the war was still raging in Europe and the Pacific, in July 1944, 730 delegates converged upon the plush Mount Washington Hotel located in the New Hampshire town of Bretton Woods. Over three weeks of intensive negotiations, they hammered out the nature and institutions of the postwar global monetary order.

They did not come to Bretton Woods spontaneously but at the behest of President Roosevelt whose New Deal administration was determined to win the peace, after almost having lost the war against the Great Depression. The one lesson the New Dealers had learnt was that capitalism cannot be managed effectively at a national level. In his opening speech Roosevelt made that point with commendable clarity:

> The economic health of every country is a proper matter of concern to all its neighbours, near and far.

The two issues that were, ostensibly, central to the conference were (a) the design of the postwar monetary system and (b) the reconstruction of the war-torn economies of Europe and Japan. However, under the surface, the real questions concerned the institutional framework that would keep a new Great Depression at bay and who would be in control of that framework. Both questions created significant tensions, especially between the two great allies represented, in the US corner, by Harry Dexter White[1] and, in the UK corner, by none other than John Maynard Keynes. In the aftermath of the conference, Keynes remarked:

> We have had to perform at one and the same time the tasks appropriate to the economist, to the financier, to the politician, to the journalist, to the propagandist, to the lawyer, to the statesman – even, I think, to the prophet and to the soothsayer.
>
> (Keynes, 1944 [1980])

Two of the institutions that were designed at Bretton Woods are still with us and still in the news. One is the International Monetary Fund (IMF), the other the *International Bank for Reconstruction and Development*, which developed to today's *World Bank*. The IMF was to be the global capitalist system's 'fire brigade'; an institution that would rush to the assistance of any country whose house caught (fiscal) fire, handing out loans under strict conditions that would ensure that the failures would be fixed and the loans repaid. As for the *World Bank*, its role would be of an international investment bank with a remit to direct productive investments in regions of the world devastated by the war and promising a decent return in the future.

However, the one institution that left the greatest mark on postwar history is no longer with us, its demise in 1971 marking the end of the *Global Plan* and the beginning of the second postwar phase which we label the *Global Minotaur*. It was the new exchange rate regime that came to be known as the Bretton Woods system. During the debate on what that new system should look like, John Maynard Keynes made the most audacious proposal that has ever reached the bargaining table of a major international conference: Create an International Currency Union (ICU), a single currency (which he even christened, naming it the 'bancor') for the whole capitalist world, with its own *International Central Bank* and institutions to match (Keynes 1980).

Keynes' proposal was not as impudent as it seems. *First*, it would not be the first time that the world would be bound together by a single currency. The Gold Standard that was killed off by the Great Depression (after having contributed handsomely to its amplification – see Chapter 7) had operated, effectively, as a means of fixing the exchange rates of different currencies (with reference to gold). Nations, thus, were already familiar with the idea of some form of monetary unification. *Second*, his proposal was designed to combine the advantages of the single currency (price stability, predictability in international trading) with remedies for the great failing of the Gold Standard: the fact that, by restricting the quantity of money in each country to a pre-specified level linked to its gold deposits, it prevented governments from dealing with catastrophic declines in effective demand (e.g. the *Crash of 1929*) by means of increased public expenditures.

Additionally, Keynes' idea was aimed at resolving another intrinsic problem that the Gold Standard had proven itself incapable of addressing: *systematic trade imbalances*. Keynes believed, correctly, that some countries or regions are in systematic deficit with other countries or regions, which enjoy an equally systematic surplus. (The European Union today is a good case in point.) Keynes' proposed ICU was designed to deal both with these problems: catastrophic crashes and systematic trade imbalances.

Having spent the previous decade studying the causes of the Great Depression, and the role of the exchange rate regime in fomenting it, Keynes' great concern about the post-war order was how to prevent a repetition of debt-deflation in countries that find themselves in a trade deficit: a downward spiral where the deficit country is forced to pay higher interest rates to service its increasing debts, reacts by cutting down its public spending, realises that these cuts put the domestic economy in a nose-dive (as national income begins to shrink) and, finally, loses all means by which to arrest this free-fall. And if other deficit countries enter the same downward cycle, e.g. as a result of a rise in the interest rates they have to pay, then these competitive devaluations will submerge a large part of the world economy under recessionary tidal waves. It takes no great imagination to conclude that this could lead to a new depression, as 'Great' as that of the 1930s. Indeed, come to think of it, Keynes might as well have been thinking about the crisis that befell the Eurozone in 2010!

Keynes' proposed remedy was simple: the ICU would grant each member country an overdraft facility, i.e. the right to borrow at zero interest from the *International Central Bank*. Loans in excess of 50 per cent of a deficit country's average trade volume (measured in bancors) would also be made but at the cost of a fixed interest rate. However, at the same time, there would be a penalty for excess trade surpluses: recognising that a systematic surplus is the other side of the problematic coin of a systematic deficit, Keynes' proposal stipulated that any country with a trade surplus exceeding a similar percentage of its trade volume would be charged interest and its currency would, therefore, have to appreciate (thus effecting a capital transfer to the deficit countries).

Lionel Robbins, an influential British economist and the pioneer behind the rise of the London School of Economics and Political Science, wrote that, upon hearing

Keynes' proposals, the conference participants were stunned. '[I]t would be difficult to exaggerate the electrifying effect on thought throughout the whole relevant apparatus of government … nothing so imaginative and ambitious had ever before been discussed.'[2]

Alas, it was not to be. The ICU did not come into being for the simple reason that the United States was neither ready to share world hegemony nor, more importantly, to accept that, in the post-war era, its trade with the rest of the world should be balanced. The New Dealers, however respectful they might have been of John Maynard Keynes, had another plan: a *Global Plan* according to which the dollar would become the effective world currency[3] and the United States would export goods *and* capital to Europe and Japan in return for direct investment and political patronage; a hegemony based on the direct financing of foreign capitalist centres in return for an American trade surplus with them.

For this reason, the US representative, Harry Dexter White, vetoed Keynes' plan[4] and, in its stead, proposed a simpler alternative: a system of fixed exchange rates with the dollar at its heart. Each currency would be locked to the dollar at a given exchange rate. Fluctuations would be allowed only within a narrow band of, plus or minus, one per cent which governments would try to stay within by buying or selling their own dollar reserves. A re-negotiation of the exchange rate of a particular country was only allowed if it could be demonstrated that its balance of trade and its balance of capital flows could not be maintained given its dollar reserves. As for the United States, to create the requisite confidence in the international system, it committed to peg the dollar to gold at the fixed exchange rate of $35 per ounce of gold and to guarantee full gold convertibility for anyone, American or non-American, wanting to swap their dollars for gold.

To address concerns about the lack of a Plan B in the case where a country or countries would land in a tight fiscal spot, and the concomitant danger that this might drag the whole world down, the New Dealers proposed the setting up of an International Stabilisation Fund, which was soon renamed the International Monetary Fund, our familiar IMF. While the IMF did have the capacity to come to the rescue of states with a deteriorating fiscal position, in the form of short- and medium-term loans, nothing was put in place to prevent the creation of systematic trade imbalances. Ironically, perhaps the greatest victim of such imbalances was the United States itself. Of course, it took another 20 years or so for this development to arise.

Notes

1 White was an ardent New Dealer and avowed Keynesian. Having earned an economics PhD from Harvard, he served in the US Treasury as assistant to Secretary Henry Morgenthau. A committed internationalist, he played a crucial role in the Bretton Woods negotiations which led, among other things, to the creation of the International Monetary Fund. White went on to represent the USA at the IMF and to act as its director. In 1947, as the Cold War was brewing, he resigned abruptly under a cloud of innuendo that he had acted as a Soviet spy. He died the following year of a heart attack.

2 Quoted in van Dormael 1978, p.35.

3 It is important to note that, as the war was coming to its conclusion, all war-torn European nations were highly indebted to the USA and transferred large amounts of gold to the USA, a fact that contributed to the latter's determination to turn the dollar into the Bretton Wood's system's central axis.

4 White's unequivocal words were: 'We have been perfectly adamant on that point. We have taken the position of absolutely no'.

at the epicentre of the capitalist world. But before it could be effected, some serious preparatory groundwork had to be done. It took another 15 years before the Bretton Woods agreement could be implemented (it finally got underway in 1959). During that period, the United States had to put together the essential pieces of the jigsaw puzzle that we call the *Global Plan*.

The *Global Plan*'s first strand was the urgency to end the dollar's monopoly by creating another two world currencies which would support the dollar and act as shock absorbers in case of another severe recession in the United States itself. Without these supporting pillars, the Bretton Woods monetary system would be hanging in mid-air. However, to shore up these two currencies, a second strand was required. To make these currencies strong or at least viable, a heavy industry had to underpin each and a surrounding trade zone, a form of *Lebensraum* or vital space, had to be conjured up so as to ensure that its manufacturing products would find buyers.

The New Dealers (see Box 11.2) thus, understood that their work was cut out for them. Had they not been energised by the experience of running the War Economy for four long years, it is doubtful whether they would have chosen to take on a task of such scope and ambition.

11.2 The rise of the fallen

It is history's wont to turn unimaginable developments into seeming inevitabilities. At war's end, with Germany still smouldering, divided into different occupation zones, devastated, despised by the whole world; with Japan still numb at the humiliation of surrender, wounded by the nuclear attacks at Hiroshima and Nagasaki, coming to terms with the immense death toll on the East Asian and Polynesian battlefields, and labouring under an American occupation… the writing of the eventual post-war script was definitely *not* on the wall!

No one had an inkling of the role that these once proud but now ruined countries would be playing in a few short years. The notion that Germany and Japan would become the pillars of the new *Global Plan* was as outlandish as it was outrageous. And yet, it was the notion on which the New Dealers converged around 1947. How did that choice transpire? The answer is: gradually.

Box 11.2 The *Global Plan's* New Deal architects

As we have referred to the New Dealers extensively (see Sections 8.1 and 9.2), we only need to turn the spotlight on the four members of the administration who played the most crucial role in fashioning the new post-war *Global Plan* which began with the brief to create, *tabula rasa*, two new monetary pillars for the dollar: one in Europe (the Deutschmark) and one in Japan (the Yen). The four men in question were, importantly, also the architects of the Cold War:[1]

- *James Forrestal*, Secretary of Defence (previously Secretary of the Navy)
- *James Byrnes*, Secretary of State
- *George Kennan*, Director of Policy Planning Staff at the State Department and renowned 'prophet' of Soviet containment
- *Dean Acheson*, Leading light in all major post-war designs (the Bretton Woods agreement, the Marshall Plan, the prosecution of the Cold War, etc.) and Secretary of State from 1949 onwards.

These four men shared a common pragmatic view that was forged during the war and emerged under the shadow of the 1930s experience with flagging domestic aggregate demand, the failure to coordinate a unified response by the different capitalist centres against the Great Depression and, not least, the crucial role of military-induced production in keeping a capitalist economy effervescent. They also shared a contempt for economic theory and a conviction that the post-war economy should be run in a manner not too dissimilar to the successful running of the War Economy: by a combination of non-economist technocrats (the *Scientists* of Chapter 8) and New Dealer policymakers.

Note
1 See also Schaller (1985).

At first, it was inconceivable that Britain would not be a central pillar of the *Global Plan*. However, the fiscal weakness of the British state, its fast declining industry, the 1945 electoral victory of the Labour Party, the clear reluctance to come to terms with the impending End of Empire and, last but not least, the slide of the Pound to eventual non-convertibility, alerted the New Dealers to the possibility that Britain was better left out of the *Global Plan*. Britain had to experience the Suez Canal trauma in 1956, not to mention the undermining of its colonial rule in Cyprus by the CIA throughout the 1950s, before realising this turn in US thinking.[1]

Once Britain was deemed 'inappropriate', its sense of having won the war being part of the problem, the choice of Germany and Japan increasingly appeared entirely logical: both countries had been rendered dependable (thanks to the overwhelming presence of the US military), both featured solid industrial bases, both offered a highly skilled workforce and a people who would jump at the opportunity of rising, Phoenix-like, from their ashes. Moreover, they both held out considerable geostrategic benefits *vis-à-vis* the Soviet Union.

Nonetheless, that realisation had to overcome a great deal of resistance grounded on an opposite instinct: the urge to punish Germany and Japan by forcing them to deindustrialise and return to an almost pastoral state from which they would never again find it possible to launch an industrial-strength war. Indeed, Harry Dexter White, the US representative at Bretton Woods (see Box 11.1), had advocated that Germany's industry be effectively removed, forcing German living standards to fall to those of its less developed neighbours. In 1946, the Allies, under the auspices of the *Allied Control Council*, ordered the dismantling of steel plants with a view to reducing German steel production to fewer than six million tons annually, that is around 75 per cent of Germany's pre-war steel output. As for car production, it was decided that output should dwindle to around 10 per cent of what it was before Germany invaded Poland.

Things were a little different in Japan. Administered as an occupied country by one man, General Douglas MacArthur or SCAP (Supreme Commander of the Allied Powers), United States policy could be dictated directly, unencumbered by the need to negotiate with other allies (as was the case in Germany). MacArthur decided that Japan should not go through an equivalent process to de-Nazification and went to great lengths to exonerate the Emperor and the Japanese political, military and economic elites. Nevertheless, during the first two years of occupation, he too had to argue vigorously with Washington policymakers against punishing Japan by destroying, or severely circumscribing, its industrial base.

The sea change against the idea of flattening Germany's and Japan's industrial sectors was aided and abetted by the increasing tension between the United States and the Soviet Union. It was George Kennan's *Long Telegram* from Moscow in February 1946 (first mentioned in Section 8.1), and the inexorable rise of the Cold War spirit, that created the circumstances for a change of heart about Germany. The pivotal moment came when President Harry Truman, who succeeded F.D. Roosevelt when the veteran President died in April 1945, announced his notorious Doctrine in 1947.

The impetus for the Truman Doctrine to contain Soviet influence, in accordance with Kennan's Long Telegram, came from the streets of Athens in December 1946. It was there that left-wing, pro-Soviet partisans clashed with the British Army and its local allies (many of them ex-Nazi collaborators) thus setting off the awful Greek Civil War of 1946–49. Soon after, the British discovered that they could not pursue that war successfully, especially in the circumstances of Britain's increasing financial difficulties at home. They thus called upon the United States (which were playing a commendably neutral role until then) with an urgent request that the Americans step into the British Army's shoes and pursue the Greek Civil War.

Thus, the United States took its baptism of fire on the mountains of Greece, in a clash-by-proxy with the Soviet Bloc and its allies. A few months later, the proxy war nearly turned into a direct confrontation when the Western occupiers in West Berlin tussled with the Soviet occupiers of East Berlin; a mêlée which led to a long air-lifting of supplies from Western Germany to West Berlin, over the lines of the Red Army. The Cold War had almost begun. What it required was an official declaration.

The official declaration came on 12 March 1947 when President Truman delivered a famous speech in which he committed substantial sums, arms and political ammunition against the Greek partisans. It was to be the first instalment in a general drive to contain the Soviet Union and its sympathisers throughout Europe and Asia. The second instalment came in the form of the Marshall Plan, (see Box 11.3) a large financial injection into the economies of Western Europe which succeeded in creating the circumstances for the enactment of the Bretton Woods agreement that had been struck back in 1944.

Box 11.3 From the Truman Doctrine to the Marshall Plan

On 12 March 1947, President Harry Truman unveiled his Doctrine, pledging military and economic aid to the Greek government in its war against the resistance fighters who had previously opposed the Nazi occupation. The bill for this monstrous civil war, that still haunts Greeks today, was 400 million dollars. However, it was only the beginning of a massive intervention to stabilise Europe and render it safe for the *Global Plan*. On 5 June 1947, Truman's Secretary of State, George Marshall addressed a Harvard audience with a speech that marked the beginning of the Marshall Plan, a massive aid package that was to change Europe.

Its formal name was the European Recovery Program (ERP), the brainchild of the *Global Plan's* architects mentioned in Box 11.2. The fact that it was meant as a game-changing intervention, the purpose of which was clearly to establish a new world order in order to save capitalism's bacon, can be gleaned from some key words employed by Marshall in that important speech: 'the modern system of the division of labour upon which the exchange of products is based is in danger of breaking down'. The point of the Marshall Plan was, put simply, to save global capitalism from collapse.

The Marshall Plan involved not only a great deal of money but also vital institutions. On 3 April 1948, Truman established the Economic Co-operation Administration and 13 days later the United States and its European allies created the Organisation for European Economic Co-operation (OEEC), with a remit to work out where to channel the funding, under what conditions and to which purpose. The first Chair of the OEEC (which later, in 1961, evolved into what we know today as the Organisation for Economic Co-operation and Development, the OECD) was Robert Marjolin, one of the three participants in the Harvard reading group dedicated to understanding Keynes' General Theory (see Section 8.1).

During the first year of the Marshall Plan, the total sum involved was in the order of 5.3 billion dollars, a little more than 2 per cent of the United States' GDP. By 31 December 1951, when the Marshall Plan came to an end, 12.5 billion dollars had been expended. The end result was a sharp rise in European industrial output (about 35 per cent) and, more importantly, political stabilisation and the creation of sustainable demand for manufacturing products, both European and American.

Not all of the New Dealers, it must be said, accepted the premise that the Truman Doctrine and the Marshall Plan was a one-way street. For instance, Henry Wallace, the former Vice President and Secretary of agriculture, who was fired by Truman for disagreeing with the Cold War's imperatives, referred to the Marshall Plan as the 'Martial Plan', warning against creating a rift with America's wartime ally, the Soviet Union, and remarking that the conditions under which the Soviet Union was invited to be part of the Marshall Plan were designed in order to force Stalin to reject them (which, of course, Stalin did). A number of academics of the New Deal generation, amongst them Paul Sweezy and John Kenneth Galbraith (also mentioned in Section 8.1), also rejected Truman's cold-warrior tactics. However, they were soon to be silenced with the witch-hunt orchestrated by Senator Joseph McCarthy and his House Committee on Un-American Activities.

As important as the dollarisation of the European economy was for restoring markets and reinvigorating industry, the Marshall Plan's relatively unsung, but equally significant, legacy was the creation of the institutions of European integration, from which the greatest beneficiary was to be the continent's defeated nation: Germany!

The Americans' condition for parting with about two per cent of their GDP annually was the erasure of intra-European trade barriers and the commencement of a process of economic integration that would increasingly be centred around Germany's reviving industry. In this sense, the Marshall Plan can be fruitfully thought of as the progenitor of today's European Union. Indeed, from 1947 onwards the US military (and in particular the Joint Chiefs of Staff at the Pentagon) called for the 'complete revival of German industry, particularly coal mining' and pronounced that the latter was acquiring 'primary importance' for the security of the United States.

However, it would be a while longer before the rejuvenation of Germany's industrial might would become an openly declared aim; for even as the Marshall Plan was unfolding, the dissolution of German factories was continuing. It is indicative of the period that the

German Chancellor, Konrad Adenauer, pleaded in 1949 with the Allies to put an end to factory liquidations.

The most resistant of the Allies to the notion of an industrialised post-war Germany was, as one might have expected, France. The French demanded that the agreement of 29 March 1946, in which the Allies had ruled that half of Germany's industrial capacity would be destroyed (involving the destruction of 1,500 plants), remained in force. It was. By 1949, more than 700 plants had been disassembled and steel output was reduced by a massive 6.7 million tons.

So, what was it that convinced the French to accept the reindustrialisation of Germany? The United States of America, is the simple answer. When the New Dealers formed the view, around 1947, that a new currency must rise in Europe to support the dollar, and that this currency would be the Deutschmark, it was only a matter of time before the destruction of German capital would be reversed. The price France had to pay for the great benefits of the Marshall Plan, and for its central administrative role in the management of the whole affair (through the OEEC), was the gradual acceptance that Germany would be restored to grace, courtesy of the United States' new *Global Plan*.

In this context, it is useful to think of the Marshall Plan as a foundation of the *Global Plan*. For as the former was running out of steam, in 1951, it was already passing the baton to phase two of the American design for Europe: integration of its markets and of its heavy industry. That second phase came to be known as the European Coal and Steel Community (ECSC), the precursor to today's European Union. The new institution was soon to provide, as was intended by the New Dealers, the vital space that the resurgent German industry required in its immediate economic environment.

Turning now to the second pillar that was intended to support the dollar on the other side of the Northern hemisphere, the restoration of Japan as an industrial power, proved less problematic for the New Dealers than Germany had. The eastern version of the *Global Plan* was helped significantly by the onslaught of Mao Zedong's Chinese Communist Party against Chiang Kai-shek's nationalist government army.

The more Mao Zedong seemed to be evading attacks against his guerrillas, and winning the Chinese Civil War, the more General MacArthur edged towards a resolution to bolster Japanese industry, rather than succumbing to pressures to weaken it. However, there was a snag: while Japanese industry and infrastructure emerged from the war almost intact (in sharp contrast to Europe's), Japanese industry was plagued by a dearth of demand. The New Dealers' original idea was that the Chinese mainland would provide the Yen zone with its much needed vital space. Alas, Mao's gains and his eventual victory threw a spanner in those works (see Schaller, 1985; Forsberg, 2000).

General MacArthur understood the problem and tried to convince Washington to embark upon a second Marshall Plan, within Japan itself. However, the New Dealers could not see how enough demand might ever be created within Japan alone, without significant trade links with its neighbours. In any case, at that time they were preoccupied with the struggle to convince Congress to keep pumping dollars into Europe (see Halevi, 2001). However, MacArthur's luck changed when on 20 June 1950 Korean and Chinese communists attacked South Korea, with a view to unifying the peninsula under their command.

Suddenly, the Truman Doctrine shifted focus from Europe to Asia and the great beneficiary was Japanese industry. Mindful of the difficulty Japan was having to develop its industry, given the lack of consumer purchasing power, the New Dealers sought ways to boost demand within Japan well before Kim Il Sung's escapade in Korea. The latter provided the architects of the *Global Plan* with the opportunity they had been seeking.

The Marshall Plan was initially to last until 1953. But the war in Korea allowed the New Dealers to alter course: they would wind the Marshall Plan down in Europe and shift funds to Japan, whose new role would be to produce the goods and services required by the US forces in Korea – a fascinating case of war-financing of an old foe!

As for the Europeans, the idea was that the first three years of the Marshall Plan dollarised Europe sufficiently and that, from 1951 onwards, cartelisation centred around Germany's resurgent industry, and in the context of the newly instituted ECSC (see Box 11.4), would generate enough surplus for Europe to move ahead under its own steam.[2]

The United States' transfers to Japan were quite handsome. From day one, they amounted to almost 30 per cent of Japan's total trade. And, just as in Europe, the United States did

---

Box 11.4 From coal and steel to the European Union

The European Coal and Steel Community (ECSC) was, technically speaking, a common market for coal and steel linking Germany, France, Italy, Belgium, Luxembourg and Holland. Not only did it involve the dismantling of all trade barriers between these countries concerning coal and steel products but, additionally, it featured supra-national institutional links whose purpose was to regulate production and price levels. In effect, and despite the propaganda to the contrary, the six nations formed a cartel over coal and steel.

European leaders, such as Robert Schuman (a leading light in the ECSC's creation), stressed the importance of this coming-together from the (pertinent) perspective of averting another European war and forging a modicum of political union. Creating a shared heavy industry across, primarily, France and Germany would, Schuman believed (quite rightly), both remove the causes of conflict and deprive the two countries of the means by which to persecute it.

Thus, Germany was brought in from the cold and France gradually accepted its re-industrialisation; a development essential to the New Dealers' *Global Plan*. Indeed, it is indisputable that without the United States guiding Europe's politicians, cajoling and threatening them, often in one breath, the ECSC would not have materialised. Contrary to the Europeans' self-adulating narrative (according to which European uni-fication was a European dream made real by means of European diplomacy and because of an iron will to put behind Europe its violent past), the reality is that European integration was a grand American idea implemented by American diplomacy of the highest order. That the Americans who effected it enlisted to their cause enlightened politicians, such as Schuman, does not change this reality.

There was one politician who saw this clearly: General Charles de Gaulle, the future President of France who was to come to blows with the United States in the 1960s, so much so that he removed France from the military wing of NATO. When the ECSC was formed, de Gaulle denounced it on the basis that it was creating a united Europe in the form of a restrictive cartel and, more importantly, that it was an American creation, under Washington's influence and better suited to serve what we call the *Global Plan* than to provide a sound foundation for a New Europe. For these reasons, de Gaulle and his followers voted *against* the formation of the ECSC in the French parliament.

not just pour money in. They also created institutions and used their global power to bend existing institutions to the *Global Plan*'s will. Within Japan, the United States wrote the country's new constitution and empowered MITI, the famed Ministry for International Trade and Industry, to create a powerful, centrally planned (but privately owned), multi-sectoral industrial sector. Overseas, the New Dealers clashed with, among others, Britain to have Japan admitted to the General Agreement on Tariffs and Trade (GATT) (the ancestor of today's World Trade Organisation). The importance of the latter cannot be underestimated, as it allowed Japanese manufactures to be exported with minimal restrictions wherever the United States deemed as a good destination for its new protégé's goods.

In conclusion, the New Dealers' central organising principle was that American global hegemony demanded generous augmentation of external sources of both effective demand and stability for the two countries that it would patronise and whose assistance it would seek in order to stabilise world capitalism.[3] For this purpose, they took audacious steps to create the Deutschmark and the Yen zones, to provide them with the initial liquidity necessary to restart their industrial engines and to ensure that the political institutions were there that would allow the green shoots to flourish and grow into the mighty pillars that the dollar zone required for long-term support. Never before in history has a victor supported the societies that it had so recently defeated in order to enhance its own long-term power, turning them, in the process, into economic giants.

11.3 The *Global Plan's* golden era

Within five years of the initial conception of the *Global Plan*, two non-dollar currency zones, founded on rejuvenated industrial sectors, had emerged in full supporting roles to the dollar's unchallenged dominion. Its architects had taken the measure of the task, adopting bold political initiatives, both in Europe and in Japan, to ensure the parallel creation of free-trade areas within these zones. Their mission? To carve out crucial vital space for the real economies 'growing around' the new currencies.

Of course, the best-laid plans, or at least parts of them, often end up lying in ruins. Whereas the European free trade zone evolved, as planned, into German industry's vital space, the *Plan* came unstuck in the Far East, courtesy of Chairman Mao. What is fascinating, however, is the way in which successive US administrations attempted to make amends in diverse and creative ways.

First, there was the Korean war which, as mentioned above, proved an excellent opportunity to inject demand into the Japanese industrial sector. Second, the United States used its influence over its allies to allow Japanese imports freely into their markets.[4] Third, and most remarkably, Washington decided to turn America's own market into Japan's vital space. The penetration of Japanese imports (cars, electronic goods, even services) into the US market would have been impossible without a nod and a wink from Washington's policymakers. Fourth, the successor to the Korean war, the war in Vietnam, was further to boost Japanese industry. A useful by-product of that murderous escapade was the industrialisation of South-East Asia, which further strengthened Japan by providing it, at long last, with the missing link: a commercial vital zone in close proximity (see Rotter, 1987).

Our argument here is not that the Cold Warriors in the Pentagon and elsewhere were pursuing the New Dealers' *Global Plan* with a view to organising world capitalism. While not innocent of the idea, as the heavy involvement of military leaders in the Marshall Plan reveals, they naturally had their own geopolitical agenda. Our point is that, while the generals, the Pentagon and the State Department were putting together their Cold War strategic

314 Modern political economics

plans, Washington's economic planners approached the wars in Korea and Vietnam from a quite distinct perspective.

At one level, as we claimed, they saw them as crucial in maintaining a continual supply of cheap raw materials to Europe and Japan. At another level, however, they recognised in them a great chance to bring into being, through war financing, the vital economic space that Mao had robbed 'their' Japan of. It is impossible to overstate the point we raised earlier (again see Rotter, 1987) that the South-East Asian 'tiger economies' (Korea, Thailand, Malaysia and Singapore, which were soon to become for Japan what France and Spain were to Germany) would never have emerged without these two US-financed wars, leaving the US as the only sizeable market for Japanese industrial output.

The United States tended to its European and East Asian creations for at least two decades. After Europe[5] and Japan[6] were politically 'stabilised' (more often than not by unwholesome means), when the two regions began to take their fledgling steps, Washington extended credit, directly or indirectly, to the German economic zone and its Japanese counterpart so as to enable them to purchase the requisite technology and energy products, fundamentally oil, as well as to attract and utilise (often) migrant labour (see Hart-Landsberg, 1998).

The United States had come out of the war with a healthy respect for the colonised and a short temper towards their European colonisers. Britain's stance in India, Cyprus, even its incitement of the Greek Civil War (as early as in 1944), was thoroughly criticised by the New Dealers. France too, Holland and Belgium, were chastised for their ludicrous ambition to remain the colonial masters in Africa, Indochina and Indonesia, despite the sorry state in which the Second World War had left them.

However, the loss of China, the trials and tribulations of Latin America, the escalation of liberation movements in South-East Asia that tended to coalesce with Mao's communists (against the French), the stirrings in Africa that gave the Soviet Union an opening into that continent; all these developments enticed the US into developing an aggressive stance against liberation movements in the Developing World which Washington soon came to identify with the threat of rising input prices for its two important protégés: Japan and Germany.

In short, the US took it upon itself to relegate the periphery, and the Developing World *in toto*, into the role of supplier of raw materials to Japan and Western Europe. In the process, American multinationals in energy and other mining activities counted themselves among the beneficiaries, as did many sectors of the US domestic economy. However, the *Global Plan*'s architects saw much further than the narrow interests of any company. Their audacious policies to promote capital accumulation in distant lands, over which they had no personal or political interest (in the narrow sense), can only be explained if we take on board the weight of history under which they laboured.

Indeed, to understand the scale of the New Dealers' ambition we must again take pause and look briefly for clues of what they were on about in their own, not too distant, past: in the Great Depression that formed their mindset. The *Global Plan*, we must not forget for a moment, was the work of individuals belonging to a damaged generation; a generation that had experienced poverty, a deep sense of loss, the anxieties engendered by the near collapse of capitalism, and a consequent war of inhuman proportions.

In addition, they were educated men (some of them with formal economics training) who understood in their bones what in this book we refer to as the economists' *Inherent Error*; that deeply ingrained cause of serious theoretical failure affecting *all* economic modelling. They had vivid memories of how the great economists of the 1930s were fiddling with their models as the labour and capital markets were melting down. They knew that economics was not a good source of advice on how to run capitalism. Some of them even understood that that was *precisely* the point of economics: to have nothing to say about really existing capitalism.

With these thoughts in their minds, and a determination in their hearts not to allow capitalism to slip and fall again under their watch, they calibrated and implemented their *Global Plan* with panache. Their thinking about what needed to be done was influenced by the writings of John Maynard Keynes, whose crucial message to them was not to trust markets to organise themselves in a manner that brings about prosperity and stability; and to distrust anyone who tells them that they have the measure of capitalism; that, through some economic model, however sophisticated, they can predict the great beast's ways.

The break from Keynes was, nevertheless, inevitable. For whereas the Englishman had become convinced that global capitalism required a formal, cooperative system of recycling surpluses, the New Dealers both wanted and were obliged to tailor-make their *Global Plan* in the context of the Cold War imperatives and in clear pursuit of American hegemony (recall the White–Keynes class at Bretton Woods; see Box 11.1). Moreover, as Brinkley (1998) so vividly illustrates, the New Dealers lost, very early in the piece, their willingness seriously to confront corporate power.

To bring to fruition their joint task, of preventing another Great Depression and of constructing a new global order (with the United States at the helm and the American multi-nationals as effective agents of the state), the New Dealers knew that they would require a lot more than simplistic tinkering with monetary and fiscal policy.

What makes their story fascinating is the combination of their sophisticated, discursive Keynesianism, their audacious initiatives and the interaction of their economic planning with the demands of the Cold War. In this sense, the *Global Plan* comprised:

(a) not only the creation of the Deutschmark and Yen zones, by means of economic injections and political interference, to benefit Germany and Japan; but also
(b) the careful management of aggregate demand within the United States, always with a clear view to its effects on these two zones, in Europe and the Far East.

Since (a) has already been discussed sufficiently, let us now turn to (b). Indeed, domestic demand was kept up at a healthy level (particularly during the 1960s) through three large public expenditure programmes, two of which were closely related to the Cold War:

- The *Intercontinental Ballistic Missile* (ICBM) programme, which we discussed in Chapter 8 in the context of John von Neumann and the *Scientists.*
- The Korean and then, in the 1960s, the Vietnam War.
- President John Kennedy's New Frontier and, more importantly, President Lyndon Johnson's Great Society.

The first two spending programmes substantially strengthened US corporations and kept them on side at a time when their own government was going out of its way to look after foreign capitalists. That strength played a role not only domestically (providing corporations with the sound basis they needed at home) but also internationally (where the said strength assisted the State Department and other US agencies in their endeavours).

The greatest benefits, of course, accrued to companies somehow connected to what President Dwight Eisenhower had disparagingly (even though a celebrated ex-army commander himself) labelled the *Military-Industrial Complex* (MIC). The latter, and its special treatment, contributed heftily to the development of the *Aeronautic-Computer-Electronics* complex (ACE); an economic powerhouse largely divorced from the rest of the US economy but central to its continuing power (see Markusen and Yudken, 1992; Melman, 1997).

Despite the sizeable positive impact of the *Global Plan* on the domestic American economy, and particularly on maintaining a high level of aggregate demand within the United States, it was an uneven impact and also an impact that may well have been a mere (however hugely desirable) *by-product* of Washington's *main policy*; namely, of the policy to prioritise energy and input supplies (at favourable prices) for the reconstruction and development of Europe and Japan.

That it was uneven is evidenced from the fact that segments of the economy not linked to the MIC and the ACE (see the previous paragraph), never recovered in step with either Germany and Japan or with the rest of the US economy.[7] That it was *not* Washington's *main* aim to bolster American companies (though it was certainly one of its aims) can be gleaned from the ruthlessness with which the United States government introduced, whenever it saw fit, harsh regulations which ultimately discriminated *against* American multinationals in pursuit of its *top* priority: the augmentation of the Deutschmark and the Yen zones via the reinforcement of German and Japanese industry (see Forsberg, 2000).

The unevenness with which prosperity was distributed within the United States, at a time of rising aspirations (not all of them income related), caused significant social tensions. These tensions, and their gradual dissolution, were the target of the Great Society spending programmes of the 1960s. At first President Kennedy and then his successor, Lyndon Johnson, pushed hard for a series of domestic spending programmes that would address the fact that the *Global Plan*'s domestic benefits were so unfairly spread as to undermine social cohesion in important urban centres and regions. To prevent these centrifugal forces from damaging the *Global Plan*, social welfare programmes acquired an inertia of their own. Box 11.5 gives a flavour.

Box 11.5 The Great Society
A New Deal in the age of the Global Plan

From 1955 until the election of President Kennedy in 1960, economic growth tailed off in the United States, a petering out that affected mostly the poor and the marginal. After eight years of Republican rule, Kennedy was elected on a New Deal-alluding platform. His New Frontier manifesto promised to revive the spirit of the New Deal by spending on education, health, urban renewal, transportation, the arts, environmental protection, public broadcasting, research in the humanities, etc. After Kennedy's assassination, President Johnson, especially after his 1964 landslide electoral victory, incorporated many of the, largely unenacted, New Frontier policies into his much more ambitious Great Society proclamation. While Johnson pursued the Vietnam War abroad with increasingly reckless vigour, domestically he attempted to stamp his authority through the Great Society, a programme that greatly inspired progressives when it put centrestage the goal of eliminating not only poverty for the white working class but also racism.

The Great Society will be remembered for its effective dismantling of American apartheid, especially in the southern states. Between 1964 and 1966, four pieces of legislation saw to this major transformation of American society. However, the Great Society had a strong Keynesian element that came to the fore as Johnson's 'unconditional war on poverty'. In its first three years, 1964 to 1966, one billion dollars were spent annually on various programmes to boost educational opportunities and to introduce health cover for the elderly and various vulnerable groups.

The social impact of the Great Society's public expenditure was mostly felt in the form of poverty reduction. When it began, more than 22 per cent of Americans lived below the official poverty line. By the end of the programme, that had fallen to just below 13 per cent. Even more significantly, the respective percentages for Black Americans were 55 per cent (in 1960) and 27 per cent (in 1968). While such improvements cannot be explained solely as the effect of Great Society funding, the latter played a major role in relieving some of the social tensions during an era of generalised growth.[1]

Note
1 For more on the Great Society see Kaplan and Cuciti (1986) and Jordan and Rostow (1986).

In retrospect, the results of the *Global Plan*'s implementation were impressive. Not only did the end of the Second World War not plunge the United States, and the rest of the West, into a fresh recession, as it was feared that the winding down of war spending would do, but instead the world experienced a period of legendary growth. Figure 11.1 offers a glimpse of these golden years. The developed nations, victors and losers of the preceding war alike, grew and grew and grew.

The Europeans and Japan, starting from a much lower level than the United States, grew faster and made up for lost ground while, at the same time, the United States continued along a path of healthy growth. However, this was not a simple case of a spontaneously growing world economy. There was a *Global Plan* behind it, one that involved a large-scale, and impressively ambitious, effort to overcome and to supplant the multiple, conflicting imperialisms that characterised the world political economy until the Second World War.

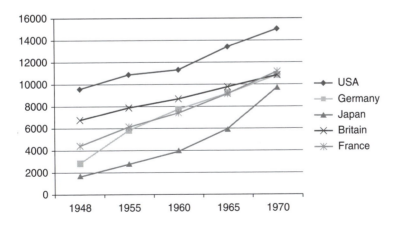

Figure 11.1 Real GDP per capita during the period of the *Global Plan*.

Table 11.1 Percentage increase/decrease in a country's share of world GDP

	USA	Germany	Japan	Britain	France
1950–72	−19.3%	+18%	+156.7%	−35.4%	+4.9%

The essence of that effort is captured nicely in Table 11.1: American hegemony was purchased as the price of intentionally bolstering demand and capital accumulation in Japan and Germany. To maintain American prosperity and growth, Washington purposefully dished out part of the global 'pie' to its protégés, Germany (an increase in its share of world income of 18 per cent) and even more so Japan (a stupendous 156.7 per cent).

To conclude this section, the preceding thoughts lead to a reassessment of post-war US dominance from the perspective of the United States' balance of payments in relation to the rest of the world. While seemingly in competition with the United States, the economies of Germany and Japan were aided and propped up by their former conqueror. Was this a form of internationalist altruism at work? The more we consider the long-term interests of American accumulation, in the light of the 1930s experience, the less credible the altruistic explanation seems.

At the heart of the New Dealers' thinking, from 1945 onwards, was an intense anxiety regarding the inherent instability of a single-currency, single-zone global system. Indeed, nothing concentrated their minds like the memory of 1929 and the ensuing crisis. If a crisis of similar severity were to strike while global capitalism had a single leg to stand on (the dollar), and in view of the significant growth rates of the Soviet Union (an economy not susceptible to contagion from capitalist crises), the future seemed bleak. Thus, these same minds sought a safer future for capitalism in the formation of an interdependent network comprising three industrial-monetary zones, in which the dollar-zone would be predominant (reflecting the centrality of American finance, and its military 'defence of the realm' in the sphere of securing inputs from the Developing World). To them, this *Global Plan* was the optimal mechanism design for the rest of the twentieth century and beyond.

In this sense, and if our analysis is correct, the notion that European integration sprang out of a European urge to create some bulwark against American dominance appears to be nothing more than the European Union's 'creation myth'. Equally, the idea that the Japanese economy grew inexorably *against* the interests of the United States does not survive serious scrutiny. However strange this may seem (especially to readers whose more recent memories of the United States are the introverted years of the 2000–08 period), behind the process of European integration and of Japanese export-oriented industrialisation lies a prolonged and sustained effort by Washington policymakers to plan and nurture it, despite the detrimental effects on America's balance of trade that the rise of Europe and Japan entailed.

The simple lesson that the *Global Plan* can teach us today is that world capitalism's finest hour came when the policymakers of the strongest political union on the planet decided to play an hegemonic role; a role that involved not only the exercise of military and political might but also a massive redistribution of surpluses across the globe that the market mechanism is utterly incapable of effecting.

11.4 The *Global Plan's* unravelling

The *Global Plan*'s path was not laid with roses. From its inception, a series of developments conspired to undermine it (with Chairman Mao's triumph delivering the first and most serious blow). But even when parts of it were overturned by the vagaries of reality, such failures prompted creative responses which maintained the *Plan*'s integrity, often as a result of unintended consequences.

The Vietnam War is a good case in point. Though it is a gross understatement to suggest that its persecution did not go according to the original plan, the silver lining is visible to anyone who has ever visited South-East Asia. Korea, Thailand, Malaysia and Singapore grew fast and in a manner that frustrated the pessimism of those who predicted that underdeveloped nations would find it hard to embark upon the road of capital accumulation necessary to drive them out of abject poverty. In the process, they provided Japan with valuable trade and investment opportunities, therefore shoring up the *Plan*'s eastern flank.

Just as Japan's economy began to grow on the back of US military spending during the Korean war, the tigers of South-East Asia were the offspring of enormous investment, paid for from the US military budget, during the lengthy, tragic conflict in Indochina (see Hart-Landsberg, 1998). Ho Chi Minh's stubborn refusal to lose the war, and Lyndon Johnson's almost manic commitment to do all it takes to win it, were crucial in creating a new capitalist region in the Far East, one that would eventually play a major role in the more recent rise of the Chinese behemoth. Nonetheless, these developments proved a bridge-too-far for the *Global Plan*. The escalation of the financial costs of that war that were to be a key factor in its demise.

As the costs of Johnson's Great Society and of the Vietnam War began to mount, the Fed was forced to take on mountains of US government debt. In effect, it was printing the necessary dollars to finance the two interrelated 'projects'. Towards the end of the 1960s, many governments began to worry that their own position, which was interlocked with the dollar in the context of the Bretton Woods system, was being undermined. By early 1971, liabilities in dollars exceeded 70 billion when the US government possessed only $12 billion of gold with which to back them up.

The increasing quantity of dollars was flooding world markets, giving rise to inflationary pressures in places like France and Britain. European governments were thus forced to increase the quantity of their own currencies in order to keep their exchange rate with the dollar constant, as stipulated by the Bretton Woods system. This is the basis for the European charge against the United States that, by pursuing the Vietnam War, it was exporting inflation to the rest of the world. In addition, the Europeans and the Japanese feared that as the quantity of dollars was rising, and with the US stock of gold constant, a run on the dollar might force the United States to drop its commitment to swapping an ounce of gold for $35, in which case their stored dollars would devalue, eating into their national 'savings'.

American dominance was, as explained earlier, built into the Bretton Woods system since it allowed the United States to be the only country that could print money at will in order to finance its global dominance. Valéry Giscard d'Estaing, who was at that time President de Gaulle's finance minister, called this the *exorbitant privilege of the Dollar*. De Gaulle and other European allies (plus various governments of oil producing countries whose oil exports were denominated in dollars) accused the United States of building its imperial reach on borrowed money that undermined their countries' prospects.

On 29 November 1967, the British government devalued the Pound sterling by 14 per cent, well outside the Bretton Woods 10 per cent limit, triggering a crisis and forcing the United States government to use up to 20 per cent of its entire gold reserves to defend the $35 dollars-to-one-ounce-of-gold peg. On 16 March 1968, representatives of the G7's central banks met to hammer out a compromise. They came to a curious agreement which, on the one hand, retained the official peg of $35 an ounce while, on the other hand, left room for speculators to trade gold at market prices.

When Richard Nixon won the US Presidency in 1970, he appointed Paul Volcker as Undersecretary of the Treasury for International Monetary Affairs. His brief was to report to the National Security Council, headed by Henry Kissinger, who was to become a most influential Secretary of State in 1973. In May of 1971, the taskforce headed by Volcker at the Treasury presented Kissinger with a contingency plan which toyed with the idea of 'suspension of gold convertibility'. It is now clear that, on both sides of the Atlantic, policymakers were jostling for position, anticipating a major change in the *Global Plan*.

In August 1971 the French government decided to make a very public statement of its annoyance at the United States' policies: President Georges Pompidou ordered a destroyer to sail to New Jersey to redeem US dollars for gold held at Fort Knox, as was his right under Bretton Woods! A few days later, the British government issued a similar request, though without employing the Royal Navy, demanding gold equivalent to $3 billion held by the Bank of England.

President Nixon was absolutely livid. Four days later, on 15 August 1971, he announced the effective end of Bretton Woods: the dollar would no longer be convertible to gold. Thus, the *Global Plan* unravelled. Soon after, he dispatched John Connally, his Secretary of the Treasury, a no-nonsense Texan, to Europe. Connally's account of what he said to the Europeans was mild and affable. He told reporters:

> We told them that we were here as a nation that had given much of our resources and our material resources and otherwise to the World to the point where frankly we were now running a deficit and have been for twenty years and it had drained our reserves and drained our resources to the point where we could no longer do it and frankly we were in trouble and we were coming to our friends to ask for help as they have so many times in the past come to us to ask for help when they were in trouble. That is in essence what we told them.[8]

In reality this is not at all what he told the Europeans, either in form or in spirit. With the reporters out of range, Connally delivered a brutal message to European leaders; one whose shocking value is still remembered in Europe's corridors of power. His real message was: *it's our currency but it's your problem!*

What Connally meant was that, as the Dollar was the reserve currency (see below) and the only truly global means of exchange, the end of Bretton Woods was not America's problem. The *Global Plan* was, of course, designed and implemented to be in the interest of the United States. But once the pressures on it, caused by Vietnam and internal US tensions that required an increase in domestic government spending, such that the system reached breaking point, the greatest loser would not be the United States itself but Europe and Japan; the two economic zones that had benefited enormously from the *Global Plan*.

It was not a message either the Europeans or Japan wanted to hear. Lacking an alternative to the dollar,[9] they knew that their economies would hit a major bump as soon as the dollar started to devalue. Not only would their dollar assets lose value but, additionally, their exports would become dearer. The only alternative was for them to devalue their currencies too but that would then cause their energy costs to skyrocket (given that oil was denominated in dollars). In short, Japan and the Europeans found themselves between a rock and a hard place.

Towards the end of 1971, in December, Presidents Nixon and Pompidou met in the Azores. Pompidou, eating humble pie over his destroyer antic, pleaded with Nixon to reconstitute the Bretton Woods system, on the basis of fresh fixed exchange rates that would reflect the new 'realities'. Nixon was unmoved. The *Global Plan* was dead and buried and a new beast was to fill in the vacuum in its wake.

11.5 Interregnum: The 1970s oil crises, stagflation and the rise of interest rates

Once the fixed exchange rates of the Bretton Woods system collapsed, all prices and rates broke loose. Gold was the first commodity to jump discretely from $35 to $38 per ounce, soon to $42 and then to float unbounded into the ether. By May 1973 it was trading at more than $90 and before the decade was out, in 1979, it had reached a fabulous $455 per ounce – a twelvefold increase in less than a decade.

Turning to a key rate for any capitalist economy, money (or nominal) interest rates rose too, from between 5 per cent and 6 per cent during the *Global Plan*'s final years to 6.44 per cent in 1973 and to 7.83 per cent the following year. By 1979, when President Carter's administration began to attack inflation seriously, average interest rates topped 11 per cent. In the following year, June of 1981 to be precise, Paul Volcker (who was appointed by Carter as Chairman of the Fed in 1979) raised interest rates to a lofty 20 per cent, and then further up again to 21.5 per cent in 1981. While this brutal form of monetary policy did tame inflation (pushing it down from 13.5 per cent in 1981 to 3.2 per cent two years later), its harmful effects on employment and capital accumulation were profound, both domestically and internationally.

And yet, despite the scorched earth aspects of the high interest rate policies of Volcker's Fed, the mission was accomplished: the United States' early 1970s problems with competitiveness and its balance of payments had disappeared. Capital flows to New York, due both to the high interest rates and the fast declining inflation rate, were allowing the US administration to emancipate itself from the deep red ink splattered all over the country's international trade balance sheet.

The United States could now run an increasing trade deficit with impunity while the new Reagan administration could also finance its tremendously expanded defence budget. The latter proved essential in curbing unemployment which, between 1979 and 1983, was getting out of control. These two deficits (the US trade deficit and the US government's budget deficit) changed the post-1970s world. In our parlance, they constituted a *Global Minotaur* whose imprint we still see around us everywhere we look. a creature whose demise in 2008 promises to shape another, the third, phase of the post-war reality.

Turning back to the 1970s again, and the predicament of the Europeans, of the Japanese and of the oil-producing countries once the fixed exchange rates of the Bretton Woods system had been and gone, at the centre of *their* crisis (recall Connally's 'It is our dollar but it is *your* crisis'!) was the devaluation of the dollar. Within two years of Nixon's August 1971 bold move, it had lost 30 per cent of its value against the Deutschmark and 20 per cent against the yen and the franc. Oil producers suddenly found that their black gold, when denominated in yellow gold, was worth a fraction of what it used to be. Members of the *Organisation of Petroleum Exporting Countries* (OPEC), which regulated the price of oil through agreed cutbacks on aggregate oil output, were soon clamouring for coordinated action (i.e. reductions in production) to boost the black liquid's value.

At the time of Nixon's announcement, the price of oil was less than $3 a barrel. Soon after, concerted effort was put into bringing about a hike. In 1973, with the *Yom Kippur* war between Israel and its Arab neighbours apace, the price jumped to between $8 and $9, thereafter hovering in the $12 to $15 range until 1979. In 1979 a new upward surge began that saw oil trade above $30 well into the 1980s.[10] It was not just the price of oil that scaled unprecedented heights. All primary commodities shot up in price simultaneously: bauxite (165 per cent); lead (170 per cent); silver (1065 per cent); and tin (220 per cent) are just a few examples. In short, the termination of the *Global Plan* signalled a mighty rise in the costs of production across the world.

Did Nixon, Kissinger and Connally miscalculate? Had they brought about a major catastrophe upon the United States and the capitalist world at large by allowing their anger towards the Europeans to create the circumstances of an economic implosion? Or was all this part of a plan of sorts? As alluded to above, there was no miscalculation. Although not all of the repercussions had been anticipated, and indeed some proved exceedingly costly, the general drift was as planned.

The conventional wisdom of what happened in the early 1970s is that, against the will of the United States, OPEC countries (because the dollar began to slide, and was no longer exchangeable for gold at a fixed rate) tried to recoup the real (or gold) price of their oil by restricting shipments and production, thus pushing oil dollar prices sky high. Taking advantage of the conflict in the Middle East, they bound the Arab and Muslim nations together, imposed an embargo on the United States and thus managed to boost oil prices and, naturally, their collective revenues. With the cost of energy scaling such heights, inflation spread to the rest of the world, nominal interest rates followed in sympathy and the developed economies were thus brought to their feet.

If all this were true, one would have expected the United States government to have regretted President Nixon's 1971 break from Bretton Woods and to have vehemently opposed anyone within OPEC trying to bring about a binding agreement to curtail oil production. But no such regrets were ever expressed. Moreover, a country that had no compunction in bringing down Mohammad Mossadegh's democratically elected government in Iran in 1953 (to prevent the nationalisation of that country's oil wells) and staging one *coup d'état* after the other for the purposes of safeguarding its interests worldwide (from Greece and Indonesia in 1967, to Chile in 1973 and almost in every other Latin American country during the 1960s, 1970s and 1980s), did not raise a finger to effect political or 'other' means that would have so easily prevented the OPEC oil price hikes.

So, why didn't they do something to stop the oil price rises? Why not undermine the regimes pushing for them? The simple reason is that the Nixon administration neither regretted the end of Bretton Woods nor cared to prevent OPEC from executing oil price rises. Why? Because these hikes were utterly consistent with the administration's very own plans for a *substantial increase in the prices of energy and primary commodities!* (see Box 11.7)

Now, this is a large claim, in need of substantiation. Thankfully, our claim comes, so to speak, from the horse's mouth. In his 1982 memoirs, *Years of Upheaval*, Henry Kissinger writes: 'Never before in history has a group of relatively weak nations been able to impose with so little protest such a dramatic change in the way of life of the overwhelming majority of the rest of mankind' (1982: 887). And why did Kissinger, a man of incredible power in the Nixon administration, not protest? It is now well accepted (see Oppenheim, 1976/7 and Box 11.6 below) that the reason why there was so little US resistance to OPEC's price increases was that US policymakers, including Kissinger, were quite happy to see oil prices quadruple. In fact, they worked diligently to push them up!

The obvious question is: why would they want to do that? Why, oh why, would the Nixon administration embark upon a strategic plan whose effect would be to increase production costs worldwide, risk hyperinflation, produce mass unemployment for the first time since the late 1930s and, generally, destabilise capitalism? For this is precisely what happened in the 1970s: for the first time in capitalist history, we witnessed a combination of inflation and

Box 11.6 Vietnam War: Counting the costs

The economic cost

The direct *accounting* cost of the Vietnam War for the United States government was a staggering $113 billion. New Deal Keynesian economist Robert Eisner (Professor at Northwestern University and a former President of the American Economic Association), computed the total *economic* cost of the Vietnam War for the United States' economy to have been closer to $220 billion. Moreover, he suggested that real US corporate profits declined by 17 per cent. At the same time, during the period 1965–70, the war-induced increases in average prices forced the real average income of American blue-collar workers to fall by about 2 per cent. 'This loss in income', wrote Eisner, 'must be a major factor in working-class malaise and tension'. In this context, President Johnson's Great Society (see Box 11.5) was also (though not exclusively) a domestic policy to counter the increasing tensions due to the Vietnam War, which Johnson pursued with such fervour.

The human cost[1]

South-East Asia

* 1,921,000 Vietnamese died
* 200,000 Cambodians died (1969–75)
* 100,000 Laotians died (1964–73)
* 3,200,000 were wounded (Vietnam, Laos and Cambodia)
* 14,305,000 were refugees (Vietnam, Laos, Cambodia) by the end of the war
* in general, approximately one out of 30 IndoChinese was killed between 1964 and 1973; one in 12 wounded; and one in five made a refugee

USA

* 2,500,000 soldiers served in the war
* 58,135 soldiers died
* 303,616 were wounded
* 33,000 were paralysed as a result of injuries
* 111,000 veterans died from 'war-induced' conditions since returning home (including at least 60,000 suicides)
* 35,000 US civilians were killed in Vietnam (non-combat deaths)
* 2,500 were missing in action

Note
1 The figures here come from the US Department of Defence and the United Nations. Eisner's estimates were reported in *Time* magazine's article "Business: The Hidden Costs of the Viet Nam War", Monday, July 13, 1970.

unemployment at once;[11] a condition that required a new label: stagflation – a moment in history when the two dragons feared most by policymakers visited every capitalist centre simultaneously. Surely, it is preposterous to believe that it was the United States government that issued the dragons' invitations!

Box 11.7 An odd 'crisis'
'Who pushed oil prices up'? – 'We did'!

With average consumer and commodity prices rising across the industrial world, the dollar price of oil stagnant, and the dollar devaluing relative to gold, OPEC began to make noises from as early as December 1970 about impending action to boost the price of oil. The Western oil companies, the so-called *Seven Sisters*, immediately demanded bilateral monopoly negotiations with OPEC. Remarkably, it was the US government that scuttled the negotiations, ensuring that the oil companies did not get a chance to negotiate with OPEC on a one-to-one (or bilateral monopoly) basis; a negotiation in which they would exercise a great deal more bargaining power than they would in piecemeal discussions. Oppenheim (1976/77) writes

> '… a split was announced in the talks in Tehran by a special US envoy, then Under-Secretary of State John Irwin, accompanied there by James Akins, a key State Department man on oil….[T]he real lesson of the split in negotiations with OPEC was that higher prices were not terribly worrisome to representatives of the State Department… the whole subject of what the negotiations were about began to focus not on holding the price line but on ensuring security of supply'.

Oppenheim also quotes extensively from an article by an advisor to the Libyan government on how the United States successfully undercut Europe's attempts to secure lower oil prices. In particular, US representatives refused to contribute to a series of initiatives proposed in various open and secret groups meeting in Paris at the OECD, the purpose of which was to work out oil-sharing arrangements in the event of an embargo. Oppenheim continues: 'In fact, the prediction, and advocacy, of higher oil prices became a common feature of statements from the Nixon administration'.

In 1972, the same Mr Akins that undermined the oil companies' bargaining position in Tehran two years previously told an audience at the 8th Petroleum Congress of the League of Arab States that '… oil prices could be expected to go up sharply due to lack of short-term alternatives to Arab oil,' a turn of phrase that was widely interpreted as an American green light on oil price increases. Akins' career continued to revolve around oil, rising to US Ambassador to Saudi Arabia. In his confirmation statement to Congress, he stated clearly that the United States was never really opposed to oil price increases.

It is important to note that all of the above transpired well before the *Yom Kippur* war and the oil embargo that ensued (during which the Arab countries restricted oil sales to Israel's Western allies). During that Arab–Israeli war and the oil (i.e. at a time one would have expected the hawkish Dr Kissinger to unleash the powers of hell against the Arab countries that were simultaneously attacking Israel and holding the United States to ransom), Kissinger continued secretly to channel foreign aid and investments to Saudi Arabia. Akins himself later testified that, in 1975, Kissinger was cajoling the Shah of Iran to let oil prices rise further.

By 1974, US officials lower down the Washington pecking order of the administration were learning, often at great personal cost, that higher oil prices, rather than a hindrance, had become a strategy. For example, the Chief of the Federal Energy Administration, John Sawhill, found this out the hard way when his efforts to reduce oil prices were blocked by persons of greater rank and authority within the Nixon administration: before he knew it, his persistence was met with a summary dismissal.

Moreover, such a choice seems to fly in the face of at least two decades of American policy in the context of the *Global Plan*; history's most impressive attempt to regulate capitalism on the basis of creating a stable environment in which all major capitalist centres prosper, with the United States maintaining the leading position. Nothing short of collective madness would explain how Washington's global stability builders would *choose* to throw such a sizeable spanner in global capitalism's works.

Are we, therefore, being disingenuous to claim that the hike in oil prices, which opened up Pandora's box and turned the 1970s into a decade of turmoil and instability, was *planned*? Not in the slightest, we submit. Our position on this delicate matter is that, naturally, no one chose stagflation, high interest rates, expensive raw materials, etc., *as such*. Rather, Washington's policymakers made a different choice under duress: one between:

(a) serious cutbacks in government spending and in the living standards of the American middle class and its elites (a decline that would have been inevitable if the United States were to cut its trade deficit); and

(b) a strategy that would allow the United States to liberate itself from the constraint of its twin deficits (the trade and the government budget deficits).

To explain this choice better, we note that, once the *Global Plan* began to unravel, the United States was facing a serious problem to which Treasury Secretary Connally alluded when he addressed the Europeans in public in September 1971:

> [A]s a nation that had given much of our resources and our material resources and otherwise to the World to the point where frankly we [are]... now running a deficit and have been for twenty years and it had drained our reserves and drained our resources to the point where we could no longer do it and frankly we were in trouble.

Connally was telling the truth, not the whole truth but the truth nonetheless: the United States' balance of payments deficit had become unsustainable, reflecting the extent to which the Vietnam War was confounding the US military's best efforts. Additionally, American industry had lost its edge. In comparison to the burgeoning productivity of German and Japanese industries, American manufacturers were falling behind, and were doing so unprotected by tariffs from the German and Japanese goods that the American government was intentionally letting into the land, as part of its plan to patronise the two former enemies' industries. With profitability dipping quickly, a large trade deficit developing, and an everincreasing public debt, the United States had to change course or forfeit its hegemony there and then.

The choice it faced was, therefore, simple. As we suggested above, it had to choose between a major reduction in the American middle and elite classes' living standards and a strategy that would, effectively, free the United States from its balance of trade and government deficit constraints. 'How could the latter be an option?', the reader will rightly ask. Is it not a little like inventing perpetual motion or squaring the circle? Surely it is not possible to liberate a country from its two major shackles: the budget and the balance of trade constraints. Only it is, when the country in question issues the world's sole reserve currency; the money that everyone uses to pay for energy and other major commodities; the currency one turns to when the dark clouds of crisis of recession gather.

Having ruled out as unacceptable the first option, the reduction in US government spending and a general fall in imports and associated living standards for well-to-do Americans, the Nixon administration embarked on a quest for an ingenious way to continue with high trade and budget deficits by making other people, foreigners, pay for them. It will be our contention in this chapter's remaining pages that the Nixon administration, and every administration that followed it since, opted for this exceptionally alluring option.

The aim of the new strategy was to redress the balance of payments situation between the three major zones on which the *Global Plan* had staked its integrity: the United States, Europe and Japan. Looking back to Table 11.1, this means a shift of the global surplus back to the United States, and away from Germany, Japan and the oil-producing countries. Two were prerequisites of that simple end:

(i) to improve the competitiveness of US firms in relation to their German and Japanese competitors; and
(ii) to attract large capital flows into the United States that would cancel out the US balance of trade deficit and pay for the US government's chronic deficit.

Prerequisite (i) could be achieved in one of two ways: either by boosting productivity in the United States or by boosting the relative unit costs of the competition. The US administration decided to aim for both, for good measure. Labour costs were squeezed with enthusiasm and, at the same time, oil prices were 'encouraged' to rise; precisely as we argued above. The basic assumption here was that, in the estimation of the US authorities, both Japan and Western Europe would find it much harder than the United States to deal with a significant increase in oil prices. How right they were!

Prerequisite (ii) was closely linked to (i). The drop in US labour costs not only boosted the competitiveness of American companies, but also acted as a magnet for foreign capital that was searching for profitable ventures. Similarly, the rise of oil prices led to mountainous rents piling up in bank accounts from Saudi Arabia to Indonesia. It was only a small step for their owners to wire them to their bank accounts in Wall Street, thus contributing to the sought after (by US administrators) capital flight *into* the United States.[12] And if oil-sourced monies were to crave a trip to Wall Street, that would also apply to the surpluses accumulating in the bank accounts of the manufacturers, Japanese and German, who owed their very existence to the now sadly deceased *Global Plan*! The vast increases in US interest rates of the later 1970s did no harm in this regard either.

In short, a new phase was beginning. Gone were the days when the United States would be financing (either directly or through war financing or totally indirectly, by the exercise of political power) Germany and Japan, hoping to create in those countries substantial markets for American high technology, military and other goods and adding, in the process, important shock absorbers (the Deutschmark and the Yen) to the international monetary system. The new era would be different. America would be importing like there was no tomorrow, and its government would splurge out unhindered by the fear of increasing deficits, with foreign investors sending billions of dollars every day to Wall Street, quite voluntarily and for reasons completely related to *their* bottom line, to make up the difference and plug the United States' twin deficits.

11.6 A *Global Minotaur* is born

The United States had neither wanted nor resigned easily to the collapse of the *Global Plan*. However, once its collapse became inevitable, US policymakers moved on very rapidly, unwilling to countenance the prospect of jeopardising global hegemony in a futile attempt to mend a broken design. By the end of the 1970s a new global order was in place. Far less stable than the *Global Plan*, without the institutionalised multilateralism of the Bretton Woods system and its paraphernalia, the new order transformed global capitalism and further entrenched American hegemony. From a system of regulated and planned international flows of trade and capital, the world was suddenly flung into chaotic flux. Then again, there was order and serious planning behind the seeming chaos.

The first spurt of chaos happened with the intentional dismantling of Bretton Woods. It took at least a decade before the resulting tumult could be beaten back into a discernible system that would transform and reconfigure America's global supremacy. In the same way that Washington had underestimated the resolve of the Viet Cong in the 1960s, in the 1970s they underestimated the chain reaction that their meddling in oil prices would engender. Nevertheless, and in spite of the many trials and tribulations experienced within and without the American economy, the United States managed to snatch an array of crucial advantages out of the jaws of a major self-initiated crisis.

To be precise, the United States succeeded in eliminating its *problem* with the twin deficits (balance of payments and government deficits) *without having to eliminate the deficits themselves*. Indeed, if anything, the deficits rose as if without bounds. Soon they started

---

Box 11.8 The Cretan Minotaur
A tale of greed, dominance and defiance

The Minotaur is a tragic, mythological figure, the result of greed, divine retribution, revenge and the progenitor of much suffering in his own right. According to the myth's main variant, King Minos of Crete asked Poseidon for a fine bull as a sign of godly approval, pledging to sacrifice it in the god's honour. Recklessly, after Poseidon obliged him, Minos decided to spare the animal, taken by its beauty and poise. The gods, never letting a good excuse for horrid retribution go to waste, chose an interesting punishment for Minos: using Aphrodite's special skills, they had Minos' wife, the Queen, fall in lust with the Cretan Bull. Using various props constructed by Daedalus, the infamous engineer, she managed to impregnate herself, the result of that brief encounter being the Minotaur: a creature half human half bull (*tauros* in Greek).

Once the Minotaur grew larger and increasingly ferocious, King Minos instructed Daedalus to build the Labyrinth, an immense maze where the Minotaur was kept. Unable to nourish itself with either corn or human food, the beast had to feast on human flesh. It proved an excellent excuse for Minos to seek his revenge on the Athenians, whose King Aegeus, a lousy loser, had Minos' son killed after the young man had won all races and contests in the Panathenean Games. After a brief war with Athens, Minos forced Aegeus to send seven young men and seven unwed girls to be devoured by the Minotaur every year (or every nine years, depending on the myth's version).

Beyond myth, historians confirm that, at the time, Crete was the economic and political hegemon of the Aegean region. Weaker city-states, like Athens, had to pay tribute to Crete regularly as a sign of subjugation. This may well have included the shipment of teenagers to be sacrificed by priests wearing bull masks. Returning to the realm of myths, the eventual slaughter of the Minotaur by Theseus, son of the King of Athens, marked the emancipation of Athens from Cretan hegemony and the beginning of a new era.

absorbing other nations' capital at tremendous rates – up to $5 billion net inflows into Wall Street per working day. The era of the *Global Minotaur* had dawned. It was as if the whole world was sending tributes to Wall Street daily in order to keep a latter day *Minotaur* satiated. For that was the New Deal: as long as the *Minotaur*'s voracious appetite was satisfied, aggregate demand for the manufactures and raw materials of the rest of the world would be maintained.

The Athenians' gruesome tributes to the Cretan Minotaur were imposed by King Minos' military might. In contrast, the tributes of capital that fed the *Global Minotaur* flooded into the United States voluntarily. Why? How did US policymakers persuade capitalists from all over the world to fund the superpower's twin deficits? What was in it for them? Our answer turns on four factors:

1. The dollar's reserve currency status and the continuing denomination in dollars of commodity prices (including oil); a status which grew in importance once the fixed exchange rates of the Bretton Woods system dissolved and uncertainty rose to unprecedented heights.
2. The *escalation of energy costs* during the 1970s that increased the relative costs of production in Germany and Japan (relative to those in the United States).
3. The *rise in US profitability* which made the United States an attractive destination for foreign investment, and which was due to:

    (a) the *squeeze on real wages* in the United States and the concomitant relatively *low rate of price inflation* in the United State (compared to its competitors)
    (b) the *advances in information technology* (IT) that were associated with the US Military-Industrial complex and the Aeronautics–Electronics–Computer sector.

4. *US military dominance* around the globe, both during the Cold War confrontation with the Soviet Union and its satellites and even more so after 1991 when the United States were the only superpower.

Let us take these factors one at a time.

Reserve currency status

While the *Global Plan* lasted, it did not matter much which currency one held, since the exchange rates *vis-à-vis* the dollar were almost fixed and the exchange rate between the dollar and gold was welded at $35 to an ounce of the gleaming metal. Nevertheless, oil magnates, German industrialists, French winemakers and Japanese bankers preferred to store their cash in dollars simply because of capital controls; that is, restrictions on how much cash one could convert to dollars or other currencies at any one time.

In the brave newer world that began on 15 August 1971, the psychological shock caused by the idea that currencies would soon be allowed to float freely, as if in a perpetual anarchic waltz around one another, created a stampede towards the dollar. To this day, whenever a crisis looms, in moments of gathering storm clouds, capital flees to the greenback. This is exactly why, as mentioned in the very first paragraph of this chapter, the *Crash of 2008* led to a mass inflow of foreign capital to the dollar, even though the crisis had begun in Wall Street. It was a far from one-off experience. Indeed, throughout the *Global Minotaur* era (1973–2008) every time the world sensed an impending downturn, a flight to the dollar ensued.

Of equal importance is the institutional fact that primary commodities are denominated in dollars. This puts the United States in a uniquely privileged position: the position of the only country whose currency's demand does not just reflect an increase in the demand of goods and services it produces. To make this plainer, consider the Singapore dollar. The only reason why the demand for it may rise is if persons holding other currencies want to buy goods or services originating in Singapore, if they wish to visit the island state or if they want to buy Singaporean real estate or shares. If Singapore's products, services and assets become less attractive to foreign buyers, or the state builds up debts which make investors fear that more Singapore dollars will be printed for the same level of output (and for the same level of demand for that currency), capital will migrate away from the Singapore dollar, its demand will fall and so will its value in terms of other currencies. That none of these constraints apply to the US dollar is the cause behind its *privileged position*!

When Singaporean, German or indeed Chinese drivers put petrol in their car, this act translates into an immediate increase in the demand for US dollars. Moreover, this is so even if the petrol is refined in a French refinery that bought the crude oil from a Libyan company and had it transported to the other side of the world in a Greek tanker, without the involvement of a single US company or national. How come? Simply because oil sales are denominated in dollars. So, the Singaporean petrol station's business translates into demand for a commodity, crude oil, whose sale from the Libyan oil well to the French refinery must involve the changing of French francs (or nowadays Euros) into US Dollars.

In short, the only currency in the world that is demanded for reasons that have nothing to do with economic activities occurring within its country of origin, is the US Dollar. This privileged status empowers US authorities to run deficits that would cause other countries to buckle under in no time. Moreover, and this is crucial to our argument below, it bestows upon US authorities another curious capability: both to engineer a crisis at the global level and, at once, to benefit from it, as foreign capital is bound to flood into the dollar zone at a whiff of such a crisis (even if the latter originates in the land of the free).

Rising energy costs

The United States' decision to accept (or, as we claim, spearhead) oil price increases as a means of arresting its deteriorating finances was largely based on the, correct, presumption that, while the US economy would suffer under the weight of rising energy costs, the relative position of the United States *vis-à-vis* Germany and Japan would be tilted back in its favour. Figure 11.2 reveals the main, albeit not the only, reason. While the US economy imported 32.5 per cent of its oil, Europe imported almost all of it and Japan imported every single drop. Even in 1980, after a great many energy-saving measures were introduced in Europe and Japan, and North Sea oil began to flow, the picture of relative dependencies did not change much.

Beyond import dependence, two more factors contributed to America's benefits from the oil crisis: first, as the oil trade was intimately linked to American multinationals, the higher oil prices meant a larger revenue base for them, higher profits and a strengthening of their capacity to diversify internationally; second, because of the dollar's reserve currency status (see above), the burgeoning revenues of oil exporters ended up back in New York in the form of investment in shares of American companies or of an increased demand for US government bonds.

Naturally, not all effects of a tumultuous train of events, like the traumatising oil crisis of the 1970s, move in one direction. Japanese and German industries reacted to the shock along

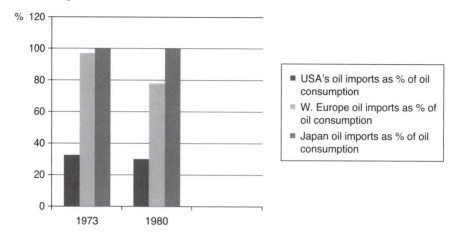

Figure 11.2 Oil dependency.

innovative paths that transformed their industrial production in ways that clawed back some of the relative gains that the United States had snatched from them by making energy so expensive. For instance, both Japan and Germany shifted their investment plans away from energy-intensive activities towards more high-tech endeavours (e.g. electronics). And even in the sectors that would always be reliant on oil and its by-products, for example the car industry, they produced a new generation of small, efficient cars which competed ruthlessly with US-produced cars.

Nevertheless, despite the conflicting effects, it can be said with a degree of confidence that the US government's plan succeeded. Higher energy prices tilted the balance back; away from Germany and Japan and in a manner that allowed the United States to continue with its deficits while maintaining (indeed bolstering) its position of global dominance. Figure 11.3 offers a snapshot of this tilting-back.

The pain caused by the crisis was real everywhere, with growth falling and prices and unemployment rising across the industrialised world. However, growth fell very little in the United States when compared with Western Europe and, in particular, with Japan.

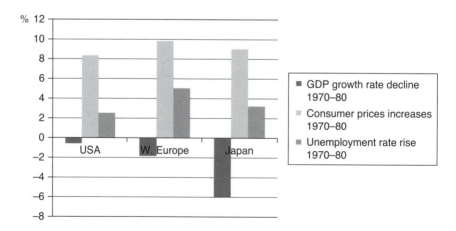

Figure 11.3 Effects of the 1970s crisis on the United States' relative position.

Similarly, inflation and unemployment costs fell disproportionately on the United States' protégés and this helped 'restore' power upon the superpower. Figure 11.6 (see Epilogue below) confirms that, as the *Global Minotaur* kept on devouring the capital tributes sent from Europe, Japan and the oil-exporting countries to its New York labyrinth, America's growth performance rose once more to dominance, for the first time since the Vietnam War scuttled the *Global Plan*.

Stagnant real wages and skyrocketing productivity

The dominant idea in the United States of the 1960s, one that permeated most shades of the political establishment, was that society had a collective task to reduce inequality of opportunity and, thus, to ameliorate social tensions through programmes that would assist the weakest in society at the expense, if need be, of higher taxes for those who could afford to pay them.

A cynic might say that this was the price the elites had to accept for co-opting the lower classes in their Vietnam War adventure. Or that, at the very least, it was the price the establishment was prepared to pay for stabilising the social order of a country that had managed, only quite recently, to dominate global capitalism. Regardless, the redistributive policies proved an important contributor to the gains made in relation to the repealing of racist institutions, the acceptance of the idea that the state had a responsibility to fund the education and health of the less well off, and the energising of a whole generation in the pursuit of social justice issues.

The 1970s crisis precipitated a major backlash. With the Vietnam War polarising society, and its impending loss signalling the end of any attempt at forging an alliance between the establishment, the lower classes and the dissidents among the young and the educated, the scene was set for new divisions between the haves and the have-nots; between capital and labour; between those who continued to think, both nationally and internationally, in terms of a *Local* and *Global Plan* (by which to regulate surplus and distribution) and those who fell back on the old idea of capitalism as a free-for-all; a playing field on which the strong do as they please and the weak bear their burdens stoically.

With energy prices rising, long queues forming at petrol stations, factories suspending production due to lack of raw materials or electricity, a new setting emerged in which all prior deals were off. Trade unions, incensed with across the board price rises, started demanding higher wages for their members. Employers were beginning to imagine a labour market without trade unions. The scene was, in other words, ready for a confrontation. In this new conflictual environment, the mighty corporations discerned a wonderful opportunity to put a lid on real wages and to strive for simultaneous increases in productivity. Figure 11.4 reports on their amazing success.

It is clear from the above table that, from 1973 onwards, something spectacular happened in the United States: in a country priding itself over the fact that, at least since the 1850s, real wages were rising steadily, thus giving every generation of workers the hope that their children would be better off than they were, real wages stagnated. To this day, they have not even recovered their 1973 real purchasing power.

Meanwhile, labour productivity accelerated. The employment of new technologies, the intensification of labour processes (often helped by the rising fear of unemployment) and the increasing investment into capital goods from abroad (e.g. German and Japanese firms that sought to boost their profitability by shifting operations to the US) gave rise to the impressively curved labour productivity graph in Figure 11.4.

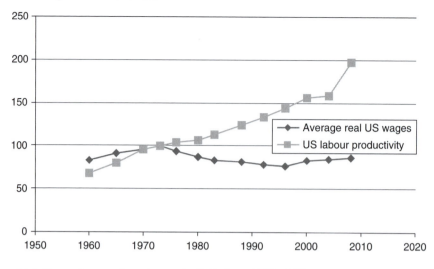

Figure 11.4 Stagnant wages, booming productivity (year 1975 = 100).

What happens when real wages fall, or remain stagnant, at a time of booming productivity? Profits reach for the sky. Figure 11.5 shows that this is precisely what happened after 1973. US corporate domestic profits rose, and rose, and rose. Increasing US profitability is the third reason why foreign (non-US) capital willingly fell on the *Global Minotaur*'s lap, migrating at great speed and in unprecedented volume from Frankfurt, Riyadh, Tokyo, Paris and Milan to New York.

Geopolitical might

Power concentrates the mind of the weak. And nuclear power concentrates it better. The very fact that the United States led the West not only in economic but also in geostrategic

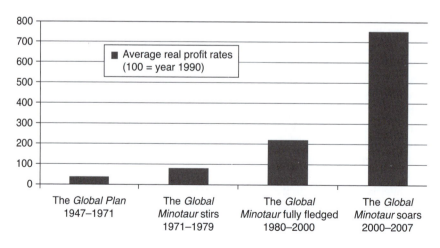

Figure 11.5 US real profits during the post-war period and prior to the *Crash of 2008*.

terms cannot be neglected when studying the mechanism by which capital readily migrated to nourish the *Global Minotaur*. Of course, if foreign capital had no expectation of accumulating faster once it made the journey via New York to the US Treasury or to some US company or financial institution, nothing could have enticed it do so. Nonetheless, geopolitical and military power played a role in shoring up the expectation of such a gain.

Boxes 11.9 and 11.10 present examples of such links between the economic and the geopolitical dimension of the *Global Minotaur*. Beyond them, it is not hard to spot a broader nexus between economic and strategic policymaking; between the arm of US government that pursued policies for strengthening US multinationals and other governmental agencies that worked scrupulously to augment the United States' political and military position. By the early 1980s, under the Reagan administration, US policy fully endorsed the import of this nexus and a consensus emerged that the balance of payments ought not be the focus of attention any more; that what mattered was the strength of US finance, founded upon the strength of its multinationals, particularly in the energy sector; on maintaining the dollar's reserve currency status (without any form of concrete payment, like gold, behind it); and, last but not least, on developing even stronger links between economic and geopolitical power, especially through the cultivation of local elites hooked in every possible way to the US administration and to the US multinationals.

Box 11.9 The *Global Minotaur*'s Guardian and his Disciples
Europe, Oil, the Developing World, *China*

Just like the *Global Plan* had some very bright minds behind it (recall Box 11.2), so did the *Global Minotaur*. Henry Kissinger (who was initially President Nixon's National Security Adviser before climbing to the position of Secretary of State in 1973) was the Minotaur's first guardian; the walking think tank that took the Minotaur by the hand and showed him how to rule the world.

In a talk he delivered on April 1973, known as the *Year of Europe* speech, Kissinger voiced the fear that, courtesy of what we call the *Global Plan* of the 1947–71 period, Europe was on the verge of turning into a power comparable to the United States. At least, that it would begin to find it possible to strike separate deals with Middle Eastern oil producers, a development that would cut out US mediation and, potentially, undermine the hitherto central role of the dollar. In this light, Kissinger's determination to see oil prices rise fast across the board, and the political clash between Arab oil exporters and the United States extend to the Europeans' relation with the Arab countries, throws additional light to the discussion in Box 11.7.

In this view, the oil crisis of 1973 bore no causal relationship with the Arab–Israeli conflict, which simply proved too good an opportunity to miss for a strategist of Kissinger's calibre. In fact, a US Senate Report (reporting mainly on US military exercises in Iran) confirms in no uncertain terms that '... the leadership within OPEC in rising prices has come from Iran and Venezuela, countries that have a minimal interest in the Arab–Israeli dispute' (cited in Chomsky 1977). At this point it must be remembered that the two countries mentioned were, at the time, two of America's staunchest geopolitical allies run by despots kept in power almost singlehandedly by the US military and the CIA: The Shah of Iran and President Suharto of Indonesia.

The two men played a major role in serving the United States' military interests in the underbelly of the Soviet Union and The People's Republic of China respectively and, at once, they were doing, according to the said Report, the United States' bidding within OPEC against Germany and Japan.

A year later, in 1974, Henry Kissinger circulated a new National Security Doctrine for the United States, through the now well-known *National Security Study Memorandum 200 (NSSM-200)*. Under the cloak of the imperative to defend the West from the encroachments of the Soviet Union and its allies in the realm of raw materials and energy, the Memorandum staked a naked claim, on behalf of the United States and US multinationals, over the mineral wealth of the Developing World. In fact, Kissinger's new 'national security' writ explicitly expressed the view that Developing World development posed a threat to United States security. Unbelievably, it even went as far as to suggest that it would might be in the interests of the United States if tens of Developing World countries were to see their populations shrink. Kissinger's neo-Malthusian penchant even named some of these countries. They included India, Turkey, Brazil, Indonesia, Nigeria and Egypt.

Henry Kissinger was not a shooting star through the night's dark sky. In the years that followed, and especially as the *Global Minotaur* was to soar (between 2000 and 2007), his thinking found worthy heirs and successors. In November 2000, Richard Hass, who was to become Director of Policy Planning in the State Department, wrote an essay advocating that the USA adopt an 'imperial' (*sic*) foreign policy. He defined the latter as '... a foreign policy that attempts to organise the world along certain principles affecting relations between states and conditions within them'. This would not be achieved through colonies but through what he termed 'informal control', which would require military might (if necessary). Global mechanisms such as international financial markets, the World Trade Organisation (WTO), the IMF, etc. were earmarked as essential devices for ensuring the dominance of US interests, with the military iron fist backing up the invisible hand of the market.

To give an additional example of the nexus between military dominance and the USA's economic comparative advantage, it is useful to recount the testimony given to a Congressional hearing on Afghanistan in 1998 by John Maresca, Vice President of oil giant UNOCAL (see Maresca, 1998). In a cheerful prophecy of the 2001 war in Afghanistan, Maresca outlined a rationale for a US invasion of Afghanistan and a future takeover of Central Asia's natural resources. His argument turned on Chinese economic development, which has to be, in his view, both abetted and controlled (just like Europe's and Japan's economic development was after the Second World War, we might add).

Maresca implied that, unlike Japan and Europe, China will not willingly liberalise its capital account and, therefore, the flow of capital from China to the USA will be impeded. In simpler words, profits by Chinese, Japanese, European and, of course, US companies operating in China will not be readily transferable to the *Global Minotaur*, Maresca lamented. Even though Maresca did not spell it out, he was hinting strongly that China's refusal to allow for free capital movements to the USA was certain to impede the process of financing the US deficit from the emerging giant. The best way to overcome China's recalcitrance, Maresca explained, would be to monopolise the supply of energy *in its vicinity*. It does not take much genius to see that if China's energy supplies are indeed successfully circumscribed, and placed under the control of US companies, it would be easier for the USA, via the WTO, IMF, etc. to force China's hand and earn concessions on the freedom of China-generated capital to flee to New York.

Nowadays, after the *Global Minotaur's* demise in 2008, and the heightened importance of Chinese capital transfers to the United States to maintain the dollar zone, these thoughts have taken on a new and urgent significance. China is continuing to fund the American budget deficit, though not the trade deficit. At the same time, it has almost taken the whole of the African continent under its wing, hoping that its large infrastructural and political investment[1] in that tragic continent will generate the oil supplies that it needs.

Note
1 It is worth noting here that, in 2007, China's investments in Angola alone exceeded the total sum lent by the IMF worldwide. The fact that Angola is now emerging as a major oil producer should not be lost on us.

Box 11.10 The Cold War's most lethal weapon: Interest rate rises

Following the swift ascent of oil prices in the 1970s, inflation took hold. Central banks, struggling to keep the lid on average prices, increased money (or nominal) interest rates. Setting aside, for the moment, the worldwide, recessionary effects of this development, the rise of interest rates proved *more effective in destroying the enemies of US foreign policy around the globe than any military operation the USA could ever imagine.* Arguably, the chain of events that led to the implosion of communism in Poland and Yugoslavia began in the 1970s with the sharp rise in interest rates soon after these countries had accepted offers of substantial loans from Western financial institutions. Similarly with Developing World countries in which national liberation movements had grabbed power, often against the West's better efforts.

From the early 1960s till 1972, Western banks (usually based in the new country's old colonial master) visited the new rulers, bearing offers of large loans at low interest rates. They also travelled to Soviet satellites, such as Poland, and communist countries that were detached or semi-detached from Moscow (Yugoslavia and Romania). Reportedly, they wouldn't take 'no' for an answer, for the simple reason that the whole period of the *Global Plan*, with its stability and low interest rates, presented the banks with few opportunities for speculative lending. Thus, African, Latin American and several Eastern Bloc states borrowed large sums from international banks, at low interest rates (even though slightly above those paid in the North). The loans were used to underwrite much needed new infrastructure, education, health systems, fledgling industrial sectors, etc. In this way, by the mid-1970s, most Developing World economies, and a number of Eastern European ones, were extremely vulnerable to interest rate rises.

So, as interest rates shot up in the mid-1970s, from between 4 and 5 per cent to between 20 and 30 per cent, the Developing World Debt Crisis began and communist

336 Modern political economics

regimes in Warsaw, Bucharest and Belgrade began to feel the pressure too. The latter, once they realised their new grave dependency on the 'capitalist enemy', gave their all to repay the debts as quickly as possible. To do so, however, they imposed particularly harsh austerity measures on their own workforce (in Romania, for example, house heating ceased for years, even during the coldest of winter months), the result being mass discontent that led to major social and political unrest. The latter turned out to be the source of legitimacy of Polish trade union *Solidarnosc*, which was soon to spearhead a chain of events leading to the first collapse of a communist regime, even before the breaching of the Berlin Wall in 1989. Yugoslavia's ills can also be traced to the debt crisis, as can the first cracks in the ironclad regime of Romanian despot Nicolae Ceaușescu.

Meanwhile, in the Developing World, countries that found themselves unable to meet their interest payments, under the new interest rates, were forced to call in the IMF (see Box 11.1). The IMF happily offered to lend money to governments for the purposes of repaying the Western banks, but at an exorbitant price: the dismantling of the public sector (including schools and clinics), the shrinking of the newly founded state and the wholesale transfer of valuable public assets (e.g. water boards, telecommunications, etc.) to Western companies. It is not at all an exaggeration to suggest that the Developing World Debt Crisis was the colonised world's second historic disaster (the first being colonisation and the slave trade); in fact, it was a disaster from which most Developing World countries never quite recovered.

In short, the oil crisis had a staggering side-effect wholly in tune with Washington's geopolitical aims: it destroyed the Developing World's dream of liberating itself from neo-colonialism and, even more, planted the seeds of destruction into the foundations of the Eastern bloc.

Box 11.11 The *Global Minotaur's* geostrategic mindset and climate change

Moving, for a moment, beyond wars and oil, President George W. Bush distinguished himself not only by invading Iraq but also by an earlier policy decision of his first administration (in 2000): the torpedoing of the Kyoto Protocol on climate change. History's kindest possible interpretation of this would be the view that his administration was focused on the oil industry (due to their well-established personal involvement in US oil multinationals) and did not care much for the environment. However, there is another, more disturbing, interpretation; one that connects the *Global Minotaur*, geopolitical concerns and climate change.

According to this more disturbing take on American policy during 2000–8, the organised undermining of the green agenda, the war waged against scientific research on climate change, the scuttling of the Kyoto Protocol, etc., were consistent with *particular* climate-related objectives of the Bush administration (as opposed to a lack of focus on climate). In 2002–3, circles in Washington were canvassing the view that global warming might be bad for most parts of the world *but not necessarily bad for the USA*. There is, indeed, speculation that US agri-business might *benefit* from an increase in global temperatures because, according to estimates based on large-scale computerised simulations, the productivity of American agriculture will rise *as long as genetically modified seeds are extensively used*. Guess who controls the production and distribution of genetically modified seeds: Monsanto, the US multinational.

These Dr Strangelovian ideas, while thankfully discarded by the Obama administration, are a useful reminder of the United States' policymakers' obsession with the project of remaining unimpeded by its balance of trade deficit. That some of them were prepare to countenance these schemes at the planet's expense is merely symptomatic of the mindset that the *Global Minotaur* occasioned.

To recap, the nexus between geopolitical power and the centrality of the dollar's role in maintaining the *Global Minotaur* grew stronger and stronger. A brief perusal of the Fed's research papers during the 1990s confirms that US authorities saw the greenback as a *strategic asset*. The drive to use political influence in order to dollarise whole foreign economies, especially in Latin America in the 1990s, is to be understood as part of the same mindset. Dollarisation meant that the dollar became the country's *de facto* local currency.

The main effect of this move, from the *Global Minotaur*'s perspective, was that the demand for dollars all of a sudden depended not only on the international transactions of other countries but on the domestic transactions of the dollarised economies as well. As dollars were increasingly demanded by foreigners also for their own domestic purposes, the United States' balance of payments played a decreasing role in shaping the dollar's value in the international money markets (see Halevi, 2002). The deep, and deeply wounding (for local societies), crises that dollarisation led to in the later 1990s were, in this sense, mere collateral losses during the process of maintaining the *Minotaur*.[13]

11.7 Epilogue

Book 1 ended with our manifesto for a thoroughly modern political economics. This chapter, the first of *Book 2*, is our attempt to put our money where our proverbial mouth is. In the Postscript to *Book 1*, we wrote: 'Equipped with the necessary, but erroneous, viewpoints provided by the different shades of political economics… we shall now attempt to synthesise them into a theory of 2008 and its aftermath'. Thus, with a panoply of failed models at the back of our minds, we took our first step towards an historical inquiry into how the post-war world was designed, by whom, to what purpose and with what effect.

Our conclusions are, no doubt, controversial. However, our exercise did produce one indubitable inference. No model or determinate abstraction stands a chance of retaining even a whiff of post-war capitalism; of a 'system' whose geometry and essence keeps evolving in a manner that is both structured and inherently unpredictable; both designed and spontaneously fashioned; an organic whole that defies all modelling attempts to second-guess it. And yet, at the very same time, we felt doubly certain that our ability to 'see' our subject matter's metamorphoses depended on having engaged previously with the *necessary errors* also known as economic models.

In the end, we settled for a specific theory of post-war global capitalism, something of our very own *Genealogy of 2008* which, in the next chapter, will develop into our account of the *Crash of 2008* and its aftermath. The simple story so far is that the post-war era can be fruitfully divided into two phases. The first was very carefully planned and lasted from around 1947 to the end of Bretton Woods in 1971. We labelled it the *Global Plan* era for the plain reason that it was both global and meticulously planned.

The basis of the *Plan* was the idea of creating a stable international monetary system in which the dollar would play the role of the effective world currency, with the Deutschmark and the Yen in a supporting role (primarily the role of shock absorbers in case of a domestic US downturn). To shore up these two currencies, and support its own export sector, the United States extended credit to Western Europe and Japan (on occasion through war financing) and used its geopolitical might to guarantee them both cheap raw materials and sizeable markets for their industries' output. In return, its protégés absorbed substantial imports from the United States (increasingly of the high tech, aeronautical and military technology type) and afforded the dollar the privilege of being the only currency whose value transcended the demand and supply of American goods, services and assets.

The second phase was nowhere near as neat and tidy. Having emerged from the catastrophic collapse of the *Global Plan* (caused largely by the explosive costs of the Vietnam War and the need to spend large sums of money within the United States in order to minimise dangerous social tensions), the second phase was, at least to the naked eye, anarchic, traumatic and precarious. Indeed, the tumult was such that, even though the new phase was largely designed in Washington, it would be wrong to call it a 'design'.

Its main feature was that, in contrast to the *Global Plan*'s express intention of balancing trade flows, capital flows, exchange rates, interest rates, energy prices, etc., the new phase was designed to defend American hegemony by doing exactly the opposite: that is, by causing energy prices to go through the roof, closely followed by interest rates, commodities prices, average prices, etc. Systematic asymmetries were the order of the day. Moreover, these asymmetries, on which the new global architecture was erected, could only be maintained if they kept deepening, accelerating, growing. In this sense, the second phase required a kind of *negative engineering*; an attempt by its architects (strategists like Henry Kissinger and Paul Volcker) to *unbalance and rule*; to *destabilise and reign;* to *unhinge and stay ahead.*

When thinking of a label for this second post-war phase, the parable of the Minotaur suggested itself. The period that began in the mid-1970s, after the eruption of the oil crisis, and ended dramatically in the *Crash of 2008*, reminded us of the Minoan reign over the Aegean states, and the system of tributes to the Minotaur that King Minos had imposed upon weaker city-states as the price of a semblance of peace and prosperity.

While the Minotaur parable is somewhat stretching historical reality, like all mythological metaphors must do, the essence of America's hegemony during the 1973–2008 period was not too dissimilar: rather than extending the protestant ethic of thrift and personal morality to the whole nation (i.e. instead of reducing its trade and government budget deficits), the United States embarked upon a project of *expanding* its deficits and of inducing an accelerating flood of foreign capital to flow into Wall Street (a modern day form of voluntary tributes). Bluntly put, the deficits would burgeon and other people's money would pay for them.

It was of course not the first time that a large and powerful hegemon succeeded in having others pay for its profligacy. Indeed, Ancient Athens exacted protection money from its 'allies'; the Ottomans from their far flung territories; Spain built palaces and cathedrals using gold plundered in the Americas; the Northern Europeans turned the process of profiting from colonialism into a fine art. Perhaps the closest parallel to the 1973–2008 phase of US hegemony was the manner in which Britain used India's trade surpluses to cover for its own balance of trade deficits in the first two decades of the twentieth century (see Box 11.12 below).

> *Box 11.12* A more recent parallel
> *Indians bearing surpluses and the* Global Minotaur
>
> From the end of the nineteenth-century until the Great War, Britain ran a considerable balance of trade deficit. However, during the same period, India was in surplus with the rest of the world. Britain, using its position as India's imperial master, took advantage of Indian merchandise surpluses. Not only did it tax India's surpluses but, even more significantly, it ensured that India's surpluses were processed through the City of London. In this manner, India was exporting to the rest of the world and its surpluses were financing Britain's balance of payments deficits either directly (through crude taxation) or indirectly (through the financial gains made by City institutions on the back of the financial flows due to Indian external trade).
>
> To some extent, this is reminiscent of the *Global Minotaur* whose *raison d'être* was to encourage capital to flow from the rest of the world to Wall Street; a financial flow that the United States used to pay for its expanding twin deficits. There is however a major difference that renders this parallel imperfect: whereas India could run a trade surplus with the rest of the world, in the process of financing Britain's balance of trade deficit, in the case of the *Global Minotaur*, the rest of the world could not run a surplus, namely the rest of the world.
>
> It is in this sense that the *Global Minotaur* imposed upon the world a policy of effective global deflation. For in the absence of inter-stellar trade, the only way that the United States could cajole the rest of the world to accept the perpetual migration of capital to its financial institutions was by eliciting, and recapitulating, a systematic drainage elsewhere. This incongruity, we shall be arguing, was a major cause of instability which constantly lurked in the shadows of the *Global Minotaur*. The *Crash of 2008* cannot be fully understood without this simple fact in mind.

And yet, there was something unique about the *Global Minotaur*. First, the influx of foreign capital into Wall Street was entirely voluntary. Unlike the Athenians' tributes, the Mayan gold and the Indian surpluses, the America-bound capital inflows of the 1973–2008 period into Wall Street were completely self-motivated, unforced, spontaneous. Second, because the tributes to the United States were coming from all capitalist centres around the globe, these systematic capital transfers meant that the rest of the world was constantly being bled of capital. The point here is that, since the rest of the world could not make up its capital account deficit with the United States by having a trade surplus with... the rest of the world, the result was that it was being steadily drained of investment and, therefore, of effective demand (see the last paragraph in Box 11.12).

With foreign capital on a perpetual *haj* to New York's stock and money markets from the 1973 oil crisis onwards, the United States' increasing balance of trade deficit (see Figure 11.6) and its government budget deficit[14] (see Figure 11.7) became sustainable. Since at least 1980, it is as if the whole globe was busily supplying the United States with (a) the capital transfers necessary to feed its twin deficits (our *Global Minotaur*) and (b) commodities at non-inflationary prices. But the more successful the United States was at attracting capital from the rest of the world the greater the forces that pulled the latter towards stagnation.

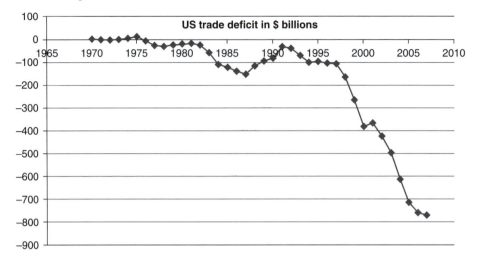

Figure 11.6 US trade deficit.

With the world economy (excluding the US) labouring under the constant threat of permanent deflation, Japanese factories found it hard to make use of their capacity and thus the Japanese economy entered a so-called lost decade; a state of perpetual recession.[15] This made Japan even more dependent on exporting to the USA. US officials, cognisant of this, allowed Japanese firms continued (albeit controlled) access to American consumers but at a hefty price: Japan had to forego any plans at developing its own international financial policy or from establishing new international bodies for the minimisation of financial volatility – especially in South-East Asia. Meanwhile, on the globe's other side, in Europe, Germany began to consider a currency union that would allow its manufacturing industry to extract

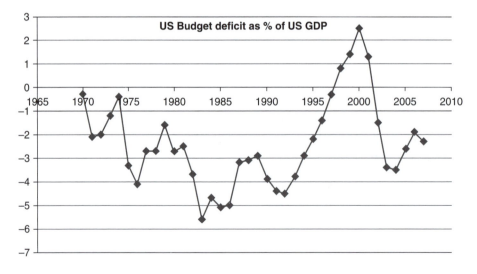

Figure 11.7 US federal government budget deficit.

surpluses within a deflationary European Union more efficiently (and with less uncertainty *vis-à-vis* exchange rate valuations).

Summing up, the second post-war phase was marked by the transformation of the world economy into a periphery from which the United States imported large quantities of capital which allowed it to run an increasing trade deficit. Of course this periphery was no homogeneous magma. It was, rather, a well-structured realm, complete with two powerful currency zones (euro-land and Japan–South-East-Asia) which themselves featured internal imbalances between chronically surplus and deficit regions (e.g. the divide between the surplus countries in the European Union, led by Germany, and the deficit countries, e.g. Spain, Portugal and Greece). When, in the mid-1990s China entered the fray as another trade surplus powerhouse, the asymmetries deepened and grew further, both at the global level and within Asian goods and capital markets.

Throughout the *Global Minotaur* years, the United States paid for its deficit (to the rest of the world) by issuing bonds and treasury bills or by attracting capital through its stock exchanges. This is the way in which the economists' traditional concern (of what to do with the deficit) was dispensed with. Low US inflation and low US wages were pivotal to this strategy.[16] Similarly, low wages translated into high corporate profitability which, in turn, made the stocks traded in Wall Street even more attractive to foreign investors.

So, from the late 1970s onwards, the main game in Washington was how to underpin and reinforce the power of US financial capital, at the inevitable cost of a deflationary environment for the rest of the capitalist world. The halcyon days of the *Global Plan*, a time when the United States would erect its hegemony on a bedrock of support for the rest of the capitalist world, were well and truly over. The moment the *Global Minotaur* took over the globe's reins, the pattern was reversed. Figure 11.8 reveals the *Minotaur*'s towering success. No commentary is needed. By the 1990s, its triumph was complete.

It is perhaps fitting to end this chapter with the words of Paul Volcker, the man whom we first 'met' earlier (see Section 11.4) when, during 1970–1, from the position of Under Secretary of the Treasury for International Monetary Affairs, he advised Henry Kissinger that the time had come to confine the *Global Plan* to history's dustbin.

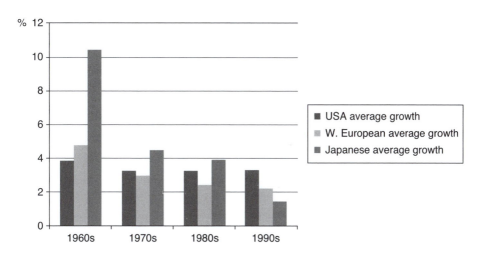

Figure 11.8 The *Global Minotaur*'s success.

By the end of the decade, in 1979, Volcker had been elevated to the Chair of the Federal Reserve, the Fed. One of the first things he did, as Fed Chairman, was to give a disarmingly honest lecture at Warwick University in 1978, which was published in the *Quarterly Review* of the Federal Reserve Bank of New York (Volcker 1978–9). In it he tells anyone who was interested to listen that:

> It is tempting to look at the market as an impartial arbiter … But balancing the requirements of a stable international system against the desirability of retaining freedom of action for national policy, a number of countries, including the US, opted for the latter …

And as if this were not loud and clear enough, Volcker added the following for good measure:

> [A] controlled disintegration in the world economy is a legitimate objective for the 1980s.

12 Crash

2008 and its legacy

12.1 The *Minotaur* in the room

On the run up to the *Crash of 2008*, almost everyone sang from the same song sheet in praise of the American economy. European policymakers in Brussels, their Japanese counterparts in Tokyo, Italian ex-communists, Eastern European born-again neo-rightists, academic economists: they all cast a lustful gaze across the great oceans and towards the land of the free, convinced that the United States was *the* model to be urgently and unequivocally emulated.

Whole forests were pulped to produce the policy papers heralding yet another 'new era'. One where American-style unregulated labour and financial markets promised new vistas of prosperity, spreading with the *élan* of Hollywood's latest blockbuster from Paris to Moscow, from Amsterdam to Athens, from Yokohama to Shanghai.

Ireland and even Britain, were held up as pioneers on this modern road to Damascus. The proverbial pot of gold was sought at the end of the Anglo-Celtic rainbow, somewhere between a Wal-Mart store and a Wall Street bankers' club, between the City of London and an East End building site on which armies of Eastern European *gastarbeiters* were building new apartments for the platoons of up and coming city workers.

The relevant keywords were 'entrepreneurship', 'competitiveness', 'flexibility', all great virtues that Europe, Japan and the rest of the world had, allegedly, 'allowed' the United States, and its fellow-travelling Anglo-Celts, to make their own. In a rendition of the 1920s (recall Chapter 7), people truly believed that poverty was a choice made by the weak and that it could easily be avoided by a conscious decision to join the power-drive to affluence. Lunch was for wimps, the market was king and queen wrapped up in one, social justice was an excuse for avoidable failure and any talk of crisis revealed a weakness for loony left narratives, or at least an incapacity to grasp the new possibilities made possible by the Anglo-American blueprint. As for governments, regulating capitalism was no longer on their radar screen. The newest mantra was about ways and means of enshrining into their ministries and institutions the urgency for pursuing the triptych: 'entrepreneurship', 'competitiveness', 'flexibility'.

For years the conference halls in which the bureaucrats met echoed with the quasi-religious hymns to the new Anglo-Celtic 'enterprise culture'. Bureaucrats and politicians were singing them *as if* to atone for prior allegiance to the welfare state, to the regulation of financial and labour markets, to the idea that capitalism ought to be kept on a leash. The European Union became the greatest producer of endless reports, green papers, resolutions, research papers, outlining the imperative of adopting the entrepreneurial logic from across the Atlantic as a prerequisite for jumping on the Anglo-Celtic bandwagon.

It was a sad literature that traded heavily on the preposterous assumption that the reasons why the US economy was steaming ahead of the European and Japanese ones had to do with the superiority of the Protestant ethic, the debilitating effects on incentives caused by over-generous safety nets and overly regulated European and Japanese goods, labour and capital markets. With a beastly *Minotaur* in the room wrecking the furniture and devouring all he could grab, Eurocrats were engaged in jejune discussions on competitiveness and the subtleties of the European Union's *Lisbon Treaty* (2000). But this silliness was not confined to Europe. Every card-carrying member of the global commentariat was on the same wavelength, refusing to acknowledge the inescapable truth about the United States' real source of dynamism.

Unable to come to terms with their *Minotaur Envy*, they pretended there was no beast in the room. Their pretence was so powerful that they hypnotised themselves into believing that, yes, it was possible for *everyone* (Europe, Japan, China, India, etc.) to achieve the same success as the United States had (since the mid-1970s) simply by adopting the American model. In a bid to provide yet another testimony to the human capacity for wishful thinking, hordes of otherwise bright people lulled themselves into a remarkable fantasy: that it was possible for *all* major capitalist centres around the world to attract, at once, a massive *net flow of capital* (in the region of three to five billion dollars per working day, which was the sum that the *Global Minotaur* had managed during its golden years); that it was feasible for all major capitalist centres not only to breed their own *Minotaurs* but also to cajole the rest of the world into nourishing them.

The reality was, as is its inclination, laughing in the face of such folly. Europe and Japan *always* regulated the supply of labour (either institutionally or conventionally) more stringently than the United States did. And yet for 30 years the European and Japanese economies were outstripping that of the United States. What changed in the early 1970s? Did no one notice what happened in 1973? Did they really believe that the oil crisis was an exogenous shock brought about by a few recalcitrant sheiks? Is the human mind that gullible?

Before 2008, conventional wisdom had it that it was all due to technological change; due to 'paradigmatic shift' which forced American capitalism to move up a gear, rendering Europe's and Japan's old ways (with job security, worker's rights, etc.) obsolete. Alas, conventional wisdom yet again confirms its poor track record at explaining historical shifts. Let us set aside the inconvenient fact that the Japanese and German producers never lagged behind their US competitors in technological innovation and expertise. And let us suppose, for argument's sake, that the US economy did, indeed, steam ahead on the strength of information and communication technologies (ICT), soared on the basis of its aeronautical, computing and electronic industries (ACE), fuelled by the spirit of American free enterprise, and propelled itself into a position of global dominance unencumbered by worker-friendly labour laws.

If this were so, the American economy ought to have become more dynamic, inventive and innovative *across all sectors involving* ICT and ACE (*vis-à-vis* their Japanese and European equivalents). It did not! The only sectors in which the Americans overtook the Euro-Japanese were those which were intimately linked to the US defence budget; a whopping powerhouse that makes European alleged statism seem like a walk in the park. And yet, Eurocrats, Japanese officials and the financial press were all quite happy uncritically to accept this 'conventional wisdom'. Mistaking an effect for a cause, they observed that in the United States more small firms (relative to Europe and Japan) showed a greater propensity to grow into medium-sized ones. And from this observation they surmised (without further explanation) that there must be something about American small business that boosts their growth rate. Then they looked closer but failed to spot the missing ingredient.

Exhausted, they concluded that the reason must be in the heads of American entrepreneurs; that it must have something to do with the greater fear of remaining uninsured in a rich country where millions have access to no proper medical care. And, regrettably, they recommended that perhaps what the Europeans and the Japanese need is a little tough medicine: fewer workers' rights, fewer social benefits, shorter holidays and, generally, a life more brutish, nastier and shorter (always in the hope that desperation will stir up waves of entrepreneurship).

What they had failed to see, even though it kept staring them in the face, is that the United States is not only the land of many small businesses but also the land of the world's largest and most numerous multinational conglomerates; that US policymakers were the most activist, foresighted, interventionist officials in human history; that US growth in the 1980s and 1990s was financed by other people's capital and domestic borrowing; so much overseas capital and so much domestic debt that if all Americans were to sell everything they owned, they could still not repay the borrowed funds.

Box 12.1 The rejuvenation of American corporate capitalism

During the *Global Minotaur* phase, American industry underwent a major growth spurt. While it is true that the US industrial sector was struggling to keep up with the US economy's overall growth, its major manufacturers were, nevertheless, having an excellent innings. The interconnections and synergies between industry and *the* truly booming 'sector', i.e. Wall Street, were crucial. The flood of foreign capital into Wall Street made rivers of cash available for traditional manufacturers such as General Motors. If foreign investors did not directly buy General Motors' shares, the Wall Street institutions that handled foreign cash would gladly lend to General Motors at very low rates. Moreover, companies like General Motors diversified, extending their tentacles into the world of finance. In that way, and as long as the financial sector was inflating, they were not only strengthening their bottom line but, additionally, were using the flood of cash (from issuing loans and then trading them for other financial 'products') to shore up their own monopoly power within their industrial sectors. One way they did this was by taking over or merging with competitors.

Consider the following example described in some detail in *The Wall Street Journal* of 14 February 2000 [See Foster (2004b)]. Following the South-East Asian crisis of 1999, the South Korean car industry was on the verge of bankruptcy. General Motors and Ford fought tooth and nail as to who would purchase Korea's number two car manufacturer, Daewoo. It was General Motors who moved first with a $6 billion offer. The question is: why bother? What was the allure of a failed company that owed $16 billion, offered very little in terms of technological innovation (valuable patents, etc.) and had disparate factories strewn all over the world in places that were not of great strategic importance to General Motors? The answer is: *excess capacity*.

Noting that both Ford and General Motors were already under-using their existing capacity (producing no more than 55 per cent of the cars their factories were capable of), they had no need for more capacity to expand production. However, to think that capacity is required only in order to manufacture products is to misunderstand the strategic role of unused capacity. The point of having a capacity to flood the market with a lot more cars (than the number one is currently producing) is an essential entry deterrent for competitors in the markets that one dominates. Thus, General Motors, in buying Daewoo, was not purchasing factories so as to use their capacity to produce more cars. Rather, it was buying a strategic card that would scare its European and Japanese competitors off; a card whose price would be worth paying as long as General Motors never had to use it.

Indeed, Daewoo's factories, after General Motors bought them, have never, to this date, produced above 30 per cent of their capacity. And yet, the purchase was considered a success. The new factories played their part in boosting General Motors' global oligopoly power for reasons that had everything to do with the cars they could potentially produce and nothing to do with the cars they were intending to produce. In essence, the *Global Minotaur* enabled General Motors to buy excess capacity abroad that increased its oligopoly power, and thus its profits, in every market around the world.

A year or two before, in 1998, the *Global Minotaur's* weight was felt in another way within the US car industry. Attracted to the United States, for the reasons Chapter 11 outlined in detail, German car giant *Daimler-Benz* decided to take an inordinate risk and take over Chrysler (even though, for reasons of tactfulness, it was presented as a merger). *Business Week* explained that the purpose of this new colossus was to achieve global dominance in a market that requires, for that purpose, a capacity to produce at least 15 million cars annually. (Note the operative word: 'capacity', as opposed to actual output.)

Summing up, we chose to tell the tale of US industry's success using as an example the US car industry for two reasons: first, car manufacture is America's most unionised industrial sector; second, its output is the least sophisticated and its production methods are verging on the paleolithic (when compared to the European and Japanese manufacturers). And yet, during the *Global Minotaur* era, US car makers were met with stunning success. Why? Where did this 'competitiveness' come from? Despite the Europeans' fantasies, it did not come from technological innovation, from offering customers advanced products or from having a labour force that is at the management's beck and call. So, what was the real reason?

The real reason was the capital inflows that were nourishing the *Global Minotaur* ever since oil prices went through the roof in 1973. For it was that streaming capital which allowed traditional US manufacturers to purchase additional monopoly or oligopoly power in places such as Korea, but also in Europe itself (*Volvo, Saab, Jaguar,* etc.). The result was greater global market share, higher profitability and an ever more complex interrelation with the world of finance, the sector that amplified the capital inflows into the United States.

Some years ago, our viewpoint caused incredulity among those who wanted to believe in the 'new paradigm'.[1] Like practising astrologists who will simply not countenance the possibility that stars do not determine one's life, almost everyone was determined to keep the faith that the post-1973 US economic miracle was due to the flexibility of its labour markets, the entrepreneurship of the average American manager and the US government's clear-headed pursuit of a free-market agenda. That Great Consensus was built not only on a false diagnosis of the causes of US growth but also of its outcomes. Europeans were insisting that American-style reforms would generate benefits that would trickle down to the average European. Where did they get that idea from? Certainly not from the United States' experience during the 1973–2008 period. We have already seen that real wages remained stagnant throughout that period of superior US growth (recall Table 11.4). The *Global Minotaur* proved rather mean towards the average American. In fact, never before have so few Americans had so much while the many had to survive on so little (see Galbraith, 1998; Varoufakis, 2002).

Beside the increasing inequality, it is important to look at the different growth rates of different sectors of the US economy. The true beneficiaries from the *Global Minotaur*'s ascent were three sectors of the US economy: (a) energy multinationals (mostly oil companies); (b) the ICT and ACE sectors hooked into the US military; and, last but definitely not least, (c) the financial institutions handling the capital flows from the rest of the world. As for the rest of the US domestic economy, its fate was identical to that of the rest of the world: condemned to live in a state of slow-burning, thinly disguised, deflationary crisis.

Another fantasy of the time was the so-called *trickle down wealth effect*;[2] the idea that if the rich get richer then, eventually, some of that wealth will slip through the cracks 'downstairs', where the poor are. In a bid to minimise any residue of guilt felt by the minority whose pay cheques were acquiring more zeros, the rich told themselves that *everyone* would benefit, including the majority on minimum wages. Well, the country where this idea gained a large following in the1980s, the United States, is also the place where the hypothesis can be empirically dismissed.

To see this consider the US sectors in which the greatest productivity gains were experienced and the highest profitability was registered. Even in these lucrative sectors, median salaries remained unchanged throughout the *Minotaur*'s best years (2000 to 2006); the same period during which productivity rose by 16 per cent, profits by a whopping 23 per cent, and the remuneration of management leapt by a stunning 85 per cent. In fact, within the depressed sectors of the US economy, median wages slipped steadily for more than 12 years.

Imagine: up to five billion dollars being pumped every day into a country for 20 long years and, at the end of the day, *its median wage earner sees none of the benefits*, even though he/she works longer hours and much more productively than ever before.[3] How is it that the living standards of a nation's hard-working labourers were falling steadily against the background of an economy that grows steadily for three decades both in absolute terms and, also, in relation to its main competitors abroad? Table 12.1 throws some additional light (to that which we saw in Chapter 11) on this puzzle.

What we see is that the period during which the United States began to attract massive capital inflows coincided with the period (1985–90) when American unit labour costs almost stayed still[4] while Germany's and Japan's were growing at a rate closer to the rate of productivity rises. By the time the capital flights from Germany and Japan to New York had begun in earnest, thus causing wages to deflate there too (in the early 1990s), the collapse of the rate of increase in labour costs in Europe and Japan could no longer match the fall in US labour costs. Seizing the opportunity that the oil crisis and the rising unemployment presented to

348   *Modern political economics*

Table 12.1 Average annual rate of change in *labour unit costs* (in $US)

	1985–90	*1990–98*
USA	1.6	0.2
Japan	10.8	1.3
West Germany	15.9	0.3
France	11.6	−2.0
Britain	11.4	1.8
Italy	14.4	−2.3
Canada	7.1	−2.3

Source: United States Department of Labor, Bureau of Labor Statistics, *International Comparisons of Manufacturing Productivity and Unit Labor Cost Trends, 1998.*

management, US corporations discovered that the bargaining power of labour unions was withering under the panic of the 1973 crisis and took instant advantage of this major development. Real median wages fell precipitously, never since to recover.

Whereas (as we argued in Chapter 11) low US labour costs were only one (relatively insignificant) factor underpinning the *Global Minotaur*, they certainly helped reinforce the capital flight to the United States. Thus, US corporate profits were buoyed by a convergence of synergistic tides in the wake of the *Minotaur*'s trail:

- Wall Street was happy to pass on the inflowing foreign capital to corporate America, which used the cash to buy itself more global oligopoly power (i.e. to purchase excess capacity at home and abroad).
- Corporations doubled in profitable financial transactions on the coat-tails of such a cash flood (recall the example of General Motors, which created a division trading in financial products that grew to be as large as its car-making units).
- Declining labour costs.

By the 1990s, on the other side of the Atlantic, the commentariat shaping public opinion was hailing Mrs Margaret Thatcher for having successfully transferred the American miracle onto European soil. Britain was the beacon on the hill and Europeans were implored to turn to it; to see its light; and to reform accordingly. The dominant story was: if Europe wants to become competitive again, it must follow the Anglo-Celtic model of deregulating labour markets and reducing unit labour costs.

The problem with that narrative was that it withstood no close scrutiny. Mrs Thatcher's government never reduced unit labour costs. What she did do was to take a machete to industrial output, 'ridding' Britain of many of its traditional industrial sectors (the 'lame ducks' as they were pejoratively called) and, in the process, of the hitherto bothersome trade unions. This she undoubtedly succeeded in doing.

What effect did the destruction of the trade unions have on British labour costs? The answer here is more complex than most commentators acknowledge. It is true that, together with the mining and steel industries, which bore the brunt of the Iron Lady's reforms, millions of full-time jobs disappeared forever. Naturally, the portion of national income that went to workers fell dramatically and whole areas of Britain were taken over by Developing World conditions. But the one thing that did *not* happen is that for which Mrs Thatcher was given credit: real wages per hour did not drop. In fact they rose considerably.

It is now clear that Mrs Thatcher's impressive electoral successes (the anti-democratic first-past-the-post electoral system notwithstanding) would have been impossible had a large proportion of workers' votes not gone her way. The reason why they did was twofold: first, because most of the 4.5 million jobless people were too glum and disgruntled to bother to vote;[5] second, the workers who *did* hang on to their jobs saw their real wages rise.[6] Mrs Thatcher gave them bonuses that roped them into a speculative mood, in tune with the financial frenzy in Wall Street and the City of London. These bonuses came in the form of (a) selling (at very low prices) to the workers the council houses in which they had been living, and (b) offering them shares in newly privatised companies (such as British Telecom, British Gas and the Trustee Savings Bank)[7] at half the estimated price. Both these offerings encouraged the still-working segments of the working class to consent to an economy that put all its eggs in the basket of speculation either on house prices or on share prices.

As anticipated, the co-opted workers sold their shares immediately to the conglomerates. The much advertised 'shareowners' democracy' lasted but a few days. They did the same thing with their council houses, in an attempt to move to better neighbourhoods and make some extra cash in the process, since much of the new house's price would be paid for with a mortgage. The newly privatised housing encouraged banks to extend mortgages to families that had never had one. The concomitant increase in the demand for houses boosted their prices and that gave the workers an illusory belief that they were getting richer. On the back of their rising 'assets', the banks fell on top of each other to lend them money to go on holiday, buy a car, upgrade their stereo, etc.

Meanwhile, the City of London's traditional strength in the realm of finance, its deregulation under the Thatcher government (also known as the Big Bang) and the City's links with Wall Street, ensured that a significant portion of the foreign capital flight to the United States passed through the City of London. That passage gave the City's institutions access to large sums of money, even if for a short space of time. Nothing excites bankers more than the challenge of making money for themselves by using transient funds. Together with the proceeds from domestic privatisations of UK industries and of the nation's stock of social housing, as well as the Great British public's mountain of borrowing (using the booming house prices as collateral), these financial streams merged into a potent torrent which allowed the City of London to prosper.

Looked upon from Brussels, Paris, Rome and Athens, this London-based prosperity seemed like incontrovertible proof that the Anglo-Celtic model was working. The common language which divides Britain from the United States was mistaken for a bridge over the Atlantic and evidence that the American and British economies, as if in honour of the *Anglo-Celtic Enlightenment* that was capitalism's precursor, were moving in unison, paving the way for the rest of the developed world towards a globalised, uniform New Economy. However, the truth, again, begs to differ and threatens to spoil a good fairy tale. Britain's competitiveness was a mirage.

Once a large segment of its population, the long-suffering British working class, had been cast into various gulags (mainly located in the Midlands and the north of England) the rest of society went on a speculative binge. Most speculated on house prices while some, the more savvy, speculated on shares and the various 'financial' products of that time. The success with which the City latched on, quite parasitically, to the *Minotaur*'s feeding frenzy, in conjunction with the home-grown bubble due to housing and privatisations, buttressed Britain's image as an entrepreneurial society. In reality, all the razzmatazz was nothing more than a gigantic bubble. Indeed, if we take the house prices and the City's paper trades out of the British economy, nothing much will be left to write home about.

The United States was a truly different proposition. While a bubble was also building up in Wall Street and in suburbia, and consumption was being fuelled by borrowing on the strength of those rising 'assets', there was also the *Minotaur*. The world's capital, while it was passing through the City of London, was only stopping over Britain, and perhaps Ireland, on its way to New York. When it got there, it reinforced the corporations that had, since the days of Edison and Ford, been the foundation of the US economy. While most Americans were not linked with the parts of corporate America that paid its employees handsome rewards, the corporations were, indeed, growing more interwoven with the financial sphere, more technologically astute and less bothered by sizeable global competitors (who lacked the *Minotaur*'s backing).

Box 12.2 America's soft power

At an aristocratic cocktail party, a man spots an acquaintance taking an ornate silver salt dispenser and, convinced that no one is watching, slips it into his pocket. The witness is incensed but wishes to avoid a scene. So, after the thieving socialite moves on to another room, the witness to the crime picks up the matching pepper dispenser and put it in his pocket. Casually, he ventures into the other room where the culprit is lounging. Making sure that no one is watching them, he approaches the thief, nods conspiratorially, takes the pepper dispenser out of his pocket, places it upon a nearby table and whispers into his ear: 'I am afraid old chap we have been spotted.' The man blushes but without a word takes the salt dispenser out, places it on the table next to its salt equivalent and steals into the night.[1]

The above is an example of *soft power*, or the power to get people to do what you want them to do with no exercise of actual coercion and no fuss. If we want to be more academic, soft power is akin to Lukes' (1974) third type of power.[2] Whatever we wish to call it, soft power is serious power and capable of doing a great deal of a hegemon's bidding. The United States of America developed a large amount of it immediately after the Second World War. The *Global Plan*, with its generous extension of credits to East and West, and with considerable assistance from Hollywood and the black musicians who shaped the postwar music scene globally, equipped the United States with important cultural power.

Though US politicians, the US armed forces and the CIA tried hard to squander it (e.g. with their demeanour in Vietnam as well as their support of odious regimes like that of the colonels in Greece, the Wahabis in Saudi Arabia and General Augusto Pinochet in Chile), the United States managed to preserve enough of that soft power throughout the 1970s. So, when the *Global Minotaur* was sweeping all in his path, it received a helping hand from this most understated, unseen but awfully potent form of power.

Much of that soft power was generated spontaneously. Figures such as Orson Welles, Jimmy Hendrix and Andy Warhol did not set out to boost American soft power. Yet, through their endeavours they did. Nevertheless, not all of that type of power was spontaneously produced. At least some small part of it was planned, just like Bretton Woods, the Marshall Plan, and the *Global Minotaur* itself were. In 1999 Frances Stonor Saunders published a remarkable book on CIA's cultural wars. Its title: *Who Paid the Piper?*[3] and its theme: how the CIA funded the production of art, cinema and literature, throughout the Cold War, with a view to splitting the European Left and promoting a better image for the United States among people that no one would have expected to use their intellectual output in this manner. In short, little was left to chance.

Notes
1 The clever strategist was none other than Winston Churchill.
2 See Steven Lukes (1974). *Power: A radical view.*
3 See Frances Stonor Saunders (1999).

Summing up, while the Europeans and the Japanese were going through an existentialist crisis, believing that they must become like the Americans to reverse their own sorry post-1973 decline, they missed the simplest of points: the US strategy for retaining world hegemony could *only* succeed if adopted by one capitalist centre. There was no room for emulation. To be born, to survive and to prosper, the *Global Minotaur* had to be the only such beast on the planet.

In less metaphorical terms, world capitalism could, and did, sustain net flows of billions of dollars of capital to New York daily. But nothing the Europeans or the Japanese could do to their labour markets or to their financial sectors would alter that. Moreover if it did, and the daily capital tributes to Wall Street were stemmed, global capitalism would collapse, taking them down with it. The best a non-American capitalist centre could hope for was to be allowed to set up shop next to the *Minotaur*'s labyrinth, hoping to prosper on the sizeable crumbs that fell on the wayside as the great beast feasted.

However, this was never an option for Germany and Japan. It required that one had to ditch its own industrial base, as Britain has done, or to start from next to no industry and become a green-field development site where American corporations build some additional excess capacity; which was Ireland's strategy. No such avenue was open to countries like Germany and Japan, with their own conglomerates spawning technologies and innovations as good as, or better than, those of the Americans.

Sadly, very few Europeans, and almost no mainstream economist, chose to see the *Minotaur* in the room. The result was a lot of boring conferences, millions of wasted report pages and lost opportunities for growth in Europe and Japan. Although their factories are still producing wonderful cars, spectacular gadgets and capital goods of immense merit, the political *nous* that is a condition for generating the aggregate demand for them was, and remains, absent.

To end this section on a light-hearted note, one hopes that, by now, Europe's leaders realise how much merriness they must have caused in Washington when they pronounced, in the context of their 2000 Lisbon summit, that they intended to turn the European Union into the world's 'most competitive economy by the year 2010'. Against the *Minotaur*'s brutish manners, and the panoply of the United States' economic, political and military advantages, the European leadership was proposing to pit microeconomic reform of its labour markets plus subsidies for its knowledge-based sectors! American officials must have been shaking in their boots!

12.2 Double-W capitalism

American officials may not have been 'shaking in their boots' when reading the Europeans' farcical policy documents, but they were worried nevertheless. As befits a true hegemon, the United States produced a no-nonsense mindset among its high and mighty that empowered them to do what the Europeans had no stomach for: to look the *Minotaur* in the eye and not blink. Paul Volcker, our acquaintance from Chapter 11 (where he featured initially as a young Undersecretary of the Treasury, suggesting to his superiors the euthanasia of Bretton Woods and then re-appeared again in 1979 as the Fed Chairman who ruthlessly increased interest rates and did his utmost to serve the *Minotaur*'s rise), had this to say in 2005:

> What holds [the US economic success story] all together is a massive and growing flow of capital from abroad, running to more than $2 billion every working day, and growing. There is no sense of strain. As a nation we don't consciously borrow or beg. We aren't even offering attractive interest rates, nor do we have to offer our creditors protection against the risk of a declining dollar… It's all quite comfortable for us. We fill our shops and our garages with goods from abroad, and the competition has been a powerful restraint on our internal prices. It's surely helped keep interest rates exceptionally low despite our vanishing savings and rapid growth. And it's comfortable for our trading partners and for those supplying the capital. Some, such as China, depend heavily on our expanding domestic markets. And for the most part, the central banks of the emerging world have been willing to hold more and more dollars, which are, after all, the closest thing the world has to a truly international currency… The difficulty is that this seemingly comfortable pattern can't go on indefinitely. I don't know of any country that has managed to consume and invest 6% more than it produces for long. The United States is absorbing about 80% of the net flow of international capital. And at some point, both central banks and private institutions will have their fill of dollars.[8]

We could not (and would not have tried to) put it better ourselves. If the *Global Minotaur* requires an introduction, the above description by Paul Volcker will do nicely. As further proof that US powerbrokers were completely aware and wary of the *Minotaur*'s massive footprint on the planet's economy, here is what Stephen Roach, the Chief Economist of investment bank Morgan Stanley, had to say in 2002 in response to fears that a bubble was building up within the US financial markets:

> This saga is not about the bubble. It is about the unwinding of a more profound asymmetry in the global economy, the rebalancing of a US-centric world… History tells us that such asymmetries are not sustainable… Can a savings-short US economy continue to finance an ever-widening expansion of its military superiority? My answer is a resounding no. The confluence of history, geopolitics, and economics leaves me more convinced than ever that a US-centric world is on an unsustainable path.[9]

Volcker and Roach were in agreement. The causes of the post-1980 take off of the Anglo-Celtic economies has nothing to do with entrepreneurship, labour market flexibility and all the nonsense that Europeans mistook for the causes of their own economies' stagnation. There was a *Minotaur* in the room whose brute power was helping the United States expand its multifarious hegemony. However, the asymmetries that were created and amplified in its wake were unsustainable. Volcker and Roach feared that when that 'unsustainability' came to the fore, as it would, the world was in for a major shock with unmanageable repercussions.

Note the profound difference between this viewpoint and the mundane talk of labour market reforms or of the fear of bubbles. While not saying so explicitly, both Volcker (the seasoned policymaker) and Roach (the Wall Street analyst) were alluding to some major changes in the foundations of capitalism that have given rise to deep asymmetries transcending the realm of labour market policy or the inevitable build up of bubbles in the financial markets. The two men were on to something bigger and more profound.

In Chapter 7 we began our account of the *Crash of 1929* with a section on a new phase of capitalism that was sweeping all in its path during the three decades that preceded the *Crash*. Using Edison and Ford as paradigmatic figures of that transformation, we told the story of how the rise of corporations changed capitalism's face; of how technological innovations led to a higher concentration of increasingly massive investment in the hands of a small number of industry moguls and of how that concentration went hand in hand with an expanding role for the stock market and of the financial institutions connected to it.

Our point there was that it is impossible to understand capitalism's worst moment (the *Crash of 1929*) without first acquainting ourselves with (a) the prior emergence of a new phase of capitalism (referred to, usually, as *monopoly capitalism, oligopoly capitalism* or *corporate capitalism*); and (b) the deeper and broader uncertainty brought about by financialisation. Precisely the same applies here today, in our inquiry into the *Crash of 2008*. Yet again, we shall be arguing, the *Crash* was preceded by the unfolding of a new capitalist phase and the onslaught of a new financialisation phase. We call the confluence of these two new phases *Double-W capitalism*. To give a hint of our argument, we start by giving away the origin of the two W's: Wal-Mart is one and Wall Street is the other.

The Wal-Mart Extractive Model

Wal-Mart is one of the largest conglomerates in the world. With annual earnings in excess of $320 billion, it is second only to oil giant Exxon-Mobile. The reason it is singled out here is because, we believe, Wal-Mart symbolises a brand new phase of capitalist accumulation, one that is central to recent developments worldwide.

Unlike the first conglomerates that evolved on the back of impressive inventions and technological innovations in the 1900s, Wal-Mart and its ilk built empires based on next to no technological innovation, except a long string of 'innovations' involving ingenious methods of squeezing their suppliers' prices and generally hacking into the rewards of the labourers involved at all stages of the production and distribution of its wares. Wal-Mart's significance revolves on a simple point: in the era of the *Global Minotaur* it traded on the American working class' frustration from having lost the *American Dream* of ever-increasing living standards (recall Table 11.4), and its related need for lower prices.

Unlike other corporations that focused on building a particular brand within a previously defined sector (e.g. Coca Cola or Marlboro), or companies that created a wholly new sector by means of some invention (e.g. Edison with the light bulb, Microsoft with its Windows software, Sony with the Walkman, or Apple with the iPod/iPhone), Wal-Mart did something no one had ever thought of before. It built a new *Ideology of Cheapness* into something of a brand that was meant to appeal at a time the American working class was frustrated by diminishing living standards.

Fishman (2006) offers an anatomy of the new industrial model that Wal-Mart introduced during our *Minotaur*'s ascent. Take his example of Vlasic pickles, a well-known brand in the United States. Wal-Mart's 'innovation' was to sell these pickles in one gallon (3.9 litre) jars for $2.97. Fishman's point is that this was not a shrewd retailer's response to market demand. No one in their right mind wanted to buy almost four litres of pickles. Few family fridges had the necessary room for such an item. The selling point was the *idea* of a huge quantity at an ultra low price. Wal-Mart's buyers, in this sense, were not buying pickles as such. They were buying into the symbolic value of cheapness; of having managed to put in their homes a large jar of pickles that Wal-Mart's monopoly power had forced producers to make available at a cut-throat price.

Most of the pickles themselves ended up in the bin, as very few families managed to consume them before they went off (since few found room for them in their fridges).[10] As Korkotsides (2007) so astutely explains in his book *Consumer Capitalism*, the working class, unable to do something about the increasing rate of extraction of its own labour by capital, at least took some pleasure in 'buying', from companies like Wal-Mart, the labour extracted from other workers. The jar of pickles in the fridge, in this reading, was no more than a small victory at a time of wholesale defeat.

Wal-Mart's strategy reverberated around the world. Take the case of Chilean Atlantic salmon that Wal-Mart sold, in 2006, for $4.84 a Pound. As Fishman (2006) explains, salmon is not native to Chile and it was only farmed there *en masse* because of Wal-Mart's mass orders which ushered in 'an industrial revolution that has turned thousands of Chileans from subsistence farmers and fishermen into hourly paid salmon processing plant workers'. Lanchester (2006) adds that 'the salmon live in huge underwater pens, and leave a "toxic sludge" of excrement and uneaten food on the ocean bed'. Similarly with Brazilian beef that Wal-Mart advertises at prices that cannot possibly be consistent with animal husbandry based on half decent practices. Lanchester's (2006) astute comment sums the situation up nicely: 'The feeling [these prices] give is a little like the one that washes over you when you see flights advertised for 99p: something just isn't right'.

Clues as to what is wrong are not hard to come by. Take Wal-Mart's domestic employees. It does not have any! At least not according to Wal-Mart which describes its employees as 'associates'. What this means is that the company does not consider itself to be bound to its workforce by means of the problematic *labour contract* (discussed in Chapters 4 and 5) but, instead, by individual contracts like those struck between two sellers. Wal-Mart effectively declares itself liberated from the *trouble with humans* (recall Chapter 4). This is no more than Orwellian language by which to explain its blanket ban on any trade union activity on its premises. The result is that Wal-Mart's 'associates' work for less than $10 per hour,[11] are habitually forced to work overtime with no additional pay and are often locked up inside the warehouses while working overnight. Lanchester (2006) reports that these practices have resulted in lawsuits in 31 states.[12]

The situation in the workshops and fields of the Developing World, where goods are grown or produced on behalf of Wal-Mart, is, as one can imagine, bordering on the criminal. Defenders of the type of globalisation imposed upon an unsuspecting world by Wal-Mart and the *Minotaur* will argue that growth has been strong for two decades internationally, a trend that seems to continue. Surely, this is good for the poor. But what this misses is the distributive effect of Wal-Mart-type practices on the poor. The United Nations report on global poverty tells us that in and around 1980, for every $100 of world growth, the poorest 20 per cent received $2.20. Twenty-one years later, in 2001, an additional $100 of world growth translated in a measly extra 60 cents for the poorest 20 per cent. And when one takes into account that disproportional rise in prices for basic commodities as well as the diminution in public services following the IMF's structural adjustment programmes (following the

Developing World Debt Crisis of the 1980s), there appears to be very little cause for celebration on behalf of our poverty-challenged fellow humans.

In Robert Greenwald's 2005 shocking documentary Wal-Mart: *The High Cost of Low Price* a woman working in a Chinese toy factory asks 'Do you know why the toys you buy are so cheap?' and then proceeds breathlessly to answer her own question: 'It's because we work all day, every day and every night'. Fishman (2006) adds to this the account of another factory worker who works in a clothes factory that supplies cheap trousers to Wal-Mart. Her *labour contract* stipulates that she must complete 120 pairs of trousers per hour, work 14 hours daily and get 10 days holiday annually. As for the incentive mechanism that keeps her productivity so high, in her own words, 'if you make any mistakes or fall behind your goal, they beat you'.

Box 12.3 Wal-Mart: A corporation after the *Minotaur*'s heart

Wal-Mart was the creation of Sam Walton who 'discovered' that low prices can be lucrative. This sounds nothing like an epiphany: any first-year economics student will tell you that, if demand for a set of goods is elastic, the best strategy to maximise revenues is to charge low prices. However, Walton's 'concept' went far beyond that: first, he worked hard to ensure that his low prices kept *falling* from year to year (or at least seemed to do so). Thus, Wal-Mart did not just concentrate on low-elasticity products, where a low price maximised profits, but, and this is crucial, cultivated in the consciousness of its customers an *ideological expectation of falling prices.* Secondly Walton set out to expand everywhere. Having started his first outlet in Arkansas in 1962, by 1970 the number of outlets rose to 32, by 1976 to 125 and by 1980 to 276 outlets netting the company annual revenues exceeding $1.2 billion. In 2007 Wal-Mart employed more than two million workers, becoming the largest employer in 35 states and expanded to Britain, Mexico and Canada. Third, Wal-Mart embarked upon a major drive to commodify labour and, just as it did with every other commodity it touched, to cheapen it.

The immediate macroeconomic effect of the Wal-Mart 'business model' (that was adopted by many other companies, e.g. Starbucks) was, quite obviously, anti-inflationary. This was essential for the *Global Minotaur's* continuing rude health since the flow of foreign capital to the United States was, partly, predicated upon US inflation trailing that of other, competing, capitalist centres. In Wal-Mart's defence one may argue that it was simply responding to the facts. As the Minotaur was gathering strength, American workers (recall, once again, Table 11.4) felt their diminishing purchasing power in their bones. Wal-Mart simply responded to this reality by providing them with basic products at prices reflecting their diminishing capacity to pay. Was this not a decent helping hand that helped American families in need from slipping into poverty?

This is the conventional wisdom, not least among the American working class itself. However, there is now plenty of evidence that the truth begs to differ; that Wal-Mart's overall effect has been quite the opposite; that wherever Wal-Mart expanded, poverty rates rose. To be more precise, the 1990s was a period of rapid growth in the United States, courtesy of the Minotaur and its astonishing capacity to attract other people's capital into the country. So, poverty rates began to decline (only to rise again after 2001). During that decade of declining poverty rates, something extraordinary happened: a series of important research papers[1] have shown that, during the 1990s, poverty rates not only proved more stubborn in towns where Wal-Mart set up shop but, indeed, in many such regions poverty rates rose; a development at odds with trend at the national level.[2]

Notes
1 See Goetz and Swaminathan (2006), Grassmueck, Goetz and Shields (2008) and Goetz and Shrestha (2009).
2 Kenneth Stone, an economics professor at Iowa State University, has published a number of reports showing that, while Wal-Mart employs a large number of workers in its gargantuan warehouses, the overall effect of its operations on employment is decisively negative. Small town stores close down when Wal-Mart comes to town and, more poignantly, total sales and total employment fall even though Wal-Mart's sales and employment levels seem impressive enough. See Stone (1988), Stone (1997) and Stone, Artz and Myles (2000).

Summing up, Wal-Mart represents more than monopoly or oligopoly capitalist industry. It represents a new guise of monopoly capitalism which evolved in response to the circumstances brought on by the *Global Minotaur*. The Wal-Mart extractive business model reified cheapness and profited from amplifying the feedback between falling prices and falling purchasing power on the part of the American working class. It imported the Developing World into American towns and regions and exported jobs to the Developing World (through outsourcing), causing the depletion of both the 'human stock' and the natural environment everywhere it went. Wherever we look, even in the most technologically advanced US corporations (e.g. Apple), we cannot fail to recognise the influence of the Wal-Mart model. The *Minotaur* and Wal-Mart rose in prominence at about the same time. It was not a coincidence.

The Wall Street money creation model

The previous chapter concluded with an account of how the reversal of global capital flows, which we refer to symbolically as the birth of the *Global Minotaur*, enabled the United States to regain its 'competitiveness' and redouble its hegemony *because of* (rather than despite) *its deficits*. In Paul Volcker's frank words, 'external financing constraints were something that ordinary countries had to worry about, not the unquestioned leader of the free world, whose currency everybody wanted'.[13]

Our argument in Chapter 11 was that the *Global Minotaur* was financed by a tsunami of capital that raced across both oceans towards the United States. Figure 12.1 focuses on the 1980 to 2008 period. The first bar in each year depicts the US current account (or trade); the second bar corresponds to the current account of both the European Union and Japan (the two former *protégés* of the United States); last, the third bar concerns the current account of Asia and the oil exporters *in toto*.

We note that, once the early 1980s recession was overcome (to a great extent as a result of a large boost of military spending by the Reagan administration), the *Global Minotaur*

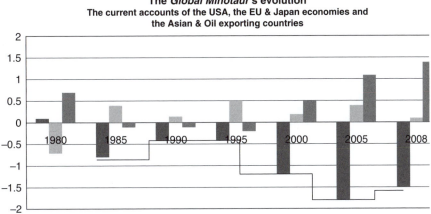

The ***Global Minotaur**'s evolution*
The current accounts of the USA, the EU & Japan economies and
the Asian & Oil exporting countries

Figure 12.1 How the EU and Japan on the one hand and Asia and oil exporters on the other financed the US current account deficit.

Note: (*First bar*: The US current account;
Second bar: The combined current accounts of EU & Japan;
Third bar: The current account of emerging Asia & oil exporters)

got underway. In 1985 it was financed almost exclusively by Europe and Japan.[14] In 1990 a mini-recession squeezed the imbalances slightly (as recessions always do) which, however, blew out again once the recovery got into its swing. By 1995 again Europe and Japan did the honours. Come 2000, Asia (mainly China) and the oil exporters began to contribute increasingly to the *Minotaur*'s upkeep. From then onwards, while Europe and Japan continued to send their capital tributes to Wall Street, the burden shifted emphatically towards China, the rest of Asia and the oil exporters. Figure 12.1 offers a more disaggregated snapshot *circa* 2003.

Figure 12.2 shows that, in 2003 (a typical year during the run up to the *Crash of 2008*, and before the crazed frenzy of the 2006–8 period), the United States *Minotaur* was devouring more than 70 per cent of global capital outflows. Japan was by far the largest contributor, followed by Germany and China. Mountains of cash flowed to Wall Street and from there to US corporations in the form of equity and loans.

To understand the way that these capital infusions into the US economy caused Wall Street to develop a new role for itself, we need three additional pieces of the jigsaw puzzle. First, there is the increasing profitability of US corporations for the reasons already seen: the constant productivity gains against a background of stagnant real wages (recall Table 11.4, from the previous chapter, and see Figure 12.3 below).

Second, at a time of stagnant wages against a background of a fast increasing pie, and of great social demands to *keep-up-with-the-Joneses*, the banks' natural instinct was to use their expanding capital inflows (from abroad but also from the accumulation of domestic profits) in order to extend *credit* to middle and working class households both in the form of mortgages and of personal loans and credit cards. Those credit facilities were taken up by the relatively low paid on the strength of the hope of rising future wages; a hope sustained by the discourse, especially in the media, of an American economy experiencing high growth rate; a hope, however, that was forever crushed by the ruthlessness of their personal, local reality.

Capital inflows in %, 2003

Capital outflows in %, 2003

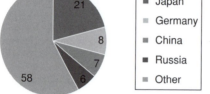

Figure 12.2 Global capital inflows and outflows, 2003.

Source: IMF *Global Financial Stability Report*
Note: The 'other' surplus countries that contributed 58% of capital exports (see lower diagram) were the following:
Norway, Sweden, Switzerland, Saudi Arabia, Singapore, Taiwan, Hong Kong, Canada

Figure 12.3 US corporate profitability (1961–1970 = 100).

The result was debt levels that were rising even faster than the corporations' profitability throughout the United States and the rest of the Anglo-Celtic world, which was attaching itself to the *Minotaur*'s coat-tails (see Figure 12.4 below).

Perhaps the most widely understood effect of the *Minotaur*'s rise was its impact on house prices. Anglo-Celtic countries, with the United States naturally leading the way, saw the largest rises in house price inflation. The combination of the capital inflows (see the lower pie chart of Figure 12.1) and the increasing availability of bank loans pushed house prices up at incredible rates. Between 2002 and 2007 the median house rose in price around 65 per cent in Britain, 44 per cent in Ireland, and by between 30 per cent and 40 per cent in the USA, Canada and Australia.

There is an interesting antinomy in the way popular culture, and the financial commentariat, treat increasing house prices. Whereas inflation is thought of as an enemy of civilisation and a scourge, house price rises are almost universally applauded. Homeowners feel good when estate agents tell them that their house is now worth a lot more, even though they know very well that this is akin to monopoly money; that, unless they are prepared to sell and leave the country (or move into a much smaller house or in a 'worse' area), they will never see that 'value'. Nevertheless, the rise in the asset's nominal value never fails to make house owners feel more relaxed about borrowing in order to finance consumption. This is precisely what underpinned the stunning growth rate in places like Britain, Australia and Ireland.

Figure 12.5 exposes the correlation between the housing price inflation rate and the growth in consumption. The Anglo-Celtic countries in which the former was strongest were also the ones in which consumption rose fast. Meanwhile, in the two ex-US protégés, Germany and Japan (the two countries that were financing the Anglo-Celtic deficits through their industrial production, which the Anglo-Celtic countries were, in turn, absorbing) house prices not only did not increase in value but, in the case of Germany, they actually dropped.

Third, the massive and asymmetrical capital flows, together with the increases in corporate profitability, caused a great wave of mergers and acquisitions that, naturally, produced

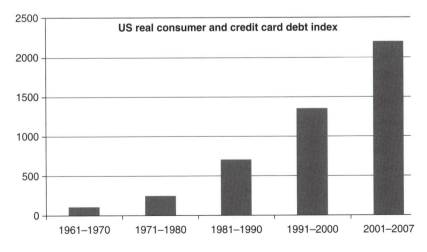

Figure 12.4 Personal loans and credit card debt of US households (1961–1970 = 100).

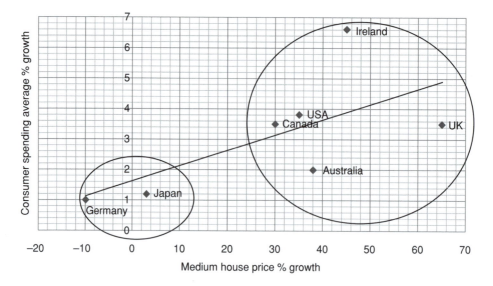

Figure 12.5 Link between median house price inflation and the growth in consumer spending, 2002–7.

even more residuals for Wall Street operators. In October 1999, Michael Mandel, the chief economic writer of *Business Week* offered the following opinion: 'The old market verities apply: as concentration increases, it's easier for remaining players to raise prices. In the copper industry, the prospect of consolidation helped drive up future prices by more than 20% since the middle of June' (cited in Foster 2004b).

Indeed, the 1990s and 2000s saw a manic drive towards 'consolidation'; a euphemism for one conglomerate purchasing, or merging with, another. The purchase of car makers like Daewoo, Saab and Volvo by Ford and General Motors (which was mentioned in Box 12.1) was just the tip of the iceberg. two periods in capitalist history stand out as the pinnacles of merger and acquisition frenzy: the first decade of the twentieth century (recall Edison and his type of enterprising innovators) and the last decade of the same century.

Reading the 1999 *Economic Report of the President,* we come across the following lines:

> Measured relative to the size of the economy, only the spate of trust formations at the turn of the century comes close to the current level of merger activity, with the value of mergers and acquisitions in the United States in 1998 alone exceeding 1.6 trillion dollars. Corporate mergers and acquisitions grew at a rate of almost 50 percent per year in every year but one between 1992 and 1998. Globally, more than two trillion dollars worth of mergers were announced in the first three quarters of 1999. The leading sectors in this merger wave have been in high technology, media, telecommunications, and finance but mega-mergers are also occurring in basic manufacturing.
>
> [*Economic Report of the President* (1999), p. 39]

Both 'consolidation' waves (of the 1900s and the 1990s) had momentous consequences on Wall Street, effectively multiplying the capital flows that the banks and other financial institutions were handling by a considerable factor. However, the factor involved in the 1990s version was much greater than anything the money markets had ever seen. The reason was the Internet. More precisely, the idea of *e-commerce* mesmerised investors and caused a great bonanza that amplified the capital flows, originally due to the *Minotaur*, beyond the computing capacities of a normal human mind. Box 12.4 offers an example borrowed from Lanchester (2009).[15]

Box 12.4 Wishful thinking
How mergers and acquisitions created fictitious value

Suppose there are two companies selling widgets: *Goodwidget* is the traditional manu-facturer with 25 years of a track record behind it and *E-widget* an upstart that has been going for only a year and is selling widgets through the Internet (unlike *Goodwidget*, which still relies on its traditional network of outlets). Suppose further that the follow-ing statistics capture the fundamentals of the two companies.

Goodwidget: (*25 years old*)

*   Earnings (E) = $500 million per year
*   Growth = 10 per cent annually for the previous 25 years
*   Stock market equity/capitalisation (K) = $5 billion
* $K / E = 10{:}1$

E-widget: (*1 year old*)

*   Earnings (E) = $200 million last year
*   Projected e-sales share in a year's time = 10 per cent of an (estimated) $1 trillion market = $100 billion
*   Stock market equity/capitalisation (K) = $10 billion
* $K / E = 50{:}1$

A prudent person might imagine that *Goodwidget* is probably a safer investment. However, that thought was routinely dismissed as fuddy-duddy; as backward looking and insufficiently tuned into *E-widget*'s bright future. So, here is how Wall Street thought: suppose *E-widget* were to use its superior equity to buy *Goodwidget*. What would be the value of the merged company? Should we just add up the two compa-nies' equities or capitalisations ($10 billion and $5 billion = $15 billion)? No, that would be too timid. Instead, Wall Street did something cleverer. It added the earnings of the two companies ($700 million + $200 million = $900 million) and multiplied it with *E-widget*'s capitalisation to earnings ratio. This small piece of arithmetic yielded a fabulous number: 50:1 times $900 million – 45 billion!

Thus, the new merged company was valued at $30 billion more than the sum of the equity or capitalisations of the two merged companies (a sudden leap of 300 per cent). Needless to say, the fees and commissions of the Wall Street institutions that saw the merger through those rose-tinted lenses was analogous to the marvellous big figure at which they had miraculously arrived.

In 1998 Germany's flagship vehicle maker, Daimler-Benz, was lured to the United States where it attempted, successfully, to take over Chrysler, the third largest American auto maker. The price the German company paid for Chrysler sounded exorbitant, $36 billion, but, at the time, it seemed like a good price in view of Wall Street's valuation of the merged company that amounted to a whopping $130 billion! According to *Business Week*, again (May 18, 1998), the aim of the new colossus was 'the emergence of a new category of global carmaker at a critical moment in the industry - when there is plant capacity to build at least 15 million more vehicles each year than will be sold'.

In this regard, it sounds like another move along the lines of oligopoly capital's games, no different in spirit from what the conglomerates were doing back in the 1900s. There is, however, a difference: for in the 1990s, Wall Street's valuations had undergone a fundamental transformation (as Box 12.4 illustrates). Motivated by the psychological exuberance caused by the *Minotaur*-induced capital inflows, Wall Street's valuations were stratospheric. When Internet company AOL (America On Line) used its inflated Wall Street capitalisation to purchase time-honoured TimeWarner, a new company was formed with $350 billion capitalisation. While AOL produced only 30 per cent of the merged company's profit stream, it ended up owning 55 per cent of the new firm. These valuations were nothing more than bubbles waiting to burst. And burst they did, just before the *Crash of 2008*. In 2007, DaimlerChrysler broke up with Daimler, selling Chrysler for a sad $500 million (taking a 'haircut' of $15.5 billion, compared to the price it had paid for it in 1998, the lost interest not included); similarly with AOL-TimeWarner. By 2007 its Wall Street capitalisation was revised down from $350 billion to... $29 billion.

On the other side of the Atlantic, in the other Anglo-Celtic economy that the Europeans so much admired before 2008, in Britain, a similar game was unfolding at the City of London. In 1976, just before the *Minotaur* matured fully, the households with the top 10 per cent of marketable wealth (not including housing) controlled 57 per cent of income. In 2003 they controlled 71 per cent. Mrs Thatcher's government prided itself for having introduced what she called an 'entrepreneurial culture', a 'shareowners' democracy'. But did she? If we take British households in the lower 50 per cent income bracket and look at the proportion of the nation's speculative capital that they owned and controlled, in 1976 that was 12 per cent. In 2003 it had dropped to 1 per cent. By contrast, the top 1 per cent of the income distribution increased its control over speculative capital from 18 per cent in 1976 to 34 per cent in 2003.

Beyond statistics, two concrete examples illustrate well the change in capitalist logic in the time of the *Minotaur*. The City of London, attached every so firmly to Wall Street, could not but emulate the spirit of financialisation that first emerged in the United States in response to the large capital inflows from the rest of the world. Take for instance Debenhams, the retail and department store chain. It was bought in 2003 by a group of investors. The new owners sold most of the company's fixed assets, pocketed a cool £1 billion and re-sold it at a time of exuberant expectations at more or less the same price that they had paid. The institutional funds that bought Debenhams ended up with massive losses.

Even more spectacularly, in October 2007 the Royal Bank of Scotland put in a winning bid of more than €70 billion for ABN-Amro. By the following April, it was clear that RBS had overstretched itself and tried to raise money to plug holes exposed by the purchase of ABN-Amro. By July 2008 the parts of the merged company that were associated with ABN-Amro were nationalised by the governments of Holland, Belgium and Luxembourg. By the following October, the British government had stepped in to salvage RBS. The cost to the British taxpayer: a gallant £50 billion.

Summing up, the *Global Minotaur* created capital flows that propelled Wall Street (and, by osmosis, the City of London) to the financial stratosphere. The flows came from three main directions: (a) foreign capital streaming into the United States; (b) US domestic profits generated by the Wal-Mart extractive sector; and (c) domestic debt created by middle and working class America founded on the misplaced faith in an escalator economy that sooner or later would push everyone onto greater heights of prosperity.

These three surging capital streams converged upon Wall Street where they formed a torrent of monies. The resident apparatchiks felt they were the masters of the universe. For at least two decades, the *Minotaur* conspired to make them believe that no valuation of theirs, however ludicrous in its optimism, could be wrong. It was as if their willpower alone could create new value. Aristotle's conviction that money making was a *telos*-less activity was lost in the cacophony of the stock exchange and the frenzied activities of the futures' markets. Greed was not only good but a prerequisite for getting out of bed in the morning.

It was during that postmodern gold fever that Wall Street aimed for a bridge too far. Its building materials had been around for a very long time but it took the *Minotaur*'s energy to bring them together into what the world later came to know as the toxic derivatives.

Double-W capitalism begets its own private, toxic 'money'

Following the *Crash of 2008*, 'derivatives' sound like something the Devil keeps in his toolbox. But to blame the *Crash of 2008* on derivatives is akin to blaming nitrogen technologies for the carnage in the trenches of the Great War. Of course they wreaked havoc and carnage but they were not the cause. Indeed, before the *Minotaur*, derivatives were cuddly 'creatures' that actually helped hard-working people find a modicum of safety in a viciously uncertain world. The *Chicago Commodities Exchange* (originally known as the *Chicago Butter and Egg Board*) allowed long-suffering farmers the opportunity to sell today their next year's harvest at fixed prices, thus affording them a degree of predictability.

The problem with derivatives is that, like all useful instruments and machines, when they are let loose in a capitalist world, they seem to develop a life force of their own. Of course, they are not to blame. For it is the human mind which, like a demented sorcerer in the clasps of some alien logic (in our case that of capital accumulation), fuses them with superhuman power which then proceeds to hijack it. It all starts in the most innocent of ways but soon the human spirit loses control and becomes the appendage of a nebulous entity with no apparent human agency. Let's take a look at this process.

Suppose that a cash-strapped artist offers you a futures contract, or 'option' to buy a painting that he/she has not yet painted. The option is worth $1,000 now and the price you will pay for the painting when the painting is complete will be determined by an independent art dealer's valuation. Once you purchase the option, you can, of course, simply sit there and wait for the painting to materialise, at which point you will need to dish out the remaining dollars for the painting itself.

Alternatively, you can sell the option to someone else for a lot more than $1,000 if, for example, an older work by the same artist has just done well at auction; and vice versa. If the artist's fortunes dip in the stock exchange of fine work, your option's market value will have dropped. This is how futures markets also work, the only difference being that the holder of a futures contract is contracted to pay a specified price, regardless of the painting's eventual valuation by the art dealer.

Defenders of the derivatives' trade never miss a chance to broadcast the view that derivatives are instruments for reducing the uncertainty that hard-working people take when engaged in producing something (from wheat to a work of art) with a long lead time. However, this is where the 'defence' usually ends. What the public is rarely told, possibly because it has no interest in the complexity involved, is what happens when derivatives are taken to another realm, one in which the risk reduction does not benefit producers at all.

Suppose for instance that the person who wants to reduce risk is not our fine young artist or the hard-working farmer but a speculator who wants to reduce the risk involved in buying a certain bunch of shares currently worth $1 million. However bullish his predictions, he/she wants to reduce his/her risk exposure and to do this he/she buys an option to sell these same shares for $80 thousand. In effect, our speculator has bought some insurance against a fall in the shares' value. Like any form of insurance, if the shares' value rises, as anticipated, the insurance policy was a waste of money. But if, say, the shares lose 40 per cent of their value, he/she can use his/her *get-me-out-of-here* option and sell the shares at the original price, thus cutting his losses substantially. This is what finance people refer to as *hedging*.

Hedging has been with us for a long time. But it was the *Minotaur* that gave it a wholly new role, and a bad reputation after 2008. At a time when the capital flows into Wall Street made its boys and girls feel invincible, masters and mistresses of the universe, it became common for options to be used for exactly the opposite purposes than hedging. So, instead of purchasing an option to sell shares as an insurance in case the shares that they were buying depreciated in value, the smart cookies bought options for *buying* even more! Thus, they bought their $1 million shares and on top of that they spent another $100 thousand on an option to buy another $1 million. If the shares went up by, say, 40 per cent that would net them a $400 thousand gain from the $1 million shares plus a further $400 thousand from the $100 thousand option: a total profit of $700 thousand.

At that point, the seriously optimistic had a radical thought: Why not buy only options? Why bother with shares at all? For if they were to spend their $1.1 million only on an option to buy these shares (as opposed to $1 million on the shares and $100 thousand on the option), and the shares went up again by 40 per cent, their profit would be a stunning $4.4 million. And this is what is called *leverage*: a form of borrowing money to bet big time, which increases the stakes of the bet monumentally. Note how the bet above converts a borrowed $1 into a cool profit of more than $4 but, when things go the other way (and shares decline by 40 per cent in value), one is stuck with an obligation to buy shares whose value has fallen, thus converting the borrowed $1 to a debt of more than $4; exactly what one's mother would have warned against.

Alas, from 1980 onwards, prudential mothers could be, more or less, safely ignored. The *Minotaur* was generating capital inflows that in turn guaranteed a rising tide in Wall Street. During that time, people 'in the know' made a great deal of so-called new financial 'products' and 'innovations'. There was of course no such thing. These 'innovations' were just new ways of creating *leverage*; a fancy term for good old debt. If Dr Faustus had known about all this, he would not have loaned his soul to Mephistopheles in exchange for instant gratification. He would, instead have taken options out on it. Of course, the result would have been the same.

Regarding the notion of 'financial innovations', the best line belongs to Paul Volcker. After the *Crash of 2008* Wall Street bosses went into damage-control mode, desperately trying to stem the popular demand for stringent regulation of their institutions. Their argument, predictably, was that too much regulation would stem 'financial innovation' with dire consequences for economic growth; a little like the mafia warning against law enforcement because of its deflationary consequences. In a plush conference setting, on a cold December 2009 New York night, all the big Wall Street institutions were assembled to hear Paul

Volcker address them. He lost no time before lashing out with the words: 'I wish someone would give me one shred of neutral evidence that financial innovation has led to economic growth; one shred of evidence'. As for the bankers' argument that the financial sector in the United States had increased its share of value added from 2 per cent to 6.5 per cent, Volcker asked them: 'Is that a reflection of your financial innovation, or just a reflection of what you're paid?' To finish them off, he added: 'The only financial innovation I recall in my long career was the invention of the ATM'.

Leveraging is so risky that it would never have survived as a systemic practice without the *Minotaur* guaranteeing a steady flow of capital into Wall Street. Sure enough, even then lots of traders lost lots of money when they overdid it. Nick Leeson, for example, was a young trader who in the early 1990s managed to bring down a venerable financial institution, Barings, which had survived through thick and thin for a good two centuries but proved too brittle to endure a young man's deals in front of a computer screen somewhere in the office maze that is Singapore.

These sudden catastrophic losses were a reminder that the potent combination of derivatives, options, computers and leverage had a great potential for amplifying risk at a time when traders felt that the *Minotaur* was keeping risks low. However, to turn fully into a WMD (a weapon of mass destruction, as investor Warren Buffet called them) the derivatives–leverage combination required something else; something that was missing before the *Minotaur* fully fledged: it required some mechanism for pricing them quickly, easily and *en masse*. That 'mechanism' or formula should use as 'inputs' the past variation in the price of assets related to the derivative in question, correlations between the prices of different assets, interest rates and some assessment of risk. Its output should be a single price for the derivative in hand. The first such workable formula appeared in the *Journal of Political Economy* in 1973. Its authors were Fischer Black and Myron Scholes.[16] The proposed formula was a major hit. A world of appreciative traders latched on to it and a roaring trade in derivatives began.

The main idea behind these trades was to use scientific methods and raw computer power by which to take advantage of the minutest of arbitrage opportunities (recall the ingenious trading in Radford's POW camp, Section 6.7, Chapter 6); that is detecting and profiting from tiny differences in prices in different markets. In fact, this is what Barings thought Leeson was doing on its behalf in Singapore: taking advantage of the fact that the average price of Japanese futures (also known as the *Nikkei 225*) was determined through electronic trading whereas its Singaporean equivalent was manual and slower to adjust. Thus arose a differential in prices, as a result of the different speeds with which prices changed in the two markets. That differential lasted for a few seconds but Leeson's job was to buy low and sell high within that fleeting window of opportunity.

In 1994, John Meriwhether, who had previously been a star trader and a former vice-chairman of the respected firm Salomon Brothers, set up a new financial firm, also known as a *hedge fund*, under the name of *Long Term Capital Management*. In fact, both labels were misleading. LTCM was neither operating on the basis of some long-term strategy for managing other people's funds (indeed, quite the opposite, it was placing extremely short-term bets on prices movements) nor was it focusing on *hedging*. The whole point about *hedge funds* is that, because they deal on a person-to-person basis with super-rich clients, who entrust large sums to them to bet on the markets, *hedge funds* are not regulated like banks are. That's their whole *raison d' être*.

Meriwhether's idea, in setting up LTCM, was to employ formulae like those that Black and Scholes had concocted, combine them with high powered computers and then invite rich people to give him their money so as to experiment with the new 'equipment' in a bid to make 'guaranteed' profits for everyone involved. The first person he employed was Myron Scholes (Robert C. Merton, who shared with him the 1997 Nobel Memorial Prize in Economic Sciences, was also on LTCM's board). With his good contacts, and some early success, Meriwhether attracted a large capital base to LTCM; an impressive $4.87 billion. However, drunk on the early successes that saw LTCM's heavy leverage strategy yield a fourfold return to its capital, Meriwhether, Scholes and Black threw everything into maximum leverage and a plethora of derivatives. A few years later, LCTM's risk exposure was somewhere in the order of $1.3 trillion. So, when in 1998 Russia defaulted on its state (or sovereign) debt to foreign financial institutions, a risk that Black and Scholes had never factored in, LCTM went belly-up. In the end, the Fed had to step in and organise LCTM's liquidation.

While LCTM ended up in ruins, it left an important legacy: the powerful combination of leverage and highly complex derivatives whose constituent parts were synthesised by mathematical formulae of an intricacy that not even the mathematicians who concocted them understood fully. However, this was beside the point. Everyone knew that the derivatives were too complex to decipher (see Box 12.5). But their appeal was not harmed by that fact in the slightest. If anything, the very idea that one was buying and selling contracts containing high-order mathematical formulae enhanced their appeal. Of course that was not the main reason why they were all the rage. The main reason was that their value was rising.

Suppose a friend bought a small black box for $100 and then found a buyer for it the next day for $400. Then the new buyer sold it on on the following day for $1,000. Later, the little black box was resold a week later for $1,800 before, a minute ago, someone offered it to you for $2,000. Would you not want it? Of course you would. Does it matter what's in it? Of course it does not. Naturally, the question remains: why did such 'little black boxes' appreciate in value consistently for two decades? That one wants one if it does appreciate is no explanation of its systematic appreciation.

While it is obvious that people who had no clue of (and cared not one iota regarding) what was hidden inside them, would want them, as long as they were appreciating in value, we still need to explain why they appreciated for so long. Our explanation is the *Global Minotaur*. In the previous chapter, and the preceding pages of the current one, we argued that the collapse of the *Global Plan* in 1971 set in train a new dynamic which attracted massive capital transfers from the rest of the world to the United States, but also caused large inflows into Wall Street from within the United States (both in the form of corporate profits and debts by the working and middle classes). These capital flows operated like a perpetual tide that kept pushing all boats up. That buoyant environment was perfect for the incredible enlargement of the derivatives' market witnessed between 1990 and 2008.

Returning to the derivatives themselves, it is helpful to focus on a new form labelled *Collateralised Debt Obligation* or CDO; the nearest Wall Street ever got to devising a Byzantine instrument. In a manner resembling Hyman Minsky's point (see Box 7.9, Chapter 7) that a low interest environment causes financial institutions to take greater risks (just like an improvement in a car's brakes encourages the driver to drive faster), when the Fed's strategy of dealing with fears of recession following the 1998–2001 various crises[17] led to low interest rates, the banks began to lend money more freely and to seek out good returns in new, exotic and some not so exotic places. With real wages under a perpetual squeeze, the greatest demand for these loans came from the have-nots, whose relative desperation translated into a greater readiness to agree to pay higher interest rates.

Of course, poor people were always ready to borrow but the banks' main principle was never to lend to anyone unless they did not need the money. So, what changed here?

Two things: first, the United States and its fellow Anglo-Celtic countries, again courtesy of our Minotaur, was experiencing the longest, unbroken period of increasing house prices in history. Second, the poor person's debt could now be 'made over', repackaged within a shiny derivative, complete with rocket science mathematics disguising its unappetising content.

The long rise in house prices led lenders to feel safe in the thought that if the poor borrowers were to find it hard to meet the repayments due, they could always sell the house and thus repay not only the initial capital plus the interest but also any additional late-payment penalties. This proved correct. But it was only one of the two reasons why the banks lent money to poor home buyers. The second was that the knowledge that, using the magic CDOs, they would not have to bear the risk that their poor customers would default.

This, as the reader will have gathered by now, is the sad tale of subprime mortgages. The story of how Wall Street, not content to process and build upon the tsunami of foreign capital and domestic corporate profits that the *Minotaur* was pushing its way, tried to profit also from poor people by selling them mortgages which they could never really afford. By 2005, more that 22 per cent of US mortgages were of this subprime variety. By 2007, this had risen further to 26 per cent. All of them were inserted into CDOs before the ink had dried on the dotted line. In raw numbers, between 2005 and 2007 alone, US investment banks issued about $1,100bn of CDOs.

The trick was to combine in the same CDO subprime with good, or prime, debt; each component associated with a different interest rate. The mathematics behind each of these CDOs was, as ever, complex enough to ensure their inscrutability. However, the mere hint that serious mathematical minds had designed their structure, combining prime and subprime components within the same 'tranche', and the solid fact that Wall Street's respected, and feared, ratings agencies had given them their seal of approval (which came in the form of AAA ratings), was enough for banks, individual investors and hedge funds to buy and sell them internationally as if they were high-grade bonds.

In terms of value, it is estimated that in 2008 the mortgage-backed bonds came to almost $7 trillion, of which at least $1.3 trillion were based mainly on subprime mortgages. The significance of that number is that it is larger even than the total size of the, arguably gigantic, US debt. But to give an accurate picture of the disaster in the making, it is important to project these vast numbers in relation to one another as well as to the level of global income. Only then can we begin to make sense of them. Figure 12.6 is a small step in that direction.

What is clear here is that, as most commentators suggested after 2008, the planet had become too small to contain the derivatives' market. Whereas in 2003 for every $1 earned somewhere in the world there corresponded $1.73 'invested' in some derivative, by 2007 the ratio had changed: almost $8 worth of derivatives corresponded to every dollar made in the real world. So, as if the *Minotaur*'s actual capital flows (handled mainly by Wall Street and the City of London) were not large enough, the derivatives market regularly experienced trade in the order of more than $1 trillion daily. Of those a small minority were related to US mortgages, and of the latter only one in five were laced with subprime mortgages. However, the inverted pyramid had grown too large and the slightest of pushes threatened to destabilise it.

Most people find it hard to understand how these derivatives grew and grew and grew; how they could end up almost eight times more 'valuable' than the whole wide world's output. One answer to that question is to try to think of derivatives, effectively, as bets. Whether one is betting that the price of pork bellies will rise next June or that a 7+ Richter

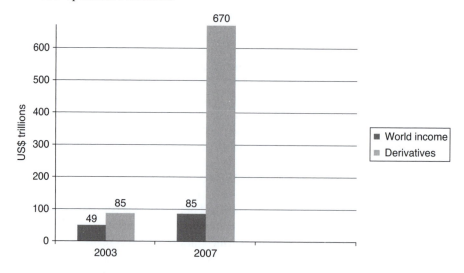

Figure 12.6 The World is Not Enough: world income and the market value of derivatives (in $US trillions) at the height of the Minotaur's reign.

Box 12.5 The *trickle-up effect* and securitisation (the ultimate financial weapon of mass destruction)

The *trickle-down effect* was meant to legitimise reducing tax rates for the rich, by suggesting that their extra cash will eventually trickle down to the poor (see Section 12.1). While all empirical evidence conspires against that hypothesis, despite a sequence of significant tax cuts for the top earners in both the United States and Europe, a quite different effect, the *trickle-up effect*, was observed in the context of the derivatives market. Securitisation of the unsafe debts of the poor (e.g. the conversion of subprime mortgages into CDOs) had the effect of making the initial lender indifferent to whether or not the loan could be repaid (for she had already sold the debt to someone else). These securitised packages of debt were then sold on and resold at tremendous profit (prior to the *Crash of 2008*). The rich, in an important sense, had discovered another ingenuous way to get richer by trading on commodities packaging the dreams, aspirations and eventual desperation (once the market crashed and the home foreclosures began) of the poorest in society.

Five years before the *Crash of 2008*, investor Warren Buffett, who was at the time the most eminent trader in insurance, said: 'In my view, derivatives are financial weapons of mass destruction, carrying dangers that, while now latent, are potentially lethal… there is no central bank assigned to the job of preventing the dominoes toppling in insurance or derivatives'. In a letter to his shareholders, he added:

If our derivatives experience… makes you suspicious of accounting in this arena, consider yourself wised up. No matter how financially sophisticated you are, you can't possibly learn from reading the disclosure documents of a derivatives-intensive company what risks lurk in its positions. Indeed, the more you know about derivatives, the less you will feel you can learn from the disclosures normally proffered you. In Darwin's words, "Ignorance more frequently begets confidence than does knowledge".

[Buffet (2010), p. 59]

So, the following question becomes increasingly pressing: why didn't enough people listen to such a consummate insider? Our answer is simple: they were too busy making money buying and selling these derivatives!

scale earthquake will hit Tokyo in 2019, some obliging broker will write down a CDO that you can buy, in essence taking this bet. Imagine now a world in which pork bellies more often than not go up in price every June, or that a 7+ Richter scale earthquake hits Tokyo almost every year. In that world, the number of derivatives changing hands would go through the roof, as they did by 2007 (see Figure 12.5). What was it that provided the 'certainty' of ever-increasing house prices and an ever-rising stock exchange? The *Minotaur*, of course.

During that time when money seemed to be growing on trees, traditional companies that actually produced 'things' were derided as old-hat. What steel producer, car manufacturer or even electronics company could ever compete with such amazing returns? All sorts of companies wanted to join in! Staid corporations like General Motors for this reason entered the derivatives racket. At first they allowed the company's finance arm, whose aim was to arrange loans on behalf of customers who could not afford the full price of the firm's product (e.g. hire purchase for cars), to stick a toe in the derivatives pond. They liked the feeling and the nice greenbacks streaming in. Soon, that finance arm ended up becoming the company's most lucrative section. So, the firm ended up relying more and more for its profitability on its financial services and less and less on its actual, physical product.

Indeed, some companies that appeared to offer important physical or traditional products and services, in fact were nothing more than purveyors of derivatives. The infamous Enron is an excellent example (see Box 12.6) of how to fraudulently employ derivatives in order to artificially increase profitability with a view to inflating the company's stock market value, and with a further view to lining management's pockets with many more millions.

Moreover, even fully legitimate companies that provided a decent service to their customers and had no intention whatsoever to mislead or cheat anyone, they too were lured into using derivatives as part of their normal operations. Northern Rock, the bank whose collapse in a sense started the ball rolling in 2008, is the obvious example (see Box 12.7).

Summing up this brief foray into the smoke and mirrors of the modern derivatives' marketplace, the reason why an initially innocuous type of contract turned into a potential weapon of mass financial annihilation is threefold.

First, while billeted as an instrument for reducing risk, it can just as easily be employed as an amplifier of gambles and an enlarger of the risks involved. Unlike the fool who has to raise money from friends and family to play at the casino, the derivative buyer can gamble now without much money but be just as readily saddled in the future with a debt that no casino can ever hope to unload on a human being.

Second, derivative trading is off the books. What this means is that there was no mechanism for even knowing what derivatives were being traded, let alone a mechanism for

Box 12.6 Enron

In the 1990s, Enron was corporate America's blue-eyed company. Voted America's Most Innovative Company six times in row, by no other than the readers of *Fortune* magazine, it exerted a powerful influence in what used to be called (prior to the Minotaur's successful push to privatise them) public utilities: electricity generation, natural gas distribution, water management and telecommunications. Connected as it was to the real, old-fashioned sectors involving cables, water pipes, etc., no one had imagined that Enron was no more than a house of cards made of derivative paper. When it went bankrupt in 2001, it had 21 thousand employees on its payroll in 42 countries. Most lost not only their due wages but also their pensions (some only months away from retirement, as the company had already used up the pension funds for other, mostly illegal, purposes).

To cut a long story short, Enron lied about its revenues, its costs and its assets thus presenting a bottom line that was as impressive as it was fraudulent. Arthur Andersen, the international accounting firm that audited its books, was successfully prosecuted by US authorities for wilfully damaging evidence of its part in Enron's false accounts. As a result, Andersen followed Enron into oblivion. Two major companies thus perished.

From the perspective of this chapter what matters is the manner in which Enron and Andersen managed to hide the truth, that the former had no clothes, for so long. They did this simply by employing derivatives that never appeared as such on the company's balance sheets. For instance, just before the annual accounts were filed, the company would package a debt as a derivative, sell it to itself and thus manage to remove that debt from the liabilities segment. Soon after the accounts were filed, it would restore it. And similarly with revenues. When planning to build a power station that would start bringing in actual revenues in ten years' time, Enron would 'create' a derivative whose present value it would immediately list in the current assets column, thus inflating its revenues and profit. As long as no one noticed, these 'beautiful numbers' boosted Enron's equity (or market value at the Wall Street stock exchange) and, as a result, Enron acquired greater power to acquire other companies (on the basis of that increased equity) to further inflate its bottom line.

Box 12.7 Northern Rock

Northern Rock is a bank doing most of its business in the north east of England. A medium-sized mortgage lender, it was doing brisk business for a while. Using the power of the Internet, it allowed customers a fast and easy service that seemed, at the time, like a great innovation. The fact that its interest rates were slightly below that of the more established banks seemed logical given its lean, digitised operation and the lower costs it faced in terms of branch rentals and staff wages. In general, Northern Rock was liked by its customers who felt better treated than they had been previously by the four big high-street banks that dominated previously.

As in the United States, so too in Britain, mortgage lenders learnt the trick of imme-diately converting the loans (given to customers to buy a house or business) into CDO-like derivatives to be sold on. Northern Rock was not at all exceptional in doing this. But it was exceptional in another regard: its *Achilles' heel* was that the bank drew less than 30 per cent of the money deposited with it by customers. The rest it was rais-ing from other banks on very, very short-term contracts. Imagine that: Northern Rock would lend Joe Bloke £100 thousand for, say, 20 years but it would do so by borrowing the money at rock bottom interest rates for a night or two, then re-borrowing it again, and again, and again. Needless to say, Northern Rock had good cause to bundle this £100 thousand into some CDO and sell it off as quickly as possible. In short, Northern Rock's continuing operation required that (a) short-term interest rates remain low, (b) other banks were happy to lend it the money from day to day and (c) the CDO market continued to absorb newly issued CDOs. Alas, in 2008 all three conditions stopped holding and the rest, as they say, is history.[1]

Note

1 Even though, unlike in the United States, in the case of Northern Rock, the underlying mort-gages were never of the subprime variety! Indeed, to this day, the vast majority of Northern Rock mortgage holders continue to meet their repayments as agreed in their contracts.

regulating them. The whole regulatory framework that the New Dealers put in place, after 1932, in order to prevent banks from speculating with their customers' hard-earned money, had been torn asunder both by the Clinton administration in the 1990s (with Larry Summers at the helm) and, quite independently, by the rise of the derivatives market; a market that is almost completely underground and shrouded in secrecy.

Third, because of both the opacity and the immensity of this market, no one could possibly know how a meltdown in parts of that market would affect the rest of the global financial system. The very size of the right-hand side bar in Figure 12.6 suggests that the mighty would easily be felled if only a small component of that market were to fail. As it turned out, it only took a little over $1 trillion of it (the subprime mortgage-backed bonds) to slip before the whole edifice came tumbling down.

The above is well known to anyone who has been following the financial press. There are, however, two crucial truths that cannot be understood satisfactorily outside the context of our *Modern Political Economics*. One is the fact that, without the *Global Minotaur*'s rise (which we have been tracking in *Book 2* in some detail), the prerequisites of the drive towards financialisation (namely the massive capital flows through Wall Street) would not have been satisfied and the last few figures would not have looked as they do. The second fact takes us back to Chapter 7 and the *Quantity Theory of Money*, of which free marketeers have been so enamoured for at least two centuries.

According to the latter, too much money flooding into the economy is a recipe for disas-ter; for hyper-inflation and the loss of the market's capacity to send meaningful signals to producers and consumers on what to produce and what to economise. The reader will also recall Friedrich von Hayek's, admittedly extreme, position that the state could not be trusted to produce money, because collective or political institutions simply lack the *nous* to determine the appropriate quantity of money (recall Box 7.12). His recommendation? To let private firms, banks and individuals issue their own money and then allow the market, through good old-fashioned competition, determine which of these competing currencies the public trusted more.

Now, consider the role of the zillions of CDOs that flooded the financial system in the decade 1998–2008. What were they? In theory, the CDOs were options or contracts. In reality, and since no one knew (or really cared to know) what they contained, they acted as a form of *private money* that financial institutions and corporations used both as a medium of exchange and a store of value. Friedrich von Hayek ought to have been pleased!

This flood of a form of *private money*, over whose quantity and worth no one had the slightest control, played an increasing role in keeping global capitalism liquid in the era of the *Global Minotaur*. So, when the plug was pulled in 2008, and all that *private money* disappeared from the face of the earth, global capitalism was left with what looked like a massive liquidity crisis. It was as if the lake had evaporated and the fish, large and small, were quivering in the mud.

12.3 The Econobubble: The *Inherent Error* in the Age of the *Minotaur*

In 1997 Robert Merton and Myron Scholes shared the Nobel Prize in Economics for developing 'a pioneering formula for the valuation of stock options. Their methodology', trumpeted the Nobel committee, 'has paved the way for economic valuations in many areas. It has also generated new types of financial instruments and facilitated more efficient risk management in society'. If only the hapless Nobel committee knew that in a few short months the lauded 'pioneering formula' would cause a spectacular multi-billion dollar debacle, the collapse of LTCM (in which Merton and Scholes had invested all their *kudos*) and, naturally, a bail-out from the reliably kind US taxpayers…

Box 12.8 Taming risk? Henri Poincaré's timely warning

Henri Poincaré (1854–1912) was a mathematician, physicist and philosopher with a talent not only for solving difficult analytical problems but also for understanding the workings and limitations of human reasoning. His basic premise was that, when faced with a problem, the mind begins with random combinations of possible answers, often generated unconsciously, before a definite, rational process of validation begins by which the solution is finally arrived at. In his schema, chance plays an important but incomplete role in understanding. However, it is futile, he thought, to try to impose upon chance the rules of certainty. In Chapter 4 of his 1914 masterpiece *Science and Method*, Henri Poincaré writes:

> How can we venture to speak of the laws of chance? Is not chance the antithesis of all law?… Probability is the opposite of certainty; it is thus what we are ignorant of, and consequently it would seem to be what we cannot calculate. There is here at least an apparent contradiction, and one on which much has already been written. To begin with, what is chance? The ancients distinguished between the phenomena which seemed to obey harmonious laws, established once for all, and those that they attributed to chance, which were those that could not be predicted

because they were not subject to any law. In each domain the precise laws did not decide everything, they only marked the limits within which chance was allowed to move. In this conception, the word 'chance' had a precise, objective meaning; what was chance for one was also chance for the other and even for the gods. But this conception is not ours. We have become complete determinists, and even those who wish to reserve the right of human free will at least allow determinism to reign undisputed in the inorganic world… Chance, then, must be something more than the name we give to our ignorance. Among the phenomena whose causes we are ignorant of, *we must distinguish between fortuitous phenomena, about which the calculation of probabilities will give us provisional information, and those that are not fortuitous, about which we can say nothing, so long as we have not determined the laws that govern them.* And as regards the fortuitous phenomena themselves, it is clear that the information that the calculation of probabilities supplies will not cease to be true when the phenomena are better known (our emphasis).

[Poincaré (1908 [1914]), pp. 64–6]

In 1900, Louis Bachelier (1870–1946), one of Poincaré's more able doctoral students, submitted a thesis entitled *The Theory of Speculation* (Bachelier 1900, 2006). In it, the young student applied stochastic processes to offer a model by which to price options taken out on the French state's bonds. In this sense, Bachelier was an early precursor of financial engineers like Black, Merton and Scholes. Poincaré passed the thesis and made some polite noises about the young man's mathematical skills but, nevertheless, was quite categorical that the class of phenomena involved in pricing options are well outside the scope of probability calculus. The reason? That they fall under (b) above, the class of phenomena over which we can say nothing precise. Or, in the language of our interpretation of Keynes (see Chapter 7): *we are damned if we know!*

It was not that Poincaré believed that humanity lies beyond the realm in which probability calculus can prove useful. For instance, in the same book he writes:

The manager of a life insurance company does not know when each of the assured will die, but he relies upon the calculation of probabilities and on the law of large numbers, and he does not make a mistake, since he is able to pay dividends to his shareholders. These dividends would not vanish if a very far-sighted and very indiscreet doctor came, when once the policies were signed, and gave the manager information on the chances of life of the assured. The doctor would dissipate the ignorance of the manager, but he would have no effect upon the dividends, which are evidently not a result of that ignorance.

[Poincaré (1908 [1914], p. 66)]

However, Poincaré understood well that pricing options or second guessing the stock exchange was a wholly different problem to that of estimating life expectancy. Whereas the latter fell under (a) above, the former was a class (b) phenomenon; one whose 'laws' are not only unknown but also unknowable.

In effect, Poincaré intuitively understood that which, in this book, we refer to as economics' *Inherent Error*. Bachelier did not. And nor did Black, Merton, Scholes and the large army of financial engineers that priced the flood of derivatives in the run up to the *Crash of 2008*.

The Nobel committee, and the whole financial sector that embraced this highly motivated madness, should have known better. At least since 1914 bright mathematicians (see Box 12.8) understood that pricing options by means of pristine formulae is fools' gold; that, although the private rewards from developing mathematical pricing models are tremendous, reality will sooner or later come knocking. Inevitably floods of tears will wash away all the gains and, with the markets in a state of shock, governments will be forced to step in to mop up.

The annals of financial economics will refer to the collapse of LTCM as the result of an exogenous shock that the 'theory' had not predicted: the fiscal crisis in Russia that caused the Moscow government to default on its debts and an avalanche of bad debts to flatten the pristine equations of Merton, Scholes, *et al*. The question is: why did these models not allow room for the possibility of a crisis occurring somewhere in the world? How on earth can one describe a fiscal crisis as *exogenous to the capitalist system*? Was it caused by a meteorite from space?

Our answer was given back in Chapter 9 (see, in particular, Box 9.10). The pricing models bestowed upon us by the wizards of financial engineering left the possibility of systemic crisis out of their equations because, over a period that began in 1950 and ended up with the demise of the *Global Plan*, mainstream economics fully adopted a particularly strong meta-axiom by which economists habitually closed their models (meta-axiom **E**). Economists who did not adopt it were expunged from the profession with an efficiency that Stalin would have marvelled at. Meanwhile, the economists who *did* espouse the offending meta-axiom lost even the remotest of connections with really existing capitalism; a loss which, paradoxically, lent them (and economics in general) immense discursive power in the universities but also in Wall Street, in the government, in the corporations' boardrooms, etc.

In practice, the meta-axioms to which the profession conceded *en masse* meant that those teaching and learning economics were adopting a mind-frame in which a crisis was simply unfathomable. Once in that mind-frame, it was 'logical' to jump to the natural inference that today's share and option prices incorporate all available 'wisdom' about future fluctuations. In technical language, current prices are a *sufficient statistic* by which to estimate future prices. Markets were, thus, meta-axiomatically conceived as efficient mechanisms that no humble intellect could plausibly doubt or second-guess.

Box 12.9 The Efficient Market Hypothesis

Bachelier's basic tenet (see Box 12.8) was that financial markets contrive to ensure that current prices reveal all the privately known information that there is. If this is so, no one can systematically make money by second guessing the market. The only way money can be made systematically is if stocks prices rise on average over a period of time. Even then, 'players' cannot hope to make more money, on average, than the average rate of stock price inflation.

The idea is simple: suppose Jill gets some information that *E-widget* will announce a rise in its profit. She will immediately respond by buying *E-widget* shares. The more certain she is of her information's reliability the more shares she will buy. But then others will notice in a split second that Jill is buying a lot of shares. They immediately think that 'she must know something'. Thus, her benefits (if her information is right) are very short-lived because the price of *E-widget* shares will escalate very quickly. Jill's insider information begets a higher price for *E-widget* shares for everyone, thus annulling the value of that information. It is as if Jill broadcast her private information to the world simply by buying these shares.

Naturally, prices may fluctuate as Jill's information is proved inaccurate causing the market to 'overshoot' (i.e. investors to buy too many of *E-widget*'s shares). This variation is, however, random noise and can be treated like a random walk around a price whose best estimate is the current price.

In the 1930s, Alfred Cowles, the founder of the Cowles Commission that played such a prominent role in Chapter 9, in his own research on Wall Street's behaviour (occasioned by his incredulity at what had happened there in 1929) hinted at the possibility that no one could consistently make money over and above the average growth in stock values, however seasoned in the art of trying to make money by 'playing' the stock exchange. In essence, this was a restatement of Bachelier's hypothesis.

In the early 1960s, another acquaintance of ours from Chapter 9, Paul Samuelson, discovered Bachelier's thesis and circulated it among colleagues. A few years later, Eugene Fama, who was to become professor at Chicago's business school, submitted his own thesis; a modern-day extension of Bachelier's original. The gist of the theory is that investors react to private and public information randomly. Some overreact, some underreact. Thus, even when everyone errs, the market gets it approximately 'right'. Those trying to bet against the market systematically, through for instance a meticulous study of past prices, will lose their shirt. The reason? Every piece of information that can be inferred from past prices has already been inferred and has been factored into the current price. Hence, prices follow a random path and no theory can predict them better than a series of random guesses.

The Efficient Market Hypothesis resembles the old joke about two economists walking down the street. One looks down and says: 'By golly, look! There is $100 note on the pavement'. The other does not even bother looking. He coolly replies: 'Can't be. If there was one, someone would have picked it up'. While this attitude makes perfect sense *on average*, and with regard to the possibility of $100 notes lying around on the pavement, to take this attitude to the financial markets as a whole is a different matter altogether.

In effect, the Efficient Market Hypothesis presupposes that there exists a unique sufficient statistic for financial asset prices towards which the market converges, albeit a noisy one. But as Poincaré knew from the outset, there can exist no sufficient statistic when it comes to radically indeterminate variables; variables that move according to 'laws' that are not only unknown but also unknowable.

To put the same point differently, the prerequisite for the Efficient Market Hypothesis to make sense is the existence of a unique and well-defined equilibrium path on which the 'economy' is guaranteed to move. But, as we have explained in *Book 1*, for such a path to exist, the economy must comprise a single sector or a single Robinson Crusoe-like individual. The Efficient Market Hypothesis, therefore, cannot possibly be sustained in a really existing capitalist world.

Chapters 8 and 9 argued that, beginning with Nash's 1950 paper at the Cowles Commission, political economics embarked upon a road with no return, following the agenda of a formalism whose theoretical results were predicated upon meta-axiomatic 'closure' by means of moves that could only engender a permanent chasm between economic theory and capitalist reality. Only in that context is it possible to explain how intelligent scholars, in living memory of the 1930s, could see the world through the prism of the Efficient Market Hypothesis, the Rational Expectations Hypothesis and, more recently, so-called Real Business Cycle Theory.

The common thread that runs through them is the determination to misapply a Nash–Debreu–Arrow type of solution to a macroeconomy. Up until the early 1970s, Nash–Debreu–Arrow models, while dominant in the academic discourse, were confined to an abstract, microeconomic, academic game that was played in universities. While the *Global Plan* stood tall, macroeconomic policy was still informed by the New Dealers' experience of at first running the War Economy and later the institutions of the *Global Plan*. A largely trial-and-error form of policymaking, based too on a strong track record, kept a firm controlling hand over global capital and trade flows.

Box 12.10 The Rational Expectations Hypothesis

The Rational Expectations Hypothesis (REH) is based on a clever argument that, under certain circumstances, makes perfect sense. Discursively, it suggests that no one should expect a theory of human action to predict well in the long run if it presupposes that humans systematically misunderstand that very theory. REH rejects the idea that a social theory can reliably expect people consistently, and at a personal cost, to misunderstand the rules that govern their own behaviour. Humanity, REH proponents believe, has a capacity eventually to work out its systematic errors. Thus, a theory that depends on the hypothesis that people systematically err, will, eventually, stop predicting human behaviour well. Put simply, as Abraham Lincoln supposedly[1] once said, 'you can fool some of the people all of the time, and all of the people some of the time, but you cannot fool all of the people all of the time'.

In neoclassical economics the REH was articulated first and most powerfully by John F. Nash, Jr. His concept of a game's (Nash) equilibrium is defined as the set of strategies, one for Jill and one for Jack, such that Jill's strategy is the best reply to Jack's and vice versa (i.e. Jack's strategy is also his best reply to Jill's). The point here is that if both choose these very strategies then, by definition, each will find that his or her predictions of the other's behaviour is confirmed. Now, consider two theories: the first theory T_1 predicts that Jack and Jill will choose their Nash equilibrium strategies (which are, by definition, self-confirming). The second, T_2, predicts that they will choose some other pair of strategies that are *not* in a Nash equilibrium. Clearly, the only way the latter can occur is if Jill, Jack or both entertain mistaken expectations about one another. The central difference, therefore, between theories T_1 and T_2 is that T_2 alone predicts well if Jill, Jack or both hold systematically mistaken predictions about the outcome. Theory T_2, by contrast, makes no such assumption. Indeed, its prediction is that the players will behave in a manner that confirms their expectations. In this sense, theory T_1 is consistent with the REH whereas T_2 is not.

In 1961, John Muth published a paper in which he assumed that when people assigned a future value to any economic variable that they cared to predict (e.g. wheat prices, the price of some share) any error they made was random; that is, that there could be no theory that systematically predicts the predictive errors of investors, workers, managers, etc.[2] Note that this is entirely equivalent to espousing theory T_1 above on the grounds that it makes no assumption of systematic predictive errors on behalf of Jill or Jack.

Muth's model was largely ignored until the *Global Plan* collapsed in 1971. Then, it was retrieved by two other Chicago economists, Robert Lucas, Jr. and Thomas Sargent, who applied the idea to their neoconservative brand of macroeconomics, which assumed that the macroeconomy is in permanent equilbrium.[3] Of course, to be able to attach a consistent neoclassical equilibrium narrative on the macroeconomy, Lucas and Sargent had to ditch complexity in favour of time. So, in conformity with the demands of the neoclassical form of the *Inherent Error*, the Lucas and Sargent macroeconomic REH-based model is confined to a single- sector inter-temporal model, one not too dissimilar to that of Frank Ramsey (see Chapter 7).

The REH allows Lucas and Sargent to get rid of Ramsey's central planner and therefore to claim that equilibrium is 'achieved' miraculously by the market itself. Since the agents' expectations are assumed always to be correct, plus or minus some random errors, there is indeed no need for a planner. In a sense, the planner's role has become obsolete courtesy of the strong version **E** of neoclassicism's third meta-axiom (recall Section 9.5, Chapter 9). Together with the Efficient Market Hypothesis (see previous box), the REH's 'policy implication' is crystal clear: government should keep off!

If the world behaves like this type of theory suggests, it is impossible for output, employment or any other variable that society cares about to be positively affected by means of government intervention. If agents *always* entertain the correct expectations (plus some random noise), then aggregate output and employment is always going to be as high as it can. Inevitably, meddling governments can only undermine perfection!

Remarkably, the REH literature dominated at a time of historically high unemployment. How did it manage that? To be consistent with their model, they had to claim that if observed unemployment is, say, 8 per cent, then 8 per cent is the level of unemployment that it is 'natural' for the economy to have at that point – the 'natural' rate consistent with agents' rational, i.e. correct, expectations. Suppose, they added, government tried to suppress unemployment to below that 'natural' level by means of 'Keynesian' meddling. The ensuing increase in the quantity of money cannot, in this context, change what people expect (in terms of actual output, employment, etc.) since everyone harbours the correct expectations. Everyone will then know in advance, on the basis of their rational expectations, that the government's effort will leave output and employment unaffected. Immediately they will surmise that prices must rise (since there is now more money in the economy chasing after the same quantity of goods and the same amount of actual labour).

378 Modern political economics

> The gist of it all is: if you accept the REH, then you want a government that does not try to manage the economy. Of course to accept the REH, you must first buy the worst guise of the economists' *Inherent Error*.
>
> Notes
> 1 While this quotation is frequently attributed to Lincoln, it is almost certain that it was uttered by someone close to him.
> 2 See Muth. (1961).
> 3 For an encyclopedic entry concerning the influential REH literature and Lucas and Sargent's role in it, see Sargent (1987).

When the *Global Plan* buckled under, for reasons discussed in Chapter 11, the game changed. In the era of the *Global Minotaur*, and in Paul Volcker's inimitable words, the disintegration of the global economy and the enhancement of global trade and capital flow asymmetries became a legitimate policy option for the US government, a tool for recovering and reinforcing US hegemony. In particular, energy price inflation, interest rate volatility, significant rises in unemployment, financial deregulation, etc. became essential in the persecution of the new ambitious project of restoring US economic and geopolitical power after the Vietnam catastrophe, and at the expense of Germany and Japan who had grown 'too competitive' during the *Global Plan* era.

The new policy of *controlled disintegration* of national economies and global capitalism alike, a form of *negative engineering* that was pursued after 1971, had to have, as all major policy twists do, a veneer of theoretical legitimacy. Now that the *Global Minotaur* required governments that stood aside while massive asymmetries were gathering pace, especially in the form of the capital flows into Wall Street that were to sustain the United States' expanding trade deficits, a new form of macroeconomics was necessary; one with a simple message: the good government is one that takes its leave; that concentrates on keeping US inflation below that of its competitors and leaves it to the market to decide everything else.

It took two steps to bring to prominence this type of free-marketeer (or new classical, or neoclassical, or neoconservative, or neoliberal) macroeconomics. First, an end had to be put to the idea of rationally managing an economy, for example, by means of fiscal and monetary policy; the idea that Paul Samuelson had cultivated in the mind of countless students, many of them in the US administration. This proved a simple task once the policy levers of the *Global Plan* (e.g. a looser fiscal policy to reduce unemployment) ceased to function in the dying days of Bretton Woods and as the massive increase in oil prices was taking hold. The straw man version of Keynes that neoclassicists like Paul Samuelson had created in the 1960s (see Section 9.3 of Chapter 9 for the argument) had outlasted his sell-by date and could be done away with by lightly blowing in its direction. Such is the fate of impostors when the winds of history change.

Second, a new type of macroeconomics had to take its place, preferably one that recommended the sort of policies needed during the *Global Minotaur*'s formative years. It was none other than the neoclassical variant of the *Inherent Error* (or, as we called it in preceding pages, the *Inherent Error on steroids*). It came in different, yet depressingly similar, forms (see Boxes 12.10 and 12.11) which did no more than apply the vulgarised versions of the Nash–Debreu–Arrow formalist method, *against its progenitor's wishes*, to macroeconomics. The great advantage of these models was that they provided exceedingly complex mathematics that only a tiny band of practitioners understood but whose conclusion was clear for all to grasp: capitalist markets are axiomatically impossible to second-guess, both at the level of individual investments (see Box 12.9) and at the level of the macroeconomy (see Box 12.10). Recessions can and do take place but only because of external shocks that society cannot do anything about through collective or state action and which are best absorbed by allowing the market free rein to respond (see Box 12.11).

Box 12.11 Real business cycles

The Rational Expectations Hypothesis, along with its bedfellow the Efficient Market Hypothesis, left the reader of that quaint literature with an impression that capitalism was a harmonious system that never caught anyone by surprise, constantly confirming everyone's expectations (give or take a few random and independently distributed errors) and permanently on the road to maximum growth and prosperity; as long as the government stayed out of its hair. Of course, reality was rather different and even true believers, such as Robert Lucas, Jr., saw the need to tell a story about fluctuations, recession, upturns and downturns. The theory of the real business cycle (RBC) was the result.

Turning necessity into virtue, RBC portrayed recessions as capitalism's rational (and 'efficient') response to external or exogenous shocks. The idea here is that the nebulous markets are working optimally in a capitalist world, which occasionally is threatened by events that occur outside its realm. Like a well-functioning Gaia that must respond to and adapt after the crashing into it of a large meteor, so does capitalism react efficiently to exogenous shocks. In neoclassical language, this translates as follows: unregulated capitalist markets maximise inter-temporal expected utility and recessions, when they occur, are part of that 'plan'; a best reply to extra-economic events that happen on the markets' periphery; e.g. a tsunami or a crazed oil producer's decision to inflate oil prices.

But what makes these business cycles real? The answer is that they are not due to some endogenous market failure but, rather, are an efficient reaction to a 'real' external shock. With this assumption under their belt, RBC theorists spend their days and nights carrying out statistical analysis (and a lot of 'filtering') of aggregate data, usually GDP and GNP data. Their purpose? To filter out of the raw data the growth trend, revealing in full view the fluctuations around the trend that can be seen as random and consistent with some external shock.

The idea that recessions (i.e. below-trend growth) are the market's way of dealing with external shocks is mainly due to Finn Kydland and Edward Prescott (1982).[1] They explain all deviations from the trend in terms of events for which the markets are neither to blame nor to commend: catastrophic weather, oil price rises, technological change, political interventions to tighten environmental legislation, etc. These external or exogenous changes cause employment, prices, output, etc. to deviate from their prior equilibrium path until a new equilibrium path is established, one that is consistent with the new external reality.

The connection with both the Efficient Market Hypothesis and the Rational Expectations Hypothesis is intimate. All three turn on the assumption that markets know best. Under the surface, however, they share something far more important: the neoclassical version of the *Inherent Error*, which forces these theorists to think of capitalism as a single sector, Robinson Crusoe-like economy where a decision to save is also a decision to invest and the possibility of coordination failure or Keynes' *fallacy of composition* is simply non-existent.

One does not need to be particularly radical to recognise the inanity of such theories. Larry Summers (1986) who became President Clinton's deregulation guru, and more recently returned as a key figure in President Obama's administration, had this to say: '[R]eal business cycle models of the type urged on us by Prescott have nothing to do with the business cycle phenomena observed in the United States or other capitalist economies'.

What Summers does not say is that RBC theorists have long stopped caring. Taking a leaf out of neoclassical economics' turn in the 1950s, following the *Formalists'* triumph, they are innocent of any concern regarding the seaworthiness of their theoretical model. Economics became a mathematised religion quite a while before REH and RBC. And like all successful religions, the fact that it was founded on a web of superstition, with nothing useful to say about how the world actually works, never counted against it.

Note
1 See also Lucas (1977) and Stokey, Lucas and Prescott (1989).

The best thing that can be said about the *Global Minotaur*'s macroeconomics is that it was a magnificent combination of higher mathematics with childish political economics. Nevertheless, it condemned a whole generation of economists to thinking of the most complex, disintegrated, precariously balanced period in the history of capitalism in terms of a universe in immaculate equilibrium. A model that applied exclusively to a single-sector, Robinson Crusoe-like economy that featured no actual markets, which some invisible hand was assumed always to keep in equilibrium ended up the parable on which humanity had to rely as a source of insights into the *Global Minotaur*'s workings.

Section 7.3 of Chapter 7 told the story of the state of political economics prior to the *Crash of 1929*. This section tells a disappointingly identical story about the state of economic theory on the cusp of the *Crash of 2008*. In the former we wrote that, just before 1929 struck, the best way of capturing the political economists' sum of understanding of the workings of capitalism would come in the form of a sentence beginning with: *we have no clue!* We then went on to say that the rest of the book will be arguing that:

> [N]othing has changed since then. Absolutely nothing! Whereas other sciences have moved in leaps and bounds, the insiders of our discipline remain wedded either to single commodity and Robinson Crusoe models (featuring amazingly complex dynamics) or

to wonderfully complex multiple commodity (or General Equilibrium) models in which time sits still. Neither variety of model allows us a glimpse of an expectations-driven world in which our expectations are capricious, not because we are not smart enough to form them rationally but, because capitalism is indeterminate.

No further comments are needed. Except perhaps for one more box that answers the question on everyone lips, concerning the spectacular failure of so many bright people to see through Wall Street's *private money* (i.e. the toxic derivatives) before the bottom fell out of that 'market', pushing the whole world into the downward spiral of debt-deflation, unemployment and negative growth. Box 12.12, therefore, completes this section with an account of the mathematics that helped create a market for a burgeoning mountain of CDOs simply by allowing traders to quote one price per CDO on offer. That mountain, and the fictitious prices CDOs were assigned, were to be the *Minotaur*'s undoing.

To recap, from the mid-1990s to 2008 the CDOs (and associated CDSs, see Box 12.12 for a definition) became a new form of *private money*. Financialised capitalism was quickly hooked. As the flood progressed with no rhyme or reason, capitalism was propelled to its worst implosion since 1929. If we look carefully at the causes of this dynamic, we shall discern, behind the generation of this ultimately destructive form of *private money*, a mighty alliance comprising

(a) the capital inflows into Wall Street and the City of London that were part and parcel of the *Minotaur*;
(b) the US government's penchant for deregulation (which started in the 1970s in a bid to disintegrate the *Global Plan* and reached a climax with the Clinton–Summers legislative moves of the 1990s);
(c) the securitisation of US mortgages into CDOs;
(d) the use by so-called financial engineers of high-order mathematical statistics and computer algorithms that turned options contracts into an impenetrable maze whose ultimate 'achievement' was to assign a single price to each CDO; and
(e) the neoclassical version of the *Inherent Error* which provided the key assumptions that 'closed' the financial engineers' pricing models under (d) above.

Box 12.12 overviews (d) and (e), two crucial links in the chain of inauspicious events. It begins with Black Monday (a bleak day in the stock markets back in October 1987), which we used in Chapter 1 as an introduction to the special difficulties involved in predicting financial storms, and tells the story of how financial institutions sought safety in numbers, in estimates of risk to be precise. These estimates, for example, the values VaR and R which Box 12.12 elucidates, attempted to do the impossible: in Poincaré's words, to discuss untameable chance using the language of certainty.

The formulae that produced these numbers, which in turn 'informed' traders during the frenzy that typified the financial markets for almost two decades, were but a fig leaf by which to cover up the nakedness of the models. But it was enough. Traders *wanted* to believe in them and, while the party lasted, they had no reason not to (except, that is, for a plethora of scientific reasons that should have prevailed upon them). Oodles of cash were being made by those who professed faith in the formulae. There is, indeed, nothing like success in the world of naked moneymaking to reinforce one's beliefs in magical formulae that look scientific and whose contents almost no one understands.

Box 12.12 Black Monday, 'Value at Risk', CDSs, Dr Li's formula and the *Inherent Error*'s latest clothes

On Monday, 19 October 1987, Black Monday as it is now known, the stock markets went into free-fall. In one day, Wall Street lost more than 22 per cent of share values. It was even worse than any single day during the *Crash of 1929*. By the end of October the City of London had lost 26.4 per cent, Wall Street followed with a 22.7 per cent fall, Hong-Kong equities were decimated by a mindboggling 45.5 per cent, with Australia not far behind dropping 41.8 per cent. It was clear that the 1980s bubble, which was inflating during the *Global Minotaur's* energetic early phase, had burst, aided and abetted by the electronic trading systems that had come on line in previous years (allowing traders to program computers to sell automatically *en masse* when the markets fell by more than a given percentage).

While the Fed and the other central banks managed to stabilise the situation and, indeed, to reverse the losses by the end of the year,[1] the shock left an indelible mark on the traders' collective psyche. In Black Monday's aftermath the Efficient Market Hypothesis looked frail and sad. Unwilling to go through another trauma comparable to Black Monday, traders started looking at ways to estimate their exposure to risk, to second-guess the market (against the edicts of the Efficient Market Hypothesis). Most analysts accepted the hypothesis that an abnormal 'point of inflection', like Black Monday, must be preceded by an increase in the 'noise' surrounding price movements just before the crash is about to hit. If that noise, or variation, could be detected in good time, then the hope was that early warning of the impending crash can help a trader salvage a great deal of money by selling up, at the expense, of course, of everyone else.

Value at Risk, or VaR, was developed fully in the early 1990s at Wall Street merchant bank J.P. Morgan. The innovation there was that price information was pooled from all of the trading desks of the company and a single number was produced that, supposedly, answered a simple question: how much does the company stand to lose in case of an adverse market move whose probability was estimated at 1 per cent? It is said that Dennis Weatherstone, J.P. Morgan's CEO, expected a piece of paper with that number every day at around the close of business (the 4.15 report). Interestingly, J.P. Morgan was possibly the only financial institution that did *not* take VaR estimates seriously, even though they developed it in-house and its CEO wanted to see it every afternoon. In fact, J.P. Morgan sold the VaR computational apparatus technology in the form of an independent business that was absorbed into a company known as *RiskMetrics Group*. The new firm did brisk business, since the demand for VaR estimates around Wall Street and the City of London was sky high.

The statistical idea behind VaR is as simple as the formulae involved are convoluted. First, one specifies the desired confidence level, usually set at 99 per cent. Then, one looks at the whole portfolio of assets (shares, options, etc.) that one trades in and asks the question: what is the smallest number x such that the probability that my loss today, say L, will exceed x is smaller than 1 per cent? The answer to that question, i.e. x, is the trader's VaR value at that moment in time. More formally, but saying exactly the same thing,

$$\text{VaR}_{1\%} = \inf\,(x \in R \mid \Pr(L > x) \le 1\%)$$

So far so good. The question then becomes: how does one compute that probability? This is where the plot thickens and the fraudulent part comes in. The only way to compute x is to approximate the probability that $L > x$ either by means of some assumed probability distribution or by some so-called parametric measure; i.e. a presumption of how many abnormal events (i.e. events whose losses cannot be defined) one can reasonably expect. Either way, the gist here is that to define x one must, effectively, assume that one knows something that is unknowable. Henri Poincaré must have been spinning in his grave.[2]

A few years later, a Chinese business statistician, Li Xianglin who later changed his name to David X. Li and worked for *RiskMetrics*, the Canadian Imperial Bank of Commerce and Barclays Capital, before moving back to China to work for CICC (China International Capital Corporation), developed another famous and, indeed fatal, formula: the *Gaussian copula function*, which proved manna from heaven for the financial institutions seeking a simple method of pricing their *Credit Default Obligations* (CDOs), which, as we postulate, played the role of private money that Wall Street created on the back of the *Global Minotaur*.[3] The reason why Li's formula (see below) became all the rage on Wall Street was that it gave banks and other institutions the illusion that it afforded them a simple, accurate way to price the options involving mortgages (prime as well as subprime).

The problem with pricing CDOs was that, as they comprise many different types of mortgages (some safer than others), to price a CDO one had first to work out an estimate of how the default probability of one type of mortgage was correlated with that of another type. Dr Li's epiphany was to model default correlations by emulating actuarial science's solution to the so-called *broken heart syndrome*: the observation that people tend to die faster after the death of a beloved spouse. Statisticians had been working for a while on how to predict the correlation between deaths on behalf of insurance companies selling life insurance policies and joint annuities. 'Suddenly I thought that the problem I was trying to solve was exactly like the problem these guys were trying to solve', said Dr Li. 'Default is like the death…, so we should model this the same way we model human life'.

Dr Li tackled this problem by employing a mathematical theorem (by A. Sklar) to model the joint distribution of two uncertain events. In technical terms, the Sklar theorem allowed Li to separate the dependence structure from the univariate margins of *any* multivariate distribution. In plain language this means that Li had come up with an ingenious way of modelling default correlation that did not require use of historical default data. Instead, he used market data about the prices of specific 'insurance policies' called *Credit Default Swaps* or CDSs.[4]

The difference between a CDS and a simple insurance policy is this: to insure your car against an accident, you must first own it. The CDS 'market' allows one to buy an 'insurance policy' on someone else's car so that if, say, your neighbour has an accident, then you collect money! To put it bluntly, a CDS is no more than a bet on some event taking place; mainly someone (a person, a company or a nation) defaulting on some debt. When you buy such a CDS on Jill's debt you are, to all intents and purposes, betting that Jill will fail to pay it back, that she will default.

CDSs became popular with hedge fund managers (and remain so to this day) for reasons closely linked to the trade in CDOs. Take, for example, a trader who invests in a CDO's riskiest slice; committing to protect the whole pool of mortgages if the holder of the riskiest mortgages in the CDO defaults on their repayments. Suppose further that our investor undertakes to cover $10 million of such default losses. Just for that pledge, in the pre-2008 days, he could receive an upfront payment of $5 million, plus $500,000 a year! As long as the defaults did not happen, he would make a huge bundle without investing anything: just for his pledge to pay in case of a default! Not bad for a moment's work – until, that is, the defaults start piling up. To hedge against that eventuality, the trader would buy CDSs that would pay him money if the mortgages in the CDOs he bought defaulted.

Thus the combination of CDSs and CDOs made fortunes for traders at a time when defaults on mortgages were rare and uncorrelated. What gave that combination a great big boost was Dr Li's idea to use the prices of CDSs in order to value the CDOs more easily and quickly! It brought tears of joy to the traders' eyes. All of a sudden, and as long as they trusted the formula's underlying assumptions, they could ignore the nearly infinite relationships between the various parts (i.e. types of mortgages) that made up a CDO. They could set aside concerns about what happens when some partial correlations between components turn negative while others turn positive. All they needed was to keep a trained eye on one, single number, one correlation R that summed up all the information relevant to pricing the derivative.

$$\Pr\left[T_A < 1, T_B < 1\right] = \Phi_2\left(\Phi^{-1}\left(F_A(1)\right), \Phi^{-1}\left(F_B(1)\right), \gamma\right)$$

The particular ingredient on which Dr Li's formula hinged is the innocuous looking γ on its right-hand side and, more importantly, the assumption that it is a *parameter*. The reader need not bother with the rest of that formula. Just focus on the γ. In plain English, the assumption that γ is constant means that traders assumed away the possibility of a sudden wave of defaults, unanticipated by the actuarial data. The mind boggles: where did Dr Li find the confidence to assume that no such wave would ever gather pace and that his γ's constancy is safe as houses (rather that a fluctuating variable connected to capitalism's unpredictable whims)?

The simple answer is: in the same place that Formalists derived the confidence to impose the third meta-axiom (see Chapter 8) every time they needed to 'close' one of their models. That place was no other than a fantasy world of economics' *Inherent Error* in which the economy operates *as if* to confirm the economists' mathematised superstitions.

Notes

1 The main reason that the markets were stabilised simply by extending credit and liquidity to the financial institutions was that, unlike in 2008, banks had not yet become replete with private money, i.e. derivatives. In 2008, things turned out very differently when the crash not only wiped out share values but also the entire derivatives market on which the financial alter ego of the *Global Minotaur* had grown so reliant.

2 Poincaré also understood that which modern financial engineers conveniently, and catastrophically, neglected: That predictions are extremely sensitive to imperceptible initial deviations. In the same book that we quoted before, he wrote: '[E]ven if it were the case that

the natural laws had no longer any secret for us, we could still only know the initial situation *approximately*. If that enabled us to predict the succeeding situation *with the same approxima-tion*, that is all we require, and we should say that the phenomenon had been predicted, that it is governed by laws. But it is not always so – it may happen that small differences in the initial conditions produce very great ones in the final phenomena. A small error in the former will produce an enormous error in the latter... The meteorologists see very well that the equilib-rium is unstable, that a cyclone will be formed somewhere, but exactly where they are not in a position to say; a tenth of a degree more or less at any given point, and the cyclone will burst here and not there, and extend its ravages over districts it would otherwise have spared...'

[Poincaré (1908 [1914]), p. 68]

3 See Li (2000).

4 When the price of a credit default swap goes up, that indicates that default risk has risen. Li's breakthrough was that instead of waiting to assemble enough historical data about actual defaults, which are rare in the real world, he used historical prices from the CDS market.

Heads of trading desks would take a look at the VaR estimate that their minnows fed them regularly and thought that they knew how much money they were liable to lose at that moment if an unlikely, harmful 'development' (a 1-in-100 'event' like Black Monday) were to occur. However, what most did not understand was that their little VaR estimate had no capacity to tell them what would happen in case of a 1-in-150, or a 1-in-200, 'event'; an event from which they would lose much, much more. Nor did they allow themselves to ask the most pertinent of questions: why might such 'abnormal' events actu-ally happen?

The reason they did not ask this question was twofold: first, because it would have got in the way of a great deal of moneymaking. Stopping to *think* in the middle of a feeding frenzy means a smaller catch for great fish and small ones. Second, because the 'best' economists in the best economics departments were winning Nobel Prizes with theories proclaiming that all unexpected events are exogenous and basically predictable; that they happen for reasons external to capitalism (and, as such, are the sort of events that cannot possibly be given an economic explanation); that capitalism is secure from global events with a probability less than one per cent. Who were they, the traders, to dispute the brightest Nobel Prize winners?

In the seven years or so before 2008, another important formula was devised: Dr Li's Gaussian copula function which, as Box 12.12 explains, was the cherry on the cake: a simple formula by which even an unsophisticated trader could 'calculate' the value of any CDO he wanted to flog off, comprising a cacophony of different tranches of mortgages and other financial assets. The explosion of the CDO market between 2000 and 2008 owed a great deal to it.

At this point it is important to remind the reader that neither VaR nor Dr Li's formula materialised from thin air. As *Book 1* went to great pains to show, from the second half of the 1950s onwards, the economics profession began to view capitalism from within the prism of the Nash–Debreu–Arrow approach. It looked nothing like the capitalism that real capitalists, workers, consumers and government officials experienced daily. But it was a powerful viewpoint. Its most enduring impact was finally and irreversibly to deny the notion of radical uncertainty that Keynes had highlighted. At around that time, scholars like Harry Markowitz[18] and James Tobin[19] introduced a notion of variability that was a total denial of the idea of indeterminacy; of Keynes' insights concerning the nature and depth of uncertainty. It was the notion that Fischer Black and Myron Scholes would harness, in 1973, to present the first formula that claimed to offer a practical way of pricing derivatives, which later morphed into VaR, before evolving into Dr Li's little toxic formula.

The direct lineage of these formulae in the formalism of the 1950s can be gleaned from their fundamental axioms: zero transaction costs; continuous trading; and, of course, the assumption of Brownian motion. The latter is what we may call the 'killer' assumption. In other words, it means that the model assumes away not only the possibility of crises but, incredibly, the possibility that changes in prices are patterned (as opposed to totally random).[20]

VaR and Dr Li's Gaussian copula formula are stunningly compatible with the rampant neoclassicism of the 1970s (see the hypotheses in Boxes 12.9, 12.10 and 12.11) which, in effect, proclaimed the end of genuine macroeconomics.[21] The pricing of the CDOs presupposed the same theoretical move that formalist neoclassicists had been making in the context of bypassing the *Inherent Error*; assumptions that fell under the umbrella of the strong version **E** of their third meta-axiom. So, a type of theory that cannot handle *time* and *complexity* together became the foundation of a fiendishly complex financialised capitalism that evolves at neck breaking pace along time's arrow. The world's largest market (by value) was founded upon a theory that could not survive outside the pages of a formalist's scribbling.

However well versed one may be in the intricacies of the story, one cannot but return to the same question, again and again: why were the prices that Dr Li's formula generated believed? Why did numerous smart, self-interested, market operators, whose livelihood depended on the constancy of Dr Li's γ parameter (see Box 12.12) never question that obviously flawed assumption? The question becomes even more pressing when it is pointed out that, just as J.P. Morgan's staff had mistrusted the VaR measures of risk they had themselves developed (possibly because they understood better than anyone what went into it), Dr Li did not really believe his own model's pricing recommendations either![22]

The answer is twofold: first, because they were captives of herd-like behaviour and would have risked their jobs if they moved against the pack;[23] second, because during the *Global Minotaur* era political economics had ridded its textbooks and leading research programmes of all dissident voices that might have warned against such assumptions. In short, the economics profession had successfully peddled a form of mathematised superstition which armed the hand of the traders with the superhuman, and super-inane, confidence needed (perhaps against their better judgement and wishes) to bring down the system which nourished them; a very contemporary tragedy indeed.

12.4 The abandoned protégés: Japan and Germany in the Age of the Minotaur

The dimming of the Rising Sun[24]

During the years of the *Global Plan*, Japan achieved enormous export-led growth under the patronage of the United States (which guaranteed Japan cheap raw materials and access to US and European markets – see Chapter 11). Japanese wages rose throughout the period but not as fast as growth and productivity. Government spending was directed to building infrastructure for the benefit of the private sector (e.g., transport, R&D, training, etc.) and minimally to the end of providing a social safety net for the population at large.

This set of priorities ensured that, in the context of the well-regulated international environment of the *Global Plan*, Japan was to grow on the back of an export drive that proceeded along the lines of three phases. At first, the emphasis was on exporting primary products and importing light industrial goods. Then, by the late 1950s, Japan moved to exporting light industrial goods and importing heavy industrial goods plus raw materials. Lastly, it matured enough to export heavy industrial goods while limiting its imports to scarce raw materials.

Production was based on large-scale capital investments yielding impressive economies of scale in the context of a highly oligopolistic industrial structure known as *keiretsu* (e.g. Mitsui, Mitsubishi and Sumitomo). These conglomerates were vertically integrated, hierarchical organisations around which revolved (through an intricate subcontracting system) countless *Small-to-Medium Sized Enterprises* (SMEs) or *chusho-kigyo*. This structure still survives today, and the SMEs account for about 80 per cent of total employment. However, their contribution to overall productivity is quite low, estimated at less than half of the average level of larger firms.

Thus, Japan's industry is bifurcated. At the centre we find the conglomerates, dominating the economy and producing its substantial productivity gains, while around these centres we observe many small business clusters that create most of the employment but little of the nation's productivity. This combination of oligopoly capital, many small businesses and a government that spends a tiny percentage of its large outlays on social programmes, lies at the heart of Japan's reliance on foreign demand for its output in order to maintain aggregate demand domestically. In short, it is the main reason why, after the *Global Plan* gave its place to the *Global Minotaur*, Japan's macroeconomy was so seriously destabilised.

Japan's banks were traditionally controlled by the state. This afforded authorities leverage over investment, the result being a relatively easy implementation of the 'national policy' of industrialisation in the post-war period. Japanese firms were actively discouraged from financialisation (from seeking their own finance through the money markets, in other words), with the Ministry of Finance performing that task on their behalf (in association with the Bank of Japan). Consequently, the flow and circulation of capital was usually directed by the banks affiliated to each respective industrial grouping.

During the *Global Plan*, and under the tutelage of the United States, authoritarian *de facto* one-party rule (by the almost invincible Liberal Democratic Party) ensured that the Japanese state maintained a high level of structural autonomy from civil society. In this sense, it is impossible to explain Japan's path without affording its policymakers a major part in the unfolding drama. After 1971, when the *Global Plan* was shredded and the *Global Minotaur* got underway, the dollar's initial devaluation forced upon Japanese officials an urgency to find ways of maintaining competitiveness. In this context, the appreciation of the Yen, which happened the moment Bretton Woods died, was effectively countered with the export of capital through foreign direct investment (FDI) and through capital outflows to the United States.

In short, to keep its oligopolistic industry going, Japan had to nourish the *Global Minotaur* with continuous transfers of capital to Wall Street. The, perhaps tacit, agreement between Japanese and American authorities was simple: Japan would continue to recycle its trade surpluses by purchasing US debt (i.e. government bonds and securities) and, in return, Japan would have privileged access to the US domestic market, thus providing Japanese industry with the aggregate demand that Japanese society was incapable of producing.

However, there was a snag. When one buys foreign assets, at some point these assets start generating income which must be, eventually, repatriated. Japan thus 'ran the risk' of ceasing to be able to remain a net capital exporter, turning into a rentier nation. This prospect was at odds with the post-oil crisis Japanese growth strategy, which was to concentrate on high-value-added, low-energy-using industries like electronics, integrated circuits, computers and mechatronics (industrial robots).

On 22 September 1985, the United States, Japan, W. Germany, France and Britain signed the *Plaza Accord*. The 'advertised' purpose of the agreement was to devalue the US dollar in an attempt to rein in the US trade deficit.[25] Our interpretation is quite different. The purpose was, at least in part, to prevent Japan from becoming a rentier nation, a development that would jeopardise both Japan's own long-term plans and the *Global Minotaur* (whose wont was to remain the undisputed global rentier).[26]

In the years that followed the rise in the Yen forced the Japanese economy into the lap of a major, sustained slowdown. Indeed, the 1990s are referred to commonly as Japan's lost decade. The slow-burning crisis was due to a flood of liquidity and over-accumulation. In an attempt to keep up the rate of investment when Japanese exports were becoming dearer in the United States, the Bank of Japan pumped a lot of liquidity into the system. The result was the largest build-up of excess liquidity in modern history. Its side effect was massive speculative activity in real estate.[27]

When that speculative bubble burst in the early 1990s, following a rise in interest rates whose aim was to limit liquidity, house plus office prices crashed. The nation's banks ended up with huge loans on their books that no one was ever to repay. Although their central location in Japan's industrial structure (the *keiretsu*s) ensured that they would not go to the wall, they nevertheless were weighed down by these non-performing loans. All injections by the Bank of Japan into the banking system were partly absorbed by these loans, thus curtailing the injections' effect on real investment. Largely because of its zombie banks, banks that were neither dead nor truly alive, the Japanese economy was caught in a liquidity trap from which it has yet to recover. No matter how far the interest rate dropped, and it was never far above zero, it failed to reignite investment.

The very structure of Japan's oligopolistic industry and its citizens' great sense of insecurity (which is reinforced by the absence of decent social welfare provisions that translate into high savings ratios) combined to deny the country the levels of aggregate demand that would have otherwise restored growth. The only components of effective demand that have been keeping the Japanese economy afloat since the early 1990s are (a) direct government expenditure on infrastructure and (b) net exports.

The most substantive global repercussion of Japan's stagnation was the effect of almost zero interest rates on capital flows from Japan to the United States. To the already large amounts of capital that the government of Japan was investing in US government debt, and the equally large amounts of capital that Japanese firms were diverting to the United States as foreign direct investment (e.g. the purchasing of American shares, whole firms or the setting up by Sony, Toyota, Honda, etc. of production facilities on US soil), a third capital flow was added: the so-called *carry trade* by financial speculators who would borrow in Japan at rock bottom interest rates and, subsequently, shift the money to the United States where it would be lent or invested for much higher returns. This *carry trade* significantly expanded the *Minotaur*'s inflows, thus speeding up the financialisation process described in the previous section.

Perhaps the greatest threat to Japanese capitalism is that, unlike the United States, Japan has not managed to cultivate a hegemonic position in relation to South-East Asia.

Box 12.13 The *Minotaur*'s little dragons
Japan and South-East Asia

Ever since the Korean and, more significantly, the Vietnam Wars caused capitalism to take root in South-East Asia, Japan began to play the hegemonic role in the region. Japan constitutes the source of both initial growth and technological progress for that part of the world. However, it would be false to argue that Japan was to South-East Asia what the United States was to Germany and Japan during the *Global Plan*. The reason is that Japan never absorbed the surpluses of South-East Asian industries the way that the United States absorbed Japan's and Germany's. Indeed, South-East Asia is in a structural (or long-term) trade deficit with Japan.

This situation was sustained on a capacity to generate net export revenues outside that part of the world. During 1985–95, the decline in the value of the dollar was accompanied by a shift of Japan's foreign direct investment towards Asia. In a few short years, Japanese oligopoly industrial capital had spread its wings over Korea, Malaysia, Indonesia and Taiwan in the form of exported capital goods used in both production and the building of new infrastructure. This development, which was always part of the intention behind the 1985 Plaza Accords, reinforced South-East Asia's trade deficit *vis-à-vis* Japan. As the Japanese were always incapable of generating sufficient aggregate demand, the pressure to find export markets for South-East Asian output *outside Japan* grew stronger.

Once again, the United States came to the rescue. For, unlike Japan, that could produce everything except the requisite demand necessary to absorb its shiny, wonderful industrial products, the United States, under the *Minotaur's* gaze, had learned the art of creating immense levels of demand for other people's goods. Thus the United States became *the* export market for the area as a whole, inclusive of Japan, while South Korea and Taiwan imported mostly from Japan.[1] This process created, perhaps for the first time, the Japanese *vital space* that the *Global Plan's* designers had imagined, but never implemented fully (because of Chairman Mao's unexpected success).

Note
1 The greatest development in the region since 2000 has, of course, been the rise of China. It is interesting to note that, if Hong Kong is included in our statistics for the period 2000–8 (and it must be since it is a major gateway for the trade of the People's Republic), the combined current account position of China *vis-à-vis* Japan is negative. In this sense, the pattern was reproduced all the way to the *Crash of 2008*.

While Korea, Taiwan, Malaysia, Singapore, etc. rely on Japan for technology and capital goods, they cannot look to it as a source of demand. The whole area remained tied to the *Minotaur* and its whimsical ways. The rise of China in the late 1990s only exacerbated the situation since it added another surplus country, and a Great Dragon one at that, to the equation. Thus, the Rising Sun, the Great Dragon and the Little Dragons remained, at least prior to 2008, wedded to the *Minotaur*, feeding it with capital in the hope that it would, in return, devour their surpluses.

Box 12.14 Prodigal Japanese savings
A return with global repercussions

Following the *Crash of 2008*, the Yen revalued substantially, giving another blow to Japan's plans for export-led growth out of the mire. The conventional wisdom is that, at a time of crisis, capital flows back to the largest economies in search of safe havens and that this is the reason why the Dollar and the Yen are rising. But that leaves unanswered the question of why the Yen was rising so fast against the Dollar. The explanation consistent with the above is that, following Japan's stagnation in the 1990s and beyond, Japanese interest rates had collapsed to almost zero. Japan thus began to export its savings, worth at least $15 trillion, in search of higher interest rates. This carry trade was partly responsible for the fast pace of financialisation in the rest of the (mainly Anglo–Celtic) world, as much of the exported savings ended up contributing to Wall Street's private money (i.e. were used up buying CDOs, CDSs, etc.).

In the panic of 2008, a mass return of Japanese capital (the part of it that did not 'burn up') back to Japan was caused by the collapse of Wall Street's private money and, of course, the fall of US and EU interest rates to the near-zero, Japanese-like levels.

The long-term effect of this 'return' of Japanese savings back to Japan is serious. On the one hand it deepens Japan's stagnation through the appreciation of the Yen. On the other, the end of the yen carry trade translates into an upward push for world interest rates, despite the central banks' efforts to push them down.

The Deutschmark's new clothes

In sharp contrast to Japan's travails during the *Global Minotaur*'s formative years (1973–80), during which Japan's average growth rate was an anaemic 0.3 per cent, W. Germany was able to protect its trade surplus from the devaluation of the dollar by exploiting its dominance of the *vital space* the United States had previously laboured so hard to create on Germany's behalf: the European Common Market, that is today's European Union (EU). The role of German exports to the rest of Europe remained that which the *Global Plan*'s US architects had envisioned: they supported a strong Deutschmark and, at the same time, played a central role in the industrial development of the rest of Europe. Indeed, German exports were not just Volkswagens and refrigerators but also capital goods essential for the normal functioning of every aspect of Europe's productive apparatus.

Nevertheless, Germany was not Europe's locomotive. From 1973 onwards, the developmental model of continental Europe has been resting on the combined effect of maintaining a powerful capital goods industry, linked through Germany to global oligopolistic corporations. However, the aggregate demand that keeps these corporations going was always scarcer in their home countries, than in their neighbours. As did Japan, so did Germany show a magnificent capacity to produce efficiently the most desirable and innovative industrial products but, at the same time, it failed miserably in endogenously generating the requisite demand for them. That demand came from Germany's European periphery, or *vital space* as we call it, and, during the *Minotaur*'s halcyon days not only from across the Atlantic but also (in the 1998–2008 decade) from China.

Much ink has been expended in recent years in discussing Europe's fundamental hetero-geneity. The latter results from the coexistence of three groupings under the EU's umbrella: (a) persistent trade surplus generating countries (Germany, Holland, the Flemish part of Belgium; to which more recently Austria and Scandinavia were added); (b) persistent trade deficit inducing countries (headed by Italy and including Greece, Spain, Portugal); and (c) France, in a category of its own, for reasons that we explain below. For short, we shall refer to (a) as the ants, to (b) as the magpies and to (c) as… France.

The ants are the producers with the best and shiniest capital goods and, as a result, the most capital intensive output. Their industries are highly concentrated oligopolies sustained by both excess capacity and technological innovations of the highest order. However, just like Japan's sparkling industry, they cannot possibly generate sufficient demand for their own wares locally and this is why, once the *Global Plan* was gone, they desperately sought institutional arrangements with their neighbouring magpies, plus France, to whom they would siphon an increasing share of their output. The European Common Market, whose creation was (as we argued in the previous chapter) a US policy decision that goes as far back as the late 1940s, was the obvious set of institutions for fostering such a link.

Turning to the magpies, while the government and entrepreneurs of countries such as Greece and Portugal dreamed of convergence with the European north, the fact is that they proved unable to generate net exports because, their export growth notwithstanding, they have weak domestic capital goods sectors, so much so that any sustained expansion in national income yields a rising import content. In that sense, convergence was a bridge-too-far for the magpies because the infrastructural work needed to support their industries required large imports of capital goods from the ants (primarily from Germany).

The only magpie that did fairly well in the convergence game was Italy which, on occa-sion, even became a trade surplus country. However, these successes, judged from a neo-mercantilist's perspective, were predicated upon the devaluation of the Italian Lira relative to the Deutschmark. Italy, in this sense, is a curious magpie in that it could occasionally transfigure itself into an ant by waving the magic wand of aggressive currency devaluations. All that, of course, came to a grinding halt with the introduction of the Euro, which turned Italy into a fully fledged magpie.

And then there is France; the outlier in the European family.[28] The French elites, its government and private sector leaders alike, consistently aimed at a trade surplus; a neo-mercantilist goal that was, alas, seldom achieved. Being the largest destination for not only German but also for Italian exports, France only attained a net surplus during 1992–3 after the collapse of the Euro's predecessor, the European Monetary System (EMS); a system whose aim was to limit fluctuations in the exchange rates between European currencies. What marks France out (e.g. from Italy) are two strengths.

First, the calibre of and expertise within its political institutions which (perhaps due to its Napoleonic past) were the nearest Europe got to a policymaking civil service that might rival that of Washington (or of London during the days before the Great War). Second, France sports a large banking sector which is more advanced than that of the ants, and of course of the magpies. Because of the *gravitas* of its banks, France achieved a central position in the facilitation of trade and capital flows within the European economy. At the same time, before the Euro's introduction, the importance of its financial sector ruled out the strategy competitive devaluations (like those of Italy) of the French government's menu of policy options. After the Euro, French banks were upgraded further as they tapped into the energy of financial waves stirred up by the *Minotaur*'s rampant impact in New York and London.

Summing up the third category of EU states, which comprises France alone, we may, perhaps unkindly (but pretty accurately) describe it as an aspiring but chronically under-achieving neo-mercantilist desperately seeking a way out of its 'special' place in the European scheme of things on the strength of its financial sector.

Back to Germany, the ants' undisputed queen, from 1985 onwards the *Global Minotaur*'s drive to expand the US trade deficit translated into a major improvement in Germany's current account or trade balance. It was the new scheme of things: the United States imported as if there were no tomorrow and Germany exported to the United States both industrial goods and the capital necessary to nourish the *Minotaur*. The improvement in Germany's trade surplus *vis-à-vis* the United States rubbed off on the rest of the EU, which saw its collective trade position go into surplus. This was the environment in which the forces that would create the common currency, the Euro, gathered pace. Each grouping had different reasons for wanting to link the currencies up.

From the 1970s onwards, Germany was keen to shore up its position in the European scheme of things, as a net major exporter of both consumption and capital goods and a net importer of aggregate demand. While the *Global Minotaur* was turning the United States into the country in which consumption-led growth exceeded the growth in domestic produc-tive capacity, German policymakers intentionally aimed for the opposite: for a growth rate that was below that of the rest of Europe but, at the same time, of a capital accumulation (or investment) drive that was harder and faster than that of its neighbours.[29]

The aim of this policy was simple: to accumulate more and more trade surpluses from within its European *vital space* in order to feed the *Minotaur* across the Atlantic so as, in turn, to maintain its own export expansion within the United States and, later, China. That was indeed Germany's response to the challenge of maintaining its surplus-led growth model after the end of the *Global Plan* and once US authorities had chosen to allow global capitalism to enter a state of partial disintegration under the menacing domination of the *Minotaur*.

The one spanner in the works of this *German Strategy* was the threat of competitive currency devaluations that Italy and other countries were using with good effect to limit their trade deficits *vis-à-vis* Germany. The idea of a monetary system to limit currency fluctua-tions grew from the ants' preference for intra-European currency stability that would kill three birds with one stone: (a) it would remove the ants' uncertainty about the Deutschmark value of their exports to the magpies; (b) it would render their cross-border production costs more predictable given that the ants were engaged in considerable FDI (foreign direct investment) in the magpies' currency area (e.g. German manufacturers setting up whole factories making Volkswagen gearboxes in Spain or washing machine components in Portugal); and (c) it would solidify the surplus position of the ants, in relation to the magpies, by locking in a permanent differential between their growth rates and the magpies' growth rates; a differential which translated into permanent infusions of aggregate demand from the magpies to the ants.

The other groupings, the magpies and France, had different reasons for embracing the idea of monetary union. Starting with the magpies, their elites had grown particularly tired of devaluations – plain and simple. The fact that the Deutschmark value of their domes-tically held assets (from the value of their beautiful villas to that of their shares in domestic banks and companies) was liable for large and unexpected falls weighed heavily upon them. Similarly, the magpies' working classes were equally tired of a cruel game of catch up. All their hard fought nominal wage gains were liable to be wiped out at the stroke of the finance minister's pen, which was the sole requirement for a loss of up to 30 per cent of the local currency's value, and an immediate increase in the price of imported goods (mainly imported from the ants) which played a central role in the basic goods basket of the workers.

As for France, it had three reasons also for seeking a lock-up between the Franc and the Deutschmark: (a) it would strengthen the political elite's bargaining position *vis-à-vis* the powerful French trade unions, in view of the moderate wage rises across the Rhine that German trade unions negotiated with employers and the Federal government; (b) it would shore up its, already important, banking sector; and (c) it would give its political elites an opportunity to dominate Europe in the one realm where French expertise was terribly advanced compared to its German counterpart: the construction of transnational political institutions.[30] For these three reasons, France and the ants discovered common ground for combining the oligopoly industrial capital priorities of the ants with the project of *la construction européenne* aspired to by France.[31]

The road to the Euro began with the ill-fated European Monetary System (EMS), a mechanism of coordinated action by the central banks whose purpose was to intervene in the currency markets in order to keep the exchange rates within a narrow band. Alas, the *Global Minotaur* was stirring up so many waves of speculation that very soon it became clear that the combined forces of the central banks had insufficient fire power in Wall Street and the City of London to impose their will over the speculators. When George Soros, along with other astute money market gamblers, recognised a weakness in the EMS, and in particular saw that the British Pound and the Italian Lira were overvalued (in comparison to the countries' trade and fiscal position), he took huge bets out that the Pound and the Lira would devalue. In a game of chicken that lasted 24 tense hours, Soros and the Bank of England fought it out by betting serious amounts of capital against one another: Soros betting that the Pound would devalue, the Bank that it would not. The question was who would blink first. Once other speculators began to think that the Bank of England was losing too much money, and would have to withdraw from this contest, they added their bets on Soros' pile and, soon after, it was game over. The Pound and the Lira exited the EMS and Soros made more than $1 billion in one night.

That traumatic experience was the harbinger Germany required to decide to give up its beloved Deutschmark, as the price it was prepared to pay for the benefits of ending currency fluctuations within its European *vital space*. The rest, magpies and France, also took fright at the sight of the unprecedented power of the money markets and decided that huddling together under a renamed Deutschmark was a good idea.

The formation of the Euro, and the period of adjustment that led to it, crystallised the preceding situation and enabled Germany and the other ants to reach exceptional surpluses in a context of deepening stagnation in the rest of Europe. These surpluses became the financial means with which German corporations internationalised their activities in the rest of the world; whether the internationalisation materialises in the form of FDI, merger and acquisitions, or mega joint ventures (such as the construction of the Beijing-Lhasa railway line, or the touted collaborative construction of the Santos-Antofagasta line) the way local capitalisms react in the post-2008 environment. Yet, the primary prerequisite for such internationalisation of the German capital goods sectors is the continued growth of the Bundesrepublik's external surpluses with the rest of Europe.

In an important sense, Germany became the *Global Minotaur*'s European *Simulacrum*;[32] an economic system fully integrated within the European sphere, courtesy of the US-sponsored *Global Plan*, which mopped up increasing quantities of the shrinking aggregate demand pie of its neighbours. In the process, it put the magpies and France into an effective slow-burning recession, which was the price the latter had to pay for hooking their currencies up to the Deutschmark.

While the *Simulacrum* was the mirror image of the *Global Minotaur* (in that it drained the rest of Europe of demand, rather than injecting demand into it), it nevertheless had a similar end outcome. Just as the *Minotaur* exported a recessionary environment to the rest of the world in order to preserve its hegemony, so did the *Simulacrum* maintain Germany's relative position during that global receding tide by exporting stagnation into its own European backyard. The mechanism for accomplishing this was the celebrated *Maastricht Treaty* (later augmented in Dublin and Amsterdam) which laid down the following rules of monetary union:

- *budget deficits* for member states capped at 3 per cent;
- *debt to GDP* ratios below 60 per cent;
- *monetary policy* to be decided upon and implemented by an 'independent' European Central Bank, the ECB, whose single objective was to keep a lid on inflation; and
- a *no transfers clause* (or no bail outs, in post-2008 parlance), which meant that, if member states ever got into fiscal trouble, they should expect no assistance from the Euro's institutions (ECB, Eurogroup, etc.).

The above stipulations were 'sold' to the European public and elites as reasonable measures for shielding the Euro from 'free riding' by member states and, thus, creating credibility for the new currency. However, there was a hidden agenda that was as crucial as it was unspoken. The *no transfers clause*, in particular, became an all-consuming ideology (that was later to be dented in 2010 with the Greek fiscal crisis) which signified the ants' determination to use the creation of the Eurozone as a mechanism by which to cast in stone the 'obligation' of the magpies (plus France) to provide the ants with net effective demand for their exports.[33]

Summing up, the difference of this *Minotaur Simulacrum* from its transatlantic cousin was that (a) it fed on other people's aggregate demand (unlike the *Global Minotaur* that fed on other people's capital and goods);[34] and (b) it remained hopelessly dependent upon the *Global Minotaur* (as the *Crash of 2008* confirmed; see below). Under these circumstances, with the *Global Minotaur* draining the world of capital and its German sidekick draining real capital from within the non-surplus EU region, it is hardly surprising that European growth rates declined during every single one of the last four decades. Meanwhile, Europe has been falling more and more under the spell of German surpluses, a predicament that was only ameliorated during the *Global Minotaur*'s halcyon days by net exports to the United States. But when 2008 struck, even that silver lining was removed.[35]

German reunification and its global significance

The collapse of the Soviet Union, which began unexpectedly around 1989, soon led to the demolition of the Berlin Wall. Chancellor Helmut Kohl moved quickly to seize this opportunity to annex the DDR, East Germany as it was more commonly known. Conventional wisdom has it that the inordinate cost of Germany's reunification is responsible for the country's economic ills and its stagnation in the 1990s. This is not our reading.

While it is undoubtedly true that reunification strained Germany's public finances (to the tune of approximately $1.3 billion), and even led it to flout the very Maastricht rules that it had initially devised to keep Europe's magpies on the path of fiscal rectitude, at the same time it conferred upon German elites new powers and novel policy levers. On the negative side,

German capitalism had to shift its focus from traditional investments in technology, innovation and engineering to more mundane things like rebuilding from scratch the East's infrastructure and environmental reconstruction. However, these burdens proved an excellent investment for reasons that go much beyond national pride from the fulfilment of an understandable dream to reunite the country's two parts after 40 years of enforced separation.

The first effect of reunification on the real economy was the reduction in labour's bargaining power.[36] The West German trade unions tried to enforce similar wages and conditions in the East. Soon they found out that the complete implosion in the East's industrial sector and social economy did not allow them room to manoeuvre. Moreover, East Germany was not the only part of the former Soviet empire that collapsed. So did Eastern Europe as a whole, from Poland to Slovakia and from Hungary to Ukraine. The effect of the availability of dirt cheap labour either within the Federal Republic's new borders or close by was to depress German wages wholesale. Thus, German industry's intra-European competitiveness rose and, by 2004, Germany had become, once again, the world's largest exporter of industrial goods.[37]

To sum up, Germany's response to the cost blowout of reunification was the pursuit of *competitive wage deflation*. In the run up to the introduction of the euro, Germany was locking into its labour markets substantially decreased wages in relation to the wages elsewhere in what was to become the Eurozone. Almost in a bid to copy the *Global Minotaur*'s domestic strategy (recall Table 11.4 in the previous chapter), the German *Simulacrum* promoted a strategy of restraining wage growth to a rate less than that of productivity growth. Once the Euro was introduced, and German industry was shielded from the competitive currency depreciation of countries like Italy, its gains from the fall in wages became permanent.

Additionally, Germany's system of collective wage bargaining, based on a corporatist-*cum*-neo-mercantilist *entente* between German capital and the German trade unions, enabled the gap between productivity and wages to be more favourable to capital compared to the rest of Europe. The gist of the matter was low growth reinforcing German export competitiveness on the back of continual real wage deflation and vigorous capital accumulation. As the *Global Minotaur* began to soar, after 2004, Germany's trade surplus took off in sympathy, capital accumulation rose, unemployment fell to two million (after having risen to almost double that) and German corporate profits rose by 37 per cent.[38] However, even though the picture seemed quite rosy for the German elites, something rotten was taking over its banking sector; a nasty virus that the *Minotaur Simulacrum* had wilfully contracted from the *Global Minotaur* itself (see Box 12.15). And when the *Crash of 2008* happened in New York and London, that virus was energised in earnest. It was to become the beginning of the Euro's worst crisis ever.

12.5 Crash and burn: Credit crunch, bailouts and the socialisation of everything

> We are now in the phase where the risk of carrying assets with borrowed money is so great that there is a competitive panic to get liquid. And each individual who succeeds in getting more liquid forces down the price of assets in the process of getting liquid, with the result that the margins of other individuals are impaired and their courage undermined. And so the process continues…. We have here an extreme example of the disharmony of general and particular interest.
>
> John Maynard Keynes, 'The World's Economic Outlook',
> *Atlantic Monthly*, (1932)

Box 12.15 Rats abandoning a sinking ship
(while German bankers were jumping aboard)

In mid-2010 the *US Securities and Exchange Commission* (SEC), whose remit is to regulate Wall Street and the financial sector in general, began legal proceedings against Goldman Sachs (GS), Wall Street's most successful merchant bank. The offence over which GS was taken to task concerns a particular CDO called *Abacus 2007-AC1* that GS 'constructed' and sold at the beginning of 2007, just as the CDO market was about to go into meltdown. The essence of the charge is that GS was knowingly flogging a dead horse. In fact, it is a little worse than that: the SEC is alleging that GS had a hand in the killing of a horse and then trying to market its carcass as a boisterous stallion!

According to the SEC, GS created *Abacus* in association with a hedge fund called John Paulson & Co. The hedge fund chose a series of unsafe subprime mortgages that it knew were about to default and asked GS to infuse them into *Abacus*. Why did it do that? Because it wanted to bet against *Abacus*, the very CDO it helped create! Rather than take the small risk of betting against an unknown CDO, it chose to have GS create a duff one, ensuring that *any* bet against it would have been lucrative (as long as no-one else, except GS and John Paulson & Co, knew that *Abacus* was dead in the water).

Technically, the bet against *Abacus* meant that John Paulson & Co took a CDS out against *Abacus* (i.e. an 'insurance policy' that would pay good money if those whose bought *Abacus* lost their money – see Box 12.12). The problem of course was to find gullible buyers that would purchase *Abacus* no questions asked. That task fell on GS, the merchant bank which, according to the SEC, recommended *Abacus* to specific clients leading them to believe that it too, GS, would be buying into *Abacus*. Of course, GS had no such intention. With their accomplice, John Paulson & Co, they took out loads of CDSs against *Abacus* netting a nice little earner when the mortgages within *Abacus* failed (as planned).

Merchant banks, with GS at the forefront, made billions creating (or 'structuring') CDOs and selling them. That was well known. The *Abacus* case reveals an even darker side of this 'market': merchant banks creating financial products that were designed to fail so that they would collect the insurance. This is no different whatsoever, at least in principle, to the following scenario: imagine an aircraft manufacturer that is approached by a friendly insurer who suggests that it builds a faulty aircraft, one that is designed to crash, while the insurer writes a policy on behalf of its passengers. Only the insurer will ensure that the insurance monies will not go to the victims' families but will be, instead, collected by the insurer himself and the aircraft manufacturer with whom they will split the payout.

Let us now turn to the German connection. One of the main institutions that bought *Abacus* was called Rhinebridge, a subsidiary, or rather a SIV (a structured investment vehicle) of German bank IKB which used to be a conservative outfit lending, mainly, to German small- and medium-sized firms. What did such a parochial little bank from middle Germany know about *Abacus*? Exactly nothing, is the honest answer. Except that it knew that those before it who had bought CDOs from GS had profited greatly. It is not that the IKB did not try to look into *Abacus* to see what was under the bonnet. Its financial engineers and accountants took a good look. But they could not work out its contents, for that was GS' great talent: to instil such mindboggling complexity into its CDOs that not even a god could decipher them.

GS was not an exception to the rule. Most, if not all, merchant banks worked closely with hedge funds to similar effect.[1] Especially in the months leading to the *Crash of 2008*, these smart operators knew that there was something rotten in the mortgage backed bonds that they had helped create. So, they went into a flurry of creating new CDOs that would unload the truly dangerous tranches of mortgages off their own books to those of unsuspecting buyers. In the process they took out CDSs to profit from the transaction on top! Infinite 'innovation' went into similar schemes; as Ford and Jones (2010) demonstrate:

> ...investment banks were interested in the possibility of using CDOs to offload the toxic risks in rivals' balance sheets on to clients. As Goldman's Fabrice Tourre put it in an e-mail to his superiors at the end of 2006, one of the big opportunities lay in 'Abacus-rental strategies... [where] we 'rent' our Abacus platform to counterparties focused on putting on macro short in the sector'. Decoded: Goldman would sell CDOs stuffed with other investment banks' toxic waste, allowing them to short it....[2] The banks didn't want to look as if they were shorting themselves,' says one subprime investor. 'So bank A helped bank B get short and then bank B helped bank C and so on. Unless you were very close to the market you wouldn't get it.[3]

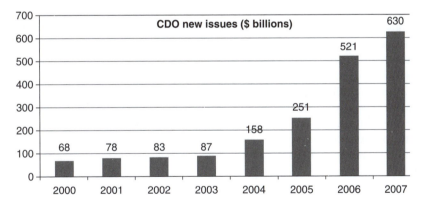

Figure 12.7 The triumph of financialisation.

Source: Securities Industry and Financial Markets Association)

When the inevitable happened, IKB ran to the German government and its parent bank (KfW) for help. The bill for keeping it alive came to €1.5 billion. It was the tip of the iceberg. The *Global Minotaur*, unbeknownst to the German people, and to most of its politicians, had infected the German capital with the virus of financialisation. When that disease became fully blown, Germany suffered considerably from the consequences. We return to this in Section 12.6.

Children learn from a young age the dynamics of piles of building blocks. They pile one cube on top of another cube and keep doing it until their little tower of cubes topples over; at which point they emit a happy giggle and start afresh. If only bankers and hedge fund managers were equally rational!

The moment one asset bubble bursts, a new one begins slowly to emerge somewhere; often in exactly the same place. But this is where the similarity with the children's game ends. While the children know full well that their new pile will come to the same end as the previous one, in asset markets the supposedly super-smart operators somehow convince themselves that *this-time-it-will-be-different*. They succeed in *believing* that they are living the dream of some *new paradigm*.[39]

The longer the rally lasts, and the more absurd their profits, the more convinced they become that it will last forever. Moreover, this growing conviction is cemented into place with the attendant belief that their new fabulous payoffs are deeply deserved and fully justified by the bout of psychic anguish they had experienced during the previous collapse. The smartest cookies in the business, who recognise first the signs of a potential fresh calamity, turn their faith in the righteousness of their cause into the most ruthless slash-and-burn practices (e.g. aggressive short-selling, financial cannibalism of the sort described in Box 12.15 above) which not only bring the next crash forward but also amplify its catastrophic force.

The story of how the *Crash of 2008* began is now the stuff of legend. Piles of books have been written on it and stacked on the shelves of university libraries, in airport news agencies, at the stalls of leftist groupings plying their revolutionary wares on street corners, etc.[40] We shall, therefore, desist a precise chronological account (see Box 12.16 for an ascetic timeline). Suffice to remind the reader that the 'deconstruction' began in the shadowy world of CDO trading, particularly those containing vast tranches of subprime mortgages.

As Section 12.3 argued, Wall Street had managed to set up a parallel monetary system, based on the use of CDOs as a form of *private money* underwitten by the capital inflows toward the *Global Minotaur*. This parallel 'monetary system' was based on a game of passing-the-parcel from one financial institution to the next, without a care in the world about what was in the parcel. Alas, the contents mattered.

When in 2001 a bubble in Wall Street burst (a bubble centred upon the so-called dot.com or New Economy craze), Alan Greenspan, Paul Volcker's successor as the Fed's Chairman, took fright that a recession would ensue (like that of the 1979–83 or the 1987, 1991 and 1998 varieties which he had himself seen off, with considerable success). He responded, quite reasonably, by loosening monetary policy substantially; exactly as he had done in 1987, 1991 and 1998. To that effect, US interest rates fell until in 2004 they were at a rock bottom 1 per cent.

Greenspan's policy seemed to make perfect sense. In fact his reputation as an artful and astute monetary policy tsar was built on his success at exactly such a move back in October 1987 (immediately after his appointment), when his quick-fire response to Black Monday (i.e. a quick reduction in interest rates and a large injection of liquidity into the financial sector), averted a recession and restored confidence in Wall Street before 1987 was out. Similar episodes in 1991 and 1998 turned him into the Fed's unrivalled sage. His 2001 seemed for a long while to have met with similar success, judging by the impressive post-2001 growth figures. By the time of his retirement, in 2007, Alan Greenspan was feted as a demi-god.

Alas, 2001 was no 1987. The main difference was that in 1987 the financial sector had not yet built up a whole new parallel system of *private money* on the back of the *Global Minotaur*. The latter had managed to stabilise the US balance of payments but had not yet created the dynamic of financialisation that, by the late 1990s, would erect a parallel monetary system on the foundations of the derivatives' market. Thus, when the Fed pumped liquidity into the financial system in 1987, it simply helped kick-start a stalled engine. In sharp contrast, in 2001, the injection of liquidity and the low interest rates, in conjunction with the *Minotaur*'s exploding vivacity, helped create a monster that was to turn on its creator very, very viciously six or seven years later.

By 2004, Greenspan had got a whiff of the growing bubble. He decided to go about its gradual deflation by increasing US interest rates slowly but steadily. Unfortunately, the parallel private monetary system had in the meantime grown too large on the strength of the *Minotaur*, the laughably large amounts of *leverage* chosen by Wall Street operators (30:1 was common) and, of course, the proliferation of securitised derivatives, that is CDOs and their offshoots. The quantity of *private money* in the global economy was so great that it became impossible to find a rate of interest rate rises that would, at once (a) deflate the *Bubble* and (b) avert a *Crash*. Thus, Wall Street's game began to unravel.

By 2006, US interest rates had risen to 5.35 per cent. The immediate effect was a downturn in the US housing sector. Some homeowners who were sitting on the most unaffordable (to them) subprime mortgages defaulted. Soon the trickle of defaults turned into a torrent; one that Dr Li's formula (given the assumed constancy of parameter γ) could not cope with. The value of CDOs crashed and soon the market for CDOs ground to a halt. Suddenly the merry-go-round game of profiting through passing CDOs from one financial institution to another turned into a desperate, cut-throat game of musical chairs, in which CDO holders (mainly the financial institutions) were going around in circles aghast at the realisation that someone had removed *all* the chairs.

In a few short weeks, the *private money* that Wall Street had created in the wake of the *Global Minotaur*'s capital flows had turned into hot ashes. The fact that the world's most venerable financial institutions had grown fully to depend on that money meant one thing: the global financial system had come to a standstill. No one would lend to anyone, fearing that the borrower had a huge exposure to the worthless CDOs. Capitalism was facing a crisis bigger than that of 1929.

It was at that point that the state, with the US state at the forefront, stepped in with the greatest government intervention humanity has ever seen. In a few months, more capitalist institutions were socialised than in Lenin's Soviet Russia. Ironically, this wave of socialisation happened at the behest of the world's strongest opponents of state intervention. At the very least, history retains its sense of humour.

Box 12.16 The diary of a Crash foretold

2007 – The canaries in the mine

April – A mortgage company that had issued a great number of subprime mortgages, New Century Financial, goes bankrupt with reverberations around the whole sector.

July – Bear Stearns, the respected merchant bank, announces that two of its hedge funds will not be able to pay their investors their dues. The new Chairman of the Fed, Ben Bernanke (who had only recently replaced Alan Greenspan) announces that the subprime crisis is serious and its cost may rise to $100 billion.

August – French merchant bank BNP-Paribas makes a similar announcement to that of Bear Stearns concerning two of its hedge funds. Its explanation? That it can no longer value its assets. In reality, it is an admission that the said funds are full of CDOs whose demand has fallen to precisely zero, thus making it impossible to price them. Almost immediately, European banks stop lending to each other. The ECB (European Central Bank) is forced to throw €95 billion into the financial markets to avert an immediate seizure. Not a few days go by before it throws a further €109 billion into the markets. At the same time, the US Federal Reserve, the Bank of Canada, the Reserve Bank of Australia and the Bank of Japan begin to pump undisclosed billions into their financial sectors. On 17 August, Bernanke reduces interest rates slightly, demonstrating a serious lack of appreciation of the scale of the impending doom.

September – The obvious unwillingness of the banks to lend to one another is revealed when the rate at which they lend to each other (*Libor*) exceeds the Bank of England's rate by more than 1 per cent (for the first time since the South-East Asian crisis of 1998). At this point, we witness the first *run-on-a-bank* since 1929. The bank in question is Northern Rock (see Box 12.7). While it holds no CDOs or subprime mortgage accounts, the bank relies heavily on short-term loans from other banks. Once this source of credit dries up, it can no longer meet its liquidity needs. When customers suspect this, they try to withdraw their money, at which point the bank collapses before being restored to 'life' by the Bank of England at a cost in excess of £15 billion. Rocked by this development, Bernanke drops US interest rates by another small amount, to 4.75 per cent while the Bank of England throws £10 billion worth of liquidity into the City of London.

October – The banking crisis extends to the most esteemed Swiss financial institution, UBS, and the world takes notice. UBS announces the resignation of its chairman and CEO who takes the blame for a loss of $3.4 billion from CDOs containing US subprime mortgages. Meanwhile in the United States, Citigroup at first reveals a loss of $3.1 billion (again on mortgage backed CDOs), a figure that it boosts by another $5.9 bn in a few days. By March of 2008, Citigroup has to admit that the real figure is a stunning loss of $40 bn. Not to be left out of the fracas, merchant bank Merrill Lynch announces a $7.9 billion loss and its CEO falls on his sword.

December – An historic moment arrives when one of the most free-marketer opponents of state intervention to have made it to the Presidency of the United States, George W. Bush, gives the first indication of the world's greatest government intervention (*including* that of Lenin after the Russian revolution). On 6 December President Bush unveils a plan to support a million of US homeowners to avoid having their house confiscated by the banks (or foreclosure, as the Americans call it). A few days later, the Fed gets together with another five central banks (including the ECB) to extend almost infinite credit to the banks. The aim? To address the *Credit Crunch*; i.e. the complete stop in inter-bank lending.

2008 – The main event

January – The World Bank predicts a global recession, stock markets crash, the Fed drops interest rates to 3.5 per cent, and stock markets rebound in response. Before long, however, MBIA, an insurance company, announces that it lost $2.3 billion from policies on bonds containing subprime mortgages.

February – The Fed lets it be known that it is worried about the insurance sector while the G7 (the representatives of the seven leading developed countries) forecasts the cost of the subprime crisis to be in the vicinity of $400 billion. Meanwhile the British government is forced to nationalise Northern Rock, Wall Street's fifth-largest bank, Bear Stearns (which in 2007 was valued at $20 billion) is absorbed by JP MorganChase, which pays for it the miserly sum of $240 million, with the taxpayer throwing in a subsidy in the order of… $30 billion.

April – It is reported that more than 20 per cent of mortgage 'products' in Britain are withdrawn from the market, along with the option of taking out a 100 per cent mortgage. Meanwhile, the IMF estimates the cost of the *Credit Crunch* to exceed $1 trillion. The Bank of England replies with a further interest rate cut to 5 per cent and decides to offer £50 billion to banks laden with problematic mortgages. A little later, the Royal Bank of Scotland attempts to prevent bankruptcy by trying to raise £12 billion from its shareholders, while at the same time admitting to having lost almost £6 billion in CDOs and the like. Around that time house prices start falling in Britain, Ireland and Spain, precipitating more defaults (as homeowners in trouble can no longer even pay back their mortgages by selling their house at a price higher than their mortgage debt).

May – Swiss bank UBS is back in the news, with the announcement that it has lost $37 billion on duff mortgage-backed CDOs and its intention to raise almost $16 billion from its shareholders.

June – Barclays Bank follows the Royal Bank of Scotland and UBS in trying to raise £4.5 billion at the stock exchange.

July – Gloom descends upon the City as the British Chamber of Commerce predicts a fierce recession and the stock exchange falls. On the other side of the Atlantic, the government begins massively to assist the two largest mortgage providers (Fannie Mae and Freddie Mac). The total bill of that assistance, takes the form of cash injections and loan guarantees of $5 trillion (yes dear reader, trillion – this is not a typo!), or around one tenth of the planet's annual GDP.

August – House prices continue to fall in the United States, Britain, Ireland and Spain, precipitating more defaults, more stress on financial institutions and more help from the taxpayer. The British government, through its Chancellor, admits that the recession cannot be avoided and that it would be more 'profound and long-lasting' than hitherto expected.

September – The City of London stock market crashes while Wall Street is buffeted by official statistics revealing a spiralling level of unemployment (above 6 per cent and rising). Fannie Mae and Freddie Mac are officially nationalised and Henry Paulson, President Bush's Treasury Secretary and an ex-head of Goldman Sachs, hints at the grave danger for the whole financial system posed by these two firms' debt levels. Before his dire announcement has a chance of being digested, Wall Street giant Lehman Brothers confesses to a loss of $3.9 billion during the months June, July and August. It is, of course, the iceberg's tip. Convinced that the US government will not let it go to the wall, and that it will at least generously subsidise someone to buy it, Lehman Brothers begins searching for a buyer. Britain's Barclays Bank expresses an interest on condition that the US taxpayer funds all the potential losses from such a deal. Secretary Paulson, whose antipathy of the CEO of Lehman's since his days at Goldman Sachs is well documented, says a rare 'No'. Lehman Brothers thus files for bankruptcy, initiating the crisis' most dangerous avalanche. In the meantime, Merrill Lynch, which finds itself in a similar position, manages to negotiate its takeover by Bank of America at $50 billion, again with the taxpayer's generous assistance; assistance that is provided by a panicking government following the dismal effects on the world's financial sector of its refusal to rescue Lehman Brothers.

When it rains it pours. The bail out of Merrill Lynch does not stop the domino effect. Indeed one of the largest dominoes is about to fall: the American Insurance Group (AIG). When it emerges that AIG is also on the brink, the Fed immediately puts together an $85 billion rescue package. Within the next six months, the total cost to the taxpayer for saving AIG from the wolves rises to an astounding $143 billion. While this drama is playing out in New York and Washington, back in London the government tries to rescue HBOS, the country's largest mortgage lender, by organising a £12 billion takeover by Lloyds TSB. Three day later in the United States Washington Mutual, a significant mortgage lender with a valuation of $307 billion, goes bankrupt, is wound down and its carcass is sold off to JP MorganChase.

On 28th of the month, Fortis, a giant continental European bank, collapses and is nationalised. On the same day, the US Congress discusses a request from the US Treasury to grant it the right to call upon $700 billion as assistance to the distressed financial sector so that the latter can 'deal' with its 'bad assets'. The package is labelled the *Paulson Plan*, named after President Bush's Treasury Secretary. In the language of this book, Congress was being asked to replace the *private money* that the financial sector had created, and which turned into ashes in 2007/8, with good, old-fashioned public money.

Before the fateful September is out, the British government nationalises Bradford and Bingley (at the cost of £50 bn in cash and guarantees) and the government of Iceland nationalises one of the small island nation's three banks (an omen for the largest 2008-induced economic meltdown, by *per capita* impact). Ireland tries to steady savers' nerves by announcing that the government guarantees *all* savings in *all* banks trading on the Emerald Isle. On the same day Belgium, France and Luxembourg put €6.4 billion into another bank, Dexia, to prevent it from shutting up shop.

The date is 29 September but this particularly recalcitrant September is not done yet. In its thirtieth day the big shock comes from the US Congress, which rejects the Treasury's request for the $700 billion facility with which Paulson is planning to save Wall Street. The New York stock exchange falls fast and hard and the world is enveloped in an even thicker cloud of deep uncertainty.

October – On 3 October the US Congress succumbs to the pressing reality and in the end passes the $700 billion 'bail out' package, after its members have secured numerous deals for their own constituencies. Three days later the German government steps in with €50 billion to save one of its own naïve banks, Hypo Real Estate. While painful for a country that always prides itself as supremely prudent, the pain comes nowhere close to that which Icelanders are about to experience. The Icelandic government declares that it is taking over all three banks given their manifest inability to continue trading as private lenders. It is clear that the banks' bankruptcy will soon bankrupt the whole country, whose economic footprint is far smaller than that of its failed banks. Iceland's failure has repercussions elsewhere, in particular in Britain and Holland where the Icelandic banks are particularly active. Many of the UK's local authorities have entrusted their accounts to Icelandic banks (in return for high-ish interest rates) and for this reason their failure adds to the malaise. On 10 October, the British government throws an additional £50 billion into the financial sector and offers up to £200 billion in short-term loans. Moreover, the Fed, the Bank of England, the ECB and the Central Banks of Canada, Sweden and Switzerland cut their interest rates at once: the Fed to a very low 1.5 per cent, the ECB to 3.75 per cent, and the Bank of England to 4.5 per cent.

Two days later, the British government decides that the banks are in such a state that, despite the huge assistance they have received, they require a great deal more to stay in business. A new mountain of cash, £37 billion, is to be handed out to the Royal Bank of Scotland, Lloyds TSB and HBOS. It is not a move specific to Britain. On 14 October, the US Treasury uses $250 billion to buy chunks of different ailing banks so as to shore them up. President Bush explains that this intervention is approved in order to 'help preserve free markets'. George Orwell, the British author of 1984, would have been amused with this perfect example of naked double-speak.

It is now official: both the United States and Britain are entering into a recession, as the financial crisis begins to affect the real economy. The Fed immediately reduces interest rates further, from 1.5 per cent to 1 per cent.

November – The Bank of England also cuts interest rates, though not to the same level (from 4.5 per cent to 3 per cent), as does the ECB (from 3.75 per cent to 3.25 per cent). The *Crash* is spreading its wings further afield, sparking off a crisis in Ukraine (which prompts the IMF to lend it $16 billion) and causing the Chinese government to set in train its own stimulus package worth $586 billion over two years; money to be spent on infrastructural projects, some social projects and reductions in corporate taxation. The Eurozone announces too that its economy is in recession. The IMF sends $2.1 billion to bankrupt Iceland. The US Treasury gives a further $20 billion to Citigroup (as its shares lose 62 per cent of their value in a few short days). The British government reduces VAT (from 17.5 per cent to 15 per cent). The Fed injects yet another $800 billion into the financial system. Finally, the European Commission approves a plan that will see €200 billion being spent as a Keynesian stimulus injection to restore aggregate demand.

December – The month begins with the announcement by the respected US-based National Bureau of Economic Research that the US economy's recession had begun as early as December 2007. During the next ten days, France adds its own aid package for its banking sector, worth €26 billion, and the ECB, the Bank of England, plus the Banks of Sweden and Denmark, reduce interest rates again. In the United States, the public is shocked when the Bank of America says that its taxpayer-funded takeover of Merrill Lynch will result in the firing of 35,000 people. The Fed replies with a new interest rate between 0.25 per cent and 0 per cent. Desperate times obviously call for desperate measures.

As further evidence that the disease which began with the CDO market and consumed the whole of global financial capital has spread to the real economy, where people actually produce things (as opposed to pushing paper around for ridiculous amounts of cash), President Bush declares that about $17.4 billion of the $700 facility will be diverted to America's stricken car makers. Not many days pass before the Treasury announces that the finance arm of General Motors (which has become ever so 'profitable' during the derivatives' reign) will be given $6 billion to save it from collapse.

By the year's end, on 31 December, the New York stock exchange has lost more than 31 per cent of its total value when compared to 1 January of this cataclysmic year.

2009 – The never ending aftermath

January – Newly elected President Obama declares the US economy to be 'very sick' and foreshadows renewed public spending to help it recover. As a stop-gap measure, his administration pumps another $20 billion into the Bank of America while watching in horror Citigroup split in two, a move intended to help it survive. US unemployment rises to more than 7 per cent and the labour market sheds more jobs than ever before since the Great Depression (see Figure 12.8 below). US imports fall and, as a result Japan, Germany and China see their trade surpluses dwindle. The *Global Minotaur* has been wounded. The question is if its wounds are fatal or not. The answer is still not clear (see Section 12.7 below).

In Britain the Bank of England cuts interest rates to 1.5 per cent, the lowest level in its 315 year history (the current rate, as these words are penned, is 0.5 per cent) and, as GDP declines 1.5 per cent, the British government offers loans of £20 billion to small firms to help tide them over during the storm. German Chancellor Angela Merkel follows suit with a €50 billion stimulus package at the same time that the ECB cuts interest rates to 2 per cent. Ireland nationalises the Anglo-Irish Bank since no amount of money given to it seems sufficient to stop its inexorable slide to oblivion.

The IMF warns that global economic growth will turn negative for the first time since 1945 and the International Labour Organisation (ILO) predicts that 51 million jobs will be lost worldwide in 2009 due to the crisis.

February – The Bank of England breaks all records when it reduces interest rates to 1 per cent (in its fifth cut since October). Soon after President Obama signs his $787 billion stimulus *Geithner–Summers Plan*[1], which he describes as 'the most sweeping recovery package in our history'. It is a pivotal moment to which we return in the main text below. Meanwhile, AIG continues to issue terrible news: a $61.7 billion loss during the last quarter of 2008. Its 'reward' is another $30 billion from the US Treasury.

March – The G20 group (which includes the G7, Russia, China, Brazil, India and other emerging nations) pledges to make 'a sustained effort to pull the world economy out of recession'. In this context, the Fed decides that the time for piecemeal intervention has passed and says it will purchase another $1.2 trillion of 'bad debts' (i.e. of Wall Street's now worthless private money).

April – The G20 meets in London, among large demonstrations, and agrees to make $1.1 trillion available to the global financial system, mainly through the auspices of the IMF, which soon after estimates that the Crash has wiped out about $4 trillion of the value of financial assets (warning that only one of these four trillions has been taken off the banks' books, thus giving the impression that their bottom line is better than it truly is). In London, Chancellor Alistair Darling forecasts that Britain's economy will decline by 3.5 per cent in 2009 and the budget deficit will reach £175 billion or more than 10 per cent of GDP.

May – Chrysler, the third largest US car maker, is forced by the government to go into receivership and most of its assets are transferred to Italian carmaker Fiat for a song. The news from the financial sector continue to be bleak, as a government probe reveals that they are still in dire straits. The US Treasury organises another assistance package to the tune of more than $70 billion.

June – It is General Motors' turn, America's iconic car maker, to go bankrupt. Its creditors are forced to 'consent' to losing 90 per cent of their investments while the company is nationalised (with the government providing an additional $50 billion as working capital). GM's own unions, who have become creditors owing to the company's failure to cover its workers' pension right, become part owners. Socialism, at least on paper, seems alive and well and living in Detroit. Over the other side of the Atlantic Pond, the unemployment rate in Britain rises to 7.1 per cent with more than 2.2 million people on the scrapheap. Another indication of the state of the global economy is that in 2008 global oil consumption falls for the first time since 1993.

Note
1 Named after Tim Geithner, the new Secretary of the Treasury who previously served as Undersecretary to the Treasury when Larry Summers was Bill Clinton's Secretary; and of course Larry Summers himself who is operating this time in his new capacity of Director of President Obama's National Economic Council.

While it is beyond the scope of this book to present a complete history of the *Crash of 2008*, the above box relates all we need for our purposes – a catalogue of wholesale failure of the deregulated financial sector that spearheaded history's greatest, deepest and most sustained intervention by the world's governments. The astonishment that this story causes us every time we revisit its twists and turns can only be surpassed by the audacity of what followed. In an effort to prove Marx's hunch that capital knows no restraint, and before the dust had settled from the nuclear explosion it had caused, the financial sector embarked upon a new project: how to recreate its *private money* using as raw materials the public money the hapless taxpayer sent it in its hour of extreme need.

From June 2009 onwards, the financial press began reporting that banks were ready to return to the state the money that they borrowed (see Box 12.17 below). Most people thought that the banks, having received oceans of liquidity from the taxpayer, made amends, pulled their socks up, tided up their business, altered their ways, stopped meddling with toxic derivatives (CDOs, CDSs and the like) and started making money legitimately, from which they now wanted to repay the taxpayer – if only…

To see what really went on, it is important to take a closer look at the *Geithner–Summers Plan*; President Obama's February 2009 own $1 trillion package for saving the banks from the worthless CDOs that were drowning them (see Box 12.16 above). The main problem the banks faced was that they were awash with the pre-2008 CDOs which no one wanted to buy at prices that would not cause the banks who owned them to declare that they were insolvent. Within these CDOs there were some solid mortgages, that homeowners continued to service and, of course, a lot of junk subprime mortgages too. What was their value? No one knew because (a) the CDOs were so complex that not even those who created them could work out their contents, and (b) the market in CDOs had perished and it was, therefore, impossible to price them by offering them for sale.

Tim Geithner's and Larry Summer's idea was simple: to set up, in partnership with hedge funds, pension funds, etc. a *simulated market* for the toxic CDOs, hoping that the new *simulated market* would start a trade going in existing CDOs that would restore enough value to them so that the banks could remove them from their liabilities column and start afresh. A sketch of their Plan follows.

Suppose *bank B* owns a CDO, let's call it *c*, that *B* bought for $100, of which $40 was *B*'s own money and the remaining $60 was *leverage* (i.e. a sum that *B* somehow borrowed in order to purchase *c*). *B*'s problem is that, after 2008, it cannot sell *c* for more than $30. The problem here is that, given that its vaults are full of such CDOs, if it sells each below $60, it will have to file for bankruptcy, as the sale will not even yield enough to pay its debt of $40 per CDO (i.e. a case of negative equity). Thus, *B* does nothing, holds on to *c*, and faces a slow death by a thousand cuts as investors, deterred by *B*'s inability to rid itself of the toxic CDOs, dump *B*'s shares whose value in the stock exchange falls and falls and falls. Every penny the state throws at it to keep it alive, *B* hoards in desperation. Thus, the great bail out sums given to the banks never find their way to businesses that need loans to buy machinery or customers that want to finance the purchase of a new home.

The *Geithner–Summers Plan* proposed the creation of an account, let's call it *a*, that could be used by some hedge or pension fund, call it *H*, to bid for *c*. The account *a* would amount to a total of, say $60 (the lowest amount that *B* will accept to sell *c*) as follows: the hedgefund *H* contributes $5 to *a* and so does the US Treasury. The $50 difference comes in the form of a loan from the Fed.[41] The next step involves the hedge or pension fund, our *H*, to participate in a government organised auction for *B*'s *c*; an auction in which the highest bidder wins *c*.

By definition, the said auction must have a reservation price of no less than $60 (which is the minimum *B* must sell *c* for if it is to avoid bankruptcy). Suppose that *H* bids $60 and wins. Then *B* gets its $60 which it returns to its creditor (recall that *B* had borrowed $60 to buy *c* in the first place) and, while *B* loses its own equity in *c*, it lives to profit another day. As for hedge fund *H*, its payout depends on how much it can sell *c* for. Let's look at two scenarios: a good and a bad one for *H*.

We begin with the good scenario. Hedge fund h discovers that, a few weeks after it purchased c for $60 (to which it only contributed $5), its value has risen to, say, $80, as the *simulated market* begins to take off and speculators join in. Of that $80, H owes $50 to the Fed and must share the remaining equity ($30) with its partner, the Treasury. This leaves H with $15. Not bad. A $5 investment became a $15 revenue. And if H purchases a million of these CDOs, its net gain will be a nice $10 million.

In the case of the bad scenario, H stands to lose its investment (the $5) but nothing beyond that. Suppose, for instance, that it can only sell CDO c, which it bought for $60 using account a, for $30 (which is what it traded for before this *simulated market*, created by the *Geithner–Summers Plan*, came into being). Then, H will owe to the Fed more than it received. However, the loan by the Fed to H is what is known as a *non-recourse loan*; which means that the Fed has no way of getting its money back.

In short, if things work out well the fund managers stand to make a net gain of $10 from a $5 investment (a 200 per cent return) whereas if they do not they will only lose their initial $5. Thus, the *Geithner–Summers Plan* was portrayed as a brilliant scheme by which the government encouraged hedge and pension fund managers to take *some* risk in the context of a government designed and administered game that *might* work; one in which everyone wins – the banks (who will get rid of the hated CDOs), the hedge and pension funds that will make a cool 200 per cent rate of return, and the government, which will recoup its bail out money.

It all sounds impressive. Until one asks the question: what smart fund manager would predict that the probability of the good scenario materialising is better than around $\frac{1}{3}$?[42] Who would think that there is more than one chance in three that they would be able to sell the said CDO *for more than $60*, given that now no one wants to touch the toxic CDO for more than $30? Who would participate in this *simulated market*? Committing one trillion dollars to a programme founded on pure, unsubstantiated optimism seems quite odd.

Were Tim Geithner and Larry Summers, two of the smartest people in the US administration, foolhardy? We think not. Their plan was brilliant but not for the stated purpose. It was a devilish plan for allowing the banks to get away with figurative murder. Here is our interpretation of what really happened or, indeed, our answer to the question who would, in their right mind, participate in the *Geithner–Summers simulated market*? *The banks themselves!*

Take bank B again. It is desperate to get CDO c out of its balance sheet. The *Geithner–Summers Plan* then comes along. Bank B immediately sets up its own hedgefund, H', using some of the money that the Fed and the Treasury has already lent it to keep it afloat (see previous box for examples). H' then partakes of the *Plan*, helps create a new account a', comprising $100 (of which H' contributes $7, the Treasury chips in another $7 and the Fed loans $86) and then immediately bids $100 for its very own c. In this manner, it has rid itself of the $100 toxic CDO once and for all at a cost of only $7, which was itself a government handout![43]

The significance of the subterfuge in the *Geithner–Summers Plan* goes well beyond its ethical or even fiscal implications. The *Paulson Plan* that preceded it was a crude but honest attempt to hand cash over to the banks no-questions-asked. In contrast, Geithner and Summers tried something different: to allow Wall Street to imagine that its cherished financialisation could rise Phoenix-like from its ashes on the strength of a government-sanctioned plan for creating new derivatives. Come to think of it, the very essence of the *Geithner–Summers Plan* was the creation of synthetic financial products (account a in the example above) with which to refloat the defunct pre-2008 CDOs. Henceforth the government

---

Box 12.17 Recovery
(but only in Wall Street and the City of London)

June 2009 – A dozen US banks claim to have turned the corner and are now able to return a portion of the money they were lent in October 2008 (which is a tiny fraction of the total taxpayers' outlay on saving them). Commentators note that this is a strategic ploy by bank management to pay themselves large bonuses. *Goldman Sachs* surprises with an unexpected announcement of an after-tax profit of $3.44 billion for the second quarter. At the same time, it announces that in the second quarter alone it has paid out $6.65 billion in pay and management bonuses. More banks announce large profit taking in the weeks that follow. Seasoned analysts, however, look on sceptically.

August 2009 – Barclays posts an 8 per cent rise in profits for the first six months of 2009, created mostly in its proprietary investment division (i.e., the department that continues to trade in derivatives and other such 'products').

Meanwhile, during the first two quarters of 2009, more American families lose their homes than ever before and whole neighbourhoods in California and the Midwest lay abandoned. Britain's unemployment tally heads for the three million mark, Japan's GDP falls by 14.2 per cent (in the first quarter of the year) and the OECD declares that the GDP of the 30 most developed countries will fall at an average rate of 4 per cent.

---

proceeded to organise a rigged auction for these CDOs in which hedge and pension funds would bid for them using the new, government sponsored, derivative-like money.

In short, the Obama administration blew a breezy wind into Wall Street sails by engineering a new marketplace for the old derivatives (which were replete with poor people's mortgage debts) where the medium of exchange was a mixture of the old (refloated) derivatives and new ones (based not on poor people's mortgages but on the taxes of those who could not avoid paying them; often the same poor people, that is). Thus, much of the banks toxic assets were moved off their accounts.

Once the banks' balance sheets were cleansed of most of the toxic CDOs, at a profit too, the banks used some of the proceeds, and some of the bail out money from the various waves of assistance received from the state, to pay the government back enough of the monies received in order to be allowed their hefty bonuses. In other words, the process of fashioning *private money* was on again after a short break of no more than a year.

In political terms, President Obama's approval of the plan constitutes a complete capitulation to Wall Street. And as is usually the case with capitulations to sinister characters, no one thanked the capitulator. Indeed, the *Geithner–Summers Plan* increased the banks' blackmailing power *vis-à-vis* the state. While President Obama's administration was busily accepting the Wall Street mantra on no fully blown nationalisations (i.e. the dodgy argument that recapitalising banks by means of temporary nationalisations, as in Sweden in 1993, would quash the public's confidence in the financial system, thus creating more instability which, in turn, might jeopardise any eventual recovery), the Street's banks were already plotting against the administration, intent on using their renewed financial vigour to promote Obama's political opponents (who offered them promises of offensively light regulation).

This twist took on added significance in January 2010 when the US Supreme Court, with a 5:4 vote, overturned the Tillman Act of 1907, which President Teddy Roosevelt had passed in a bid to ban corporations from using their cash to buy political influence. On that fateful Thursday the floodgates of Wall Street money were flung open as the Court ruled that the managers of a corporation can decide, without consulting with anyone, to write out a cheque to the politician that offers them the best deal, especially regarding regulation of the financial sector in the aftermath of 2008.

President Obama's reaction to this 'betrayal' was to use his anger smartly. He empowered Paul Volcker, who was still going strong in his eighties, to author the regulatory legislation under which Wall Street will have to labour in the future; and to write it in such a manner as to tighten the authorities' grip over Wall Street in important ways. Volcker, in his new capacity as head of the *Economic Recovery Advisory Board* (ERAB), came up with the *Volcker Rule* which the administration seems, at the time of writing, determined to push through Congress. The *Volcker Rule* revives the New Dealers' Glass–Steagall Act, which Larry Summers had done away with in the 1990s. It prohibits banks from doubling in derivatives and other exotic financial products. Volcker's basic idea is that banks that accept deposits and are insured against failure by the state ought not to be allowed to participate in either the stock market or the derivatives' trade.

Having to face one of the *Global Minotaur*'s early prophets and minder during its 1980s adolescence (recall Volcker's role from Chapter 11), has given Wall Street bankers a few sleepless nights. However, it would be foolhardy to bet against the Street's capacity to overcome *any* regulatory constraints it finds in its way; especially after having recovered from its near-death 2008 experience.

So far, the above account of the *Crash* moved within the smoke and mirrors of Wall Street and its hazardous games. Let us conclude this section with some hints regarding the real costs of the *Crash* as experienced by real people whose job involves hard work but no gambling with other people's money.

Figure 12.8 uncovers the true cost in units of anguish that the *Crash of 2008* visited upon the long-suffering American working class. After three decades of living in the *Global Minotaur*'s world, with real wages that never rose above their early 1970s levels, of working

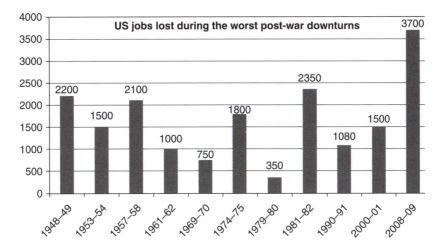

Figure 12.8 US job losses (in thousands) during the 12-month period around the worst post-1945 recessions.

more and more hours and achieving remarkable productivity levels for no tangible benefits, suddenly they were literally turned into the streets in their millions. Almost four million Americans lost their jobs while, according to the US *Mortgage Bankers Association*, it is estimated that 1 in 200 homes was repossessed by the banks. Every three months, from 2008 to 2010, 250,000 new families had to pack up and leave their homes in shame. On average one child in every US classroom was at risk of losing his or her family home because the parents could not afford to meet their mortgage repayments.

In the aftermath of 2008, American families are growing more desperate at the time of Wall Street's celebrated tax-fuelled recovery. According to the US-based *Homeownership Preservation Foundation*, which surveyed 60 thousand homeowners, more than 40 per cent of American households are getting further and further into debt every year. Sometimes the most insightful data come from unexpected sources. Figure 12.9 plots the average height of US office buildings against time. It is uncanny how the plot picks up all the troughs and peaks of the economic cycles. The *Crash of 2008* comes across this graph as a true successor to the calamity that was 1929.

Beyond the United States, it is often said that the Developing World was relatively unscathed by the *Crash of 2008*. While it is true that China successfully used simple Keynesian methods for delaying the crisis through spending more than $350 billion on infra-structural works in one year (and close to twice that by 2010), a study by Beijing University shows that poverty rates actually increased while the rate of private expenditure fell (with public investment accounting for the continuing growth). Whether this type of Keynesian growth is sustainable without the *Global Minotaur* remains to be seen.

Countries like Brazil and Argentina, which as we have seen export large quantities of primary commodities to China, weathered 2008 better than others. India too seems to have managed to generate sufficient domestic demand. Nevertheless, it would be remiss not to take into consideration the fact that the Developing World had been in deep crisis, caused by escalating food prices, for at least a year before the *Crash of 2008*. Between 2006 and 2008 average world prices for rice rose by 217 per cent, wheat by 136 per cent, corn by

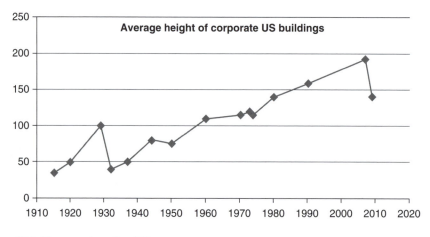

Figure 12.9 The recession of ambition.

Source: The Netherlands Architects Association Annual Report 2010.

125 per cent and soybeans by 107 per cent. The causes were multiple but also intertwined with the *Global Minotaur*.

Financialisation, and the ballistic rise of options, derivatives, securitisation, etc. led to new ways of speculation at the Chicago Futures' Exchange over food output. In fact, a brisk trade in CDOs, comprising not mortgages but the future price of wheat, rice and soybeans, gathered steam in the run up to 2008. The rise in demand for bio-fuels played a role too, as they displaced normal crops with crops whose harvest would end up in 4x4 monsters loitering around Los Angeles and London.

Add to that the drive by US multinationals like Cargill and Monsanto to commodify seeds in India and elsewhere, the thousands of suicides of Indian farmers caught in these multinationals' poisonous webs and the effects of the demise of social services at the behest of the IMF on its special adjustment programmes (SAPs), etc., and a fuller picture emerges. In that picture, the *Crash of 2008* seems to have made a terrible situation (for the vast majority of people) far worse.[44] Tellingly, when the G20 met in London in April 2009, and decided to bolster the IMF's fund by $1.1 trillion, the stated purpose was to assist economies worldwide to cope with the *Crash*. But those who looked more closely saw, in the fine print, a specific clause: the monies would be used exclusively to assist the global financial sector. Indian farmers on the verge of suicide need not apply. Nor should capitalists interested in investing in the real economy.

Glancing at the world in its totality, it is hard to miss the significance of 2008. Figure 12.10 offers a useful comparison of the *Crash of 2008* with the *Crash of 1929*. Based on the assumption that the two calamities began in June 1929 and April 2008, it normalises data so that both the 1929 and the 2008 numbers are arbitrarily set equal to 100 for the relevant starting point of each *Crash* (June 1929 and April 2008 respectively). The first graph concerns world output, the second graph looks at the total value of shares in all the stock exchanges of the world (global equities) and the third graph plots the total volume of global trade (measured in discounted dollars).

One thing becomes apparent. By all three measures, the *Crash of 2008* was significantly worse during the first year. In the second year, recovery has been stronger. This is clearly due to the large stimulus packages (quite separately from the injections of money into the banks) that governments unleashed onto world capitalism in a gallant attempt to save it from itself. However, it is also clear that the recovery is a relative one. The world is still producing less than in 2007 even though China, India, Brazil and a number of other countries have been growing quite well. When we take into consideration the distributional aspects involved, it is not hard to see that the *Crash of 2008* is having devastating effects on those at the sharp end worldwide.

Moreover, two menacing dark clouds are hanging over the world economy. First, there is the question that the *Greek crisis* posed in 2010 (see next section for more). Now that public money has replaced the burnt out *private money* of Wall Street, and the public debt of various governments has risen sharply, should we anticipate a new *Credit Crunch* or even a new financial storm to spring out in the market for government debt? Second, what will we do without the *Global Minotaur*? After all, that callous beast kept up the aggregate demand of the surplus nations (Germany, Japan and China). Now that the beast is wounded by the *Crash of 2008*, and US trade deficits are not the vacuum cleaners (sucking in mountainous imports) that they used to be, what will play its role?

There is no better place to start looking into these questions than in Europe's heartland. The next section takes us there, to the axis linking Berlin, Frankfurt and Brussels with Athens, Lisbon, Rome and Madrid.

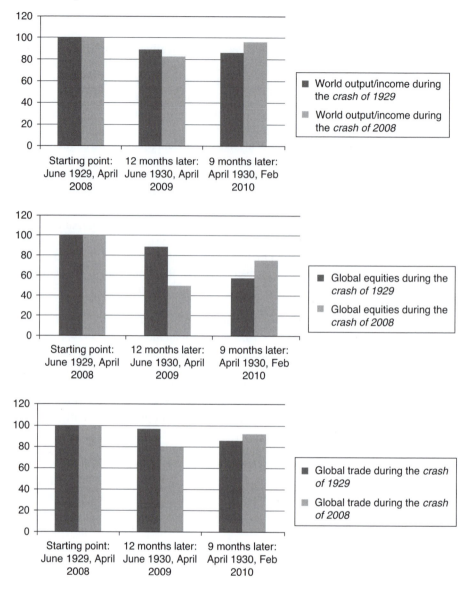

Figure 12.10 A comparison of the *Crash of 1929* with the *Crash of 2008*.[1]

Note: See Barry Eichengreen and Kevin O'Rourke (2010) 'What do the new data tell us', *mimeo*, March

12.6 First as history then as farce: Europe's crisis in context

Saving the banks – European style

The demise of the *Global Plan* in the 1970s had dealt a powerful blow at Europe. Somehow, Europe managed to recover by adapting to the new regime, the *Global Minotaur*. It learned the art of nourishing the transatlantic fiend with steady capital flows in return for a healthy trade surplus, particularly in manufactures.[45] At the same time, its own financial sector, especially the French and German banks (not to mention, of course, the City of London which was closer to Wall Street than New Jersey), jumped on the financialisation gravy train from which it too drew substantial benefits (see Section 12.4).

When the *Crash of 2008* hit, and the *Global Minotaur* was seriously wounded, Europe was destabilised. On the one hand, it had lost a critical source of aggregate demand while, at once, its banks faced meltdown as the American CDOs bursting out of its vaults, turned to ash. Despite European gloating that this was an Anglo-Celtic crisis, and that its own banks had not been taken over by financialisation's equivalent to a gold fever, the truth soon came out.

When the crisis struck, German banks were found out: for they had, secretly, reached an average *leverage ratio* (i.e. the ratio of money borrowed for the purpose of speculation to own money used) of 52 to 1; a ratio much higher than the already exorbitant ratio common in Wall Street and London's City. Even the most conservative and stolid state banks, the Landesbanken, 'proved bottomless pits for the German taxpayer', once the CDO market collapsed.[46] Similarly in France; from 2007 to 2010 French banks had to admit that they had at least €33 billion invested in CDOs that are, post-2008, worth next to nothing.[47]

Additionally, the Bank for International Settlements (the body representing the world's central banks) recently disclosed that European banks are terribly exposed to the debts of precarious economies from Eastern Europe and Latin America, not to mention around €70 billion of bad Icelandic debts. Austria's exposure to so-called 'emerging markets' amounts to 85 per cent of the Alpine country's GDP, and most of it is owed by countries about to melt down (e.g. Hungary, Ukraine and Serbia). Spanish banks, in particular, lent $316 billion to Latin America, almost twice the lending by all US banks combined ($172 billion).

The European Central Bank (ECB), the European Commission (the EU's effective 'government') and the member states rushed in to do for the European banks that which the US administration had done for Wall Street. They shoved in the banks' direction quantities of public money the size of the Alps, so as to replace the 'departed' *private money* with fresh public money borrowed by the member states. So far, this seems identical to the US experience; only there were two profound differences.

The first difference is that the Euro is nothing like the Dollar, as Chapter 11 made clear. While the Dollar remains the world's reserve currency, the Fed and the US Treasury can write blank cheques knowing that it will make very little difference on the value of the dollar, at least in the medium term. Indeed, IMF data show that the dollar's share of global reserves was 62 per cent at the end of 2009 and has, since then, been rising in response to Europe's post-2010 sovereign debt crisis (see below).

The second difference concerns the *way* that European banks succeeded in emulating Wall Street by using the post-2008 infusion of public money in order to start a new process of 'minting' fresh *private money*. As the previous section showed, Wall Street did this by utilising the *Geithner–Summers Plan* which, with the connivance of the US government, created from scratch a new type of financial instrument that allowed US banks to shift the toxic CDOs from their balance sheets at the taxpayers' expense. The European banks did the same; only without the direct cooperation, or even knowledge, of the state (either of nation-states or of the EU). This is how they did it.

Between 2008 and 2009, as mentioned above, the ECB, the European Commission and the EU member states socialised the banks' losses and turned them into public debt. Meanwhile, the economy of Europe went into recession, as expected. In one year (2008–9) Germany's GDP fell by 5 per cent, France's by 2.6 per cent, Holland's by 4 per cent, Sweden's by 5.2 per cent, Ireland's by 7.1 per cent, Finland's by 7.8 per cent, Denmark's by 4.9 per cent, Spain's by 3.5 per cent. Suddenly, hedgefunds and banks alike had an epiphany: why not use some of the public money they were given to *bet* that, sooner or later, the strain on public finances (caused by the recession on the one hand, which depressed the governments' tax take, and the huge increase in public debt on the other, for which they were themselves responsible) would cause one or more of the Eurozone's states to default?

The more they thought that thought, the gladder they became. The fact that Euro membership prevented the most heavily indebted countries (Greece, Portugal, Spain, Italy, Ireland, Belgium) from devaluing their currencies, thus feeling more the brunt of the combination of debt and recession, focused their sights upon these countries. So, they decided to start betting, small amounts initially, that the weakest link in that chain, Greece, would default. As London's famous bookmakers could not handle multi-billion bets, they turned to the trusted CDSs; insurance policies that pay out pre-specified amounts of money if someone else defaults.

The reader will notice the subtle but important difference from the pre-2008 US-centred CDOs: whereas the latter constituted a bet that homeowners would pay back their debts, the EU-centred CDSs of the post-2008 era were naked bets that some EU state would *not* be able to pay its bets back. Soon, the issuers of these CDSs discovered, with glee, that their new 'products' sold like hot cakes. They had emerged as the new *private money* of the post-2008 world!

Of course, the greater the volume of trade in this newfangled *private money* the more the capital was siphoned off both from corporations seeking loans to invest in productive activities and from states trying to refinance their burgeoning debt.

In short, the European variant of the banks' bail out gave the financial sector the opportunity to mint *private money* all over again. Once more, just like the *private money* created by Wall Street before 2008 was unsustainable and bound to turn into thin ash, the onward march of the new *private money* was to lead, with mathematical precision, to another meltdown. This time it was the *sovereign debt crisis*, whose first stirrings occurred at the beginning of 2010 in Athens, Greece.

Greeks bearing debts

In October 2009, the freshly elected socialist government announced that Greece's true deficit was in excess of 12 per cent (rather that the projected 6.5 per cent, already more than double the Maastricht limit). Almost immediately the CDSs predicated upon a Greek default grew in volume and price, thus pushing the interest rate the Greek state had to pay to borrow in order to refinance its €300 billion debt (more than 100 per cent of GDP) above 4.5 per cent (when, at the same time, Germany could borrow at less than 3 per cent). By January 2010 it had become clear that the Greek government would be in trouble meeting its repayments during the next 12 months. The task it was facing was indeed herculean: to pay back maturing bonds to the tune of more than €60 billion and borrow more to finance a large annual budget deficit; and all this in the midst of a recession that depleted its effective tax base.

Informally, the Greek government sought the assistance of the EU. What it asked for was not cash as such but some form of statement on the part of the EU or the ECB that Greece's Eurozone partners would stand behind any new loans that Greece took out. Such a guarantee, if issued in January or February 2010, would have ensured that Greece would borrow at manageable interest rates and might, therefore, avoid both defaults without having to go to Europe cap in hand for real money. However, this request was turned down by Chancellor

Angela Merkel who issued her famous *nein*-cubed: *nein* to a bail out for Greece; *nein* for interest rate relief; *nein* to the prospect of a Greek default.

The triple no was unique in the history of public or even private finance. Imagine if Secretary Paulson had said to Lehman Brothers, in October 2008, the following: 'no, I am not going to bail you out' (which he did say); 'no, I shall not organise for you low interest rate loans' (which he may have said, but to no avail); and 'no, you cannot file for bankruptcy' (which he would never have said). The last 'no' is unthinkable. And yet this is precisely what the Greek government was told. Mrs Merkel could fathom neither the idea of assisting Greece nor the idea that Greece would default on so much debt held by the French and German banks (about €75 billion and €53 billion respectively).

The result was that from January to April 2010 Greece continued to borrow at increasing interest rates, sinking deeper and deeper into the mire, while new CDSs were issued placing increasing bets on a Greek default and netting the banks indecently large profits. On 11 April, and after a major altercation with President Sarkozy of France, Mrs Merkel relents and announces a joint venture with the IMF for 'rescuing' Greece. According to that plan, the Eurozone (EZ) and the ECB would offer €30 billion, the IMF would chip in another €15, and Greece would have to accept draconian austerity measures to qualify for the loans.

While the Greek government sighed with relief, the financial markets did not take long to decide that, despite the IMF-EZ-ECB package, it was still worth betting on a Greek default. They were right: Greece had to find a lot more money than there was on the table; the offered interest rates were shockingly high;[48] and the austerity policies to be introduced were so savage that the Greek economy would go into a tail-spin once they were introduced.

Soon after, and especially when Mrs Merkel appeared reluctant to commit even to this package (before a key state election in Germany was out of the way), the hedgefunds and the banks decided it was time to bet even more on a Greek default, to churn out a lot more such CDSs. In short order, the Greek government saw the interest rate, that the money markets were demanding in order to lend it cash, skyrocket to above 12 per cent. It immediately declared that it was withdrawing from the money markets and that it would request loans from the announced (but not finalised) IMF-EZ-ECB package.

By itself, the Greek government's request would not have swayed Germany. Mrs Merkel seemed prepared to let Greece twist in the wind until the very last moment, when it would have to step in in order to prevent the Eurozone's first default. That moment came in early May of 2010. Under pressure from France and the ECB, Germany succumbed not only to validating the original IMF-EZ-ECB package but, astonishingly, to boosting its size from €35 billion to €110 billion for Greece alone. Nevertheless, even that was not enough to avert the gathering storm clouds.

Within days, the world's financial system went into something close to the *Credit Crunch* of 2008. Starting with the market for government bonds, which at least in Europe seized up completely, the world's stock exchanges began to tumble. Hedge funds and banks continued betting against not only Greek debt but against an assortment of European state debts. So, four days after the €110 billion IMF-EZ-ECB package had been announced, a new startling announcement was made: (a) the IMF-EZ-ECB package would rise to €750 billion (€500 by the EZ-ECB and €250 by the IMF) and extend to all eurozone deficit countries; and (b) the ECB would start buying (second-hand) member state bonds (i.e. debt).

Thus, the Euro area changed overnight. The strict separation of monetary policy (the ECB's remit) from fiscal policy (that was left to member states, under the Maastricht conditions) ended the moment the whole of the Eurozone (in association with the IMF) were made responsible for bailing each other out and, more importantly, by having the ECB cross into the area of debt management. These two moves tore up the Maastricht treaty without, however, putting some other, rational, architecture in its place. Instead, following those momentous developments, the only discussion in Brussels on institutional reform concerns a further tightening of budgets across Europe; even on instilling a legal obligation to run balanced budgets in the constitutions of member states.

The banks and the hedge funds responded, first, by easing their bets on Greece, once a Greek default was delayed by at least two years. However, they looked closely at the figures and realised that the pledged $750 billion of the IMF-EZ-ECB mechanism would not solve the problem. For the austerity package that went along with it was more likely than not to exacerbate the recession, especially in the deficit countries, lessen their tax take and spearhead another debt crisis further down the road. Would the surplus countries be able to put together another loan package in two years' time, before their own bonds got attacked by the infamous CDSs?

Thus, shortly afterwards, the speculators took their eyes off Greece and began to issue new CDSs, no longer based on a Greek default but, this time, on a falling and faltering Euro. Thus, *private money* continues to grow by draining the life out of the very public purses that sustained it. Incredibly, this growth spurt at the expense of the Eurozone was massively assisted by the IMF-EZ-ECB package itself. The reason is that the €440 pledged by the Eurozone to the IMF-EZ-ECB loan package would come in the form of a euphemistically named *Special Purpose Vehicle*; if this sounds like a *Special Investment Vehicle* (which, before 2008 were the outfits the banks created to issue derivatives, like the CDOs) it is because it *is* one. Box 12.18 explains.

Box 12.18 A European *Geithner–Summers Plan* for bailing out Europe's banks

In May 2010 the EU created a so-called Special Purpose Vehicle (SPV) whose aim will be, purportedly, to help deficit Eurozone countries, such as Greece, Spain, etc., avoid defaulting on its debts in case the money markets refuse to lend them more at manageable interest rates (as was the case with Greece in April–May of 2010). Many commentators celebrated this turn of events as the beginning of a European Monetary Fund, a first step in the post-Maastricht era and down the path that leads to genuine economic integration.

The SPV will take the form of a company called the European Financial Stability Facility (EFSF) and will begin life with a capital base of €60 billion made available from the EU's own budget and €250 from the IMF. Additionally, it will be able to borrow up to €440 billion from the financial markets and institutions. Unlike the IMF–EZ–ECB package for Greece, which is based on bilateral parliament-sanctioned agreements between Greece and all other EZ countries, the EFSF will lend at the behest of the EZ governing group, the so-called Eurogroup. This will speed up its capacity to intervene without the added uncertainty and delay of 16 separate parliamentary debates.

So far so good. While the EFSF does not address the root causes of the crisis, at least it seems like a decent response to its symptoms. Until, that is, one scratches the surface of the €440 billion part of the fund which the EFSF is meant to raise on the markets. Conventional wisdom tells us that the trick to the EFSF's potential success is that it borrows by issuing its own bonds (let's call them EFSF bonds) which are supported by collateral provided by all the EZ countries in proportion to the size of their economy. In other words, Germany and France put up most of the collateral. This should encourage investors to buy the EFSF bonds at low interest rates.

The problem, and worry, here is that this bears an uncanny similarity with the circumstances that gave rise to the dodgy CDOs in the United States and, later, their European counterparts. Looking back to the US-issued mortgage-backed CDOs, we find that the trick there was to bundle together prime and subprime mortgages in the same CDO, and to do it in such a complicated manner that the whole thing looks like a sterling investment to potential buyers. Something very similar had occurred in Europe after the creation of the Euro: CDOs were created that contained German, Dutch, Greek, Portuguese bonds, etc. (i.e. debt), in such complex configurations, that investors found it impossible to work out their true long-term value. The tidal wave of private money created on both sides of the Atlantic, on the basis of these two types of CDOs, was the root cause, as we have seen, of the *Crash of 2008*.

Seen through this prism, the EFSF's brief begins to look worrisome. Its 'bonds' will be bundling together different kinds of collateral (i.e. guarantees offered by each individual state) in ways that, at least till now, remain woefully opaque. This is precisely how the CDOs came to life prior to 2008. Banks and hedgefunds will grasp with both hands the opportunity to turn this opacity into another betting spree, complete with CDSs taking out bets against the EFSF's bonds, etc. In the end, either the EFSF bonds will flop, if banks and hedge funds stay clear of them, or they will sell well thus occasioning a third round of unsustainable private money generation. When that private money turns to ashes too, as it certainly will, what next for Europe?

Just as the *Geithner–Summers Plan* of 2009 sought to solve the problem with the toxic derivatives by issuing new state-sponsored derivatives (recall the previous section), so too the IMF-EZ-ECB package (see Box 12.18) creates new derivative-like bonds that will be sold to the banks and hedge funds in return for money that will be passed on to member states which will then be returned to the banks (that hold the member states' debt) which are already profiting from issuing their own derivatives (the CDSs) whose value depends on the member states (separately or together, as the entire Eurozone) fail use…

Is it any wonder that in 2010 Europe entered a crisis from which it seems incapable of escaping? Which bring us to the main question: does Germany's leadership not see this? Why is the Eurozone reacting so sluggishly and so weakly to the challenge? Why have they failed to take the crisis' measure?

The conventional answer is that Europe suffers from a simple coordination failure. Too many cooks spoiling the broth; too many small countries that insist on holding on dearly to their small country mentality and, therefore, failing to create a Europe with a mentality fit for its size and proper role. Though there is some truth in this, with sixteen different fiscal policies, no centralised supervision and lowest common denominator leaders, it is not *the* reason. The reason is different and has to do with the analysis in Section 12.4.

A New Versailles

Section 12.4 argued that the formation of the Euro crystallised a situation that had emerged since the rise of the *Global Minotaur* in the 1970s and enabled Germany to reach unprecedented surpluses in a context of deepening European stagnation. Figuratively, we labelled the German economy, with its heavy reliance on both the United States and the rest of Europe as sources of aggregate demand for its industrial output, the *Minotaur's Simulacrum*.

The *Crash of 2008* shook both pillars of Germany's successful strategy for living happily within the Eurozone. The United States drastically reduced its imports and the German banks fell to the ground. The *Simulacrum* was on skid row. Profoundly worried about this unexpected twin blow, Germany's leadership hardened its neo-mercantilist stance and unilaterally decided to rewrite the rules of the game.

Following the events of May 2010, and the creation of the IMF-EZ-ECB mechanism, plus the ECB's new role in the bond market, many commentators heralded these developments as a step towards a new *Rational Plan for Europe*; one that brings the Eurozone area closer to federalism (at least at the level of Economic policy). So far, it is nothing of the sort. Germany seems hell bent on forcing the Eurozone members to embark upon a series of competitive austerity drives. Having 'won' such a game in the 1990s (see Section 12.4, and in particular the subsection on German reunification), Mrs Merkel wants to play the same game and by the same German rules. This is why no one is even allowed to discuss alternative policies for handling Europe's debt crisis in its entirety, that is, tackling *at once* the twin problems of (a) its indebted member states *and* (b) its banking system (which is, once again, hooked on unsustainable *private money*).

Box 12.19 A modest proposal for Europe

Each and every response by the Eurozone (EZ) to the galloping sovereign debt crisis that erupted at the beginning of 2010 has consistently failed to arrest the fall. This includes the quite remarkable formation of a €750 billion IMF–EZ–ECB Special Purpose Vehicle (SPV) for shoring up the fiscally challenged Eurozone members. The reason is simple: the EZ is facing an escalating twin crisis but only sees one of its two manifestations. On the one hand we have the sovereign debt crisis that permeates the public sector in the majority of its member countries (France and the countries we called 'magpies' in Section 12.4). On the other hand we have Europe's private sector banks many of whom find themselves on the brink. Yet, the EZ remains in denial, pretending that this is solely a sovereign debt crisis that will go away as long as everyone tightens their belt.

The €750 billion SPV has failed to convince that it will, in itself, stave off defaults. The reason is that it offers no comprehensive solution to an all-embracing problem. For instance, it was agreed that the Greek state will be lent up to €110 billion over three years to help it deal with its €330 billion debt, which it owes mainly to European banks that are, themselves, facing a serious challenge to their continued existence. While the banks themselves borrow from the ECB at less than 1 per cent interest rate, Greece borrows from the SPV at close to 5 per cent to pay back the banks at an interest rate well in excess of 6 per cent. All this, against the background of a shrinking national income (Greek GDP will shrink by 5 per cent in 2010) and with a commitment to undertake fiscal tightening measures that will accelerate further the loss of national income and, thus, constraining Greece's tax base further. Naturally neither the markets nor the banks trust that Greece will be able to repay its loans (the old as well as the new ones it is currently borrowing from the SPV), especially after the SPV is wound down in 2013 (if everyone goes to plan). Thus, the CDSs on a future Greek default divide and multiply.

This is a textbook case of how *not* to run a 'bail out'. Is it a puzzle that few really believe in the SPV's chances of solving the Eurozone's sovereign debt crisis? How could the SPV be organised differently? Is there an alternative? The question grows in pertinence now that the SPV will be extended to other countries such as Portugal, Spain, etc. An outline of a modest proposal for an alternative SPV, let's call it SM (support mechanism) is offered below.

Just IMF and EZ–ECB representatives visited Athens in May 2010 to strike a deal (in the context of talks that can be thought of as the SPV's precursor), another such Grand Bargain can be organised in Brussels, one that may mark a modern European Bretton Woods, with the following participants:

(a) representatives of all high deficit countries that will, potentially, use SM;
(b) the IMF;
(c) the ECB and head of the Eurozone (EZ); and
(d) representatives of all the main European banks holding the majority of the high deficit countries' bonds.

The proposed Grand Bargain must seek three different, but interrelated, covenants:

1. *A covenant with Europe's banks* according to which (a) the European Banks will restructure the debt of the high deficit countries, through both a postponement of repayments and a reduction of the average interest rate to a level not exceeding Libor,[1] *and* (b) the IMF–EZ–ECB will use part of the $750 billion to extend credits and liquidity to the European banks when necessary.[2]
2. *A covenant with high deficit countries* according to which (a) the IMF–EZ–ECB will use their collective clout to effect covenant 1 above while (b) the high deficit countries undertake a drastic reduction in all manners of unproductive public spending (e.g. military procurements) and a concomitant increase in public sector efficiency (a task that requires a redistribution of public pay towards the more socially necessary parts of the public sector employees, without however reducing the state's total wage bill, since such a reduction would be, at the present juncture, highly deflationary and, thus, counterproductive *vis-à-vis* overall debt reduction).

Such a Grand Bargain would bear the following benefits for the Eurozone:

(a) It would force Europe's banks to assist with the overcoming of the present sovereign debt crisis, while guaranteeing them, on condition that they will change their ways regarding the indiscriminate issuing of short-lived private money, i.e. CDOs,

CDSs and the like, easy access to liquidity and possible injections in case the threat of insolvency rears its ugly head again.

(b) It would encourage Europe's high-deficit states to commit to sustainable debt-reduction programmes – programmes that do not insist, as the present SPV does, that they cut their noses to spite their faces.

(c) It will motivate the EZ to face up, at long last, to its responsibility to undertake the task of managing the Euro area's aggregate public and private debt, as well as its aggregate demand – exactly like Washington does in that other, arguably more successful, currency union on the Atlantic's other side.

Notes

1 *Libor* stands for London Inter Bank Offered Rate, and is a daily estimate of the interest rates at which banks are glad to loan to one another.

2 In other words, on the one hand banks will be required to drop their expectations regarding the interest payments of the high deficit countries (and wait longer to collect the capital plus *Libor*) while, on the other, they can expect *direct* assistance from SM. Instead of the SPV handing monies to Greece, Portugal and Spain at 5 per cent, so that the latter can make repayments to the banks at much higher interest rates, SM will guarantee the banks' liquidity in the long run as long as the banks reduce their claims on the high deficit states' income. This way, the latter will find it much easier to stay within their budget, and to avoid the spending cuts that are *guaranteed* to derail the current SM package of austerity measures. At the end of the day, direct assistance of the banks will be both cheaper for the IMF–EZ–ECB than the existing SPV and less recessionary within the high deficit countries.

So, back to our question: why is Germany so reluctant to countenance anything other than a Herbert Hoover type of policy for the Eurozone at a time of recession and when a real danger of a fatal debt-deflationary cycle is haunting Europe?[49]

To answer this we need a little more psychology than political economics usually admits. Returning to our Section 11.4 'terminology', Europe's ants see the magpies as insufferable spendthrift over-reachers. After the eruption of the Greek debt crisis, the ants turned on the magpies with a vengeance explainable only in terms of their own deep uncertainty at a time when they cannot rely on anyone anymore, not even on the *Global Minotaur*. The Germans, in particular, are incensed. Hard working, well drilled, innovative, technologically advanced and with a history of substantial belt-tightening when their country faced a serious decline in its products' competitiveness (e.g. in the 1990s following the country's reunification), the German people became furious that a small nation's profligacy should shake violently the very foundations of that to which they have invested their collective post-war energies: *the stability of their currency*.

Their wrath is all the more understandable when placed in an historical context. When the German nation surrendered after the Great War, the allies exacted their Pound of flesh from its collective body: no mercy, no compunction, no magnanimity for the vanquished. The *Versailles Treaty* imposed heavy reparations on the already defeated and decimated nation and let its people fend for themselves, after the nation's wealth was stripped by the victors.

While the rest of the developed world was rejoining the Gold Standard, the single currency of that era (recall Chapters 6 and 7), Germany was forced to stay outside (since it had no gold left after its ignominious defeat) and print its own money. Starved of investment, and forced to pay reparations between two per cent and three per cent annually to the victors, its currency began inexorably to devalue. The result was a hyper-inflation that wiped out the German middle class' hard-earned savings and paved the ground for the Nazi takeover, which followed after the shockwaves of 1929 had reached the already devastated country. The rest of the story need not be told here.

Since then Germany has resolved, almost in one voice, never to allow a similar descent to destitution caused by a currency collapse. While happy to contribute heftily to the European Union's budget, and to pick up large bills whenever some European project demanded it, the one thing they will not fathom is any violation of the austere set of monetary policies that keeps their Deutschmark strong and which was meant to be carried over to its new, pan-European reincarnation – the Euro.

In September 2009, after the newly elected Athens government announced that Greece's deficit was double what the previous government was reporting, Germans pinched themselves; for they could not believe that even a southern European state could engage in such a game of subterfuge. A few months later, when the banks and the hedgefunds ganged up against Greek bonds, many Germans felt that the Greeks had got their comeuppance.

Retribution was the order of the day, especially in the mindset of a nation that, over the past century, has accepted its collective punishment gracefully and managed to rise out of the mire through sheer hard work and extensive reform. Greece should pay for its sins too, they opined. For Germans, the cost of saving the Greek state from the clutches of the money markets was not the issue. The issue was that Greece should suffer a deserved punishment for putting at risk a club which gallantly bent the rules to have it admitted as its member. And when the said club is the one issuing the currency in which the German people trade, save and take collective pride in, that punishment took on the significance of a crucial bonding ritual.

Though the above sentiments are understandable, the problem with moral outrage is that it is rarely a sound basis for decent political economics. Personal virtue is important but it is an unsafe guide for dealing with a crisis and a poor historian of its causes. A good example is the aforementioned 1919 *Versailles Treaty* which condemned Germany to years of reparations. At the time, the victors felt morally justified to impose heavy penalties on a country that had started the most murderous war hitherto.

But was it wise? No, it was not, as John Maynard Keynes knew. The reader may recall that one of the first pieces on economics Keynes wrote was on the *Versailles Treaty*. His conclusion was that the victors had imposed a treaty upon the losers that was not just pitiless towards them but that it was self-defeating from the perspective of the victors as well. In that sense, retribution was exacted at a price that the victors miscalculated; a price that was just as steep for the vanquished as it was for the punishers. And by golly was Keynes right!

As discussed in Chapter 7, the reparations proved insufficient to mend the finances of France and Britain but perfectly adequate for draining the German economy of life and, thus, creating the circumstances for the hyper-inflation that softened its society up for Hitler's meteoric rise. After 1929, and the momentous Wall Street crash, the countries that enjoyed low inflation during the 1920s courtesy of the Gold Standard suddenly realised that, in deflationary times, a common currency is like a ball and chain attached to the sinking person's leg. Unable to coordinate economic policies, they started jumping ship, one after the other; abandoning the single currency (the Gold Standard) and embarking upon a deflationary war of all against all.

The result of all this inability to come to terms with a simple truth, namely that forcing the deficit countries to deflate was a plague on the house of the (until then) surplus countries, translating into wholesale poverty for everyone and a real war that humanity has since been trying to put behind it. In Keynes' words:

> the insincere acceptance... of impossible conditions which it was not intended to carry out [made] Germany almost as guilty to accept what she could not fulfil as the Allies to impose what they were not entitled to exact.[50]

If Versailles teaches us anything it is that the strong do not always impose upon the defeated a treaty that is in its own interests. Sometimes they get carried away by their urge to punish, flex their muscles a little too energetically and in so doing end up punishing themselves. This is how we see the conditions imposed upon the Eurozone's deficit countries that will be forced to resort to the IMF-EZ-ECB €750 billion loan package from the new SPV formed in the context of the 2010 sovereign debt crisis.

This is what Keynes wrote on the consequences of the *Versailles Treaty*:

> Moved by insane delusion and reckless self-regard, the *Greek* people overturned the foundations on which we all lived and built. But the spokesmen of the European Union have run the risk of completing the ruin, which *Greece* began, by a *financial assistance package* which, if it is carried into effect, must impair yet further, when it might have restored, the delicate, complicated organisation, already shaken and broken by *the 2008 crisis*, through which alone the European peoples can employ themselves and live.[51]

These are, of course, not exactly Keynes' words. But they are not far off! All we did was to replace some of his words with the ones appearing in bold above. Indeed, Keynes might have just as well have been writing about the Greek fiscal calamity and the IMF-EZ-ECB package that was, effectively, imposed upon the bankrupt Greek state and subsequently extended to the rest of Europe's magpies.

Summing up, the IMF-EZ-ECB package is a most peculiar sort of punishment. Indeed, it is an irrational sentence both because

(a) it constitutes a cruel and unusual punishment[52] and
(b) it is bound to hurt the punishers disproportionately more compared to a fairer punishment for Greece.[53] Ironically, from this perspective, it is not very dissimilar to the original *Versailles Treaty*!

Whither Europe?[54]

* *Quidquid id est, timeo Danaos et dona ferentes* (Or in a popular German rendering: *Vorsicht vor falschen Freunden*)[55]
* *The problem, as always, was what to do with Germany*[56]

The Germans are right to think that Greece is a problem for the Euro. But, at the same time, Germany is an equally large problem for the common currency. In a sense, Greece and Germany are two sides of the same problematic coin.

History is something which all countries have but some have more than others. The Greeks have too much of it; but the Germans make up for their history's relative brevity with a great deal of historical gravitas. While one can easily imagine a European Union without

Greece, one without Germany is unimaginable. Having said that, Germany would never have become as central to Europe if it were not for the minnows (plus France) that kept its industries in business during the crucial years of the *Global Plan*. Even during the *Global Minotaur*'s reign, the magpies provided German capital with surpluses which assisted it greatly in globalising and thus improving its position relative to both the *Minotaur* and the *Dragon* (NB the Chinese hunger for German capital goods).

The Maastricht Treaty was not a treaty imposed by the bankers, as many on the European left had claimed. It was more than that: a charter for the German dominance of the Eurozone; a monetary manifestation of the *Minotaur's Simulacrum*. Locked into the single currency and the fiscal rules of Maastricht, and with the German real wage controlled by the country's functioning corporatist institutions,[57] the Euro area was the new Imperial Preference Area for German dominance.

Since 2008, the ECB and the Eurozone's ant-based leadership have put all their energies into serving a two-item agenda. First item on the agenda was, as in the United States, the salvation of the banking system. Thus, they risked transferring all of the latter's sins onto the public accounts. Second item on the agenda was the preservation of the spirit of Maastricht, an imperative that had nothing whatsoever to do with the stated purpose of keeping the lid on inflation and everything to do with the paramount task of preserving the *status quo*, according to which the ants grow by expanding their trade surpluses while the magpies are forced into whatever fiscal posture is necessary to manage their debt levels.

The reasons why this kind of Europe is currently unravelling is not at all a mystery. For the two-item agenda above became unsustainable once the *Global Minotaur*, severely injured by 2008, lost its appetite for the ants' exports and the Chinese *Dragon* turned inward.[58] In short, the Eurozone of 2000–08 is not viable post-2008. The former could soldier on, despite the imbalances between the deficits and surplus countries, as long as the Eurozone enjoys a large trade surplus with the rest of the world. But when the United States and China dried up as a source of excess demand for European manufactures, the ants had to rely more and more on the magpies for their surpluses. Doing so while immediately insisting that the magpies rein their deficits in defied logic. The financial markets got a whiff of that incongruity and started issuing new piles of *private money*, in the form of CDSs betting against Greece, Portugal, Spain, the Euro itself.

Back in 1944, the New Dealers faced the very same problem: the United States was facing a future in which it would have to occupy a surplus position *vis-à-vis* the rest of the world and it was a matter of concern that the aggregate demand for its exports should come from somewhere and not be undermined either by competitive currency devaluations or by competitive wage deflation. The *Global Plan* (i.e. Bretton Woods, the Marshall Plan and all the interventions during the 1944–71 period discussed in Chapter 11) was meant to address this concern. It did so for a decade before the *Plan* began to unravel and then, in August 1971, die. The reason, as we saw, was that the hegemon behind it went into deficit too quickly and had to react somehow to retain its hegemony; the *Global Minotaur* being the outcome.

The creation of the Euro, and the Maastricht Treaty underpinning it, were not a manifestation of the continent's *esprit communautaire*, as Europeans like to think, but rather a negation of both the supranational and the communitarian ideological principle. It was an instance of power imposing a dogma.[59] The fact that Germany's leaders seem unable to reconcile with is that that power withered the moment the *Global Minotaur*, upon which it was predicated, fell seriously ill. If they continue to live in denial, the project of European integration will surely wither too.

So what? Let Europe wither, we hear some Germans say. The problem, however, is that Germany is not doing that either! On the one hand, it blocks any serious debate on rationalising the Eurozone, in fear of losing its surpluses, and, on the other, it does not even come out and courageously declare the whole thing a bad idea with a proposal to dismantle the Euro. Instead, it keeps countries like Greece in intensive care, administering enough medicine to keep it going but not enough to help it recover.

In effect, the ants of Europe are turning the magpies' terrains into sun-drenched wastelands (except for Ireland, which will return to its pre-tiger sodden, mulchy past) and are, consequently, pushing the whole deficit area of the Eurozone into an accelerating debt-deflationary downward spiral. But this is a most efficient way of undermining Germany's own economy in the post-2008 world. Assuming, for argument's sake, that Greece is getting its just deserts, do the hard-working German workers deserve a political elite that quick-marches them straight into economic catastrophe?

We believe not. But it has happened before and it may happen again unless Germany grasps, as the United States did in 1947, the subtle difference between authoritarianism and hegemony. To quote Keynes' 1920 book on the *Versailles Treaty* one last time:

> Perhaps it is historically true that no order of society ever perishes save by its own hand.[60]

12.7 A (Chinese) future for the beast?

We closed Chapter 11 with Paul Volcker's dictum, *circa* 1979, that US hegemony required the disintegration of the global economic order. Volcker was summing up the end of the *Global Plan* which begot the *Global Minotaur*, a beast that drew its primal energy from the crisis in the real economy (spearheaded by the US-sponsored oil crisis of the 1970s that Volcker had a small part in designing) and served the purpose of allowing the US middle and upper classes to live, quite sustainably, beyond their means for three whole decades.

The 1970s crisis, which was overcome as late as in the mid-1980s, threatened capitalism's monetary system (through the unpredictable escalation of inflation) and quickly spread from the real economy into the world of finance. Volcker, as the Fed's Chairman during the crucial 1979–87 period, ruthlessly increased interest rates in order to quash inflation and transfer capital from the rest of the world into the United States. Once the flow of other people's goods and capital into the United States started in earnest, the Fed eased interest rates substantially. To that effect it was helped significantly by Asia and, in particular, the South-East Asian crisis of 1998.

What happened in 1998 was a nightmare for South-East Asia's and Argentina's people. However, the crisis, while reflected in similar meltdowns in Mexico and Russia, did not manage to contaminate Wall Street, the City of London or the EU, although the IMF's heavy-handed intervention, with its stringent, inhuman austerity that it imposed on these countries (in return for loans of dubious benefit to the average citizen), left an indelible mark on Asia's and Latin America's consciousness: *'never again!'*, they screamed inside their heads. Never again will we find ourselves in a state of dependence on the IMF and the rest of the West's institutions.

The result was a rise in the rate at which Asian savings were sent to Wall Street to buy assets that would act as a buffer in case of another crisis.[61] This flood of capital into Wall Street (in addition to the influx of *carry trade* into New York, Europe and London caused by zero per cent Japanese interest rates) pushed US interest rates down and kept them there for a very long while. We have already seen how this process depressed US interest rates, strengthened the *Minotaur* and reinforced financialisation.

In 2008 when that bubble burst and a crisis that began in the murky world of real estate and finance spread to the real economy, the United States responded robustly with unheard of spending programmes (which Keynes, one imagines, would have approved without necessarily thinking of as sufficient). Europe, in contrast, found itself in a bind and followed only reluctantly. Not only had its Eurozone architecture never contained a Plan A (let alone a Plan B) in case of a crisis, largely due to the success of neoclassical economists (the Econobubble, as we call it) in convincing policymakers in Brussels (as they had done elsewhere) that crises were obsolete, but its currency, the Euro, lacked reserve currency status as well.[62]

So, while the US administration (of both political persuasions) felt at liberty effectively to throw trillions of dollars (that it never actually owned) at the crisis, the Europeans were loath to follow suit. Organising such bold steps via a consensus of 16 parochial administrations was tough going, especially in view of their division between the ants, the magpies and, somewhere in the middle, France. Thus a crisis which had begun in the United States threatened to bring down the Eurozone; echoes of Treasury Secretary John Connally's infamous 1971 message to the Europeans: 'it is our currency but it is your problem.' All that Tim Geithner, the current US Treasury Secretary, needs to do when addressing today's European leadership is replace the word 'currency' with the word 'crisis'.

We now come to the trillion dollar question: is the *Global Minotaur* a spent force? That it is seriously wounded is beyond doubt. The top graph of Figure 12.10 shows the large drop in the US current account deficit, the *Minotaur*'s calling card. This drop, as explained in the previous section, is the cause of Europe's and Japan's travails, and the reason why China's own stimulus packages (which keep the Chinese factories going on the basis of accelerating infrastructural projects) are the only thing that prevent the rest of the world from falling into a large hole.

But is the *Global Minotaur* really on its last legs? Or will it bounce back? Are we entering the third post-war phase of US hegemony? Or is a brave new phase beginning that features no definitive hegemon? Granted that the backbone of what the world grew accustomed to think of as *Globalisation*[63] was the United States' capacity to generate enough aggregate demand for the exports of the great surplus countries (mainly, Germany, Japan and, lately, China), the *Minotaur*'s decline may well signal a new world order. Perhaps then Europe's crisis, Japan's stagnation and China's desperate experimentation with alternative sources of demand, are all mere symptoms of the birth pains of some new order. If this turns out to be so, the decade beginning in 2010 will resemble the 1970s, in the sense of being pregnant with a new twist in the 300-year story of capitalism.

On the other hand, the announcement of the *Minotaur*'s passing may prove premature. The middle and bottom parts of Figure 12.10 harbour some clues. The middle graph and the bottom graph allow us to juxtapose the fluctuations of capital flows into the United States by (a) foreign governments and (b) the foreign private sector respectively. An interesting choreography is apparent. When foreign private capital seems reluctant to feed the *Minotaur*, foreign governments rush in to fill the gap. This is almost a truism. Still, it is useful to observe the emerging pattern and the timing of the turning points.

We note that, during the *Minotaur*'s 'childhood' years (1971–80), the US deficit was not yet solidified and the two flows go up and down: at the collapse of Bretton Woods, foreign governments step away from dollar assets but the foreign privateers immediately step in,

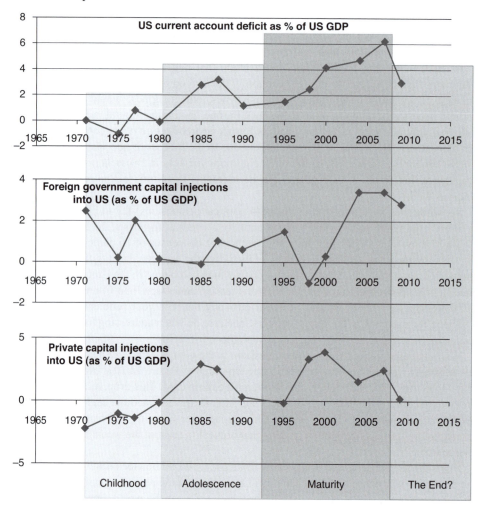

Figure 12.11 The *Global Minotaur*: a life.
Source: Bureau of Economic Analysis (BEA)

only to step aside after 1975 and let the governments step in with higher tributes to the *Minotaur* (who does not really get established before 1977 – see top graph). During its 'adolescence', the governments take their leave and the private sector begins to send more and more capital to Wall Street. Then, after Black Monday (October 1987), the *Minotaur* slows down and the flow of foreign private sector capital is reduced to a trickle. During 1996–99 President Clinton's project of reining in the government budget deficit depresses the *Minotaur* too and deters foreign governments. However, at the same time (and possibly because Wall Street begins the financialisation process), private foreign capital again flows in large sums. Then, at around 2000, the *Minotaur* enters maturity with particularly boorish energy. Interestingly, it is foreign governments that pour their 'savings' into Wall Street with the foreign private sector being considerably more hesitant.

After 2008, the *Minotaur* goes into sharp decline. Nonetheless, it has certainly not exited the scene but only receded, in 2009, to levels it had scaled in 1998. While it is early days yet,

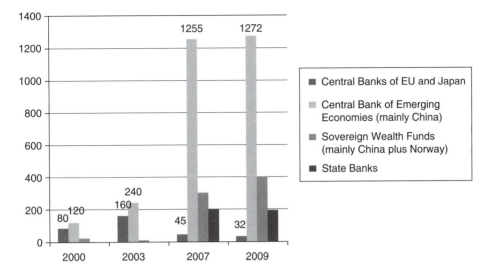

Figure 12.12 Increase in US assets (in $ billion) OWNED by foreign state institutions.

there are some signs of a possible *Minotaur* comeback. Throughout the crisis the Dollar's reserve currency status has strengthened, thanks to a large extent to the mess the Europeans made with their crisis 'management' (which is only a euphemism for what ought to be referred to as crisis amplification). Moreover, the United States seems to attract capital from foreign governments that go well beyond the levels the latter require to safeguard their own monetary and financial stability (see Figure 12.11) which reports on the new US assets (expressed in dollars) acquired by various state-backed foreign institutions in each of the given years.

The first bar in each year corresponds to the central banks of the two main US protégés from its *Global Plan* years: the ECB and the Bank of Japan taken together. While both central banks continue to nourish the *Minotaur*, their relative importance as its feeders fades after 2003. In contrast, China's Central Bank steps to the fore (see the second bar) and makes this role its own. Poignantly, even in 2009, when the *Minotaur* receded, and thus required less capital to be satiated, the Central Bank of China increased its tributes, even though slightly. This observation is strengthened further by data on capital inflows into Wall Street from sovereign wealth funds (mainly Chinese), the third bar and from (again mainly Chinese) state-owned banks, the fourth bar.

The gist of Figure 12.10 is that China has taken it upon itself to keep the *Minotaur* alive, at least for now. For not only does the *Minotaur* continue to offer China the only real prospect of renewed aggregate demand for its manufacturing sector, but, in addition, if the *Minotaur* dies it is very likely that the US assets that China already owns will devalue, thus causing it to lose a substantial portion of its hard-earned savings.

Will China continue to keep the beast alive? As long as the Chinese leaders entertain the hope that the *Minotaur* will get better soon and will start absorbing its output once again at the pre-2008 level, they will continue to nourish it. The mystery question is: at what rate? The gravest medium-term danger for global capitalism is not that China may stop sending its tributes to New York but the prospect that, while it is doing so, the *Minotaur*'s recovery will be too limp to restore aggregate demand to something resembling pre-2008 levels. For if the

Chinese capital that flows into Wall Street is *not* counterbalanced by analogous volumes of manufactures crossing from the rest of the world into the United States, and in view of Europe's love affair with austerity, our world threatens to become less and less stable.

We conclude this, unavoidably inconclusive, section with a few thoughts on the impact on the rest of the world of China's relationship with the injured *Global Minotaur*. China's startling growth affected not only its relationship with the still hegemonic United States but also with the other developing nations. Some were devastated by the competition but others were liberated from a relationship of dependence on the West and its multinational corporations. Mexico was among the first group of countries to have suffered from China's rise. Because it had chosen to invest much energy into becoming a low-wage manufacturer on the periphery of the United States (and a member of the US–Canada–Mexico free trade zone known as NAFTA), China's emergence was a nightmare for Mexican manufacturers. However, it was a miracle for countries ranging from Australia (which in effect put its vast mineral resources at the disposal of Chinese firms) to Argentina and from Brazil to Angola (which received in 2007 more funding, as direct investment mainly into its oil industry, than the IMF had lent to the whole world).

Latin America is possibly the one continent that was changed forever by China's emergence into the *Global Minotaur*'s major feeder. Argentina and Brazil turned their fields into production units supplying 1.3 billion Chinese consumers with foodstuffs, and also dug up their soil in search of minerals that would feed China's hungry factories. Cheap Chinese labour and China's market access to the West (courtesy of World Trade Organisation membership) is allowing Chinese manufacturers to undercut their Mexican and other Latin American competitors in the manufacture of low value-added sectors such as shoes, toys and textiles. This two-pronged effect causes Latin America to deindustrialise and return to the status of a primary goods producer.

These developments have a global reach. For if Brazil and Argentina turn their sights towards Asia, as they already have started doing, they may abandon their long-term struggle to break into the food markets of the United States and Europe, from which they have been barred by severe protectionist measures in favour of American, German and French farmers. Already, Latin America's shifting trade patterns are affecting the orientation of a region which has hitherto been thought of as the United States' backyard.

Latin America's governments choose not to resist their countries' transformation into China's primary goods producers. They may not like deindustrialisation much but it is a far cry from the prospect of another crisis like that of 1998–2002 and another visit from an IMF seeking to exact more Pounds, if not tons, of flesh from their people. The only government that protests is that of the United States. For some time now, Washington has been pressurising Beijing to revalue its currency. The main reason is not so much an ambition to sell to Chinese customers more US-produced goods but, rather, to preserve the profits of US multinationals which, since the 1980s, had set up production facilities in countries like Mexico and Brazil, and which are now under threat from severe Chinese competition.[64]

China has so far steadfastly resisted US pressures. Though not ideologically opposed to the idea of revaluing its currency, it has learned well from Japan's experience of bowing to American pressure to revalue the Yen – recall the *Plaza Agreement* of 1985. A latent stand-off of sorts is therefore gathering pace. However, it is a curious tiff between two parties whose fortunes are so intimately intertwined and who know full well that if it comes to a head, both stand to lose enormously.

China has invested hugely in US assets and would see its people's accumulated hard labour lose much of its worth were the United States to be hit by another serious crisis.

Similarly, the United States' living standards are predicated upon continuing capital gifts from China. The US government would love to push China into a Plaza-type Agreement, like it did Japan in 1985, but lacks the clout it once had when the *Minotaur* was exploding with youthful energy. China bides its time, certain that time is on its side. America knows that too but its stranglehold on the world's reserve currency, which is not totally unrelated from the fact that it stations US troops in 108 countries, gives it hope that global hegemony will remain in its grasp.

An uneasy US–China liaison is thus the *Minotaur*'s poignant legacy to the post-2008 world. 'The trend has the potential to be more divisive than any issue since the collapse of the Soviet Union', says Walter Molano, an analyst with BCP Securities. We suspect that the future of this affair will be determined neither in China nor in the context of the US–Chinese diplomatic game but *within* the guts of the American social economy itself. If we are right, the post-2008 world will come to reflect the way that the *Minotaur* mutates, in response to external stimuli, into a new, currently unpredictable, creature.

12.8 Epilogue

The trouble with humans is that we cannot desist from celebrating our indeterminacy while at the same time trying our best to suppress it. Our political economics has always strived to place capitalism in a theoretical straitjacket which is nonetheless shredded into bits (at the level of theory) by our discipline's *Inherent Error* and (in practice) by reality itself. That was our conclusion to *Book 1*.

In *Book 2* the same process manifested itself differently but only slightly so. We like the sound of binary oppositions and seek to position ourselves on one of their opposing sides. We imagine some almighty clash between the 'free market' and collective action, between the individual and the state, between on the one hand liberty and on the other hand equality or justice. In policy discussions we are consumed by arguments for greater regulation that clash with conflicting views in support of greater reliance on market forces. But it is all a mirage; our binary oppositions have dissolved before they were formed and live on only in our imagination. *Capitalism has always been a system founded on state power where wealth was collectively produced and privately appropriated.*

The real question, as Lenin liked to say, is *who does what to whom?* Its answer is a complex coalescence of grey zones, lacking the clear dividing lines of black and white. It is the sort of question that cannot, ever, be answered dogmatically but only with a sense of history aided by a critical engagement with the *necessary errors* of the social sciences. Those who care for the truth cannot begin with dogmas and must delve into *lost truths* that the more confident once understood better. Above all else, they have a duty to keep a watchful eye out for the economists' *Inherent Error*.

Political economics can only begin with open-ended questions and any attempt to button them down constitutes an assault on common sense. The question for those wishing to make sense of the post-2008 world, thus, cannot be whether we should have more or less regulation of the banks? Should labour markets become more flexible? Should governments turn to tighter monetary policy or adopt looser fiscal rules? We need different questions like *how can we prevent our artefacts (i.e. machines, derivatives, even ideas) from taking us over? Why do some people seem to have everything while most have next to nothing?* On those who claim to have answers rooted in some 'closed' model, we ought to turn our back in a hurry.

Ever since capitalism shifted gear in the first decade of the twentieth century, when corporations acquired immense economic power, our market societies have been oscillating like an irregular yo-yo between tighter and looser regulatory regimes for reasons that have precious little to do with 'scientific' analyses or even purely economic arguments. The 1920s establishment economists were not as certain regarding the merits of unbridled capitalism as we might now think; nor were the New Dealers dead keen on bashing Wall Street, regulating banks and planning the economy. If this is how history panned out, it is because of force of circumstance beyond their wishes.

Keynes *believed* that he had a simple solution to capitalism's tendency to stumble, fall and refuse to pick itself up without a helping hand from the state. He thought that through judicious fiscal and monetary adjustments it was possible to prevent, or at least mend, depressions. He was wrong. Capitalism cannot be civilised, stabilised or rationalised. Why? Because Marx was right. Increasing state power and benevolent interference will not do away with crises. For the more the state succeeds in bringing about stability, the larger the centrifugal forces that will eventually tear that stability apart. Crises cannot be massaged out of capitalism because, as Marx pointed out, labour creates the machines which then auto-reify, take over the human spirit and turn into its manic slave. Moneymaking reifies its own premises and the means become the end. When that happens, capitalism itself is destabilised. The liberal state, at that juncture, can only look on in stunned disbelief as the whole edifice falls apart, and gleaming machines end up idle while workers keen to labour remain jobless.

Marx too thought that he had a simple answer for capitalism's troubles. Convinced that its own deep contradictions would, effectively, force it to commit suicide, he *believed* that a new rational order (one that does not constantly undermine itself, by turning workers and capitalists into capital's slaves and confining generations of workers to the unemployment scrapheap in the process) was inevitable. He, too, was wrong. Capitalism will not just go away under the strain of its admittedly titanic incongruities. Why? Because it has Keynes (or someone with similar ideas) on its side. In its bleakest moments, Keynesian interventions give capitalism a second wind; and a third and a fourth, if need be. Regulation and state intervention do save capitalism from itself, in the limited sense of preserving property rights and buying time for capital to overcome the authorities' renewed ambition to rein it in.

The post-war period, with its two phases, is an apt illustration. The *Global Plan* was the offspring of the Great Depression and the War Economy. It sought to impose a rational set of rules onto the global capitalist game. Never before had such a wide-reaching plan been thought up and implemented by so few for the benefit of so many (give or take a few million Vietnamese, Indonesians, etc). It kept both inflation and unemployment to levels hardly detectable by the naked eye and promoted sustained growth that no one had thought possible before. However, its success was its worst enemy.

The hegemon minding the shop decided to help itself to the till. At first that transgression stabilised the *Plan* and reinforced the tendency to play fast and loose with the rules. However, little by little the stability and trust eroded and gave their place to suspicion and tumult. The hegemon felt threatened and, to preserve its hegemony, it chose the path of partially controlled disintegration of the global order (or the proverbial shop). Through orchestrated energy price hikes and monetary crises, it brought into being a new asymmetrical, unplanned order which, nevertheless, guaranteed it a medium-term capacity to live beyond its means, courtesy of other people's money. Like a *Global Minotaur*, it buttressed a unique form of stable disequilibrium in which a heavily asymmetrical growth pattern was accommodated and financed by large daily capital tributes from the rest of the world.

Once the new quasi-stable disequilibrium was established, instead of letting things be, the beast spawned a new phenomenon: *financialisation* – a reaction to the combination of

(a) great capital flows (rushing into New York to provide for the *Minotaur*) and (b) extremely low interest rates, reflecting both the procured stability and the fact that, since everyone wanted to supply the hegemon with capital, the latter could afford to reduce the price of borrowing inordinately. Thus, the banks inundated the globe with their *private money* and promoted unsustainable growth rates, especially in unproductive assets like real estates and derivatives.

Then the bubble broke, the *private money* burnt out (see Box 12.20 for a description) and a ping-pong game began with private losses turning into public debt (as state officials, often ideologically committed against *any* form of government intervention, were compelled to intervene), and public debt becoming the field on which cunning financiers planted the seeds of new, short-lived, *private money*. The problem with this type of cycle is its irregularity. Like an out of control pendulum, it threatens to exhaust the state's capacity to come to the market's rescue and, vice versa, to deplete the market's ability to bounce back because of a collapse of the state's financial position.

Could the authorities have prevented this vicious circle that is, clearly, spinning out of control and threatening the world with a new variant of the 1930s? There is no doubt that the authorities could have done better. However, it is not our view that government could have, however brilliant, stood in the way of the *Minotaur* and prevented the vicious circle itself. Alan Greenspan, the iconic Chairman of the Fed (from which he retired just before the *Crash of 2008*) put it ever so succinctly in a recent article:

> I do not question that central banks can defuse any bubble. But it has been my experience that unless monetary policy crushes economic activity and, for example, breaks the back of rising profits or rents, policy actions to abort bubbles will fail. I know of no instance where incremental monetary policy has defused a bubble.[65]

We agree wholeheartedly with Greenspan. Just as there is no such thing as an optimal degree of income redistribution that can deliver social justice without pushing the rate of capital accumulation below that which is necessary to sustain capitalism's vigour and growth,[66] there is no such thing as an optimal monetary–fiscal policy mix that can deflate the forming bubbles (at a time of disequilibrium quasi-stability) without crushing economic activity and employment.

Box 12.20 The *Crash of 2008* summarised by Alan Greenspan (Fed Chairman 1987–2007)

Global losses in publicly traded corporate equities up to that point were $16,000 bn (€12,000 bn, £11,000 bn). Losses more than doubled in the 10 weeks following the Lehman default, bringing cumulative global losses to almost $35,000 bn, a decline in stock market value of more than 50 per cent and an effective doubling of the degree of corporate leverage. Added to that are thousands of billions of dollars of losses of equity in homes and losses of non-listed corporate and unincorporated businesses that could easily bring the aggregate equity loss to well over $40,000 bn, a staggering two-thirds of last year's global gross domestic product.

Why not? Our answer is the same as the one we gave in Chapters 4 and 5 to the question of why labour cannot be quantified and reduced to a mere input analytically equivalent to electrical power, and to the question in Chapters 7, 8 and 9 on the reasons why investor risk and uncertainty cannot be captured by some mathematical model. It is because we live in a world combining (i) a system of private appropriation of collectively produced wealth *with* (ii) the *ontological indeterminacy* (see Chapter 10) springing from the human animal's curious penchant for

(a) producing in a manner that no mathematical function can capture without missing the essence of human creativity *and*
(b) creating a higher order form of uncertainty (through the infinite feedback effect between human belief and action) which no mathematical function incorporating well-defined probabilities can encapsulate.

Thus to believe the idea that prudent governments and tight regulation could have prevented the *Crash of 2008* is to seriously misunderstand the irrepressible tumult that is capitalism; the unavoidable turbulence that just happens when we mix liberty with private property; creativity with expropriation; doing things for their intrinsic value and reducing every value to its market determined price; a robust *Global Plan* for organising capital and trade flows worldwide with conglomerates that are motivated solely by a primordial search for monopoly power and machine-like labour.

Alas, this very basic point about an elemental clash at the very foundations of our social order is so hard to keep on our intellectual radar screen, especially when most people (if not all) who spend serious time scrutinising the current crisis have been trained to think about capitalism within a mindset in which capitalism is impossible.

Box 12.21 Why regulation cannot prevent crises: A rather modern view

An ignorant and mistaken bank legislation, such as that of 1844–45, can intensify this money crisis. But no manner of bank legislation can abolish a crisis [...] In a system of production, in which the entire connection of the reproduction process rests upon credit, a crisis must obviously occur through a tremendous rush for means of payment, when credit suddenly ceases and nothing but cash payment goes... At the same time, an enormous quantity of these bills of exchange represents mere swindles, and this becomes apparent now, when they burst. There are furthermore unlucky speculations made with the money of other people. Finally, they are commodity-capitals, which have become depreciated or unsalable or returns that can never more be realized. This entire artificial system of forced expansion of the reproduction process cannot, of course, be remedied by having some bank, like the Bank of England, give to the swindlers the needed capital in the shape of paper notes and buy up all the depreciated commodities at their old nominal values. Moreover, everything here appears turned upside down, since no real prices and their real basis appear in this paper world...

Karl Marx, *Capital* Volume 3, part V, Chapter 30,
Marx (1894 [1909]), pp. 575–6

Box 12.22 Failure pays

Nothing perseveres like privilege's determination to reproduce itself. During the *Global Minotaur*'s undisputed rein the free market promoted the notion of choice by parents, students, patients, defendants, etc. In practice it meant that children were increasingly selected at the best schools on the basis of their parents' income, the sick received treatment more and more in tune with their wealth, justice was denied to those who came from the wrong part of town. Similarly with macroeconomic management: during the Clinton administration, Larry Summers' policy decision to deregulate Wall Street completely and utterly contributed to the financial sector's uncontrolled gallop into near oblivion. At the time Timothy Geithner was his Under-secretary. Guess who was to be summoned to clean up the mess when President Obama came to power eight years later? Summers and Geithner of course! The explanation? Who else could be trusted with such a big job and all the privileges it brings to its bearers? Once capitalism grows sufficiently complex, failure pays. Every crisis boosts the incumbent's power because they appear to the public as the only good candidates for mopping up the mess. Think of not only the *Geithner–Summers Plan* of 2009 but also the IMF–ECB–EZ mechanism (see Box 12.18) that is meant to sort out the post-2010 European debt crisis. The trouble is that the 'solutions' implemented by the original creators of the problem create even more centralisation and complexity which, in turn, further boosts the culprits' indispensability... does any of this remind the reader of something from *Book 1*? Perhaps the sciences' most peculiar failure – a discipline whose discursive power grows as it goes from one sad theoretical failure to another?

Summing up, capitalism does indeed go through cycles. Not of the 'real business' variety (see Box 2.11), which pack as much analytical power as a hen packs flying power, but cycles between periods when regulation is tight (usually after the horses have bolted) and periods when government applies a 'light touch' (when stability seems to be the order of the day); between periods of active state planning and periods of negative macroeconomic engineering. Arguably, the post-war period saw the most violent swing from one to the other as the unprecedented *Global Plan* gave its place to the matchless *Global Minotaur*.

The swing was so violent that something else, something brand new, emerged from the guts of that transition: *financialisation*. It upped the stakes by allowing institutions that produced nothing tangible to generate almost as much *private money* as there was public money. The monetary explosion distorted everything within the global social economy, causing all sorts of cycles to increase in amplitude. The higher the cycle went the harder the fall. Of course, those who hit the floor hardest where not the same people who had benefitted from the upswing.

The *Global Minotaur* era, and its end in the *Crash of 2008*, has added another wrinkle to our story in *Book 1*. Chapter 4 expounded our hypothesis that humans are constantly taken over, at least in spirit, by their mechanical artefacts but, because the takeover can never be complete (due to humanity's stubborn resistance to turn *fully* into an automaton), crises erupt periodically. The *Global Plan* was meant to iron out these crises, by means first touted by

Keynes and then developed by the New Dealers. It failed, perhaps for reasons von Hayek (among others) had important things to say about; mainly, the twin ideas that:

(a) no *plan*, however brilliant, can reflect its constituents' ever-changing capacities and needs; *and*
(b) no government, national or local, can be trusted to act in the public interest because public interest is as ill-defined as labour's, industrial capital's and speculative capital's sentiments are grossly indeterminate.

What the *Minotaur* added to the story is a capacity for the theoretically inept neoclassical models of macro and financial economists to lend a helping hand in the manufacture of *private money*; a process that has added substantially to capitalism's fully endogenous instability. At last, neoclassical economics became part and parcel of the *Spirit of Capitalism*, exacerbating its inherent propensity for unsustainable booms and recessionary sojourns. The economics functional to the *Minotaur*'s interest consequently evolved from theories that were, at worst, quaintly irrelevant to techniques essential in the manufacture of financial weapons of mass destruction. Thus, capitalism's endogenous failures at last joined forces with economics' *Inherent Error* to produce crises bigger, juicier and more catastrophic than ever before.

We ended the last chapter with Paul Volcker's effective announcement of the *Minotaur circa* 1979. We end this chapter with the words of his successor at the Fed, Alan Greenspan which, to us, sound like the *Minotaur*'s eulogy. In this extract Greenspan is addressing the Congressional Committee for Oversight and Government Reform on 23 October 2008, presided over by California Democratic Senator Henry Waxman.[67] Waxman conducted the hearing in an aggressive manner, at a time when the American public were seething at what had gone down, demanding of Greenspan to explain the degree to which it would be true to say that the Fed, under his stewardship, had set the stage for the *Crash of 2008*.

GREENSPAN: Well remember that what an ideology is, is a conceptual framework with the way people deal with reality. Everyone has one. You have to, to exist, you need an ideology. The question is whether it is accurate or not. And what I'm saying to you is, yes, I found a flaw. I don't know how significant or permanent it is, but I've been very distressed by that fact.
WAXMAN: You found a flaw in the reality?
GREENSPAN: A flaw in the model that I perceived is the critical functioning structure that defines how the world works, so to speak.
WAXMAN: In other words, you found that your view of the world, your ideology, was not right, it was not working?
GREENSPAN: That is – precisely. No, that's precisely the reason I was shocked, because I have been going for 40 years or more with very considerable evidence that it was working exceptionally well.

We believe that Greenspan was being perfectly sincere in uttering, under stress, the above words. The model of the world that he courageously calls 'his' was the dominant paradigm that began life in or around 1950 (see Chapter 8) and which ended up the official ideology of those who saw it as their life's work to do the *Minotaur*'s bidding. In this book, we have also (unkindly perhaps) called it, among other things, the Econobubble; the economists' *Inherent Error* on steroids; a mathematised religion, etc. Along with the derivatives market and the rest of the financial and real estate bubbles, the Econobubble, Greenspan's model-*cum*-ideology, burst too in 2008.

We feel a sense of pride in *Greenspan's Confession*. Of all the confessions we have encountered by powerful men caught up in the whirlpool of historical reversals, his was the most sincere and intellectually robust; a downright affirmation of truth's ultimate importance. It is particularly helpful for younger minds who need role models, examples of intelligent people who change their minds drastically against the forces of ideological inertia and even at significant personal cost. It is a rare phenomenon and as such must be cherished.

It is also helpful because it points to the origin of the dogma that supported countless individual and institutional choices that led the world to crash in 2008. It was the same dogma that gave mainstream economists the conviction to 'close' their models by means of untestable meta-axioms (recall Chapters 7, 8 and 9); the same pool of elixir that the financial engineers used in order to mask the stench of the parameters within the formulae with which they priced the CDOs; the same song sheet on which paeans to the markets were written in the language of the *Formalists* who scored such an unexpected triumph in US economics departments from 1950 onwards; the same mindset that informed decision makers in Brussels, Washington, the World Bank and the IMF to script policy papers which ended up diminishing the life prospects of so many and for so little sustainable gain.

If we were to point to a single silver lining from the calamitous developments of the post-2008 world, *Greenspan's Confession* will do nicely.

ADDENDUM

The Recycling Problem in a Currency Union[1]

by George E. Krimpas

PROLEGOMENON: the recycling problem is general, not confined to a multicurrency setting: whenever there are surplus and deficit units, i.e. everywhere, real adjustment must be either upward or downward, the question is which. An attempt is made to formulate the recycling problem in terms of EMU. But while the problem seems clear the resolution is not. A minimalist solution is proposed through a detour consistent with the Maastricht rules. Inadequate as this is, it highlights the limits of technical arrangements when confronted with political economy, namely the inability to set operational rules of the game from within a set of axiomatically predetermined constraints dependent on the fact and practice of sovereignty. Even so, an attempt at persuasion through clarification of the issue may be a useful preliminary, in particular by highlighting the distinction between recycling and transfers. Some of the paper's evocations, notably on 'oligopoly', may be taken as merely heuristic.

The only economy which does not have an external surplus or deficit problem is the closed economy and, since Robinson Crusoe time, there aren't any. By contrast, the situation of any open economy is eternally asymmetric; if in surplus it can carry on merrily, at least until something untoward, exogenous or perhaps internal, turns up; while, if in deficit, it is under pressure both externally and internally, additionally to any exogenous event.[2] Keynes (1980: 27) put the problem succinctly in his very first official memorandum, dated 8 September 1941, on the proposal of a Clearing Union, thus:

> It is characteristic of a freely convertible international standard that it throws the burden of adjustment on the country which is in the *debtor* position on the international balance

of payments, – that is on the country which is (in this context) by hypothesis the *weaker* and above all the *smaller* in comparison with the other side of the scales which (for this purpose) is the rest of the world. [emphasis in the original]

A definition of the problem and its resolution which was half-scuttled on the tortuous way to Bretton Woods, nevertheless functioned reasonably until abandoned some 25 years later.

Keynes himself, having 'lost' the decisive argument for *symmetrical adjustment* of fixed but adjustable exchange rates in his own, multicurrency clearing union, did not further argue the case of a fully-fledged single currency union's possible additional or alternative internal arrangements. Yet after the nameless, dogmatic years in the doldrums between the Smithsonian and Maastricht, such a currency union eventually turned up in a tiny part of the globe called Europe, partly in response to the abandonment of Bretton Woods but also, crucially, subsequent to the grand design of Europe led by the Marshall Plan and some peculiar pairs[3] of Enlightened European statesmanship constructing the Franco-German integrating dynamic, the rest following.

But the Euro-Maastricht architects constructed an EMU with the 'E' effectively left out. The intra-union imbalance problem was thought settled by the fiscal rules; it was not, and not because the fiscal rules were in practice inoperative; it would have turned up even if they were. The nominal uni-currency national accounts do not account for differential intra-union competitiveness, only at best indicate it afterwards. 'Real' as distinct from now non-existent nominal exchange rates, conventionally proxied by intra-union differential unit labour costs [but see further below on 'oligopoly'], remain to create 'external' intra-union imbalances within the union even with balanced [fiscal] budgets. To focus the argument on fundamentals, not accounting devices, this latter condition will be assumed to hold throughout – it is, perhaps, when taken by itself, the least constraining of the Maastricht rules, neither preventive cure nor remedy for the recycling problem.

To illustrate the oddity of the 'internal' imbalance notion, imagine a sub-lunar visitor to China where he/she observes a Chinaman holding a dollar note. The visitor immediately knows where that one came from: 'it' has crossed a monetary border. As for its destination he/she may ask the bearer, who being a law-abiding person is already on his/her way to the office where the foreign body in his/her hands is to be exchanged for what in his country is called 'money'. The receiving authority will then do its mediating job, likely ending up by holding an alternative asset yielding some return, most usefully American treasuries, thus recycling the value of the item, helping the world to sustain deficits elsewhere – Adam Smith might have said this was no part of anybody's intention, in the present context falsely. But what if the sub-lunar visitor were to land in Germany there to observe a German person holding a Euro note? Nobody, including the bearer, would have the means to know where that token body came from; it is not 'it' but just *money*. Borderless transition of the token of value annuls the question of its origin; its destination is as mystical. Who and by what observing instrument can tell whether that Euro note is on the wing or heading for a temporary abode or plain hoard, in principle immune from the necessity of intermediation? Yet in this one-money sub-lunar world there are still surpluses and deficits and their myriad offshoots; the problem is their implications when the surplus and deficit units are sovereign states. So what precisely is the *internal*, intra-union 'external' imbalances 'problem'; what rules might be devised to meet it in a union-wide acceptable form? The ongoing and perhaps deepening crisis is not crucial to the argument that follows, though it serves as backdrop and certainly as origin for concentrating the mind wonderfully.[4]

It is convenient to think of country-members of a currency union as composed of differentially powerful *oligopolists*,[5] the predicate 'power' leading one to think in terms of (partial equilibrium) 'neo-mercantilist' or 'vent for surplus' national strategies, though eventually coming up against those ultimately constraining (General Equilibrium) identities – for we cannot all be simultaneously successful neo-mercantilists.[6] The stylised facts of the currency union disequilibrium case are then summarised thus:

(a) The definition of the problem is assisted by the fact that EMU is only marginally in surplus with the rest of the world: to the extent that some member countries are in surplus with the rest of the world, that part of their overall surplus can be ignored as being someone else's problem, so the effective stylised fact is that there is no rest of the world; all 'external' imbalances are internal to the currency union.
(b) The currency union *regime* thus being the whole world is only a union insofar, positively, as *free and stable* – a tall order (for labour markets even taller) – *markets* rule the game, but also, negatively, insofar as oligopoly,[7] as the prevalent subspecies thereof, induces a dynamic asymmetry of endogenous action and response which *regime* rules allow but cannot handle, thus triggering the equivalent of Keynes' diagnostic statement quoted above: thus, ultimately, insofar as – though in merely accounting terms – fiscal imbalances are concerned, the rules can only work downwards, the asymmetry is dynamically part of the system and cannot be corrected. The otherwise unseeable (by the national accounts) 'causal' imbalances in the real economy will be reflected in falling real wages and employment.

Without naming names, the currency union equilibrating game is thus intra-union competitively disinflationary: taking unit labour cost as the proxy metric, oligopolistic power will turn up on either the numerator falling or the denominator rising – real wages must fall or productivity must rise. Oligopoly is precisely the power to do either or both, differentially. It is also the differential power to enforce unemployment or anything else interfering with the 'vent for surplus' overarching objective, the ultimate *raison d'être* of any respectable oligopolist. But the resulting deflationary underemployment equilibrium is dynamically unstable, asymmetrically affecting the currency union's members, a game without endogenous issue till vanishing point, a subzero equilibrium solution eventually detrimental to the surplus unit – if only the world could wait for it.

The question of the present exercise is, given the Maastricht–EMU rule-book as is, can there be an acceptable mechanism for *recycling surpluses* so as to offset the deflationary impact of deficits? – the answer being, if not plainly 'no', then decidedly unpleasant unless some additional not incompatible rule may be devised and accepted. To investigate this we must look at the flow of 'external' surpluses once earned and trace the path of their eventual destination.

Since by definition, in a currency union all flows are denominated in the same currency, it will simplify investigation to assume that the union consists of two countries, one in surplus, one in deficit, taking the most favourable benchmark for the exercise: both countries have zero fiscal deficits and are, however mediately, equally financially served (in terms of collateral, etc.) by the single currency union central bank called the CUB, assumed subject to present European Central Bank (ECB) rules.[8] The 'single market' in everything then implies a 'single price' for everything insofar as everything is the same – which it is not[9] – thus, in the oligopolistic setting of the modern world, also differential markups and margins therefore profits, the surplus country being the differentially high profit country. Tracing the path of profits is then tracing the path of surpluses.

The question now is: where do these profits go? Is there financial intra-union but inter-country intermediation of profits or are differential profits so to say 'oligopolistically' intra-country retained, effectively intra-country 'hoarded' thus ruling out surplus recycling?

But the private sector financial system is itself ruled by asymmetry, surplus units are ever more creditworthy than are deficit units, etc., therefore the dynamics work out so that surplus country profits are retained by the surplus country and cannot be recycled to the benefit of the deficit country (net of foreign investment plus transfers of all kinds by the surplus to the deficit country). The original deflationary impact on the deficit country is thus not recyclable.

In this case, Keynes' Essential Principle of Banking[10] is nullified; there can be no recycling since there is hoarding prior to banking. So the question becomes, can the currency union's CUB act *anti-asymmetrically* to offset this bias – can the 'lender' turn round to become 'spender', let alone, in crisis, the before-the-last resort lender and presently the first resort spender?

It possibly can, if it subsumes the functions now entrusted to the European Investment Bank (EIB), with the latter's rules as they now stand – the EIB can lend to both the private and the public sector of any currency union country as well as others, *not on collateral but rather on prospective yield*; noting also that public borrowing from this source need not, by present rules, be counted in the national debt.[11]

This institutional twist represents a novel degree of freedom for the adjustment process, a window of opportunity akin though more proactive to the conventional discount window of a standard central bank in normal times. The CUB–EIB thus reconstructed is then more than a lender of last resort to the financial system – though by rule explicitly not currency union governments – it is also *'like' a fiscal authority* to the extent that it is a spender of first resort, albeit *on commercial rather than distributional criteria*: the principles of Maastricht–EMU are not disturbed. But EIB finance is also hereby undisturbed, its credit worthiness is if anything enhanced, it can directly and indirectly draw surplus profits arising from external surplus into proper and appropriately prudential intermediation directly aimed at productive profit-yielding investment.

To the extent that such an institutionally based recycling device is effective, it obviates the deficit government's investment needs to borrow from the market, by construction on terms more onerous than those available to the surplus government's country. For the CUB–EIB construct, apart from borrowing on its own creditworthiness, which should be similar if not on the grounds of scale superior to the creditworthiness of the surplus country, can, as part of its primary inflation targeting mission, expand credit autonomously just like any central bank can within its remit; but in this case CUB–EIB credit expansion in the form of enhanced liquidity would be linked to and locked by the extent to which the deflationary impact of un-recycled surplus works against the CUB's inflation target.

There is here implicitly a growth-and-employment objective which has slipped into the argument: but is this not ever so in the reality of actual practice? And, this being the case, is it not enticing for formalist enthusiasts to devise the right rule transforming, say, output gaps and the like (e.g. 'foreign gaps', let alone unit labour cost gaps) into algorithmic solutions concerning the CUB's accommodating finance to his/her EIB brother/sister, perhaps 'modelling' these two on the fantastic Washington twins?

Not necessarily, in this line of thinking. The revolving fund of finance which is at the back of the preceding argument does not preclude the notion of growing financial support for a growing currency union economy hopefully aiming at stable full employment, not rule-based but judgement-based, a political matter here taken as exogenous.

This may be taken as fudging the issue: it is not an original thought that the EIB should be brought into the picture, it has already been so – nor, which is perhaps more important, have the orders of magnitude being taken into account other than in qualitative terms: what proportion of imbalance should EIB finance offset that would correspond to a re-cyclical revolving fund equilibrium? – here tempting the algorithmic response above rejected. The issue now and beyond is rather not how much but to what purpose, in regard particularly to *the problem of institutionally evolving towards the solution of recycling surpluses*, not to the current short-term problem of boosting investment expenditure, immensely necessary as this is. Immiseration, either in the form of falling real wages or unemployment is the road to destruction of what still bears the name of Europe. In a nutshell, the EMU must start on the long road to bring the 'E' to conjoin the 'MU'. This all has to do with investment, not consumption. Only this can be the offset for oligopolistically crippling vent for surplus. *Recycling is thus not a redistributive transfer, let alone bailout, from the surplus to the deficit fiscal authority, but a straightforward application of the banking principle.*

It would mean that the effective EIB spending leg of the CUB–EIB construct has a lower-than-the-market financing cost, as dictated by the CUB's intervention rate which is the prime instrument directed to achieving the counter-inflation target. By being consonant with this would also help to enrich the CUB's armoury *vis-à-vis* the yield curve, thus enhancing the non-inflationary growth prospects of the currency union as a whole. If the argument is correct, it may be only an acceptable beginning, perhaps in a small way, but it may instruct the course for the future. *In fine*, an otherwise desired sound financial policy would be compatible with a non-deflationary mechanism of adjustment. The policing rules of the mechanism are simple and should be obvious; but these fall under the head of politics.

Notes

1   Thanks for a positive response are due to the authors of this book plus especially to Victoria Chick; but also to Mark Hayes, on whose initiative the paper is posted on the Post Keynesian Study Group site and to Dimitri Papadimitriou on whose initiative the paper is published as a Levy Economics Institute Working Paper (wp 595).
2   The obvious *ceteris paribus* qualification is implicit here; surpluses are necessarily matched by deficits so untoward feedback is certainly lurking somewhere, but this is in the 'long run', etc.
3   Monnet-Schuman, de Gaulle-Adenauer, Giscard- Schmidt, Mitterand-Kohl.
4   Recall Dr. Johnson's dictum, that *if a man knows he will be hanged, it concentrates his mind wonderfully*. (NT: In his journal entry for 19 September 1777, Boswell noted that a friend of Johnson's told the great man he suspected Dodd didn't write the piece himself, because it was so good: 'Why should you think so?' responded Johnson. 'Depend upon it, Sir, when a man knows he is to be hanged in a fortnight, it concentrates his mind wonderfully'.)
5   This tack is more in line with an earlier theory, due to Kałecki rather than Keynes (misemployed in a stable equilibrium context, e.g. in Kaldor's MkIII growth model) where price markup and margin, profit size, rate and share, with positive feedback on profitable accumulation, etc., thus taking the argument beyond the simple unit labour cost proxy for differential competitiveness.
6   For the revived neo-mercantilist notion invoked here I am pleasurably indebted to Joseph Halevi and Yanis Varoufakis, also belatedly to Jörg Bibow, 'The Euro and its Guardian of Stability', Levy Economics Institute, Working Paper 583. (NT again adds: exchange in mercantilism was always perceived, in modern terminology, as a zero-sum game [Heckscher 1935, II: 25–8].)
7   Note that 'oligopoly' is here understood as more particularly macro-agent or entity; it is akin to Kalecki rather than Keynes; it is but another name for 'vent for surplus' – differential profit is part and parcel of dynamically differential market share.
8   Though not ideology, a real-world dimension from which I am tortuously attempting to abstract.
9   Ignoring Polish plumbers and the like, whatever other than geographical this may mean; given product and factor differentiation, the relatively powerful oligopolist is the one who in

man-to-man competition always wins, comparative advantage yields to absolute advantage, however transient – how else to explain the obfuscated notion of 'competitiveness' in a world where congruent demands and supplies are hierarchically (perhaps better, lexicographically or at least semi-lexicographically) as well as price determined: 'value for money' is but a mystical expression. Measurement in terms of relative unit labour costs remains, unfortunately, the only plausible quantitative benchmark.

10 This will be a long footnote: The expression '*essential principle of banking*' turns up apropos – in a credit money economy – in the first instance in Keynes's second draft of the proposal of what he still then called a Currency Union (18 November 1941), thus:

> The idea underlying my proposals for a Currency Union is simple, namely to generalise the essential principle of banking, as it is exhibited within any closed system … This principle is the necessary equality of credits and debits, of assets and liabilities. If no credits can be removed outside the banking system but only transferred within it, the Bank [sole intermediating agent] *itself* can never be in difficulties. It can with safety make what advances it wishes to any of its customers with the assurance that the proceeds can only be transferred to the bank account of another customer. Its problem is solely to see to it that its customers behave themselves [*sic!*] and that the advances made to each of them are prudent and advisable from the point of view of its customers as a whole.
>
> (Keynes, (1980), p. 44, emphasis in original)

This is repeated in the third draft, still calling the project a Currency Union, insisting that 'its members behave themselves' but expanding on the rules *vs* discretion problem of the management of the mediating authority, this being 'a typical problem of any super-national authority' (Keynes, (1980), p. 73).

The fourth draft [25 January 1942] is more forthright on the objective of the exercise, thus:

> The plan aims at the substitution of an expansionist, in place of a contractionist, pressure on … trade … A country is in credit or debit with the Clearing Union [note the shift of nomenclature] as a whole. This means that the overdraft facilities, whilst a relief to some, are not a real burden to others. For credit balances … represent those resources which a country voluntarily chooses to leave idle. They represent a potentiality of purchasing power, which it is entitled to use at any time. Meanwhile, the fact that the creditor country is not choosing to employ this purchasing power would not necessarily mean … that it is withdrawn from circulation and exerting a deflationary and contractionist pressure on the whole world including the creditor country itself ['vent for surplus' countries, underline this last one]. No country need be in possession of a credit balance unless it deliberately prefers to sell more than its buys (or lends); no country loses its liquidity or is prevented from enjoying its credit balance whenever it chooses to do so; and no country suffers injury (but on the contrary) by the fact that the balance, which it does not choose to employ for the time being, is not withdrawn from circulation. In short, the analogy with a national banking system is complete. No depositor in a local bank suffers because the balances, which he leaves idle, are employed to finance the business, of someone else.
>
> (Keynes, 1980)

The revolving fund of finance doctrine thus settled, he goes on:

> Just as the development of national banking systems served to offset a deflationary pressure which would have prevented otherwise the development of modern industry, so by extending the same principle into the international [including intra-currency union arrangements] field, we may hope to offset the contractionist pressure which might otherwise overwhelm in social disorder and disappointment the good hopes of our modern world.
>
> (Keynes, 1980, p. 113)

But there is more:

> The proposal put forward … aims at putting some part of the responsibility for adjustment on the creditor country as well as on the debtor … The object is that the creditor should not be allowed to remain entirely passive. For if he is, an intolerably heavy task may be laid on the debtor country, which is for that very reason in the weaker position.
>
> (Keynes, 1980, p. 117)

And [the dates no longer matter]:

> In short, the analogy with a national banking system is complete. No depositor in a local bank suffers because the balances, which he leaves idle, are employed to finance the business of some-one else. Just as the development of national banking systems served to offset a deflationary pressure which would have prevented otherwise the development of modern industry, so by extending the same principle into the international field we may hope to offset the contractionist pressure which might otherwise overwhelm in social disorder and disappointment the good hopes of the modern world. *The substitution of a credit mechanism in place of hoarding would have repeated in the international field the same miracle, already performed in the domestic field, of turning a stone into bread.*
>
> (Keynes, 1980, p. 177, emphasis added)

The '*potential miracle*' yet suffers the eternal threat of the eternal evil spirit:

> *The world's trading difficulties in the past have not always been due to the improvidence of debtor countries. They may be caused in a most acute form if a creditor country is constantly withdrawing international money from circulation and hoarding it, instead of putting it back into circulation, thus refusing to spend its income from abroad either on goods for home consumption or on investment overseas.*
>
> (Keynes, 1980, p. 273, emphasis added)

concluding with a warning, in a private letter, his persuasive Golgotha [as if this were aesthetically possible within his 'open' paradigm] with:

> In all this you have to bear in mind that there were some quarters who confidently believed until recently that all these plans would die a natural death. Since it now seems possible that nature cannot be relied on to do the work, it is felt, not [to]put it more strongly, that there is no need officiously to keep alive any conception of any kind of an international scheme.
>
> (Keynes, 1980, p. 394)

and, the by now chastised adventurer–reformer turned Stoic philosopher nonetheless hopefully noting [in a private letter again] that:

> You will see that *the arts of government as we understand them* are not [practiced] in this [who?] country. *It may be that some other art, which we have difficulty in apprehending,* is being employed. Indeed, if it were not so the final outcome must be a great deal worse than it actually is. Anyhow, it is important to bear in mind the total absence of the arts of government as we understand them. For otherwise we are led to impute to malice or unfriendliness what is in fact due to nothing of the kind.
>
> (Keynes, 1980, p. 370, emphasis added)

therewith ending the sermon....

11 For this enlightened if intriguing detail I am indebted to Stuart Holland.

13 A future for hope

Postscript to *Book 2*

13.1 Living in truth

The abiding memory of life under Soviet rule was the wretchedness of having to live a lie. Except for a minority who were imprisoned, tortured, killed and maimed by the Greek colonels or by the monster going by the name of Augusto Pinochet, the worst violation for most was the compulsion to pretend to mistake naked propaganda for self evident truth. The passing of these regimes was largely due to a certain intolerance that humans have towards a life of wilful acquiescence to falsity.

Which is why *Condorcet's Secret* is so poignant. The worst form of slavery is that to which the slave consents. And the fiercest irrationality comes wrapped up in a package that appears to us as the epitome of efficiency. Whereas the Soviet Union, Pinochet's Chile and the Greek junta collapsed because their naked coercive power at some point waned, more robust tyrannies manage to reproduce themselves by harnessing the never-ending capacity of victims unconsciously to reproduce the circumstances of their victimhood.

The *Crash of 2008* marks a turning point in human history. It signalled the end of a composite lie that infected our minds for decades and, while so doing, fashioned extraordinary social power for some and a growing sense of insecurity for most. The composite lie in question fused the ideology of financialised capital with the economists' *Inherent Error*.

Capitalism was always predicated upon a 'creation myth' (i.e. a lie): the idea that profit is the return to brave, risk-taking entrepreneurs which is necessary to keep society on the frontier of its potential growth path. *Financialisation* added another layer to the lie by instilling in global society's collective mind the notion that wealth could spring out of energetic paper shuffling motivated by greed, naked ambition and a deep-seated nastiness. Of course, ambition, greed and genuine nastiness have always been around. The central trait of the *Global Minotaur* age, however, went well beyond their mere presence. For the first time in human history, we became *incapable* of imagining that anything other than avarice and malice might rule the world efficiently. Thus a deeply irrational system came to pass as the epitome of efficiency.

Once in that mind-frame, the *Minotaur*'s work was done and *Condorcet's Secret* had reached its apotheosis. We had *all* become accomplices of the beast (even those of us who proposed an alternative economic model). The word 'opportunism' shed any negative connotations it once had and acquired a positive ring to it, becoming a synonym to 'savvy'. Even old-fashioned entrepreneurs, who continued to believe in the value of prudence, abstinence and the production of tangible values, were left behind; taken over; discarded as has-beens; a spent force.[1] While not everyone *agreed* with the new creed, almost all lost any sense of outrage when encountering it, even in its crudest form.

Bereft of any sign of some alternative way of getting on with life, even the weakest tried their hand at the main game. They bought at rock bottom prices jars of pickles from Wal-Mart that represented an inordinate amount of someone else's labour. They bought houses that they could not really afford, banking on house prices rising and their making a sort of killing.

Labour always had a dual nature (recall Chapter 4) in the sphere of production. Now, it acquired another dual nature in the sphere of speculation. Before financialisation, workers faced one type of risk alone: hardship due to unemployment. In the *Minotaur*'s era, with decreasing real wages against a background of rapid growth, they were lured into taking on board another type of risk: to commit part of their future wages to the financial/housing sectors in the hope of participating in the financialisation bonanza.

In this sense, the subprime crisis is part and parcel of the way in which capitalism evolved, giving more and more 'choices' to the majority of people whose real social power was shrinking.[2] The meek would no longer inherit the Earth but, instead, they would be free to lose in more ways than were available to them prior to the *Minotaur*'s rise.

Back in the nineteenth-century, Friedrich Engels (1845) painted in the gloomiest colours the portrait of the British working class. More recently, it was the sweatshops employing legal or illegal migrants in Mexico, China, even New York, that conveyed a similar feel. In the post-2008 world, it became possible to paint a sweatshop story of a very different kind; one in which the goings-on are a cross between Arthur Miller's *Death of a Salesman*, David Mamet's *Glengarry Glen Ross* and Charles Dickens's *Christmas Carol*. Box 13.1 relates one such story.

Economics played a crucial role in the ideological transformation that was both an effect and a prerequisite for the *Minotaur*'s evolution into the planet's dominant force. Our discipline has always been prone to an *Inherent Error*, as *Book 1* sought to demonstrate. However, it was only recently that it dealt with its *Inherent Error* not by attempting to overcome it (however ineffectually) but by engaging it in a power-waltz that spun the whole of mainstream economics faster and faster around its axes, until the profession, in its entirety, overcame reality's gravity and free-floated towards a rarefied universe that bears no relationship to our capitalist reality. The resulting theoretical economics, aided and abetted by its econometric

---

Box 13.1 A very modern sweatshop

This was a classic sweatshop, a small outfit being paid by an obviously failing corporation to unload cheap stocks. These fat chain-smoking salesmen would say anything to their victims …. In their own way these bucket shops are specialists. They have no clients from whom to protect their reputation. They also have no reputation to defend. They just get out there and sell stocks and bonds they often know full well are worthless, and to hell with the consequences …. All [my boss] wanted me to do was locate guys with cash and then sell them, jam them into worthless penny stocks with promises or anything else that worked. From my view across that hellhole of an office, just picking up the merest snatches of conversation, I could work out that this was an underworld operation, selling stock in fake shells of corporations to raise cash, which was tantamount to ripping investors off, stealing them blind.

Extract from Larry McDonald's 2009 book *A Colossal Failure of Common Sense: The Inside Story of the Collapse of Lehman Brothers*

appendages, became the secular religion that consecrated the spirit and legitimised the practices of financialisation.

It was not by choice that economists played that role. They simply adapted to a replicator dynamic which they learned at first to tolerate and later enthusiastically to espouse. While the *Minotaur* was flourishing, this new variant of the *Inherent Error* afforded *Condorcet's Secret* such a revival that anyone who stepped out of its (neoclassical) fold was branded a dissident, ostracised to some peripheral economics department and condemned to a life of toying around with different (admittedly less toxic) versions of the *Inherent Error* (e.g. tinkering with little Marxist or post-Keynesian models; theoretical exercises which were next to useless in helping one gain a better handle on developments).

As for the tiny minority of dissidents who managed to escape economism and say something useful about really existing capitalism, their dissenting voices were muffled by the overwhelmingly boisterous celebrations coming from the boardrooms, the bankers' clubs, the university authorities (who nowadays know which side their bread is buttered), the students themselves (who, over the years, developed a fine ear for the sermons most likely to bolster their career prospects). The list is endless.

Just as the industrial revolution would never have happened if people had to vote for it in a referendum, the world would never have liberated itself from the potent brew of financialised capitalism and the economists' obfuscation by an act of collective will. It took the *Crash of 2008* to give us a chance of liberation from the staunchest variant of *Condorcet's Secret* since the Middle Ages.

The ancient Athenians, we are told, worshipped at the altar of the unknown god (*Acts* 17:22–23). Economists taken by the Nash–Debreu–Arrow method of the early 1950s revered the unknown source that equilibrated their models.[3] Everyone else, since the collapse of the *Global Plan* in 1971, eventually learned to deify the unknown source of *private money*. Placing their trust in the lap of the veracity of appearances, they believed that if it looked like a system that worked, it must have been a system that was designed to work – in perpetuity.

Encouraged further by the Leibnizian models that had acquired totemic status in economics departments, they trusted the stability of a 'system' which treated steel mills as passé, considered real estate to be 'productive', and got hooked on the exponentially lucrative trade in CDOs, CDSs and other such exotica.

Unknown gods tend to be very useful. Especially to those who invoke their name in order to legitimise great wealth transfers to themselves and, additionally, to their attendant priesthood that performs the relevant rituals. And since the history of religion is so rich in prose that it can be plundered readily by the *nouveau riche*, the *Global Minotaur* did not even have to come up with a new hymn. Matthew 25:29 would have done nicely: 'For unto every one that hath shall be given, and he shall have abundance; but from him that hath not shall be taken away even that which he hath' (King James' version).[4]

Of course, the punishment of unknown gods is that, sooner or later, it becomes apparent that they were nothing but apparitions. The *Crash of 2008* was such a revelatory moment. Above all else, it allowed us a glimpse of what *living in truth* might be like;[5] a mere peek that, nevertheless, is only available to those willing and ready to treat all economic theories as *necessary errors*.

13.2 Democracy versus Trapezocracy[6]

T.H. Huxley (1880: 229) once said that 'it is the customary fate of new truths to begin as heresies and to end as superstitions'. The grave danger of our post-2008 era is that of creating a mythical explanation of the causes of the *Crash*. Financialisation was not the cause. Nor was ineffectual regulation of banks. Greed was not the culprit. Nor was globalisation the perpetrator. The Fed's policies did not initiate the crisis. Nor did they prevent it. Europe's monetary union was flawed. But it was not responsible for the catastrophe. All these were but co-determined symptoms of a general dynamic to which they contributed.

The rise of the conglomerate in the late 1890s and early 1900s gave rise to the world as we now know it. The 1920s gave us the first example of the exuberance that was to return with the *Global Minotaur* and also deepened the one great scarcity afflicting capitalism: the scarcity of sustainable demand for the goods that the new conglomerates could churn out.

The Great Depression gave us pause and the New Deal which, in turn, yielded the first attempt at a *Global Plan* for rationalising the irrational; for managing trade and capital flows and maintaining global demand at a planetary scale; for bringing order to the chaos that is capitalism, especially of the corporate, financialised variety. It also gave us the Cold War, the Military–Industrial Complex, Vietnam and a host of other malignancies.

The New Dealers' misfortune was that they never came to terms with capitalism's profound illiberalism, especially during the era of oligopolised, corporatised accumulation. The hands-down winner of the post-war period was not the individual, as rumour had it, but the corporate entity and its capacity to enter into a cosy embrace with the powers that be at a global level. The New Dealers' design did not make any provisions either for the instability that this coalition would bring to its *Global Plan* nor for the threat it would constitute to basic, human liberty. The paranoia occasioned by the Cold War did not help much in that regard either.

When the *Global Plan* dissolved, under the pressure of an out of control war and of the internal tensions that destabilised the planned monetary system, the coalition of corporate and state operatives moved on to a new phase in which the new plan would be to have no plan, save for a myriad little plans that constituted the *Global Minotaur*'s blueprint.

The new regime was to rely on a controlled disintegration of the world economy and be one in which the coalition between private interests and public offices would preach competition, but beget monopoly; speak the language of balanced budgets, but organise the largest deficits in history; advocate democracy, but, in reality, spread tyranny. Double-speak never had it so good.

Box 13.2 The liberal and the beast
Extracts from the correspondence between Professor Milton Friedman and General Augusto Pinochet[1]

April 21, 1975

Dear Mr. President,

During our visit with you on Friday, March 21, to discuss the economic situation in Chile, you asked me to convey to you my opinions about Chile's economic situation and policies .... This letter is in response to that request .... The key economic problems of Chile are clearly twofold: inflation, and the promotion of a healthy social market economy ... The source of inflation is crystal clear: government spending .... There is only one way to end inflation: by reducing drastically the rate of increase in the quantity of money …. There is no way to end the inflation that will not involve a temporary transitional period of severe difficulty, including unemployment …. Such a shock program could end inflation in months, and would set the stage for the solution of your second major problem – promoting an effective social market economy. This problem is not of recent origin. It arises from trends toward socialism that started 40 years ago, and reached their logical – and terrible – climax in the Allende regime. You have been extremely wise in adopting the many measures you have already taken to reverse this trend …

Sincerely yours
Milton Friedman

May 16, 1975

Distinguished Mr. Friedman,
    I am pleased to acknowledge receipt of your courteous letter of this past April 21 in which you gave me the opinion you formed about the situation and economic policy of Chile after your visit to our country …. The valuable approaches and appraisals drawn from an analysis of the text of your letter coincide for the most part with [my] National Recovery Plan …. Along with reiterating my gratitude for your personal contribution to an analysis of the economic situation of my country, I am also taking this occasion to express my highest and most respectful regard to you.

Courteously yours

Augusto Pinochet Ugarte
General of the Army
President of the Republic

Note
1 Reproduced in the book by Friedman and his wife Rose, (1998, p. 591) with the title 'Two lucky people' [and many unlucky Chileans].

The capital flows that the *Minotaur* thrived upon *and* heightened, created the conditions for a remarkable hybrid: a global monetary system in which good old public money was coexisting with *private money* created almost at will by the financial sector on the back of the *Minotaur*-induced capital flows.

Public money traces its history in IOUs; pieces of paper on which a jeweller would certify that Jill had left with him a quantity of gold. In contrast, our *private money* grew out of contracts that were, in essence, bets on other people's debts. The addition of *private money* to the pool of public money made available by governments was enough to preserve global demand at high levels, to oil the old-fashioned machinery strewn all over the globe and to generate great levels of surplus value.

High as global demand was, there was something rotten in its distribution and, therefore, in the distribution of the surplus value it generated. Capitalism was always predicated upon a distribution that was at odds with its founding Protestant ethic. Imbalances and inequities are as old as rain. Whereas the official ideology advocated that wealth is the just reward of hard work, from the days of the dark satanic mills onwards those who did not work prospered and those who slaved were consigned to poverty. But the imbalances and inequities of the *Minotaur* had a very special feature.

While the United States created the global demand necessary to keep the industries of Japan, Germany and China gainfully employed, and received in return the lion's share of world capital, the rest of the world had to produce more with less capital. Worldwide growth, in this sense, went hand in hand with the draining of capital and the consequent stagnation of the off-centre centres of capitalist accumulation (e.g. Germany and Japan).

Like shifting sands in a desert storm, capital moved inexorably in every conceivable direction. But there was a definite pattern that survived for three decades. It shifted the top soil from the American working class' backyards to the green and pleasant suburbs; it carried mountain ranges worth of the earth's riches to Wall Street; it forced the planet's most productive industries (in Germany and Japan) to send its profits in the same direction and to find ways of passing the curse of stagnation onto their neighbours; it caused the end of hope in the Developing World. The earth became collectively richer but it was hard to find any place untainted by new, more sinister forms of insecurity, frustration, alienation and poverty. A major fresh paradox became the age's trademark and lived happily along with all the other paradoxes that traditionally typified capitalism (and which we described in Chapters 4, 5 and 7).

An unbalanced dynamic system, as any mechanic knows, requires more energy to keep it going than a more balanced one. A badly calibrated bicycle takes more out of its rider because he/she must make up with extra effort that which the contraption lacks in poise; similarly with the *Minotaur*'s globalising capitalism. Having to expand, deepen and amplify imbalances (both across continents but also within the national economies) in order to keep going, its requirements in terms of the necessary aggregate demand were constantly increasing.

What kept the show on the road, despite the swelling paradoxes within, was indeed the growth of *private money*. But like false gods, known or unknown, its days were numbered. The world was being told that risk had been tamed; that the new financial instruments (e.g. the Credit Default Swaps, CDSs) would act as early warning systems, warding off all danger. Crises had been engineered out of capitalism. Double-speak at its best!

In truth, the 'invention' of CDOs and other instances of securitisation, *private money* for short, did precisely the opposite: it exacerbated the forces leading to crisis, ensuring that when it hit it was larger than life, and lulled everyone who counted into a false sense of security. Meanwhile, those whose opinion did not 'count', the population at large, had been distanced from any decision-making process that might have made a difference.

Liberalism, we tend to forget, was traditionally inimical to the idea of democracy. If anyone is in doubt, think of Thomas Hobbes, Immanuel Kant, G.W.F. Hegel: liberals who equated rule by the *Demos* with a living nightmare. And if a more recent example is preferred, we suggest a look at the so-called central bank credibility literature in monetary economics which, effectively, concludes that the central bank, and monetary policy in general, are too important to be left to the democratic process.[7] The guardianship of public money should be given, we were told, to unelected ex-bankers or academics who (once allowed into the enchanted circle of serious money) quickly learn to aspire to becoming real bankers (upon their retirement from the central bank).

Suppose we accept this argument. Why then not hand fiscal matters over to unelected officials too? Why stop at monetary policy? The answer is that the elites would gladly do so if it were not so damned hard to accomplish politically. For it is one thing to persuade pliable parliamentarians to vote away their control of interest rates and quite another to persuade them to give up their power to tax or spend. But it did not matter much.

The solution to that little problem came in the form of (a) using the oligopolised press to ensure that any proposal to increase taxes on those who can afford to pay them is strangled at birth; and (b) imposing stringent limits on spending that was not in the interests of the conglomerates, the banks and those who could have afforded to pay more taxes but were never asked to because of (a).

Thus, economic policy was removed from public scrutiny and both public and private money creation was divorced from the democratic process. Central banks were meant to control both but, after the developments in the world of derivatives (discussed in the previous chapter), they ended up controlling nothing, except the interest rate lever which they used only in reaction to some major downturn (e.g. the bursting of the dot.com bubble in 2000).

At a time when *private money* had the best moves, remaining in control of public money alone must have been very frustrating even for unelected central bankers who had retained a soft spot for what was once known as the Public Interest. Alan Greenspan (see the last page of Chapter 12) conveys the central banker's frustration dilemma vividly: once the *Minotaur* was out of control, he told us, the central banker had a choice between killing the economy by killing the beast or letting the economy die by not tackling it. This is the stuff of moral philosophy Phil101 lecturers: 'A runaway train is about to crush fifty people; would you throw the fat guy on the rails to stop it (especially if you do not know if it would work)?'

When the bubble burst, and the banks proved too big to fail, we discovered that capitalism's basic rules did not apply. Once upon a time, we were told that capitalism promotes efficiency by the force of failure; that bankruptcy is to capitalism what hell is to Christianity; that conglomerates are OK because, even though they have a great deal of monopoly power, some upstart will force them along the evolutionary path to extinction.

But then, post-2008, we found out that conglomerates cannot die. Like zombies they will be maintained by the flesh of the living, spoon-fed by unelected central bankers who turn their unfreedom to tackle the banks into an audacious campaign to convince a dumbfounded public that the solution to the never-ending debt-deflationary crisis is more austerity for workers, less public spending and fewer services to the poor.

Politics being war by other means (to reverse von Clausewitz's famous dictum), we should not be surprised. Central bankers are there not just to regulate the supply of public money and its value in the money markets but to act out their role as major political players. Unelected, but as highly political as it is possible to be, they, more than anyone else, understand that our liberal, Western societies, were designed from the outset so that the rule of the majority was never really about *Rule by the People*. At best it was about fashioning an oligarchy who would gain sufficient legitimacy so as to portray its practices as a form of *Rule on Behalf of the People*.

In this sense, the original idea of democracy (as a collective decision-making mechanism founded on *isegoria*)[8] was designed out of the 'system' from the inception of the 'Western' or the 'Free' World. Its standard invocation of the *People* as the ultimate legitimiser of public policy may sound like an appeal to democracy but, in fact, has a different lineage. Morgan (1988), for instance, argues that the Founding Fathers invented the *idea* of the American People, and of their 'sovereignty', as a means of imposing upon them a stable government over which the People would have no direct control (Morgan 1988).

Though representatives were to be elected, the Federalists were particularly wary of a ruling *Demos*. Indeed some of their texts could have been written by Plato (or some of his anti-democratic disciples). The multitude was to stay out of political deliberation and be content that they are represented in Congress by their social superiors. Who were these to be? Unlike Plato, who thought that the ideal *Republic* ought to be run by the philosophers, the Federalists had another category in mind: *the merchants*.[9] Well, nothing much has changed except that, post-2008, the merchants have given their place to the *bankers*.

The clear blue water between the pre-*Minotaur* and the post-2008 worlds lies in the essential difference between the merchants and the bankers. The former at least had the habit of going to the wall in droves with every crisis, allowing capitalism a modicum of rejuvenation, both economically and politically. The post-*Minotaur* bankers, however, are made of sterner stuff.

Being the custodians of the capital flows that keep the *Minotaur* alive, albeit injured and somewhat diminished, and in full control of the machinery that creates wave upon wave of short lived, highly toxic *private money* (on the back of the state's strengths and weaknesses), the too-big-to-fail financial institutions have put humanity on a path with only one possible destination: *ruin*.

Able to secure guarantees that their losses will always be socialised by panicky politicians (whose only degree of freedom is to socialise these losses), the bankers spend their days taking unfathomable risks with the world at large and pursuing those that owe them money (especially if too poor to be bailed out or a country in deficit).

Back in the 1900s, when Thomas Edison and Henry Ford were wielding a monopoly of socio-economic power, at least the little people understood that these men had put together huge factories producing the instruments of progress. After the war, in the years of the *Global Plan*, the little people could at least fall back on the soothing thought that their rulers were managing a system that could, potentially, be seen as a rational design in which most could maintain hope for a better tomorrow: working class and management, American bankers and Japanese automakers, French farmers and German precision machinists.

Even under the *Global Minotaur*, the end of the Cold War incited hope that an open society might just be possible; growth seemed like a tide that might, one day, lift all boats; the rise of China was a portent of autonomous development, unmediated by some external imperial entity.

The *Crash of 2008* and its aftermath ended all this. Just like 1929 meant curtains for the swinging 1920s, and the beginning of a long depression with tragic consequences, 2008 threatens to be the end of post-war hope and the beginning of a long drawn-out period of introversion, of a race to the bottom, of beggar-thy-neighbour economic policies; of the final retreat from the idea of a Good Society.

What can be done to avert a triumph of pessimism and the privatisation of hope at a global level? Regulation, fiscal stimuli, belt tightening, productivity enhancement, etc. are all beside the point. What matters is who has the power, how he/she uses it and how it can be redistributed.

Today's unassailable power is held in the hands of people who (as Paul Volcker incisively put it) have not innovated since the late 1970s, when they gave us the first ATM. The result of their almost infinite power, not dented in the slightest by the *Crash of 2008*, is that the world has become more unstable than ever before. This must change.

In short, the world faces a stark choice. Not between socialism and capitalism, not between the Anglo-Celtic capitalist model and some Eurasian alternative, but between democracy and trapezocracy.[10] Oligarchy we tried. It gave us the Great Depression, the *Global Plan*, the *Global Minotaur* and, following the latter's *Crash*, circa 2008, it now is on the verge of pushing us into the clasps of *trapezocracy*.

The problem, of course, is that these days democracy has almost as bad an image problem as socialism did after the Berlin Wall was breached. In large parts of the world, it rings hollow, as it was the rallying call of murderous invading armies whose interest in democracy was akin to Genghis Khan's concern for human rights. Elsewhere, the world over, the sound of the word that once inspired people to die for its realisation causes waves of apathy on behalf of electorates. This is a rational response by citizens to the complete devaluation of political goods during the *Minotaur*'s rein; to their transformation from their nations' citizens into the *Minotaur*'s subjects. Why struggle for control of political office when political power lies elsewhere?

Hope may not, currently, shine brightly. The light on the hill may be dim, imperceptible. But if there is a light, it comes from the original idea of democracy as the only possible antidote to trapezocracy and to the calamities that it has in store for us. The task is simple and at once, supremely hard: to utilise the crises that trapezocracy cannot help itself from generating in order to revitalise a global drive towards regaining collective control over our economic system.

It may never happen. But unless it does, humanity will end up like an idiotic virus that destroys its own host.

13.3 Liberty in the shade of a *Globalising Wall*

Before the 'discovery' of the autonomous individual, the ancient polis constantly dreamed of demolishing its walls or, at least, of never having to keep its gates closed. When a son of an ancient Greek city won an Olympics event, the elders ordered the demolition of part of the city walls. Only at times of crisis or degeneracy were the gates ordered shut. Unlike today in North Korea or the southern states of the USA, open gates were, then, a symbol of power. Hadrian and the Chinese Emperors built great walls, but never with the intention of freezing human movement. They were porous walls, mere symbols of their Empires' self-imposed limits and a form of early warning system.

Fences took on a new role and character at the time European feudalism was running out of steam. Under the strain of the commodification that was to lead later, to the industrial revolution and capitalism's rise, the English commons were cut up, fenced off, privatised. Thus the Enclosures 'liberated' the peasants from access to the land of their mothers and the free labourer was born. It was the birth of the *labour contract*, that source of unending indeterminacy in the bosom of market societies.

The American Constitution, a beacon of hope for a still darkened world, revelled in the light of Reason and Liberty while erecting all sorts of fences whose purposes were to cast in legal stone rights of man defined purely in terms of freedom from interference; fences that would keep the riff-raff out and, of course, keep the State and the executive at bay; constitutional fences marking the autonomous realm of the liberal bourgeois individual.

Soon after, the idea of nationhood sprang up in the rest of the Americas by Creole elites fashioned by English and Spanish influences, and in juxtaposition to the American Revolution. Europe, in good time, pirated New World models and embraced the nation-state wholeheartedly. Border fences, in this manner, became synonymous with Modernity in Europe, while in Africa, in the Caribbean, in parts of the American West and of course in Australia, the fence remained for decades the handmaiden of slavery, expropriation and genocide.

Meanwhile, at the level of Theory, for at least three hundred years now, Reason is being defined as the absence of Unreason; *as if* a mighty fence is separating the two, with Reason maintaining a unique narrative to offer to Unreason courtesy of, on the one hand, the economists' *Inherent Error* and, on the other, psychiatry. In the same manner, Freedom is defined almost instinctively as the instrument that demarcates the self and pushes back the interfering others; whether they are foreign armies, migrant workers, one's own employees, the homeless, even one's nearest and dearest.

The very notion of personhood that emerged out of Anglo-Celtic capitalism hinges on the idea of 'well defined' spaces within the 'walls' that exclude. Our concept of Liberty and Progress is, thus, contingent on the prior colonisation of 'alien' others, while our splendid cosmopolitanism is bought at the price of parochial divides that mindlessly cut the Earth's face, giving shape to the map of a world divided, supposedly neatly, into nation-states.

Modernity, in short, spawned fences, walls and fortifications fit for an exciting variety of new roles: they liberated the individual from the tyranny of the 'other'; gave rise to the proletariat, thus massively expanding the productivity of labour; pacified the colonised; marked the nation-state's territory; imprisoned the alien; exterminated inconvenient peoples; institutionalised the weird and, lately, prevented labour mobility in the age of 'Globalisation'. In short, the fence helped destroy the silly old world and gave a hand to the construction of Modern Empires that the Romans could not have imagined.

It was the twentieth century and the dissolution of the great Empires that sped up the Fence's evolution into a *new species of division*. The Great War invented the trench; a cruel quasi-permanent division, dug deeply into the ground, complete with underground quarters, razor sharp wires, minefields. On the one hand the Great War's trenches inaugurated cuts into the land that no land-bound creature could transgress while, in the larger scheme of things, it undid Tsarist Russia, gave birth to the Soviet Union, unravelled the Ottoman and Austro-Hungarian Empires and forced Germany to retreat into an unsustainable Republic behind mutilated borders.

The Second World War brought down what was left of the European empires, and spawned history's greatest peacetime *trench, fault line, division, binary opposition*; one that cut across Eurasia from Finland to the Aegean, from Palestine to Kashmir, through the streets of Nicosia, to the thirty-eighth parallel of the Korean peninsula – the *Iron Curtain* in its various guises. With a persona sinister beyond the imagination of a world full of hope at the end of the war that was meant to end all wars, it spread like a bushfire from continent to continent; each time with added ferocity, as if in order to make amends for the crumbling European Empires.

The post-war *Global Plan* was symbiotic with this division. The origins of its demise coincide with the forces which destabilised the *Global Plan* and paved the ground for the *Minotaur*'s coming. When one of the two sides of the division dissolved, sometime between 1989 and 1991, 'Globalisation' was heralded as the process to dismantle all borders in a universal bid for openness.

It has done no such thing. If anything, the divisions are getting stronger, the walls taller, the fortifications more impenetrable than ever before. To illustrate this, suppose we take a map of the world and draw on it a crude line that:

(a) encircles the Schengen area of Europe (extending it to the parts of Morocco where Europe's fences prevent African migrants from entering the promised land, and taking in the area on the western side of Sharon's Wall in Palestine);

(b) jumps across the Atlantic to include North America, while cutting Mexico off with the brutal determination of the US-Mexican border; and finally

(c) leaps over the Pacific to include Japan, Australia and New Zealand (countries also cut off from their neighbours by an invisible but equally impenetrable wall).

What will we end up with? With a walled part of the world which, in fact, is literally shielded by a wall, a fence, a minefield, a gunboat ready to fire at ramshackle boats full of exhausted humans! All these borders are hermetically sealed *vis-à-vis* their neighbouring regions. The *Globalising Wall* sprang up during the era of the *Global Minotaur*. It was not coincidence.

In fact, its bits and pieces have almost merged into one large *Globalising Wall* that is slithering across the planet's surface with an unparalleled determination to divide, to sepa-rate, to create greater insecurity in people's lives; always in the name of security.[11]

If we look at the economic footprint of this *Globalising Wall* (Figure 13.1), we find that, *circa* 2008, around 15 per cent of the world's population lived within it. Their income? A whopping 74 per cent. Had we looked in 1971, we would have found a different mix: 28 per cent within those same borders sharing only 59 per cent of world GDP.

While the *Minotaur* expanded its dominion, trade and capital were liberated from border controls. But at the same time, the fences and dividing lines that separate people keep getting less porous, taller, more intimidating. They are becoming a pandemic.

Besides the *Wall*'s main presence, its tentacles spread far and wide, like rivulets that flow into the main river. In places, they reinforced older divisions that emerged like fault lines from the Cold War (e.g. the divisions in Cyprus, Kashmir, Palestine, Korea) or from even further back (e.g. the former Yugoslavia). In other regions, new cracks that soon developed into fault lines crept up on the soil, mostly the result of tensions brought on by the growing imbalances caused by the *Minotaur*'s footprint.

From Botswana to the streets of Baghdad, from Mitrovica to the valleys of Chechnya, Allah and God are often blamed but, in truth, they are just scapegoats for purely secular forces that would never even allow the competing gods the impossible task of drawing 'just' borders between their people.

Therein lays another wrinkle to the Grand Paradox that is our post-2008 world: the *more* we develop reasons for dismantling the dividing lines the *less* powerful the forces working to dismantle them. Deep divisions, patrolled by merciless guards, seem to be the homage that our supposedly enterprise culture pays to misanthropy.

The end of the *Global Plan* at first, the rise of the *Global Minotaur* and the subsequent demise of the Cold War later caused disarray among the elites worldwide. The generalised

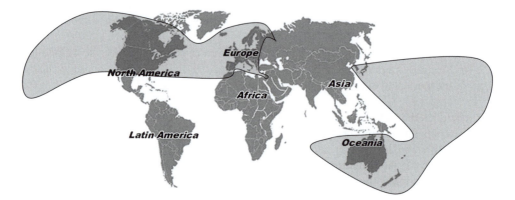

Figure 13.1 The *Globalising Wall*.

In 2008 the shaded area contained 15% of the world's population whose income amounted to 74% of world income. More importantly, however, the shaded area is divided *physically* from the rest by a *Globalising Wall*; a sequence of fences, fortifications, walls, minefields etc. whose explicit purpose is to keep the 'others' at bay.

Box 13.3 Tyranny matters!

And I am bringing you the news:
In India
In the city of Calcutta
they stopped on his way.
A man who was walking
and they chained him.

And I don't bother anymore
to lift my head toward the bright skies.
If the stars are far,
if the earth is small
I don't care at all
I don't mind....

I want you to know that I find
more astonishing
more powerful
more mysterious and gigantic

THIS MAN
stopped on his way
and chained

A poem by Nâzım Hikmet [Microcosm 1934, in Hikmet (1954)]

---

global deflation that was burning slowly under the cover of the *Minotaur*-powered growth of the pre-2008 years created social tensions within most societies that had to send Wall Street its daily capital tributes. The Wall grew stronger and more brutish in response to the tension on both of its sides.

The elites themselves were divided. Parts of them failed to join in the financial capital's migratory routes towards the *Minotaur*. Even those who joined failed to understand what was going on. The irrationality of the world's order, especially after the loss of ideological illusions about being on the side of Liberty, in the struggle against Totalitarianism, begat confusion, doubt, loss of direction. A tide of fear threatened to drown all. Fear of the migrant, the terrorist, the different, the 'other'. It spread from the workplace to the airport, from the schoolyard to the shopping mall.

In places where no walls existed, all sorts of divisive fears were invented. The streets of Bradford, the Northern beaches of Australia, the ports of Sicily became new battlegrounds where insecure states took their anxieties out on wretched migrants. On the old Cold War faultiness, the existing walls were reinvented. They remain the only fixed point now that the Soviet influence is gone and the US withdrew, concerned solely with the feeding of its *Minotaur*.

Then, in 2008, the *Minotaur* fell seriously ill. Confusion was added to confusion. How will the *Globalising Wall* react, especially if and when the emerging trapezocracy causes further crises, lower growth, greater instability, deeper insecurity? During the past few decades the *Wall* became the only certainty in a shifting ocean of doubt and against the background of a global economy that everyone *feels* was on the brink of something nasty. It offered a precious link with a past that seemed better than the present, and idyllic compared to the murky future. Its future will depend on whether a new truly *Global Plan* emerges that will settle the world's nerves and recreate hope of stability, security and a chance for empowerment that comes neither from the barrel of a gun nor from access to *private money*.

In the midst of such anxieties, it is well worth recalling that crises are the laboratory of the future. They fashion new opportunities that the past could never have imagined. The *Minotaur*'s recent weakness may well spawn the circumstances for a world free of systemic divisions. As long as humanity remains indeterminate, hope's candle will continue to burn brightly. After all, Yeats taught us that no humanism can be authentic that has not passed through its own negation.[12] The *Minotaur* years, as well as the menacing trapezocracy, may well turn out to have been our negation.

13.4 Epilogue

The *Crash of 2008*, and the subsequent economic crisis, has exposed, among other things, the irrelevance of the economists' mindset. As our verdict on economic theory was summed up in the Postscript to *Book 1* (see Chapter 10), we shall say no more here other than to remark on the sad insignificance of the pre-2008 contest between 'monetarists' and the so-called 'Keynesians'; between those favouring inflation targets and those against the fans of zero inflation; between advocates of microeconomic reform in the labour markets and others paying more attention to the credibility of central banks. All these debates, it turns out, were beside the point. The world was on a trajectory that moved from post-war centrally planned stability, to designed disintegration in the 1970s, to an intentional magnification of unsustainable imbalances in the 1980s and, finally, to the most spectacular privatisation of money in the 1990s and beyond.

Presently, the world is precariously balanced. At the time of signing off this book, the global economy is on the verge of a new recessionary spin, following the sovereign debt crisis that ensued in 2010, after the financial sector was propped up with public money. The reader, by the time these lines are read, will know more than we do about how the short term panned out. We shall simply note that the announcement of 'recovery' seems to have been terribly premature. For even if only 25 per cent of the income the world lost in 2008–9 proves permanent, the long-term value of these losses for humanity will come to more than 70 per cent (some say 90 per cent) of annual world income.

Meanwhile, we cannot even seek solace in the thought that the *Crash of 2008* had some redemptive effects on the world economy in terms of returning us to a more stable situation. It has not! Rather, it has simply transferred more of the burdens of systemic failure onto the shoulders of public authorities; which are now tempted to follow Herbert Hoover (see Chapter 7) in cutting deficits at a time of looming recession.

Whether they do or do not follow Hoover's risible policies, the sands of time are counting down to the moment when the exorbitant privilege of the United States (i.e. the Dollar's unquestionable reserve currency status) will be challenged. Ironically, the Dollar's status may be the only thing that stops us currently from sliding into a new 1930s style depression. However, the imbalances are due to grow stronger and the only way that a crisis can be averted (one that may even acquire non-economic manifestations) is by means of a major re-jigging of world capitalism.

In this reading, the *Crash of 2008* was not just an act of nemesis but a warning of what is to come. It gave us a glimpse of an underlying reality that could only laugh loudly when in proximity to the economists' theories. Those who want to take advantage of this 'glimpse' will discern an international political economy alive with an ultimately geopolitical contest between surplus and deficit sovereign entities. Within those entities themselves, other, more traditional, distributional contests continue and a series of feedback effects are running back-wards and forwards between the global and the local contests. The only certainty we have is that the manner in which the *Crash of 2008* was dealt with, by infusions of trillions of dollars of public money, has arrested the collapse, has restored the power of the financial sector and has created the circumstances for greater instability.

In short, our hunch is that the world is spinning out of control, despite the better efforts of the powers that be to stabilise it. Just like Greenspan's interest rate rise came too late to deflate the pre-2008 bubble, so will the crop of regulatory changes that will be introduced shortly do nothing to change the dynamic. The only hope for a rational future is a massive transfer in social power away from the 'markets' (i.e. the banks) to those who cannot be captured by them because they are too many to bribe, threaten and extort: *Global Labour*.

Labour must come to see that the *Minotaur* has extinguished the post-war dream of a Good Society sustained by balanced growth and social justice. The crisis of social democ-racy is nothing but a side-effect. Old recipes for social justice and economic growth stand no chance in the post-2008 world. Neither the nation-state nor the market can help labour claim the share of the global pie that will stabilise the world we live in. The narrative of empower-ment through education is bogus; the older idea that trade unions are about wrestling a higher percentage of the surplus from specific bosses grossly inadequate; the hope that new legislation will avert environmental disaster quixotic; the promise of progress through free trade a pipedream.

The new task ahead is as simple as it is daunting: to create a *New Global Plan*. However, this time there are no New Dealers to design it on our behalf. Judging by what happened when they did, and despite its many successes, it is perhaps a good thing that we cannot bank on the New Dealers' successors today. The *New Global Plan* will have to be democratic, if only because nothing else seems to last. But what does democratic really mean?

It means that those who earn by actually *working* (and who do not rely on speculating with other people's money or default probabilities), independently of whether they live in the United States, China, India, Africa or Europe, will have to have a say in the *New Plan*'s constitution; that on that basis they must be allowed to tap into the almost infinite wealth doing the rounds in the international capital markets daily. In the long run, there may not be another way of taking out the *Minotaur* and his helpers and of imposing the rule of Reason on our grossly irrational market societies.

And what would the *New Global Plan* look like? We are tempted to use our favourite line in this book: *we are damned if we know!* However, a book inspired by the *Crash of 2008* that began with Aristotle, ended with Greenspan, and warned that the future demands a clash between democracy and trapezocracy, is a book that ought not to end without a sketch of an idea of a vision of what a future *New Global Plan* might look like. Given that the *Minotaur* and the associated trapezocracy will not lie down and die, a fight is in the offing. But is there a future socio-economic arrangement worth fighting for? Can this question be answered in brief without instantly confining the answer to the too-hard, too-utopian basket?

In his little book, *The Meaning of Life*, Terry Eagleton (2007: 171–4) faced a similarly daunting task: to capture, in brief, the meaning of life. His answer was: a band like the Cuban *Buena Vista Social Club*; that's the meaning of life! Eagleton's point was that such a band illustrates the dialectic at its best: a 'community' with a clear, unifying tune towards which each 'individual' contributes by improvising. Its members do not mechanically play from some given score, written by a despotic musical mind (however brilliant that mind might be), but, rather, integrate their own private freedom into a collective pursuit which enhances the experience of each of its members. Their improvisation confirms their private freedom not by having each note whimsically selected by autonomous players but, rather, when all the various pieces of improvisation fall into place, as if by the nod of some invisible conductor.

Our parable for the *New Global Plan*, for a social economy that we think is worth fighting for, also comes from the Americas: the US National Football League! Think of it: the NFL is a paragon of aggressive competitiveness. On the pitch, extremely well prepared players give their all for victory, wealth and glory. Teams pull no punches to win. The road to the Grand Final is littered with injured bodies, broken egos but, in the process, a great deal of satisfaction and camaraderie is shared by everyone, winners and losers, both on and off the pitch.

Meanwhile, the League is based on a Central Plan. Teams cannot spend highly differential amounts on salaries and the best new players are *forced* to sign with the weakest teams. The market works but to do so it must be severely circumscribed by the Common Pursuit. The constraints liberate the true spirit of competition, preventing the successful from monopolising the best players and killing off the interest of most matches.

Thus, planning and competition are fused into a League that minimises predictability and maximises excitement. Socialist planning lives in sin with unbridled competition right under the spotlight of American showbusiness!

All we need do is think of a way to organise the game of human life along the NFL's lines, merely substituting the goal of maximising the audience's excitement with that of minimising humanity's chances of ending up like a dim, self-defeating virus.

Notes

2 *Condorcet's Secret*: On the significance of classical political economics today

1 See Westfall (1980), Dobbs (1991) and of course Keynes (1947).
2 'When there are disputes among men, we can simply say: Calculate, without further ceremony, to see who is right.' « Projet et Essais pour arriver à quelque certitude pour finir une bonne partie des disputes et pour avancer l'art d'inventer » in Couturat (1903) pp. 175–82, at p. 176.
3 Examples: Karl Marx 'In France and in England the bourgeoisie had conquered political power. Thenceforth, the class struggle, practically as well as theoretically, took on more and more outspoken and threatening forms. It sounded the knell of scientific bourgeois economy. It was thenceforth no longer a question, whether this theorem or that was true, but whether it was useful to capital or harmful, expedient or inexpedient, politically dangerous or not. In place of disinterested inquirers, there were hired prize fighters; in place of genuine scientific research, the bad conscience and the evil intent of apologetic.' (1873) Afterword to the Second German edition of *Capital*, Vol. 1.), John Bates Clark: 'While there is no danger that any theory may establish a permanent reign of practical socialism, there is a general and not unfounded fear of agitations and attempts in this direction; and systems of economic science must submit to be judged, not merely by their correctness or incorrectness, but by their seeming tendency to strengthen or to weaken the social fabric. In this view can that theory be the one desired which in any way obscures the action of moral forces in originating, developing and sustaining the institution of property, and which tends, however remotely, to place that institution again on a *de facto* basis?' Clark 1883, p. 363. Böhm-Bawerk: 'to-day [1884, exploitation theory] forms the theoretical focal point around which move the forces of attack and defence in the struggle of organising human society.' (Böhm-Bawerk (1884 [1921]) p. 318.) Some, like Hayek (*Road to Serfdom*) unconvincingly pretend to separate the political from the economic.
4 To give an example: much has been made of the inability of Marxian theory to solve the so-called transformation problem and its unrealistic hypothesis of a uniform organic composition of capital (see Sweezy 1949). But when the same criticism was levelled against the neoclassical capital theory nothing much happened (see Harcourt, 1972).
5 As Galileo noted in 1632 'in the natural sciences, whose conclusions are true and necessary and have nothing to do with human will, one must take care not to place oneself in the defense of error, for here a thousand Demostheneses and a thousand Aristotles would be left in the lurch by every mediocre wit who happened to hit upon the truth for himself'. Galileo Galilei, *Dialogue Concerning the Two Chief World Systems, Ptolemaic & Copernican*, (1632 [1967]) pp. 53–4.
6 'And it is of these goods that riches in the true sense at all events seem to consist. For the amount of such property sufficient in itself for a good life is not unlimited (*apeiros*, infinite), as Solon says that it is in the verse. "But of riches no bound has been fixed or revealed to men" for a limit has been fixed, as with the other arts, since no tool belonging to any art is without a limit whether in number or in size, and riches are a collection of tools for the householder and the statesman. Therefore that there is a certain art of acquisition belonging in the order of nature to householders and to statesmen, and for what reason this is so, is clear. But there is another kind of acquisition that is specially called wealth-getting (*chrêmatistikê*), and that is so called with justice and to this kind it is due that there is thought to be no limit to riches and property' *Politics* 1256b30–42. Aristotle goes on to condemn wealth-getting chrematistics as contrary to nature. In the process of doing so makes the distinction between what later would be called 'value in use' and 'value in exchange', or rather use of a thing

for the purpose it has been created and use of a thing for exchange (1257a). This exchange, however, must be done only to attain self-sufficiency.

7 Before Aristotle, Xenophon in his *Oeconomicus* reports an attempt by Socrates to define what things are useful and what are not. Socrates, however, aborts the endeavour since it is the virtuous life we should seek, not the usefulness of things. Interestingly enough, after Socrates has shown that the whole exercise of defining the task of an 'economist' (*oikonomos* i.e. an estate manager) is philosophically impossible, Xenophon embarks on explaining the art of good estate management. Even more interestingly we find out that the model of an *oikonomos* and perfect Athenian gentleman, Ischomachos, has relegated the task of estate management to his teenage wife, who remained nameless, and she in turn gave that task to a virtuous and able slave woman. See Xenophon (1994).

8 Aristotle's theory of value as part of a *reciprocal* exchange assumed also that exchange was *equivalent*. This aspect of his theory was preserved in classical political economy and Marx, but it was anathema to neoclassicists. See the comments of Georgescu-Roegen about a 'physicalist explanation' and von Mises about an 'inveterate fallacy' (in Theocarakis (2006), pp. 41 and 46).

9 We are using June Barraclough's translation Condorcet (1955 [1979]), p. 30. Admittedly, the French original [and the 1795 English translation] is less dramatic but the spirit of the text is preserved in the translation we use. The original reads: 'et la force comme l'opinion ne peuvent forger des chaînes durables, si les tyrans n'étendent pas leur empire à une distance assez grande pour pouvoir cacher à la nation qu'ils oppriment, en la divisant, le secret de sa puissance et de leur foiblesse'. Condorcet (1794), p. 53. Equally the more faithful English translation of 1795 reads 'and force as well as opinion could forge no durable chains, if tyrants did not extend their empire to a distance sufficiently great to be able, by dividing the nation they oppressed, to conceal from it the secret of its own power and of their weakness'. Condorcet (1795) pp. 49–50. The work was edited posthumously, but Condorcet must have written it in hiding during the last year of his life (1794).

10 There was of course commodity exchange under feudalism. But the 'economic' theory of the period was more concerned with the 'just price' that should be paid. This mainly ethical theory developed by the scholastic theologians was more concerned with setting up a price so that those who paid it and those who charged it would live in a manner consistent with the existing social – god ordained – hierarchy. This view may have been challenged by modern historiography but we believe that this is the more plausible one. We also know that we greatly simplify here in order to make the point that political economy was created when there was a need to explain how surplus is distributed when market is the dominant form of economic organisation. After feudalism we have the period of mercantilism where the modern states have been created, and we moved from a situation where the economy and society was divided to create nation states and national economies. (See Schmoller, (1884 [1896]) and Heckscher, *Mercantilism*, (1935 [1994]). The theory of value of this period was more directed to explain the factors that determine buyers' preferences, and was not concerned with the distribution of surplus, since profits were made mostly by buying cheap and selling dear outside the realm. It was a period of state control of the economy and early laissez faire economists, like Boisguilbert, at the beginning of the eighteenth century, were concerned with breaking the state's grip over the economy. Adam Smith's Book IV of the *Wealth of Nations* is the most well known critique of mercantilist policies. On the role of this period for the birth of capitalism (see Box 2.2) on the commercialisation thesis.

11 Indeed, Adam Smith in his *Wealth of Nations*, argues that in order for the division of labour to be observed, we have to study it in 'trifling manufactures' (1776 [1981], I.i. p. 14) since it is lost in society at large.

12 The reader may protest that workers, in reality, are paid after they work. This is not the point. The issue here is that capitalists are contracted to pay wages in the short term (e.g. at the end of the working week) *independently of the timing of the output's market sale*. On the same question, the demanding reader may raise the point that feudal lords can also be thought of as paying wages in advance, in the form of goods (such as meals) that they made available to peasants before the work was done and the harvest was in. Be that as it may, just like it is always true that pre-capitalist societies featured markets *without being market societies*, equally, some portion of the feudal surplus was advanced to peasants without, however, altering the fact that the bulk of the surplus was distributed *ex post*.

13 Even those who did not leave the countryside were now employed as rural wage labourers.

14 Recall the title of Bernard Mandeville's 1714 book: *The Fable of the Bees: or, Private Vices, Publick Benefits* (Mandeville (1714 [1924])). The provocative title of the book met with a huge reaction from the moralists of the day. Mandeville was a mercantilist and the point he was making was different from Smith's. The difference between him and the Scottish philosopher, however, was that Smith thought that it was self-interest tempered by moral qualities that was responsible for the realisation of the common good through commerce. The attribution of civilising qualities to 'sweet commerce' calmed the moralists; and instead of exculpating greed, elevated 'self-interest' to the moral high ground. German authors of the nineteenth-century could not understand how the moral philosopher and author of *The Theory of the Moral Sentiments* could also write the encomium of self-interest in the *Wealth of Nations*; hence they called the conundrum *Das Adam Smith Problem* (See Oncken 1897, 1898).

15 Keynes writes about Silvio Gesell in Chapter 23 of his *General Theory* that his 'main book is written in cool, scientific language, though it is suffused throughout by a more passionate, a more emotional devotion to social justice than some think decent in a scientist'. (Keynes 1936, p. 219). We share Keynes' sarcasm and we think that scientific decency is enhanced by concern with justice.

3 The odd couple: The struggle to square a theory of value with a theory of growth

1 The fact that most ancient Greek texts were initially transmitted through Arab translations into the West is well documented, despite recent attempts to discredit Islamic scholarship (e.g., Gouguenheim, 2008). Averroes' commentaries on Aristotle were translated into Latin quite early and a printed edition was available in the sixteenth century. It was, however, after proper translations into Latin from the Greek originals in the thirteenth century that the West used Aristotle extensively, to an extent that most scholarship was Aristotelian. If anything, the seventeenth century in the West had a love–hate relationship with Aristotle. Our point here, however, is that the Islamic concept of Paradise is one where affluence of goods is opposed to a measly terrestrial existence and that concept set images of possible surpluses.

2 Indeed, Richard Cantillon, an author who had strongly influenced the Physiocrats entitled a chapter of his book, *Essai sur la nature du commerce en général*: "All Classes and Individuals in a State Subsist or are Enriched at the Expense of the Proprietors of Land" [Cantillon (1755 [1931]), Part I, Chapter XII]. This posthumous work that has been called by Jevons 'the cradle of political economy' was written by an international financier and not a landlord, so strong was the imprint of the importance of land on people's minds, even though Cantillon was more impressed by the right of property of the land than by its cultivation.

3 Indeed, just after the physiocratic movement petered out, the post-physiocratic engineer Achylle-Nicolas Isnard, in his *traité des richesses* (1781) has constructed a model in which surplus was generated in all sectors of the economy (Berg 2006). See Kurz and Salvadori (2000).

4 For the physiological metaphors in Quesnay, see Foley (1973) and Christensen (1994).

5 The *tableau economique* purported to show that it is possible for an economy to reproduce itself – without the need for regulation – only through the material and monetary flows between the three sectors. For various editions of the *tableau* see: Quesnay (1758 [1972]). In other physiocratic works the *tableau* was used, by changing its parameters, to derive more sophisticated models of growth, particularly in Mirabeau (1762). On the importance of the *tableau* for the Physiocrats see Higgs (1897).

6 In the original *tableau*, even though Quesnay speaks of classes, he has sectors in mind. Only after the greatest French economist of the eighteenth century, Jacques Turgot, the analysis of classes became more sophisticated within the physiocratic paradigm. See Anne Robert Jacques, Turgot, *Reflections on the Formation and Distribution of Wealth*, Condorcet, trans.(?), London: E. Spragg. 1793 [Original first French edition 1766].

7 We are referring to Marx's discussion of the Physiocrats in his *Theories of Surplus Value* (see Box 3.2) and, in particular, to Volume 2 of *Das Kapital* (1885), where reproduction is the major theme. The numerical examples are worked out in Chapter 20. John von Neumann's famous growth model is Neumann (1937 [1998]). English translation by Neumann (1945–6). For Wassily Leontief, see Leontief (1936, 1966). For Piero Sraffa, see Sraffa (1960). For the history of these schemes see Kurz and Salvadori (2000). See also the Appendix 'On Reproduction Schemes' by Shigeto Tsuru in Sweezy (1942 [1970]).

8 This is, of course, our own rendering of the *tableau*, which is somewhat different from that commonly found in History of Economic Thought textbooks. The original device was much more convoluted and difficult to work with it. A physiocratic *tableau économique* would look like this

Reproduced from Mirabeau 1767. See Loïc 2004.

9 All of modern mainstream (or neoclassical) economics posits a society comprised of individuals who belong to no social class and enjoy identical rights, privileges as well as institutional, political and market power. Our divided and deeply inegalitarian world is, thus, theorised as if it were a specimen of radical egalitarianism in action. (See Chapter 5 and Book 2) for more on this.

10 In Box 3.1 we hinted at this by working out the logical conclusion of the input–output model embedded in the physiocratic tradition in the form of two inequalities. If surplus is to be generated in both the agricultural and the industrial or artisanal sectors, these inequalities pinpoint the minimum prices per unit of output consistent with a positive profit; which is equivalent to a positive overall surplus.

11 See Box 2.1 in the previous chapter.

12 For a detailed account of the impact on values when labour's share of the surplus changes, in connection to the theories of Adam Smith and David Ricardo, see Sylos-Labini (1984).

13 Or, as Adam Smith puts it in the famous passage on the 'invisible hand' (*Wealth of Nations*, Smith (1776 [1981]) IV, ii, p. 456) 'I have never known much good done by those who affected to trade for the publick good. It is an affectation, indeed, not very common among merchants, and very few words need be employed in dissuading them from it.'

14 Marx is actually quoting Smith: 'Industry, indeed, provides the subject which parsimony accumulates' (*Wealth of Nations*, 1776, II. iii., p. 337) even though something is lost in translation from English to German and back (see Box 3.3).

15 Free market zealots often forget that Adam Smith is not just the author of the *Wealth of Nations* in 1776 but that person who authored the *Theory of Moral Sentiments* in 1759. In the latter he discussed the conditions that must hold *before* the market mechanism can be counted upon to turn self interest into social welfare. The primary condition for this to happen, Smith argued, is that society has already established the social conventions that cultivate further the natural sympathy for one another that we come to the world with. In this sense, Smith would not have been at all surprised that the overnight transition from communism to free markets in the ex-Soviet Union and its satellites, in a vacuum of 'moral sentiments', resulted in a market economy emulating the worst excesses of the most heinous Mafia.

16 Another assumption that would have had a similar analytical result is the assumption that capital intensity is the same across all sectors of the economy. Thomas Robert Malthus explicitly argued this in his critique of David Ricardo's economics. Smith may have predicted that critique and concluded that it is less unrealistic to presume a constant distribution of income than to assume that all production processes, from farming to needle manufacturing to shipbuilding, etc., involved the same degree of capital intensity.

17 Ricardo cut his political teeth in Parliament, arguing vehemently for the repeal of the *Corn Laws* which restricted the importation of corn into Britain, laws that the aristocrats had actively worked to implement in order to maintain their high wartime rents.

18 The *corn model* appeared in Ricardo (1815 [1951]).

19 As capital migrates out of the less profitable sector, supply in that sector declines, prices rise and consequently the profit rate increases. In contrast, the more profitable sector towards which capital flows experiences an increase in supply, a reduction in prices and a drop in the profit rate. This movement was expected to continue until the profit rates across the two sectors are equal, at which point capital movements would end. Notice a nice analytical repercussion of this assumption: all of a sudden the inequalities in Box 3.1 can now be turned into equality simply by adding on the right-hand side a profit term such that the profit rate is the same across the sectors. Once the inequalities have thus become equalities, it is possible to solve like a system of equations for the relative prices. This is indeed what we do in the next chapter (see Section 4.2).

20 As in the previous note only this time the factor of production that migrates is labour. As workers move from lower to higher wage sectors, wage rates tend to equalise throughout the economy.

21 Ricardo (1815 [1951]) p. 21.

22 Recall the inequality between ratios R_1 and R_2 when the production processes yielding two goods involve different degrees of capital intensity. Indeed, in the case of David Ricardo, it was Thomas Robert Malthus who first pointed out this incongruity, an incongruity which we refer to throughout this book as economics' *Inherent Error*.

23 The standard edition which combines the three editions (1817, 1819 and 1821) of Ricardo's *Principles* is Vol. 1 of the 11-volume edition *The Works and Correspondence of David Ricardo*, edited by Piero Sraffa; with the collaboration of M.H. Dobb. Ricardo (1817/1819/1821 [1951]).

24 Note that Malthus' point is neither here nor there in the Box 3.4 model. The reason, of course, is that in that model there was no machinery. Analytically, this is equivalent to assuming a constant capital intensity.

4 The trouble with humans: The source of radical indeterminacy and the touchstone of value

1 Recall their tale in which a magic pot producing porridge goes out of control, spewing rivers of porridge into the village's houses and streets and refuses to be shut down unless the magic words are uttered. Like Prometheus' liver which is renewed in perpetuity to prolong his punishment, the pot

punishes the user by refusing to cease producing that which she had craved. 'The sweet porridge' (*Der süße Brei*) is a fairy tale of the 'magical mill' type (Aarne-Thompson-Uther Type 565) of which 'how the sea became salty' and capitalism are its most famous examples (see Chapter 2, Box 2.4). The tale first appeared in the second volume of the *Kinder und Hausmärchen* of the Brothers Grimm in 1815. It is tale number 103 of the standard edition. See Grimm (1843), p. 104.

2   We are referring to *The Terminator* series of movies that gave Arnold Schwarzenegger memorable lines such as 'I will be back' and the public persona which helped him become Governor of the State of California. The first of the series, *The Terminator*, was released in 1984, followed by *Terminator 2: Judgment Day* in 1991 (both directed by John Cameron) and *Terminator 3: The Rise of the Machines* in 2003 (dir. Jonathan Mostow). The fourth instalment in 2009 was without Schwarzenegger who was by then Governor. The *Blade Runner* was released in 1982 and it was directed by Ridley Scott. Its script was loosely based on Philip K. Dick's 1968 novel *Do Androids Dream of Electric Sheep?*

3   We say 'usual' because the idea of machines unleashing nuclear rockets in order to destroy their human 'masters' is a common ploy science fiction uses as a precursor to the post-apocalypse world where its narratives unfold, e.g. *The Terminator* movies.

4   Solving (4.6) given these parameter values yields:

$$p = \frac{(1-w) + \sqrt{(w-1)^2 + 40}}{10}$$

since $p \geq 0$.

5   Note that we do not enter coefficients for goods that are free such as air or water.

6   To see the derivation, set $w=0$ into the equation of endnote 4 above to get

$$p = \frac{1 + \sqrt{41}}{10} \approx 0.74$$

Substituting this value into the growth rate equation for the assumed values of the parameters we get

$$g = \frac{p(1-\alpha) - q\beta}{p\alpha + q\beta} \approx 49.22\%$$

This is the growth rate of our economy for both sectors. We can also see that this the rate at which both N and M grow as follows. Note that in every period of our economy the output of one period is the input for the next. The two sectors of the economy must work at different intensities or scales in order for this condition to apply. Since we are interested only in relevant intensities we can make the intensity of *sector 2* equal to one and we must solve for the intensity of *sector 1*. *Sector 2* will produce one unit of M with δ units of N and ε units of M: $\delta N + \varepsilon M \rightarrow M$. For *sector 1*, the equivalent equation is $\alpha N + \beta M \rightarrow N$, but since it works at intensity x, everything is multiplied by that, so we have $\alpha N x + \beta M x \rightarrow N x$. For the total economy the output then is xN for N and xM for M. The input requirements for N of the next cycle are $\alpha N x$ for *sector 1* and δN for *sector 2*, that is a total of $\alpha x + \delta$ units of N. These produce x units of N. Therefore the growth rate of N is $\frac{x}{\alpha x + \delta} - 1$ which must be equal to the growth rate of the economy g. Hence $\frac{x}{\alpha x + \delta} - 1 = g \Rightarrow x \approx 1.85$. Equally, the input requirements for M of the next cycle are $\beta M x$ for *sector 1* and εM for *sector 2*, that is a total of $\beta x + \varepsilon$ units of M. These provide one unit of M giving a growth rate equal to $\frac{1}{\beta x + \varepsilon} = g \approx 49.22\%$. This is the gist of the von Neumann (1937) growth model. In the latter, things are more complicated since each production process is visualised as a number (less or equal to n) of inputs producing a number of outputs (also less or equal to n, where n is the total number of goods in the economy). For example, a very elementary von Neumann economy would be one with two goods (chicken and eggs) and two processes (laying and hatching). In the laying process, one chicken (the input) could lay 12 eggs and the output would be 1 chicken (the original) and the 12 eggs. In the hatching process one can have as inputs one chicken and 4 eggs and get as output 5 chickens (the hatched eggs and the original); see Kemeny *et al.* (1966).

7 Which can be easily computed as $g_H = \dfrac{p(1-\alpha)-\beta-w\gamma}{p\alpha+\beta} = \dfrac{(1-\varepsilon)-p\delta-w\zeta}{p\delta+\varepsilon}$

8 The mathematics are tedious but straightforward. Since,

$$g_H = \frac{p(1-\alpha)-\beta-w\gamma}{p\alpha+\beta} \Rightarrow w = \frac{(1-\alpha(g_H+1))p - \beta(g_H+1)}{\gamma}$$

or in our numerical example $w = (1-0.4(g_H+1))p - 0.2(g_H+1)$

Since $\dfrac{p(1-\alpha)-\beta-w\gamma}{p\alpha+\beta} = \dfrac{(1-\varepsilon)-p\delta-w\zeta}{p\delta+\varepsilon}$

we get that

$$w = \frac{[p(1-\alpha)-\beta](p\delta+\varepsilon)-[(1-\varepsilon)-p\delta](p\alpha+\beta)}{[\gamma(p\delta+\varepsilon)-\zeta(p\alpha+\beta)]}$$

which in our numerical example becomes

$$w = \frac{5p^2 - p - 2}{-p}$$

and get a more complicated expression for p.

$$p = \frac{[1+0.2(g_H+1)] + \sqrt{[1+0.2(g_H+1)]^2 + 8[5+(1-0.4(g_H+1))]}}{2[5+(1-0.4(g_H+1))]}$$

which for $g_H = 0$ gives a p of around 0.714 and a w of 0.229. Note that if g_H is higher than 49.22%, w becomes zero and 49.22% is the upper bound for the growth rate of the economy.

9 In equations 4.1 and 4.2 the inequalities become equalities, i.e. $p = p\alpha + q\beta + w\gamma$ and $q = p\delta + q\varepsilon + w\zeta$. You could check by substituting our numerical examples noting that $p \approx 0.714$, $w \approx 0.229$ and $q = 1$.

10 This is nicely consistent with the film's theme of a wholesale war launched by killer machines against the band of human rebels who plot to rescue their brothers and sisters from the *Matrix*, thus (one presumes) making human heat available to machines more scarce.

11 This is due to the fact that this particular *Matrix Economy* is assumed to rely more on the machinery produced in *sector 1* than those in the second sector (recall that $\alpha = 4/10$ and $\beta = 2/10$ whereas $\delta = 5/10$ and $\varepsilon = 3/10$).

12 A somewhat different criticism of the Ricardian labour theory of value was raised by proto-Marginalist economists like Nassau W. Senior, who asked whether 'wine in a cellar, or oak in its progress from a sapling to a tree' were also creating value (Senior 1836, p. 152). Indeed, the whole discussion about 'natural agents' that led to the definition of 'factors of production' was inspired by an attempt to dethrone labour and ascribe value creating properties to 'natural agents'. But as Marx (1875 [1962], p. 15) wrote: 'Labour is not the source of all wealth. Nature is ... [But] to the extent that man from the beginning behaves towards nature, the first source of all means and subjects of labour, as an *owner*, treats her as belonging to him, *his labour becomes the source of use values*, and also of wealth' (emphasis in the original). See Theocarakis (2010). So natural processes in themselves do not create value.

13 When astronomers are speculating regarding some distant planet where a kind of murky atmosphere may be maintained by bacteria and other relatively simple organisms, by the ebb and flow of gamma rays emitted from its sun and by various other organic and inorganic forces, they too speak

of the *function* that each of these life forms and inorganic factors play. Nothing would be added to their analysis by bringing into the discussion the concept of *value*.

14 This does not mean that our position is shared by all. Indeed, a common mathematical structure of certain problems leads some to conclusions that their essence is similar. In the natural world this may lead to the so-called *pathetic fallacy*: ascribing consciousness to inanimate objects. In economics it can be the reverse: to assume that economic problems are problems similar to those of the natural world. The great Paul Samuelson was fascinated by the mathematical structure of economics and attempted to make maximisation under constraint almost tantamount to the definition of our science. See in particular his 1970 Nobel Prize Lecture: 'Maximum principles in analytical economics' (Samuelson 1970) and the striking opening paragraph of his *Foundations of Economic Analysis* (Samuelson 1947): '*The existence of analogies between central features of various theories implies the existence of a general theory which underlies the particular theories and unifies them with respect to those central features* ... It is the purpose of the pages that follow to work out [this fundamental principle's] implications for theoretical and applied economics'. In linear programming, for example, the same tools were used for a variety of different uses. It is in fact ironic that the most supposedly strategic branch of the social sciences, Game Theory, still has a JEL classification which bears the historical marks of its being perceived through its mathematical structure, rather than through its strategic insights. In neoclassical economics, after Robbins redefinition of our science as 'the science which studies human behavior as a relationship between given ends and scarce means which have alternative uses' (Robbins 1932, p. 16), one has the impression that the human economy of free agents is a *Matrix Economy* brought about by its human slaves. The inevitability of rationality coupled with an obsession with harmonious efficiency, makes a centrally planned economy tantamount to a perfectly competitive one in its results, like the body of Leviathan that was composed of 300 homunculi in the famous frontispiece of Hobbes' *magnum opus* created by Abraham Bosse.

15 Just as nothing would have changed in Ricardo's corn model if the gold turned into dust every now and then – recall Box 3.5.

16 In chess, the German term *Zugzwang* applies to situations where a player would be at a disadvantage when it is their turn to move. In some cases a move is forced. In checkmate you just lose. In Ken Loach's *The Navigators* (released in 2001) Gerry, a British Rail (former) employee, plays chess against himself. When Fiona asks him 'who's winning?' he replies 'Checkmate'. Fiona asks again: 'Checkmate, what's that mean?' to get the reply 'Whatever move you make, you lose.' Fiona then chuckles and says 'Story of my life'.

17 'Life has been integrated into the market as easily as could be imagined because it has been a progressive process. It started with something that was symbolically far removed from mankind, the vegetable domain; from there it passed to the micro-organism, then to the most rudimentary forms of animal life like the oyster. The whole of the animal kingdom is now targeted and we are on the verge of the human, weighed down with precedents which ensure the closure of the system and make any resistance difficult. The work of man, which must be remunerated, claims repayment from the whole realm of nature which has traditionally been free of any property claims.' Edelman (1988 [1997]), p. 197.

18 'in a perfectly competitive market, it really doesn't matter who hires whom: so have labor hire "capital"', Samuelson (1957, p. 894).

19 When one agrees to buy apples or generators for a given price, the moment this agreement is concluded signals the end of the economic relation between buyer and seller. In the case of the labour contract, its signing signals the very beginning of the economic relation between employer and employee.

20 Speaking of complex mathematical functions, there is no dearth of explanations in which 'effort', 'diligence' or 'performance' has been attempted to be determined as a result of a complicated mathematical formula. Once the mainstream economic theory decided to extend its scope to the black box of the labour process and allow for asymmetry of information and uncertainty in its assumptions, it proposed the so-called agency model in which the employer, as the principal, and the employee, as the agent, attempt to enter into a mutually acceptable contract in which the employer will pay the wage in such a specific manner that it would be rational for the worker to apply the specified level of effort, thus escaping the dreaded indeterminacy. This research programme has created a veritable sub-industry in modern labour economics with dumbfounding mathematical sophistication (see for an advanced textbook treatment Cahuc and Zylberberg, 2004, Ch. 6. For a survey of the literature see Malcomson, 1999.) The new branch of 'personnel

economics' has been extremely fruitful (see Lazear, (1999) and Lazear and McNabb 2004). The Human Resources literature is naturally even more voluminous. The problem with such attempts is that they insist in an asocial model in the determination of effort. On the contrary, what the industrial relations and the industrial sociology literature has demonstrated time and again is that of work literature which shows that the determination of effort is either hard to quantify (e.g. Baldamus, 1961) or that workers react strategically to attempts by management to set rules by which the latter try to control them. This literature goes way back in time (see e.g. Goodrich, 1920 [1975]; Mathewson, 1931; Roy, 1952; Lupton, 1963; Burawoy, (1979); Arthur Marsh (1979, p. 37) offers a litany of names for restricting output: 'ca'canny, go-slow, slow-gear strikes, lazy strike, folded arms strike, stay-in strike, working without enthusiasm, restrictive practices, protective practices, craft control, quota restriction, gold bricking'. Geoff Brown in his *Sabotage* (1977) studied conscious attempts by workers to disrupt production even if there was no rational reason to do it. For a more plausible view of managing remuneration and productivity see especially the work of William A. Brown (1979, 1989, Brown and Nolan 1988). Moreover, issues of trust, not contractually achievable, become paramount (Fox, 1974). In the industrial relations literature it is a commonplace that the motivation of workers is not achieved through the labour contract, however skilfully managed. Notions of fairness, unrelated to the rational opportunistic worker, are important in the process of motivation (Hyman and Brough, 1975). Job evaluation schemes, for example, are less linked to the external labour market and more aimed at creating a wage and salary structure that respects norms of fairness of the employees (Doeringer and Pior, 1971; Theocarakis, 1991, ch. 5). Research from experimental economics demonstrates that in labour contexts notions of instrumental rationality do not apply (Fehr and Gächter, 2000). Ideologies at large in society serve to bolster the authority relationship (see Bendix, 1956).

21 Marx's exact words were: 'Capital is thus the governing power over labour and its products'.

22 Again, we have paraphrased. His own words are: 'Modern bourgeois society with its relations of production, of exchange and property, a society that has conjured up such gigantic means of production and of exchange, is like the sorcerer, who is no longer able to control the powers of the nether world whom he has called up by his spells.' (*The Manifesto of the Communist Party*, Marx and Engels (1848 [1998]), p. 41.

23 Marx here speaks specifically of Political Economy rather than Capital, but it is clear from his discussion that his analysis concerns both.

24 Lenin wrote in 1913 that the 'Marxist doctrine ... is the legitimate successor to the best that man produced in the nineteenth-century, as represented by German philosophy, English political economy and French socialism'. ('The Three Sources and Three Component Parts of Marxism' in *Collected Works*, 1977, Vol. 19, pp. 21–8.) We believe that the influence of Ancient Greek philosophy was as important.

25 See G.W.F. Hegel (1807 [1931] p. 103). Ten years later he expanded on the theme thus: 'The concrete return of me into me in the externality is that I, the infinite self-relation, am as a person the repulsion of me from myself and have the existence of my personality in the being of other persons in my relation to them and my recognition of them which is mutual.' Hegel *Enzyklopädie der philosophischen Wissenschaften: III. Philosophie des Geistes* (1817, 2nd 1827, 3rd 1830) Hegel 1894, §490.

26 To be fair to Smith, he did not suggest that human nature was immune to all experiences. For example, he was worried that his cherished division of labour might turn human labourers into automata. To combat this danger Smith prescribed education as an antidote to such alienation. Nevertheless, along with David Hume, Smith held to the belief that, systematically adverse situations notwithstanding, human nature was more or less fixed and only the social norms governing behaviour changed in response to changing circumstances.

27 David Hume, (1748 [1902]) Sec. VIII, Part 1, §65.

28 Hegel (1894) I. The Logic, §131.

29 All the quotations in this paragraph are from *The Manifesto of the Communist Party*, by Karl Marx and Friedrich Engels, published in 1848. In the same passage Marx and Engels extol the bourgeoisie's contribution to the demise of the old, anachronistic ways; of the stagnation that typified the Middle Ages. 'The bourgeoisie', they wrote, 'cannot exist without constantly revolutionising the instruments of production, and thereby the relations of production, and with them the whole relations of society. Uninterrupted disturbance of all social conditions, everlasting uncertainty and agitation distinguish the bourgeois era from all other ones.' Marx and Engels 1848 [1998], p. 38.

30 Paul MacCready was, amongst other things, the inventor of the solar powered airplane. A committed environmentalist, he argued vehemently about the unsustainable imbalance between the biomass under our control and the biomass in the 'wild'. The figure reported here is part of that argument. MacCready's figure concerns the mass of land animals, that is, of terrestrial vertebrates. He did not include insects, worms or the fish in the sea. What he found was that humans plus their livestock overtook wild animals (in weight) at the beginning of the twentieth century. Humans alone (without livestock) began out-weighing wild animals only after World War II. In the past decades the combined footprint of humans and cattle has all but eclipsed all other land-based animals.

31 Paul B. MacReady, (2004) p. 8 [emphasis in the original].

32 In this context, it is possible to argue that twentieth-century communism committed precisely this type of fundamental error: it concentrated on the top-down Central Plan while ignoring the ways in which bottom-up 'natural selection' (i.e. decentralised activity by individuals) would alter, affect and, eventually, undermine the Plan. They behaved like genetic engineers who unleash their designer organisms in the ecosystem on the assumption that they will neither mutate nor interact unpredictably with existing organisms.

5 Crises: The laboratory of the future

1 'In the market, as the owner of the commodity "labour-power", [the worker] stood face to face with other owners of commodities, one owner against another owner. The contract by which he sold his labour-power to the capitalist proved ... that he was free to dispose of himself. But when the transaction was concluded, it was discovered that he was no "free agent", that the period of time for which he is forced to sell his labour-power is the period of time for which he is forced to sell it, that in fact the vampire will not let go ' "while there remains a single muscle, sinew or drop of blood to be exploited"' Marx, *Capital.*, Vol. 1, (1867 [1976]), p. 416. Marx quotes from Engels' "Die englische Zehnstudenbill" [The English ten-hour bill].

2 Marx in *Wage-Labour and Capital*, (1849 [1902]), p. 58.

3 Marx in *Grundrisse*, (1857 [1973]), p. 361.

4 Neoclassical economics denies the fact that there is an essential difference between the two. In a famous article Armen Alchian and Harold Demsetz argue that the difference between the pairs 'grocer–customer' and 'employer–employee' is in the 'team use of inputs and a centralized position of some party in the contractual arrangement of all other inputs' [Alchian and Demsetz (1972), p. 778]. In the *Markets and Hierarchies* paradigm Oliver E. Williamson argues that due to the existence of uncertainty, adaptation is needed for the changing circumstances and therefore the need for flexible contracts arises. There are four types of possible contracting modes: (1) 'contract now for the specific performance of X in the future' (a *sales contract*); (2) 'contract now for the delivery of X_i contingent on event e_i obtaining in the future' (contingent claims contract); (3) 'wait until the future materializes and contract for the appropriate (specific) X at the time' (sequential spot contract); (4) 'contract now for the right to select a specific X from within an admissible set X, the determination of the particular X to be deferred until the future' (authority or employment contract). [Williamson *et al.* (1975)]. Ronald Coase in a celebrated article made efficiency decide where the limits are set between markets and firms. The limits of the authority relationship are set according to this view by transaction costs (Coase (1937)).

5 In the next section we discuss the reason why the labour market must be Jill's only *fallback position*; her only *outside option*. If she has alternative options, e.g. can go into business for herself, she has no reason to accept a *labour contract* of the form discussed here.

6 In Section 4.5 we explained that workers are offered a *labour contract* only when they work in the context *of social production* such that the link between Jill's output and her *labour input* is opaque (see also Box 4.8). If this link is transparent, we claimed, there is no reason why the employer would want to employ Jill on a *labour contract*, as opposed to contracting work out to her; effectively turning her into a sub-contractor.

7 This point was made powerfully by Sue Himmelweit in her 1995 paper entitled 'The Discovery of Unpaid Work: The Social Consequences and the Expansion of Work', Himmelweit (1995).

8 Marx, *Capital*, Vol. 1, (1867 [1976]), p. 932.

9 Referring to E.G. Wakefield's account of capitalism in the colonies, Marx writes: 'First of all, Wakefield discovered that in the Colonies, property in money, means of subsistence, machines, and other means of production, does not as yet stamp a man as a capitalist if there be wanting the

correlative – the wage-worker, the other man who is compelled to sell himself of his own free-will. He discovered that capital is not a thing, but a social relation between persons, established by the instrumentality of things'. Marx, Capital, Vol. 1, (1867 [1976]), p. 932.

10 Seaford's address was partially reprinted in Seaford (2009).

11 Seaford (2009) relates another pertinent Greek myth according to which a man called Erysichthon 'cut down a sacred grove to make himself a banqueting hall and is punished by being made insatiable. No food is enough – whether from land, sea, or air – to satisfy him. He is driven to sell his daughter in marriage, from which she returns to him, and the process is constantly repeated. In the end he eats himself'. Money, therefore, is spreading its poisonous web, making it impossible for mortal men to satiate their cravings, commodifying trees and women alike, consuming everything in its path, including the very flesh and blood of the man who craves it the most.

12 See Marx's *Economic and Philosophical Manuscripts*, 1844, and in particular the chapter on 'The Power of Money' where he also writes: 'If you suppose man to be man and his relation to be a human one, then you can only exchange love for love, trust for trust'. Money on the other hand 'changes fidelity into infidelity, love into hate, hate into love, virtue into vice, vice into virtue, slave into master, master into slave, stupidity into wisdom, wisdom into stupidity. It is the universal confusion and exchange of all things, an inverted world'. Marx (1844 [1977]), p. 111.

13 Karl Marx. 1856, April 19th, 'Speech at the anniversary of the *People's Paper'*, in Marx and Engels 1969, p. 500.

14 Shaw, 1949, p. 19.

15 *The Manifesto of the Communist Party*, by Karl Marx and Friedrich Engels, (1848 [1998]), p. 37.

16 Marx in *Wage-Labour and Capital*, (1849 [1902]), p. 58 [original emphasis].

17 *Supra-intentional causality* refers to a social process culminating into a social outcome that was not part of the intentions which led the various actors to the actions that brought it about. *Sub-intentional causality*, on the other hand, refers to a process internal to the agent (i.e. one that operates at the level of psychology or of the subconscious) culminating in the motives and beliefs behind their acts.

18 Addressing the *First International Working Men's Association*, June 1865. His talk was later published as *Value, Price and Profit*. Marx (1865 [1969]).

19 Note that Marx and Ricardo are speaking with one voice here. The Ricardian profit rate equation (3.4), in Box 3.4 and Marx's own equation (5.2) tell a similar story: whenever the wage rate w rises, the profit rate suffers. This is not to say that Marx did not recognise that some prices would rise, following a wage increase. In *Value, Price and Profit* he agrees that the price of basic goods (that workers buy with their wages) will increase as workers have more money to spend. However, the profit rate in the relatively more labour-intensive sector (i.e. the *capital goods* sector) will fall, dragging employment down in that sector. Then workers will migrate to the other sector(s), which are growing. Thus the wages in the other sector(s) will dip a little (as labour supply there rises) and increase a little in the capital goods sector. The overall effect will be a long-term increase in the economy-wide wage (but not as much as the initial rise in the basic goods sector) and an economy-wide drop in the profit rate. All in all, commodity prices will be, in the long term, left unaffected.

20 Maxwell 1890, Vol. 1, p. 500.

21 The interested reader may consult Paul Sweezy, (1942 [1970]) Chapter 10, pp. 162–3.

22 An assumption we made also in the context of the *Matrix Economy* (see Box 4.5). Another way of grasping the importance of assuming that profit rates tend to equalise is to go back to our depiction of the Physiocrats' model in Box 3.1. The inequalities at the end of that box cannot, by definition, be solved as a system that yields the prices consistent with growth. To do that, these inequalities had to be expressed as equalities. Since the difference between the left-hand side and the right-hand side of these inequalities is profit per unit of output; the assumption that profit rates are equal allows one to add the same profit component to the right-hand side of the inequalities in Box 3.1 thus turning them into equalities before solving the two as a system of equations for the prices of the two goods. Clearly, without the assumption of Ricardo and Marx that profit rates tend to equalise, there can be no determinate theory of prices or values.

23 See in particular the Appendix to Ch. 5 of his *Lectures on the Theory of Production*. Pasinetti (1977).

24 The validity of Marx's iterative procedure in moving from values to prices has also been shown by Anwar Shaikh in 'Marx's Theory of Value and the Transformation Problem', in Schwartz (1977), pp. 106–39.

25 Recall Hegel's *dialectical* argument, so influential in Marx's thought, that no one can be free in a society where some are enslaved. History, being the factory of irony, many decades later in the communist Poland of the 1980s, would produce a piece of dissident anti-communist graffiti that proclaimed (in opposition to the threat of a Soviet invasion) that 'No country that threatens to invade another can be free'. Marx was being used, quite correctly, to lambast Soviet socialism. While we think that he would have sided with the graffiti writer, this incident underscores the Left's massive political and moral twentieth century failure.

26 Piero Sraffa, *Production of Commodities by Means of Commodities: Prelude to a Critique of Economic Theory*. Sraffa (1960).

27 As opposed to the ratio of labour inputs bestowed (during production) into the commodities under exchange.

28 Relative prices are determined by equation (4.5) solved explicitly in note 4 of Chapter 4. The interpretation of *w* in the present context is as the economy's wage rate expressed in units of the *numéraire* that *labour input* is to be paid for per unit. The relationship between the economy's uniform (across the sectors) *growth rate* (which is the same as the *profit rate*) and the wage rate can be computed by plugging the value of *p* above into equation (4.6). Note that in the original context of the *Matrix Economy*, *w* was not the wage but the relative weight attached by that economy's *Overlord Program* to the only natural resource: human heat.

29 Sraffa's rationale is that labour is the only input not produced by some sector of the market economy and, for this reason, its price, the wage rate *w*, cannot be computed by the model. Indeed, all the model can do is tell us which *profit rate* corresponds to which *wage rate* (recall Box 4.6, Chapter 4), with the two variables being inversely related. This inverse relation captures the contest, or struggle, between the classes over the distribution of the surplus. Noting that it is fully consistent with Ricardo's mode [see equation (3.4) in Box 3.4 of Chapter 3], Sraffa's approach is understandably referred to as *neo-Ricardian*. So, in one sense, the idea of *social power* is preserved since the model itself suggests that the distribution of the surplus between capital and labour is not an economic matter, as it cannot be determined mathematically by the economic model. Distribution, thus, remains in the ambit of politics and, once history, politics and sociology has determined who gets which part of the surplus (i.e. the particular combination of π and *w*) economics kicks in and determines relative prices. For the strongest argument in favour of a Sraffian, physical output based, notion of extraction, exploitation and social power, see Garegnani (1984).

6 Empires of indifference: Leibniz's calculus and the ascent of Calvinist political economics

1 We assume here that capital utilisation, or the organic composition of capital (the *k*'s in equation (5.8)), differ across sectors. Indeed, only by a rare fluke would they not differ.

2 E.g. (i) the conversion of a piece of metal into a magnet by passing electrical current through it and (ii) the fact that light exhibits wave-like properties in some, but not all, experiments.

3 Hegel in his *Philosophy of History* called it *Zeitgeist*; a stand-in for humanity's collective consciousness.

4 To the sectors with higher profit rates.

5 Away from sectors with higher extraction rates.

6 E.g. due to the temporary effects of some innovation, before it spreads to many competing firms, or of geographically determined conditions of monopoly, like those experienced by rural communities served by a single petrol station.

7 Note that the *power of firms* (or *market power*, as economists call it) differs crucially from the power that is, in Marx's mind, *capital*. *Capital* is a mighty force whose origins lie in the peculiarities of the *labour contract* (see Section 4.5) and which survives perfectly well in a fully competitive world where everything sells at its value and no one can profit from buying and selling commodities. The *power of firms*, in contrast, goes beyond that and is related to insufficient competition; e.g. when firms enjoy a degree of monopoly in the market for products or monopsony in the market for *labour power*.

8 Keynes in his famous essay on Alfred Marshall provides another difference between physics and economics. He writes: 'Professor Planck, of Berlin, the famous originator of the Quantum Theory, once remarked to me that in early life he had thought of studying economics, but had found it too

difficult! Professor Planck could easily master the whole corpus of mathematical economics in a few days. He did not mean that! But the amalgam of logic and intuition and the wide knowledge of facts, most of which are not precise, which is required for economic interpretation in its highest form is, quite truly, overwhelmingly difficult for those whose gifts mainly consist in the power to imagine and pursue to their furthest points the implications and prior conditions of comparatively simple facts which are known with a high degree of precision' (Keynes, (1924 [1972]) p. 186, n. 2). The preceding footnote in Keynes' essay is also scathing on the lure of mathematics 'Mathematical economics often exercise an excessive fascination and influence over students who approach the subject without much previous training in technical mathematics. They are so easy as to be within the grasp of almost anyone, yet do introduce the student, on a small scale, to the delights of perceiving constructions of pure form, and place toy bricks in his hands that he can manipulate for himself, which gives a new thrill to those who have had no glimpse of the sky-scraping architecture and minutely embellished monuments of modern mathematics' (*ibid.*). Modern mathematical economics have gone a long way since Keynes's days but the thrill of toy bricks remains intact.

9 *Simplistic* in the sense that the multiple identities that classical political economics allowed for (e.g. of capitalist, landowner, productive or unproductive worker, etc.) are replaced by the juxtaposition of buyer and seller. *Dualist* because of the impossibility of a dialectical account of the sort explained in Box 4.10. Tony Aspromourgos (2009) in his book *The Science of Wealth: Adam Smith and the Framing of Political Economy* uses the acronym SAD for 'supply and demand'. Francis Edgeworth speaks of the 'catallactic molecule' (1881, p. 31), whereas Bishop Whately suggested that the proper name for political economy should have been 'CATALLACTICS or the "Science of *Exchanges*"' (Whately 1831, p. 6, emphasis in the original). No wonder that Marx (*Capital*, Vol. I, (1867 [1909]), p. 196) speaks of the 'sphere of simple circulation or of exchange of commodities, which furnishes the "Free-trader *vulgaris*" with his views and ideas'.

10 Ludwig von Mises (1949 [1996]), pp. 203–4. For an early discussion of the impossibility of calculating value in its own terms but only in ratios of exchange between things, see A.R. Jacques Turgot (1769 [1919]), p. 96.

11 Known to economists as *consumer surplus*. Note how this notion of surplus, first suggested by Marshall in his *Principles* (1890), although 50 years earlier (1844) the French engineer Jules Dupuit described the concept, quickly moves from a material basis that it had in classical political economics (taking the form of corn or other material goods that society produces over and above the levels necessary to replenish the stocks consumed during the production period) to a purely subjective one in neoclassical theory (where a mere increase in Jack's desire for something boosts his consumer surplus, even though nothing extra was actually produced).

12 Note that the logic here is similar to that of English auctions: the winner pays a price slightly above the valuation of the second keenest bidder but below his/her own. In 'normal' markets (as opposed to auctions where only one unit is usually for sale), it is the *least keen buyer* whose appraisal of the *last unit* determines the price at which *all* units will sell. However, there is a condition for this: that competition prevents sellers from charging different prices for different units. For if the seller could sell lemons at higher prices to Jack than to Jill, the 'law of one price' implied here will not hold. Competition usually enforces that 'law' simply because if Jack got whiff of the fact that Jill buys lemons more cheaply, he could always ask her to buy some for him too (and pay her a small premium for the service). So, as long as the seller cannot stop re-selling (i.e. the establishment of a secondary market), one price will emerge and it will reflect the lowest *marginal* valuation (that is, Jill's valuation of the *marginal*, or last, lemon). W. Stanley Jevons in his *The Theory of Political Economy* (1879, p. 99) suggested the law of one price, or 'The Law of Indifference' as he called, i.e. '*in the same open market, at any one moment, there cannot be two prices for the same kind of article*' (emphasis in the original). This law is 'one of the central pivots of the theory'.

13 Consider: 'To be "on the margin" has implied exclusion from "the centre". But social, political and economic relations which bind peripheries to centres, keep them together in a series of binary relationships, rather than allowing complete disconnection. In this way, "margins" become signifiers of everything "centres" deny or repress; margins as "the Other" become the condition of possibility of all social and cultural entities'. Shields, 1991, p. 276.

14 The young abbé Ferdinando Galiani in his *Della moneta* (1751) described value as a ratio of utility and scarcity: 'Value, then, is a ratio (*ragione*), and this ratio is composed of two ratios, the names thereof I express with *utility* (*utilità*) and *scarcity* (*rarità*). (…) It is obvious that the air and the water, which are elements extremely useful for human life, have no value whatsoever, because they

lack scarcity. On the contrary, a small bag of sand from the shores of Japan would be a rare thing, but since it has no particular utility, it would have no value.' (Galiani 1751 [1803] Vol. III at p. 59.) Galiani was closer to the subjectivists but he saw *fatica* (labour) as the main source of scarcity.

15 Classical authors, of course, did not reject the importance of utility. But they did not see it as a *determinant* of value. Adam Smith spoke of the water and diamond paradox: 'Nothing is more useful than water: but it will purchase scarce any thing; scarce any thing can be had in exchange for it. A diamond, on the contrary, has scarce any value in use; but a very great quantity of other goods may frequently be had in exchange for it' (*Wealth of Nations*, (1776 [1981]) Book I, ch. IV, pp. 44–5). Ricardo wrote 'Utility then is not the measure of exchangeable value, although it is absolutely essential to it.' (Ricardo (1817/1819/1821 [1951]), p. 11). Marx gives short shrift to utility as a measure of value in the beginning section of *Capital*, Vol. 1 (1867 [1909], p. 46): 'The utility of a thing makes it a use value. But this utility is not a thing of air. Being limited by the physical properties of the commodity, it has no existence apart from that commodity. A commodity, such as iron, corn, or a diamond, is therefore, so far as it is a material thing, a use value, something useful. This property of a commodity is independent of the amount of labour required to appropriate its useful qualities. (…) Use values become a reality only by use or consumption: they also constitute the substance of all wealth, whatever may be the social form of that wealth. In the form of society we are about to consider, they are, in addition, the material depositories of exchange value'. He also makes the observation in a footnote that 'In English writers of the 17th century we frequently find "worth" in the sense of value in use, and "value" in the sense of exchange value. This is quite in accordance with the spirit of a language that likes to use a Teutonic word for the actual thing, and a Romance word for its reflexion'.

16 See for example Senior (1836, p. 138) 'if all the commodities used by man were supplied by nature without any intervention whatever of human labour, but were supplied in precisely the same quantities as they now are, there is no reason to suppose either that they would cease to be valuable, or would exchange in any other than their present proportions'. Note also that the first edition of Walras, *Elements d'économie politique pure*, 1874, was simply an exchange model with no production. The most extreme case of this inversion is the entry by J. Trout Rader in *The New Palgrave* (Rader 1987).

17 In the case where the Internet makes it possible to distribute an infinite number of copies at zero cost to the producer (i.e. endless downloads), one would expect that the utility of the last available copy of the particular video game will tend to zero. Then, its price would tend to zero too. But is this not what we observe? Video game producers, for this reason, strive for ways either to stop free downloads or to create online games which can only be played by logging on to some website. In the latter case, the software for playing the game is downloadable free of charge but access to the online site comes at a price. Which price? According to the Marginalists, the price is given by the utility of access to the least motivated (or marginal) player.

18 See Book V, Chapter II, §1 of Alfred Marshall (1890). *Principles of Economics*. This example was there from the very first edition (at p. 390). Behind the vivid example lies, of course, a mathematical theory of differential calculus. In Note XII of the Mathematical Appendix he provides the necessary mathematics: 'If, as in Note X., v be the discommodity of the amount of labour which a person has to exert in order to obtain an amount x of a commodity from which he derives a pleasure u, then the pleasure of having further supplies will be equal to the pain

of getting them when $\dfrac{du}{dx} = \dfrac{dv}{dx}$.

If the pain of labour be regarded as a negative pleasure; and we write $U \equiv -v$; then $\dfrac{du}{dx} + \dfrac{dU}{dx} = 0$,

i.e. $u+U$ = a maximum at the point at which his labour ceases'. A similar analysis was provided by Jevons in his *Theory of Political Economy*, 1871 (Chapter 5, Theory of Labour).

19 That is, the more units of X we have the less utility we get from our last (or our marginal) unit of X.

20 Note the hidden assumption here: every dollar corresponds to the same amount of utility, irrespective of how many dollars Jill has. This is, clearly, too restrictive. Surely, the richer (or poorer) you are the different your subjective valuation of your last penny. However, it is not too hard, with a little mathematical wizardry, to correct for this. Since nothing much changes in the essence of the arguments here, we shall skip such complications.

21 Those unfamiliar with utility considerations may ask: Why would Jill buy this unit when she gets the same utility as dis-utility? This is no different from saying that you are prepared to pay up to $300 thousand for an apartment and then find out that the lowest price the seller is willing to accept is ... $300 thousand. Then, you buy it at that price.

22 The formal proof is as follows: Let Jill's utility from X and Y be given by the function $U=U(X,Y)$. Her total expenditure on X and Y must be such that the money in her pocket, M, must equal her expenditure on X and Y: $M = p_X X + p_Y Y$. Thus, Jill is looking for the combination of quantities (X^*, Y^*) that will maximise U within her budget. This is, mathematically, equivalent to maximising without any constraints the function $U(X,Y) + \lambda(M - p_X X + p_Y Y)$, where λ is a mere constant (known as the *Lagrange multiplier*). Differentiating the above function subject to X and Y, and setting these derivatives equal to zero, respectively yields: $MU_X = \lambda p_X$ and $MU_Y = \lambda p_Y$. Dividing the first equation by the second we get this new version of the *equi-marginal principle*: $MU_X/MU_Y = p_X/p_Y$, which is equation (6.1) above. This is the famous Gossen's second law, first proposed 20 years before the Marginalist revolution by Hermann Heinrich Gossen in his *Entwicklung der Gesetze des menschlichen Verkehrs und der daraus fließenden Regeln für menschliches Handeln* (1854). It appeared also in Jevons (1871). The usual formulation is that the ratio of marginal utility divided by the price of each good is the same across all goods.

23 For a detailed critique of utility calculus and the claim that rationality is synonymous with a capacity for utility maximisation, see Varoufakis (1998), Chs 3 and 4 in particular.

24 This is no exaggeration. The hapless Gossen put Schiller's *Ode to Joy* at the beginning of his 1854 book, while Walras in 1905 asked his friends to propose him for the Nobel Peace Prize (See Sandmo (2007). He complained later to a friend that Ted Roosevelt 'm'a soufflé le prix Nobel' (snatched the Nobel prize from me).

25 Or perhaps Beethoven's ninth. See the previous note on Gossen.

26 Hayek (1945).

27 That has been established quite early on by mercantilist writers. See in particular Jean Bodin (1568 [1934]). Also O'Brien (2000).

28 Hayek 1976.

29 This point was made by Joan Robinson, 1971, pp. 4–6.

30 See Radford (1945).

31 There must have been at least a few prisoners who thought that there was something slightly amiss with the sight of hundreds of officers and privates indulging in profiteering, under the watchful eye of Nazi guards, and not too far from other camps where countless less privileged skeleton-like prisoners were queuing up to enter the gas chambers. Arbitrage in the midst of the most crucial conflict humanity has ever staged against the forces of genuine evil may boost utility and be pretty disgusting at the same time.

32 Prisoners who, against their better judgement, would sell their food rations for more cigarettes.

33 In Marx's mind, a society that has overcome scarcity and reached a condition of plenty is one in which: 'nobody has one exclusive sphere of activity but each can become accomplished in any branch he wishes; society regulates the general production and thus makes it possible for me to do one thing today and another tomorrow, to hunt in the morning, fish in the afternoon, rear cattle in the evening, criticise after dinner ... without ever becoming hunter, fisherman, herdsman or critic'. Karl Marx and Friedrich Engels. *The German Ideology* (1845 [1932] [1998]).

34 The manna from heaven metaphor was evoked by C.E. Ferguson in his best-selling textbook *Microeconomic Theory*. Goods fall like *m* different types of manna from heaven on each trader's parcel of land (Ferguson 1966, p. 354).

35 Though an embryonic labour market emerged (usually some unlucky person willing to perform laundry services at two cigarettes a garment), the POW camp was as close to a pure exchange economy as it is possible to imagine.

36 Note that this is precisely the same problem as the difficulty with different degrees of capital utilisation intensity in the economy's different sectors first encountered by David Ricardo (and pointed out by Thomas Robert Malthus) (see Chapter 3, Section 3.4) and then again by Karl Marx who realised that his theory of value lacked consistency when different sectors or firms were characterised by a different *organic composition of capital* (see Chapter 5, Section 5.4).

37 Knut Wicksell (1901 [1934]).

38 Note that this resonates perfectly with all three incarnations of the *equi-marginal principle*; equations (6.5) and (6.1): *The ratio of marginal utilities (from supplying capital) equals its*

relative price. In (6.1) the relevant exchange was units of X and Y; in (6.3) it was the labour required to clean someone else's shirt in exchange for 2 teabags; and in (6.5), as interpreted by Wicksell here, it is monetary units of capital invested for units of monetary capital saved.

39 Suppose that, for some unspecified reason, capital has become scarcer than labour. Then the interest rate will rise. This condition means that *all* the firms and branches of production in the economy must simultaneously use a more labour intensive (and thus a less capital intensive) production technique. Moreover, this *rate of substitution* must be common to all firms.

40 The book was originally published in French in 1838 under the title *Recherches sur les principes mathématiques de la théorie des richesses*. See Cournot (1838 [1897]) Chapter VII (pp. 79–89) for the relevant passage.

41 We say 'partly' because Cournot's scheme, as pointed out earlier, requires that firms do not set prices *and* output, but only output. This led to the famous Bertrand critique who raised '(u)ne objection péremptoire' against Cournot's assumption. (Bertrand (1883), p. 503).

42 For more on this, see Hargreaves-Heap and Varoufakis (2004).

43 The original idea was to preserve Jeremy Bentham's principle of the greatest utility for the largest number of people (*An Introduction to the Principles of Morals and Legislation*, 1781, influenced by Cesare Beccaria's *Of Crimes and Punishments* (1764) where the principle appears as 'the greatest happiness for the greatest number' (*la massima felicità divisa nel maggior numero*). Beecaria (1764 [1768]) p. 2 (emphasis in the original) However, Bentham's principle was highly charged politically, since it allowed for comparisons between the utility the ultra-rich derive from their last dollar with the utility of the poorest from an additional dollar. Assuming diminishing marginal utility (which is necessary for the Marginalist calculus to make sense), this comparison led to a simple policy recommendation. Take the last dollar of the rich and give it to the poor, for this redistribution will increase average or social utility. To eradicate such a political implication, Marginalists abandoned the idea that Jill's utility could be compared to Jack's. Utility, therefore, became a private metric, or variable, which could not be compared across persons. (See Varoufakis (1998), chs 2, 3 & 4). While this move de-radicalised the calculus of utility, it killed off any chance Marginalism had to define the common good in an analytically defensible manner. Kenneth Arrow's 1953 theorem that has come to be known as the *Impossibility Theorem* put the final nail in that coffin (for an account, see Varoufakis, 1998, chs 8, 9 & 10).

44 Notably, Mises, (1922 [1951]); Hayek 1935; Schumpeter, 1942. For a sympathetic view see Boettke (1998).

45 According to anthropologist Evans-Pritchard, the Azande (first mentioned in Chapter 1) do not distinguish between the present and the future. In their mindset, one's future health and happiness depend on future conditions that are regarded as already existing. Consequently it is believed that the mystical forces which produce those conditions can be tackled here and now. When the soothsayer predicted ominously that a man would fall ill in the near future, it was as if his illness was already present, his future already incorporated into present time. (Evans-Pritchard (1976 [1937]). In a later study, Evans-Pritchard reports on another people, the Nuer, who have no equivalent for the word time. They cannot speak of it as something that passes or that can be either saved or wasted. Events follow a logical order but are not controlled by an abstract system. It seems that neoclassicism does possess a lineage. (Evans-Pritchard (1940)).

46 Elsewhere it has been argued that neoclassicism's discursive power is, in fact, enhanced by its absurdity. See Yanis Varoufakis and Christian Arnsperger (2010).

47 It is useful to note here that Adam Smith, the patron saint of free market economic thinking, never used the term *demand and supply*. Instead he referred to *supply to demand*. See Aspromourgos 2009.

48 Indeed, Kenneth J. Arrow and Frank H. Hahn usher in the chapter on increasing returns in their book *General Competitive Analysis* (Arrow and Hahn 1971, p. 169) with the following lines from Milton's *Paradise Lost:* 'A gulf profound, as that Serbonian bog | Betwixt Damiata and mount Casius old, | Where armies whole have sunk'.

49 Walras (1874–1926 [1954]).

50 We are referring of course to the Walrasian *deus ex machina,* the fictitious announcer of prices, whom Walras calls *crieur* and who is mistranslated into English as the 'auctioneer' but who does not perform an auction.

51 This the process of 'groping' or *tâtonnement*.

52 Note that if out-of-equilibrium trading were allowed between rounds, every transaction would invalidate the previous round's information gathered by the program (as those who buy at the out-of-equilibrium prices will reduce their demand in the next round in ways that the program cannot anticipate). We would have 'false trading'. This is no different from the problem that Cournot hit upon in 1838, which he 'solved' by assuming myopics firms. Walras' solution was to ban time; just like John Nash Jr did in 1950 in order to prove his remarkable theorems about the Nash equilibrium in non-cooperative games and the theorem according to which there exists a unique solution to the *Bargaining Problem*. We return to the significance of Nash in Chapter 8. Hargreaves-Heap and Varoufakis (2004) present the theorems mentioned above is some detail.

53 Time and neoclassical price theory, as we have already shown, are like oil and water: they cannot mix. But what of space? If spatial distance is allowed between firms, and consumers are spread out over that distance, then some firms are closer to some consumers and, in principle, can exercise a modicum of market power over them. For example you may be prepared to pay a little more at the local store rather than travel to the nearest supermarket. But this means that distance is inconsistent with *perfect competition* since it contradicts the assumption of zero power over prices. How does neoclassicism respond to that? – by assuming distance away. In short, in its model of capitalism it is as if all firms and all consumers are living on a pin's head, or on a proton to be more precise. And since time has also been reduced to a single moment, the space–time continuum is but a point.

54 Note that the mathematics of the original Walrasian General Equilibrium left much to be desired. 'Counting equations and unknowns' did not provide a solution. It was the mathematicians and economists such as Abraham Wald, Karl Schlesinger and John von Neumann of the Vienna mathematical Colloquium who salvaged mathematical respectability from the Walrasian system.

55 Okonogi (2008); or as *The Telegraph* put it in his obituary (14 Dec 2009) 'he became disillusioned with Chicago where, even in the middle of the Depression, finer economic principles seemed to matter more than the dole queues'. Telegraph (2009).

56 Marx's phrase from *The Manifesto of the Communist Party*, by Karl Marx and Friedrich Engels, (1848 [1998], p. 38).

57 Here we borrow Joseph Schumpeter's famous term from his *Capitalism, Socialism and Democracy*. (1943 [1994], Chapter VII "The Process of Creative Destruction").

58 Sraffa, (1960), p.v.

59 But, for reasons already explained, end up creating single-person models as a price for retaining real time within their analysis.

60 The quotation comes from Marginalist Chicago economist, and 1982 Nobel Prize winner, *George Stigler* (1911–91). It was quoted in Clotfelter (1997), p. 95.

61 Alfred Marshall tried to steer a middle course. He focused on a single firm, which he thought of as representative of the average capitalist enterprise. This *representative firm* would embody the normal behaviour of every firm in the economy. Likewise, the industry to which the firm belonged was to be taken as the *representative industry* which he evoked to represent the behaviour of the whole economy. Thus, Marshall teetered on the edge of Marginalism, struggling not to fall headlong into the neoclassical, Walrasian paradigm. He understood the centrality of productivity increases, of increasing returns, of time. Alas, his Marginalism left him nowhere to turn to and he ended up sitting on the proverbial fence incapable of turning back to classical political economics and unwilling to join the rampant neoclassicists.

62 The strategy is simple: first, they define preferences statically and assume that they are: (a) impervious to private experience (i.e. that what Jill does does not affect what she craves) and (b) independent of other people (i.e. that what Jack feels or does has no direct effect on Jill's preferences). Then, they define as 'special cases' situations where (a) is relaxed (they call these *endogenous preferences*) or where (b) is 'violated' (they refer to interaction between Jill's preferences and Jack's utility/actions as *externalities*). Some play around with Marginalist calculus that permits departures from (a) and (b) before recoiling back (in horror at the impossible indeterminacy of the mathematics) to the 'standard model' where (a) and (b) are restored. In effect, typical features of human behaviour are defined as 'special cases' and the most extreme special case (a 'static' Jill bleached of all sociality and denied anything we would recognise as human psychology) is presented as the 'standard model'. And all this because Marginalism cannot handle the mathematical complexity unleashed by real temporal change.

63 Suppose Jill is indifferent between basket X (2 kg of coffee) and basket Y (1 kg of tea). Then her preferences are convex if there exists a third basket Z combining some coffee (<2 kg) and some tea (<1 kg) that is equally desirable to X. Such convexity is indispensable for the Marginalist price theory of equation (6.1) since, without it, the ratio of marginal utilities on the right-hand side of that equation is indefinable. Similarly with production theory: if the firm produces 100 widgets either by utilising a combination X of machines and labour (e.g. 1 machine and 10 person hours) or combination Y (e.g. 3 machines and 2 person hours), there must also exist an in-between combination (e.g. 2 machines and 5 person hours) that also produces 100 widgets. If not, no Marginalist theory of profit and wages is forthcoming. Marginalist price theory, therefore, requires that goods and factors of production are seen as infinitely substitutable by their 'consumers' (consumers and firms respectively) along a non-linear, convex *indifference curve* first posited by Edgeworth (see Box 6.5).

64 For a complete account, see Hargreaves-Heap and Varoufakis (2004).

65 The very same 'escape' route was forced upon thinkers of a Marginalist disposition again and again. A celebrated example is that of John Nash Jr and his bargaining solution: The only way he could prove the existence of a uniquely rational agreement between bargainers was to abstract from any actual negotiations that, in reality, would yield the agreement. In Chapter 8 we shall be arguing that this 'solution' by the young Nash changed the course of post-war economics. Until then, the interested reader can turn to Chapter 4 in Hargreaves-Heap and Varoufakis (2004) for an account of Nash's theorem.

66 There were 11 letters in all exchanged by the two men between 1873 and 1875. See Jaffé, 1965. See also Kolm (1968).

67 Walras wrote: '..we have proceeded in opposite directions. You start from monopoly to arrive at indefinite competition. I thought I had to start from indefinite competition, which I consider to be the general case, to arrive at monopoly, which seems to be a special case. This way is more difficult, but I believe it to be more beautiful and more complete'.

7 Convulsion: 1929 and its legacy

1 Harmony theories of the economy existed before the advent of Marginalist economics. Frederic Bastiat and the French liberals are the best known examples. But with neoclassical economics we have the pretence that class harmony is the result of some immutable scientific law that comes as reliably as Neptune does from the tip of Le Verrier's pen. The harmony of the *mécanique céleste* is paralleled with the equilibria of the *mathématique sociale*.

2 His name was Samuel Morse (1791–1872) and his invention was, of course, the electric telegraph.

3 *The Tempest*: Act 5, Scene 1.

4 *George Westinghouse Jr* (1846–1914) had made his name as an electrical and mechanical engineer. To this day, the air brakes used on railways and many trucks are his invention. However, he made his fortune by betting on alternative current as opposed to the direct current favoured by Edison. See Hughes (1983).

5 E.g. contest between VHS and Beta video tapes (in the 1970s and 1980s); competing high definition TV formats; Nintendo, Sony and Microsoft gaming consoles, Blue Ray and HD, DVD, etc.

6 Westinghouse was, naturally, livid. To stop Edison's negative marketing involving the AC-powered electric chair, he refused to sell Edison's company the AC generator that was necessary to fire up the electric chair. Edison and Harold Brown (the engineer who worked on the electric chair project for Edison) had to place a fake order for such a generator on behalf of some Latin American university laboratory. As a result, the generator that powered the first execution by electric chair had to travel via Latin America before returning home to do its murderous deed. See also Moran (2002).

7 DC current can only travel for about three kilometres from the power generating station, making it incredibly expensive to deliver to customers outside a city centre.

8 See Hobsbawm (1999).

9 The term 'abstinence' was first used as an alternative name for capital as a factor of production by Nassau W. Senior [*An Outline of the Science of Political Economy*, 1836, p. 153]. But as Alfred Marshall complained in his *Principles* [(1890 [1920]), IV, vii, §8, fn. 99] 'Karl Marx and

his followers have found much amusement in contemplating the accumulations of wealth which result from the abstinence of Baron Rothschild, which they contrast with the extravagance of a labourer who feeds a family of seven on seven shillings a week; and who, living up to his full income, practises no economic abstinence at all.' Hence Marshall adopted the more neutral term '*Waiting*' which he wrote 'was given by Macvane in the Harvard *Journal of Economics* for July, 1887.' Marshall (1890 [1920], IV.vii, §8, p. 233, n. 1). He notes in the text of the same page that we may 'say that the accumulation of wealth is generally the result of a postponement of enjoyment, or of a *waiting* for it'.

10 See the papers in Kates (2003).
11 See Robert Sobel (1968), *Panic on Wall Street: A History of America's Financial Disasters*. Since panics are recurrent, there is a tendency for good books on the subject to be reissued with an addendum after a new episode. Sobel is no exception. In 1988 it was reissued under the title *Panic on Wall Street: A Classic History of America's Financial Disasters with a New Exploration of the Crash of 1987*. See also Kindleberger and Aliber (2005).
12 This quotation comes from a footnote by Engels in his edition of Marx's *Capital Vol. 3*, Chapter 30 [Marx (1894 [1909]), pp. 574–5].
13 Hobson and Mummery (1889).
14 See Rosa Luxemburg (1913 [1951]), p. 334.
15 Recall Section 6.11 of the previous chapter.
16 As all economics undergraduates know, textbook economics is Robinsonian; i.e. devised to explain the economy built by Daniel Defoe's hero. Robinson Crusoe, the said character, is producer, consumer, investor, saver, worker and employer (of his own labour) *all at once*. His little economy is analytically equivalent to Ricardo's *corn model*. For whereas Ricardo imagined a populous economy in which everyone consumed or produced corn and nothing but corn, Robinson produces many different things (catches fish, repairs his clothes, builds a shelter, etc.). However, in the Marginalist mindset, all these 'things' are reducible to one: Robinson's *utility*. So, as long as the 'economy' under investigation contains either one commodity or one person, the analysis is the same and it does not evoke the *Inherent Error*. It makes no difference whether value is measured in terms of the quantity of corn in Ricardo's *corn model* or in terms of Robinson's utility. In fact, one of the more honest and outspoken neoclassicists, Philip Wicksteed is proud of the fact. In his critique of Marx's *Capital*, Vol. 1, [Wicksteed (1884)] he writes: '"All the mystery" says Marx, "of the world of wares, all the false lights and magic which play about the creations of labour when produced as wares, disappear at once when we have recourse to other forms of production. And since Political Economy delights in Robinsoniads, let us begin with Robinson on his island". I accept this invitation, and proceed to make my own observations on what I see. Robinson, then, has to perform various kinds of useful work … and although he does not ever exchange things against each other, having no one with whom to exchange, yet he is perfectly conscious of the equivalence of utility existing between certain products of his labour, and as he is at liberty to distribute that labour as he likes, he will always apply it where it can produce the greatest utility in a given time.' However, the moment Friday comes into the picture, the *Inherent Error* rears its ugly head. Is it not interesting that economists using the Crusoe parable keep Friday out of the narrative? An interesting exception is Edgeworth where he introduces Friday with Robinson Crusoe in the initial presentation of what later has been called the Edgeworth Box [Edgeworth (1881 [2003]) at p. 28]. But as he acknowledges in the next page 'This simple case brings clearly into view the characteristic evil of indeterminate contract, *deadlock*, undecidable opposition of interests' and ends the sentence with a phrase in Greek from Demosthenes' 'On the crown' [*De corona*, 18) '*akritos eris kai tarachê*' meaning 'confused strife and disorder' [Edgeworth (1881 [2003]) pp. 29 and 162]. An interesting film on the Crusoe–Friday relationship is *Man Friday* (1975), directed by Jack Gold with Richard Roundtree and Peter O'Toole.
17 We have already mentioned the *Quantity Theory of Money* as one of the Marginalists' dogmas, the fourth to be precise, in Box 6.6 of the previous chapter.
18 See David Hume (1752 [1955]). Following Hume, classical political economists like David Ricardo (1773–1823), James Mill (1773–1836) and J.R. McCulloch (1789–1864) were firm believers in the *Quantity Theory of Money*.
19 I.e. the theory that this rate of exchange (or relative price) reflects, in the first instance, the ratio of Jill's utility from her last slice of bread over her utility from her last croissant and, in the second instance, Jill's utility from hiring Jack's last hour of labouring.

20 Note also the distributional impact of expectations caused by the fact that non-smokers would take the full brunt of any inflation (as they could not gain utility directly from cigarettes).

21 From Chapter 25 of *The Grapes of Wrath* (1939), John Steinbeck's remarkable novel whose plot unfolds during the Great Depression.

22 Stigler (1963 [1986]), p. 350.

23 Roosevelt even nationalised all the gold held by American citizens and tore up all contracts binding the US government to pay loans back in gold. Thirty-eight years later, another US President, Richard Nixon, was to echo Roosevelt's decision by tearing up a post-Second World War version of the Gold Standard, thus ending any connection currencies had with the precious metal.

24 While the banks were falling likes dominoes, the surviving ones were beginning to cash in their paper money reserves, acquiring gold from the government as an insurance policy against the falling value of their cash holdings both domestically and internationally. The Fed reacted the only way it knew, within the logic of the Gold Standard and the underpinning *Quantity Theory of Money*: it increased interest rates to stem the outflow of gold from its vaults. Insult was therefore added to injury: in an economic quicksand, where jobs, investment and prices were sinking without trace, this increase in the interest rate was the last straw.

25 John Maynard Keynes (1920), *The Economic Consequences of the Peace*.

26 During the crisis, the Soviet Union advertised in New York for about six thousand jobs, seeking Americans willing to migrate to the USSR. They received 100,000 applications!

27 As the people of Nanjing were to find out at great human cost, before the bombing of Pearl Harbor alerted the West to the threat that was Imperial Japan.

28 From 1937 to 1938 industrial output fell by 37%, 7 million additional souls were driven into unemployment and average income subsided by 15%.

29 The main cause of the hike in prices once the war was won was the end of price controls that were ruthlessly enforced by the US government during the war years.

30 I.e. that government cannot stimulate a flagging economy by printing paper money, a policy that will *only* increases average prices, *via* the inflationary effect on people's expectations.

31 John Maynard Keynes (1932), 'The World's Economic Outlook', *Atlantic Monthly*.

32 Here we are succumbing to a popular attribution. According to Justin Fox (2008) the phrase "we are Keynesians now" was the in the cover of *Time* magazine in 1965 and it quoted Milton Friedman, Keynes' arch-enemy. Fox writes: 'Friedman later objected that it was taken out of context – all he meant was that everybody used Keynesian language and concepts. But the phrase stuck. It's often attributed these days to Republican President Richard Nixon, but what Nixon actually said, in 1971, was the less expansive "I am now a Keynesian".' Be that as it may, Nixon uttered the phrase in order to suggest that his Republican administration would not rock the boat by cutting spending at a time of flagging employment and investment.

33 Bertrand Russell (1872–1970), Keynes's contemporary at Cambridge, wrote about Keynes and his circle of friends that '[t]hey aimed at a life of retirement among fine shades and nice feelings, and conceived of the good as consisting in the passionate mutual admirations of a clique of the elite'. Quoted in Ray Monk's (1999) biography of Russell. Beyond his lofty social and academic status, Keynes was also a successful player in the money and futures' markets, famously gambling his College's funds – with success. Unlike our Section 7.2 rebels, when Keynes spoke, it came from the horse's mouth.

34 Until the *Depression* is over and variable Q in equation (7.1) bounces back to a level consistent with the economy's productive capacity.

35 See his essay on Malthus, Keynes (1933 [1972]). The quote appears on pp. 100–1.

36 Malthus made his name by prognosticating that population growth would outstrip the Earth's resources, despite our better efforts, and therefore that famine was an essential 'equilibrating' mechanism. As a man of the cloth, he explained this as part of God's design: the suffering of the masses, the swollen tummies of the emaciated children and the exhausted faces of the grieving mothers were a divinely afforded opportunity for humans to embrace good and fight evil.

37 Recall Section 3.6 where we first encountered Malthus' valid criticism of Ricardo's theory; a criticism based on the fact that, for the *labour theory of value* to work, each commodity had to be produced by the same technique of production involving the same proportions in the use of the various inputs.

38 See Box 7.1 where the debate between Malthus and Ricardo on the validity of *Say's Law* was discussed.

39 That is demand backed up by the spending power which makes it effective, as opposed to a mere craving.

40 Keynes (1932).

41 The precise quotation is: 'When my theory has been duly assimilated and mixed with politics and feelings and passions, I can't predict what the final upshot will be in its effect on action and affairs. But there will be a great change, and, in particular, *the Ricardian foundations of Marxism will be knocked away*' (emphasis added). Keynes (1982), p. 42.

42 See the *General Theory*, Chapter 16 (1936, p. 212).

43 Keynes, of course, never used the term which was coined by Herbert A. Simon in a different context of simplifying rational decisions.

44 To see this, it is best to work backwards: to get to the twentieth match first, Jack needs to collect the seventeenth match first. For if he does, then whatever Jill does, he will win: if she picks only the eighteenth, Jack will pick both the nineteenth and the twentieth. If she picks both the eighteenth and the nineteenth, again Jack will pick up the twentieth when his turn comes. Now, notice that the same logic guarantees that he will get to the seventeenth match first if he manages to arrive at the fourteenth first. And so on. It is now easy to confirm that if he picks two matches at the beginning he can jump on the bandwagon that takes him to the fifth, eighth, eleventh, fourteenth, seventeenth and twentieth matches first. His opening move, therefore, must be to pick two matches. QED.

45 For a more sympathetic view of the 'animal spirits' see Dow and Dow (1985), pp. 46–65. Recently a book by that title by two eminent economists subsumed under the rubric 'animal spirits' all kinds of psychological factors [Akerlof and Shiller, 2009].

46 Indeed, the anti-Keynesian turn of the 1970s and beyond, which re-established the dominance of the neoclassical school in macroeconomics, was self-styled as *The Rational Expectations' Revolution*. [See e.g. Miller (1994)]. The implication was that economics had rid itself of the Keynesian assumption that people are less than rational and thus began to model economic outcomes as the results of rational choices under beliefs that were no less rational and foresighted than those of the model itself. See next chapter for more.

47 Tragically, it seems we are getting closer to a situation where humanity's beliefs about its own impact on the Earth's weather begin to influence the weather, just as on our fictitious Ambience, at least in the longer run when climate change, and our response to it, takes firm hold.

48 (Keynes 1936, p. 156). The last three quotations were from Chapter 12 of the *General Theory*.

49 The tumult inside Keynes' mind, caused by his break from his own Marginalist upbringing, is evident in Chapter 11 of the *General Theory*. Throughout the chapter he tries to relate his views of the determinants of investment in terms of the *equi-marginal principle* (discussed here in Chapter 5). However, in later chapters it transpires that Keynes has no intention of going the neoclassical way and assuming that the marginal expected returns of capital (or the marginal efficiency of capital) can be fixed within a determinate economic model. The more Keynes discussed the fickleness of investment the closer he got to seeing that the *equi-marginal principle* had next to no analytical gravitas.

50 See Lovejoy (1936).

51 Or perhaps it was the influence of G.E. Moore's *Principia Ethica* on Keynes' thought. See 'My early beliefs' Keynes (1938 [1972]).

52 During a recession, as prices deflate, previous debts grow in Real terms; that is, in terms of the new, lower prices. Thus, indebted people, firms and countries find themselves in a perfect storm: a growing debt at a time of a falling income.

53 Marx's redrafting of Ricardo's *labour theory of value* started life as a brilliant statement of the vivifying role of human productive activity and the impossibility of objectifying it. But once Marx began to sense the gravitas of his *Das Kapital*, he smuggled into the story what was effectively an immanent Newtonian gravitational law with which he fixed the rates of exchange between commodities. In contrast, the 'we are damned if we know' attitude of Keynes, and his outright distancing from the *Inherent Error*, is here compared to the impact of the Fifth Solvay Conference that took place in October 1927 in Brussels. For it was at the conference that modern quantum mechanics emerged and a major break in particle physics took place. From then onwards physicists began to accept that, at the micro level, the very act of measurement causes the set of probabilities to collapse to the value defined by the measurement. An idea not too dissimilar to Keynes' suggestion that capitalism turns on average opinion about capitalism.

54 King Canute was an eleventh-century Danish King of England. An able king by all accounts, he is mostly remembered for the tale of placing his throne on the shore instructing the incoming tide

to desist. One interpretation of the story is that he was taken in by sycophantic couriers who never ceased praising him for his omnipotence. Another, more kindly, interpretation is that he did this to demonstrate to them the limits of his powers.

55 Keynes (1932).

56 See Karl Marx (1852, 1937), *The Eighteenth Brumaire of Louis Bonaparte*.

57 In the following chapters this book argues that the post-war era is split into three phases. Phase 1 begins around 1947 and ends in 1971 – we call it the era of the *Global Plan*. With the collapse of Phase 1, a second phase began around the mid-1970s which we refer to as the *Global Minotaur*. We believe that that phase ended in 2008. If we are right, we are now in Phase 3 of the post-war period.

8 A fatal triumph: 2008's ancestry in the stirrings of the Cold War

1 Available from http://www.ourdocuments.gov.

2 The extent of their will to prevail upon Wall Street was confined to the passing, in 1933, of the *Glass-Steagall Act*. It was an important piece of legislation which, in a bid to prevent another 1929, forced a separation between (a) normal bread-and-butter banks, which took deposits from the common man and woman; and (b) investment banks, which were allowed to gamble on shares, futures, commodities, etc. but banned from taking deposits. The idea was that normal banks should be prevented from gambling with other people's money, from being exposed to high default risks, and from becoming so large that their bankruptcy might threaten the rest of the economy with another 1929. As for investment banks, they could do as they pleased: sink or swim in an ocean of high risks. The *Glass-Steagall Act* was set aside in the 1990s by the Clinton administration. Following 2008, the Obama administration has touted a similar regulatory device known as the *Volcker Rule*. Its fate remains to be seen.

3 We call this instinct 'natural' because, as argued in the previous chapter, the dominant mindset tended to the *Inherent Error* which, in a neoclassical context, forces our mind to think of capitalism as a simple generalisation of a representative firm (e.g. some fictitious Robinson Crusoe economy) and to conclude with the corner-store's dictum: *When in trouble, cut spending to make ends meet.* That this mindset is still with us can be witnessed daily just by listening to politicians, economists, commentators, European Central Bankers, etc. regurgitate the argument that our post-2008 world's main task is to convince governments (from Greece and Spain to the USA and the UK) to cut their recession-induced deficits.

4 'Remarks by the President on Financial Rescue and Reform', Federal Hall, New York, NY, The White House, Office of the Press Secretary. Available at http://www.whitehouse.gov/the_press_office/remarks-by-the-president-on-financial-rescue-and-reform-at-federal-hall/.

5 Alan Brinkley (1998).

6 The obvious example here is Harvard economist Larry Summers who, in 2009, was appointed by President Obama to the crucial post of President of the *Council of Economic Advisers*. Previously, Summers had served as Secretary to the Treasury under President Bill Clinton. In that capacity, he steered the adoption by Congress of the *Gramm-Leach-Bliley Act* of 1999. The significance of this Act was that it repealed the New Dealers' 1933 *Glass-Steagall Act* (see note 1 above). It was this act of 'deregulation' that allowed banks to become not only gargantuan but also hugely interconnected with various shady markets (e.g. derivatives). So, when the *Crash of 2008* hit, the government had to come up with trillions of dollars to prevent another collapse of the entire banking sector. Back in 1999 Summers was celebrating his dismantling of the New Dealers' constraints on banks with the following flourish: 'Today Congress voted to update the rules that have governed financial services since the Great Depression and replace them with a system for the twenty-first century. This historic legislation will better enable American companies to compete in the new economy.' In 2008 his new 'system' lay in ruins. His reward? The presidency of the most influential economic institution of the US government, courtesy of President Obama who, puzzlingly, had castigated the repeal of the *Glass-Steagall Act* as a significant contributor to the *Crash of 2008*. Such is political life...

7 In January 2010 the Supreme Court's five-member conservative majority voted to grant corporations (including of course Wall Street) the same rights to donate to political candidates that citizens enjoy. The decision was based on a ruling that limiting the campaign funding of corporations imposed 'constitutionally unacceptable limits on free speech'. Thus, the citizen's right to talk and write freely was equated with the right of Citigroup, Goldman Sachs, AIG, etc. to donate taxpayer

funds, given to it by the Obama administration, to opposition Republican candidates who promise that, if they win, they will allow the banks, once again, to run riot.

8   See the opening line of Marx's *The Eighteenth Brumaire of Louis Bonaparte*, 1852.

9   Breaking up the cartels, or trusts, had been a radical slogan since at least the turn of the century. Indeed, this anti-monopoly mood had led Congress to pass the *Sherman Anti-Trust Act*. Teddy Roosevelt, Franklin's cousin, had in fact run in the 1912 Presidential election on a platform which promised a 'course of supervision, control and regulation of these great corporations'.

10   See Parker (2005).

11   As is well known, in reality there is no Nobel Prize in Economics. Rather, there is a prize set up by the Bank of Sweden in honour of Alfred Nobel which, cunningly, managed to attach itself, as least in the public's mind, to the Nobel Prizes proper. In this book we spare the reader this distinction by referring to its recipients as Economics Nobelists. Samuelson's textbook [*Economics*, New York: McGraw-Hill] was so successful that it underwent 19 editions from 1948 to 2010, the last eight with William D. Nordhaus.

12   Hansen (1938).

13   *An Economic Program for American Democracy, by Seven Harvard and Tufts Economists: Richard V. Gilbert; George H. Hildebrand Jr.; Arthur W. Stuart; Maxine Yaple Sweezy; Paul M. Sweezy; Lorie Tarshis and John D. Wilson.* [Gilbert *et al.* (1938)]. Maxine Yaple was the wife of Paul Sweezy. There were also other economists involved in the project but they did not sign the program because of their government involvement. See John Bellamy Foster (2004a).

14   Both their books appeared in 1942: Schumpeter (1942 [1994]) and Sweezy (1942 [1970]).

15   Many years later Samuelson recalled 'the interchange of wit, the neat parrying and thrust, and all made the more pleasurable by the obvious affection that the two men had for each other despite the polar opposition of their views'. Samuelson (1969 [1981]), p. 8. Galbraith too was to refer to Sweezy as 'a dominant voice' in the debates on stagnation and the future of capitalism of the 1930s. Both quotes appear in Foster 2004.

16   In his 1936 electoral campaign he said: 'I admit I am a New Dealer, and if [the New Deal] takes money from the few who have controlled the country and gives it back to the average man, I am going to Washington to help the President work for the people of South Carolina and the country'.

17   In February 1946 Kennan sent a long telegram from Moscow, where he was number two at the US embassy, with an intricate analysis of the Soviet Union. It concluded that Soviet power had to be contained. A year later he published an article entitled 'The Source of Soviet Conduct' [Kennan (1947)]. Together with his telegram, this piece is thought of as the beginning of the Cold War 'containment' doctrine which was to dominate, albeit not in a manner that Kennan approved, US policy for decades to come.

18   In 1946, as mathematical adviser to the US Air Force Comptroller, he was challenged by his Pentagon colleagues to see what he could do to mechanise the planning process, 'to more rapidly compute a time-staged deployment, training and logistical supply program'. In those pre-electronic computer days, mechanisation meant using analog devices or punch-card machines. ('Program' at that time was a military term that referred not to the instruction used by a computer to solve problems, which were then called 'codes', but rather to plans or proposed schedules for training, logistical supply, or deployment of combat units. The somewhat confusing term 'linear programming', Dantzig explained, is based on this military definition of 'program'.)

19   The motto was changed to *Theory and Measurement* in 1952. See 'Cowles Commission' in Segura and Rodríguez Braun 2004, at p. 52. For the history and role of the Foundation see the papers by Debreu, Solow, Malinvaud and Arrow at the 50th Anniversary celebration (June 3–4, 1983) in Cowles Commission/Foundation for Research in Economics (1983). See also Christ (1952).

20   Indeed, to this day, a considerable portion of the formalism that von Neumann introduced remains the standard framework for most mathematical expositions of quantum mechanics.

21   See Neumann (1928 [1959]) and Neumann and Morgenstern (1944).

22   See Gödel (1931 [1967]).

23   The other professors were J.W. Alexander, Albert Einstein, Marston Morse, Oswald Veblen and Hermann Weyl.

24   Interestingly, in 1940 von Neumann mediated (together with Einstein and Veblen) to appoint Gödel to one of the Institute's chairs, as well as to sponsor his application for US citizenship. Gödel, an Austrian refugee from the Anschluss, took up the appointment and also spent the rest of his days at Princeton.

25 In fact, the first computer to be built *in situ* at RAND, where von Neumann spent many years, was named JOHNNIAC in his honour (***John** von Neumann **N**umerical **I**ntegrator and **A**utomatic **C**omputer*).

26 At Los Alamos von Neumann was very taken with electrically stimulated jellyfish, which he appears to have viewed as doing some kind of continuous analogue of the information processing of an electronic circuit. In any case, by about 1947, he had conceived the idea of using partial differential equations to model a kind of factory that could reproduce itself, like a living organism.

27 See Neumann (1937 [1998]) and (1945–6).

28 Wages and labour are not explicitly modelled in the von Neumann growth model. He assumes that the workers involved in the processes are paid with wage goods which are reproducible commodities within the system of equations. Workers appear in the processes only through the goods they consume.

29 In fact, von Neumann, by positing processes that will possibly not be used and goods that will be possibly free goods he wrote dismissively about Walras' mathematically low-brow method of 'counting equations and unknowns', though he did not explicitly mention him.

30 Boxes 3.1, 3.4, 4.4 and 5.14 discussed holistic classical economic models which are close in spirit to von Neumann's, and just as alien to the Marginalist-*cum*-neoclassical type of modelling. Heinz D. Kurz and Neri Salvadori have also argued that von Neumann's economic analysis was of the classical political economics variety – see Kurz and Selvadori (1993). We wholly agree with this interpretation, even though it is not the dominant one. It is interesting to note that in a Cowles Foundation Discussion Paper the von Neumann model is described as dealing 'with the growth of the economy through "production of commodities by means of commodities" (Sraffa), leaving the mechanism of consumption almost completely aside' [Łoś and Wycech-Łoś (1974). Then the authors construct a von Neumann model 'with labour and consumption' to make the comparison possible defeating the whole purpose of the model.]

31 A set of tokens in which to express relative prices but lacking any capacity to play a significant role in influencing the economy's path.

32 Arguably, von Neumann's two economic contributions (his 1928, 1944 game theoretical work as well as his 1937 equilibrium growth models) started life as applications of linear programming, a field where Koopmans had also excelled. Indeed, his own first seminar presentation at Cowles [December 13, 1943] was entitled 'Dynamic economic systems'.

33 These seven papers came out all at once, presented as they were between January and April of 1949. The order in which they were presented was: (January 9) L.J. Savage, 'The Theory of Games: Zero-Sum Games'; (January 20) Kenneth J. Arrow, 'The Theory of Games: Multi-Person Games'; and (February 17) 'The Theory of Games: Applications to Economics'; (March 3), Jacob Marschak, 'The Theory of Games: Measurable Utility'; (March 10) M.A. Girshick, 'The Theory of Games: Continuous Games'; (March 31) L.J. Savage, 'The Theory of Games: Application to Statistical Inference'; (April 14) Herbert A. Simon, 'The Theory of Games: Application to Politics and Administration'. They are reported in Cowles Commission for Research in Economics (1943–54). Of these, Arrow and Simon eventually collected Nobel economics prizes.

34 In fact, von Neumann's Game Theory can only provide advice to players engaged in constant-sum games. See below for a discussion of whether this is a weakness of the theory or not. For a critical account of Game Theory, see S. Hargreaves-Heap and Y. Varoufakis (2004).

35 The title of the presentation was 'The Extended *Bargaining Problem*'. Hollywood, always on the lookout for dramatic tales of historical significance from which to profit, told Nash's story in the 2002 film *A Beautiful Mind*, directed by Ron Howard and featuring Russell Crowe as Nash.

36 See Weintraub and Mirowski (1994).

37 As Debreu himself wrote 'I had become interested in economics, an interest that was transformed into a lifetime dedication when I met with the mathematical theory of general economic equilibrium, founded by Léon Walras in 1874–77, in the formulation given by Maurice Allais in his book, *A la recherche d'une discipline economique,* 1943'. Since then Debreu always kept an eye out for interesting mathematical depictions of economic relations.

38 A Japanese mathematician working at Princeton, where Nash was a doctoral student.

39 See Debreu (1983), p. 90.

40 Quoted from his Presidential address delivered at the 103rd meeting of the *American Economic Association*, on 29th December, 1990, in Washington, DC. See Debreu (1991).

41 Mirowski and Weintraub (1994) refer to Debreu's following conception of an 'economy' as 'visual' evidence of his Bourbakism: 'Economy E is defined as follows. $\forall$ agent $i = 1,...,m$, $\exists$ a non-empty subset $x_i \subset \Re^l$ completely pre-ordered by, and at least as desirable by i, such that $\forall$ agent $j = 1,...,n$ a non-empty subset $Y_j \subset \Re^l$ and some point $w \in_j \subset \Re^l$ is an $(m+n)$-tuple of points $\subset \Re^l$.'

42 Recall that this was precisely Nash's method for 'solving' the *Bargaining Problem*. Just as Nash abstracted from (that is, ignored) the bargaining process that leads to the final agreement or bargain, Debreu abstracted from (that is, also ignored) the process by which prices are formed. And just as Nash had simply posited certain conditions or axioms that the final agreement must be characterised by, so did Debreu posit conditions or axioms which 'ought' to typify an economy in General Equilibrium. Last, but not least, Debreu's proof utilised the same *fixed point theorem* as the one Nash had used in his paper.

43 See Koopmans (1957) and Debreu (1959).

44 See Mirowski (2002).

45 Unlike von Neumann, whose tragedy is figurative, Nash's was real and due to schizophrenia [see Nasar (1994)]. Because of it, one may speculate, he did not have the opportunity to become involved in the uses of his method to economics-proper (that is, to the General Equilibrium results of the 1950s). Nevertheless, it is still rather unseemly how very few people, even among leading economists, acknowledge his pivotal influence on the General Equilibrium work by Debreu and Arrow. It is our view (which derives from a personal conversation with Nash that one of us had) that he was, in the end, far less convinced than those who utilised his method (jettisoning von Neumann's) of the superiority of his approach to that of von Neumann's. Those of a romantic disposition may even read something of significance in the heart-wrenching description of John Nash, at the height of his illness in 1959, wandering around the Princeton campus insisting that he be addressed as Johann von Nassau...

46 His bargainers were utility maximisers taken straight out of the Marginalists' models. In fact, an attempt at an *ante litteram* Nash solution can be found even in Turgot [1769]. See Theocarakis (2006).

47 From the perspective of political economics, one thing matters, namely, this paragraph: the confirmation that, when one begins with a Marginalist model of economic behaviour, the only way of ending up with a 'result', and thus bypassing the *Inherent Error*, is to assume time away. At that moment, it becomes a technical problem, easily addressed by technical means, to close the model; to find a 'solution' simply by pinpointing certain conditions on the functions that typify one's agents which, if assumed, will lead to that 'solution'.

48 For it is one thing to put together examples of model economies where it is possible to derive all (equilibrium) prices, as Walras had done in the nineteenth-century, and quite another to *prove* (that under certain conditions) such a set of prices can be computed for *any* feasible economy.

49 At the beginning of the second post-war phase, which we refer to as the *Global Minotaur* (see Chapters 11 and 12).

9 A most peculiar failure: The curious mechanism by which neoclassicism's theoretical failures have been reinforcing their dominance since 1950

1 See the CEA website at http://www.whitehouse.gov/administration/eop/cea/about/Former-Members.

2 Rather obligingly, once Keyserling succeeded Nourse to the CEA's chairmanship, he pushed for *National Security Council Resolution No. 68* which, in April 1950, asserted that increasing the military budget would not affect American living standards or risk the 'transformation of the free character of our economy'.

3 And when an academic economist was included, it was in spite (rather than because) of the fact that he was an economist.

4 Acheson had conceived and implemented the American/British/Dutch oil embargo that cut off 95 per cent of Japanese oil supplies and escalated the crisis with Japan in 1941, in the full knowledge that it might incite war between the USA and Japan.

5 Acheson played a central role at the Bretton Woods conference, in the design of the Marshall Plan, and was a great supporter of George Kennan and the latter's view on 'containment' of the USSR. Soon after, Acheson spearheaded the Truman Doctrine and designed the US position *vis-à-vis* the French in Vietnam (a strategy of simultaneously supporting and undermining them). During the Cuban Missile Crisis (a while after his formal retirement), he was brought back by President Kennedy to join his inner circle of advisors. Even Kennedy's successor, President Johnson, utilised his skills by asking him to pen a plan for resolving the Cyprus conflict; a plan whose core (proposed) solution reeked of the Cold War's logic.

6 As CEA Chair he advised President Kennedy and proved quite influential during the Johnson years. He left his mark by pushing, successfully, for augmenting the US domestic economy through tax cuts (accompanied by wage controls for the purposes of controlling inflation). He also suggested to President Johnson a *War on Poverty*, which Johnson enthusiastically espoused and turned into the Great Society initiative.

7 Arthur M. Okun (1928–80) held that position from 15 Feb 1968 to 20 Jan 1969. He was a member of CEA from 16 Nov 1964. See his Okun (1975). Paul A. Samuelson writing Okun's obituary for *Newsweek* in 1980 [Samuelson (1980 [1986]), p. 826] refers to an often cited saying by President Harry S. Truman who mistrusted academic economists: 'Harry Truman is sometimes quoted as saying, "What I want is a one-armed economist, who won't pussyfoot with 'on the one hand this, on the one hand that'." With respect this is foolish. What he'd have is a cripple. Or one-armed economists in two dogmatic varieties, those with a right arm only and those with only a left. And then you need a two-armed eclectic to adjudicate between them. Arthur Okun looked at both sides of an issue, and then, in striking his judicious compromise, he employed a cool hand in the service of a warm heart'.

8 In fact, the *Sveriges Riksbank Prize in Economic Sciences in Memory of Alfred Nobel 1975* was awarded jointly to Leonid Vitaliyevich Kantorovich (1912–86), a Soviet mathematician involved in planning problems and Tjalling C. Koopmans 'for their contributions to the theory of optimum allocation of resources'. (See http://nobelprize.org/nobel_prizes/economics/laureates/1975.)

9 Indeed, Kenneth Arrow, when commenting on policy issues, repeatedly adopted a social democratic, quasi-Keynesian tone.

10 Samuelson was mentioned in Section 8.1 of Chapter 8, as a member of a small study group of Harvard students whose purpose was the dissection of Keynes' *General Theory*. His textbook which was entitled, simply, *Economics*, is currently in its nineteenth edition, with William D. Nordhaus, a Yale economist, who has been its co-author since the twelfth edition (Samuelson, 1997). Samuelson, soon after acceptance of his doctoral thesis, moved to MIT where he built the economics department around him. After he had taught there for six decades, the elite ranks of the economics profession were filled with his former students, including Jagdish Bhagwati and Greg Mankiw, two younger economists destined to write influential textbooks of a mould similar to Samuelson's 1948 original. [Bhagwati wrote more on International Trade and Underdevelopment, e.g. Bhagwati, 1966. Mankiw was quite prolific in writing textbooks. See Mankiw (1998 [2009]), (1998 [2009]a), (1992 [2010]).

11 This and the next quotation are from an interview Paul Samuelson gave Kiyoshi Okonogi in November 2008 at his MIT office, where he was working almost until the end of his life in December 2009. The interview was published in the Japanese newspaper *Asahi Simbun* under the title: 'Financial Crisis: Work of 'Fiendish Monsters'.

12 In a later edition he observed, 'No longer does modern man seem to act as if he believed "That government governs best which governs least"' (8th edition, p. 140). In keeping with his Keynesian past, he writes that a large government provides 'built-in stabilizers' to the economy, through taxes, unemployment compensation, farm aid and welfare payments that tend to rise during a recession (8th edn: 332–4). In 1947, writing in a volume edited by Seymour E. Harris on the New [i.e. Keynesian] Economics a chapter on *General Theory* he describes the influence of the *General Theory* on his generation: 'I have always considered it a priceless advantage to have been born as an economist prior to 1936 and to have received a thorough grounding in classical economics. It is quite impossible for modern students to realize the full effect of what has been advisably called 'The Keynesian Revolution' upon those of us brought up in the orthodox tradition. What beginners today often regard as trite and obvious was to us puzzling, novel, and heretical.

   'To have been born as an economist before 1936 was a boon – yes. But not to have been born too long before!'

> *Bliss was it in that dawn to be alive,*
> *But to be young was very heaven!*

(Samuelson, 1947a: 145) The verses are from William Wordsworth's poem *The Prelude* written in 1805 on the French Revolution. The message is clear.

13 See Samuelson (1947). The thesis was submitted in 1941 and in the same year it won Harvard's David A. Wells Prize for best publishable thesis. But publication came six years later. See Samuelson (1998).

14 Pareto initiated Samuelson's interest in reformulating demand theory and the treatment of utility and the notion of social welfare. His attitude towards the maximising principle, the similarity between production and consumption theory was there. Equally we find in Pareto, as in Samuelson, the need for a mathematisation of economic science culminating in his 1911 article in the *Encyclopédie des sciences mathématiques* (Pareto, 1911) See also Pareto (1909). Nevertheless, Samuelson himself argued that his greatest influence came not from Pareto and Slutsky but through Willard Gibbs (Samuelson 1986, p. 836). In another paper he writes that 'All the more credit is due to the youthful Schumpeter, since after 1900 the moon of Pareto was serving to eclipse the sun of Walras. All hats off to Pareto, but as Lagrange lamented in eulogising Newton, there is alas only one system of the economic world to discover and Walras had already done that when Pareto was still a schoolboy.' (Samuelson, 1981, p. 8) He doth protest too much, we think. Samuelson was a major economist, but a major post-Paretian.

15 Samuelson always wanted to be the unifier. In his contribution on Schumpeter he writes: 'Marshall, despite his reputation as a synthesizer, was in fact primarily a *miniaturist* who lacked the energy and the will to shape a coherent masterwork in analytical economics. It went against the grain to admit that Schumpeter was right in elevating Leon Walras above Marshall and the rest as the Newton of economic who discovered the system of the world in his paradigm of General Equilibrium' (Samuelson, 1981: 8).

16 See the Mathematical Appendix to Marshall 1890. Further down, however, he qualifies his qualms: 'It is a danger which more than any other the economist must have in mind at every turn. But to avoid it altogether, would be to abandon the chief means of scientific progress: and in discussions written specially for mathematical readers it is no doubt right to be very bold in the search for wide generalizations'.

17 Where IS implies the assumption that the real economy is characterised by an equality between savings (S) and investment (I) while the money markets are also in equilibrium, with the supply of money (L) equalling M: the sum of (a) the demand for money for speculative purposes plus (b) demand for money for transaction purposes. For a history of the IS-LM diagram see Young (2010).

18 'In recent years 90 per cent of American Economists have stopped being "Keynesian economists" or "anti-Keynesian economists". Instead they have worked toward a synthesis of whatever is valuable in older economics and in modern theories of income determination. The result might be called neoclassical economics and is accepted in its broad outlines by all but about 5 per cent of extreme left wing and right wing writers.' [*Economics*, 1955, 3rd edn, p. 212.]

19 In this task he was ably assisted by Don Patinkin, a Chicago economist with strong roots at the Cowles Commission. See, for instance, his influential articles (Patinkin, 1948, 1949): (1948) 'Price Flexibility and Full Employment', American Economic Review 38(4): 543–64; and (1949) 'Involuntary Unemployment and the Keynesian Supply Function', Economic Journal 59(235): 360–83. His book (Patinkin, 1956) remained a classic for many years.

20 Money illusion is the idea that people think of money in nominal rather than in real terms. They do not realise for example that their wages buy less even if there is a wage increase when the prices of goods have increased by a larger proportion.

21 The fact that Keynes did refer to *money illusion* and to the resistance of wages to downward pressures has added to the confusion. While he certainly believed that people often do mistake average price changes for relative price shifts (the essence of *money illusion*), and that workers care more about their wage relative to the wages of similar professions (one possible cause of wage rigidity), he certainly did not explain capitalism's incapacity automatically to exit a depression by reference to these phenomena. Indeed, as explained in Chapter 7, he thought that an end of wage rigidities (i.e. wage reductions) would exacerbate a depression, rather than spearhead growth.

22 Nasar (1995). Nasar provides no attribution for the quote. Her article is a very interesting description of the market for introductory economics textbooks after Samuelson.

23 E.g. with Joan Robinson, Luigi Pasinetti and Piero Sraffa over the so-called 'capital controversies', which we discussed in Chapter 6 (and to which we return below, or with Marxist economists over the 'transformation problem' of Chapter 5.

24 That Samuelson never seemed to grasp the New Dealers' *Global Plan* is evidenced from the fact that the Text, while expansive on global aspects of economic development, has very little to say about Germany and Japan; the two economies that, according to Chapter 11 below, were such an important element of the *Plan*. From the 2nd to the 14th edition, Samuelson incredulously attributes Germany's recovery to currency reform and the removal of price controls (2nd edn: 36; 14th edn: 36). More surprisingly, he offers nothing on Japan, except for a throwaway line in the 8th edition: 'Japan's recent sprint has been astounding' (8: 796). In the 1980s and 1990s, even while many textbooks offered a more global approach, the Text still, to all intents and purposes, ignored Japan.

25 For a thorough presentation of this argument, on how Nash's four papers, published between 1950 and 1953, set off a chain reaction of attempts to unify at first all of political economics and later the whole gamut of social theory (using Nash's method), see Hargreaves-Heap and Varoufakis (2004).

26 For instance, David Colander and John Davis are among authors who point out that the percentage of economists engaging in Nash–Debreu style analysis is shrinking fast; that the majority of academic economists are turning to computational methods, behavioural economics, statistics and laboratory experiments. While it is true that the proportion of academics involved directly with formalism is small, we reject the point. Our reason is that formalism was always practised by a minority. However, it was this minority that produced the dominant economic paradigm. Despite the proliferation of non-formalist practices mentioned by these authors, formalism is still the source of the dominant economic paradigm. In short, to this day, if you were to ask academic economists how they envision the market mechanism, the vast majority will answer in a manner reflecting Debreu, Arrow and perhaps Nash. For more see Colander *et al.* (2004a); Davis (2006); Varoufakis and Arnsperger (2009). The Colander *et al.* article is reprinted in the 2008 spring issue (Vol. 7(1)) of *The Long Term View* which is devoted to the subject 'How Economics is Changing'.

27 For they think of what they do as scientific economics. The history of the term 'neoclassical' is discussed in Aspromourgos (1986).

28 Victorian values and practices evolved through time and meant different things in different sub-periods; e.g. the late Byzantine era resembled its earlier more 'Roman' phase very little indeed. This dynamic complexity, however, does not detract from the usefulness of an overarching characterisation such as 'Byzantine' or 'Victorian'.

29 A good example of such axiom-based definitions are Becker (1976), Blaug (1992), Vilks (1992), Hodgson (1999) and Colander (2005a). They define neoclassicism in terms of their *assumptions*. To take the most recent attempt to do so, Colander (2005a) defines neoclassicism thus: the 'holy trinity' of rationality, greed and equilibrium. Notice that, in terms of his definition, all it takes for a theory to step outside neoclassicism is a minor relaxation of any of these axioms (a relaxation that every self respecting graduate student can perform in their spare time). It was, therefore, inevitable that Colander (2005b) would conclude that neoclassical economics is dissolving. In contrast, our meta-axiomatic definition accommodates evolving axioms which, while in flux, remain within what we think is a particular and highly distinctive method; one that not only 'survives' these relaxations, but in fact one that strengthens its stranglehold over the profession as it evolves. In this sense, our line of argument is more in tune with Dow (1995) and Fine (2008). We say more on this in the next section.

30 For an excellent account see Philip Mirowski (1989).

31 See also Hodgson (2007); Udéhn (2001, 2002).

32 The predilection of mainstream economics for closed explanatory systems is also discussed in Lawson (2003).

33 John Geanakoplos and two other colleagues offer an excellent case in point. By allowing an agent's utility to depend directly on his/her second-order beliefs regarding his/her own choice, as is the case more often than not for all of us (e.g. Jill's utility from passing an examination differs depending on whether she thought that Jack expected her to pass or not) they enrich the model of individual agency. However, this enrichment comes at the price of indeterminacy even when the agent acts alone and under perfect information, namely all relevant data (e.g. Jill's decision may belong to violently different equilibria; in one she studies hard expecting that Jack thinks she will pass, an expectation that she wants to fulfil; in another she thinks he is not expecting her to pass, a thought

that makes her less eager to want to invest in this examination). See J. Geanakoplos, D. Pearce and E. Stacchetti (1989). Philip H. Wicksteed, one of the initial neoclassical economists, argued that egoism is not required by the theory, my motives for exchange may not be selfish. What is required, however, is 'non-tuism', i.e. disregard for the effect of the trade on the other trader. Justly Israel Kirzner (1976: 66) calls this an 'ingenious artificiality'.

34 See also Fine (2008).

35 To mention a few, social norms have been allowed to 'infect' a worker's preferences in a manner that explains wage rigidity and even the decision to join a strike (see Akerlof, 1980 and Varoufakis, 1989); preferences are formed endogenously (see Bowles, 1998); macroeconomic events influence individual motives (see Akerlof, 1982, 2007); social evolution determines private actions (see Weibull, 1995); what others think has a direct impact on what we want (see Rabin, 1993), etc.

36 For an introduction to Evolutionary Game Theory close in spirit to this book's narrative, see Hargreaves-Heap and Varoufakis (2004), Chapter 6. Some non-neoclassical readers will protest that Evolutionary Game Theory is not neoclassical. While we understand the hope this theory has given to many non-neoclassicists, and at the risk of wrecking it, we shall be arguing in the next section that Evolutionary Game Theory remains firmly neoclassical (at least given the present section's definition of neoclassicism).

37 Once upon a time, we could have instead talked of *methodological rationalism* as the dominant narrative centred on agents acting rationally. But since ordinal utilitarianism took over, there is no sense in narrating behaviour in terms of agents acting rationally. Instead, rationality is reduced to the consistency of one's preference ordering which, by definition, determines that which agents will do. See Arrow (1994) and Varoufakis (1998, Ch. 4).

38 See Varoufakis (2008) for the argument that such models are, essentially, ahistorical.

39 See David Hume (1740 [1888]).

40 However, while S's roots are Humean, Hume would have objected strongly to it. Our Reason, he would have thought, is too timid to tell us what is best in a social context, while our Passions are too unruly to fit neatly into some ordinal or expected utility function. It took the combined efforts of the late nineteenth-century Marginalists to build upon Jeremy Bentham's reduction of all the Passions to a single one (the passion for utility) before they tamed it sufficiently, bleached it of all psychology and sociality, thus reducing it to a unidimensional index of preference ordering which is expressible as a smooth, double differentiable ordinal utility function. Indeed, Jevons (1871), the most Benthamite of the Marginalist triad, had to fit all dimensions of utility as discussed by Bentham into one in order to derive the basic results of the theory.

41 In this sense, rather than being explained as the result of some complex calculus of the locals' desires, the logic of driving on the left in Gloucestershire, or on the right in South Maine, is to be found in some adaptation mechanism that followed on from a random event (or mutation), whose trace is often lost in the past, and which yielded a dominant evolutionary equilibrium.

42 'In every system of morality which I have hitherto met with ... I am surprised to find, that instead of the usual copulations of propositions, *is* and *is not*, I meet with no proposition that is not connected with an *ought* or an *ought not*. This change is imperceptible; but is, however, of the last consequence.' David Hume (1739/40 [1888]: III, i, 1.)

43 While the neoclassicists' technical sophistication has taken off since the time of Cournot (and even of Arrow and Debreu), one truth remains: stability analysis is a fig leaf to cover up the dearth of any consistent theory of how a market equilibrium might emerge on the basis of historically situated acts of self interested buyers and sellers. In fact, as Mantel (1974) and Sonnenschein (1972, 1973) have famously shown, such a demonstration is impossible. Analogously, in Game Theory, the theorists' favourite equilibrium concept (sub-game perfection) is also impossible to rationalise logically except under very special, atypical, circumstances (see Varoufakis, 1991, 1993).

44 Consider, for example, von Neumann's input–output analysis (von Neumann, 1937; a model that, as Kurz and Salvadori, 1993, suggested (and we mentioned in Chapter 8), fits nicely in the classical economics tradition). See also the standard Sraffian model of determining prices in the context of joint production (Sraffa, 1960); Goodwin's dynamic equilibrium yielding a stable pattern of oscillating inflation and unemployment (Goodwin, 1967); Marxist schemas of reproduction (Halevi, 1998), etc. They all 'discover' the equilibrium state or path on the basis of their primitive data and some pre-specified selection mechanism (e.g. the assumption that profit rates will equalise across sectors).

45 For example, John von Neumann's Game Theory (see Neumann, 1928, and Neumann and Morgenstern, 1944), while fully Marginalist, invariantly contained complete explanations of the

reasoning that would lead players to equilibrium. Similarly with Marshall (1890), for whom equilibration was a process that required a comprehensive exegesis that is best attempted at a partial equilibrium level of abstraction.

46 See Debreu (1959) and Arrow and Debreu (1954).

47 General Equilibrium theory's divorce from convergence analysis is well understood (see also note 44). Less appreciated is that a similar problem has been afflicting Game Theory ever since the Nash equilibrium became its foundational stone: while the simple, static Cournot–Nash oligopoly equilibrium requires no more than **e** to be arrived at, the moment the interaction acquires a more realistic structure (e.g. consists of a sequence of moves or is repeated) **e** does not suffice and **E** must be introduced urgently (and usually through the back door). See Hargreaves-Heap and Varoufakis, 2004, Chs 2 and 3.

48 Take for example models of markets in which N firms compete. Neither the assumption of profit driven managers nor perfect information on demand, costs, etc. can lead to firm predictions regarding price, output or profit levels. The theorist must introduce constraints on what moves firms are allowed to make (e.g. set prices, set output or both), as well as what one firm believes about the other's predictions regarding one's own strategy, etc. In this context, it is not possible rationally to argue that these beliefs are uniquely rational. They could have been otherwise. By smuggling into the analysis the *assumption* that these are the relevant beliefs, the theorist derives a determinate solution; a form of theoretical 'closure' equivalent to the introduction of **E**, the strong version of the third meta-axiom.

49 Our hypothesis here will be that the scholars who care about the logical coherence of the offered analysis are often not the same people who have the training to recognise the meta-axiomatic shift that goes on underneath the models' surface. Meanwhile, those who have the formal training usually lack the intellectual interest in the model's value as a piece of social science and, often, have too much riding on maintaining that research programme to expose its logical incoherence.

50 See Davis (2006), Colander (2005a, 2005b) and Colander *et al.* (2004a, 2004b).

51 Once upon a time, Marginalism's *Homo Economicus* was a simple lad (yes, a lad – see Hewitson, 1999). He liked what he bought and bought what he liked, loathed work, knew all he wanted to know (given the price of information), and cared not an iota either for his neighbours or for what they thought of him. As for the sort of economics built upon him, Marginalism-*cum*-neoclassicism was typified by a familiar melange of theoretical practices: labour markets which would return to equilibrium if the troublesome unions and the meddling government let them; a habitual recourse to *Say's Law*; interest rates which never failed to equalise investment and savings; a constant array of well behaved production and utility functions; etc.

52 Here we refer to *Expected Utility Theory*, which was developed by leading *Scientists* (see Neumann and Morgenstern, 1944; Savage, 1954) before the *Formalists* borrowed it in its entirety.

53 For surveys see Sugden (1991) and Starmer (2000).

54 That is, rendered consistent with *infinite order common knowledge rationality*; see Bernheim (1984) and Pearce (1984).

55 See Binmore (1989), Pettit and Sugden (1989) and Varoufakis (1993).

56 Another form of *we are damned if we know* result that we attributed to Keynes in Chapter 7 (recall Section 7.5). E.g. when a *prisoner's dilemma* is played again and again by the same players, the *Folk Theorem* shows that *anything may happen*. Players may cooperate, they may defect, or they may oscillate between cooperation and defection in patterns of infinite complexity. By extension, neoclassicism has nothing to say regarding the formation or otherwise of cartels in oligopolistic markets: they may form, break down, reform at will and in ways that no neoclassical model can pin down analytically. For more, see Hargreaves-Heap and Varoufakis (2004), Ch. 5.

57 The sheer convenience (for the modeller) of sticking to the assumption that rational agents must remain on the equilibrium path is aided and abetted by the fascinating, provocative, but ultimately deeply flawed, argument in Aumann (1976).

58 One such acknowledgment came from Levhari and Samuelson who in 1966 published a paper beginning with the admission that the neoclassical position was false: 'We wish to make it clear for the record that the non-reswitching theorem associated with us is definitely false. We are grateful to Dr Pasinetti ...' quoted in Burmeister (2000).

59 See Cohen and Harcourt (2003). See also Bliss (2005) for an illustration not only of the neoclassicists' readiness to ignore perfectly good scientific challenges but to take pleasure in taunting the challengers as well. He writes: 'If one asks the question: What new idea has come out of Anglo-Italian thinking in the past 20 years? one creates an embarrassing social situation. This is because

it is not clear that anything new has come out of the old, bitter debates. Meanwhile mainstream theorising has taken different directions. Interest has shifted from General Equilibrium style (high-dimension) models to simple, mainly one-good models.' In one paragraph, Bliss depicts the challengers' incredulity that their perfectly valid challenge had no impact on the profession as well as the latter's recoiling behind the original neoclassical position of, effectively, bowing to the *Inherent Error* and recoiling in the *corn model* or the Robinson Crusoe economy.

60 See Bishop (1964) who tried to breathe a bargaining process, borrowed from Zeuthen (1930), into Nash's axiomatics. However, such attempts had the same basic flaw as that of Cournot's 1838 original oligopoly dynamics (recall Chapter 6): they assumed that agents would make assumptions that required a deep misconception of the model itself.

61 Debreu was always clear in his mind that out-of-equilibrium formalism is impossible. So much so that he, in fact, also rejected stability analysis: '(W)hen you are out of equilibrium, in economics you cannot assume that every commodity has a unique price because that is already an equilibrium determination' (in Weintraub 2002, p. 146). Nash, on the other hand, harboured hope that his formalism would be vindicated by some form of evolutionary analysis. In his PhD thesis he had a famous section on the "Motivation and Interpretation" of his results in which he alluded to the idea of confirming his axiomatic derivation of equilibrium by positing players (drawn from a large population) who interact repeatedly (against a different opponent each time) without assuming that they 'have full knowledge of the total structure of the game, or the ability and inclination to go through any complex reasoning process' (Nash 1950a, p. 21).

62 For an anthology of the most significant papers of Game Theory's *Refinement Project*, see Yanis Varoufakis (2001).

63 Assuming that delays in reaching agreement were costly to both bargainers.

64 Hence the authoritative textbook on *Microeconomic Theory* by Mas-Colell, Whinston and Green (1995) presents the theorem under the title 'Anything goes' (Section 17E).

65 See Binmore (1989), Pettit and Sugden (1989) and Varoufakis (1993).

66 In a nutshell, rational agents have no reason not to stray from 'the' equilibrium path (be it deterministic or stochastic) in a bid to subvert the expectations of their opponent for their own potential benefit. See Varoufakis (1991), Sugden (2000) and Chapters 3, 4 and 5 of Hargreaves-Heap and Varoufakis (2004) for the complete argument.

67 See Arrow (1951). For a simple illustration of *Arrow's Impossibility Theorem*, and a discussion of its significance from the perspective of political economics, (see Chapters 8, 9 and 10) of Varoufakis (1998).

68 This is, of course, a line that Austrian Marginalists, like Friedrich von Hayek (see Chs 6 and 7), would have been more than happy with, as it strengthens their case for the disappearance of the state. It is a also a line actively pursued by American free-market philosopher Robert Nozick (1974).

69 Here we have a cacophonous crowd, espousing this second interpretation, ranging from Marxists to neo-Kantian philosophers such as John Rawls (1971). See also Amartya Sen's (1977) short but excellent article.

70 That is, a society in which there is more than one sector and where its citizens may have different preferences.

71 By *Homo Economicus* we imply the model of men and women consistent with the strong versions of methodological individualism and methodological instrumentalist (meta-axioms **D** and **S** respectively).

72 (See Chapters 2, 3 and 5) of Hargreaves-Heap and Varoufakis (2004).

73 Under (A) he is defecting on the common understanding that she will be doing likewise.

74 Suppose Jill predicts that Jack will cooperate. Under CKR, her only rational explanation is that Jack is prepared to sacrifice utility in order to benefit her. Her expectation that he is being kind to her puts her in a new type of dilemma: For if she defects, she will be profiting by trampling upon his kindness; a thought that may incur psychological costs for her. And if these costs are high enough, her best reply to his cooperative move is to cooperate too. On the occasion that both players hold similar beliefs, they may well find themselves in a new type of psychologically supported cooperative equilibrium which operates at three levels: actions, first order beliefs and second order beliefs.

75 Note that the direct reliance of players' utility function on second order beliefs is a departure from both the first meta-axiom (which demands a one way trajectory from *agency* to *structure*) and, derivatively, the second meta-axiom (which assumes an individuated index of behavioural success).

76 We call it that because **E** must now impose equilibrium not only between acts and beliefs but also between acts, beliefs and beliefs about beliefs! And it does this before the players get a chance to peruse the interaction. Thus the label **E on steroids** … *Methodological equilibration* (meta-axiom 3), in this context, is no longer prior to *methodological individualism* and *instrumentalism* (meta-axioms 2 & 3), as is the case in standard consumer theory, Game Theory or new classical macroeconomics; the axiomatic imposition of equilibrium is now necessary not just in order to predict the interaction's outcome but also in order to define the instrumentally rational agents' preferences! (See Chapter 7 of Hargreaves-Heap and Varoufakis, 2004, and Fehr and Gächter, 2000).

77 Notice how even this ultra-strong version of **E** has not defeated all the indeterminacy caused by the added psychological sophistication: in the end, the prisoner's dilemma, even after a priori assuming full alignment of actions, first and second order beliefs, now possesses two equilibria: one is the standard *mutual defection* outcome while the other is the cooperative outcome corresponding to mutually kind intentions (Jill expects Jack to cooperate in order to benefit her, thinking that she wants to do likewise; a thought which she is happy to confirm by cooperating herself).

78 The said leap is none other than the assumption that first- and second-order beliefs are aligned a priori. It is, arguably, impossible to rationalise such an assumption as there is no logical explanation of how such alignment would ever come about (with commonly known certainty) in a static game.

79 It is less defensible because the version of the third meta-axiom it relies on stretches credulity beyond the limits of even the most impressionable neoclassicist. At the same time, it gains unprecedented discursive power due to the combination of: (a) the claims that neoclassicism no longer needs to posit psychologically unsophisticated agents; and (b) the immense complexity (which is necessary to model equilibrium behaviour in this type of analysis) which makes it *impossible* for anyone other than 'experts' even to understand the mathematical structure of the new type of model. The 'exclusion' of 'outsiders' lends power to the 'insiders' and evokes feelings of awe among the 'outsiders', including some who are usually critical of neoclassicism.

80 See Maynard Smith (1974) and Dawkins (1976).

81 The vindication came from the demonstration that populations of mindless agents (who simply copy the more successful behaviour in their midst) converge onto equilibria that neoclassicists can only axiomatically impose on populations of hyper-rational agents. Nothing pleases the theorist more than the demonstration of a result's generality, especially when the same result is reached through wholly different avenues.

82 Non-neoclassicists were seduced not only by the dropping of instrumental rationality and its extensions but primarily by the demonstration that evolutionary adaptation mechanisms can yield hierarchies and discrimination on the basis of nothing more than *arbitrary* differences between agents. It took a small leap of the imagination to recognise this approach's potential for constructing a theory of institutionalised discrimination, even exploitation, within human society. See Hargreaves-Heap and Varoufakis (2002) for more on the joint evolution of conventions and discrimination.

83 See Davis (2003), (2006); Colander *et al.* (2004a), (2004b), Colander (2005a), (2005b).

84 To mention two relevant papers, Foster and Young (1990) acknowledge that politics is what happens when mutations are coordinated into aggregate shocks which test the established conventions while Kandori *et al.* (1993) examine the impact of rational experimentation in finite and discrete populations.

85 See Bergin and Lipman (1996).

86 For a fuller account see Hargreaves-Heap and Varoufakis, 2004, Ch. 6.

87 It did this in practice by focusing exclusively on evolutionary models where the *mutation mechanism* is utterly independent of the *adaptation mechanism* and agents are not allowed to attempt to pattern their mutations (either at the individual or the social level). This is equivalent to the Harsanyi-Aumann doctrine in Game Theory (see Hargreaves-Heap and Varoufakis, 2004); to ignoring the *Sonnenschein–Debreu–Mantel* theorem in General Equilibrium; to turning to single agent models in macroeconomics; and so on. In short, it is another form of version **E** of the third meta-axiom.

88 The discursive power from claims to having established the evolutionary turn of neoclassical equilibria would, of course, crumble under the weight of critiques like the one we presented above. However, neoclassicism is shielded from the force of such arguments due to their complexity. By elevating its failures at a higher level of abstraction, neoclassicism hides them from the eyes of all but a small minority who are keen (and able) to delve into the hidden axioms.

89 The resemblance between mainstream economists and the Azande is striking: whenever economists fail to predict properly some economic phenomenon (which is more often than not), that failure is accounted for by appealing to the same mystical economic notions which failed in the

first place. Occasionally new notions are created in order to account for the failure of the earlier ones. For instance, the notion of *natural* unemployment was created in the 1970s in order to explain the failure of the market to engender full employment and of economics to explain that failure. More generally, unemployment and excess demand (or supply) is 'proof' of insufficient competition which is to be fought by the magic of deregulation. If deregulation does not work, more privatisation will do the trick. If this fails, it must have been the fault of the labour market which is not sufficiently liberated from the spell of unions and government social security benefits; and so on – the original mystical notions beget new mystical notions.

90 See Coase (1988, p. 24).

91 See Blaug (1992); Keen (2001); Stiglitz (2002); Fullbrook (2003, 2004) for a small sample.

92 E.g. to allow for preferences not only to be endogenous but also contingent on expectations and social norms that are themselves comprised of higher-order expectations and beliefs.

93 Colander (2005b), for example, writes: 'previous views considered heterodox are moving into the mainstream, as the analytic and computing technology is allowing young researchers to develop these ideas in ways that will lead to institutional advancement ... Because of these changes, today one would no longer describe modern economics as neoclassical economics'. (For more references along these lines see note 83.) Turning to capitalism, the respective line has for a while been that, due to technological and social change, the traditional analytical categories 'capital' and 'labour' have evolved to such an extent that it no longer makes sense to define capitalism in the traditional manner.

10 A manifesto for *Modern Political Economics*: Postscript to *Book 1*

1 The *Inherent Error*, naturally, keeps returning every time economists attempt to 'close' their model ('evolutionary' or not) through the importation of the usual meta-axiom. *Evolutionary* Game Theory is a good example of how formalism uses up evolutionary ideas before emptying them of content and consigning them to the dustbin, once it has justified its own 'solution' concepts by giving them a (fake) evolutionary interpretation. (For more details on this, see Varoufakis, 2008.) But there is nothing new here. Karl Marx ended up emptying his own formidable dialectics of content when he tried to 'close' his model of capitalist growth and value (see Chapter 5). It is the price every economist pays for replacing indeterminacy with 'closure'.

2 Olivier Blanchard, in the French newspaper *Libération*, 16 October 2000. The article is entitled 'En défense de la science économique' (our translation).

3 Although, to be fair to Walras, Debreu and Arrow, they never in fact claimed to be mathematising Smith's argument, but Mas-Colell *et al.* (1995) do.

4 Kirman (1989, p. 138) adds the following to capture the neoclassicists' recoiling behind simplistic models: 'It is not mere chance that one assumption that leads to strong results as to uniqueness and stability is that society should behave like an individual ... There is no more misleading description in modern economics than the so-called microfoundations of macroeconomics which in fact describe the behaviour of the consumption or production sector by the behaviour of one individual or firm.'

5 These are, naturally, broad brushstrokes by which to paint the portrait of major intellectuals. One might plausibly argue, for instance, that by the time Keynes had finished his *General Theory* very few of his roots in Marshall's Marginalism remained, at least when thinking of the macroeconomy. In this sense, the two ticks in Keynes's row ought to be fainter than the corresponding ticks in the rows of the Austrians or the Marginalists.

6 This is not to say that they did not acknowledge the special features of human nature in other writings. Adam Smith, for instance, did so extensively in his *Moral Sentiments*. Our point here is that human labour and decision making is rendered mechanistic in their writings on political economics.

7 T.S. Eliot, 'Little Gidding' (1942), the last of his *Four Quartets*.

8 The *Oxford Concise Dictionary* defines the parallax phenomenon as follows: 'Apparent displacement of object, caused by actual change of point of observation.' See also Žižek (2006) in which the author makes a similar point with regard to debates regarding binary oppositions in political philosophy.

11 From the *Global Plan* to *a Global Minotaur*: The two distinct phases of post-war US hegemony

1 It was at that point that successive British governments began clutching at straws, namely, the 'Special Relationship', which turned the UK into a minor executor of US policy in exchange for

privileged access to the US market for British multinationals and the linkage of the City of London to Wall Street.

2 In a radio interview some years ago, linguist and political activist *Noam Chomsky* pointed out an interesting fact about the Marshall Plan, one that links the United States, France, and Holland with European imperialism in Asia (Chomsky 2003). A large part of France's share of Marshall Plan aid went to re-colonising Indochina, a prelude to the Vietnam War that was, eventually, to have such catastrophic effects on everyone involved but, also, for the *Global Plan* itself (see below). Another example is Holland. It used its portion of Marshall Plan aid to re-conquer Indonesia, a Dutch colony that had managed to liberate itself from Japan towards the end of the war. Interestingly, the United States, quite furious with the Dutch, leaned on them heavily in 1950, pressurising them to send troops to Korea (so as to make amends for the misuse of Marshall Plan, for the purpose of its delusions of colonial grandeur).

3 There is ample evidence that US policymakers were well aware of the importance of generating high foreign effective demand for US output *by political means* since at least the last decade of the nineteenth-century. See US State Department memorandum circa 1895, quoted in Zinn (1998:5).

4 A good example is Japan's application to join the Organisation for Economic Cooperation and Development (OECD) (the OEEC's successor) in 1964. Washington went out of its way to sign a dozen trilateral treaties allowing European countries greater access to US markets, provided they waived the right to use GATT's clause 35 against Japan.

5 With the persecution of the Greek Civil War, the appeasement of Franco and Salazar regimes in Spain and Portugal, and the safeguarding of the iron curtain's impenetrability.

6 Through a long and comprehensive occupation involving the writing of the country's new constitution.

7 This bifurcation of the US economy into two segments, one attached to the MIC and ACE, the other not, deepened inequality among American workers and communities; an inequality that is still evident today. The segmentation is palpable when one considers that the US features on the one hand space-age industries and on the other sectors that differ little from Developing World standards.

8 In a BBC Radio 4 Documentary 'The Dollar and Dominance' [Presenter: Ngaire Woods; Producer: Chris Bowlby; Editor: Hugh Levinson. Broadcast date: 23 October 2008]. Transcript available at http://news.bbc.co.uk/nol/shared/spl/hi/programmes/analysis/transcripts/23_10_08.txt.

9 It was then that different ideas came to the fore for an alternative to the Dollar. For instance, there was thought of a new role for the Yen or the Deutschmark or some new form of world money linked to the value of commodities, e.g. butter, wheat, rubber, steel; 'butter money' as it was disparagingly called. The reason, of course, that none of these transpired, and the dollar remained as the reserve, or privileged, currency, was the simple truth that no currency can rise internationally as a dominant unit of exchange if it is not backed by substantial political power.

10 Interestingly, despite the massive increase in oil's Dollar price, there was not much increase in terms of its gold value. Hammes and Wills (2005) remark: 'Between January 1970 and December 1979, 13.5 barrels of oil exchanged for one ounce of gold, on average. The minimum was 7.91 barrels per ounce in mid-1976, and the maximum was 34 barrels per ounce in mid-1973. Most often (that is, plus or minus one standard deviation of the mean), the range was from 9.25 to 17.7 barrels per ounce.' See Hammes and Wills (2005).

11 During the Great Depression in the 1930s (recall Chapter 7), the scourge of unemployment was accompanied (and intensified) by declining prices (or deflation). Policymakers used to think that at least they only had to slay one of capitalism's dragons at a time, not both: either inflation or unemployment, and never both at once. However, in the 1970s this segmentation ended. In 1971 the inflation and unemployment rates were 5.6% and 5.5% respectively. In 1974 inflation had risen to 12% and unemployment to 6.8%. By the end of the decade, in 1979–80, inflation scaled the 13% mark while unemployment climbed to 8%.

12 Along an identical line, a 1973 annual report of the White House *Council on International Economic Policy*, quoted by Oppenheim (1976–77) notes that: 'the United States stood to gain from higher oil prices and the resulting surplus of OPEC's investible funds... The United States is likely to receive a large share of those funds'.

13 It is for this reason that the 1998–2002 crisis in Argentina was an important turning point. After years of IMF-led attempts to maintain the Peso–Dollar, one-to-one, exchange rate, the arrangement collapsed. The IMF kept pumping loans into Argentina ostensibly to maintain the Dollar–Peso equivalence. All it did was to buy time for the elites and the multinationals to liquidate their

Argentinean assets and move them, in dollars, to Wall Street. Once the exodus was complete, the loans dried up and guess who was left with the bill of more than $80 billion? The lower middle class and the working class whose labour is, to this day, repaying those loans. The tragedy was most palpable for the Argentinean middle class: they lost everything, their savings wiped out in a manner reminiscent of mid-war Germany. However, it was also a blow for our *Minotaur* since, from that moment onwards, the Argentinean economy decoupled from the United States and was co-opted by China who sourced much of their soya and meat imports from Latin American countries, mainly Argentina and Brazil.

14 Note the brief period during President Clinton's administration, when the US budget deficit disappeared, turning into a good surplus. It coincided with the heightening of the Minotaur's capacity to devour foreign capital and a massive expansion in the US trade surplus (see Figure 11.5). It is true to say that the Clinton administration put a great deal of effort into curbing the budget deficit. However, at the same time, under the tutelage of the then Treasury Secretary Larry Summers, Wall Street was freed from all regulatory constraints. It was the beginning of the financial bubble that was to explode in 2008. Thus, while the budget deficit was eliminated for a few years, this was accomplished by strengthening the Minotaur both in terms of the capital inflows and the drive to financialisation. For more see the next chapter.

15 Halevi and Lucarelli (2002) write: 'No systematic synergies exist any longer between Japan and its area of influence. In this respect Japan and East Asia constitute the most vulnerable point of the international political economy of US imperialism. On one hand, this area is fully tied to the American economy; on the other hand, it contains two countries of world importance: Japan, as a productive core, and the People's Republic of China. The external surpluses of these two countries and of Taiwan represent a major part of the US deficit. Thus the surpluses must be channelled to the financing of the international position of the United States. By the same token the two trillion dollar savings in Japan's deposits must be opened up to the hedge funds and other institutions mainly operating from, or in conjunction with, Wall Street.'

16 This is because, if there is relatively high inflation, the asset values and financial assets purchased by incoming capital would have declined in value.

12 Crash: 2008 and its legacy (with an addendum by George Krimpas entitled 'The Recycling Problem in a Currency Union')

1 We found this out back in 2003 after publishing our basic argument. See Halevi and Varoufakis (2003a and 2003b).

2 The trickle-down theory is an old chestnut. It is actually the initial version of Adam Smith's 'invisible hand' argument. In his *Theory of Moral Sentiments* (1759) Adam Smith writes: 'The rich only select from the heap what is most precious and agreeable. They consume little more than the poor, and in spite of their natural selfishness and rapacity, though they mean only their own conveniency, though the sole end which they propose from the labours of all the thousands whom they employ, be the gratification of their own vain and insatiable desires, they divide with the poor the produce of all their improvements. They are led by an *invisible hand* to make nearly the same distribution of the necessaries of life, which would have been made, had the earth been divided into equal portions among all its inhabitants, and thus without intending it, without knowing it, advance the interest of the society, and afford means to the multiplication of the species. When Providence divided the earth among a few lordly masters, it neither forgot nor abandoned those who seemed to have been left out in the partition. These last too enjoy their share of all that it produces.' Smith (1759 [1982]), IV.i.10, pp. 184–5 (emphasis added).

3 For the relevant supporting tables, see Chapter 11. For additional evidence see Bernstein and Allegretto (2007) who demonstrate that, in the unregulated US labour market, hard work and investment in one's human capital does not buy one a ticket out of poverty and into a higher social stratum. According to the latest figures from official US sources, *social mobility is less correlated with educational accomplishment than ever before*! Mischel, Bernstein and Allegretto (2007). See also Rick Wolff for further supporting evidence: Wolff (2010).

4 Indeed, if we look at the 1977 to 1998 period, the real hourly wage of American workers (excluding the wages of corporate managers) fell by 14 per cent!

5 When unemployment broke the one million mark in 1975 this was a cultural shock in the UK. Thatcher in her election campaign promised to reduce unemployment with the famous Saatchi poster of a dole queue with the not too subtle pun 'Labour isn't working'. Eventually after endless

massaging of the unemployment statistics, 17 changes in all, of which only three were neutral and the rest reduced the number of unemployed statistically, unemployment trebled reaching in 1986 an all-time-post depression height of more than 10 per cent at 3 million unemployed with the massaged data.

6 Table 12.1 confirms that unit labour costs in Britain rose fast, more than 11 times as fast as in the United States. Even in the 1990s, British labour costs rose faster than in all other major developed countries.

7 These were essentially 'stag' issues that were heavily oversubscribed and hence rationed. TSB did not even belong to the British Government. In some cases, as with BP, the advisors to the government were also the underwriters of the issue; and disaster following a stock market crash prior to the scheduled IPO was averted by the government guaranteeing the price of the share. The public was encouraged to buy through mass TV advertisement (The 'Tell Sid' campaign of British Gas, for example). Joe Q. Public soon cashed his profits by selling the stocks which reverted to the hands of the usual investors thus ending the dreams of public capitalism. For a history of privatisation in the Thatcher era see David Parker (2009).

8 Volcker 2005.

9 Extracts from a speech given by Stephen Roach in New York on 12 May 2002, entitled 'World Think, Disequilibrium and the Dollar'. We first read that speech on Morgan Stanley's website, which no longer lists it. Quoted in Chesnais (2006), p. 50.

10 See also Lanchester (2006), Fishman (2006) and the 2005 documentary by Robert Greenwald entitled 'Wal-Mart: The High Cost of Low Price'.

11 Which, although higher than the minimum wage in the United States, means that its workers live permanently under the poverty line.

12 Moreover, in a curious case of misogyny, Wal-Mart seems unwilling to promote its female workers. Apparently, the largest private lawsuit in US history involves Wal-Mart's underpayment and failure to promote more than 1.5 million women workers.

13 Quoted from a radio interview in December 2008.

14 Figure 12.1 somewhat underplays the extent of Europe's and Japan's financing of the *Minotaur* by including Britain in the European camp, given that Britain was running (just like the United States).

15 See John Lanchester (2009).

16 See Black and Scholes (1973).

17 These include the Russian default of 1998, which we already mentioned, the collapse of LTCM in the same year, the contemporaneous major crisis in South-East Asia and, finally, the implosion of the dot.com or New Economy bubble in 2000–1.

18 See Markowitz (1952).

19 Toin (1958).

20 In effect, Black and Scholes openly threw out of court an economist's approach, replacing it with an actuarial perspective. The Latins have an apt saying on this: *Quod ab initio vitiosum est non posset ex post convalescere.*

21 Li grew up in rural China in the 1960s. He studied economics at Nankai University before moving to Canada to complete an MBA at Laval University. Then he took an MA in Actuarial Science and gained a PhD in Statistics, both from the University of Waterloo. By the time the East Asian crisis was destroying LCTM, in 1997, he started working for the Canadian Imperial Bank of Commerce. In 2004 he moved to Barclays Capital where he proceeded to build from scratch its quantitative analysis department.

22 In an interview he gave to Mark Whitehouse (see *The Wall Street Journal*, 12 September, 2005), well before the *Crash of 2008*, Dr Li said that 'the most dangerous part [of his formula], is when people believe everything coming out of it ... [V]ery few people understand the essence of the model.' Whitehouse (2005).

23 Doubt about the constancy of γ would have cost them their jobs, especially so given that their supervisors did not really understand the equation but were receiving huge bonuses while it was being used.

24 The following subsection draws heavily from two articles published in *Monthly Review*: Halevi and Lucareli (2002) and Halevi and Varoufakis (2003a).

25 Indeed, from 1985 to 1987, the dollar devalued relative to the yen by more than 50 per cent.

26 The other purpose of *Plaza* was to accommodate the United States' determination that its multinationals should play a larger role in the global electronics market that Japan and Germany threatened to dominate.

27 Indeed, during the period of real estate bubble the richest man in the world in Forbes list was a Japanese real estate magnate, Yoshiaki Tsutsumi. By 2007 he was removed from the billionaire's list.

28 As for Britain, we leave it outside this taxonomy for reasons already alluded to above. Following its deindustrialisation, under the Thatcher government, the only thing standing between Britain and the magpies was the City of London; its pivotal position in the world of finance. In the aftermath of 2008, perhaps it is time to include it in the magpies, albeit in a category of its own in view of the retention of its own currency.

29 France too was not very keen on sustained growth because successive governments, including the socialist administration of President Mitterrand, feared that growth would lead to further wage demands.

30 Recall (from Chapter 11) how in the 1940s and 1950s the Americans decided to set up the European branch of the institutions supporting the *Global Plan* in Paris, rather in the territory of their main protégé (Germany). The OEEC, which later turned into the OECD, is a case in point.

31 The *actual* plan for a common currency was essentially drafted by President Mitterrand and his ex-minister of finance, Jacques Delors, who had become (perhaps the only influential) head of the European Commission. Their motivation was to use the creation of the Euro as a means of getting around the ants' neo-mercantilism and of exercising a modicum of control over Germany's stringently deflationary monetary policies.

32 French philosopher Gilles Deleuze (1968) defines a simulacrum as the avenue by which an authority occupying a globally privileged position may be 'challenged and overturned'. In his reading, a simulacrum is a 'system ... in which different relates to different by means of difference itself. What is essential is that we find in these systems no prior identity, no internal resemblance'. See Gilles Deleuze (1968), pp. 372–3.

33 Wolfgang Münchau reported in the *Financial Times* of 21 March 2010 that: 'Rainer Brüderle, economics minister, said last week there was nothing the government could do about demand because consumption was a decision taken by private individuals. A senior Bundesbank official even compared the Eurozone to a football league, in which Germany proudly held the number one slot.' It is impossible to believe that anyone who has even thought of macroeconomics, let alone studied it, would draw such an inane comparison. Every single German economics minister, from the 1950s to this day, set out to ensure that aggregate demand is managed in such a way as to ensure that domestic consumption remains more or less constant (as a percentage of German income) and the additional aggregate demand that is necessary to maintain German capital accumulation is imported from the rest of Europe. Brüderle's comments are simply a cynical statement symbolising Germany's authoritarian refusal to enter into a sensible debate on the EU's macroeconomy.

34 The import dependency on technology sectors and also on durable goods is such that past pre-euro devaluations did not help improve the external position of these countries. Both Spain and Greece, but not Portugal, experienced higher than EU average growth rates. Spain's growth was due to the insertion of the country into the international real estate market via the City of London. In the case of Greece its fiscal deficit enabled it to sustain an import oriented growth. In both instances the growth of domestic demand led to higher activity entailing yet more imports per capita.

35 At a time that Europe's magpies and France had to reckon also with growing deficits with Asia.

36 See also Jörg Bibow (2009).

37 Meanwhile, the East of Germany had entered terminal decline. Bibow (2009) explains: 'A population of 16 million in 1989 had collapsed to 12.5 million by 2008, and was set to fall further – perhaps much further – with the exodus of young women to the West. Between 1993 and 2008, no less than two-thirds of 18- to 29-year-olds born in the East had abandoned it. In the DDR, a leading writer from the region has remarked that buildings rotted, but they contained people who had work; now the buildings are brightly refurbished, and the people are dead or gone.'

38 The reader may point out that wages also rose in that same period by about 4 per cent. While this is a true *average* figure, it hides the fact that from 1995 to 2008 the bottom 25 per cent of workers (in terms of wages) saw a 14 per cent decline in their wages.

39 See Reinhart and Rogoff (2009).

40 Of all those books, we pick two at random to recommend to the reader: Kansas (2009) and Soros (2009).

41 The Treasury's equity contribution of the $5 would actually come from something called TARP (the *Troubled Assets Relief Program*) whereas the Fed's $50 would come from the FDIC (the *Federal Deposit Insurance Corporation,* founded by the New Dealers, as part of the *Glass–Steagall Act of 1933,* in order to guarantee to depositors their savings in case of a bank failure). The *Geithner–Summers Plan* set aside $150 billion for TARP, $820 billion for FDIC and expected the private sector (hedge and pension funds) to chip in $30 billion of their own money.

42 If the *good scenario* materialises, *H*'s return equals $15. If the bad *good scenario* materialises, *H*'s returns are zero. Should it take part in this simulated market gain? The entry cost is $5. Suppose that the probability of the *good scenario* is p (where $0<p<1$). *H*'s expected returns from participating equal $15p + 0(1-p) = 15p$. Its cost from participating is a fixed $5. Clearly, it is on average a good idea to participate if $15p > 5$, i.e. if $p>1/3$. But if hedge funds estimate p to be less than $1/3$, they would stay out.

43 Moreover, if by some miracle its subsidiary *H'* can sell *c* for more than $100, it will stand to gain an extra sum.

44 Vandana Shiva (2005), an Indian physicist and ecologist who directs the Research Foundation on Science, Technology, and Ecology offers a compelling explanation of the food crisis that had erupted in the developing nations just before the *Crash of 2008.*

45 In 2008, just before all hell broke loose, the EU had an annual trade surplus with the United States in manufactures of €64 billion (with another €6 billion in services) while the net capital transfer from the EU to the United States came to €104.6 billion. While these figures pale into insignificance when compared to the zillions pumped by governments into the financial system in 2008, they reflect real money (as opposed to the monopoly money bandied about by Wall Street, central banks and governments in the context of financialisation and the states' attempt to save it).

46 See Theil (2009).

47 The French banks, it must be noted, took advantage of the US government's bailout of the financial sector. The bailout of AIG in particular saved their bacon, since a collapse of the American insurer would have translated into a French write off of hundreds of billions of dollars. This can be gleaned from what followed Lehman's collapse. BNP-Paribas claimed around $1.3 billion dollars from the US government fund that oversaw the dismantling of Lehman Brothers; Societe Generale $800 million and Dexia $400 million.

48 While the IMF was to charge less than 3 per cent for its €15 billion, the EZ–ECB loans (at Germany's insistence) would be given at an interest rate of 5 per cent. In effect, a net transfer of wealth was being proposed from Athens to Berlin, since Germany would be able to borrow that money at less than 3 per cent and then re-lend it to Greece at 5 per cent. There is nothing like European solidarity to bring a tear to an outsider's eye ...

49 The reader is reminded that Herbert Hoover was the US President in 1929, whose response to the *Crash* was a policy of belt-tightening; a policy that turned the *Crash of 1929* into the Great Depression of the 1930s.

50 'Dr Melchior: A Defeated Enemy', Keynes (1949 [1972]), p. 428.

51 We have replaced 'Greek' for *German;* 'European' for *French and British;* 'Greece' for *Germany;* 'financial assistance package' for *Peace;* 'the 2008 crisis' for *war.* See the 'Introduction' to John Maynard Keynes's *The Economic Consequences of the Peace.* New York: Harcourt Brace, 1920.

52 Why do we claim that the EU–ECB–IMF package constitutes punishment, when all it reportedly does is to save Greece from bankruptcy? Because, we suggest, it does no such thing. With the exorbitant interest rates that it charges, and given its steadfast resistance to any renegotiation of Greece's existing debt, it pushes Greece further into insolvency. Just as a cruel doctor might administer enough medicine to keep the patient alive for a while longer so that he/she keeps suffering more excruciating pain, but not enough medicine to prevent him/her from shuffling off the mortal coil, so too the EU–ECB–IMF package, as it stands, only prolongs the Greek state's agony without preventing the inevitable bankruptcy. And when the bankruptcy comes, it will come at a time of a smaller national income and a higher overall debt level. It is not, therefore, unreasonable to describe this package as a punishment that is as cruel as it is unusual.

53 E.g. letting Greece default and allowing the ECB to bail out the banks (Greek, French and German).

54 We owe the *problématique* of this subsection, its title and quite a few complete sentences to George Krimpas.

55 From Virgil's *Aeneid* (II.49). The most common English translation is 'Whatever this is, beware of the Greeks even if they are bearing gifts'. The popular German translation quoted here paraphrases Virgil to say: 'Beware of false friends'.

56 See A.J.P. Taylor (1954).

57 In particular the readiness of the German trade unions, post-unification, to accept collective bargains that would limit pay in exchange for higher employment rates.

58 China's orders for German capital goods dropped by more than 50 per cent in the 2008–10 period as the Beijing government chose to maintain the growth rate by means of a stimulus package that is aimed at domestically produced capital goods.

59 While penned by French bureaucrats and politicians, the Maastricht Treaty, as is all Treaties, a compromise, was nonetheless a German Treaty, a Westfalian treaty in reverse: an imposition on Europe of the German Order, an exportation of the internal German order; an order that required no military divisions but only hard monetary reserves.

60 Chapter VI, p. 238, *The Economic Consequences of the Peace*, New York, Harcourt Brace, 1920.

61 Latin America too reacted both politically (by electing left wing governments) and also by turning to China for sources of both investment and demand.

62 The IMF reported that in 2007 alone developing economies (primarily China, but also India, Brazil and Argentina) attracted $600 billion in net private capital inflows. At the same time, they ran a $630 billion current account surplus. To alleviate this gross imbalance, their central banks bought dollars and amassed $1.24 trillion in dollar and Euro exchange reserves. Their governments' sovereign funds (whose purpose is to buy shares abroad as a form of national investment) added approximately another $150 to the total. While more is going to sovereign funds, the vast majority remains with the world's central banks.

63 Which was no more than the spread of US-style financialisation to the four corners of the world under the tutelage of the *Global Minotaur*.

64 In an Australian Broadcasting Company (ABC) radio interview, Mexican economist Rogelio Ramírez de la O stated in 2009: 'Even strong companies that are subsidiaries of international firms are very, very discouraged at the way their volumes have fallen and their margins have been totally squeezed. The China effect is kind of overwhelming.'

65 Alan Greenspan, 'We need a better cushion against risk', *Financial Times*, 26 March 2009.

66 See Varoufakis (2002–3).

67 See PBS (2008).

13 A future for hope: Postscript to *Book 2*

1 In Norman Jewison's 1991 film *Other People's Money*, such an old-style entrepreneur is played by Gregory Peck whose old-fashioned factory comes under attack by Larry the Liquidator, played by Danny DeVito, not for the productive value of the factory but for its asset stripping potential. The speeches by the two men at the General Assembly of the shareholders, who vote in favour of Larry, typify the old and the new ethic.

2 See Bryan and Rafferty (2006).

3 Which, as we saw in Chapter 9, was the strong version of neoclassicism's third meta-axiom.

4 See Bertolt Brecht's *Threepenny Novel*, where the parable is part of the plot (Brecht, 1956: 374 ff).

5 The definition of the dissident as a person 'living in truth' is due to Vaclav Havel, the Czech dissident playwright who later became President of Czechoslovakia. His own life is a cautionary tale of how heroic dissidence can shrivel and die once in power. Havel's own demeanour, once he became President, offers insights.

6 John Lanchester in an article in November 2009 in the *London Review of Books* with the title 'Bankocracy' wrote 'In the meantime, perhaps we should try and think of a name for the new economic system, which certainly isn't capitalism: that, remember, is all about "creative destruction", and the freedom to fail. That's exactly what we don't have. The most accurate term would probably be "bankocracy"'. Since two of us are Greeks we may suggest the better term 'trapezocracy' for rule by the banks (*trapeza* in Greek, ancient and modern, means *bank*) instead of the anglo-latin hybrid. As, however, an astute reader of the article (Mazen Labban, 2010) observed the term was already in use by Marx in *Capital*, vol. 1, ch. 31. The term is *Bankokratie* in German and can also be found in *Capital*, Vol, 1, ch. 27, *The Class Struggles in France*, etc. Alas, even in trapezocracy we are not the first. Googling the term produced a single result by an erudite but anonymous reader of Lanchester's article who in deep cyberspace objected to the term *bankocracy* and suggested *trapezocracy* instead.

7 It is called 'Mitigating Credibility Problems through Institutional Design' (Rogoff, 1986).

8 As the ancient Athenians knew only too well, the lynchpin of democracy is isegoria, that is, equal say in the final formulation of policy independently of whether one is rich, comfortably off, or indeed a pauper eking a modest existence out of manual labour (see Herodotus, 5.78. The Greek dictionary of Liddell, Scott & Jones defines it as '*equal right of speech*, and generally, *political equality*'). In this reading, the key figure in classical Athens was not Pericles, or orators of stunning talent like Demosthenes, but, rather, the anonymous landless peasant who, despite his propertyless-ness, had a voice in the Assembly of equal weight to that of the great and the good. See also Wood (1988).

9 The plebs (e.g. workers, mechanics; i.e. Aristotle's *banausoi*) 'are sensible that their habits in life have not been such as to give them those acquired endowments without which, in a deliberative assembly, the greatest natural abilities are for the most part useless … *We must therefore consider merchants as the natural representatives of all these classes in the community*.' Alexander Hamilton, *Federalist*, 35 (emphasis added). See Wood (1995), ch. 7 entitled 'The Demos versus "We, the People"'.

10 *Trapeza,* which is, as we said above, Greek for bank, is a good antonym for *Demos*, we feel.

11 To give just one example, the US–Mexico border fence is being built by Israeli companies that cut their teeth building the Wall in Palestine.

12 His poem *Second Coming* written after the First World War (1919) [Yeats 1920, p. 19] is even more apposite to the present situation. We quote:

> *Turning and turning in the widening gyre*
> *The falcon cannot hear the falconer;*
> *Things fall apart; the centre cannot hold;*
> *Mere anarchy is loosed upon the world,*
> *The blood-dimmed tide is loosed, and everywhere*
> *The ceremony of innocence is drowned;*
> *The best lack all conviction, while the worst*
> *Are full of passionate intensity.*

Bibliography

Akerlof, G.A. (1980). 'A Theory of Social Custom of which Unemployment may Be One Consequence', *Quarterly Journal of Economics*, 94: 749–75.

Akerlof, G.A. (1982). 'Labor Contracts as Partial Gift Exchange', *Quarterly Journal of Economics*, 96: 543–69.

Akerlof, G.A. (2007). 'The Missing Motivation of Macroeconomics', *American Economic Review*, 97: 5–36.

Akerlof, G.A. and R.J. Shiller (2009). *Animal Spirits: How Human Psychology Drives the Economy, and Why it Matters for Global Capitalism*, Princeton, NJ: Princeton University Press.

Alchian, A. and H. Demsetz (1972). 'Production, Information Costs, and Economic Organization', *American Economic Review*, 62: 777–85.

Allais, M. (1943). *A la recherche d'une discipline économique, 1e partie, L'économie pure*, Tome 1, Paris: Impr. Ateliers Industria.

Allais, M. (1953). 'Le comportement de l'homme rationnel devant le risque, critique des postulats et axiomes de l'ecole americaine', *Econometrica*, 21: 503–46.

Aristophanes (1924). *The Lysistrata, The Thesmophoriazusae, The Ecclesiazusae, The Plutus*, with the English translation of Benjamin Bickley Rogers, London: Heinemann.

Aristotle (1926). *Nicomachean Ethics*, with an English translation by H. Rackham, London: Heinemann.

Aristotle (1932). *The Politics*, with an English translation by H. Rackham, London: Heinemann.

Arnsperger, C. and Y. Varoufakis (2003). 'Toward a Theory of Solidarity', *Erkenntnis*, 59: 157–88.

Arnsperger, C. and Y. Varoufakis (2006). 'What Is Neoclassical Economics? The Three Axioms Responsible for Its Theoretical Oeuvre, Practical Irrelevance and, thus, Discursive Power', *Post-Autistic Economics Review*, 38: 2–12.

Arrow, K.J. (1951 [1963]). *Social Choice and Individual Values* (2nd edn), New Haven, CT: Yale University Press.

Arrow, K.J. (1959). 'Towards a Theory of Price Adjustment', in M. Abramovitz (ed.), *Allocation of Economic Resources,* Stanford, CA: Stanford University Press.

Arrow, K.J. (1994) 'Methodological Individualism and Social Knowledge', *American Economic Review (Papers and Proceedings)*, 84: 1–9.

Arrow, K.J. (2009). 'Some Developments in Economic Theory since 1940: An Eyewitness Account', *Annual Review of Economics*, 1:1–16.

Arrow, K.J. and G. Debreu (1954). 'Existence of an Equilibrium for a Competitive Economy', *Econometrica*, 22.

Arrow, K.J. and F.H. Hahn (1971). *General Competitive Analysis*, San Francisco, CA: Holden-Day.

Arrow, K.J., S. Bowles and S. Durlauf (eds) (2000). *Meritocracy and Economic Inequality*, Princeton, NJ: Princeton University Press.

Aspromourgos, T. (1986). 'On the Origins of the Term Neoclassical', *Cambridge Journal of Economics*, 10: 265–70.

Aspromourgos, T. (2009). *The Science of Wealth: Adam Smith and the Framing of Political Economy*, London: Routledge.

Atwood, M. (2008). *Payback – Debt and the Shadow Side of Wealth*, CBC Massey Lecture.

Aumann, R. (1976). 'Agreeing to Disagree', *Annals of Statistics*, 4: 1236–9.

Bachelier, L. (1900). *Théorie de la spéculation*, Paris: Gauthier-Villars.

Bachelier, L. (2006). *Louis Bachelier's Theory of Speculation: The Origins of Modern Finance*, translated and with commentary by Mark Davis and Alison Etheridge, Princeton, NJ and Oxford: Princeton University Press.

Baldamus, W. (1961). *Efficiency and Effort*, London: Tavistock.

Baumol, W. (1997). 'J. B. Say on Unemployment and Public Works', *Eastern Economic Journal*, 23: 219–30.

Beccaria, C. (1764 [1768]). *Dei delitti e delle Pene*, Paris: Cazin.

Becker, G. (1976). *The Economic Approach to Human Behavior*, Chicago, IL: University of Chicago Press.

Bendix, R. (1956). *Work and Authority in Industry: Ideologies of Management in the Course of Industrialization*, Berkeley, CA: University of California Press.

Bentham, J. (1781 [1843]). *An Introduction to the Principles of Morals and Legislation* in *The Works of Jeremy Bentham*, published under the Superintendence of his Executor, John Bouiring, Edinburgh: William Tait, 11 Vols (1838–1843), Vol. 1. Reproduction New York: Russel & Russel, Inc., 1962.

Berg, R. van den (ed.) (2006). *At the Origins of Mathematical Economics: The Economics of A.N. Isnard, 1748–1803*, London and New York: Routledge.

Bergin, J. and B.L. Lipman (1996). 'Evolution with State-dependent Mutations', *Econometrica*, 64: 943–56.

Bernanke, B. (2004). *Essays on the* Great Depression, Princeton, NJ: Princeton University Press.

Bernheim, D. (1984). 'Rationalizable Strategic Behavior', *Econometrica*, 52: 1007–28.

Bernoulli, D. (1738 [1968]). 'Specimen Theoriae Novae de Mensura Sortis,' *Commentarii Academiae Scientiarum Imperialis Petropolitanae,* 5: 175–92. Trans. L. Sommer (1954), 'Exposition of a New Theory on the Measurement of Risk,' *Econometrica*, 22: 23–36. Rev. trans. 'Exposition of a New Theory of Risk Evaluation' in W.J. Baumol and S.M. Goldfeld (eds), *Precursors in Mathematical Economics: An Anthology*, London: London School of Economics.

Bernstein, M. and S. Allegretto (2007). *The State of Working America 2006/7*, Ithaca, NY: ILR Press (an imprint of Cornell University Press).

Bertrand, J. (1883). 'Théorie des richesses', *Journal des savants*, September: 499–508.

Bhagwati, J.N. (1966). *The Economics of Underdeveloped Countries*, London: Weidenfeld and Nicolson.

Bibow, J. (2009). 'The Euro and its Guardian of Stability: The Fiction and Reality of the 10th Anniversary Blast', *Skidmore College and The Levy Economics Institute*, Working Paper No. 583.

Bini, P. and L. Bruni (1998). 'Intervista a Gerard Debreu', *Storia del Pensiero Economico*, 35: 3–29.

Binmore, K. (1987–88). 'Modelling Rational Players: Parts I and II', *Economics and Philosophy*, 3: 179–214; 4: 9–55.

Binmore, K. (1989). 'Social contract I: Harsanyi and Rawls', *Economic Journal* (Suppl.), 99: 84–103.

Bishop, R.L. (1964). 'A Hicks-Zeuthen Theory of Bargaining', *Econometrica*, 32: 410–17.

Black, F. and M. Scholes (1973). 'The Pricing of Options and Corporate Liabilities', *Journal of Political Economy*, 81: 637–54.

Black, R.D.C., A.W. Coats and C.D.W. Goodwin (eds) (1973). *The Marginal Revolution in Economics: Interpretation and Evaluation*, Durham, NC: Duke University Press.

Blake, W. (1804 [1993]). *Milton a Poem: and the Final Illuminated Works: The Ghost of Abel, On Homers Poetry [and] On Virgil, Laocooün*, edited with introductions and notes by Robert N. Essick and Joseph Viscomi, London: William Blake Trust and Tate Gallery.

Blanchard, O. (2000). 'En défense de la science économique', *Libération*, 16 October.

Blaug, M. (1962 [1997]). *Economic Theory in Retrospect*, Cambridge: Cambridge University Press, 5th edition.

Blaug, M. (1992). *The Methodology of Economics: Or How Economists Explain* (2nd edn), Cambridge: Cambridge University Press.

Blaug, M. (1997). 'Ugly Currents in Modern Economics', paper presented at plenary session, *Fact or Fiction? Perspectives on Realism and Economics*, Rotterdam 14–15 November. Revised version in U. Mäki (ed.), *Fact and Fiction in Economics: Models, Realism and Social Construction*, Cambridge: Cambridge University Press, 2002.

Bliss, C. (2005). 'Introduction: The Theory of Capital: A Personal Overview', in C. Bliss, A. Cohen and G.C. Harcourt (eds), *Capital Theory, Vol.1*, Cheltenham: Edward Elgar.

Bodin, J. (1568 [1934]). *La response de Maistre Jean Bodin Advocat en la cour au paradoxe de monsieur de Malestroit, touchant l'encherissement de toutes choses, & le moyen d'y remédier*, Paris: Martin le Jeune; in J.Y. Le Branchu (ed.), *Écrits notables sur la monnaie, XVIe Siècle, De Copernic à Davanzati*, Paris: Librairie Félix Alcan.

Boettke, P.J. (1998). 'Economic Calculation: The Austrian Contribution to Political Economy', *Advances in Austrian Economics*, 5: 131–58.

Böhm-Bawerk, E. von (1884 [1890]). *Capital and Interest: A Critical History of Economical Theory*, trans. William Smart, London: Macmillan.

Böhm-Bawerk, E. von (1884 [1921]). *Kapital und Kapitalzins. I: Geschichte und Kritik der Kapitalzins – Theorien*, Jena: Gustav Fischer, 4th edition, Vol 1.

Böhm-Bawerk, E. von (1889 [1891]). *Capital und Capitalzins: Zweite Abtheilung: Positive Theorie des Capitals*, Innsbruck: Wagner. Trans. William Smart, *The Positive Theory of Capital*, London: Macmillan.

Böhm-Bawerk, E. von (1896 [1898]). 'Zum Abschluß des Marxschen Systems', in Otto von Boenigk (ed.), *Staatswissenschaftliche Arbeiten. Festgaben für Karl Knies zur fünfundsiebzigsten Wiederkehr seines Geburtstages*, Berlin: Haering Trans. A.M. Macdonald, *Karl Marx and the Close of his System: A Criticism*, London: T. Fisher Unwin.

Borden, W. (1984). *The Pacific Alliance*, Madison, WI: University of Wisconsin Press.

Bowles, S. (1998). 'Endogenous Preferences: The Cultural Consequences of Markets and Other Economic Institutions', *Journal of Economic Literature*, 36: 75–111.

Bowles, S. and H.A. Gintis (1975). 'The Problem with Human Capital Theory – A Marxian Critique', *American Economic Review*, 65: 74–82.

Bowles, S. and H.A. Gintis (1976). *Schooling in Capitalist America: Educational Reform and the Contradictions of Economic Life*, London: Routledge & Kegan Paul.

Brecht, B. (1956). *Threepenny Novel*, trans. D.I. Vesey and C. Isherwood, New York: Grove Press. First published in German in 1934 as *Dreigroschenroman*, Amsterdam: A. de Lange.

Brinkley, A. (1998). *Liberalism and its Discontents*, Cambridge, MA: Harvard University Press.

Brown, G. (1977). *Sabotage*, Nottingham: Spokesman.

Brown, W.A. (1979). 'Social Determinants of Pay', in G.M. Stephenson and C.J. Brotherton (eds), *Industrial Relations: A Social Psychological Approach*, Chichester: Wiley.

Brown, W.A. (1989). 'Managing Remuneration', in K. Sisson (ed.), *Personnel Management in Britain*, Oxford: Blackwell.

Brown, W.A. and P. Nolan (1988). 'Wages and Labour Productivity: The Contribution of Industrial Relations Research to the Understanding of Pay Determination', *British Journal of Industrial Relations*, 26: 339–61.

Bryan, D. and M. Rafferty (2006). *Capitalism with Derivatives: A Political Economy of Financial Derivatives, Capital and Class*, London: Palgrave Macmillan.

Buffet, W. (2010). *Warren Buffett on Business: Principles from the Sage of Omaha*, Selected and Arranged by Richard J. Connors, Hoboken, NJ: Wiley.

Burawoy, M. (1979). *Manufacturing Consent: Changes in the Labor Process under Monopoly Capitalism*, Chicago, IL: University of Chicago Press.

Burmeister, E. (2000). 'The Capital Theory Controversy', in H.D. Kurz (ed.), *Critical Essays on Piero Sraffa's Legacy in Economics*, Cambridge: Cambridge University Press.

Cahuc, P. and A. Zylberberg (2004). *Labor Economics*, Cambridge, MA: MIT Press.

Cantillon, R. (1755 [1931]). *Essai sur la nature du commerce en général*, (edited with an English translation and other material by Henry Higgs), London: Macmillan.

Cass, D. (1965). 'Optimum Growth in an Aggregative Model of Capital Accumulation', *Review of Economic Studies*, 32: 233–40.

Chesnais, F. (2006). 'The Special Position of the United States in the Finance-Led Regime: How Exportable is the US Venture Capital Industry?' in B. Coriat, P. Petit and G. Schméder (eds), *The Hardship of Nations: Exploring the Paths of Modern Capitalism*, Cheltenham, UK and Northampton, MA: Edward Elgar, pp. 37–67.

Chomsky, N. (1977). 'Oil Imperialism and the US-Israel Relationship: Noam Chomsky interviewed by Roger Hurwitz, David Woolf & Sherman Teichman', *Leviathan*, 1:1–3, pp. 6–9.

Chomsky, N. (2003). 'A conversation with Noam Chomsky: Telling the Truth about Imperialism. Interviewed by David Barsamian', *International Socialist Review*, 32, November–December. available from http://www.isreview.org/issues/32/chomsky.shtml (retrieved December 2010).

Christ, C.F. (1952). 'History of the Cowles Commission 1932–52', in *Economic Theory and Measurement: A Twenty Year Research Report*, Chicago: Cowles Commission for Research in Economics, pp. 3–65, available at http://cowles.econ.yale.edu/P/reports/1932-52.htm#History (retrieved June 2010).

Christensen, P. (1994). 'Fire, Motion, and Productivity: The Proto-energetics of Nature and Economy in François Quesnay', in P. Mirowski (ed.), *Natural Images in Economic Thought: Markets Read in Tooth and Claw*, Cambridge: Cambridge University Press.

Clark, J.B. (1883). 'Recent Theories of Wages', *New Englander and Yale Review*, 42: 354–64.

Clark, J.B. (1891). 'Distribution as Determined by a Law of Rent', *Quarterly Journal of Economics*, 5: 289–318.

Clark, J.B. (1894). "Distribution, Ethics of" in Inglis Palgrave (ed.), *Dictionary of Political Economy*, London: Macmillan, Vol 1, pp. 596–9.

Clotfelter, C.P. (ed.) (1997). *On the Third Hand: Wit and Humour in the Dismal Science*, Ann Arbor, MI: Michigan University Press.

Coase, R.H. (1937). 'The Nature of the Firm', *Economica*, 4: 386–405.

Coase, R.H. (1988). 'The Nature of the Firm: Meaning', *Journal of Law, Economics, and Organization*, 4: 19–32.

Coase, R.H. (1994). *Essays on Economics and Economists*. Chicago, IL: Chicago University Press.

Cohen, A.J. and G.C. Harcourt (2003). 'Retrospectives: Whatever Happened to the Cambridge Capital Theory Controversies?', *Journal of Economic Perspectives*, 17: 199–214.

Colander, D. (2005a). 'The Making of an Economist Redux', *Journal of Economic Perspectives*, 19: 175–98.

Colander, D. (2005b). 'The Future of Economics: The Appropriately Educated in Pursuit of the Knowable', *Cambridge Journal of Economics*, 29: 927–41.

Colander, D., R. P. F. Holt and J.B. Rosser, Jr (2004a). *The Changing Face of Economics: Interviews with Cutting Edge Economists*, Ann Arbor, MI: University of Michigan Press.

Colander, D., R. P.F. Holt and J.B. Rosser, Jr (2004b). 'The Changing Face of Economics', *Review of Political Economy*, 16: 485–99.

Coleman, J. (1990). *Foundations of Social Theory*, Cambridge, MA: Harvard University Press.

Condorcet, M. de (1794). *Esquisse d'un tableau historique des progrès de l'esprit humain* ([publ. par P.C.F. Daunou et Mme M.L.S. de Condorcet], Paris: Agasse, L'An III. de la République [i.e., 1794].

Condorcet, M. de (1795). *Outlines of an Historical View of the Progress of the Human Mind: Being a Posthumous Work of the Late M. de Condorcet,* London: Johnson.

Condorcet, M. de (1955 [1979]). *Sketch for a Historical Picture of the Progress of the Human Mind*, translated by June Barraclough, with an introduction by Stuart Hampshire, Westport, CT: Hyperion Press.

Cournot, A-A. (1838 [1897]). *Recherches sur les principes mathématiques de la théorie des richesses*, Paris: Hachette. English trans. Nathaniel T. Bacon, *Researches into the Mathematical Principles of the Theory of Wealth*, New York: Macmillan.

Couturat, L. (ed.) (1903). *Opuscules et fragments inédits de Leibniz*, Paris: Félix Alcan.

Cowles Commission for Research in Economics (1943–54). Seminars 1943–1954, available at http://cowles.econ.yale.edu/archive/events/seminars-cc.htm (retrieved June 2010).

Cowles Commission/Foundation for Research in Economics (1983). 50th Anniversary Cele[b]ration, June 3–4, 1983 [Abstracted from Cowles Fiftieth Anniversary Volume, edited by Alvin K. Klevorick], available at http://cowles.econ.yale.edu/archive/events/50th/index.htm (retrieved June 2010).

Darwin, C. (1859 [1996]). *The Origin of Species*, edited with an introduction and notes by Gillian Beer, Oxford: Oxford University Press. [Originally published as *On the Origin of Species by Means of Natural Selection, or the Preservation of Favoured Races in the Struggle for Life*, London: John Murray.]

Dasgupta, P. (2002). 'Modern Economics and Its Critics', in U. Mäki (ed.), *Fact and Fiction in Economics: Models, Realism and Social Construction*, Cambridge: Cambridge University Press.

Davis, J.B. (2003). *The Theory of the Individual in Economics: Identity and Value*, London and New York: Routledge.

Davis, J.B. (2006). 'The Turn in Economics: Neoclassical Dominance to Mainstream Pluralism?', *Journal of Institutional Economics*, 2: 1–20.

Dawkins, R. (1976). *The Selfish Gene*, Oxford: Oxford University Press.

Dawkins, R. (1980). 'Good Strategy or Evolutionarily Stable Strategy?', in G.W. Barlow and J. Silverberg (eds), *Sociobiology: Beyond Nature/Nurture?* Boulder, CO: Westview Press.

Debreu, G. (1959). *Theory of Value: An Axiomatic Study of Economic Equilibrium*, New York: Wiley.

Debreu, G. (1974). 'Excess Demand Functions', *Journal of Mathematical Economics,* 1: 5–21.

Debreu, G. (1983). 'Economic Theory in the Mathematical Mode', *Nobel Memorial lecture*, 8 December, available at http://nobelprize.org/nobel_prizes/economics/laureates/1983/debreu-lecture.pdf (retrieved June 2010).

Debreu, G. (1986). 'Theoretic Models: Mathematical Form and Economic Content', *Econometrica*, 54: 1259–70.

Debreu, G. (1991). 'The Mathematization of Economic Theory', *American Economic Review*, 81: 1–7.

Defoe, D. (1719 [1994]). *Robinson Crusoe: An Authoritative Text, Contexts, Criticism*, edited by Michael Shinagel, New York: Norton, 2nd edition. [Originally published as *The life and strange surprizing adventures of Robinson Crusoe, of York, mariner*, London: Printed for W. Taylor at the Ship in Pater-Noster-Row.]

Deleuze, G. (1968). *Difference and Repetition,* trans. Paul Patton, New York: Columbia University Press.

Dennett, D. (2001). 'In Darwin's Wake, Where Am I?' APA Presidential Address, *Proceedings and Addresses of the American Philosophical Association*, 75: 2, 13–30 November. Reprinted (2003) in J. Hodge and G. Radick (eds), *Cambridge Companion to Darwin*, Cambridge University Press, pp. 357–76.

Dick, P.K. (1968). *Do Androids Dream of Electric Sheep?*, Garden City, NY: Doubleday.

Dickens, C. (1843 [2006]). *A Christmas Carol and other Christmas books*, edited by Robert Douglas-Fairhurst, Oxford: Oxford University Press. [Originally published as *A Christmas carol: in prose: being a ghost story of Christmas*, London: Chapman & Hall.]

Dobb, M.H. (1973). *Theories of Value and Distribution since Adam Smith*, Cambridge: Cambridge University Press.

Dobbs, B.J.T. (1991). *The Janus Face of Genius: The Role of Alchemy in Newton's Thought*, Cambridge: Cambridge University Press.

Doeringer, P. and M. Piore (1971). *Internal Labor Markets and Manpower Analysis*, Lexington, MA: D.C. Heath.

Dorfman, R. (1987). 'Marginal Productivity Theory', in J. Eatwell, M. Milgate and P. Newman (eds), *The New Palgrave: A Dictionary of Economics, Vol.3*, London: Macmillan, pp. 323–5.

Dormael, A. van (1978). *Bretton Woods: Birth of a Monetary System*, London: Macmillan, pp. 323–5.

Dow, A. and S. Dow. (1985). 'Animal Spirits and Rationality', in T. Lawson and H. Pesaran (eds), *Keynes' Economics: Methodological Issues*, London: Croom Helm for Cambridge Journal of Economics.

Dow, S. (1995). 'The Appeal of Neoclassical Economics: Some Insights from Keynes's Epistemology', *Cambridge Journal of Economics*, 19: 715–33.

Dupuit, J. (1844 [1952]). 'On the Measurement of the Utility of Public Works', trans. R. H. Barback in *International Economic Papers* no. 2. [Originally published as « De la mesure de l'utilité des travaux publics », *Annales des ponts et chaussées, Mémoires et Documents*, série 2, 8: 332–75.]

Eagleton, T. (2007). *The Meaning of Life*, Oxford: Oxford University Press.

Eatwell, J. and C. Panico. (1987). 'Sraffa, Piero', in J. Eatwell, M. Milgate and P. Newman (eds), *The New Palgrave: A Dictionary of Economics, Vol.3*, London: Macmillan, pp. 445–452.

Economic Report of the President (1999). *Economic Report of the President, transmitted to the Congress, February 1999; Together with the Annual Report of the Council of Economic Advisers*, Washington, DC: United States Government Printing Office.

Edelman, B. (1988). 'Entre personne humaine et matériau humain: le sujet de droit', in B. Edelman and M.A. Hermitte (eds), *L'Homme, la nature et le droit*, Paris: Christian Bourgois. Trans. John Frow (1997) *Time and Commodity Culture: Essays in Cultural Theory and Postmodernity*. Oxford: Clarendon Press.

Edgeworth, F.Y. (1879). 'The Hedonical Calculus', *Mind*, 4 (15): 394–408.

Edgeworth, F.Y. (1881 [2003]). *Mathematical Psychics and Further Papers on Political Economy*, ed. P. Newman, Oxford and New York: Oxford University Press.

Edgeworth, F.Y. (1904 [1925]). 'The Theory of Distribution', *Quarterly Journal of Economics*, 18: 2, pp. 159–219. Reprinted in *Papers Relating to Political Economy*, London: Macmillan.

Eichengreen, B. and K. O'Rourke (2010). 'What Do the New Data Tell us?', *mimeo*.

Eliot, T.S. (1942). *Little Gidding*, London: Faber & Faber.

Ellsberg, D. (1956). 'Theory of the Reluctant Duellist', *American Economic Review*, 46: 909–23.

Ellsberg, D. (1961). 'Risk, Ambiguity and the Savage Axioms', *Economic Journal*, 64: 643–69.

Elster, J. (1982). 'Marxism, Functionalism and Game Theory', *Theory and Society*, 11: 453–82.

Engels, F. (1845 [1994]). *The Condition of the Working Class in England: From Personal Observation and Authentic Sources*, introduction by E. Hobsbawm, Chicago, IL: Academy Chicago Publishers. First German edn (1845) as *Die Lage der arbeitenden Klasse in England. Nach eigner Anschauung und authentischen Quellen,* Leipzig: Otto Wigand. First English trans. (1887), New York: J.W. Lovell.

England, P. (1993). 'The Separative Self: Androcentric Bias in Neoclassical Assumptions', in M.A. Ferber and J.A. Nelson (eds), *Beyond Economic Man: Feminist Theory and Economics*, Chicago, IL: University of Chicago Press.

Epstein, S.S. (1998). *The Politics of Cancer, Revisited*, Fremont Center, NY: East Ridge Press.

Evans-Pritchard, E.E. (1937 [1976]). *Witchcraft, Oracles and Magic among the Azande*, Oxford: Clarendon.

Evans-Pritchard, E.E. (1940). *The Nuer: A Description of the Modes of Livelihood and Political Institutions of a Nilotic People*, Oxford: Clarendon.

Fehr, E. and S. Gächter (2000). 'Fairness and Retaliation: The Economics of Reciprocity', *Journal of Economic Perspectives*, 14: 159–81.

Ferguson, C.E. (1966). *Microeconomic Theory*, Homewood, IL: R.D. Irwin.

Ferguson, T. and J. Rogers (1986). *Right Turn*, New York: Hill and Wang.

Fine, B. (2008). 'The General Impossibility of Neoclassical Economics: Or Does Bertrand Russell Deserve a Nobel Prize for Economics?', *mimeo*.

Fisher, I. (1911). *The Purchasing Power of Money: Its Determination and Relation to Credit Interest and Crises*, New York: Macmillan.

Fishman, C. (2006). *The Wal-Mart Effect: How an Out-of-Town Superstore Became a Superpower*, London: Allen Lane.

Flux, A.W. (1894). 'Review of Knut Wicksell's *Über Wert, Kapital und Rente* and P.H. Wicksteed's *Essay on the Co-ordination of the Laws of Distribution'*, *Economic Journal*, 4: 303–13.

Foley, V. (1973). 'An Origin of the *tableau economique*', *History of Political Economy*, 5: 121–50.

Ford, J. and S. Jones (2010). 'Derivatives: A Tricky Pick' *Financial Times*, June, 9, available at http://www.ft.com/cms/s/0/b62bed3a–73fb-11df-87f5-00144feabdc0.html#axzz1Bu63JuQB (retrieved June 2010).

Forsberg, A. (2000). *America and the Japanese Miracle: The Cold War Context of Japan's Postwar Economic Revival, 1950–1960*, Chapel Hill, NC and London: University of North Carolina Press.

Foster, D. and H.P. Young (1990). 'Stochastic Evolutionary Game Dynamics', *Theoretical Population Biology*, 38: 219–32.

Foster, J.B. (2004). 'Memorial Service for Paul Marlor Sweezy (1910–2004) available from http://www.monthlyreview.org/paulsweezy.htm (retrieved June 2010).

Foster, J.B. (2004a). 'The Commitment of an Intellectual: Paul M. Sweezy (1910–2004)', *Monthly Review*, 56(5): 5–39.

Foster, J.B. (2004b). 'Monopoly Capital at the Turn of the Millennium', *Monthly Review*, 51 (11): 1–18.

Fox, A. (1974). *Beyond Contract: Work, Power and Trust Relations*, London: Faber.

Fox, J. (2008). "The Comeback Keynes", *Time*, Thursday, October 23, available from http://www.time.com/time/magazine/article/0,9171,1853302,00.html (retrieved January 2011).

Friedman, M. and R.D. Friedman (1998). *Two Lucky People: Memoirs*, Chicago, IL and London: University of Chicago Press.

Fullbrook, E. (2003). *The Crisis in Economics. The Post-Autistic Economics Movement: The First 600 Days*, London: Routledge.

Fullbrook, E. (2004). *A Guide to What's Wrong with Economics*, London: Anthem Press.

Galbraith, J. (1998). *Created Unequal. The Crisis in American Pay*, New York: Free Press.

Galiani, F. (1751 [1803]). *Della moneta, libri cinque*, in P. Custodi (ed.), *Scrittori Classici Italiani di Economia Politica, parte moderna*, Vols III and IV, Milan: G.G. Destefanis, vol. III.

Galilei, G. (1632 [1967]). *Dialogue Concerning the Two Chief World Systems, Ptolemaic and Copernican* (2nd edn), trans. Stillman Drake, Berkeley, CA: University of California Press. [Original Italian edition *Dialogo sopra i due massimi sistemi del mondo*, Florence: G.-B. Landini.]

Garegnani, P. (1984). 'Value and Distribution in the Classical Economists and Marx', *Oxford Economic Papers*, 36: 291–325.

Geanakoplos, J., D. Pearce and E. Stacchetti (1989). 'Psychological Games and Sequential Rationality', *Games and Economic Behaviour*, 1: 60–79.

Gilbert, R.V. *et al.* (1938). *An Economic Program for American Democracy, by Seven Harvard and Tufts Economists: Richard V. Gilbert, George H. Hildebrand Jr., Arthur W. Stuart, Maxine Yaple Sweezy, Paul M. Sweezy, Lorie Tarshis and John D. Wilson*, New York: Vanguard Press.

Gödel, K. (1931 [1967]). 'Über formal unentscheidbare Sätze der Principia Mathematica und verwandter Systeme I', *Monatshefte für Mathematik*, 38(1): 173–98. English translation: 'On Formally Undecidable Propositions of Principia Mathematica and Related Systems I', in J. van Heijenoort (ed.), *From Frege to Gödel: A Source Book in Mathematical Logic 1979–1931*, Cambridge, MA: Harvard University, pp. 596–616.

Goethe, J.W. von (1832 [2007]). *Faust: a tragedy in two parts*; with the unpublished scenarios for the Walpurgis Night and the Urfaust, translated, with an introduction and notes, by John R. Williams, Ware, Hertfordshire: Wordsworth Editions. [Originally published: First part 1808: *Faust. - Eine Tragödie von Goethe*, Tübingen: Cotta'sche Verlagsbuchhandlung. Second part 1832: *Faust. Der*

Tragödie zweyter Theil in fünf Acten. (Vollendet im Sommer 1831), Stuttgart: J.G. Cotta' sche Buchhandlung.]

Goetz, S. and H. Swaminathan (2006). 'Wal-Mart and Family Poverty in US Counties', *Social Sciences Quarterly*, 83: 211–25.

Goetz, S. and S. Shrestha (2009). 'Explaining Self-employment Success and Failure: Wal-Mart vs Starbucks or Schumpeter vs Putnam', *Social Science Quarterly*, 91: 22–38.

Goodrich, C. (1920 [1975]). *The Frontier of Control: A Study in British Workshop Politics*, London: Pluto Press.

Goodwin, R. (1967). 'A Growth Cycle', in C.H. Feinstein (ed.), *Socialism, Capitalism and Economic Growth*, Cambridge: Cambridge University Press, pp. 54–8. Specially revised and enlarged for E.K. Hunt and J.G. Schwartz (eds), *A Critique of Economic Theory*, Penguin, Harmondsworth, 1972, pp. 442–9.

Gossen, H.H. (1854 [1983]). *Entwick(e)lung der Gesetze des menschlichen Verkehrs, und der daraus fließenden Regeln für menschliches Handeln*, Braunschweig: F. Bieweg. English trans. Rudoplh Blitz as *The Laws of Human Relations: And the Rules of Human Action Derived Therefrom*, Cambridge, MA: MIT Press [With an introductory essay by Nickolas Georgescu-Roegen].

Gouguenheim, S. (2008). *Aristote au Mont-Saint-Michel. Les racines grecques de l'Europe chrétienne*, Paris: Le Seuil (L'univers historique).

Grassmueck, G., S. Goetz and M. Shields (2008). 'Youth Out-migration from Pennsylvania: The Roles of Government Fragmentation vs the Beaten Path Effect', *Journal of Regional Analysis and Policy*, 38: 77–88.

Greenspan, A. (2009). 'We Need a Better Cushion against Risk', *Financial Times*, 26 March available at http://www.ft.com/cms/s/0/9c158a92-1a3c-11de-9f91-0000779fd2ac.html#axzz1Bu63JuQB (retrieved May 2010).

Gregory, C. (1982). *Gifts and Commodities*, London and New York: Academic Press.

Grimm, J. and W. (1843). *Kinder- und Hausmärchen; Gesammelt durch die Brüder Grimm; Zweiter Band; Grosse Ausgabe; Fünfte, stark vermehrte und verbesserte Auflage*, Göttingen: Druck und Verlag der Dieterichischen Buchhandlung.

Groenewegen, P. (1995). *A Soaring Eagle: Alfred Marshall 1842–1924*, Cheltenham: Edward Elgar.

Gul, G. and H. Sonnenschein (1988). 'On Delay in Bargaining with One Sided Uncertainty', *Econometrica*, 56: 601–11.

Halevi, J. (1998). 'Capital and Growth: Its Relevance as a Critque of Neo-classical and Classical Economic Theories', *Indian Journal of Applied Economics*, 7: 79–98.

Halevi, J. (2001). 'US Militarism and Imperialism and the Japanese Miracle', *Monthly Review*, 52(September).

Halevi, J. (2002). 'The Argentine Crisis', *Monthly Review*, 53(11): 15–23.

Halevi, J. and B. Lucarelli (2002). 'Japan's Stagnationist Crisis', *Monthly Review*, 53: 24–36.

Halevi, J. and Y. Varoufakis (2003a). 'The *Global Minotaur*', *Monthly Review*, 55 (July–August): 56–74.

Halevi, J. and Y. Varoufakis (2003b). 'Questions and Answers on the *Global Minotaur*', *Monthly Review*, 55 (December): 26–32.

Hall, A.R. (1980). *Philosophers at War: The Quarrel between Newton and Leibniz*, Cambridge: Cambridge University Press.

Hammes, D. and D. Wills (2005). 'Black Gold: The End of Bretton Woods and the Oil-price Shocks of the 1970s', *Independent Review*, 9: 501–11.

Hansen, A. (1938). *Full Recovery or Stagnation?*, New York: Norton.

Harcourt, G.C. (1972). *Some Cambridge Controversies in the Theory of Capital,* Cambridge: Cambridge University Press.

Hargreaves-Heap, S. and Y. Varoufakis (2002). 'Some Experimental Results on the Evolution of Discrimination, Co-operation and Perceptions of Fairness', *Economic Journal*, 112: 678–702.

Hargreaves-Heap, S. and Y. Varoufakis (2004). Game Theory: *A Critical Text*, London and New York: Routledge.

Hart-Landsberg, M. (1998). *Korea: Division, Reunification and US Foreign Policy*, New York: Monthly Review Press.

Hayek, F.A. von (ed.) (1935). *Collectivist Economic Planning. Critical Studies on the Possibilities of Socialism,* London: G. Routledge & Sons.

Hayek, F.A. von (1945). 'The Use of Knowledge in Society', *American Economic Review*, 35: 519–30.

Hayek, F.A. von (1976). *Denationalisation of Money: The Argument Refined – An Analysis of the Theory and Practice of Concurrent Currencies*, London: Institute of Economic Affairs.

Heckscher, E.F. (1935 [1994]). *Mercantilism,* London: Routledge. [Originally published in Swedish 1931].

Heertje, A. (ed.) (1981). *Schumpeter's Vision: Capitalism, Socialism and Democracy after 40 Years,* New York: Praeger.

Hegel, G.W.F. (1807 [1931]). *The Phenomenology of* Mind, trans. J.B. Baillie, London: Macmillan. [Original German edition: *System der Wissenschaft. Erster Theil, die Phänomenologie des Geistes,* Bamberg/Würzburg: Verlag Joseph Anton Goebhardt.]

Hegel, G.W.F. (1894). *Hegel's Philosophy of Mind: Translated from the Encyclopaedia of the Philosophical Sciences,* trans. W. Wallace, Oxford: Clarendon. [The original edition in Hegel's lifetime is the 3rd part of the *Encyclopädie der philosophischen Wissenschaften im Grundrisse: zum Gebrauch seiner Vorlesungen,* Heidelberg: Oßwald, 1817. The first standard edition on which the English translation is based is the 2nd part of the 7th volume of Hegel's *Works*: L. Boumann (ed.), *Siebenter Band. Zweite Abtheilung. Encyklopädie der philosophischen Wissenschaften im Grundrisse. Dritter Theil. Die Philosophie des Geistes in Georg Wilhelm Friedrich Hegels Werke. Vollständige Ausgabe durch einen Verein von Freunden des Verewigten,* Berlin: Duncker und Humblot, 1845.]

Herrnstein, R. and C. Murray (1994). *Bell Curve: Intelligence and Class Structure in American Life,* New York : Free Press.

Hewitson, G. (1999). *Feminist Economics: Interrogating the Masculinity of Rational Economic Man,* Cheltenham: Edward Elgar.

Hicks, J.R. (1932). *Theory of Wages*, London: Macmillan.

Hicks, J.R. (1934). 'Léon Walras', *Econometrica*, 2: 338–48.

Hicks, J.R. (1985). *Methods of Dynamic Economics*, Oxford: Clarendon Press.

Higgs, H. (1897). *The Physiocrats: Six Lectures on the French Economists of the 18th Century,* London: Macmillan.

Hikmet, N. (1954). *Poems by Nazim Hikmet,* translated from the Turkish by Ali Yunus, with an introduction by Samuel Sillen. New York: Masses & Mainstream, Inc.

Himmelweit, S. (1995). 'The Discovery of Unpaid Work: The Social Consequences and the Expansion of Work', *Feminist Economics*, 1: 1–19.

Hobsbawm, E. (1999). *Industry and Empire: From 1750 to the Present Day* [edition revised and updated with Chris Wrigley], New York: New Press.

Hobson, J.A. and A.F. Mummery (1889 [1992]). *The Physiology of Industry: An Exposure of Certain Fallacies in Existing Theories of Economics.* London: J. Murray. Reprinted as Vol. 1 in J.A. Hobson: *A Collection of Economics Works* (6 vols), London: Routledge.

Hodgson, G.M. (1999). *Evolution and Institutions: On Evolutionary Economics and the Evolution of Economics*, Cheltenham: Edward Elgar.

Hodgson, G.M. (2007). 'Meanings of Methodological Individualism', *Journal of Economic Methodology*, 14: 211–26.

Hollis, M. (1998). *Trust within Reason*, Cambridge: Cambridge University Press.

Howey, R.S. (1960). *The Rise of the Marginal Utility School: 1870–1889*, Lawrence, KS: University of Kansas Press.

Hughes, T. (1983). *Networks of Power: Electrification in Western Society, 1880–1930,* Baltimore, MD: Johns Hopkins University Press.

Hume, D. (1739–40 [1888]). *Treatise of Human Nature*, ed. L.A. Selby-Bigge, Oxford: Oxford University Press.

Hume, D. (1748 [1902]). 'An Enquiry Concerning Human Understanding', in *Enquiries Concerning the Human Understanding and Concerning the Principles of Morals,* ed. L.A. Selby-Bigge, Oxford: Clarendon Press.

Hume, D. (1752 [1955]). 'Of the Balance of Trade' in *Writings on Economics*, ed. Eugene Rotwein, Edinburgh: Nelson.

Hutcheson, F. (1753). *A Short Introduction to Moral Philosophy, In Three Books, Containing The Elements of Ethicks and the Law of Nature*, Glasgow: Robert and Andrew Foulis, 2nd edition.

Huxley, T.H. (1880 [1899]). 'The Coming of Age of the "*Origin of Species*"', in *Darwiniana, Essays by Thomas H. Huxley, Vol. II*, London: Macmillan, pp. 227–43.

Hyman, R. and I. Brough (1975). *Social Values and Industrial Relations: A Study of Fairness and Inequality*, Oxford: Blackwell.

Ibn Khaldun (1967). *The Muqaddimah: An Introduction to History*, trans. Franz Rosenthal, Bollingen Series XLIII, Princeton, NJ: Princeton University Press.

Jaffé, W. (1965). *Correspondence of Léon Walras and Related Papers* (3 vols), Amsterdam: North-Holland for the Royal Netherlands Academy of Sciences and Letters.

Jefferson, T. (1801). *Notes on the State of Virginia, with an Appendix*, Boston, MA: David Carlisle, 8th American edition.

Jevons, W.S. (1862 [1866]). 'Brief Account of a General Mathematical Theory of Political Economy', *Journal of the Royal Statistical Society, London*, XXIX(June): 282–7.

Jevons, W.S. (1871[1879]).*The Theory of Political Economy* (2nd edn), London: Macmillan.

Jevons, W.S. (1914 [1933]). 'The Scope and Method of Political Economy in the Light of the "Marginal" Theory of Value and Distribution', *Economic Journal*, 24(93). Reprinted in Wicksteed *The Common Sense of Political Economy*, Vol.II, London: George Routledge & Sons.

Jordan, B.C. and E.D. Rostow (eds) (1986). *The Great Society: A Twenty Year Critique,* Austin, TX: Lyndon B. Johnson School of Public Affairs.

Kalecki, M. (1939 [1973]). *Essays in the Theory of Economic Fluctuations,* in M. Dobb, *Theories of Value and Distribution since Adam Smith*, Cambridge: Cambridge University Press, p. 222.

Kandori, M., G. Mailath and R. Rob (1993). 'Learning, Mutation, and Longrun Equilibria in Games', *Econometrica*, 61: 29–56.

Kansas, D. (2009). *The Wall Street Journal Guide to the End of Wall Street as We Know It*, New York: HarperCollins.

Kaplan, M. and P.L. Cuciti (eds) (1986). *The Great Society and Its Legacy: Twenty Years of US Social Policy,* Durham, NC: Duke University Press.

Kates, S. (ed.) (2003). *Two Hundred Years of Say's Law: Essays on Economic Theory's Most Controversial Principle*, Cheltenham: Edward Elgar.

Keen, S. (2001). *Debunking: The Naked Emperor of the Social Sciences*, London: Zed Books.

Kemeny, J.G., J.L. Snell and G.L.Thompson (1966). *Introduction to Finite Mathematics* (2nd edn), Englewood Cliffs, NJ: Prentice-Hall International.

Kennan, G. ["Mr. X."] (1947). 'The Source of Soviet Conduct', *Foreign Affairs* 25(4): 566–82.

Keynes, J.M. (1920). *The Economic Consequences of the Peace*, New York: Harcourt Brace.

Keynes, J.M. (1925 [1972]). *The Economic Consequences of Mr. Churchill.* London: Leonard and Virginia Woolf at the Hogarth Press. Reprinted in D.E. Moggridge (ed.), *The Collected Writings of John Maynard Keynes*, Vol. IX: *Essays in Persuasion*, London: Macmillan for the Royal Economic Society.

Keynes, J.M. (1930 [1972]). 'Ramsey as an Economist', *Economic Journal.* Reprinted in D.E. Moggridge (ed.), *The Collected Writings of John Maynard Keynes, Vol. X: Essays in Biography.* London: Macmillan for the Royal Economic Society, Chapter 29.

Keynes, J.M. (1932). 'The World's Economic Outlook', *Atlantic Monthly*, 149 (May): 521–6.

Keynes, J.M. (1933 [1972]). 'Robert Malthus: The First of the Cambridge Economists', in D.E. Moggridge (ed.), *The Collected Writings of John Maynard Keynes, Vol. X: Essays in Biography*, London: Macmillan for the Royal Economic Society.

Keynes, J.M. (1936). *The General Theory of Employment, Interest and Money*, London: Macmillan.

Keynes, J.M. (1938 [1972]). 'My early beliefs', paper read on 11 September to the Bloomsbury Memoir Club, in *Two Memoirs*, London: Hart-Davis, 1949. Reprinted in D.E. Moggridge (ed.), *Collected Writings of John Maynard Keynes*, Vol. X: *Essays in Biography*, London: Macmillan, pp. 433–50.

Keynes, J.M. (1944 [1980]). 'Closing Speech, Bretton Woods Conference, 22nd July 1944', in D.E. Moggridge (ed.), *Collected Writings of John Maynard Keynes, Vol. XXVI, Activities 1941–1946; Shaping the Post-War World, Bretton Woods and Reparations*, London: Macmillan for the Royal Economic Society.

Keynes, J.M. (1947). 'Newton, the Man', in D.E. Moggridge (ed.), *Collected Writings of John Maynard Keynes*, Vol. X: *Essays in Biography*, London: Macmillan, for the Royal Economic Society, pp. 363–4.

Keynes, J.M. (1949 [1972]). 'Dr Melchior: A Defeated Enemy', in *Two Memoirs*, London: Hart-Davis. Reprinted in D.E. Moggridge (ed.), *Collected Writings of John Maynard Keynes*, Vol X: *Essays in Biography*, Cambridge: Macmillan and St. Martin's Press for the Royal Economic Society.

Keynes, J.M. (1924 [1972]). 'Alfred Marshall 1842–1924', in D.E. Moggridge (ed.), *Collected Writings of John Maynard Keynes*, Vol X: *Essays in Biography*, London: Macmillan for the Royal Economic Society.

Keynes, J.M. (1980). *Collected Writings of John Maynard Keynes, Vol. XXV: Activities 1940–1944. Shaping the Post-War World: The Clearing Union*, edited by D.E. Moggridge, London: Macmillan for the Royal Economic Society.

Keynes, J.M. (1982). *Collected Writings of John Maynard Keynes, Vol. XXVIII: Social, Political and Literary Writings*, edited by D.E. Moggridge, London: Macmillan for the Royal Economic Society.

Kindleberger, C.P. and R.Z. Aliber (2005). *Manias, Panics, and Crashes: A History of Financial Crises* (5th edn), Hoboken, NJ: John Wiley & Sons.

Kipling, R. (1901 [1987]). *Kim*, London: Penguin Classics. [First published as a book in London: Macmillan and Co.]

Kirman, A. (1989). 'The Intrinsic Limits of Modern Economic Theory: The Emperor Has No Clothes', *Economic Journal*, 99: 126–39.

Kirzner, I.M. (1976). *The Economic Point of View: An Essay in the History of Economic Thought*, edited with an introduction by Laurence S. Moss, Kansas City, KS: Sheed and Ward, 2nd edition. [First edition Princeton, NJ: D. van Nostrand Co., 1960.]

Kissinger, H. (1982). *Years of Upheaval*, Boston, MA: Little, Brown & Co.

Kolm, S-C. (1968). 'Léon Walras' Correspondence and Related Papers: The Birth of Mathematical Economics: A Review Article', *American Economic Review*, 58: 1330–41.

Koopmans, T.C. (1957). *Three Essays on the State of Economic Science*, New York: McGraw-Hill.

Koopmans, T.C. (1965). 'On the Concept of Optimum Economic Growth', in *The Economic Approach to Development Planning*, Amsterdam: North-Holland.

Korkotsides, A.S. (2007). *Consumer Capitalism*, London: Routledge.

Kriesler, P. (1997). 'Keynes, Kalecki and the General Theory', in G.C. Harcourt and P.A. Riach (eds), *A 'Second Edition' of the General Theory, Vol. 2*, London: Routledge.

Krimpas, G.E. (1975). *Labour Input and the Theory of the Labour Market*, London: Duckworth.

Kuntz, D. (1997). *Butter and Guns*, New York: Free Press.

Kurz, H.D. (ed.) (2000). *Critical Essays on Piero Sraffa's Legacy in Economics*, Cambridge: Cambridge University Press.

Kurz, H.D. and N. Salvadori (1993). 'Von Neumann's Growth Model and the "Classical" Tradition', *European Journal of the History of Economic Thought*, 1: 130–60.

Kurz, H.D. and N. Salvadori (2000). '"Classical" Roots of Input–Output Analysis: A Short Account of its Long Prehistory', *Economic Systems Research*, 12: 153–79.

Kydland, F. and E. Prescott (1982). 'Time to Build and Aggregate Fluctuations', *Econometrica*, 50: 1345–70.

Labban, M. (2010). 'Agiotage etc', Letter to the *London Review of Books*, 32 (7), 8 April, available at http://www.lrb.co.uk/v32/n07/letters (retrieved August 2010).

Lanchester, J. (2006). 'The Price of Pickles', *London Review of Books*, 28(12): 22 June.

Lanchester, J. (2009a). 'It's Over', *London Review of Books*, 31(10): 28 May.

Lanchester, J. (2009b). 'Bankocracy', *London Review of Books*, 31(21): 35–6.

Lanchester, J. (2010). *Whoops! Why Everyone Owes Everyone and No One Can Pay*, London: Allen Lane.

Lawson, T. (1997). *Economics and Reality*, London and New York: Routledge.

Lawson, T. (2003). *Reorienting Economics*, London and New York: Routledge.

Lazear, E.P. (1999). 'Personnel Economics: Past Lessons and Future Directions', *Journal of Labor Economics*, 17: 199–236.

Lazear, E.P. and R. McNabb (eds) (2004). *Personnel Economics, Vols I and II*, Cheltenham: Edward Elgar.

Leibniz, G.W. (1714 [1898]). *The Monadology, and Other Philosophical Writings*, translated with introduction and notes by Robert Latta, London: Oxford University Press.

Leibniz G.W. (1714 [1991]). *La Monadologie*, précédée d'une étude de Jacques Rivelaygue, « La Monadologie de Leibniz »; suivie d'un exposé d'Emile Boutroux, « La Philosophie de Leibniz », Paris: Librairie Générale Française [Le Livre de poche (Classiques de la philosophie)]

Leibniz, G.W. (1991). *Discourse on Metaphysics and Other Essays*, edited and translated by Daniel Garber and Roger Ariew, Indianapolis, IN: Hackett.

Leijonhufvud, A. (1968). *On Keynesian Economics and the Economics of Keynes: A Study in Monetary Theory*, Oxford: Oxford University Press.

Lenin, V.I. (1917 [1948]). *Imperialism, the Highest Stage of Capitalism*, London: Lawrence and Wishart.

Lenin, V.I. (1929 [1964]). *War and Revolution*, first published April 23th, 1929, No. 93. Reprinted (1964) in *Collected Works, Vol 24*, Moscow: Progress Publishers, pp. 398–421.

Lenin, V.I. (1977). 'The Three Sources and Three Component Parts of Marxism', in *Collected Works, Vol 19*, Moscow: Progress Publishers, pp. 21–8.

Leontief, W. (1936). 'Quantitative Input and Output Relations in the Economic Systems of the United States', *Review of Economics and Statistics* [then *Review of Economic Statistics*], 18: 105–25.

Leontief, W. (1966). *Input–Output Economics*, New York: Oxford University Press.

Levhari, D. and P.A. Samuelson (1966). 'The Nonswitching Theorem is False', *Quarterly Journal of Economics*, 80: 518–519.

Levi-Straus, C. (1966). *The Savage Mind*, London: Weidenfeld and Nicholson.

Li, D.X. (2000). 'On Default Correlation: A Copula Function Approach', *Journal of Fixed Income*, 9: 43–54.

Loïc, C. (2004). 'The *tableau economique* as Rational Recreation', *History of Political Economy*, 36: 445–74.

Łoś, J. and M. Wycech-Ło (1974). 'The Walrasian and Von Neumann Equilibria: A Comparison', *Cowles Foundation Discussion Paper* No. 373.

Lotka, A.J. (1925). *Elements of Physical Biology*. Baltimore, MD: Williams and Wilkins.

Lovejoy, A.O. (1936). *The Great Chain of Being: A Study of the History of an Idea,* Cambridge, MA: Harvard University Press.

Lucas, R.E. Jr (1977). 'Understanding Business Cycles', *Carnegie-Rochester Conference Series on Public Policy*, 5: 7–29.

Lukes, S. (1974). *Power: A Radical View*, London: Macmillan.

Lupton, T. (1963). *On the Shop Floor: Two Studies of Workshop Organization and Output,* Oxford: Pergamon Press.

Luxemburg, R. (1913 [1951] [2003]). *The Accumulation of Capital,* trans. A. Schwarzschild, London: Routledge Classics. [Original German edition as *Die Akkumulation des Kapitals: Ein Beitrag zur ökonomischen Erklärung des Imperialismus*, Berlin: Buchhandlung Vorwärts Paul Singer G.m.b.H.]

McCloskey, D. (1985). *The Rhetoric of Economics*, Madison, WI: University of Wisconsin Press.

MacCulloch, D. (2009). *Reformation: Europe's House Divided 1490–1700*, London: Allen Lane.

McDonald, L. with P. Robinson (2009). *A Colossal Failure of Common Sense: The Inside Story of the Collapse of Lehman Brothers*, London: Ebury Press.

McPherson, C.B. (1973). *Democratic Theory: Essays in Retrieval*, Oxford: Clarendon Press.

MacReady, P. (2004). 'Aerodynamics and Other Efficiencies in Transporting Goods', in R. McCallen, F. Browand and J. Ross (eds), *The Aerodynamics of Heavy Vehicles: Trucks, Buses, and Trains*, Berlin and Heidelberg: Springer Verlag.

Maddison, A. (2008). *Contours of the World Economy 1–2030 AD: Essays in Macro-economic History*, Oxford: Oxford University Press.

Mahan, A.T. (1890). *The Influence of Sea Power upon History, 1660–1783*, London: Sampson Low and Co.

Malcomson, J. (1999). 'Individual Employment Contracts', in O. Ashenfelter and D. Card (eds), *Handbook of Labor Economics*, Amsterdam: North-Holland.

Mandeville, B. (1714 [1924]). *The Fable of the Bees or Private Vices, Publick Benefits*, With a Commentary Critical, Historical, and Explanatory by F.B. Kaye, 2 vols, Oxford: Clarendon Press. [Text of 1732 edition].

Mankiw, N.G. (1998 [2009]). *Principles of Economics*, Mason, OH: South-Western, 5th edition.

Mankiw, N.G. (1998 [2009]a). *Principles of Microeconomics*, Mason, OH: South-Western, 5th edition.

Mankiw, N.G. (1992 [2010]). *Macroeconomics*, New York: Worth, 7th edition.

Manning, A. (2003). *Monopsony in Motion: Imperfect Competition in Labor Markets*, Princeton, NJ: Princeton University Press.

Mantel, R.R. (1974). 'On the Characterization of Aggregate Excess Demand', *Journal of Economic Theory*, 7: 348–53.

Maresca, J. (1998). 'US interests in the Central Asian Republics', Hearing before the Subcommittee on Asia and the Pacific of the Committee on International Relations, House of Representatives, One hundred fifth Congress, Second Session, February 12, 1998. available at http://www.house.gov/international_relations/105th/ap/wsap212982.htm (retrieved July 2010).

Markowitz, H.M. (1952). 'Portfolio Selection', *Journal of Finance*, 7: 77–91.

Markusen, A. and J. Yudken (1992). *Dismantling the Cold War Economy*, New York: Monthly Review Press.

Marlowe, C. (1604 [1907]). *The tragical history of Doctor Faustus: a play*, written by Christopher Marlowe, edited with a preface, notes and glossary by Israel Gollancz, London: Dent. [Originally published as *The tragicall history of D. Faustus: As it hath bene acted by the right honorable the Earle of Nottingham his seruants*, London: Printed by V. S. for Thomas Bushell.]

Marsh, A. (1979). *Concise Encyclopedia of Industrial Relations*, Aldershot: Gower.

Marshall, A. (1890). *Principles of Economics,* London: Macmillan.

Marshall, A. (1890 [1920]). *Principles of Economics*, London: Macmillan, 8th edition.

Marshall, A. and M. Paley Marshall (1879). *The Economics of Industry*, London: Macmillan.

Marx, K. (1844 [1977]). 'Economic and Philosophical Manuscripts' in *Selected Writings*, edited by D. McLellan, Oxford: Oxford University Press, pp. 75–112.

Marx, K. (1849 [1902]). *Wage-Labour and Capital, first published in the Neue Rheinische Zeitung*, April 5–8 and 11, 1849. [Delivered as lectures in 1847.] Edited with an introduction by Friedrich Engels in 1891. Trans. Harriet E. Lothrop, New York: Labor News Company.

Marx, K. (1852 [1937]). *The Eighteenth Brumaire of Louis Bonaparte*, in *The Collected Works of Karl Marx and Friedrich Engels*, Moscow: Progress Publishers.

Marx, K. (1857 [1973]). *Grundrisse: Foundations of the Critique of Political Economy (Rough Draft)*, trans. Martin Nicolaus, Harmondsworth: Penguin.

Marx, K. (1862–3 [1969]). *Theories of Surplus Value, Volume IV of Capital, Part 1*, Moscow: Progress Publishers.

Marx, K. (1862–3 [1968]). *Theories of Surplus Value, Volume IV of Capital, Part 2*, Moscow: Progress Publishers.

Marx, K. (1862–3 [1971]). *Theories of Surplus Value, Volume IV of Capital, Part 3*, Moscow: Progress Publishers.

Marx, K. (1865 [1969]). *Value, Price and Profit*, New York: International Co.

Marx, K. (1867 [1909]). *Capital: A Critique of Political Economy. Volume I: The Process of Capitalist Production*, Trans. from the 3rd German edition, by Samuel Moore and Edward Aveling, ed. Frederick Engels. Revised and amplified according to the 4th German ed. by Ernest Untermann, Chicago: Charles H. Kerr and Co.

Marx, K. (1867 [1962]). *Das Kapital, Kritik der politischen Ökonomie. Erster Band, in Karl Marx – Friedrich Engels Werke*, edited by the Institut für Marxismus-Leninismus beim ZK der SED, Berlin (DDR): Dietz Verlag, Vol 23.

Marx, K. (1867 [1976]). *Capital: A Critique of Political Economy, Vol 1*, translated by Ben Fowkes, introduced by Ernest Mandel, Harmondsworth: Penguin Books in association with New Left Review.

Marx, K. (1875 [1962]). *Kritik des Gothaer Programms, in Karl Marx – Friedrich Engels Werke*, edited by the Institut für Marxismus-Leninismus beim ZK der SED, Berlin (DDR): Dietz Verlag, Vol 19.

Marx, K. (1885 [1910]). *Capital: A Critique of Political Economy. Volume II: The Process of Circulation of Capital*, ed. Frederick Engels. Trans. from the 2nd German edition by Ernest Untermann, Chicago: Charles H. Kerr and Co.

Marx, K. (1885 [1992]). *Capital: A Critique of Political Economy, Vol 2*, translated by David Fernbach, introduced by Ernest Mandel, London: Penguin Books in association with New Left Review, c1978.

Marx, K. (1894 [1909]). *Capital: A Critique of Political Economy. Volume III: The Process of Capitalist Production as a Whole*, by Karl Marx. Ed. Frederick Engels. Trans. from the 1st German edition by Ernest Untermann, Chicago: Charles H. Kerr and Co.

Marx, K. (1972). *Capital: Vols I–III*, London: Lawrence and Wishart.

Marx, K. and F. Engels (1845 [1932] [1998]). *The German Ideology*, Amherst, NY: Prometheus.

Marx, K. and F. Engels (1848 [1998]). *The Communist Manifesto: a modern edition*; with an introduction by Eric Hobsbawm, London: Verso.

Marx, K. and F. Engels (various years). *The Collected Works of Karl Marx and Friedrich Engels*, Moscow: Progress Publishers.

Marx, K. and F. Engels (1969). *Marx/Engels Selected Works*, Moscow: Progress Publishers.

Mas-Colell, A., M.D. Whinston and J.R. Green (1995). *Microeconomic Theory*, Oxford: Oxford University Press.

Mathewson, S. (1931). *Restriction of Output among Unorganized Workers*, New York: Viking.

Maxwell, J.C. (1890). *The Scientific Papers of James Clerk Maxwell*, ed. W.D.Niven, Cambridge: Cambridge University Press.

Maynard Smith, J. (1974). 'The Theory of Games and the Evolution of Animal Conflict', *Journal of Theoretical Biology*, 47: 209–21.

Meikle, S. (1995). *Aristotle's Economic Thought*, Oxford: Clarendon Press.

Melman, S. (1997). 'From Private to State Capitalism: How the Permanent War Economy Transformed the Institutions of American Capitalism', *Journal of Economic Issues*, 31: 311–30.

Menger, C. (1871). *Grundsätze der Volkswirthschaftslehre*, Vienna: Braumüller.

Menger, C. (1871/2004). *Principles of Economics*, translated by J. Dingwall and B.F. Hoselitz, Ludwig von Mises Institute electronic online edition, available from http://mises.org/Books/Mengerprinciples.pdf (retrieved September 2009).

Menger, C. (1883). *Untersuchungen über die Methode der Socialwissenschaften, und der politischen Oekonomie insbesondere*, Leipzig: Dunker und Humblot.

Menger, C. (1884). *Die Irrthümer des Historismus in der deutschen Nationalökonomie*, Vienna: Alfred Hölder.

Menger, C. (1888). "Zur Theorie des Kapitals", [Conrad's] *Jahrbücher für Nationalökonomie und Statistik*, n.s., 17: 1–49.

Menger, C. (1892). 'On the Origins of Money', *Economic Journal*, 2: 239–55.

Menger, K. (ed.) (1929–37 [1998]). *Ergebnisse eines Mathematischen Kolloquiums*, as reprinted in E. Dierker and K. Sigmund (eds), *Karl Menger: Ergebnisse eines Mathematischen Kolloquiums*. Berlin and New York: Springer Verlag.

Miller, P.J. (ed.) (1994). *The Rational Expectations Revolution: Readings from the Front Line*, Cambridge, MA: MIT Press.

Minsky, H. (1986 [2008]). *Stabilizing an Unstable Economy*, New York: McGraw-Hill.

Mirabeau, V.R. marquis de (1762). *L'ami des hommes: tableau économique avec ses explications, septième partie*, Hamburg: Chrétien Herold.

Mirabeau, V.R. marquis de (1767). *Élémens de la philosophie rurale*, La Haye: Les libraires associés.

Mirowski, P. (1988). *Against Mechanism: Protecting Economics from Science*, Totawa, NJ: Rowman & Littlefield.

Mirowski, P. (1989). *More Heat than Light: Economics as Social Physics*, New York: Cambridge University Press.

Mirowski, P. (2002). *Machine Dreams: Economics becomes a Cyborg Science*. New York: Cambridge University Press.

Mises, L. von (1922 [1951]). *Socialism: an economic and sociological analysis*, translated by J. Kahane from the 2nd (1932) German edition, New Haven, CT: Yale University Press. [Original German edition as *Die Gemeinwirtschaft: Untersuchungen über den Sozialismus*, Jena: Gustav Fischer.]

Mises, L. von (1949 [1996]). *Human Action: A Treatise on Economics* (4th rev. edn), ed. Bettina B. Greaves, Irvington-on-Hudson, NY: Foundation for Economic Education. [Expanded version of the German work: Nationalökonomie: Theorie des Handelns und Wirtschaftens, Geneva: Editions Union, 1940.]

Monk, R. (1999). *Bertrand Russell, Vol. I: 1872–1920 The Spirit of Solitude*, London: Vintage.

Moore, G.E. (1903 [1993]). *Principia ethica*, edited and with an introduction by Thomas Baldwin, Cambridge: Cambridge University Press.

Moran, R. (2002). *Executioner's Current: Thomas Edison, George Westinghouse, and the Invention of the Electric Chair*, New York: A.A. Knopf.

Morgan, E.S. (1988). *Inventing the People: The Rise of Popular Sovereignty in England and America*, New York: Norton.

Morishima, M. (1973). *Marx's Economics*, Cambridge: Cambridge University Press.

Münchau, W. (2010). 'Gaps in the Eurozone "football league"', *Financial Times*, March 21, available at http://www.ft.com/cms/s/0/6165e3b6-3510-11df-9cfb-00144feabdc0.html#axzz1Bu63JuQB (retrieved March 2010).

Murphy, A.E. (1997). *John Law: Economic Theorist and Policy-Maker*, Oxford: Clarendon.

Muth, J.F. (1961). 'Rational Expectations and the Theory of Price Movements', *Econometrica*, 29: 315–35.

Nasar, S. (1994). '*A Beautiful Mind*', New York: Simon and Schuster.

Nasar, S. (1995). 'Hard Act to Follow?', *New York Times*, 14 March. available at http://www.nytimes.com/1995/03/14/business/a-hard-act-to-follow-here-goes.html (retrieved June 2010).

Nash, J. (1950). 'The *Bargaining Problem*', *Econometrica*, 18: 155–62.

Nash, J.F., Jr (1950a). *Non-Cooperative Games; A Dissertation Presented to the Faculty of Princeton University in Candidacy for the Degree of Doctor of Philosophy; Recommended for Acceptance by the Department of Mathematics, May 1950*. available at http://www.princeton.edu/mudd/news/faq/topics/Non-Cooperative_Games_Nash.pdf (retrieved December 2010).

Nash, J. (1951). 'Non-cooperative Games', *Annals of Mathematics*, 54: 286–95.

Neumann, J. von (1928 [1959]). 'Zur Theorie der Gesellschaftsspiele', *Mathematische Annalen*, 100: 295–320. Reprinted (1959) as: 'On the Theory of Games of Strategy', in A. Tucker and

R. Luce (eds) *Contributions to the Theory of Games, Vol. 4*, Princeton, NJ: Princeton University Press.

Neumann, J. von (1937 [1998]). 'Über ein ökonomisches Gleichungssystem und eine Verallgemeinerung des Brouwerschen Fixpunktsatzes', in K. Menger (ed.), *Ergebnisse eines Mathematischen Kolloquiums*, 8. Reprinted in E. Dierker and K. Sigmund (eds.), *Karl Menger: Ergebnisse eines Mathematischen Kolloquiums,* Berlin and New York: Springer Verlag.

Neumann, J. von (1945–6). 'A Model of General Economic Equilibrium', *Review of Economic Studies*, 8: 1–9. [English translation by G. Morgenstern of Neumann 1937].

Neumann, J. von and O. Morgenstern (1944). *Theory of Games and Economic Behaviour*, Princeton, NJ: Princeton University Press.

Nozick, R. (1974). *Anarchy, State and Utopia*, New York: Basic Books.

Obama, B.H. (2009). 'Remarks by the President on Financial Rescue and Reform', Federal Hall, New York, NY, 14 September 2009, *The White House, Office of the Press Secretary*, available at http://www.whitehouse.gov/the_press_office/remarks-by-the-president-on-financial-rescue-and-reform-at-federal-hall (retrieved January 2010). available from http://www.pragoti.org/node/2503 (retrieved January 2010).

O'Brien, D.P. (2000). 'Bodin's Analysis of Inflation', *History of Political Economy* 32: 267–92.

Okonogi, K. (2008). 'Paul Samuelson: Financial Crisis Work of "Fiendish Monsters"', *Asahi Shimbun*, interview October. available from http://www.pragoti.org/node/2503 (retrieved January 2010).

Okun, A.M. (1975). *Equality and Efficiency: The Big Trade Off*, Washington, DC: Brookings.

Oncken, A. (1897). 'The Consistency of Adam Smith', *Economic Journal*, 7: 443–50.

Oncken, A. (1898). 'Das Adam Smith Problem', [Parts I-III], *Zeitschrift für Socialwissenschaft*, 1: 25–33, 101–8, 276–87.

Oppenheim, V.H. (1976–77). 'Why Oil Prices Go up: We Pushed Them', *Foreign Policy*, 25: 32–3.

Pack, S. (2010). *Aristotle, Adam Smith and Karl Marx: On Some Fundamental Issues in 21st Century Political Economy*, Cheltenham: Edward Elgar.

Pais, A. (1986). *Inward Bound: Of Matter and Forces in the Physical World*, Oxford: Oxford University Press.

Pareto, V. (1906 [1909] [1927] [1972]). *Manuale di economia politica. Con una introduzione alla scienza sociale*, Milano: Società editrice libraria (1906). French edn: *Manuel d' économie politique / par Vilfredo Pareto, traduit sur l' edition italienne par Alfred Bonnet (revue par l'auteur)*, Paris: V. Giard & E. Brière (1909); Second French edn (1927); English edn (1972): *Manual of Political Economy*, trans. Ann S. Schwier (from the 2nd French edn), London: Macmillan.

Pareto, V. (1911). « Économie mathématique », in J. Monk (ed.), *Encyclopédie des sciences mathématiques pures et appliquées*, Vol. 4, book. 1, pp. 591–640. Paris: Gauthier-Villars. English translation as "Mathematical economics", in W.J. Baumol and S.M. Goldfeld (eds.) (1968), *Precursors in Mathematical Economics: An Anthology*, London: London School of Economics.

Parker, D. (2009). *The Official History of Privatisation: vol. 1*, London: Routledge.

Parker, R. (2005). *John Kenneth Galbraith: His Life, His Politics, His Economics*, New York: Farrar, Straus, and Giroux.

Pasinetti, L. (1977). *Lectures on the Theory of Production*, New York: Columbia University Press.

Pasinetti, L. (1983). 'The Accumulation of Capital', *Cambridge Journal of Economics*, 7: 405–11.

Patinkin, D. (1948). 'Price Flexibility and Full Employment', *American Economic Review*, 38: 543–64.

Patinkin, D. (1949). 'Involuntary Unemployment and the Keynesian Supply Function', *Economic Journal*, 59: 360–83.

Patinkin, D. (1956). *Money, Interest, and Prices: An Integration of Monetary and Value Theory*, Evanston, IL: Row, Peterson.

Patokos, T. (2005). 'On the Evolutionary Fitness of Bounded Rationality Heterogeneous Populations in Antagonistic Interactions', *American Journal of Applied Sciences*, 2: 61–72.

PBS (2008). 'Greenspan Admits 'Flaw' to Congress, Predicts More Economic Problems', *PBS*, Originally Aired: October 23, 2008, available at http://www.pbs.org/newshour/bb/business/july-dec08/crisishearing_10-23.html (retrieved May 2010).

Pearce, D. (1984). 'Rationalizable Strategic Behaviour and the Problem of Perfection', *Econometrica*, 52: 1029–50.

Pettit, P. and R. Sugden (1989). 'The Backward Induction Paradox', *Journal of Philosophy*, 86: 169–82.

Petty, W. (1662 [1899]). *A Treatise on Taxes and Contributions* in C.H. Hull (ed.), *The Economic Writings of Sir William Petty, together with The Observations upon Bills of Mortality, more probably by Captain John Graunt*, Cambridge: Cambridge University Press.

Pigou, A.C. (1920 [1932]). *Economics of Welfare* (4th edn), London: Macmillan.

Poincaré, H. (1908 [1914]). *Science and Method*, translated by Francis Maitland; with a preface by the Hon. Bertrand Russell, London: Thomas Nelson [s.d.]. Original French edition, *Science et méthode* , Paris: Flammarion.

Polybius (1922). *The Histories, with an English translation by W. R. Paton*, Cambridge, MA: harvard University Press and London: Heinemann.

Proctor, R. (1991). *Value-free Science? Purity and Power in Modern Knowledge*, Cambridge, MA: Harvard University Press.

Quesnay, F. (1758 [1972]). *Quesnay's tableau économique*, edited, with new material, translations and notes, by Marguerite Kuczynski & Ronald L. Meek, London: Macmillan and New York: A.M. Kelley for the Royal Economic Society and the American Economic Association.

Rabin, M. (1993). 'Incorporating Fairness into Economics and Game Theory', *American Economic Review*, 83: 1281–302.

Rader, J.T. (1987). 'Production as Indirect Exchange', in J. Eatwell, M. Milgate and P. Newman (eds), *The New Palgrave: A Dictionary of Economics, Vol 3*, London: Macmillan, pp. 1000–2.

Radford, R.A. (1945). 'The Economic Organisation of a POW Camp', *Economica*, 12: 189–201.

Ramsey, F.P. (1928). 'A Mathematical Theory of Saving', *Economic Journal*, 38: 543–59.

Rawls, J. (1971). *A Theory of Justice*, Cambridge, MA: Harvard University Press.

Rediker, M. (2007). *The Slave Ship: A Human History*, London: John Murray.

Reinhart, C.M. and K.S Rogoff (2009). *This Time is Different: Eight Centuries of Financial Folly*, Princeton, NJ: Princeton University Press.

Ricardo, D. (1815 [1951]). *An Essay on the Influence of a Low Price of Corn on the Profits of Stock*, London: John Murray, in P. Sraffa (ed.) (with the collaboration of M.H. Dobb), *The Works and Correspondence of David Ricardo, Vol. 4: Pamphlets and Papers, 1815–1823*, Cambridge: Cambridge University Press for the Royal Economic Society.

Ricardo, D. (1817/1819/1821 [1951]). *On the Principles of Political Economy and Taxation*, London: John Murray, in P. Sraffa (ed.) (with the collaboration of M.H. Dobb), *The Works and Correspondence of David Ricardo*, Vol. 1: *On the Principles of Political Economy and Taxation*, Cambridge: Cambridge University Press for the Royal Economic Society.

Ricardo, D. (1952). *The Works and Correspondence of David Ricardo*, ed. Piero Sraffa with the collaboration of M.H. Dobb, *Vol 9, Letters July 1821–1823*, Cambridge: Cambridge University Press for the Royal Economic Society.

Ricardo, D. (1951–73). *The Works and Correspondence of David Ricardo*, ed. Piero Sraffa, with the collaboration of M.H. Dobb, Cambridge: Cambridge University Press for the Royal Economic Society, 11 vols.

Rikovski, G. (2003). 'Alien Life: Marx and the Future of the Human', *Historical Materialism*, 11: 121–64.

Robbins, L. (1932). *An Essay on the Nature and Significance of Economic Science,* London: Macmillan.

Robinson, J. (1971). *Economic Heresies*, London: Macmillan.

Roemer, J.E. (1985). 'Rationalizing Revolutionary Ideology', *Econometrica*, 53: 85–108.

Roemer, J.E. (ed.) (1986). *Analytical Marxism*, Cambridge: Cambridge University Press.

Rogoff, K.S. (1986). 'Social Institutions for Overcoming Monetary Policy Credibility Problems', paper presented at the American Economic Association Meetings, New Orleans, December [Robert Barro, Chair], available at http://www.economics.harvard.edu/files/faculty/51_Social_Institutions.pdf (retrieved June 2010).

Roncaglia, A. (2000). *Piero Sraffa: His Life, Thought and Cultural Heritage*, London: Routledge.

Roosevelt, F.D. (1936). 'We Have Only Just Begun to Fight', *Campaign Address at Madison Square Garden*, New York City, available at http://www.ourdocuments.gov (retrieved January 2010).

Rotter, A.J. (1987). *The Path to Vietnam: Origins of the American Commitment to* South-East Asia, Ithaca, NY: Cornell University Press.

Roy, D. (1952). 'Quota Restriction and Goldbricking in a Machine Shop', *American Journal of Sociology*, 67: 427–42.

Rubinstein, A. (1982). 'Perfect Equilibrium in a Bargaining Model', *Econometrica*, 50: 97–109.

Rubinstein, A. (1985). 'A Bargaining Model with Incomplete Information about Preferences', *Econometrica*, 53: 1151–72.

Russell, B. (1900). *A Critical Exposition of the Philosophy of Leibniz: with an appendix of leading passages*, Cambridge: Cambridge University Press.

Samuel, B. (1998). 'Endogenous Preferences: The Cultural Consequences of Markets and Other Economic Institutions', *Journal of Economic Literature*, 36: 75–111.

Samuelson, P.A. (1947). *Foundations of Economic Analysis*, Cambridge, MA: Harvard University Press.

Samuelson, P.A. (1947a). 'General Theory (3)' in S.E. Harris (ed.), *The New Economics: Keynes' Influence on Theory and Public Policy*, New York: Knopf, pp. 145–60.

Samuelson, P.A. (1948, 1952, 1955, 1958, 1961, 1964, 1967, 1970, 1973, 1976, 1980). *Economics: An Introductory Analysis*, New York: McGraw-Hill, 1st to 11th editions.

Samuelson, P.A. (1957). 'Wages and Interest: A Modern Dissection of Marxian Economic Models', *American Economic Review*, 47: 884–912.

Samuelson, P.A. (1969 [1981]). 'Memories', *Newsweek*, 73: 22 (June 2). Reprinted in Heertje (1981), pp. 1–21.

Samuelson, P.A. (1970). 'Maximum Principles in Analytical Economics', Nobel Memorial Lecture, December 11, available from http://nobelprize.org/nobel_prizes/economics/laureates/1970/samuelson-lecture.pdf (retrieved January 2011).

Samuelson, P.A. (1980 [1986]). "Arthur Okun, 1928–1980", Newsweek, 7 April 1980. Reprinted in K. Crowley (ed.), *The Collected Scientific Papers of Paul Samuelson*, Vol 5, Cambridge, MA and London: MIT Press.

Samuelson, P.A. (1981). 'Schumpeter as an Economic Theorist' in Helmut Frisch (ed.), *Schumpeterian Economics*, Eastbourne: Praeger, pp. 1–27.

Samuelson, P.A. (1986). 'Forewords to the Japanese edition of *The Collected Scientific Papers of Paul A. Samuelson*' in K. Crowley (ed.), *The Collected Scientific Papers of Paul* A. Samuelson, Vol 5, Cambridge, MA and London: MIT Press.

Samuelson, P.A. (1987). 'Sraffian Economics', in J. Eatwell, M. Milgate and P. Newman (eds), *The New Palgrave, A Dictionary of Economics, Vol. 3*, London: Macmillan, pp. 452–61.

Samuelson, P.A. (1988). 'Mathematical Vindication of Ricardo on Machinery', *Journal of Political Economy*, 96: 274–82.

Samuelson, P.A. (1989). 'Ricardo Was Right!', *Scandinavian Journal of Economics*, 91: 47–62.

Samuelson, P.A. (1998). "How *Foundations* Came To Be", *Journal of Economic Literature*, 36: 1375–1386.

Samuelson, P.A. and W.D. Nordhaus (1985, 1989, 1992, 1995, 1998, 2001, 2005, 2009). *Economics*. New York: McGraw-Hill, 12th to 19th editions.

Sandmo, A. (2007). 'Retrospectives: Léon Walras and the Nobel Peace Prize', *Journal of Economic Perspectives*, 21: 217–28.

Sargent, T. (1987). 'Rational Expectations', in J. Eatwell, M. Milgate and P. Newman (eds), *The New Palgrave, A Dictionary of Economics, Vol. 4*, London: Macmillan, pp. 76–9.

Savage, L.J. (1954). *The Foundations of Statistics*, New York: Wiley.

Say, J.B. (1803 [1850]). *A Treatise on Political Economy; or the Production, Distribution, and Consumption of Wealth*, ed. C.C. Biddle, trans. C.R. Prinsep from the 4th edn of the French, Philadelphia, PA: Lippincott, Grambo & Co.

Say, J.-B. (1803 [2006]). *Traité d'économie politique*, variorum edition by C. Mouchot in J.-B. Say, *Œuvres Complètes*, Vol 1, Paris: Economica.

Schaller, M. (1985). *The American Occupation of Japan: The Origins of the Cold War in Asia*, New York: Oxford University Press.

Schelling, T.C. (1960 [1980]). *Strategy of Conflict*, Cambridge, MA: Harvard University Press, revised edition.

Schelling, T.C. (1978 [2006]). *Micromotives and Macrobehavior*, New York: Norton, new edition with a new preface and the Nobel Lecture.

Schmoller, G. von (1883). "Menger und Dilthey. Zur Methodologie der Staats- und Sozialwissenschaft", *Jahrbuch für Gesetzgebung, Verwaltung und Volkswirtschaft im Deutschen Reich*, 7(3): 975–94.

Schmoller, G. von (1884 [1896]). *The Mercantile System and Its Historical Significance: Illustrated Chiefly from Prussian History: Being a Chapter from the* Studien über die wirthschaftliche Politik Friedrichs des Grossen, trans. W.J. Ashley, New York: Macmillan.

Schumpeter, J.A. (1908). *Das Wesen und der Hauptinhalt der theoretischen Nationalökonomie*, Munich and Leipzig: Duncker and Humblot.

Schumpeter, J.A. (1942 [1994]). *Capitalism, Socialism and Democracy*, introduction by Richard Swedberg, London: Routledge.

Seaford, R. (2009). 'Money Makes the (Greek) World Go Round: What Ancient Greek Anxiety about Money Has to Tell Us about Our Own Economic Predicaments', *Times Literary Supplement*, 17 June.

Segura, J. and C. Rodríguez Braun (eds) (2004). 'Cowles Commission' in *An Eponymous Dictionary of Economics: A Guide to Laws and Theorems Named after Economists*, Cheltenham and Northampton, MA: Edward Elgar.

Sen, A.K. (1977). 'Rational Fools: A Critique of the Behavioral Foundations of Economic Theory', *Philosophy and Public Affairs*, 6: 317–344.

Senior, N.W. (1836). *An Outline of the Science of Political Economy*, London: W. Clowes & Sons.

Shaikh, A. (1977). 'Marx's Theory of Value and the Transformation Problem', in J. Schwartz (ed.), *The Subtle Anatomy of Capitalism*, Santa Monica, CA: Good Year Publishing.

Shaw, G.B. (1949). *Sixteen Self Sketches*, London: Constable.

Shenn, J. and M.J. Moore (2010). 'Morgan Stanley CDOs Were Doomed Even at Low Default Rates', *Bloomberg*, May, 14, available at http://www.bloomberg.com/news/2010–05–14/morgan-stanley-shorted-doomed-baldwin-cdos-lacking-natural-curbs-on-risk.html (retrieved June 2010).

Shields, R. (1991). *Places on the Margin: Alternative Geographies of Modernity*, London: Routledge.

Shiva, V. (2005). *Earth Democracy: Justice, Sustainability, and Peace*, Cambridge, MA: South End Press.

Smith, A. (1759 [1982]). *The Theory of Moral Sentiments*, in D.D. Raphael and A.L. Macfie (eds), *Glasgow Edition of the Works and Correspondence of Adam Smith, Vol I*, Indianapolis, IN: Liberty Fund. [First edition "Printed for A. Millar, in the Strand; And A. Kincaid and J. Bell, in Edinburgh".]

Smith, A. (1776 [1981]). *An Inquiry Into the Nature and Causes of the Wealth of Nations*, in R. H. Campbell and A. S. Skinner (eds), *Glasgow Edition of the Works and Correspondence of Adam Smith, Vol II*, Indianapolis, IN: Liberty Fund. [First edition "London: Printed for W. Strahan and T. Cadell, in the Strand".]

Smith, R.P. (1977). 'Military Expenditures and Capitalism', *Cambridge Journal of Economics*, 1: 61–76.

Sobel, R. (1968). *Panic on Wall Street: A History of America's Financial Disasters*, New York: Macmillan.

Sobel, R. (1988). *Panic on Wall Street: A Classic History of America's Financial Disasters with a New Exploration of the Crash of 1987*, New York: Truman Talley Books/Dutton.

Sonnenschein, H. (1972). 'Market Excess Demand Functions', *Econometrica*, 40: 549–63.

Sonnenschein, H. (1973). 'Do Walras' Identity and Continuity Characterize the Class of Community Excess Demand Functions?', *Journal of Economic Theory*, 6: 345–54.

Soros, G. (2009). *The Crash of 2008 and What It Means: The New Paradigm for Financial Markets* (rev. edn), New York: Public Affairs.

Sraffa, P. (1960). *Production of Commodities by Means of Commodities: Prelude to a Critique of Economic Theory*, Cambridge: Cambridge University Press.

Starmer, C. (2000). 'Developments in Non-expected Utility Theory: The Hunt for a Descriptive Theory of Choice under Risk', *Journal of Economic Literature*, 38: 332–82.

Steinbeck, J. (1939). *The Grapes of Wrath*, New York, Viking Press.

Stigler, G.J. (1963 [1986]). 'The Alarming Cost of Model Changes: A Case Study', in *The Intellectual and the Marketplace*, in K.R. Leube and T.G. Moore (eds), *The Essence of Stigler*, Stanford, CA: Hoover Institution Press, Stanford University.

Stiglitz, J.E. (2002). 'There is no Invisible Hand', *The Guardian*, Friday 20 December available at http://www.guardian.co.uk/education/2002/dec/20/highereducation.uk1 (retrieved April 2010).

Stokey, N., R.E. Lucas Jr and E. Prescott (1989). *Recursive Methods in Economic Dynamics*, Cambridge, MA: Harvard University Press.

Stone, K. (1988). 'The Effect of Wal-Mart Stores on Business in Host Towns and Surrounding Towns in Iowa', *mimeo*.

Stone, K. (1997). 'Impact of the Wal-Mart Phenomenon on Rural Communities', *mimeo*.

Stone, K., G. Artz and A. Myles (2000). 'The Economic Impact of Wal-Mart Supercentres on Existing Businesses in Mississippi', *mimeo*.

Stoner Saunders, F. (1999). *Who Paid the Piper? CIA and the Cultural Cold War*, London: Granta.

Sugden, R. (1991). 'Rational Choice: A Survey of Contributions from Economics and Philosophy, *Economic Journal*, 101: 751–85.

Sugden, R. (2000). 'The Motivating Power of Expectations', in J. Nida-Rümelin and W. Spöhn (eds), *Rationality, Rules and Structure*, Amsterdam: Kluwer, pp. 103–29.

Sugden, R. (2001). 'The Evolutionary Turn in Game Theory', *Journal of Economic Methodology*, 8: 113–30.

Summers, L. (1986). 'Some Sceptical Observations on Real Business Cycle Theory', Federal Reserve *Bank of Minneapolis Quarterly Review*, 10: 23–7.

Sweezy, P.M. (1942 [1970]). *The Theory of Capitalist Development*, New York: Oxford University Press. Reprinted, New York: Monthly Review Press.

Sweezy, P.M. (ed.) (1949). *Karl Marx and the Close of his System*, New York: Kelley.

Swift, J. (1726 [1995]). *Gulliver's Travels: Complete, Authoritative Text with Biographical and Historical Contexts, Critical History, and Essays from Five Contemporary Critical Perspectives*, edited by Christopher Fox, London: Palgrave Macmillan. [First edition: *Travels into Several Remote Nations of the World: In Four Parts. By Lemuel Gulliver, first a Surgeon, and then a Captain of several Ships*, London: printed for Benj. Motte.]

Sylos-Labini, P (1984). *The Forces of Economic Growth and Decline*, Cambridge, MA: MIT Press.

Taylor, A.J.P. (1954). *The Struggle for Mastery in Europe 1848–1918*, Oxford: Clarendon Press.

Telegraph, The (2009). 'Finance Obituaries: Paul Samuelson", 14 December 2009, available from http://www.telegraph.co.uk/news/obituaries/finance-obituaries/6811985/Paul-Samuelson.html (retrieved January 2010).

Theil, S. (2009). 'The German Banks are Toxic too', *Newsweek*, 12 June.

Theocarakis, N.J. (1991). *An Investigation of the Relationship between Responsibility and Pay*, PhD thesis, University of Cambridge, [Author's name appears as Theocharakis].

Theocarakis, N.J. (2006). 'Nicomachean Ethics in Political Economy: The Trajectory of the Problem of Value', *History of Economic Ideas*, 14: 9–53.

Theocarakis, N.J. (2010). 'Metamorphoses: The Concept of Labour in the History of Political Economy', *Economic and Labour Relations Review*, 20(2): 7–38.

Tobin, J. (1958). 'Liquidity Preference as Behavior Towards Risk', *Review of Economic Studies*, 25: 65–86.

Turgot, A.R.J. (1766 [1793]). *Reflections on the Formation and Distribution of Wealth*, London: E. Spragg.

Turgot, A.R.J (1769 [1919]). 'Value and Money', in R.L. Meek (ed.), *Precursors of Adam Smith*, London: Dent and Totowa, NJ: Rowman and Littlefield, 1973. Original French 'Valeurs et monnaies', in Gustave Schelle (ed.) (1919) *Œuvres de Turgot et documents le concernant avec biographie et notes, Vol. III, Turgot intendant de Limoges, 1768–1774*, Paris: Librairie Félix Alcan, pp. 79–98. [This 'project of an article' was presumably written in 1769 and published for the first time in 1919.]

Udéhn, L. (2001). *Methodological Individualism: Background, History and Meaning*, London and New York: Routledge.

Udéhn, L. (2002). 'The Changing Face of Methodological Individualism', *Annual Review of Sociology*, 28: 479–507.

Varoufakis, Y. (1989). 'Worker Solidarity and Strikes', *Australian Economic Papers*, 28: 76–92.

Varoufakis, Y. (1991). *Rational Conflict*, Oxford: Blackwell.

Varoufakis, Y. (1993). 'Modern and Postmodern Challenges to Game Theory', *Erkenntnis*, 38: 371–404.

Varoufakis, Y. (1998). *Foundations of Economics: A Beginner's Companion*, London and New York: Routledge.

Varoufakis, Y. (ed.) (2001). *Game Theory: Critical Concepts in the Social Sciences, Vol 2, Refinements*, London: Routledge.

Varoufakis, Y. (2002). 'Deconstructing Homo Economicus? Reflections on an Encounter between Postmodernity and Neoclassical Economics', *Journal of Economic Methodology*, 9: 389–96.

Varoufakis, Y. (2002–3). 'Against Equality', *Science and Society*, 66: 448–72.

Varoufakis, Y. (2008). 'Capitalism According to Evolutionary Game Theory: An Essay on the Impossibility of a Sufficiently Evolutionary Model of Historical Change', *Science and Society*, 72: 63–94.

Varoufakis, Y. (2009). 'Pristine Equations, Tainted Economics and the Postwar Order', paper presented at the *Cold War and the Social Sciences* workshop, Heymann Centre for the Humanities, Columbia University, 10 April.

Varoufakis, Y. and C. Arnsperger (2009). 'A Most Peculiar Failure: On the Dynamic Mechanism by which the Inescapable Theoretical Failures of Neoclassical Economics Reinforce Its Dominance', *mimeo*. available at http://www.econ.uoa.gr/UA/files/1139148722..pdf (retrieved June 2010).

Vilks, A. (1992). 'A Set of Axioms for Neoclassical Economics and the Methodological Status of the Equilibrium Concept', *Economics and Philosophy*, 8: 51–82.

Visser, H. (1974). *The Quantity Theory of Money*, London: Martin Robertson.

Volcker, P.A. (1978–9). 'The Political Economy of the Dollar', *FRBNY Quarterly Review*, winter: 1–12. [Fred Hirsch Lecture at Warwick University, Coventry, 9 November 1978].

Volcker, P.A. (2005). 'An Economy On Thin Ice', *Washington Post*, Sunday, April 10, Page B07.

Voltaire (1759 [2006]). *Candide, or, Optimism*, translated and edited by Theo Cuffe, with an introduction by Michael Wood, London: Penguin.

Volterra, V. (1926). 'Variazioni e fluttuazioni del numero d'individui in specie animali conviventi', *Mem. R. Accad. Naz. dei Lincei*, 2, 31,113.

Wachowski, L. and A. Wachowski (1998). The *Matrix*, Numbered Shooting Script, 29 March 1998, available from http://www.dailyscript.com/scripts/the_matrix.pdf (retrieved June 2010).

Walras, L. (1874/7 [1926] [1954]). *Éléments d'économie politique pure, ou théorie de la richesse sociale*. [Edition définitive, revue et augmentée par l'auteur], Paris: R. Pichon & R. Durand-Auzias.

1st edn in two parts 1874 (on exchange), and 1877 (on production), Lausanne: L. Corbaz; Paris: Guillaumin; Bale: H. Georg. 2nd edn (1889): Lausanne: F. Rouge; Paris: Guillaumin; Leipzig: Duncker & Humblot. 3rd edn (1896): Lausanne: F. Rouge; Paris: F. Pichon; Leipzig: Duncker & Humblot. 4th edn (1900): Lausanne: F. Rouge; Paris: F. Pichon. English trans. William Jaffé: *Elements of Pure Economics, or the Theory of Social Wealth,* London: Allen and Unwin.

Weber, M. (1905 [2002]). *The Protestant Ethic and 'The Spirit of Capitalism',* London: Penguin Books. [First published as, Die protestantische Ethik und der Geist des Kapitalismus', *Archiv für Sozialwissenschaft und Sozialpolitik,* 20(1): 1–54 (1904) and 21(1): 1–110 (1905).]

Weibull, J. (1995). *Evolutionary* Game Theory, Cambridge, MA: MIT Press.

Weintraub, E.R. (2002). *How Economics Became a Mathematical Science,* London and Durham, NC: Duke University Press.

Weintraub, E.R. and P. Mirowski (1994). 'The Pure and the Applied: Bourbakism Comes to Mathematical Economics', *Science in Context,* 7: 245–72.

Weiss, A. (1995). 'Human Capital vs Signalling Explanations of Wages', *Journal of Economic Perspectives,* 9: 133–54.

Westfall, R.S. (1980). *Never at Rest: A Biography of Isaac Newton,* Cambridge: Cambridge University Press.

Whately, R. (1831). *Introductory Lectures on Political Economy,* London: B. Fellowes.

Wicksell, K. (1898 [1936]). *Geldzins und Güterpreise: Eine Studie über die den Tauschwert des Geldes bestimmenden Ursachen,* Jena: Gustav Fischer. First English trans. R.F. Kahn: *Interest and Prices: A Study of the Causes Regulating the Value of Money,* London: Macmillan.

Wicksell, K. (1901 [1934]). *Lectures on Political Economy, Vol. 1: General Theory,* trans. from the Swedish by E. Classen; ed. L. Robbins, London: George Routledge. [First Swedish edition: *Föreläsningar i nationalekonomi, första delen: Teoretisk nationalekonomi,* Lund: Gleerups Förlag.]

Wicksteed, P.H. (1884). '*Das Kapital*: A criticism', *Today,* October, 388–411.

Wicksteed, P.H. (1894). *The Coordination of the Laws of Distribution,* London: Macmillan.

Wicksteed, P.H. (1910 [1933]). *The Common Sense of Political Economy,* London: George Routledge and Sons.

Wicksteed, P.H. (1914 [1933]). 'The Scope and Method of Political Economy in the Light of the 'Marginal' Theory of Value and Distribution', *Economic Journal,* 24 (93), reprinted in Wicksteed *The Common Sense of Political Economy,* London: George Routledge & Sons), Vol II, pp. 772–96.

Wieser, F. von (1889 [1893]). *Der natürliche Werth,* Vienna: A. Hölder. English trans. Christian A. Malloch as *Natural Value,* London: Macmillan.

Williamson, O.E., M.L.Wachter and J.E. Harris (1975). 'Understanding the Employment Relation: The Analysis of Idiosyncratic Exchange', *Bell Journal of Economics,* 6: 250–80.

Wittgenstein, L. (1921 [1972]). *Tractatus logico-philosophicus*: the German text of Ludwig Wittgenstein's Logische-philosophische Abhandlung, with a new edition of the translation by D.F. Pears and B.F. McGuinness and with the introduction by Bertrand Russell, London: Routledge & Kegan Paul, 2nd edition, reprinted with corrections.

Wolff, R. (2010). *Capitalism Hits the Fan: The Global Economic Meltdown and what to Do about it,* Northampton, MA: Olive Branch Press.

Wood, E.M. (1988). *Peasant-Citizen and Slave: The Foundations of Athenian Democracy,* London: Verso.

Wood, E.M. (1995). *Democracy against Capitalism: Renewing Historical Materialism,* Cambridge and New York: Cambridge University Press.

Wood, J.C. (ed.) (1995). *Piero Sraffa: Critical Assessments,* London: Routledge.

Wordsworth, W. [1805 [1888]]. 'The Prelude, or, Growth of a Poet's Mind; An Autobiographical Poem' in *The Complete Poetical Works,* with an introduction by John Morley, London: Macmillan.

Xenophon (1994). *Oeconomicus*: *A Social and Historical Commentary*, with a new English translation by Sarah B. Pomeroy, Oxford: Clarendon Press.

Yeats, W.B. (1920). *Michael Robartes and the Dancer*, Churchtown, Cuala Press. Facsimile edition Shannon: Irish University Press, 1970.

Young, W. (2010). 'The IS-LM diagram', in M. Blaug, and P. Lloyd (eds), *Famous Figures and Diagrams in Economics*, Cheltenham: Edward Elgar, pp. 348–55.

Zeuthen, F. (1930). *Problems of Monopoly and Economic Warfare*, London: George Routledge and Sons.

Zinn, H. (1998). *The Twentieth Century. A People's History*, New York: HarperPerennial.

Žižek, S. (2006). *The Parallax View*, Cambridge, MA: MIT Press.

Index